9th Annual Edition
KNIVES '89

Edited by
Ken Warner

DBI BOOKS, INC.

STAFF

EDITOR
Ken Warner

ASSOCIATE EDITORS
Robert S.L. Anderson
Harold A. Murtz
Deborah Warner

ASSISTANT TO THE EDITOR
Lilo Anderson

EDITORIAL/PRODUCTION ASSISTANT
Maria L. Connor

COVER PHOTOGRAPHY
John Hanusin

MANAGING EDITOR
Pamela J. Johnson

PUBLISHER
Sheldon L. Factor

DBI BOOKS INC.

PRESIDENT
Charles T. Hartigan
VICE PRESIDENT & PUBLISHER
Sheldon L. Factor
VICE PRESIDENT — SALES
John G. Strauss
TREASURER
Frank R. Serpone

THE COVER KNIVES

The unmistakable Nolen Brothers' way with a knife lies across the top of our photo in stainless steel and turquoise this year. And clockwise below it we show a distinctive Lynn Sampson folder in polished mastodon ivory; a Mike Franklin gents knife with titanium bolster and stag scales; a tour-de-force Bowie by Richard Essegian in gold and ivory and blued steel, all work by the maker; a Jot Khalsa uptown dagger in jade, blued steel, gold, nickel Damascus blade, engraving and gold inlay by Lynton McKenzie; and a Bob Conley skinner with both his characteristic blade in the handle and his characteristic first class trimmings. Once more, of course, the photography is by John Hanusin.
KW

CONTENTS

CONTENTS

INTRODUCTION

PERSPECTIVES are changing on us fast. What was state-of-the-art ain't; stuff from 10 years ago is back; there are new realities every day. Cheap is still cheap, and big tickets are big, but the scale changes. For instance:

● Thousands of people are paying $400 and $500 for knives they carry and use.

● The not-inconsiderable sum of $1,000 is not now a lot of money for a knife. There are many knifemakers whose base price for a plain-vanilla knife is $650 to $950. That's the *bottom* for these fellows.

● For $50 to $75 or $95, you can buy a pretty good hand-ground high carbon stainless steel knife that, if it suits you, will last you from now on.

● Scrimshaw, which is relatively inexpensive, is not nearly so much used as it was, and engraving, now cheaper than it was but still not cheap, is everywhere.

● To exhibit and sell at a Japan Knifemakers Guild show in Tokyo will run, for a couple who knows how to hold down non-essential spending, such as for food, right at $12,000 for a four-day trip. And there are American knifemakers showing there, nearly every time.

● Folding knives were not in the picture at all; then there came along a lot of big jackknives; now the folders seem to have about half the attention and two-thirds the money of knife buyers.

● The varieties of pattern-welded steel have become near infinite and handsome beyond the dreams of its modern beginnings. Had this stuff been around then, it would have sold for well over $100 an inch for a finished blade. Now you can get *very* nice Damascus at more like $25 an inch.

● Westinghouse has quit making Micarta, once the staple of the handle end of the business. Hardly anyone is noticing.

● Even sawteeth are disappearing.

No, the knife field is not disintegrating. On the contrary, in fact. However, the buyers and the sellers and the makers are all moving faster. And the innovators are sometimes *way* out front.

It will come to pass, in the next 24 or 36 months, that the hunting knife will no longer be the staple pattern in belt knives. For a while it looked as if the boot knife was going to beat out the hunter, but the boot fell off the pace. The survival and camp patterns didn't really have much of a shot—too big. Same goes for fighters and tantos.

So what then? Well, as much as anything, I think the drop-point hunter will get modified toward all-purpose use. This is not the "dropped hunter" in the Loveless pattern, but rather a somewhat pointy almost-spear-point. Other designs will move way along toward a slim belt knife under 8 inches long overall, sheathed for use daily.

Are you saying that sounds like a large lockback folder that doesn't fold? Perhaps it does. Depends on your perspective.

And that will change.

Ken Warner

Knives

Left: Hudson's Bay Company scalping knife by Jukes Coulson & Co., Sheffield, ca. 1850-60. Good condition handle appears to be birch. Center: Scalper blade found in a Wahpeton Sioux village site in Minnesota. Marked "William Nowell." Period 1830-40. Right: Rare scalper blade marked "P.C.J. & CO./Cast Steel" (for Pierre Chouteau Jr. & Co., St. Louis). A surface find in central Wyoming. (Museum of the Fur Trade photo)

in the Fur Trade

by STEVEN DICK

THE WORDS "Mountain Man" for most of us conjure up a lone wilderness hunter camped some place along the "Seeds-Ke-De" river. Grazing quietly beside him is a saddled Appaloosa he got in a trade with the Nez Perce and two pinto mustangs loaded down with prime beaver pelts. The hunter is clothed in buckskin and furs from his coonskin cap to his elk hide moccasins. His red hair is braided Indian fashion but his long beard is wild and bushy. Cradled in his arms is his most prized possession, a big-bored Hawken plains rifle. On his belt is a tool nearly as important as the rifle to his livelihood, a long Russell Green River butcher knife.

So what if I told you most mountain men wore wool clothing when they could get it, and that even Davy Crockett wasn't particularly fond of coonskin caps? Or that rather than a pure race of Anglo-Saxon giants, the trappers were a mixed bunch of French-Canadians, Spanish, English, Americans and displaced eastern Indians? Or that many stayed as clean-shaven as they could so as not to offend their Indian hosts? Or that the Hawken rifle was never common in the Rockies 'til a decade after the trade in beaver pelts had disintegrated? And finally that the Russell Green River knife wasn't put into production 'til after the beaver trade was over?

Well, that's all true.

The beaver trade started almost immediately after the New World was discovered, and it was often the primary reason for exploration. Along with the French and English, the Spanish, Russians, Portuguese, Swedes, Dutch, and Danes all staked claims to the fur trade wealth. Once in Europe, the fur was stripped from beaver pelts and processed into a highly durable felt. Hats made from this felt were often passed down from father to son and there was a thriving trade in second- and even third-hand hats. For close to 300 years beaver felt had remained the preferred headgear of Europe when in the 1820s it was discovered that South American nutria could be processed into felt equal to

beaver at much less cost. This was the start of a rapid decline in the beaver trade which was only accelerated by the introduction of the silk hat and the greatly reduced stocks of wild beaver. By 1840, the beaver trade was basically dead.

The first 250 years of the fur trade were dominated by the French and the English with the Spanish controlling the Southwest, the Russians parts of the Northwest and the rest in small enclaves along the East Coast. Trade goods and cutlery within each nation's sphere of influence tended to be limited to that supplied by the mother country's industry. Each had knife patterns unique to their cultures, though basic utility knife styles overlap to a certain degree. Other than a limited number of knives turned out by blacksmiths and a handful of one-man cutlery shops, the American Colonialists depended almost totally on imports for their needs. The Revolution didn't change this basic fact of life, and it was the mid-19th century before the U.S. cutlery industry really competed with imported goods.

While a handful of American traders, trappers, and "long hunters" had been involved in the beaver trade all along, it was the Louisiana Purchase in 1803 and the Lewis and Clark expedition of 1803-06 that opened the Rockies to the American fur trade and created the "Mountain Man." When compared to the total history of the beaver trade, the American mountain man was but a brief phenomenon at the very end of the cycle.

For the most part, popular images of mountain men can be traced back to four sources. George Frederick Ruxton's novel *Life in the Far West* published in 1848 was probably the first effort to glamorize the mountain man. Lewis H. Garrard's adventures in the Southwest during the Mexican War, *Wah-To-Yah and the Taos Trail*, published in 1850, came next. Practically every historical fur trade novel written since these two books will show signs of one or both. Attend a modern black-powder rendezvous, and you'll find buckskin-clad indi-

Modern replica of the fur trade "Scalper" made by Wendall Fox. This knife displays the classic diamond-section handle found on so many of the early knives.

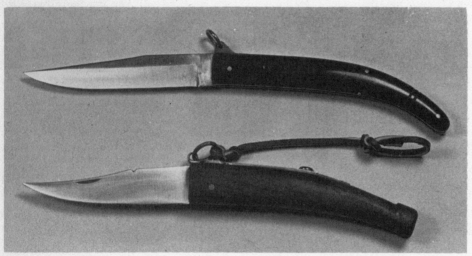

Two ring-pull French clasp knife replicas from G. Gedney Godwin Inc. Large numbers of these knives were used in the early fur trade as both tools and weapons.

viduals speaking pure mountain man lingo straight from the pages of both books: "WAUGH!"; "See which way the stick floats"; "Gone Under"; and naturally, "Give it to them up to GREEN RIVER!"

More visual are the paintings of Frederick Remington (1861-1909) and Charles Russell (1864-1926). It would take someone more versed in art than myself to explain why, but those earlier artists who actually traveled with the mountain men used a blurred-image style of painting that doesn't provide much detail for the viewer. Remington and Russell, on the other hand, painted very lifelike images of the Far West.

The public's image of the mountain man has of course been influenced to some extent by Hollywood, for example *Jeremiah Johnson* and his big Bowie. The trouble with any of these references is that none actually came from firsthand experience with the tools and weapons of the beaver trade.

Of the everyday tools used in the beaver trade none came anywhere near seeing as much use as the knife. One moment it might be skinning the day's catch, the next cutting out moccasins or horse tack, making shavings for a fire, butchering game, dicing Camas roots for stew, building shelters, furnishing log cabins, or in hard times, stripping willow bark for the horses to eat. Constant resharpening wore blades out quickly and hard use frequently broke them. Most wilderness hunters carried spare knives among their gear and the average blade probably didn't last more than one season in its original form.

The two most frequently mentioned styles of knives in period literature are the "butcher" and the "scalping." Before 1800 the term "butcher" simply meant any large, plain, utility knife used for butchering animals. If the knives I have observed from various archaeological digs are any indication, these 18th cen-

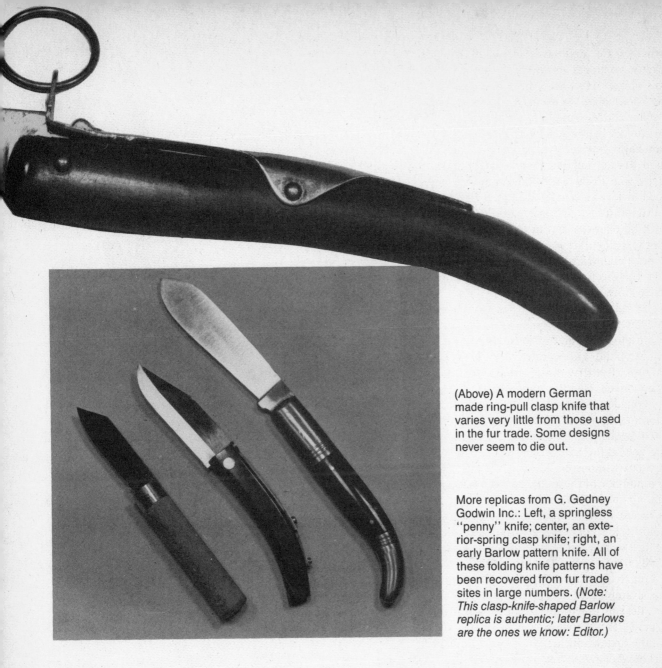

(Above) A modern German made ring-pull clasp knife that varies very little from those used in the fur trade. Some designs never seem to die out.

More replicas from G. Gedney Godwin Inc.: Left, a springless "penny" knife; center, an exterior-spring clasp knife; right, an early Barlow pattern knife. All of these folding knife patterns have been recovered from fur trade sites in large numbers. (*Note: This clasp-knife-shaped Barlow replica is authentic; later Barlows are the ones we know: Editor.*)

tury butchers tended to look a lot like modern steaking knives—long, wide, slightly curving blades with sharp points. In the early part of the 19th century Sheffield cutlers started using the term "butcher" for a style of knife with a relatively straight blade and an upswept rounded or short clip-point. This blade pattern quickly became very popular on the frontier and it remains today the most common form of butcher knife. I. Wilson, established in 1750, seems to have been the most popular brand in the mountains, but many other Sheffield companies supplied knives to the fur trade.

Many times in the past it's been said "scalping" knives were simply cheap butcher knives, but modern research has found the term was used in Sheffield for a separate type of blade. The common scalper normally had a straight backed blade around 6 inches long with the edge curving up to the point. Handle construction consisted of a half tang set in a slotted one-piece wood

grip thus helping to keep the price down. Often scalper handles were diamond shape in cross section which greatly improved the gripping qualities of the straight unguarded handle.

In the early 1960s the Minnesota Historical Society and the Canadian government searched many of the fur trade canoe routes with divers. One of the finds in Ontario's French River was a bundle of diamond-shaped knife handles with the blades rusted away. Another scalper of this pattern was found near Jackson Hole and is in the National Park Service Teton collection. Again, using archaeological finds as a reference, I think it is safe to say the scalper pattern knife was the hands-down favorite all through the beaver trade.

Surviving fur company records tend to bear this out. In 1827 alone, American Fur Co. ordered 11,160 scalpers in various blade lengths and handle materials from their Sheffield suppliers. Hudson Bay Co.,

North-West Co. and the other fur trading groups were marketing scalpers in similar quantities. Though the term "scalper" has been dropped, many modern wide bladed boning knives are basically the same pattern.

French cutlery suppliers never made the Sheffield-style butcher in any quantity. Their version of this utilitarian knife was very close to the standard scalper, though French butchers are more likely to have full tangs. Some French-style butchers also have handles shaped to form a handguard much like those used on modern professional meat cutting knives. While the French butcher lost out to the Sheffield pattern in the wilderness, it still remains popular in France and other European countries today. Modern cutlery catalogs refer to the French butcher as a "European style" butcher knife.

Other knives that saw wide use in the beaver trade include the cartouche, belduaque, hand or beavertail dag, buffalo knife, and various styles of folding knives. The cartouche was a relatively small, lightweight, spear-point, utility knife similar to many modern kitchen knives. Handles normally have a forged bolster and are made of wood, bone, or cast brass. Along with the forementioned 1827 order for scalpers, American Fur Co. requested 3600 cartouche knives which ranks it just behind the butcher and scalper in general popularity. The Minnesota Historical Society divers recovered a number of these knives from trade route rivers, including one with a fancy cast brass handle.

In the Spanish-dominated areas of the country, the standard trade knife was a variation of the Mediterranean dirk or peasant's knife. Known as a belduaque or "broadknife," it closely resembled a narrow 20th century French chef knife. Those familiar with the still existing examples of Rezin Bowie's personal "Bowie knife" designs might note they are basically fancy "belduaques." This shouldn't be too much of a surprise given the Spanish influence on early Louisiana.

The hand dag, beavertail stabber, or Hudson Bay dag was primarily an Indian trade item. This was an ultra-wide double-edged dagger-shaped knife that was traded both with and without handles. Unhandled blades could be made into knives, mounted on warclubs or used as spear-points. Northern Hudson Bay trading posts stocked the unhandled blades in 7- and 9-inch lengths right up to the end of the 19th century. Supposedly they were preferred by the Eskimos for hunting spears.

Buffalo knives or as they are sometimes called "Hudson Bay camp knives" were large and heavy clip-point multipurpose tools. When butchering large animals, they served as knife, cleaver and hatchet. Jukes Coulson, Stokes and Co., a wholesale dealer in Indian trade goods, seems to be the most common stamping found on the buffalo knife. George Wostenholm and a few other Sheffield concerns also turned out the pattern at various times.

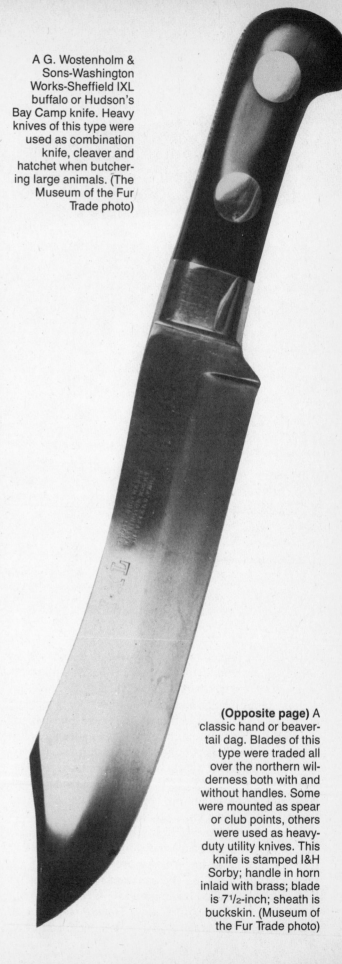

A G. Wostenholm & Sons-Washington Works-Sheffield IXL buffalo or Hudson's Bay Camp knife. Heavy knives of this type were used as combination knife, cleaver and hatchet when butchering large animals. (The Museum of the Fur Trade photo)

(Opposite page) A classic hand or beavertail dag. Blades of this type were traded all over the northern wilderness both with and without handles. Some were mounted as spear or club points, others were used as heavy-duty utility knives. This knife is stamped I&H Sorby; handle in horn inlaid with brass; blade is 7½-inch; sheath is buckskin. (Museum of the Fur Trade photo)

Replicas of the Spanish Beduaque made by Joe De La Ronde. The Spanish once controlled a large part of the western U.S. and knives of this type were a common trade item.

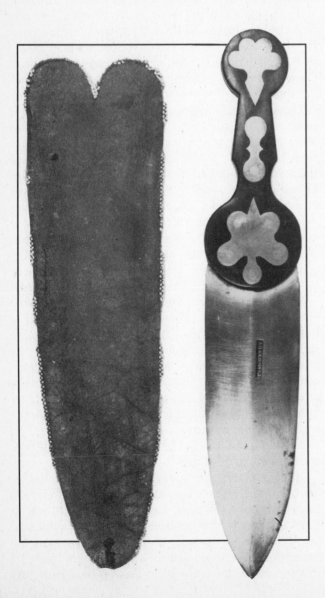

Contrary to what some authorities have stated, there seem to have been large numbers of simple folding knives in use during the beaver trade. The most popular pattern in the early days of the trade was the single blade French claspknife (sometimes called a Spanish claspknife). Most are found with an unlined horn handle, a simple flat spring mounted on the exterior of the handle, and a ring pull to release the blade lock when open. The majority of blades were of a long straight clip-point pattern. Large numbers of French claspknife blades were found during digs at both the Gubert Site, an Illinois Kaskaskia Indian village, and at Fort Michilimackinac in Michigan. Others were recovered by divers from the fur trade canoe routes in Minnesota and southern Canada. In 1702 there was a request from the Catholic missions to the Kaskaskia for a gross of "horn handled clasp knives." Along with the French trappers and traders, some Yankee trappers preferred this knife pattern. In 1832 fur trader Nathaniel Wyeth requested three dozen "Spanish" claspknives with 5½-inch locking blades from his New York jobber.

Along with the French (or Spanish) claspknives a wide variety of other folding knife styles turn up in fur trade archaeological sites. The early forms of the Barlow knife and cheap springless penny knives are probably the most common, but about any kind of folding knife in use during the period found its way into the wilderness at one time or another.

One form of frontier knife conspicuously absent from this list is the Bowie. The Bowie first came to the public's attention after Jim Bowie's 1827 Vidalia Sandbar free-for-all and reached its height of use during the early days of the Civil War. This allowed only a few short years of rising popularity before the beaver trade ended. For the most part, the Bowie was thought of as a weapon first and a tool second. The primary market for the Bowie was in the lawless semi-settled frontier areas along the Mississippi and the old South rather than with wilderness hunters.

Most of the recorded Bowie knife duels took place between drunks in backwoods taverns; there are actually very few recorded instances of mountain men going hand-to-hand with the Indians. The fur company records speak for themselves; even though the Bowie and a wide variety of other fighting-type knives were available from Sheffield, the vast majority of knives sent west were simply lightweight utility tools. It would appear the mountain man was not overly concerned about the weapon potential of his sheath knife.

Charles Hanson, curator of The Museum of the Fur Trade, tells me he has found records of Bowies being offered for sale in St. Louis during the early 1830s, so it is possible a few hard-core individualists carried the big fighters west. Most early mentions of the Bowie in the western mountains concern its use by assorted greenhorns, pilgrims, survey parties, miners, and military expeditions. One of the characters in Ruxton's book was an English sportshunter carrying a double-barrel rifle and a large Bowie. No doubt most of these tenderfeet thought the Bowie would be necessary for the expected hand-to-hand battles with the savages and miscellaneous grizzly bears.

Another frontier knife that has received a lot of attention in recent years is the crude primitive blade normally forged from a file. Backwoods settlers were almost always short on hard cash, and worn-out tools were never discarded if they could be recycled into something useful. Basic blacksmithing skills and tools were a necessity on the homestead, so it was only natural that large numbers of the knives used on the early frontier were homemade. During the first half of the 19th century, the territory bordering the Mississippi was still plenty wild. The last buffalo in Illinois was shot in 1837 after the beaver trade had pretty much run its course. It was on these backwoods homesteads that most of the mountain men grew up and I would be surprised if large numbers didn't head west with deer-horn-handled knives forged from files in their belts. Given the demands life in the mountains put on a knife, the first blade probably didn't last more than a season. As a rule mountain men didn't have access to blacksmithing tools, but they did have a relative abundance of hard cash once a year. Their life-style demanded knives in large quantities and the commercial fur trading industry supplied them with Sheffield's finest. Backing up this theory is the fact that the majority of primitive knives still in existence seem to have Eastern origins.

As for the famous Russell Green River knives, the company didn't start making knives until the late 1830s and the earliest known fur trade purchase was in 1843. Very early knives were not marked "Green River," and I haven't been able to discover when they first started using the legendary stamping. Russell's first catalog was printed in 1883; before that salesmen depended on samples and written descriptions of the knives. The majority of the knives in the 1883 catalog bear the Green River mark, though a few have the economy line "J. Ward, Atlas Works" stamp.

If you are like me, you have probably wondered about that "give it to them up to Green River!!" battle cry of the mountain men. For starters, very few butcher knives are stamped at the handle, most are marked a third to half-way up the blade. Is this a battle cry for doing something half-way? That the mountain men predate the Russell Green River knife has been explained—not quite away—by saying early Sheffield knives were stamped G.R. for "Georgius Rex." This was supposedly interpreted by the mountain men as standing for the Green River of Wyoming. One such scalping knife made by Furnis is in the National Park Service's Grand Teton collection, but again it's marked well up the blade. It's possible the entire "up to Green River" legend was started by George Ruxton in his *Life in the Far West*.

While Russell may not have made knives for the beaver trade, there is no reason to discount its significance in American history. Russell was the first cutlery company to challenge Sheffield's near-monopoly on the American cutlery market. Two of their knife patterns, the "hunter" and "Dadley," quickly replaced the Sheffield-style butcher as the preferred wilderness blade among backwoodsmen.

Though the records aren't clear, Russell's first knife, designed specifically for the Western market, seems to have been the model they simply called the hunting knife. The blade spreads from a narrow waist at the handle to a wide clip-point. As a rule, the blade thickness ran a little heavier than the standard butchers of the day though all are light compared to period Bowies. Russell made the hunter in dozens of handle variations and blade lengths from 5 to 10 inches. Before the end of the 19th century, this was the standard hunting knife of the West and practically every cutlery manufacturer made copies. After the turn of the century, Marble-style hunting knives replaced it in popularity. The 1902 Sears catalog called the Russell pattern hunter a "hunting style butcher knife." Today, the pattern is still made by Russell in a 5-inch version for commercial fish processing and in a 6-inch knife for the modern blackpowder shooter.

The second knife pattern associated with Russell is what modern knife buffs call the "Dadley." No one seems to know where that term came from, though some have said it was an English pattern before Russell popularized it. Period catalogs call it a "heavy hunting knife" or again simply "hunting knife." In its classic form the Dadley is a straight-sided knife with a spear-point and no handguard. Usually the blade stock is much heavier than the forementioned hunting knives and butchers. Like the hunting knife, many cutlery companies copied the Dadley and the line between butchers sticking knives and Dadleys is often blurred.

After the beaver trade died out, those trappers who chose to remain in the mountains were forced either to trap less desirable furs, market hunt for the mining camps, scout for the military, guide wagon trains, or hunt buffalo for the hides. Hide hunting called for large quantities of skinning knives and Russell was one of the primary suppliers of these radically curved butcher knives. Collectors call the knives "buffalo skinners" though they are normally known as "beef skinners" in the cutlery trade. Russell Green River skinners still see wide use in the meat packing industry.

Another American cutlery pioneer is Lamson & Goodnow. Lamson & Goodnow first ventured into the knife business in 1842 and was a direct competitor with Russell for the western trade through most of the rest of the century. A good example of this is the cargo of the sternwheeler Bertrand that sank in the upper Missouri River in 1865. In recent years the National Park Ser-

Top: Russell Green River butcher; bottom: I. Wilson butcher. Old butchers like these are hard to date but these are probably early 20th century. Very few utility knives have survived from before the Civil War. Both are classic Sheffield butcher patterns.

Top knife — J. Ward Atlas Works. J. Ward was an early economy mark of John Russell that may have been acquired from an earlier Sheffield firm. I know at least one J. Ward knife marked "Green River Works." At bottom is a WWII British military kitchen knife; it isn't handforged, but follows the older "cartouche" pattern.

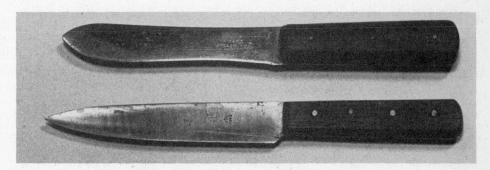

Modern reproductions of the knives that made John Russell's Green River trademark famous. The upper is a Dadley; the bottom a hunter pattern. The name "Dadley" might be a modern invention as I have not found the term in period catalogs so far. These two patterns were copied by many cutlery companies from the 1860s on.

Like John Russell, American cutlery pioneers Lamson & Goodnow are still in business. The top knife is a beef skinner and the bottom a butcher's sticking knife. Butcher's sticking knives are very similar to Dadleys, but are usually made of lighter blade stock.

vice salvaged the cargo of the steamer. Among the assorted cutlery on board was a shipment of Lamson & Goodnow hunter and Dadley pattern knives bound for the trading posts of Montana. There were also a quantity of traditional Sheffield-style butchers stamped J. Sanger, a stamping I haven't been able to uncover any information on. The Indian Department bought huge quantities of Lamson & Goodnow knives for annuity payments to western Indian tribes. One order in the early 1870s included 18,852 butcher, scalper and hunting knives; another in 1877 included 13,392 butchers. For a period of time in the mid-19th century, Lamson & Goodnow was the largest manufacturer of cutlery in the U.S., making large quantities of Bowie-style hunting knives, machetes and kitchen cutlery along with the basic utility knives of the western trade.

After the Civil War, the American cutlery industry began a rapid expansion that forever displaced the Sheffield products from the U.S. market. Charles Landers, later Landers, Frary & Clark, soon was competing with John Russell and Lamson & Goodnow head on. In 1879, the Indian Department took their business

to Landers, buying 10,005 butchers and 4,932 hunting knives. Others soon followed on their heels, but the day of the wilderness hunter, trader, and trapper was pretty much over.

I would like to add at this point that anyone with a serious interest in the tools and weapons of the fur trade owes himself a visit to The Museum of the Fur Trade in Chadron, Nebraska. I would also highly recommend a subscription to the *Museum* quarterly.

While the mountain man's rifle may have been more important to keeping him alive, the knife was the tool he used most frequently. The fact he chose a simple wood-handled butcher or scalper over the fancier hunters, Bowies, and fighters available to him was a decision based on pure utility. Rather than a Russell Green River, the knife was more likely to be an I. Wilson or similar Sheffield brand. There is also a good chance that he was carrying a French clasp or other folding knife in his possibles bag or pocket. In this day of marketing hollow-handled sawbacked shortswords as "wilderness survival knives," maybe we can yet find a lesson to be learned from the men of the beaver trade.

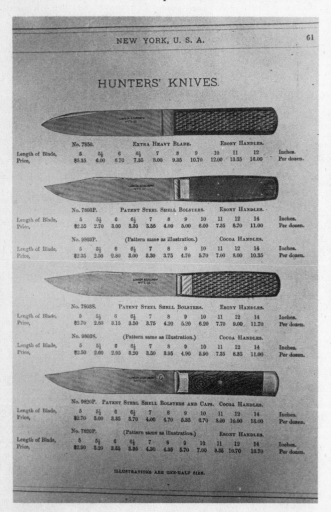

A page from the Lamson & Goodnow Mfg. Co. 1883 catalog. Note Dadley and Hunter pattern knives were offered in a wide variety of blade lengths. (Courtesy: Lamson & Goodnow)

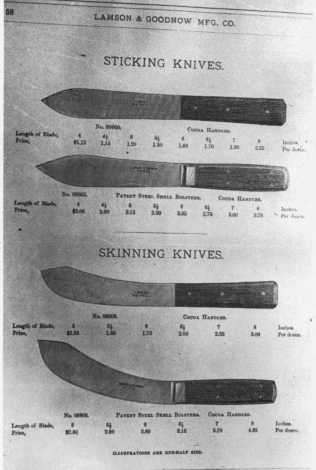

This page from the 1883 catalog shows sticker and skinning knives. The line between stickers and Dadleys was more blurred during the early days, it would seem.

Norwegian Knives Today

by AJAS KIAER

This file-worked *tolle kniv* in the modern vein is silver-ferruled and its sheath is silver-trimmed. Made by Harald Sellevold.

THE KNIFE is valued in Norway as a tool, an antique and a collectors' item. The idea of the knife as a weapon has never been primary here. The axe was the weapon the old Norsemen used to defend themselves against two- or four-legged enemies.

The best knifemakers today are artists as well as craftsmen. Without stepping on anybody's toes, I think it is fair to say that the most attractive knives come from the district of Telemark in south central Norway, but there are fabulous knifemakers in other parts of the country as well.

In Agder, a district in the south, there have been about 100 knifemakers registered and anybody owning a Mostad knife can be proud, as I am.

On the west bank of lake Mjosa lies Toten, a district with a long tradition in knifemaking. Early in the last century, Toten developed a cutlery industry. In fact, the leader was awarded prizes and official recognition. Toten knives are easily recognized by their distinctive sheaths.

Knives of the type we are concerned with here are known as sheath-knives or *tollekniv*. The prefix *tolle* means to whittle and a tool is what the knife was meant to be. But man's inherent need for beauty and ornamen-

These are Damascus blades by Peter Ytsebo destined for high-quality tollekniven.

Ytsebo finished knives are very much 20th century style without losing the practical nature of the form.

Norse insistence that the sheathed knife look good forces knifemakers to follow through as here.

tation brought forth an additional type: the knife for festive occasions, a pendant to holiday accouterments.

In the old days, the knife and especially the sheath played an important role in the engagement ceremony in some parts of Norway. When a girl reached marriageable age, her father took her to church and paraded her up and down the aisle while he chanted in a low voice: "My daughter wants to marry." If a boy desired her, he put his knife in the empty sheath she carried attached to her belt. It was a sad family if the girl repeatedly came back without a knife in her sheath!

Still today, there are young couples who exchange knives instead of rings when they marry. These are richly ornamented knives crafted by artists. Hers is small and his a bit larger. They are only worn on very special occasions; for the rest of the time they have honored places on the wall.

A knife was considered to be so much of a necessity and so much part of daily life, that early laws declared that even slaves should own knives.

There are an endless number of sayings that document the importance of being "knived." One of the juicier states that a man without his knife is like a lady of the night without her primary asset.

Although the knife was primarily a tool for everyday use, there are records of people being killed in knife fights. These are exceptions. People have been killed by hammers too, but this does not alter the hammer's classification as a tool. I know of no *tolle* knife which has been made primarily as a weapon. There are individual knives known as killer knives, but this is because they have been used for such a purpose, not made for it.

Until about 150 years ago, iron was produced from bog-ore on many Norwegian farms. Bog-ore is an iron deposit found in swamps in Scandinavia and as far south as nothern Germany. *(And in New Jersey — Editor.)* The ore was reduced to iron in pits dug in the ground. Wood was burned for heat. This type of ore cannot stand the temperatures used in modern steel making.

When the slag had been melted away, the lump of iron was taken out of the pit and hammered on a large stone while white-hot. To make steel, the operation was repeated at a higher temperature.

Iron and steel made in this way can be welded together by hammering when at the exact correct temperature. This is probably the forerunner of the present method of forming the blade by putting the steel between two pieces of iron and welding them together in such a way that the steel protrudes beyond the iron bits and forms the cutting edge of the knife.

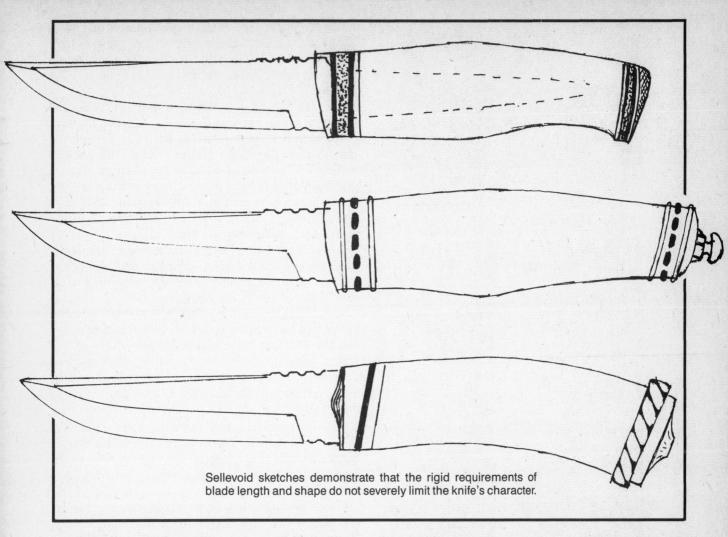

Sellevoid sketches demonstrate that the rigid requirements of blade length and shape do not severely limit the knife's character.

The blade of the Norwegian sheath knife is generally between 3 and 4 inches long, the exception is a big knife made by the Lapps in northern Norway. Those are used much like a machete in the jungle, to cut down small trees and branches.

Norwegian knifemakers do not put the same emphasis on a mirror-like finish on the blade as do their American counterparts. A nice finish is desired and achieved, but you do not get the mirror effect from the iron which borders the steel cutting edge.

The tang of a Norwegian sheath knife is almost always narrow and tapered and fits into a hole in a one-piece handle. You never see a full tang with the handle pieces fastened with rivets.

There is a typical Trondelag knife—Trondelag being the district around Trondheim in the middle of the country. The Morseth knife of the U.S.A. has its origins in this locality. Henry—or Harry—Morseth emigrated to the U.S. in the 1920s and settled in the state of Washington. He made very good and inexpensive knives. His heirs sold the firm to A.G. Russell of Springdale, Arkansas, where knives with the Morseth brand are still being made.

The custom of branding the knife with the name or initials of the maker makes the detective work of tracing a knife's heritage much easier. Not all knifemakers do the whole job themselves. Some buy the blade from some superior 'smith and do the rest themselves; and again others might buy the sheath. There are all possible types of assembly combinations in this business.

The handle is generally made from wood—birch, maple or another species with pleasing markings—and there are also handles made from horn, ivory, bone, leather or bark. In some instances, the tang goes all the way through the handle and is secured with a nut at the butt end, but there are also handles where the tang is forced into a tapered hole and fastened there by pressure, heat or other tricks of the trade. Wedges aren't used as they tend to work loose.

Very often the handle is ferruled at both ends, the ferrule being made from silver, brass or German silver and frequently engraved. Some very fine knives have silver and mother of pearl inlaid in the handle.

You hardly ever find hand guards on a Norwegian knife. They are found to be in the way when the hand is moved forward on the back of the blade for extra control in fine knife work.

Bone-handled knives are often engraved or scrimshawed, but this is thought to give the knife an impression of more novelty than seriousness. Where the tang

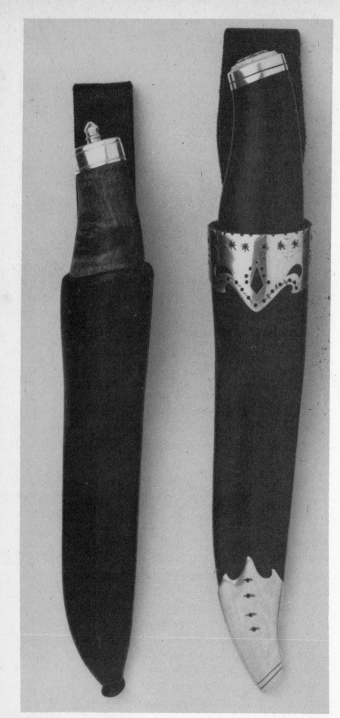

comes out at the butt of the handle the securing nut is always given an artistic appearance. This nut may have dual purposes: First to hold the blade tight and second as a button for a leather strap securing the knife in the sheath.

The sheath itself is an object of as much care as the rest of the knife. The seam is almost always on the back of the sheath which is formed over a last giving it the special shape the maker desires. You do find sheaths without any ornamentation, but more often you see that a pattern has been pressed into the moist leather. Some sheaths have silver tips at the bottom and ferrules around the tops and these may be decorated by really artistic silversmiths-cum-knifemakers.

Wooden sheaths, as well as those made from bone, generally come in two halves which are joined together with the aid of metal bands or ferrules, some of great artistic value. Simple rivets are also used.

Even the strap which attaches the knife and sheath to the bearer's belt is the result of much trial and error, and the different knifemakers swear by their special way of doing it. The importance of this can readily be understood by one who has lost a good knife and a dear friend just because the strap wasn't secured properly to the sheath.

In some parts of the country one can find special sheaths with room for two or more knives. This ensures the bearer the use of sharp knives, or he may carry different knives for the different tasks he would have to perform that special day.

Good handmade knives are becoming very popular and there is a growing interest in the art of knifemaking. Every fall there is a conference and exhibition of knives at the Museum of Forestry, Hunting and Fishing in Elverum (100 miles northeast of Oslo) and these meetings are very well attended. So far there is no Norwegian Knifemakers Guild, but it will probably come soon.

It is estimated that there are at least 350 active knifemakers in Norway today and that is an impressive number when one notes that the total population of Norway is only 4.5 million. If you should have proportionally the same number in the U.S., there should be 21,000 knifemakers. Are there?

Other dressed-up tollekniven from Sollevold employ tropical hardwoods, sterling silver, good leather for a rich, if relatively conservative, appearance.

Morseth knives from A.G. Russell are still made with Norwegian laminated blades from the same mill Harry Morseth used. (Weyer photo)

. . . And Elsewhere in Scandinavia

Axehead with inlays by Lundstrom is hafted with a curved handle like Frankish throwing axes.

Silver-inlaid laminated blade by Jan-Ake Lundstrom strives for and attains Viking-era character.

Copper and silver decoration are traditional styles; runes are the smith's name. This is Lundstrom work.

This is Jan-Ake Lundstrom himself, looking very much the Viking.

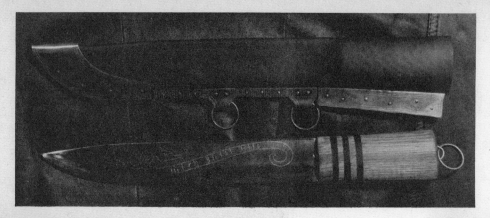

Large puuko-shaped blade must also be traditional, since Lundstrom made it.

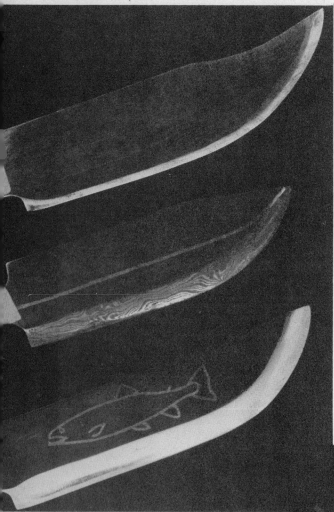

Anders Thorn, another Swedish knife-maker, says no machines touched this knife. The blade, in flame Damascus, is by Kaj Embretsen. The haft and sheath involve ebony, leather, elephant ivory, sterling silver and 18K gold as well as turquoise and amber. It's expensive, says Thorn, but good.

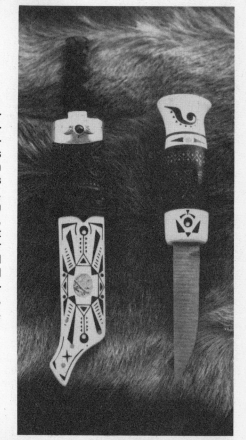

Lundstrom blades for modern carrying knives.

This Peteri Laiti knife is all work. A Lapp, he makes them to order through the Suomi shop here.

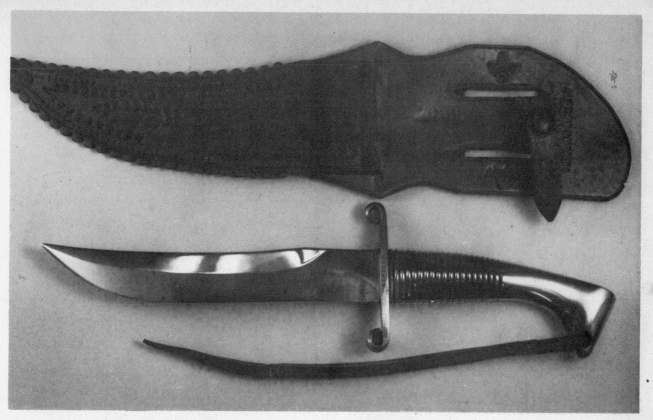

The all-out Nichols fighter looked like this, was furnished with an Alfred Cornish sheath.

THE FIGHTING KNIVES OF FLOYD NICHOLS

This sculptor did his bit in World War II, making fighting knives for our fighting men.

by

HARLAN SUEDMEIER

WOODCARVER, welder, sculptor, knifemaker—all describe the multi-talented Floyd Nichols of David City, Nebraska. A man of unlimited talents and vocations, these are the ones he advertised. From a metal and welding shop, his artistic ability led to the development of unusual forms of art, best known among them his use of an acetylene torch and bronze welding rod to create sculptures.

Nichols led a very adventurous life, starting with breaking wild horses at the young age of 14. Still in his teens, he strapped his gear behind the saddle, buckled on his gun belt and revolver, and headed for Wyoming to homestead. His road led to some memorable acquaintances and experiences. He worked at haying in the sandhills of Nebraska before continuing into the Badlands of South Dakota. Several weeks were spent with a band of Indians. Severe storms forced him to lie side by side with his horse, covered with a blanket.

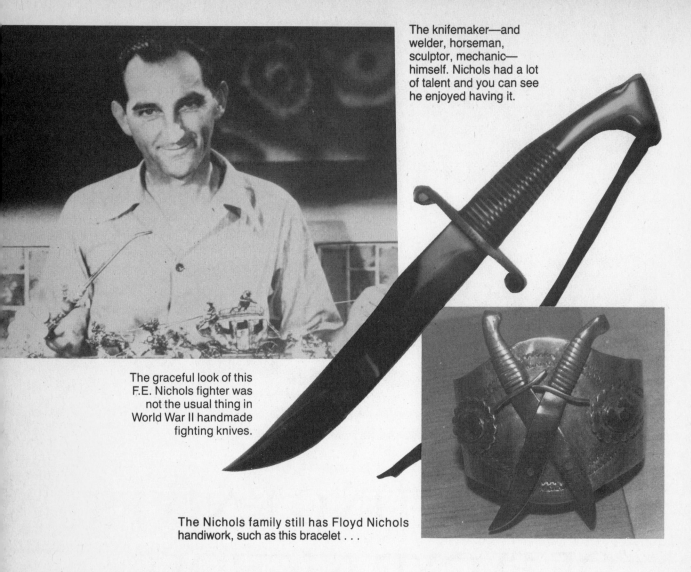

The knifemaker—and welder, horseman, sculptor, mechanic—himself. Nichols had a lot of talent and you can see he enjoyed having it.

The graceful look of this F.E. Nichols fighter was not the usual thing in World War II handmade fighting knives.

The Nichols family still has Floyd Nichols handiwork, such as this bracelet . . .

When he got to Wyoming, where he stayed with an uncle, he proceeded to apply for Homestead rights. Before he could obtain the land, World War I broke out. He enlisted in the military and was sent to Lincoln, Nebraska, for motorcycle training as a messenger courier.

After serving overseas, he returned to Nebraska and met and married Stella Staroscik in 1920. Floyd worked as a mechanic in the beginning—for a while on aircraft in Omaha, then as an auto mechanic in David City. Later he started his own welding and repair shop. It was then he started to make small metal figurines with a welding torch.

The figurines were well accepted because they were so detailed. Most were western, such as horses, stagecoaches, Indians, cowboys and wagons in various action poses. As his skills improved and his fame spread, his works were displayed in many cities: New York, Philadelphia, and Vancouver and Toronto in Canada were some. Two short documentary films also featured his works.

He turned down an invitation to tour for the USO during World War II, directing his talents instead to knifemaking. He had made a few knives prior to this

time, mainly in hunting style. He designed a fighting knife in response to the government's appeal for knives to be used in the war.

Several innovative ideas were incorporated into this knife. It had a long slender, yet stout, blade that would easily pierce a torso, sharpened more than halfway down the back for slashing. The bevel was ground on only one side of the blade on most of them. Some fancier and better finished examples have equally ground bevels. The blade material was a manganese steel, forged to a rough shape, then ground to final dimensions. They were heat-treated softer than his normal knives. The reason for this he stated, "It is better to come out of a fight with a bent knife than a broken knife."

A metal guard with a small loop forged on each end was made to slip over the tang. The handle was formed by wrapping 1/8-inch bronze or steel welding rod around the tang. The butt was formed of brass and welded on. It was this brass buttcap that produced the standout characteristic of the knife, because an Indian-head penny for "good luck" or a buffalo nickel, in reference to the maker's name, was welded into the upper

This is one of the few hunting knives Nichols made.

Author (and collector and knife-maker) Suedmeier is so intrigued with Floyd Nichols he has begun to make some knives in the Nichols style.

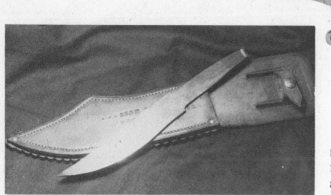

. . . and unfinished blades and unused sheaths as well.

side of this buttcap. Nichols sometimes stamped his name in a semi-circle around the coin. Some knives were produced without a coin, only the brass butt.

Another feature of Nichols' design was a leather strap fastened to the loops on the guard. This gave the user the capability to hang the knife from the wrist, leaving the hand free. This feature apparently did not catch on too well as most knives found have no thong.

The maker also stamped the serviceman's name, serial number or hometown on the edge of the guard. Many knives found will have this ground off, the explanation being, in case of capture there were no ties to endanger his family back home. And most Nichols knives were equipped with a very sturdy sheath made by Alfred Cornish of Omaha, Nebraska.

The Nichols production was about three knives per day. With the help of family members and old ledgers maintained by Mr. Nichols, we can document the production of around 1,200 knives. Several hundred letters from servicemen from all over the United States and some foreign countries are still in the possession of the Nichols family. The colorful and uniquely designed military stationery, combined with the stories they tell,

make very interesting reading. Some long-lasting friendships continued from some of these letters, long after the war was over.

An interesting sidelight to this story has come about. While following up a lead on a Nichols knife in central Iowa, I was given some current addresses of Army personnel who were also known to have owned Nichols knives. Two of these addresses were in Arizona, so I forwarded these two names to a good friend and fellow knife collector in Phoenix, Brad Watts. He located one in Yuma, the other in the Phoenix area, and found they had been best friends all through World War II, but had lost track of each other. Brad supplied them with each other's current address, which is a very good example of one of the many fine benefits of knife collecting. Incidentally, they both still had their Nichols knives.

Nichols continued his sculpture work and made a few hunting knives after the war. In 1950, he became ill with cancer. Bedridden, cared for by his wife Stella, he died Nov. 17, 1958. Stella continued to live in David City until her death in June of 1987.

A daughter, Ruth, continues the family art legacy with her paintings and bronze sculpting. It was with her help that much of this information has been compiled. I also had the pleasure of helping her obtain one of her father's knives as there were none retained in the family except for an unfinished blade.

Floyd Nichols was an exceptionally talented person in many areas. His legacy still lives and continues to grow as the interest in his artwork and knives increases.

NOT MUCH FOR

by BERNARD R. LEVINE

A two-blade barlow, with the pen blade honed thin and the master blade given a tougher edge, is up to most cutting chores.

The layout of the typical Barlow makes it a good tool.

This Russell Barlow counter box tells the whole story of the barlow knife's appearance.

GENUINE RUSSELL BARLOW JACK KNIFE

Not much to look at—But the blade stays sharp

price

A GOOD STRONG KNIFE MADE FROM FINEST STEEL

GET ONE NOW

FOR FIFTY YEARS THE BEST BLADE VALUE IN JACK KNIVES

WHEN YOU get down to basics, what is it you really want out of a knife? Sometimes we get so caught up in the pattern of a pocketknife, the romance of a Bowie, the workmanship of an art knife, or the versatility of a survival knife we forget that all we wanted the thing to do for us was to cut. Indeed, most of the time, when we reach for a knife, we just want to cut something. If the knife cuts easily and cleanly, and if the blade stays sharp a long time and resharpens without too much resistance, then we are so satisfied we probably don't give the humble thing a second thought. Most of the times one wants a knife, all one really cares about is this deep but unphilosophical question: Will it cut?

All around the world, people who work to earn their livings tend to be intensely practical about things. They won't spend more on tools than is necessary to get the job done. Working folks, even if they can afford some frills, just don't want them on their working tools. They may be willing to spend a little extra on quality — in an axe, a hammer, or a pocketknife — but cannot see how it makes any sense to spend money on fancy mate-

LOOKS, MAYBE. . . .

. . . . but knives for the working class must have quality in the blade.

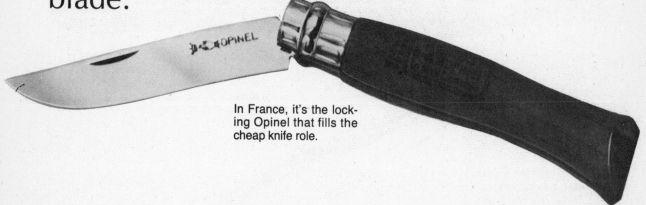

In France, it's the locking Opinel that fills the cheap knife role.

rials or a fine finish on a tool they plan to use hard.

Besides this tough-minded practicality, farmers and working men tend to have a deeply puritanical world view. A lot of them not only think frills are impractical, they go even further and believe them to be downright immoral. A man or woman of this stripe may sometimes spend extra money to obtain extra utility or durability, but believes it is always wrong — even sinful — to spend hard-earned coin on cosmetic frills. This outlook is broadly philosophical rather than purely religious and is shared by many who have never darkened the door of any sort of house of worship.

Knifemakers and cutlery manufacturers throughout the ages have known these practical and puritanical customers are a big part of their market, although almost by definition they are not a very profitable part of the knife company's market. However, since there are a lot of them out there, it is possible for a knife company, as my old economics professor Walter Falcon used to put it, "to lose a little bit on each one, but to try and make it up on volume."

Not the oldest but probably the best known of the American pocketknife types made for the hard-headed, cost-conscious consumer is the barlow. A barlow knife is a regular or sleeveboard jackknife with long front bolsters and no cap bolsters. Although some barlows have been dressed up in all sorts of odd and fanciful ways (ornate bolsters, file-work, even pearl handles), the basic barlow had plain steel bolsters and liners combined with flat undyed and unjigged bone handles.

For more than half a century (1875-1917; 1924-1941) the standard American barlow was the J. Russell, made in a couple of dozen variations in central Massachusetts (in Turner Falls until the mid-1930s, then in Southbridge). In its 1928 catalog, Russell summed up the essence of the barlow knife and of all plain and practical folders this way: "NOT MUCH FOR LOOKS BUT QUALITY IN THE BLADE."

Although the Russell was long the American standard barlow, most other cutlery firms doing business in the United States also offered a selection of them, since the barlow is a plain stout knife that can be sold at a modest price. Most of these firms followed Russell's example and stamped their name or trademark in their barlow's big bolsters. I guess their philosophy was: "If we can't make any money selling these low-priced knives, at least we can get some advertising benefit from them."

Many a young American, even before the days of Tom Sawyer and Huckleberry Finn, acquired a barlow as his first very own pocketknife. The makers hoped that each of these future consumers would feel loyal to the firm whose name was boldly stamped on the big bolsters of his first knife. Of course some barlows, such as the Imperial I bought new in 1963 for 49 cents, just say BARLOW on the bolsters, which in that case were stamped out of sheet steel. Its carbon steel blades, however, in the venerable barlow tradition, were really of very good quality.

Long strong bolsters, as used on barlows, seem to go back in history at least as far as we can trace metal-bladed knives. I have seen them on medieval knives dredged from the bottom of the Thames River in London. However, *barlow* knives under that name were

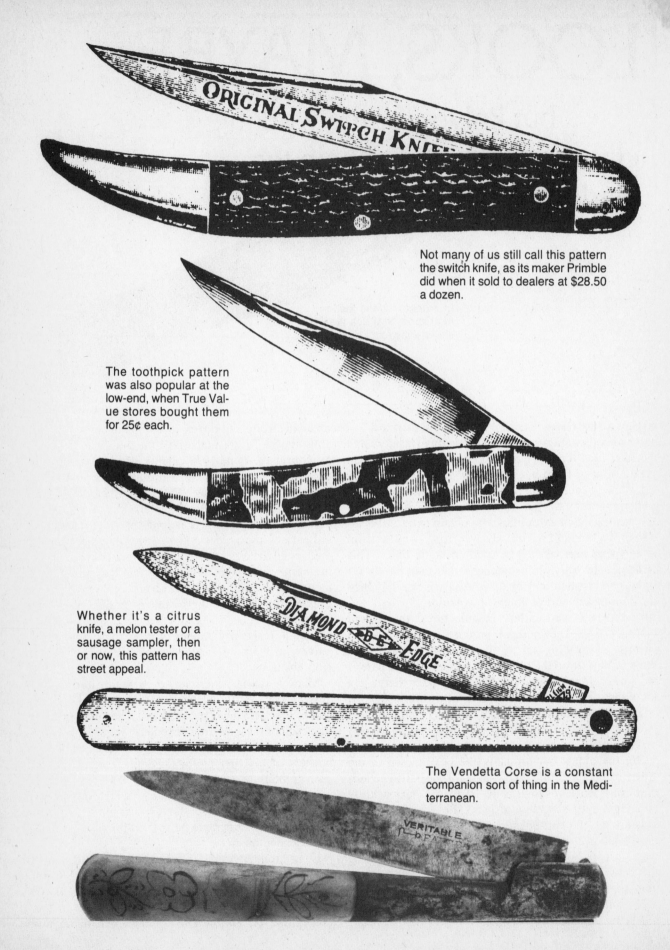

Not many of us still call this pattern the switch knife, as its maker Primble did when it sold to dealers at $28.50 a dozen.

The toothpick pattern was also popular at the low-end, when True Value stores bought them for 25¢ each.

Whether it's a citrus knife, a melon tester or a sausage sampler, then or now, this pattern has street appeal.

The Vendetta Corse is a constant companion sort of thing in the Mediterranean.

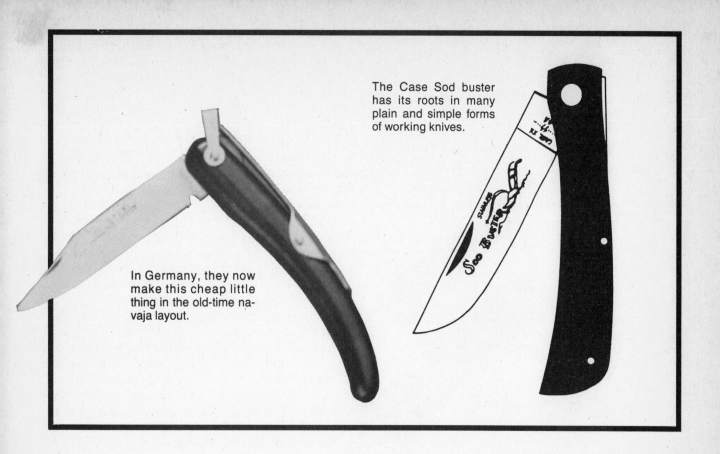

The Case Sod buster has its roots in many plain and simple forms of working knives.

In Germany, they now make this cheap little thing in the old-time navaja layout.

first made by cutlers named Barlow (or Barlowe) in Sheffield in the mid-1600s. Actual people named Barlow, with more or less exclusive claim to use of the name, made Barlow knives up until about the 1830s. The earliest known illustrated cutlery catalog distributed in the United States, Smith's 1816 *Sheffield Manufactories,* showed a couple of these real Barlows. Those examples have the long bolsters characteristic of all barlows, but short slim blades and curved pistol-grip handles make them look more like quill knives.

In recent years, the leading contender in the plain, practical, no-frills, hard-working pocketknife category is the mid-size lockback clasp-type folding hunter with molded reinforced plastic handles. The first of these frugal (under $20) high-tech knives, and still for my money the best engineered, is the Gerber LST. It comes in basic black, like a Model-T Ford, and also in red and blaze orange and green-leaf camouflage. Camo is really a bad idea for a field knife, because if you drop it in grass or leaves, you will never find it again. Out in the woods orange is the most practical, but around town black is more discreet. The new red color must be the middle ground.

Most of the other major players in the cutlery game now make relatively inexpensive plastic-handled knives of this general type. I guess the best-looking is the Coleman-Western 526, but being a plain, practical parsimonious person myself, I'll stick with my Gerber.

On the dark side of cheap and practical American

pocketknives are the patterns and styles favored for "social" occasions. Earlier in this century, the pocketknife pattern most in vogue on the wrong side of the tracks was the tickler or powder-horn pattern, known among others as the chaser, the tango, or the switch knife, and among still others as a fishing knife. This is an American interpretation to the basic southern European clasp knife, right down to the pointed handle end, which on the original was the tip of a cow or sheep horn.

Most such "switch" knives were not real switchblades, but they could be opened just as fast. The traditional mode of carry was to wedge a matchstick into the handle under the belly of the blade, so that the point would protrude a little. As the knife was drawn then, the point could be caught on a seam or pocket, and the blade pulled open with lightning speed.

More recently the cheap pocketknife pattern most favored for mayhem, especially in the Southwest and California, is the long slim melon or sausage tester. Enough melon tester blades have turned up snapped off in the bodies of murder victims that some firms have voluntarily discontinued distributing them. There is nothing especially wrong or dangerous about melon testers unless you are a melon; they just happen to be the cheapest long-bladed pocketknife on the market right now. Many are given away as free advertising premiums by fruit packing concerns.

The average European peasant or working man is at

The cat knife has been made in Germany for 80 years at least.

Author's choice for the everyday knife today, his pick of the litter, is the Gerber LST.

least as tight-fisted and hard-headed as the most puritanical American. When you talk *plain* knives, they don't get much plainer than some of the Old World types.

The very plainest of the plain are what I call "penny" knives. A penny knife consists of a light gauge blade, a slotted one-piece handle of wood or horn, a single rivet, and maybe a sheet metal ferrule. Knives of this general type have been made all over Europe (and Asia, too) for centuries, and probably millennia. Some are still made the old-fashioned way, hand forged and assembled, such as by an outfit called Bofil in the town of Vich, in the province of Barcelona, in the region of Catalonia, which is reluctantly, Catalans say, in Spain.

In fact, Bofil's methods would have seemed old-fashioned 200 years ago. I have on microfilm a remarkable treatise written in France in the 1770s on the factory mass-production of "common" folding knives. The factory shown has such modern conveniences as water-driven trip hammers and bellows. These allowed penny knives to be produced more economically there than anywhere else in the world at that time.

Modern penny knives, incorporating the slick "new" Virobloc locking mechanism, invented around 1900, are made by Opinel in Cognin, Savoie, in the Alpine region of France. Opinels are imported to the United States by Gutmann, and are sold in fancy mail-order catalogs as "picnic knives," but in France they occupy the niche long held by the barlow knife here: the favorite of boys, dirt farmers, and day laborers.

Opinels and other penny knives are light in weight and thus suited only for careful cutting. Down in Corsica, where knife fighting is a way of life, the locals have a plain style of knife called the *Vendetta Corse*. It has a straight, stout, sharp-pointed blade made for stabbing, long self-guard steel bolsters, and smooth bone or plastic handles. Most have a sort of semi-lock that discourages the blade from folding accidentally, but that must be forcibly "broken" to close the knife. A real *Vendetta Corse* has no lock release.

Northern Europeans, too, have favored styles of plain and practical folding knives. Leading in popularity today, and since the late 1950s, are simple lockbacks with black or bright-colored plastic handles. These styles pre-date the recent era of reinforced composite plastics, so most have two separate molded handles affixed to metal liners or frame pieces.

One German firm, Heinrich Kaufmann & Soehne, still makes an inexpensive, all-steel, self-guard, lockback, first introduced before World War I. This K55K Mercator "Black Cat" is the grandaddy of all modern all-steel lockbacks, and is still a better design than most of them. A friend of mine, a third-generation cutler from Romania who stocks dozens of every knife in current production, still carries a Black Cat in his own pocket in preference to all others.

Other German firms, especially Freidrich Herder Abr. Sohn, make a big, low-cost, bolsterless, wood handled folder with a light-gauge blade. This style knife was the direct antecedent of Case's plastic-handled Sod-Buster, and was at least part of the inspiration for Buck's seminal Model 110 Folding Hunter.

In Sweden a century ago, the plain inexpensive "folding" knife for ordinary use was the barrel knife. I put "folding" in quotes, because this stout *sloyd*-type knife had to be laboriously taken apart to open or close its blade, but at least one never had to worry about its closing accidentally on one's fingers. Of course, Swedes and other Scandinavians most often carried small sheath knives as work knives.

Most other countries also had, and have, their traditional everyman's knives. The English had jackknives with "Real Lambfoot" blades. Irish farm laborers still ask Dublin cutlers if they sell the "Ere a (ERA) Barber" knife. Mexicans have favored, of late, big lightweight hawkbills for work in the fields. The Japanese liked little springless folders with laminated blades and stamped sheet steel handles, that look to us more like straight razors.

As long as people continue to use knives, there will always be demand for plain no-frills folders. Hardly anyone gets rich selling these pedestrian knives — real money is more readily made in catering to people who already have real money. Still, if you come up with a good simple practical design, the world might just beat a path to your doorstep, and with luck you might be able to "make it up on volume."

This handsome Ralph Harris Big Bear, decoration apart, is very, very close to the Loveless knife. It was made in 1987 or 1988. (Long photo)

This graceful curved fighter by John Fuller is several design generations from Loveless. You can see it — the heel of the handle, the choice of grind line along the back — but you have to know how to look. (Long photo)

THE ESCAPE FROM LOVELESS

The clones are starting to fade away

by KEN WARNER

BOB LOVELESS did it; he got away from Randall. Now it looks as though some other guys are going to do it: they are going to get away from Loveless. As time moves along, fewer and fewer of the young whipper-snappers are voting the straight Loveless ticket as so many did for so long.

Perhaps you remember? All of a sudden, from rooms full of tables filled with clones of Randall knives, we jumped—those of us who went to the very few knife shows there were—straight into rooms full of tables full of knives designed by Robert Loveless. It was legitimately awesome. Seldom have so many owed so much to so few, to steal a phrase. The earth moved; I swear it did.

That was 20 years ago. And 20 years is a long time in the world of design. In those worlds where design is everything—fashion, advertising, housewares, automobiles, you name it—there just aren't very many 20-year phenomena. It may take Mercedes 20 years to get

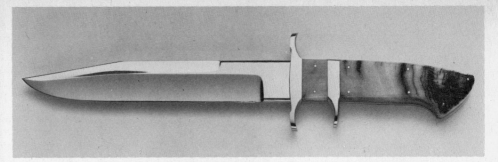

Lloyd Pendleton, all unabashed and by-permission Loveless follower, gets his Big Bears straight, too. (Weyer photo)

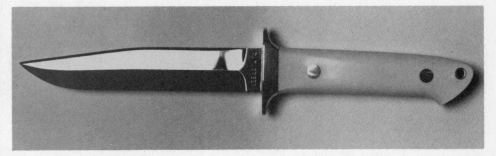

Loveless could not get a Big Bear closer to his standard than Hank Kubaiko. (Long photo)

Roger M. Green here collects the full Loveless score in a boat knife, made in the last year or so.

Tom Mayo just made this Big Bear for a Karate black belt who doesn't want to use his ivory-handled Loveless Big Bear in demonstration.

These Wayne Clay Loveless-pattern fighters take a few liberties, but very few. (Long photo)

from one look to another; it probably takes Rolls Royce 30 years to do it; I don't profess to know how things like prestige watches and such change; I do know about guns and they have to be a special case because a fair share of the most commercially successful guns of recent decades have been those which most successfully mimicked the best features of guns from the past.

So there we have Bob Loveless, the guy who, to quote him, can "make them look a little sexier than the rest." He is still selling at very good prices every knife he makes, seated firmly on a throne that suits him.

And now, finally, knifemakers are beginning to design knives more or less from scratch again. That is important. Loveless knives were liberating influences on the one hand and provided both foil and counterfoil on a couple of other hands. Were it not for the ubiqui-

tous Loveless patterns, it might be that bladesmithing over a hot forge would not be quite so attractive as an alternative; and the Loveless patterns have, for some audiences, left a market behind, a market being filled very nicely by those who still admire and use and can put together knives in the designs of Randall.

There is, right this moment as it happens, a new candidate for a few of the Loveless laurels as a basic designer of modern knives. A number—reaching into the dozens—of craftsmen who make high-class folders have chosen to adopt the Michael Walker lock and, indeed, the general Walker shape and style of knives and sell them with their own names on them. It is probably going to bemuse Mr. Walker over some considerable length of time; certainly, it will bemuse many a knife buyer to attend a knife show and see three and four

The only constants in Michael Walker's knives — and here are 12 recent ones — are his eye for line, high technical proficiency and the liner lock, except sometimes he experiments with locks. (Weyer photo)

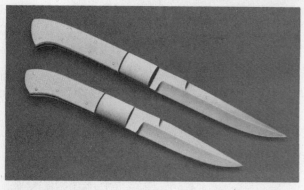

These Patrick Donovan fighters have blades ground like Loveless blades, but the rest is Donovan. (Weyer photo)

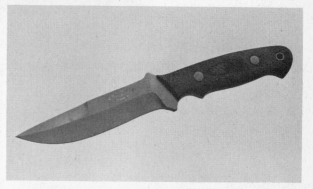

W.C. Davis makes a lot of these fighters, and most every line is Bill Davis. (Long photo)

This is R.W. Loveless' newest design — the two-edges-on-the-same-side Pro Hunter. It will be produced, with bolster and tapered tang, as a Beretta-Loveless. Maybe Loveless is getting away, too. (Long photo)

This Loveless knife is called a Stiff Horn. Loveless had a great deal to do with Jess Horn's folder design, liked this profile, and has made quite a few. (Long photo)

knifemakers from all points of the compass lined up in a row, each showing his near-to-the-original Michael Walker locker. And most of them giving full credit, though not, it may be presumed, much of the proceeds.

Several knifemakers have had a run at being copied. Bob Lum, for example, pretty well set the style for the tanto. That phenomenon came on so quickly that Lum did not get his seal so completely on the tanto as Michael Walker has with his style of liner lock.

The Walker liner lock is nothing like the little piece of brass found so often on fishing knives and electricians' knives and the TL 29 military tool knife. The Walker lock is far more positive, and the lock may very well be the feature that has swung so many people over to making Walker lockers. A series of tests was performed on a wide variety of locking designs and the

results given some small circulation among the experts in these matters and in that test the Walker locker performed better than almost all of them, which included in addition to the standard articles of trade such esoterica as the Poehlmann knife and the Boyd knives and Ray Appleton's intricate little lockblade devices.

Regardless of all that, there is Michael Walker being copied—in fact, there is already a commercial copy which doesn't work very well out there. Others are planned, to the point where Michael Walker himself may be participating with one or another. If these can get the Walker style as well as sound Walker locks, they will be very salable.

The experience of being such a design leader is no doubt going to be a mixed blessing for Mr. Walker. The knife is certainly a very good knife, and many examples

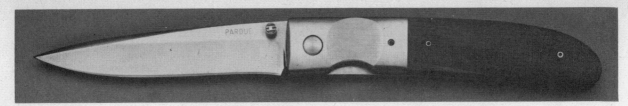

Mel Pardue's liner-locker looks just like its design daddy; Pardue advertises its lock is Walker's development. (Weyer photo)

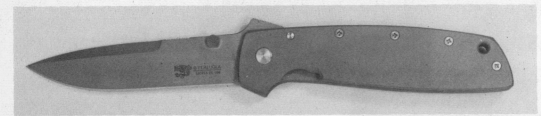

Bob Terzuola went to Walker to learn to make the lock, does his knives, though, to suit his military-type buyers.

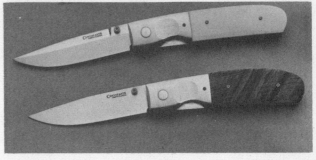

Howard Viele, who can make any profile his own with his sense of line, has decided to make liner lockers, acknowledges Walker. (Weyer photo)

Frank Centofante is trying a few liner locks, does them very nicely. (Weyer photo)

Randall Gilbreath seems to fall, in these patterns, somewhere between Pardue and Terzuola, but that locking system is a Walker-type. (Long photo)

Martial artist Ernest Emerson believes the Michael Walker knife — its action, its lock, its low weight-to-size ratio — to be the best personal protection design.

of it have been seen in these pages over the years. Why select the Walker locker to copy? Well, as we have said, it is a very good knife. The other thing is that Michael Walker himself has never wavered from this design once he found it. He has been leading the parade for a long time and they have only now caught up. And that is how this design leadership thing works.

There will not again occur the impact of a Loveless not anytime soon, and there will probably never again be the creative staying power of a Randall. The field has now so many practitioners, so many individual platforms on which to rest careers at the grinding wheel or in the forge, that the future is likely to be ruled by people doing their own thing, shaped and influenced, of course, but principally their own thing, without relationship in the design sense to others.

There are exceptions. Certainly the leader of the bladesmithing faction is one. Bill Moran however did not triumph—and he did triumph—in the design sense. He made things happen with a process, with the assertion of a technical difference. And that is a different story.

It is a good thing that Loveless patterns are less intrusive on every hand than once they were. It opens up the eyes of the people who plan the knives to patterns and shapes of their own.

Once you get past some essentials, such as sharpness and comfort in the hand and suitability to the cuts being made, a knife can be a nearly infinitely variable tool. When there are very strong design leaders, new practitioners have a way mapped, but they get it at the cost of individuality. When there is not so obviously a top gun, the new guys have to get their patterns where they can.

That is a good thing, as you can see here.

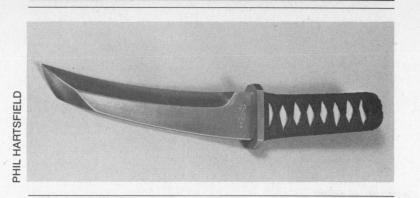

PHIL HARTSFIELD

There could be dozens of subdivisions of this view of knives. We're trying to provide both in-depth views of what is happening in the mainstream of knifemaking, and also look at the fringes. We think some of those will become mainstream soon.

We're showing mostly hand or benchmade knives here, made one at a time and usually hand-ground and hand-finished without jigs or fixtures. some knives, folders particularly, benefit from machine work or other precision techniques and so there are some such here. Some commercial knives fall into our categories, as well, either for their functional design or particular good looks.

These are the trend-setting knives, as we see them.

Ken Warner

Tut, Tut, and All That
Bush Swords
All Kinds of Hunters
Two Blades? Three? More?
Scagel Returns
Kukris Yet Again
Multi-Blade Straight Knives
The Folding Standards
Straight Standards
Leather and Such
Handmade for $50 or So
Ever the Twain Shall Meet
The Working Straight Edge
Sword Play
Easy Riders
The Land of the Small
Knives of the Year
Miscellany

TRENDS
TUT, TUT, AND ALL THAT

IT WOULD SEEM that it is going to be a while before anyone, including Buster Warenski, tops the remarkable Warenski rendition of the gold dagger of the Egyptian King Tutankhamen. Much has been made of this tour-de-force in the creation of a heavy money knife as well it should have been.

If the pictures you see do not do the Warenski knife justice, there is no way this poor typewriter is going to do it. The knife and the efforts and the knifemaker have already been the subject of several thousands of well-chosen words appearing in magazines for the past year. It took lots and lots of hours, the development of specific skills few of us have even heard of—such as first creating and then teaching little balls of gold to stay put on a flat surface—and then making it all hold together so that the replication turns out to be absolutely in the same class as the original.

It may be some time, as we have said, before this is topped, but that doesn't mean that the boys aren't out there trying. You can see here some really elaborate big-ticket items created for what we call "serious" collectors. A serious collector is a fellow who'll pay thousands of top dollars for a single knife.

I suppose the knives shown on these pages demonstrate the egalitarian nature of America. Throughout history, such creations were destined to influence the thinking of kings and emperors, to shape the fate of nations, even to shepherd the soul of a man-god into eternity as it rested beside him in a tomb buried beneath the sands of Egypt. Now, we just do it for cash and for all comers, but we do it very well.

Ken Warner

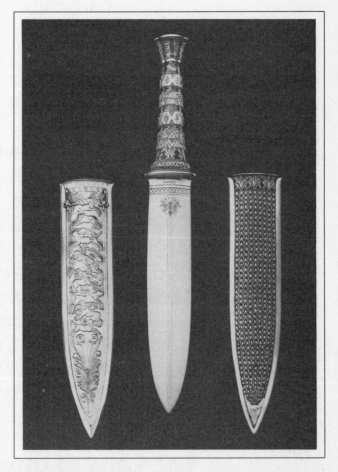

Double exposure shows the Buster Warenski Tut knife and both sides of its sheath. One man did this; scores probably worked on the original; both are very colorful. (Weyer photo)

Phil Lobred, who commissioned this extraordinary event, is shown with the knife's display at left and Warenski at right. (Weyer photo)

With C. Peterson's Damascus steel and horn and Julie Warenski gold inlay, Warenski is now making some less effortful knives like this high-end dagger. (Weyer photo)

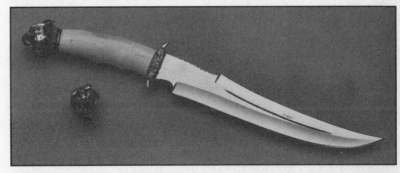

Ivory and about a pound of sterling silver and a nice concept make this Norman Bardsley Sabertooth dagger a collector special. (Weyer photo)

This is H.H. Frank doing what he does in gold and ivory and pearl and steel. You're looking at over $10,000 worth of knives.

(Right) Alaskan jade, his own Damascus, and Lynton McKenzie engraving and inlaying, make this lady's boot knife by Jot Khalsa a strong ticket, even if it is only 8¼ inches long.

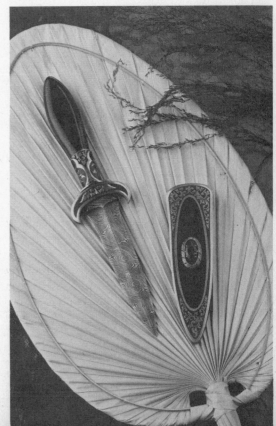

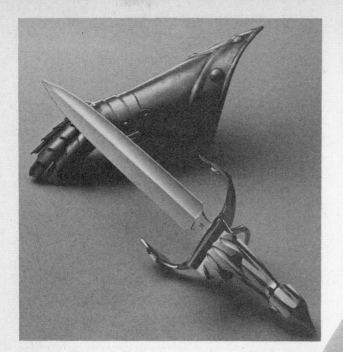

It doesn't have to be either traditional or crusted with gold if it has that big buck appeal which this Chris Miller large-scale stainless steel dagger did. (Weyer photo)

T.M. Dowell did this integral hunter in 440C and Ron Skaggs did the gold and engraving work—a non-flashy gem. (Weyer photo)

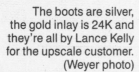

The boots are silver, the gold inlay is 24K and they're all by Lance Kelly for the upscale customer. (Weyer photo)

(Left) Jim Ence made the dagger in Damascus, ivory and gold; Gary Blanchard sculpted the eagle dancer out of the solid blade. Such work ain't cheap. (Weyer photo)

TRENDS
BUSH SWORDS

THE WONDERMENT in watching factories and individual makers of knives try to stay just a little bit ahead of consumer interest in knives is to see the forms and the functions get mixed and matched. In the present instance, several trends of the past few years have mixed and matched to create something that can only be called a bush sword. Indeed, some examples are cataloged thus by purveyors of militaria.

The non-connoisseur might conclude from a glance at these pictures that the bush sword is a big knife. Things are not so simple. A camp knife is a big knife; a machete is a big knife, a kukri is a big knife; a bush sword is that and more.

These are not swords, either. (It is not necessary to point out that a sword is not a big knife, regardless of what all those Indians thought?) A sword is a weapon of both offense and defense, intended for use against enemies of a certain size, ranging from stags and such, for which there are such designs as hunting swords and *hirschfangen* and hangers to people, against which the swordsmen of the ages have been able to bring scores and hundreds of separately and distinctly designed swords.

No, the bush sword is in its, however narrow, own role. It is designed to work and to fight. It is also designed to be very impressive. The bush sword is distinctly a tough, rough-looking number.

It may take any of several forms. Notable in recent memory has been Tom Maringer's "combat machete"

which he did not know was a bush sword. It was a falchion-shaped 24-inch (or so) high-tech heavy hitter.

Another in the forefront of the bush sword design race has been Chris Reeve, the South African. One could actually call the Chris Reeve bush sword a big knife, since it is simply scaled up from Reeve's famous one-piece edged combat tools. When we say scaled-up, we mean *really* scaled-up, since the Reeve bush sword is about 3 inches across in the blade, which is double-edged and perhaps 18 inches long. This is a nasty instrument.

You can see others close at hand. I suppose the principal practical distinctions between what we are here calling a bush sword and a big knife or a work knife is, first, a sword-like look, and then the potential for delivering a thrust (as well as several other kinds of blows) and finally size which is just about as big as such instruments can be and still be expected to accomplish useful work. To that point, it ought to be noted that a bush sword is heavier than a real sword or an ordinary sword or a regular sword or whatever. A genuine sword is normally as light as its makers can make it. Not so the bush sword.

You will see hereabouts a few recent examples. There may well be more in the future, but perhaps not. Necessarily, a bush sword is a relatively expensive piece of equipment, which generally means that, barring overriding need perceived by consumerdom, no real commercial market ever develops.

Ken Warner

This is, of course, a flaming bush sword, indeed, a Maringer flamer which we know because that is Tom Maringer holding it. (VerHoeven photo)

(Below) this super-machete with point is a working bush sword. Tom Maringer who made it (with an 18-inch blade of ATS34) regards it as a Vorpal sword, simply part of his regular line. (VerHoeven photo)

This is Frank Vought's 12-inch *golok,* a Filipino shape and a good work knife with a good point and a Kydex sheath.

This is a Vought 18-inch *golok* straightened out into something else—a flat-out bush sword of considerable merit.

These Barteaux and Sons cutlasses are heavy-weight brush cutters, but that handle and just enough point takes them out of the machete class. They come in straight or stainless. (Warner photo)

(Left and right) This is Pat Tomes' lady-size machete which has proven also to be a boy-sized bush sword, proven on bushes by one Joseph Warner. (Warner photo)

You can get this Marauder from Blackjack Knives in several lengths. This is the longest.

(Above, right and far right) These three 12-inch knives from (top down) Tom Enos, Bob Lum, and Fred Roe are already *short bush* swords; at 16 inches these patterns would be in the big leagues.

If these handsome DiGangi 14-inch carving knives are any clue, this maker could start making bush swords tomorrow.

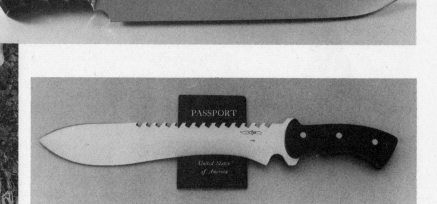

Tom Enos borrowed the lines and features of this big one from several sources.

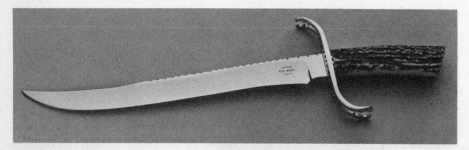

Curiously enough, a forged Sabatier 12-inch slicer is another bush dirk, more fragile no doubt than it should be, but it will cut light green brush. (Warner photo)

Jack Crain's big Predator movie knife is a pretty heavy-duty bush sword—it's 12-inches long overall. (Weyer photo)

Ken Ward's short hanger, or hunting sword, is a somewhat dressy response to the brush sword function. (Weyer photo)

Paul Sheehan's straightened kukri offers a useful point and a curved edge. (Weyer photo)

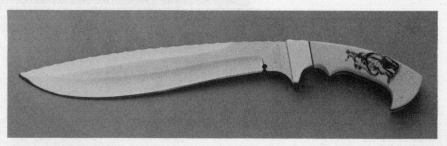

ALL KINDS OF HUNTERS

HUNTING is the reason most of us can claim a use for belt knives in the United States. There are, of course, more hunting knife owners than there are hunters, but that is a different discussion.

Handmade knife design and construction possibilities and techniques have, in the main, trickled down from the benches of those who sought, first of all, to make American sorts of hunting knives. If you prefer to believe the techniques and knowhow have trickled *up* from farm boys and shade tree mechanics who were just getting a usable knife together the best way they could — OK. Whatever.

Either way, where we are is with seven or eight clearly defined types of hunting knives commonly handmade here today. They have the following sorts of blades: drop point, straight, trailing point, clipped point, skinning, semi-skinning, and pelting and caping blades. Because human ingenuity is big in knives, there is another category called *other*.

And that is how we display them here, type by type. If you cannot find an appealing hunting knife among these five dozen knives, you are very, very picky.

Ken Warner

Stout Jesse Davis straight hunter is close to everyman's idea of a good belt knife. (Long photo)

A Butch Beaver semi-skinner in ATS34 and ironwood engraved by Fred Harrington is a good start on how upscale a hunter can get. (Weyer photo)

D'Alton Holder knows where all the lines are for the irreproachable drop hunter. (Long photo)

The classic hollow-ground blade graces this handsome Steve Johnson drop-point. (Long photo)

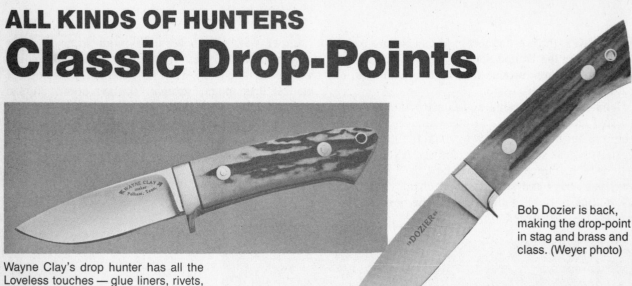

ALL KINDS OF HUNTERS
Classic Drop-Points

Wayne Clay's drop hunter has all the Loveless touches — glue liners, rivets, handle profile, hollow grind — in fine style. (Long photo)

Bob Dozier is back, making the drop-point in stag and brass and class. (Weyer photo)

Prizewinning T.M. Dowell drop-point in D2 boasts integral guard and pommel, ironwood grip. (Weyer photo)

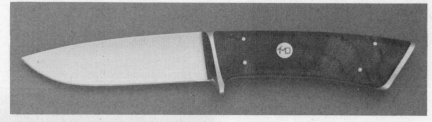

From way down in New Zealand, Bill Reddiex weighs in with as American a drop-point as ever was. (Scadlock photo)

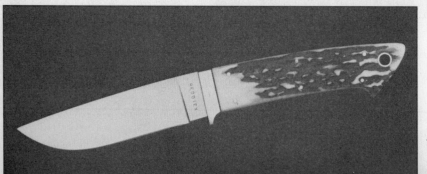

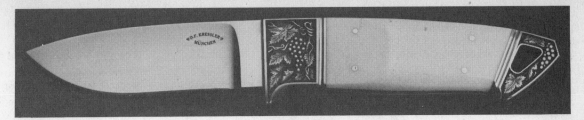

D.F. Kressler works the full integral side of the street to take classic drop hunters about as far as they can go. (Weyer photo)

Franz Becker can carry out the classic drop-point in full integral style, too. (Weyer photo)

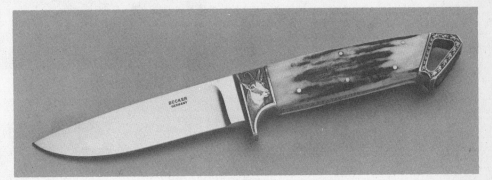

ALL KINDS OF HUNTERS
Classic Drop-Points

The point on this Rudy Wehner drop hunter is finer and the mirror finish isn't furnished, but it's a knife in the classic mode.

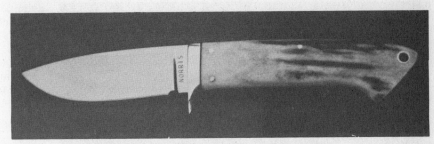

Short Mike Norris drop-point has all the tapers, and nickel silver and stag, classic fashion.

Frank Lampson understates the classic profile, but it is all there in this hunter.

This Roger Green drop-point hunter gets right after it, nicely proportioned.

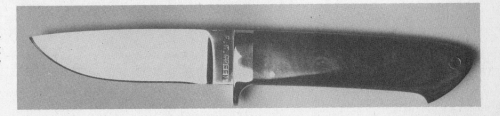

In Yuma, the Vikings who hang around D.E. Weiler's forge think a Damascus drop-point should have a *real* handle. (Allen photo)

Greg Dion's deluxe hunter has the dropped point, but its silhouette is different.

This prizewinner for Frank Vought rings some different changes on the drop-point theme.

ALL KINDS OF HUNTERS
Other Drop-Points

Bob Enders did a rope trick on this hunter's blade, and that's Fred Harrington engraving. (Weyer photo)

Bob Crowder's sheephorn-handled drop-point has a handsomely curved profile, George Sherwood engraving. (Rice photo)

Corbet Sigman has, in this hunter, dropped the point quite far, added finger placements to the handle. (Long photo)

It's very contemporary, but this Mike Wesolowski stainless-and-bocote knife is a 3¹/₂-inch straight hunter. (Weyer photo)

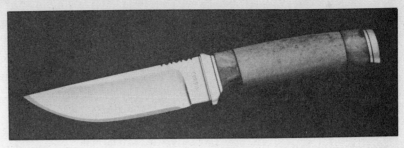

A no-nonsense blade dressed up with a handle compounded of oosic and amber makes a handsome straight hunter from Corbin Newcomb. (Scadlock photo)

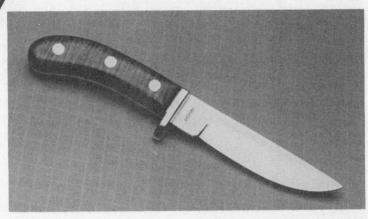

A real working handle gives this Rick Shuford knife a lot of appeal.

ALL KINDS OF HUNTERS
Straight Hunters

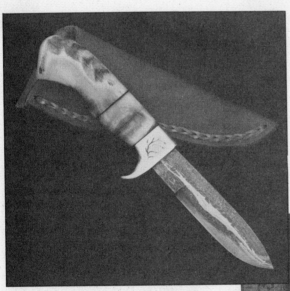

Terry Knipschield makes a very graceful bolster-cum-guard on his straight hunter model.

Ed Fowler uses ramshorn and forged cable for this hunter. (Scadlock photo)

Morris Pulliam forged this one, hafted it simply, making it a very straight, straight hunter. (Kelley photo)

This pair by Stewart G. Rowe, who also calls himself House of Kogatana, use the same pattern, made differently in half a dozen details.

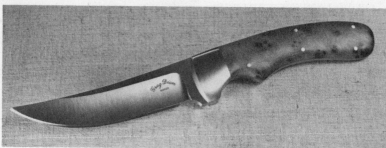

Deep hollow grinds and strong backs come easily to trailing-point blades like this Jerry Snell hunter.

HUNTERS OF ALL KINDS
Trailing-Points

Bob Lum's rendition of the old Woodcrafter pattern looks every bit as useful as the original.

This Greg Dion hunter has a high point and a very usable handle.

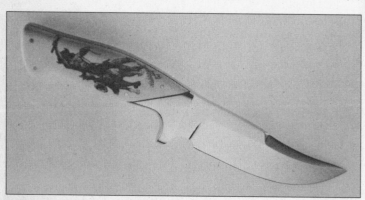

Norm Levine calls this trail-point, scrimmed by E.W. Schulenburg, an extra heavy-duty hunter.

H&W are two guys from Pace, Florida, who do clean work.

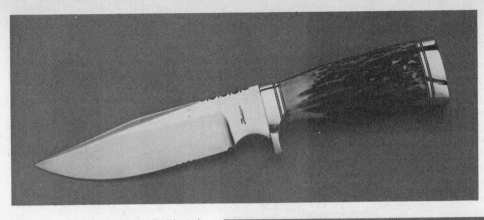

This Ed Thuesen clip-point hunter is a big knife — that's a 6½-inch blade of D2. (Weyer photo)

Bill DeFreest calls his sub-hilt (very understated) hunter Big Muddy, furnishes its 6½-inch blade of ATS34 with a clipped point. (Weyer photo)

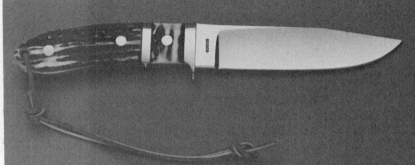

This Larry Page clip-point design provides a lot of slicing edge in ATS34

HUNTERS OF ALL KINDS
Clip-Points

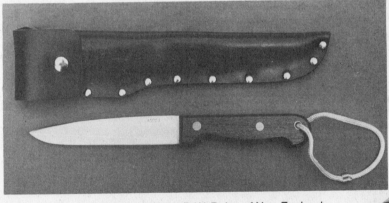

Serviceable clip-point by B.W. Baker of New Zealand is a low-cost plain vanilla belt knife. (Warner photo)

Ivory and 440C and a very smooth clip to a fine point make this Willie Rigney hunter sleek. (Weyer photo)

This Rudy Wehner clip design moves a fine point and the edge down below the knuckles when in work.

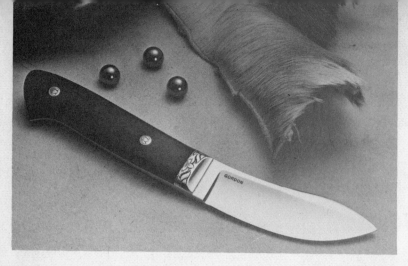

(Left) Modern classic Green River pattern by Bill DeFreest, touched up with a graver by Scott Pilkington, is as clean as it can be. (Long photo)

(Below left) Vernon Davis sticks to the tried and true and good-looking in this heavy-duty skinning knife.

(Below) Tony Taglienti puts a lot of features into his skinner, dresses them up with contrasting satin and mirror finishes. (Scadlock photo)

ALL KINDS OF HUNTERS
Skinners

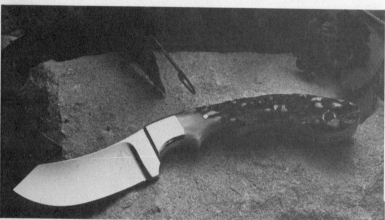

Much-imitated Larry Harley skinner puts the edge below the hand. (Long photo)

(Below) The longest of these lightweight Micarta-handled skinners by Billy Mace Imel is just 8 inches overall, but each has a lot of curved edge. (Weyer photo)

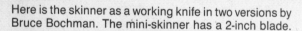
Here is the skinner as a working knife in two versions by Bruce Bochman. The mini-skinner has a 2-inch blade.

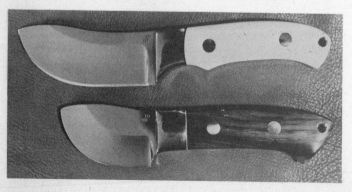

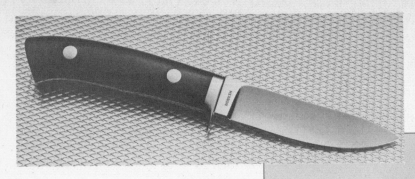

George Herron's semi-skinner classically straightens the curved skinning blade to get a woods-useful tool. (Long photo)

Tom Mayo stretches a point here to get to a very sharp end in the semi-skinner pattern.

This 4-inch semi-skinner by Randy Phillips has all the classic stuff, including stag. (Fitzgerald photo)

ALL KINDS OF HUNTERS
Semi-Skinners

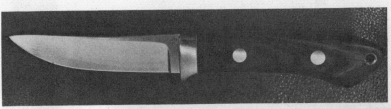

This Bruce Bochman semi-skinner has hand-rubbed metal, cocobolo; he calls it a utility hunter.

Gary Gouker jazzes this one up with mirror-polished bolsters, and a mammoth ivory inlay in the ironwood grip. (Weyer photo)

Behind all the classy touches — the shaped butt cap, for instance — this Rudy Wehner semi-skinner is a good tool.

Pete Forthofer's differently styled semi-skinner offers bighorn sheep handle and Tony Lageose engraving.

This superb very small skinner by Steve Johnson offers 1³/₄-inch blade, 2¹/₂-inch handle. (Long photo)

Sid Birt chose Damascus blades and bone handles for this set of game management tools. (Weyer photo)

This Steve Price caper set is small enough to carry and shaped for the whole job. (Fedorak photo)

ALL KINDS OF HUNTERS
Small Hunters and Capers

Frank Gamble forged this cute 3-inch skinner shape from an 01 round bar to be a bird and trout knife. (Weyer photo)

This high-style shape, here from J.D. Clay, can work in hard-to-reach places.

Don Norton's clip-point skinner is another little one, has Cape buffalo horn scales.

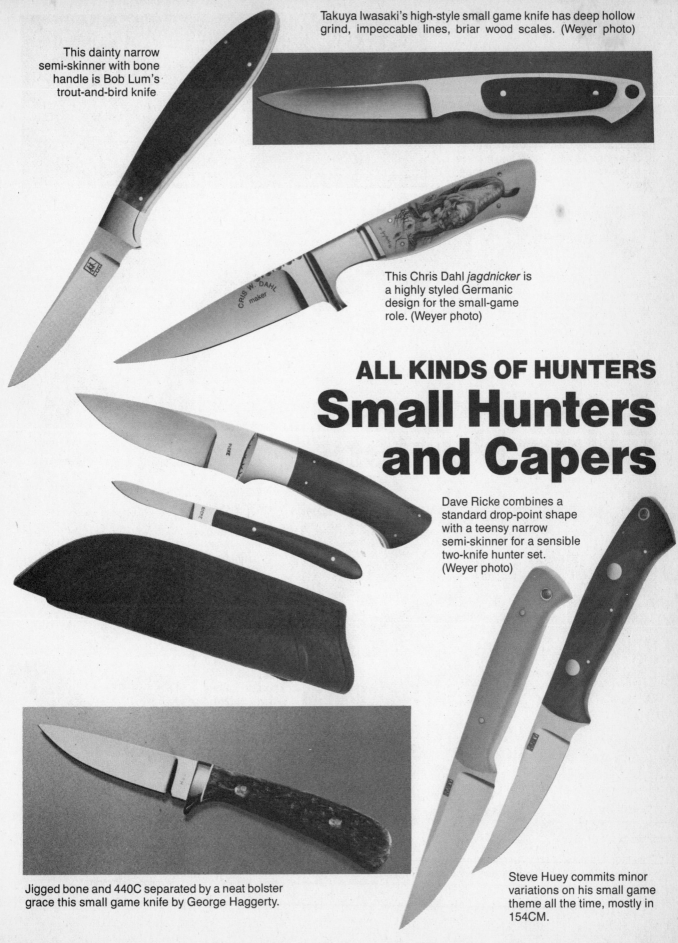

Takuya Iwasaki's high-style small game knife has deep hollow grind, impeccable lines, briar wood scales. (Weyer photo)

This dainty narrow semi-skinner with bone handle is Bob Lum's trout-and-bird knife

This Chris Dahl *jagdnicker* is a highly styled Germanic design for the small-game role. (Weyer photo)

ALL KINDS OF HUNTERS
Small Hunters and Capers

Dave Ricke combines a standard drop-point shape with a teensy narrow semi-skinner for a sensible two-knife hunter set. (Weyer photo)

Jigged bone and 440C separated by a neat bolster grace this small game knife by George Haggerty.

Steve Huey commits minor variations on his small game theme all the time, mostly in 154CM.

Harold Brown gets his collector grade knives on a Jody Samson shape up like this thuya burl and Tom Leshorn engraving.

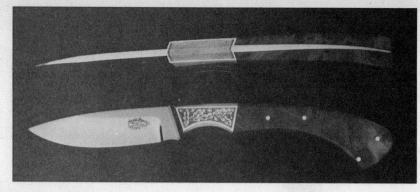

Eldon Courtney builds this 4-inch utility double-edge in 5160 steel for hunters who like the chisel grind of the upper edge.

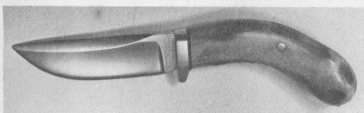

ALL KINDS OF HUNTERS
Other Hunters

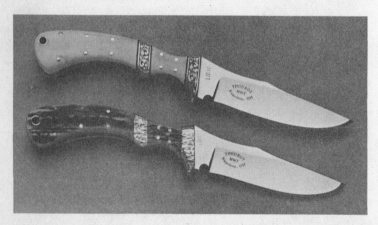

Why Patrick Donovan calls this highly individual shape "Scandinavian" must have an Irish answer. (Weyer photo)

Subhilts and complex blade grinds and deluxe materials and D2 are all in these Mike Thourot hunters. (Weyer photo)

This individual solution to the skinner blade shape is by Gerome Weinand and makes a tough-looking knife.

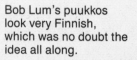

Bob Lum's puukkos look very Finnish, which was no doubt the idea all along.

TWO BLADES? THREE? MORE?

ONCE BEYOND three blades to a side, folding knives get a little complex in use if we are talking about four or five *cutting* blades. (Utility or camp or — yes — Swiss Army types are different.) I believe four-blade and five-blade patterns were, way back, mostly for people who did some kind of knife work — whittling or carving or some such — and had specific cuts for each blade. And, it follows, they used all the blades all the time.

Enough of that speculation. We can simply look at the knives. The special problems of making several blades nest, the considerations of spring tensions, which vary according to the leverage each blade might exert on the spring, the placement of pins — it is hard to realize that so many multi-blade designs were worked out in an age before computers. Complexity went along with the simplicity of having one tool with two or three cutting edges. Working out those relationships of several blades with several springs took time and skill.

Once the question of layout of blades is settled, two-blade and three-blade knives are all pretty much made alike. There is an occasional tricky pattern like the common whittler style, in which a pair of springs serve three blades — at one end, each of two small blades has its end of a spring; at the other end, the one big blade is sprung by the other ends. Such aside, they are all pretty much alike.

Handmade multi-blade knives are somewhat pricey from one point of view because they are difficult to make and are often compared to factory products rather directly; on the other hand, considering the know-how involved compared to other handmade knives, they are

The epitome of the American two-blade jackknife, this Gene Langley-made trapper is in ATS34 and good old jig bone.

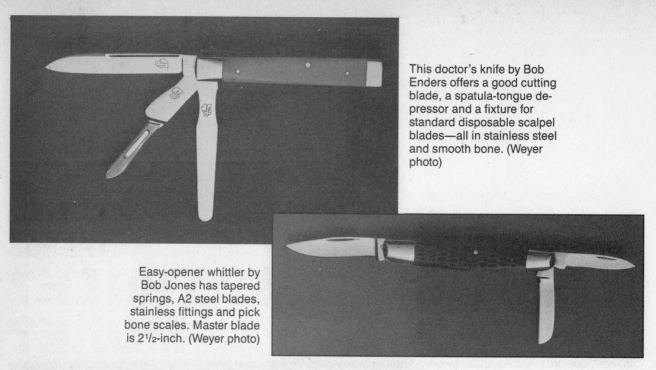

This doctor's knife by Bob Enders offers a good cutting blade, a spatula-tongue depressor and a fixture for standard disposable scalpel blades—all in stainless steel and smooth bone. (Weyer photo)

Easy-opener whittler by Bob Jones has tapered springs, A2 steel blades, stainless fittings and pick bone scales. Master blade is 2¹/₂-inch. (Weyer photo)

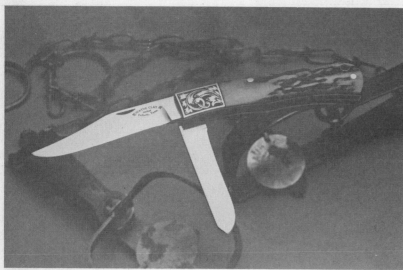

Wayne Clay makes these trappers plain and fancy. This one is fancy, has Old Dominion Engravers embellishment. (Long photo)

This is a gunstock and a sowbelly at 3-inch and 3³/₄-inch by Dennis Burton. Blades and springs are 440C; bolsters, liners and pins are nickel silver. (Below) This is a Wharncliffe whittler made the hard way by Lowell Oyster with stainless steel.

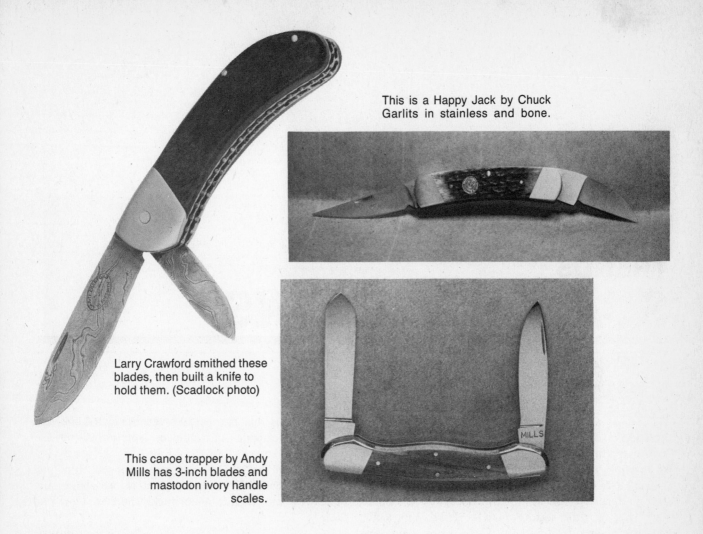

This is a Happy Jack by Chuck Garlits in stainless and bone.

Larry Crawford smithed these blades, then built a knife to hold them. (Scadlock photo)

This canoe trapper by Andy Mills has 3-inch blades and mastodon ivory handle scales.

not all that expensive. However, standards for handmade multi-blades are about the same as standards for factory knives — they range from magnificent down to barely usable — handmade does not mean first-cabin automatically. You have to look at the knife.

For some of us, the variety of patterns is all the fun. Those traditional knives with neat old names like Tobacco jack and premium stock and whittler and such are more and more fun to think about than stuff like clip points and saber-ground and sub-hilted, which is the sort of stuff one must consider in straight knives.

To learn about folders, there is no substitute for looking at a lot of folders. You go to the flea markets and the knife shows and you find fellows with lots of folders and you look at them. You don't mess with the mint specimens and you get permission and you, beyond all, never mess with a deal going on. It helps to spend some money and it helps to make some unwise decisions in the spending of that money because those you never forget.

Once you know something of the first-rate factory folders of the past, you are in a position to judge the handmades of today. Today you can find new knives

better than any, ever; you can find excellent tools; and then there are some ordinary knives—OK, but ordinary.

There are books, of course, that can help in that specialized business of finding out what there is to know about multi-blade knives, at least from the price and value and collectability status points of view. High on our list around here is DBI's own *Levine's Guide To Knives And Their Values*. In the pure tradition Levine's guide represents, there are books by John Goins, and the Fergusons and Parker and Voyles and a bunch of price guides. These straight-out price guides, which are pretty well concentrated on the most popular collectibles like Case and Ka-Bar and Winchester and Remington are long on model numbers and dating and prices, but don't get into much discussion.

It is funny about the multi-bladed knife. Lots of us have carried a three-blade or four-blade knife our whole life while we got very very interested in other sorts of edged things, all the time using — and probably abusing — one of the most interesting types right in our own pockets.

Ken Warner

TRENDS
SCAGLE RETURNS

WILLIAM Scagle is pretty high on the list of great old-time knifemakers. No less than W.D. Randall, Jr. credits Scagle and his unmistakable knives with quickening the knifemaking urge in the Randall breast.

And so, in celebration of his own 50th year as a knifemaker, Randall chose to produce a Scaglesque Randall knife. Knives in that series, which Randall sold for $350, now bring upwards of $1,000, which is one thing. An-

other thing is that the the 50th-year Randall knife has spawned a veritable—in handmade knife terms—torrent of Scagleish knives.

We present here a few examples, dipped from the stream somewhat like salmon. That is, we show only those we could reach from our rock. There are more out there.

Ken Warner

Yet another Randall phenomenon, the 1938-1988 knife has doubled and tripled in price. Its Scagle styling didn't hurt. (Long photo)

Frank Gamble has worked in the Scagle style often, has now produced this Scagle suite, ranging up to the big 9-inch bladed camp knife. The handle material, Gamble reports, is from Scagle's scrap bin. (Weyer photo)

(Below) Charles Ochs forged this Scagle camp knife. It handles very like the original. (Scadlock photo)

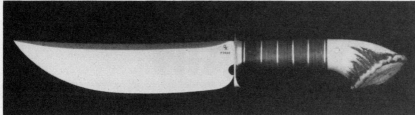

(Below left and below) The romantic Scagle handle treatment appeals to Al Woodworth. He used it for both this fighter and the one-of-a-kind knife he calls the Trickster.

(Below) North and Prater put together this close likeness of Randall's 50-year knife. (Long photo)

Gamble calls this the James Holmes hunting set, but doesn't get too far from the Scagle approach. (Weyer photo)

TRENDS
KUKRIS YET AGAIN

NO, KUKRIS will not go away, either. Neither will kopises or the other down-curved instruments of basic Greco-Nepalese origin.

One who knows how can hit hard with a kukri. I know that. One who knows how can hit quick with a kukri and Hank Reinhardt says he knows that. Whether or not those are the real attractions of the kukri, this writer cannot tell.

A kukri of the size generally carried by ghurka troops, of the size commonly sold by Atlanta Cutlery as GI (from a sub-continental point of view) puts a useful amount of weight into a relatively short package. So that's one thing in its favor. Then, the weight-forward shape of the kukri permits sensible chopping, using motions quite familiar to anyone who ever had a Boy Scout hatchet. So far, so good.

It is that edge that curves twice that gives most of us

who come late in life to the kukri fits. That takes some studying.

Even a little reflection will convince one that if you could learn how to use it, each point on that curving edge would lend you a specific advantage for some particular kind of cut that you are probably making anyway. Reflection, however intense, does not provide one with the hand-eye coordination required to make the kukri come alive in one's personal hands.

The kukri is one of those cases where what comes from the mysterious East may actually be mysterious. A fellow named John Masters, an officer of Gurkhas who carried a kukri for much of his working life, used to write of the kukri's people when he was puzzled "Hiyo, Gurkhali" and, without any license, so shall I.

Ken Warner

These kurkris were forged of 5160 steel and fitted with black Micarta handles by Jay Hendrickson for Prince Abdullah Hussein of Jordan. (Adkins photo)

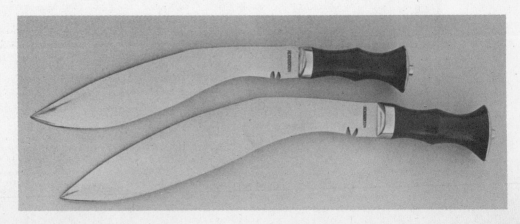

This is the Cold Steel kukri-to-be with 12-inch blade and redesigned handle. Lynn Thompson says it will be forged in the U.S.A. of Carbon V steel.

W.C. Davis keeps right on making his curved-edge military type blades. (Long photo)

Larry Harley calls this his Recurve Hunter, but a short kopis is what it is, with a 6½-inch blade. (Long photo)

Chuck Stapel likes the kopis-style curve, does it up with all sorts of handles and with Bruce Shaw engraving. (Fitzgerald photos)

One would not think the kukri could be straightened out, but James Porter did it in curly maple and W1. That's an 8¼-inch blade. (Weyer photo)

Bashful George Benjamin Jr. calls this design a cross between a kukri-Bowie and a fighter and has named it "The Finger of God." (Weyer photo)

TRENDS
MULTI-BLADE STRAIGHT KNIVES

AS THINGS usually went, during the history of personal cutlery, a fellow who wanted more than one shape of blade at hand either carried several straight knives or he found a folding knife with several blades in it to suit him. For a small group of people early on and in ever-increasing numbers now, there are very interesting multi-bladed straight knives to be found both commercially and made privately.

Someday, a clever fellow is going to accomplish a whole article about the systems and patented devices by which one changes blades for a straight knife quickly and easily and still retains a stout and solid cutting instrument. In most modern cases, that is exactly what happens. It may very well be in those devices and systems that the theoretical has come to be practical.

Leaving aside the question of utility, one of the failings of the multi-blade idea of the past has been the ease or lack of ease with which any change was made and the other failing was that once the change was made you didn't have as stout a knife as you might have had in the first place if you hadn't fooled around with all this mess. The new locking devices are pretty good. The knives resulting are quite rigid and the likelihood of wear loosening them up unduly is slim for most every design we have seen.

Long ago, when people still went hunting by train, and if long johns and a pair of Malone pants couldn't keep you warm, you put on another pair of Malone pants, lots of multi-blade straight knives went to the Big Woods. They had names on them like Case, and KaBar and Western and the other blade was a lightweight hatchet. You could always tell a real hunter because the edges of the sheath that held his hatchet-knife, as we call them, were all rumpled and water-soaked and tough-looking. I don't know that anyone ever actually faked this appearance, as rich kids are reported to do by putting new sneakers in any convenient creek, but it could have happened.

Anyway, multi-blade knives are not new. There are, however, new multi-blade knives around. Case has one called the XX-CHANGE; several factories are following suit. Others are in wide variety from a number of individual craftsmen.

This is a case, of course, where fascination may surpass need. There is some question whether one actually needs all those patterns at all, and another question that if one does need a couple of patterns, does he need four? Putting the shoe on the other foot, it is plain to see that having done all the big stuff on a given animal, it would be very useful to be able to switch to a blade better suited for doing all the little stuff. So long as the technical problems of making the switch have been solved, and we believe they have been in several ways by several sets of people, it doesn't really seem to make any difference and the whole idea of a multi-blade knife is appealing without doubt.

Some of these multi-blades are actually folding knives with hinges gone public, you might say, and there are such things as straight hunting knives with little blades folding out of the handles and over there, in another part of the forest, there are a lot of multi-bladed knives that we all call pocketknives. But looking around you here in this section of this edition, you can see a few of the current solutions to the problem called the multi-bladed straight knife.

Ken Warner

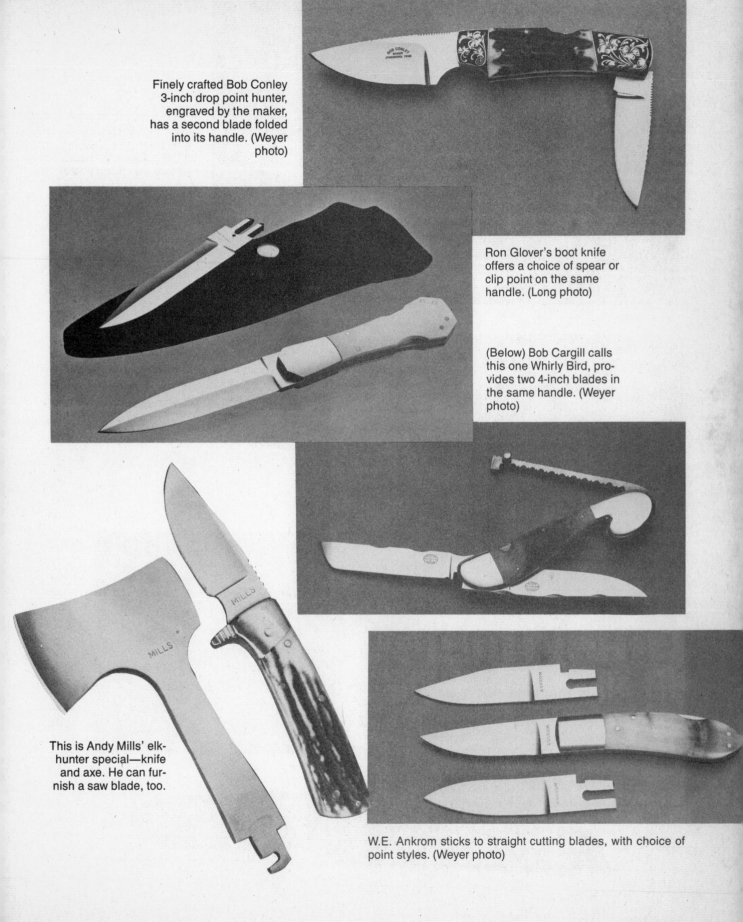

Finely crafted Bob Conley 3-inch drop point hunter, engraved by the maker, has a second blade folded into its handle. (Weyer photo)

Ron Glover's boot knife offers a choice of spear or clip point on the same handle. (Long photo)

(Below) Bob Cargill calls this one Whirly Bird, provides two 4-inch blades in the same handle. (Weyer photo)

This is Andy Mills' elk-hunter special—knife and axe. He can furnish a saw blade, too.

W.E. Ankrom sticks to straight cutting blades, with choice of point styles. (Weyer photo)

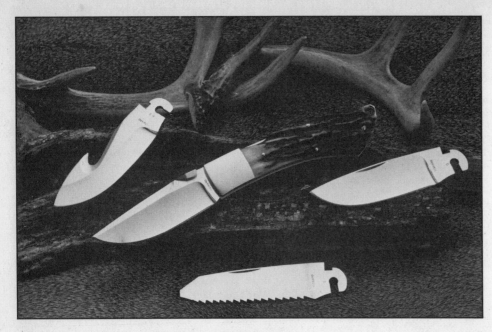

Durvyn Howard's multi-blade skips the axe, but not the guthook, and adds a screwdriver. (Long photo)

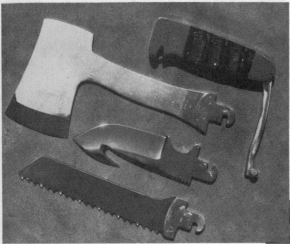

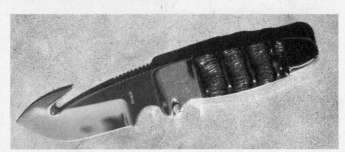

(Above, above right, right and below) This Tom Hilker combination offers everything—even a guthook.

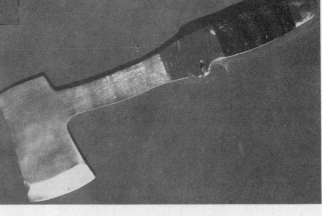

TRENDS
THE FOLDING STANDARDS

RIGHT HERE on these pages you are going to see over a dozen systems for folding and unfolding and locking and unlocking folding knives. There are levers and buttons and swinging handles. And there are plain (and fancy) flat-spring-tensioned slip-joint knives.

Does this mean there is a lot of folder going on? You bet. That part of the knifemaking craft is in a positive ferment, bubbling and steaming. Indeed, these 14 pages of pictures don't cover the whole thing, not hardly.

In another part of the book, we discuss two and three-bladed knives, and in another the remarkable liner lock frenzy. And beyond those, we also do a little something or two in Factory Trends on commercial folders.

Right here and now, just look at how really handsome nearly every one of six or seven dozen handmade folding knives is. To a fellow who remembers clearly his first handmade folder, a rude and crude Alaska-made knife, just 20 years ago, this is really something.

Ken Warner

Dean of the new folder age, Ron Lake still does his interframe thing. (Weyer photo)

Jesse Davis dresses up his working-type lockers now and again. (Long photo)

Nickel-silver handle is the ground for Buster Warenski engraving on a Buster Warenski folder. (Weyer photo)

This Steve Lawson gent's locker has the right touch. (Weyer photo)

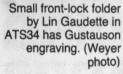

The folding hunter by James Schmidt is cut with clean lines in fossil walrus ivory, nickel Damascus, and Damascus. (Weyer photo)

Small front-lock folder by Lin Gaudette in ATS34 has Gustauson engraving. (Weyer photo)

THE FOLDING STANDARDS
Fancy Lockers

(Above) Steve Mullin did it all here—made the knife, file-cut the liners and engraved the bolster.

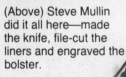

The eagle on this Harumi Hirayama nickel-silver interframe is made of 50 inlays. (Weyer photo)

This is the T.R. Overeynder Model 11 interframe front-lock folder and fully up to whatever standard you might set. (Chase photo)

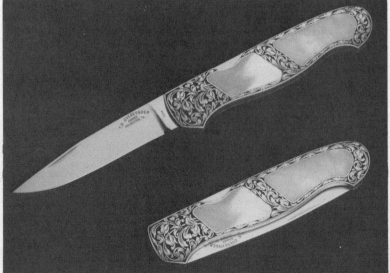

Hugh Bartrug here combines nickel silver, abalone, Damascus and Joe Kastlenik engraving around a 2¾-inch blade. (Weyer photo)

E.G. Peterson meets the time-tested tradition in this small ivory-and-silver folder, engraved by Tony LaGeose. (Rice photo)

THE FOLDING STANDARDS
Fancy Lockers

Australian Kurt B. Simmonds made this folding sgian dubh. The release is at the pommel.

The R. Spinale touch in a gent's folder of traditional pattern is clear here, African motif and all.

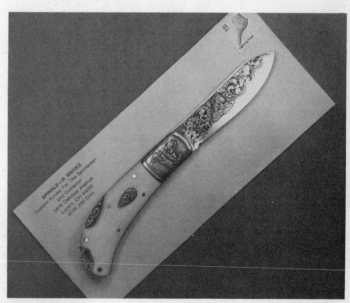

Choice of materials—here mastodon ivory, and carefully wrought Damascus—can make a knife as fancy as engraving. This is a Barry Davis example. (Weyer photo)

Plain doesn't mean low-priced, as this severe Ron Lake interframe clip-point no doubt demonstrates. (Long photo)

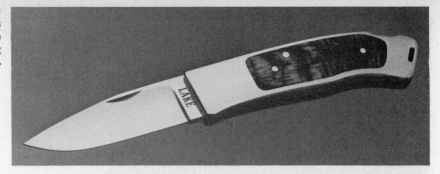

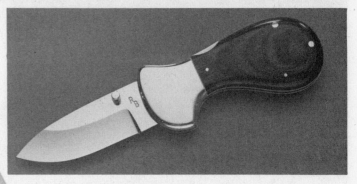

That's stag in Gene Gonzalez' interframe in aluminum. (Weyer photo)

Yep. This is Ray Beers' old palm hunter as a folder with a 3-inch 440C blade. (Weyer photo)

TRENDS
PLAIN LOCKERS

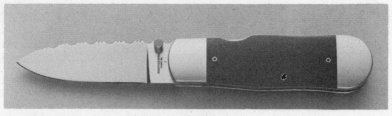

Forceful looking Phil Boguszewski folder has integral frame and African blackwood and a 4-inch blade in 440C. (Weyer photo)

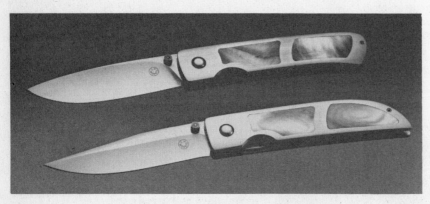

Individually styled interframes by C.H. Morris are 20th century stuff. (Long photo)

This middle-locked Bill Harsey knife is designed as a trout knife, Australian mother-of-pearl notwithstanding. (Lam photo)

Red Smith rear-locked big-enough folder has Micarta scales and a working look. (Long photo)

This is a new profile in a using-size pocket locker by Glenn L. Smith.

TRENDS
PLAIN LOCKERS

Personal shapes in bolster and profile, along with stag and filework, mark this 3½-inch folding hunter by Y.R. Yunes. (Weyer photo)

W.C. Davis chose paper Micarta scales to set off the clean shapes of this folding hunter. (Long photo)

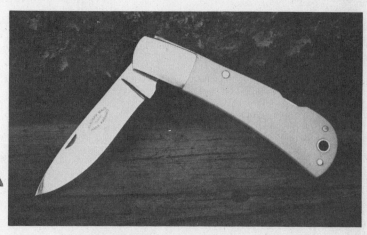

Very straightforward folder styling is evident in this Alaskan Maid model by Hank Kubaiko.

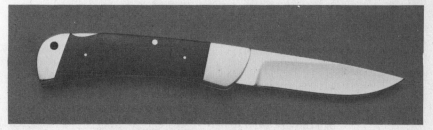

Jim Siska calls this the Model 14, made this one in 416 and 440C steels with African blackwood and a 3½-inch blade. (Weyer photo)

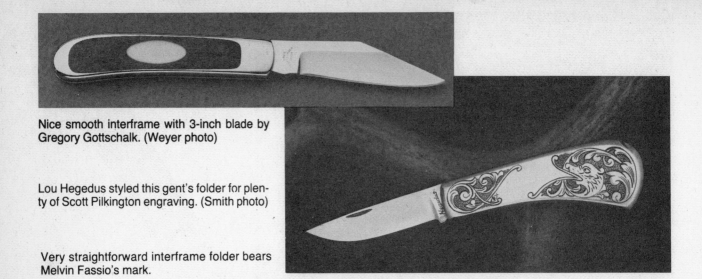

Nice smooth interframe with 3-inch blade by Gregory Gottschalk. (Weyer photo)

Lou Hegedus styled this gent's folder for plenty of Scott Pilkington engraving. (Smith photo)

Very straightforward interframe folder bears Melvin Fassio's mark.

THE FOLDING STANDARDS
Slip-Joints

Ron Gaston group offers (from top): coral—apple and angel wing—sting ray and oosik. (Weyer photo)

Clifton Polk's handsome folder combines white gold liner and bolsters engraved by Mel Wood with brushed yellow gold scales.

Brass liner and bolster with pearl scales and Damascus blade make this Jim Crowell folder rather colorful. (Weyer photo)

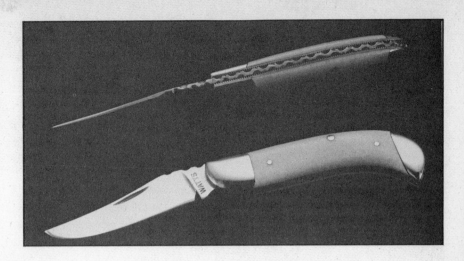

Very curvy and very dressy Wally Watts folder has ivory and filework. (Long photo)

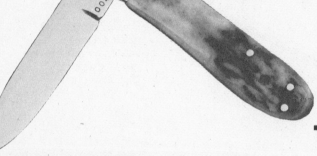

Severe Alan Bloomer folder offers nice stag-and-pin arrangement. (Weyer photo)

THE FOLDING STANDARDS
Slip-Joints

Dress-up 5-inch folder in ivory, nickel silver and 440C is by Paul Myers, with scrim by Mary Talley and engraving by Ron Smith. (Weyer photo)

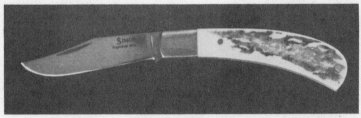

Bill Simons stag folder has a genuine American profile.

(Below) Red bone and Sornberger engraving look good on this clean Jay Harris folder. (Weyer photo)

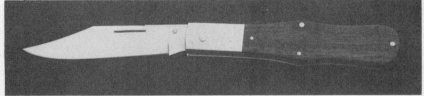

Big coke-bottle hunter is by Lowell Oyster, cleanly ground.

Fish-shaped Ray Appleton push-button folder is all hardened A2 steel and style. (Weyer photo)

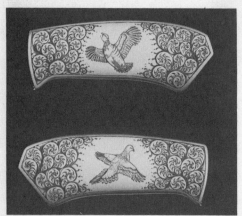

Leon Pittman's unmistakable Worm folder looks good in nickel silver engraved by Simon Lytton. (Weyer photo)

Dave Longworth does a fanciful reverse interframe with his own lever lock system. (Scadlock photo)

THE FOLDING STANDARDS
Other Folders

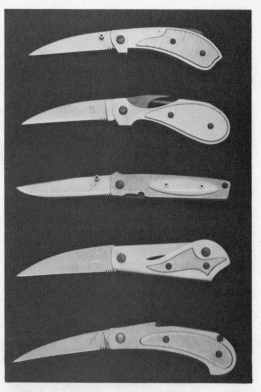

Five different locking arrangements by Gary Barnes explore the possibilities. (Klinefelter photo)

(Above left) Red Smith's swinging liners make a flat locking folder. (Long photo)

(Left) David Pitt's rendition of the old-time Neft-patent folder is cleanly finished. (Weyer photo)

Jerry Rados' immaculate Turkish Damascus pattern graces a rear-locked folder with impala horn scales. (Weyer photo)

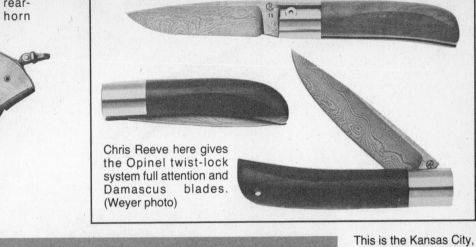

Chris Reeve here gives the Opinel twist-lock system full attention and Damascus blades. (Weyer photo)

This is the Kansas City, by Judy Gottage, with abalone, stainless steel, Harrington engraving and a special lock and spring. (Weyer photo)

THE FOLDING STANDARDS
Other Folders

(Below) Chuck Stewart's convertible coil-springed button lock folder offers stainless steel Damascus blades. (Weyer photo)

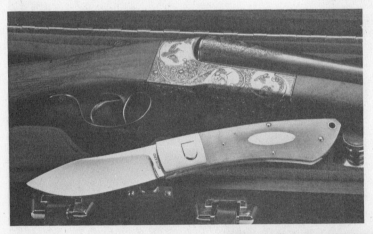

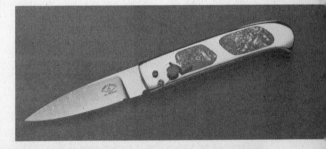

Side-lock-release skinner by Durvyn Howard is a slick handful. (Long photo)

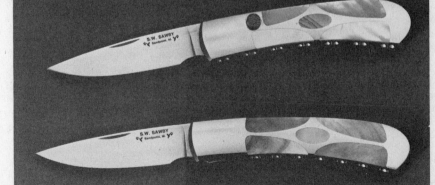

This is Scot Sawby's Robin model with choice of locks—the Sawby self-lock and a button lock.

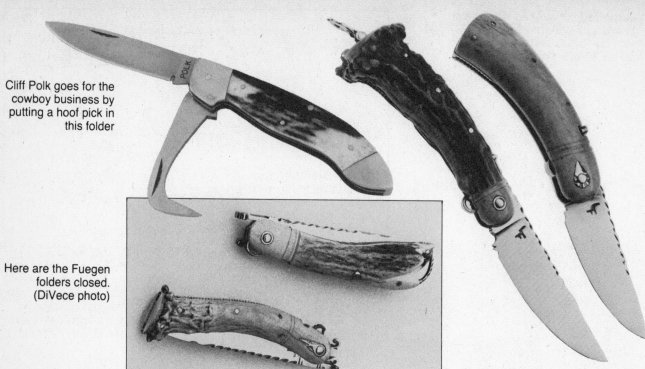

Cliff Polk goes for the cowboy business by putting a hoof pick in this folder

Here are the Fuegen folders closed. (DiVece photo)

(Above) Larry Fuegen forges these scroll folders; they are springless and good-looking. (Weyer photo)

THE FOLDING STANDARDS
Other Folders

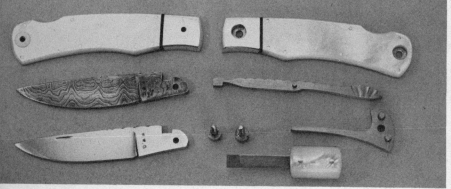

Bill Green can furnish a takedown locker with two blades and a square-handled screwdriver.

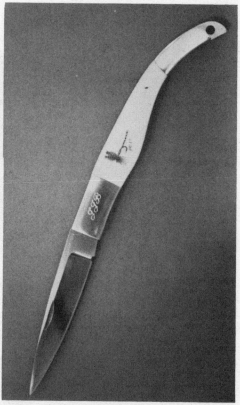

Jack Crockford's new clasp knife design carries a scrimmed trout fly.

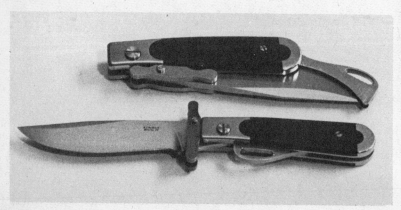

(Left) This version of an old Marble's belt knife is by A.J. Hubbard.

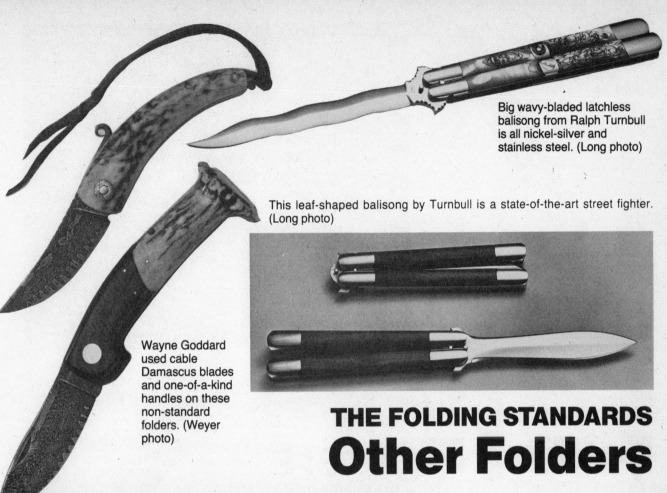

Big wavy-bladed latchless balisong from Ralph Turnbull is all nickel-silver and stainless steel. (Long photo)

This leaf-shaped balisong by Turnbull is a state-of-the-art street fighter. (Long photo)

Wayne Goddard used cable Damascus blades and one-of-a-kind handles on these non-standard folders. (Weyer photo)

THE FOLDING STANDARDS
Other Folders

Eric Erickson makes dress-up butterfly knives, here using Damascus bar stock from Wayne Valachovic. (Weyer photo)

On the balisong front, Ken Largin does decorative numbers like these.

Harvey McBurnette calls this a semi-frame, fitted it with African blackwood, then engraved it. (Weyer photo)

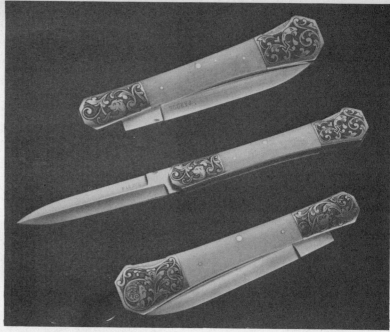

Mildly 19th century scroll by Scott Pilkington complements Mel Pardue's ivory handled pocket dirk. (Long photo)

THE FOLDING STANDARDS
Folding Fighters

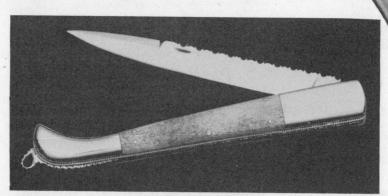

This unusual conception by Ed Lary is all stainless steel and moose horn. (Scadlock photo)

Wayne Valachovic makes a lot of fighters that look like this in Damascus and fossil ivory because people like 'em. (Weyer photo)

Joe Kious says this good-looker is a ¾-bolster fighter. Brett Irby engraved it.

Paul Fox's single-edged fighter looks as good as ever. The titanium handle makes it, naturally, the Silver Fox. (Weyer photo)

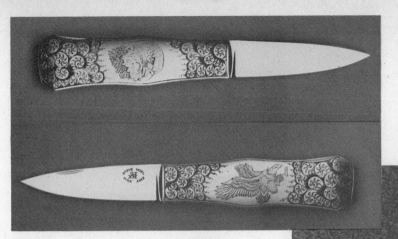

(Left) One advantage of 416 stainless steel as a handle is you can have the Hoel thing engraved by Simon Lytton. (Weyer photo)

Old-time coffin shape and slick blade button are typical Dur-vyn Howard touches. (Long photo)

Integral frame and wire wrap are only two of the neat things about this Boguszewski folder. (Weyer photo)

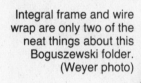

THE FOLDING STANDARDS
Folding Fighters

Left-handed Damascus easy-opener by Zollan McCarty has old-timey Pilkington scroll. (Long photo)

Chuck Stewart's fine Italian hand is clearly at work here. (Weyer photo)

Ken Steigerwalt's interframe 4¼-inch fighter has what the maker calls a "thumber" on the blade. (Weyer photo)

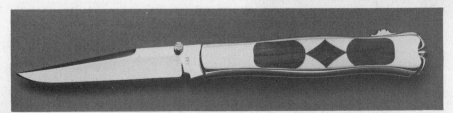

Ralph Harris's choice of blade profile makes this interframe fighter a tough looker. (Long photo)

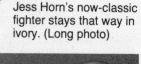

This is the Kolke Special by Seiichi Tasaki. Pins and escutcheon are gold. (Weyer photo)

THE FOLDING STANDARDS
Folding Fighters

Jess Horn's now-classic fighter stays that way in ivory. (Long photo)

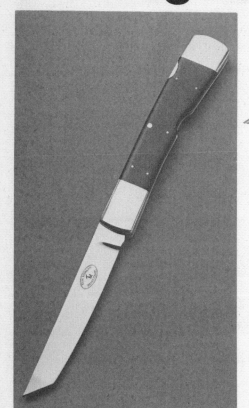

This smoothed-off interframe coke bottle dirk is in gold pearl and 440C. Koichi Kagawa is the maker. (Weyer photo)

That's a 4¼-inch blade and greenbone over ATS34 in this pocket poker by Jay Harris engraved by Howard Mendenhall. (Weyer photo)

This is a big one. Tom Morlan stretches this tanto out to 13-inch overall with integral 7075 T6 liners and bolsters. (Weyer photo)

STRAIGHT STANDARDS

GIVEN THAT we discuss hunters and the wide variety of oriental designs elsewhere, this presentation of photos of straight knives of more or less standard type has been confined to just six kinds of knives: daggers, Bowies, fighters, utility, seagoing knives.

Of course, there are several kinds of daggers and fighters and two of Bowies. That seems to make some sense of a complex presentation.

People, they are getting better and better and better at it all, including the photography. So this reporter will step aside and let you look.

Ken Warner

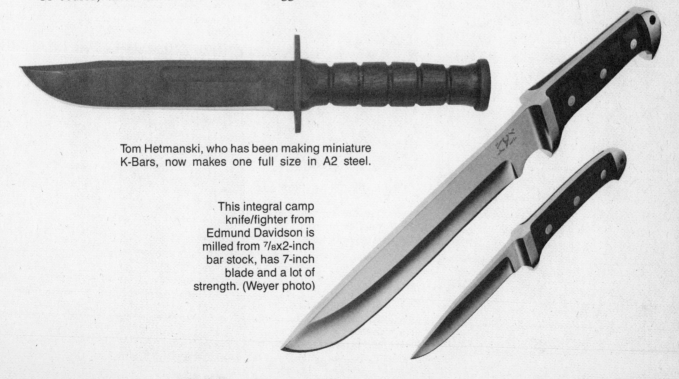

Tom Hetmanski, who has been making miniature K-Bars, now makes one full size in A2 steel.

This integral camp knife/fighter from Edmund Davidson is milled from $7/8$x2-inch bar stock, has 7-inch blade and a lot of strength. (Weyer photo)

Ivory handle and sheath, gold wire-inlaid, shows off Mel Wood 24K gold engraving and Damascus blade in this Tommy Lee dagger. (Weyer photo)

Wolfe Loerchner's finely scaled dagger is all stainless — 440C blade, 316 and 304 fittings — and ivory with, of course, stainless steel wire wrap. (Weyer photo)

STRAIGHT STANDARDS
Upscale Daggers

Not only classic, but classic Fred Carter, this all-steel dagger in gray and rich blue-black is engraved and gold-inlaid by the maker. (Weyer photo)

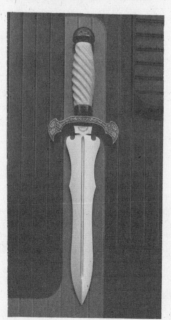

(Below) This 10-inch nicely shaped 440C blade is surmounted by stainless fittings and carved ivory. Fred Slee made it; Hank Bonham engraved it. (Weyer photo)

(Above) Intricately profiled Curt Erickson 440C 10-inch blade has carved ivory and blued steel trimmings, gold-inlaid. (Weyer photo)

(Left) All there is to this Jot Khalsa dagger is lapis-lazuli, 18K gold wire, 24K gold inlays, Damascus by the maker, and Lynton McKenzie engraving. (Weyer photo)

Slim integral Damascus dagger by Mick Langley is severe and handsome in line.

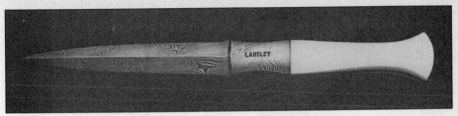

Large spear-point single-edged Damascus dagger by Steve Brooks has full-length narrow tang, cylindrical horn handle, Damascus fittings.

Bold Keith Kelly Damascus blade is complemented by stout and graceful double guard and antler crown. (Long photo)

STRAIGHT STANDARDS
Plain Daggers

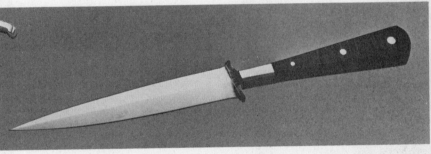

This small Daniel Winkler forged dagger with curly maple was probably a file in its first life, is distinctly 19th century American. (Long photo)

This nicely scaled and laid out Damascus dagger by J.P. Sigman is 10½-inch overall, has a 19th century look.

Simple Charles Lapen dagger offers gold fittings to the lean and clean rosewood grip and Damascus blade.

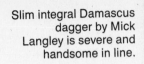

(Above) Grind and blade pattern and careful fitting make this stag-handled J. Harmon dagger fancy. (Long photo)

(Right) Ray Beers played ivory, horn, blued steel, nickel silver and African blackwood (the sheath) for all they were worth in this single-edged curved dagger. (Weyer photo)

STRAIGHT STANDARDS
Fancy Daggers

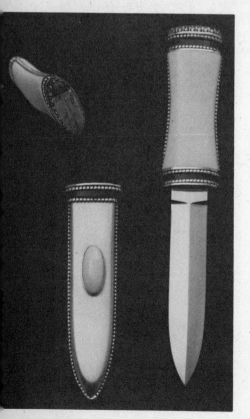

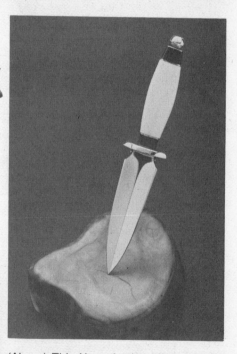

(Above) This Norm Levine blade and Richard DiMarzo handle in ivory, horn and gold add up to under 6 inches of nifty. (Weyer photo)

(Far left) Patrick Donovan assembled this 10-inches of 440C, ivory, sterling silver, turquoise and blackwood. (Weyer photo)

(Middle) Long no-nonsense blade permits fanciful cast guard and fender's grip of Ken McBain dagger. (Hodge photo)

(Left) That's probably a stainless Damascus blade in this D.F. Kressler foot-long ivory-handled dagger. (Weyer photo)

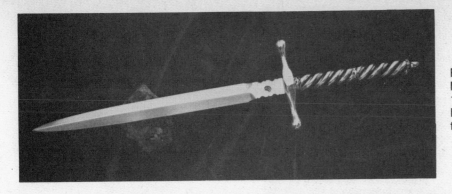

Forged 154CM? Yes. Sean McWilliams forged this blade of 154CM, forged and twisted the handle of 416 stainless. He does that sort of thing.

Trav Winn's little sticker is 440C, nickel-silver, ivory Micarta and no nonsense.

Paul Holloway's left-hand dagger — 9-inch blade — is all stainless steel. (Scadlock photo)

STRAIGHT STANDARDS
Classic Daggers

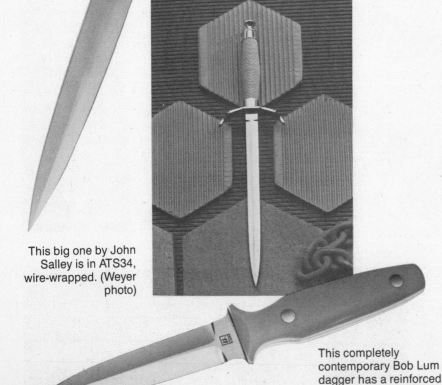

This big one by John Salley is in ATS34, wire-wrapped. (Weyer photo)

This completely contemporary Bob Lum dagger has a reinforced point and some elegance.

Forthwight Bob Hajovsky got up this forthright 10-inch dagger in ATS34 and stag. (Weyer photo)

Stunning rendition of the Rezin Bowie Searles pattern in 154CM, blued and grayed 4340 steel and African blackwood was executed by Tom Overeynder. (Weyer photo)

This replicated elaborate 1XL Bowie was done by Earl Black, as it so plainly states. (Weyer photo)

STRAIGHT STANDARDS
Classic Bowies

Fred Carter makes this bolster define itself and gets a new look into an absolutely classic profile. (Weyer photo)

This Sheffieldian classic was brought to us by Bill Reddiex from New Zealand. (Scadlock photo)

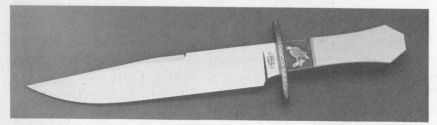

San Francisco may be back. Steve Rapp did these West Coast classics with 6¼-inch 440C blades, nickel silver-wrapped ivory and gold shields. (Weyer photo)

Gray Taylor did the knife at 14 inches, overall, fitted a blackwood handle and Simon Lytton did the rest. (Weyer photo)

Right out of the 19th century, this Chris Marks Bowie looks authentic in spite of its bright-work.

Gordon Chard's 9½-inch 440C hand-finished blade, ivory handle and blued steel fittings add up to an English Bowie. (Scadlock photo)

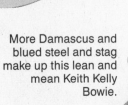

(Below) Jim Fister calls this 11 inches of forged cable a mountain man Bowie, which it certainly looks like.

More Damascus and blued steel and stag make up this lean and mean Keith Kelly Bowie.

STRAIGHT STANDARDS
Frontier Bowies

This big one by Gary Little has a bronze backstrap, guard and pommel, cocobolo grip; Larry Cole engraved it. (Weyer photo)

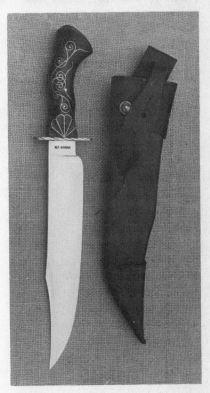

Yep. That's 11 inches of blued 01 steel and a split and rivetted stag crown by Webster Wood making in all about as frontier a Bowie as you can get. (Weyer photo)

Of course, a Bill Moran Bowie, forged of W2 if he hasn't run out of it, fitted with silver-wired curly maple and a serious sheath. (Holter photo)

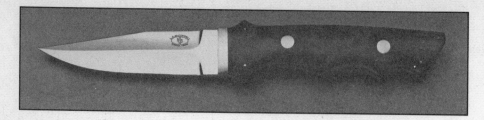

Boot-sized fighter by L.A. McConnell has neat bolster, and a self-guard covered by the ironwood scales. (Weyer photo)

Here is a 5¹/₂-inch 440C Gurganus fighter, and it too has a lot of sharp upper edge.

In the clip-point double-edge tradition is this double-hollow-ground boot-sized fighter by Terry Knipschield. Has ATS34, taper tang, red fiber lines, linen Micarta — everything.

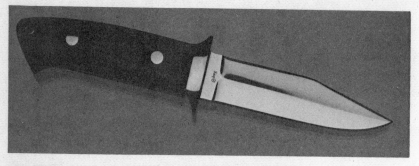

With 7-inch laminated blade, the Morseth sub-hilt fighter is back. (Weyer photo)

STRAIGHT STANDARDS
Classic Fighters

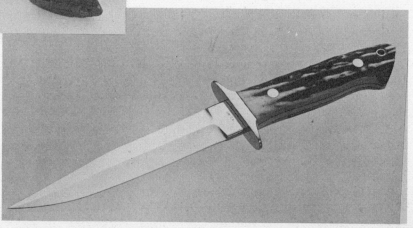

Stephen Terrill's sub-hilted short fighter has ivory and engraving and tapered tang, and the really right profile.

W.C. Davis doesn't have to work with Parkerized blades, as he proves with this finely ground stag-handled fighter. (Long photo)

Even a slightly old-timey look doesn't keep this Keith Stegall boot knife from looking like a chute knife.

(Right) The "all-out chute knife," you could call this T.R. Overeynder full integral with interframe handle. It's a tour-de-force. (Chase photo)

In his own treatment, Paul LeBatard hangs onto chute knife essentials in bead-blasted ATS34 and Micarta.

STRAIGHT STANDARDS
Chute Knives

Steve Johnson was probably there when chute knives were first patterned, and certainly hasn't forgotten how the blade should look. (Long photo)

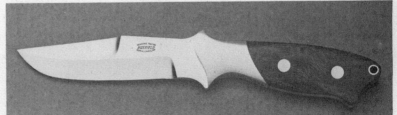

This sturdy Jim Turecek chute-shape in D2 and Micarta looks as if it will stay the distance.

Jack Busfield likes his chute knives sculpted, did this one in ATS34, 416, and desert ironwood. (Weyer photo)

Eldon Courtney admits this is bad ugly, but says the 5160 steel is tough and the shape works.

Nice quiet 440C and black Micarta with neat thonghole rivets and good serviceable finish details in these Walt Harless fighters. (Long photo)

STRAIGHT STANDARDS
Service Fighters

Chris Reeve's one-piecers remain very high on most anyone's list of serviceable knives. (Stephenson photo)

Dark and forbidding Harold Pierce fighters are passivated 440C and Micarta. (Weyer photo)

No-fooling straight-at-it style in this fighter comes from Steve Bumpus.

Colin Cox goes with integral guards, marble Micarta and Teflon for this tough-looking 7-inch fighter. (Weyer photo)

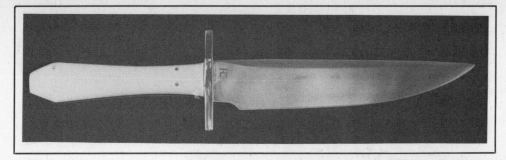

This clean-ground coffin-handled single edge by Howard Clark has good looks and an interesting ricasso.

This Bill Green fighter in Damascus has been peeled away to just knife.

Cris Dahl's fighter in ivory and tightly patterned Damascus is handsomely scrimmed with a tiger by Guy Dahl. (Weyer photo)

STRAIGHT STANDARDS
Frontier Fighters

The village blacksmith normally won't work this classy—in Damascus and ivory and all—but Jim Crowell does. (Weyer photo)

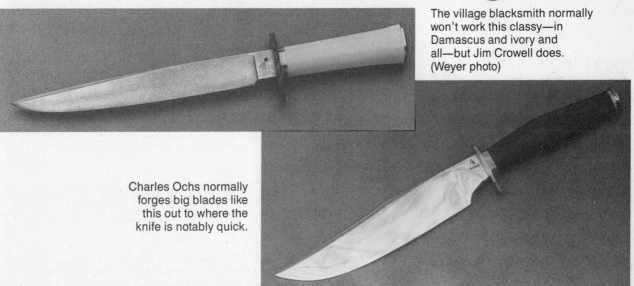

Charles Ochs normally forges big blades like this out to where the knife is notably quick.

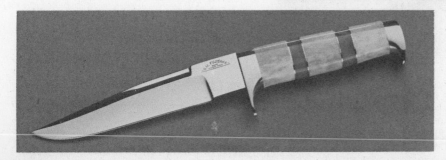

This smart Stanley Fujisaka fighter offers stag and amber and nickel-silver to go with its 6½-inch 440C blade. (Weyer photo)

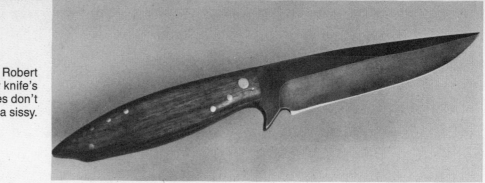

Tough-looking Robert Coogan utility knife's dress-up touches don't make it a sissy.

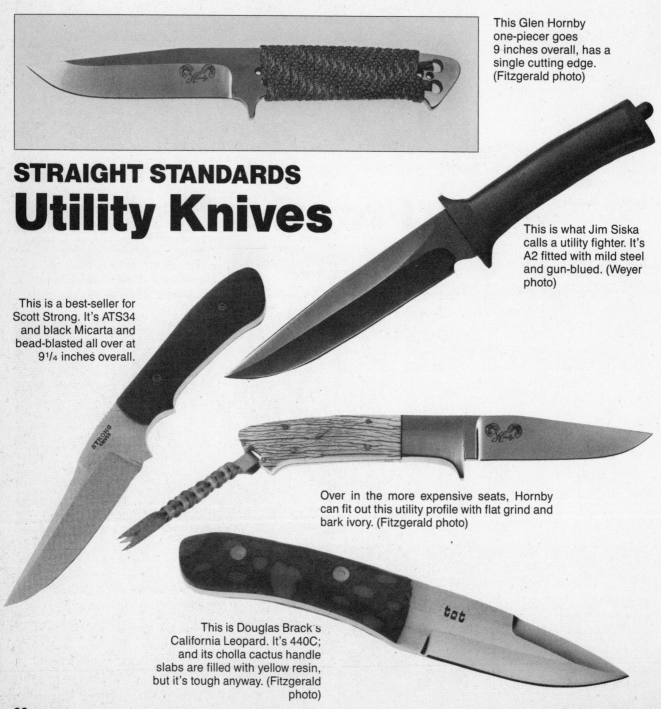

This Glen Hornby one-piecer goes 9 inches overall, has a single cutting edge. (Fitzgerald photo)

STRAIGHT STANDARDS
Utility Knives

This is what Jim Siska calls a utility fighter. It's A2 fitted with mild steel and gun-blued. (Weyer photo)

This is a best-seller for Scott Strong. It's ATS34 and black Micarta and bead-blasted all over at 9¼ inches overall.

Over in the more expensive seats, Hornby can fit out this utility profile with flat grind and bark ivory. (Fitzgerald photo)

This is Douglas Brack's California Leopard. It's 440C; and its cholla cactus handle slabs are filled with yellow resin, but it's tough anyway. (Fitzgerald photo)

Robin Golding's standard diver has 8-inch blade in ATS34, has all the diver goodies, including a Kydex sheath.

A customer designed this Glen Hornby diving knife. Handle is hollow. (Fitzgerald photos)

State of the art has to be Wenoka's Sea Style Layer Blade with replaceable blades in a high impact plastic frame.

STRAIGHT STANDARDS
Seagoing Knives

This R.G. Glover diver goes 14 inches overall out of ¼-inch 440C with Micarta and is stout and styled both. (Weyer photo)

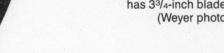

This is a boater's utility knife by Red Royal — has 3¾-inch blade. (Weyer photo)

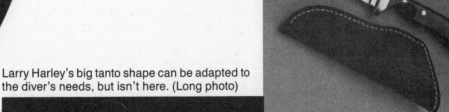

Larry Harley's big tanto shape can be adapted to the diver's needs, but isn't here. (Long photo)

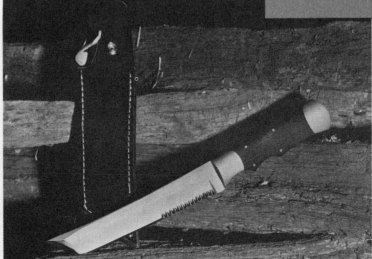

A properly sized camp knife, like this by V.J. McCracken, is a serious tool.

There are 10 inches of $^3/_{16}$-inch ATS34 in this blade. Knife by Mike Allen has brass guard, Pakkawood scales.

Shiva Ki went right to basics in Damascus and oosic for this 8$^1/_2$-inch camp-style knife. (Weyer photo)

STRAIGHT STANDARDS
Camp Knives

Nearly the latest mode in the camp knife genre is this shape by C.E. Haynes.

This, Steve Schwarzer says, is his gent's camp knife in Damascus and ivory with 9$^1/_2$-inch blade. (Weyer photo)

There are 10 inches of high carbon steel in this Crowell camp knife. The handle is ebony; the pins are silver. (Weyer photo)

TRENDS
LEATHER AND SUCH

ONCE, all we had to say was "leather," and that covered the whole subject of knife sheaths. Not so now. Mostly, sheaths are leather, but they are also rather commonly wood, Micarta, Kydex and a variety of animal parts besides skins.

And what those materials are being used to make is a far cry from say, five years ago. There is improvement in two directions—utility and style. However, it is not often we see both improvements in the same sheath.

So, one at a time then:

Knifemakers and leather people are learning about utility. Flatness is put in where needed; belt hitches are better; and design for function is taking the search into new materials. The best evidence for this is the burgeoning use of Kydex. This reporter remembers watching Tom Maringer working out Kydex technique six or seven years ago all by himself in Springdale, Arkansas.

Now—well, there's a lot of it out there.

Over on the style front, we're looking at richness, with exotic leathers (try, for instance, ostrich leg) leading. It will probably be a while before tooling and ornamentation catch up. And longer than that before *new* style catches on.

It's a big design problem, the knife sheath. First, knives are a lot of different shapes. And, second, the people who ever wear knives are very different. And, finally, knives are *knives*—they are sharp and dangerous and they have to just sit there safely and then, maybe, come out of there quickly.

One fellow thinks there are some things to be done right away. His name is Brian Katz and you can read his views on page 128.

Ken Warner

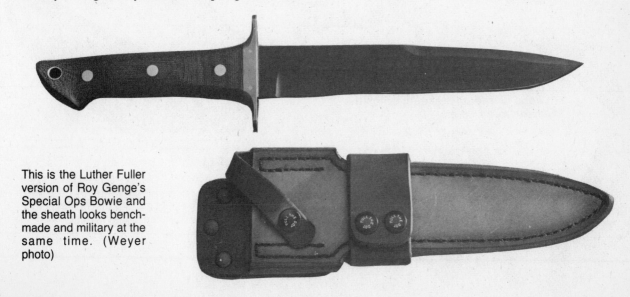

This is the Luther Fuller version of Roy Genge's Special Ops Bowie and the sheath looks bench-made and military at the same time. (Weyer photo)

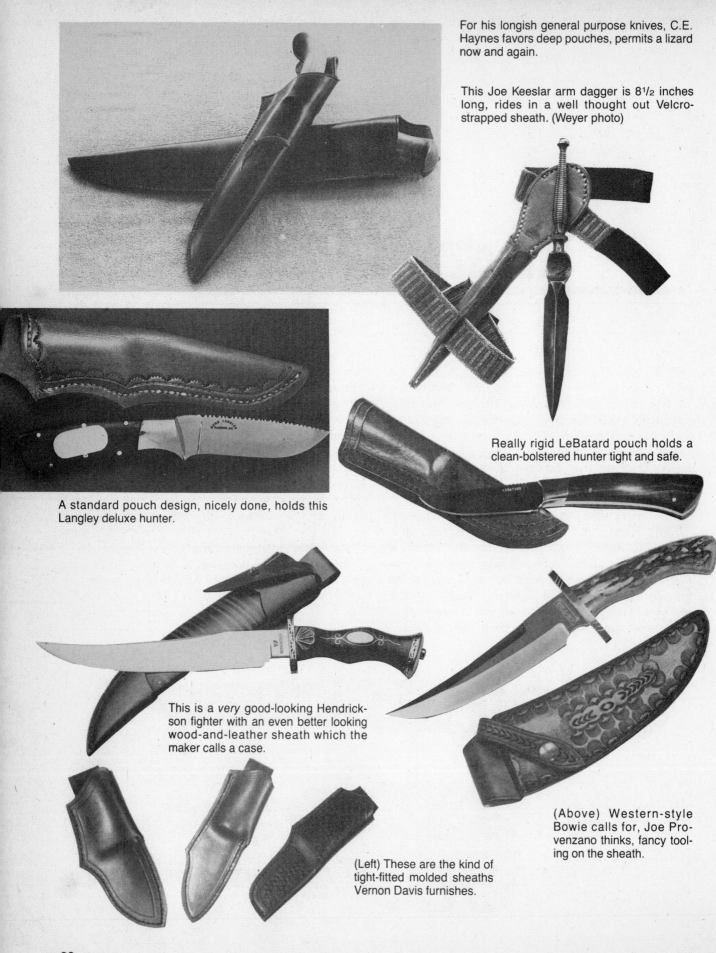

For his longish general purpose knives, C.E. Haynes favors deep pouches, permits a lizard now and again.

This Joe Keeslar arm dagger is 8½ inches long, rides in a well thought out Velcro-strapped sheath. (Weyer photo)

A standard pouch design, nicely done, holds this Langley deluxe hunter.

Really rigid LeBatard pouch holds a clean-bolstered hunter tight and safe.

This is a *very* good-looking Hendrickson fighter with an even better looking wood-and-leather sheath which the maker calls a case.

(Above) Western-style Bowie calls for, Joe Provenzano thinks, fancy tooling on the sheath.

(Left) These are the kind of tight-fitted molded sheaths Vernon Davis furnishes.

The two knives and seven alligator leather items here are all from Cattle Baron leather.

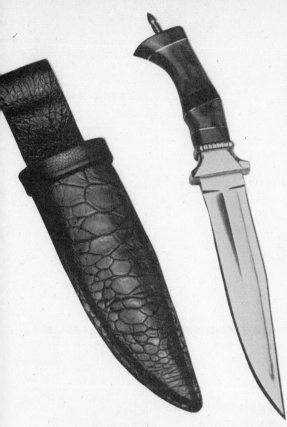

(Left) Malachite and black in this Norm Bardsley knife go well with the black alligator sheath strapped with lizard skin.

A J.N. Cooper hunter is being fitted for a pigskin sheath on the Charles Clements workbench.

(Above) Robert Schrap shows three tooled cowhide sheaths with exotic leather overlays. From left: alligator, ostrich, horned lizard.

(Right) Gil-Valasquez put this kind of no-leather, no-metal sheath together for divers out of fiberglass, Velcro, web straps.

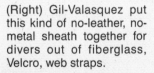

Tom Maringer will Kydex most any knife. This is a big bush sword set up for fast draw. (VerHoeven photo)

TRENDS
HANDMADE FOR $50 OR SO

YEP, THEY are there. There are people out there making knives one at a time and selling them for about $50. There seem to be a lot of them, in fact. At virtually any gun show you go to, you are likely to find a knifemaker unheralded in the public press sitting there happy as a clam turning over perfectly stout and serviceable hunting knives with sheaths for $50.

A lot of my more professional knifemaking readers won't like it, but there it is. They are knives; they are handmade knives; sometimes they are awfully good value. And, so far as my now-upscale knifemaking buddies are concerned, I guess I have to observe that a bunch of them started out selling hunting knives for $50 and glad to do it.

All the enlightened folks know absolutely that these fellows cannot make any money doing this. There is no way, they say, a fellow can grind on a piece of steel enough to make it a knife and work on it in such sophisticated fashion that it becomes properly hard and put a reasonable handle on it by any of the commonly accepted methods and come out of there if he is trying to be under $50 and throw in a sheath. I am afraid that this is a little bit like the aeronautical specifications for a bumble bee which plainly state the thing cannot fly.

What I think is happening is that a fellow who loves knives and has a certain talent with his hands spends a deal of his spare time with about $6 to $10 worth of materials and in 3 or 4 or 5 hours, maybe more, creates a knife. At this point he is a clear winner — he has a knife, he has enjoyed making it, and he doesn't have a lot of money in it. If he does that once or twice a week for 5 or 6 weeks and then spends a weekend at a gun show he'd be going to anyway and sells eight or nine of those knives and brings home $300 or $400 to go against the rent bill or the next batch of knives or whatever, what in the world could be wrong with that?

I don't believe anything is wrong with it and that is why you see here a number of photographs of handmade knives for which the makers charge $50 or so. These makers are guys who are not so far from their gun show sales days as others you see in this book, but hardly any of them are those anonymous fellows selling knives at the small shows who pay no attention to books like this one.

Ken Warner

Mike Yurco uses 440C and Pakkawood on his #7A finger-groove skinner and gets $55 for one with sheath.
(Jon Sob photo)

This is called a derringer skinner by Mike Yurco. It's 5 ¼-inch overall, sells for $50. (Jon Sob photo)

Lowell Oyster will sell you any one of these hunting knives for $55, with sheath.

Daniel Winkler forges a small skinner from a file and fits an antler handle for $50. Knife is 5 inches overall.

The top two of these Ken Largin knives are under $50; the bolstered short hunter is under $65; all with sheaths.

Rather different finger skinner by R.V. Alverson is $40.

This Oyster hunter—brass bolstered—is $55 plus the extra cost of the stag.

For these fancy Lotus gents knives Frank Vought gets over $100, but he makes the same knife in plain-vanilla sandblast and Micarta for right at $50.

TRENDS
EVER THE TWAIN SHALL MEET?

RUDYARD Kipling wasn't talking about knife design when he said that East is East and West is West. Having done more things to traditional Japanese knife design in a decade than had happened to it in the previous 300 years, we are off and running on other things Oriental, high among them the Persian.

We have not stopped mistreating Japanese design as a glance hereabouts will show you. We call "tanto" everything from eel-skinning knives—yes, I am more or less reliably informed that the popular chisel-point tanto shape is identical with a knife favored in the eeling industry along several of Japan's rivers—to an all out wakizashi, or even a katana. The word *tanto* has become a generic. And whatever the shape, the tanto is

still a standard item among American knifemakers and you will see some of them close at hand here.

The Chinese influence, spearheaded as much by Bob Lum as by anyone else, is beginning to appear. The knives are interesting shapes, but somehow there is not nearly the mystique and sense of history involved with the Chinese shapes as there has been with the Japanese shapes.

Other oriental things include the kukri, treated elsewhere, together with that wild menagerie of kinds of knife shapes we call Persian.

It is plain to see that the twain have met and are not going to detwain any time soon. Enjoy.

Ken Warner

This Kenneth Guth short dagger has a "dambrasscus" blade—a brass-steel lamination with 01 center—plus rayskin and mokume gane trimmings. (Weyer photo)

This basic American tanto is by Steve Price in ironwood and ivory. (Fedorak photo)

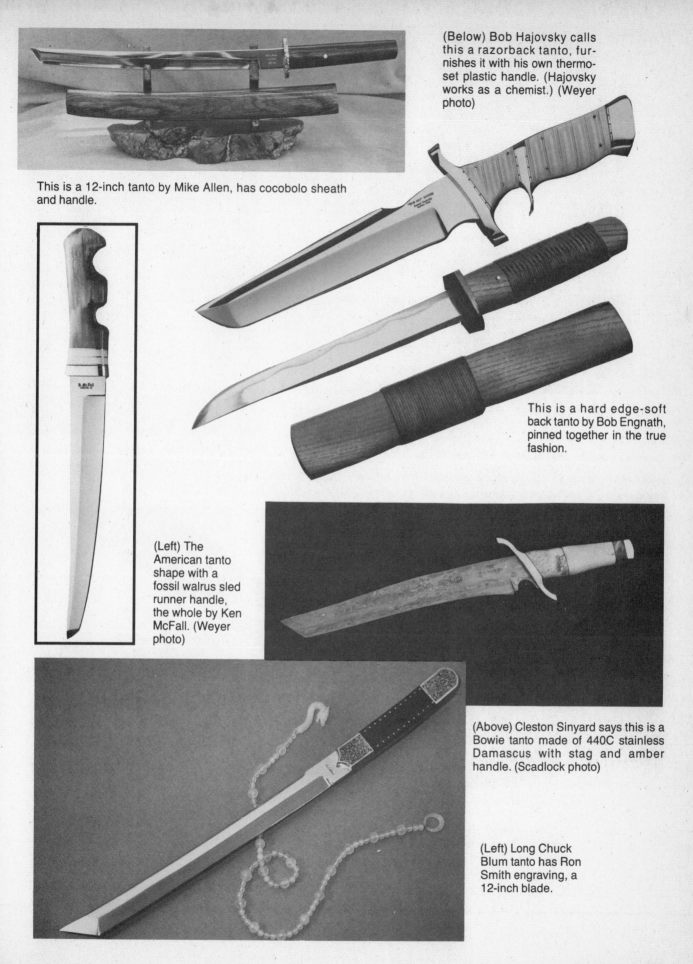

(Below) Bob Hajovsky calls this a razorback tanto, furnishes it with his own thermo-set plastic handle. (Hajovsky works as a chemist.) (Weyer photo)

This is a 12-inch tanto by Mike Allen, has cocobolo sheath and handle.

This is a hard edge-soft back tanto by Bob Engnath, pinned together in the true fashion.

(Left) The American tanto shape with a fossil walrus sled runner handle, the whole by Ken McFall. (Weyer photo)

(Above) Cleston Sinyard says this is a Bowie tanto made of 440C stainless Damascus with stag and amber handle. (Scadlock photo)

(Left) Long Chuck Blum tanto has Ron Smith engraving, a 12-inch blade.

This double-edged aikuchi by Bud Nealy is just 3½-inch short, is 01 and ivory Micarta with a copper bolster, and very stout. (Petro photo)

Persian fighter pattern by James Porter has a 7-inch blade, sterling silver fittings and bark ivory handles.

Straightforward tanto hunter by Jim Turecek has an interesting pin-and-tube handle pattern.

(Right) Gorgeous horsehead Persian dirk by Leroy Besic is 440C, blued steel and ivory with a 12½-inch blade. The gold inlay is by Byron Burgess. (Weyer photo)

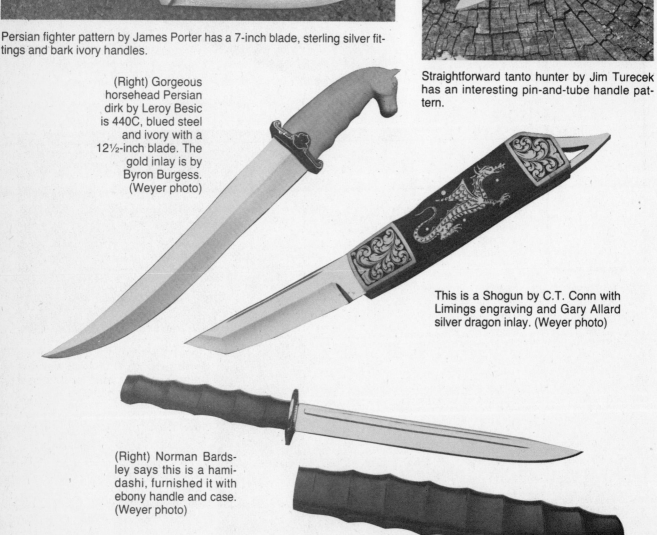

This is a Shogun by C.T. Conn with Limings engraving and Gary Allard silver dragon inlay. (Weyer photo)

(Right) Norman Bardsley says this is a hami-dashi, furnished it with ebony handle and case. (Weyer photo)

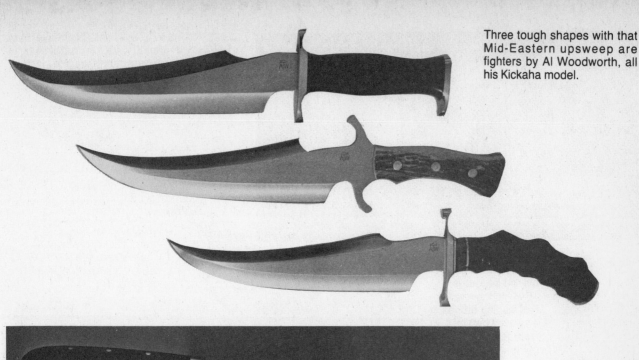

Three tough shapes with that Mid-Eastern upsweep are fighters by Al Woodworth, all his Kickaha model.

Here are two H&W tanto designs, very different one from the other.

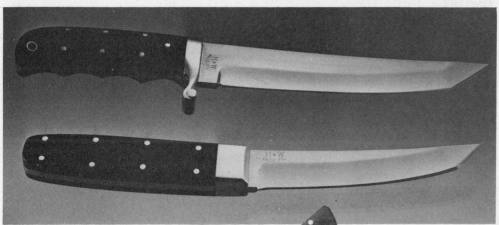

Characteristic Persian shape by Ken Ward has atypical guard. Steel is Parker Edwards Damascus; blade is 7½-inch. (Weyer photo)

Steve Jernigan's Persian style here borrows from the future or the movies, but is very cleanly accomplished for a knife nearly 18-inch long. (Weyer photo)

Butch Beaver made this kris at 18¼-inch total length, gave it a mildly Malaysian handle. (Weyer photo)

(Left) Max Harvey says this is a jambiya made 12¼-inch overall in 440C with stainless fittings in the ivory Micarta. (Macarlino photo)

Steve Likarich says this prizewinner is his Persian razor, made it 8-inch overall in ATS34 and ivory. (Weyer photo)

Ron Frazier's wavy-bladed dagger is 16½-inch, overall, has sterling fittings engraved by Tim George. (Weyer photo).

Much farther East, the wavy blade is favored and Fred Slee likes it, too, in his 11½-inch (overall) kris-style fighter. (Weyer photo)

(Left and above) Decoration for this Persian shape by Ed Brandsey is merely two turquoises, an impala horn and nickel silver fittings engraved by Mel Wood — no gold. (Weyer photo)

(Right) Bob Hardin's fight of fancy in roundly curved profile is as Mid-Eastern as a camel.

TRENDS
THE WORKING STRAIGHT EDGE WORKS

IT SEEMED at first time to give this subject a rest, but some interesting things and some interesting knives happened and so here it is again. It may be the working straight edge will arrive in the consciousness of the knife fancy after all.

Some of the interesting things were the photos you see here. If there is, for instance, a meaner looking fighter around than Paul Holloway's straight edge, it must be a junkyard dog. Curtis Jones's little worker looks like one. And there are Peterson and Benson straight edges that look as tough as the Holloway knife.

And then, thanks to Harlan Suedmeier, both a gener-ation-old working American straight edge knife and its story showed up and you can see them here. A highly respected Puget Sound fisherman named Bill Nifores made straight-edged bait knives in the '50s and '60s and owning one was a mark of fishing excellence. They're called—and marked—Bill The Greek knives.

Apparently, some knifemakers are giving the straight edge some thought. They won't go far wrong if they adopt some of the straightforward profiles you see here. You have to try it to believe it, but that long straight edge works.

Ken Warner

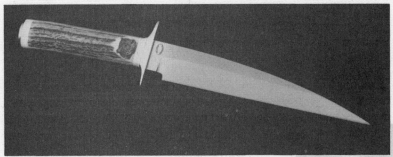

Paul Holloway straight edge fighter looks a serious cutter—it's ATS34 with stag and a tiger scrimmed by Linda Erickson. (Scadlock photo)

A customer designed and bought several of these double-edged straight edges from Lowell Oyster, who calls the pattern "thumb-splitter."

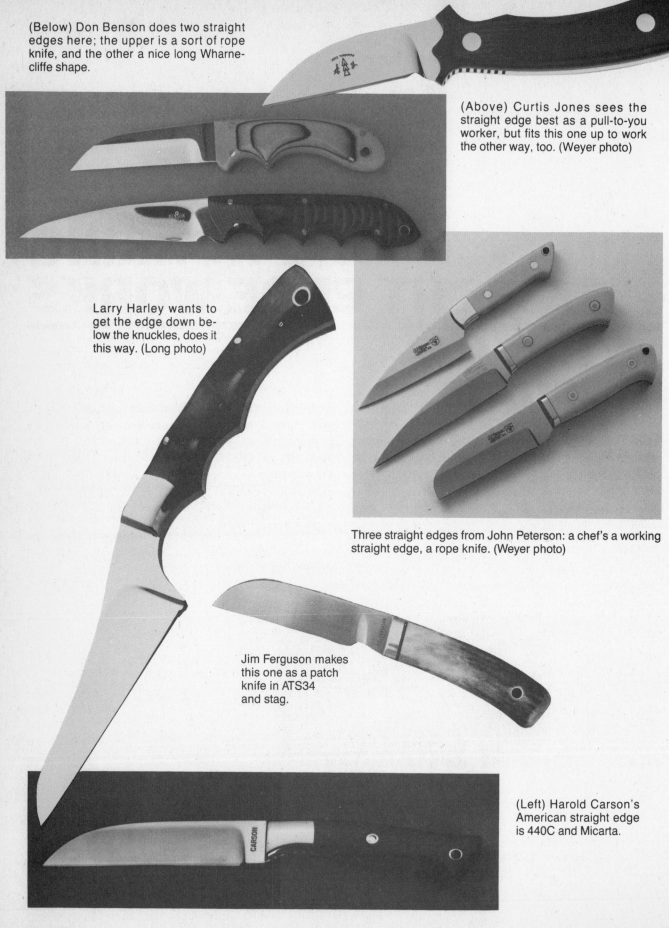

(Below) Don Benson does two straight edges here; the upper is a sort of rope knife, and the other a nice long Wharnecliffe shape.

(Above) Curtis Jones sees the straight edge best as a pull-to-you worker, but fits this one up to work the other way, too. (Weyer photo)

Larry Harley wants to get the edge down below the knuckles, does it this way. (Long photo)

Three straight edges from John Peterson: a chef's a working straight edge, a rope knife. (Weyer photo)

Jim Ferguson makes this one as a patch knife in ATS34 and stag.

(Left) Harold Carson's American straight edge is 440C and Micarta.

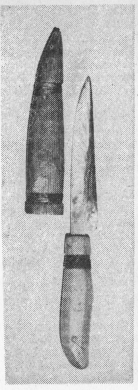

The Steve Brooks straight edge is photographed on sheath-maker Charles Clements' bench. (Cutts photo)

(Above and right) Here is a Bill the Greek knife from the 70s and a look at the late Bill Nifores. The knife is very lightly constructed, very comfortable, very sharp. (Warner photo)

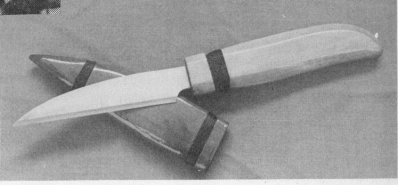

(Left) This is Howard Hitchmough's patch knife design in stag and a straight edge.

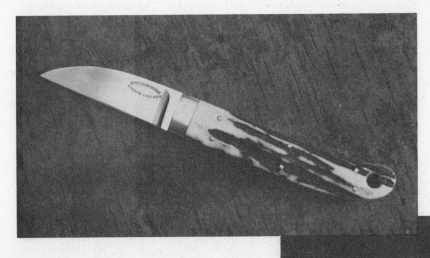

This John Bartlow straight edge is just 6-inches long. (Scadlock photo)

TRENDS
SWORD PLAY

IT GETS more and more difficult to write an introduction to a display of photographs of swords when one hasn't handled the swords. It is in the hand that you can tell nearly all there is to know about a sword and, regrettably, the opportunity just does not arise. So we have to talk of the swords we see here in profile, as it were.

One thing is sure and that is that more and more swords are being commissioned these days. That has a sort of see-saw history. In the recent beginning of the selling of handmade swords, those first fellows had to make the swords and then find customers. Having found some customers, a lot of makers found that they could commission—make the swords to order. Then, it evolved that there was more of a market for high-priced handmade swords than there had been and so it was less of a risk for a fellow to go ahead and make a sword and a lot of them did. And now I think the see has sawed once more and we are back on the made-to-order side of the fence.

Another thing that is true is that we rarely see, from American swordmakers, swords that match the style or the detailing of the swords of yore. Quite correctly, there is considerable interpreting going on. In some cases, this is functional interpretation; in others, it can be called nothing except artistic.

A Swedish swordmaker and smith named Jan-Ake Lundstrom has weighed in with a criticism, well-meant, no doubt, of American swordmakers: "They make a sword blade worthy of a king and put on hilt and knob that only a peasant boy who has not been on his first journey would accept."

All is not lost, however. The adventure called Museum Replicas, which was begun by Atlanta Cutlery, continues to serve the "real" sword market, providing what they call "combat ready" replications of swords of the past. The range is great—from the falchion to that form of rapier which immediately preceded the small sword, from trusty Viking blades to the armor-piercing broadswords of not so long ago.

There are a lot of new swords around these days. There just isn't as much swordplay as there used to be. Possibly, that is a good thing.

Ken Warner

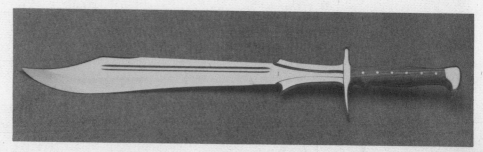

This two-hand falchion by Tim Cross would suit any barbarian who didn't demand double edges. (Lester photo)

Grand ensemble by Virgil England would warm any barbarian heart. Includes, of ironwood, rosewood, ebony, mammoth bone and WE-4, a lance, axe, saber and dagger. (Weyer photo)

(Below) Short broadsword is by Doug Casteel, nicely conceived and made. (Long photo)

Doc Hagen made this beautifully patterned 22¼-inch blade, handled it with twisted wire. (Weyer photo)

The 24-inch blade and the quillons and 21st century basket hilt style are all from Dan Keyes' private stock in 440C and ebony. (Weyer photo)

Really clean Damascus work and profiling mark this handsome ivory-handled Steve Brooks sword.

Here is a Viking sword by the Swedish smith Jan-Ake Lundstrom who does not provide hilts and knobs for peasant boys.

The Eldon Courtney's sense of style has here produced a nasty 22-inch blade of L6 Steel coupled to a three-handed stag handle.

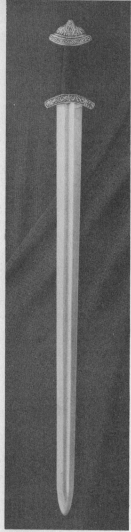

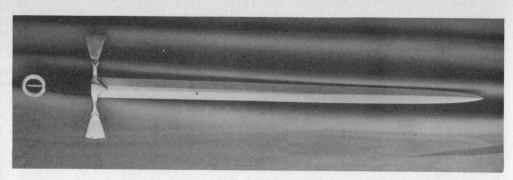

The Irish knights of today can get their Celtic-styled hardware from Museum Replicas.

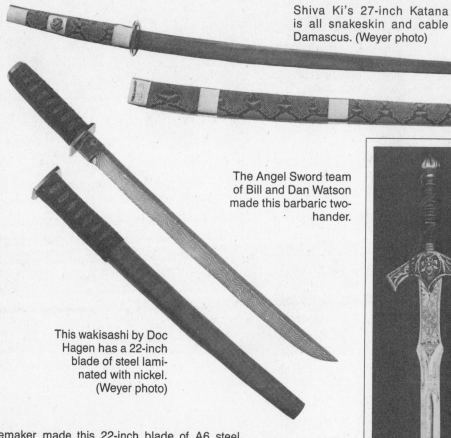

Shiva Ki's 27-inch Katana is all snakeskin and cable Damascus. (Weyer photo)

The Angel Sword team of Bill and Dan Watson made this barbaric two-hander.

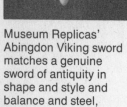

Museum Replicas' Abingdon Viking sword matches a genuine sword of antiquity in shape and style and balance and steel, the company says.

This wakisashi by Doc Hagen has a 22-inch blade of steel laminated with nickel. (Weyer photo)

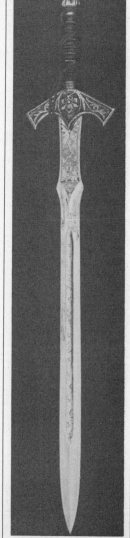

Scott Shoemaker made this 22-inch blade of A6 steel, fitted it with twisted wire over hickory. (Pfahler photo)

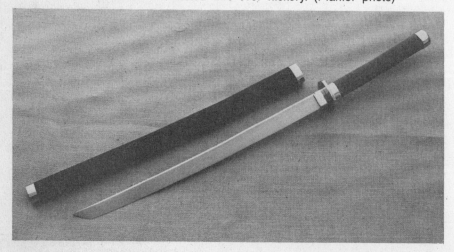

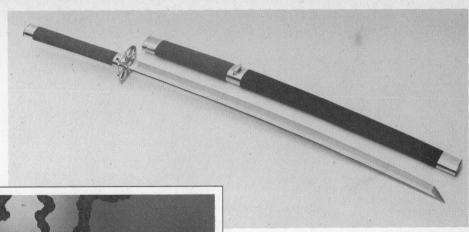

This Tom Maringer Katana is made of D2, has the full twisted wire treatment and an 8-lobed tsuba, but still has the bamboo peg. (VerHoeven photo)

(Above) Working Katana by Phil Harts-field is 36-inch overall — tool steel and black-and-white cord handle. (Weyer photo)

(Above and left) Another source of replica swords is Military Replica Arms of Tampa, now getting into Confederate items.

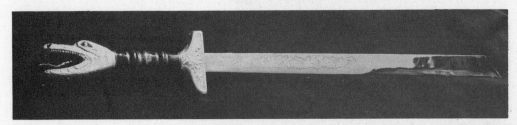

Angel Sword here takes minor liberties with a traditional Moro sword pattern.

For gentlemen who walk and fence, Chuck Stewart often makes things like this bladed stick with warthog tusk handle. (Weyer photo)

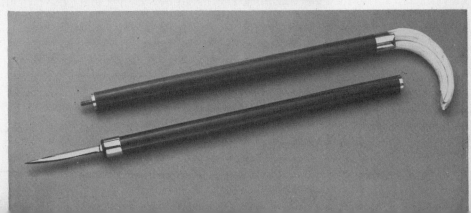

TRENDS
EASY RIDERS

AROUND the Warner house easy riders are in great demand. That is, folding knives that are very, very light in weight and very, very flat, and very, very easy to manipulate and big enough to accomplish something are great favorites. One of us did not know until she grew up that the pockets of blue jeans were for carrying things and consequently whatever goes in those pockets must be the very lightest and slimmest that will get a job done. So, we do not carry wallets, we carry only individual keys when we need them, and we carry easy riders all the time.

It is not, by the way, such an exclusive club, this easy rider unit. Nearly everyone has taken to making easy riders. Specific easy riders of note lately have included offerings from Gerber, Buck, Schrade, several individual makers, and even, or perhaps especially, A.G. Russell.

One two-blade folder of this writer's acquaintance is an easy rider. Very few "traditional" knives can be easy riders, unless they are constructed to be so by some individual cutler. Well, actually that is a rule which is occasionally broken by such things as the bareheaded muskrat trapperjack exemplified by Case No. 61049. That, which is a pattern repeated by almost everybody, is an only slightly bulky easy rider.

It is the bigger such folders that have the most appeal. That is probably where A.G. Russell's One Hand Knife shines, because he sensibly made it with a 3¼-inch blade which gives you a lot of cutting edge for not much bulge. That means that the One Hand Knife gets to go along a lot of the time.

The several models of small lockblade folders with all-plastic handles are high on the lists for constant toting. None of them has failed at getting the job done over the last couple of years, either. Some like one—Deborah Warner favors the Gerber, for instance—and some another—this writer really likes the Western-Coleman No. 526—but they seem to be functionally interchangeable on the basis of more than a few months' use. When it comes to easy riders, it is carrying that counts so long as the cutting holds up.

Ken Warner

Don't know who sells this maroon-handled dude anymore — this one came from Atlanta Cutlery and Bill Moran sharpened it — but somebody ought to. It is a whole lot of knife in a small package. (Warner photo)

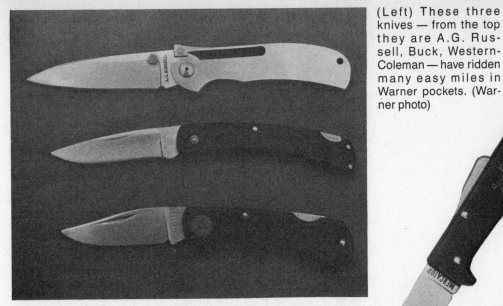

(Left) These three knives — from the top they are A.G. Russell, Buck, Western-Coleman — have ridden many easy miles in Warner pockets. (Warner photo)

(Right) These profiles have been easy riders for generations. The cat knife is a German favorite; whether it's a toothpick or a fish knife or an upscale custom job, a yellow-handled knife shaped like this carries nice. (Warner photo)

Tekna Corp. shapes nearly its whole production to attain the status of easy riders, this "invisible" blade being a fine example of the policy.

It ain't glamorous, but this Buck Creek Senator from Taylor Cutlery shape is a lot of knife in a slim and easy package. (Warner photo)

(Right) Al Mar knives are in the easy rider end of it, too. This one has gone along lots of times. (Warner photo)

(Below) This is a Chuck Stewart locking knife of a type he makes a lot of for gents who don't want to be seen with a knife. (Warner photo)

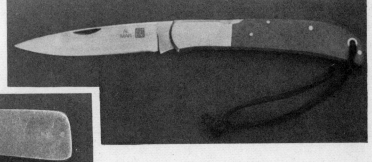

THE LAND OF SMALL

MINIATURE knives have tickled fancies and scratched itches for both makers and collectors. They have also set some makers, embellishers, and photographers to the pulling of hair. And miniatures rarely fail to bring smiles to all who see them.

That's quite a commotion over such small things. They seem to trigger the imagination of all those involved, so much so that some folks have tried to use miniatures for things better left to full-sized knives. So again we caution: Unless your height is between 8 to 18 inches, let the miniatures do what they do best — SHOW OFF. Actually using miniature knives should be left to the micro-folks of our imaginations.

You'll see here material from one miniature maker's brochure. Some makers furnish humor with their miniatures. They are almost as creative as the knives. We also show some wee folks with knives at work, brought to the world by Stanley S. Grossman. He not only makes miniature knives and swords, but the people and settings to go with them.

Deborah Warner

Joe Warner checks out a Stanley Grossman swordsmith at close range. (Warner photo)

The Executive Edge has produced its own commercial miniature, or perhaps just the smallest in their line. (Warner photo)

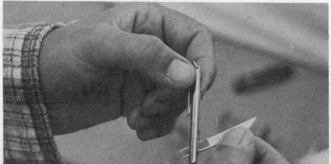

(Below and right) Grossman "scenes" include sword fights, a headsman and his client, knife throwers and their targets, all just right for desk or shelf. He also makes a lot of ordinary astonishing miniatures. (Warner photos)

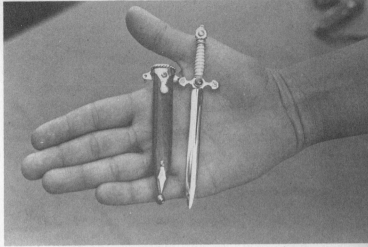

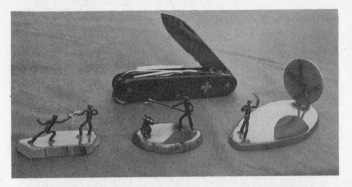

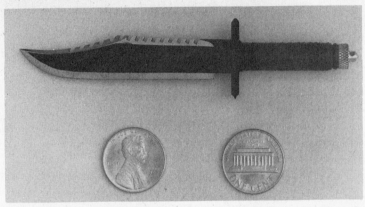

Jimmy Lile will do you a Rambo miniature, just like the ones the big boys play with. (Kiehl photo)

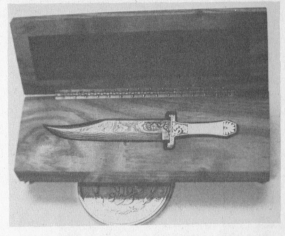

James Whitehead cased his little Damascus Bowie, which means the hinge is *really* tiny.

(Left) Jack and Yvonne Peterson of Nanaimo, B.C., do these cuties — all teeny and all replicas.

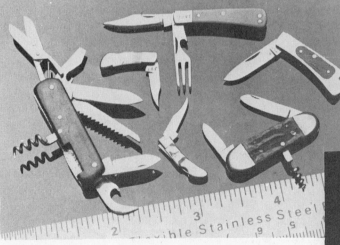

These are all small and all by Doug Casteel. (Long photo)

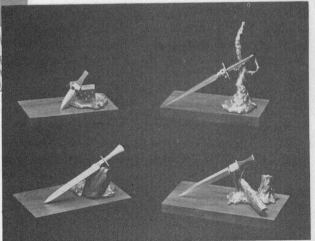

It's hard to think of a tiny Corbet Sigman, but here are three of them. (Weyer photo)

Mike Wesolowski Bowies have that big knife look. (Weyer photo)

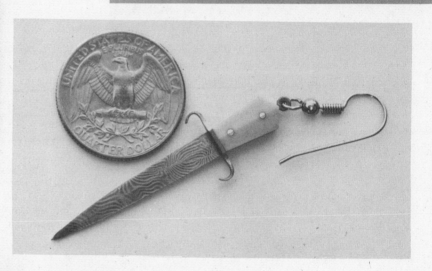

Harry Stalter says this is a functional miniature. (Kelley photo)

(Right) Earrings? Sure. Thomas A. Counts (2924 McNair Ave., St. Louis, MO 63118) made this using Damascus steel from a shotgun barrel. (Kelley photo)

(Left) Ken Ward says he had some help from Pat Donovan with one sheath here, but the rest is all his. (Weyer photo)

Is it easier to make small versions of your own designs? Larry Harley should know — he made all these from his big-knife patterns. (Weyer photo)

(Above) There are, they say, miniatures and micro-miniatures, and here we see one of each by Terry Kranning. (Kelley photo)

This delight to the eyes is just two inches long. The blade by Wayne Hensley is 154CM; DiMarzo carved the ivory handle. (Weyer photo)

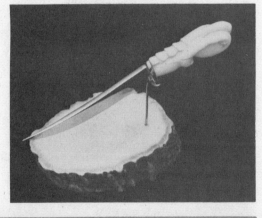

Survivalists,

If you're shorter than 1'3'' it takes both hands to wield a First Blood. Mercenaries, embarrassed because your Bowie drags on the ground behind you? Soldiers, can't get that bayonet out of it's sheath without standing on a rock? Police and SWAT teams, does your boot knife keep you from bending your leg? Do your compatriots laugh behind your back? Your girlfriend blush when you carry a pocket knife? Be a man among men, carry your weapon proudly (and without a hernia). I make miniature fighting knives for tiny warriors.

These swords are made form high-carbon steel cement nails by Ronald Blum. (Weyer photo)

Earl Witsaman does the 19th century again in two kinds of Bowie. (Weyer photo)

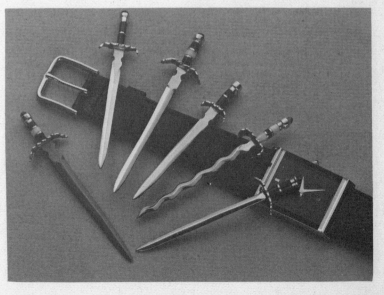

TRENDS
KNIVES OF THE YEAR

A ROYAL year, it seems, is upon us. From Tokyo to the Middle East, the handmade knife has been used to illuminate people and occasions. A Prince of Japan has a set, and so does a Prince of Jordan.

And then the events: there's a knife for the Centennial of—hang in there, now—golf in America and another celebrating Smithsonian's display of a Big Daddy Garlits vehicle and—well, you get the idea.

It's that kind of year. Enjoy it.

Ken Warner

(Above) This Happy Jack folder commemorates Don Garlits' Swamp Rat XXX.

This Ralph Harris Bowie is clearly inscribed ''Golf In America.'' (Long photo)

This handsome set in 440C, 154CM, silver, gold and ivory was presented during 1988 to a prince of the royal family of Japan. Shiro Furukawa made the knives.

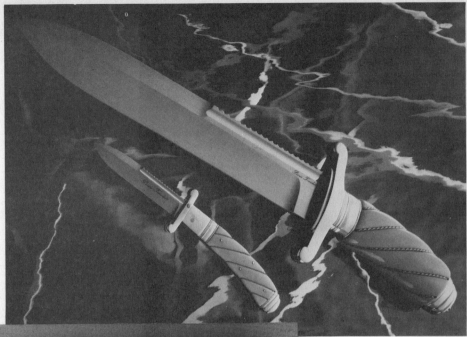

(Below) Gov. Harris of Georgia proclaimed April Georgia Knife Collectors month, so the Flint River Knife Club commissioned this Rade Hawkins knife engraved by Fred Henderson.

(Below) Prince Hussein of Jordan is shown here with his new Moran knife and with Margaret and Bill Moran.

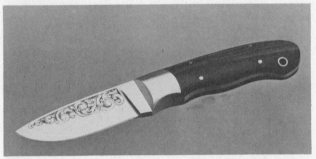

(Above) This is marked "1 of 1 — Tennessee Knifemakers Association." Larry Harley made it; Billy Bates engraved it. (Long photo)

(Below) The tardiest of the Texas Sesqui-Bowies was built by Robert W. Hudson, but it's a biggie.

(Below) Glen Hornby makes a SWAT knife for the L.A. Sheriff's Dept. — SEB means Special Enforcement Bureau. (Fitzgerald photo)

TRENDS
MISCELLANY

IT IS obligatory that we show here both razors and patch knives, and we do. Also, we should get onto these particular pages a few examples of especially interesting, even peculiar, knives that fit nowhere else and we do.

Some years back, it was in Miscellany we began to show what we later gave their own pages as fantasy knives. Somehow, this year has not produced a wide assortment of the fantastic, so we are tucking a couple noteworthy such in right here.

As for the rest—well, all the usual things: a forged Damascus bud vase, a pizza cutter, an obsidian blade or two, interchangeable D-guards. Ho hum.

Ken Warner

Shane Sloan really deluxed this 440C pizza cutter—the blade runs in Camden bushings. (Weyer photo)

(Right) Wayne Valachovic could not resist forging a Damascus bud vase nor could we resist its picture. (Weyer photo)

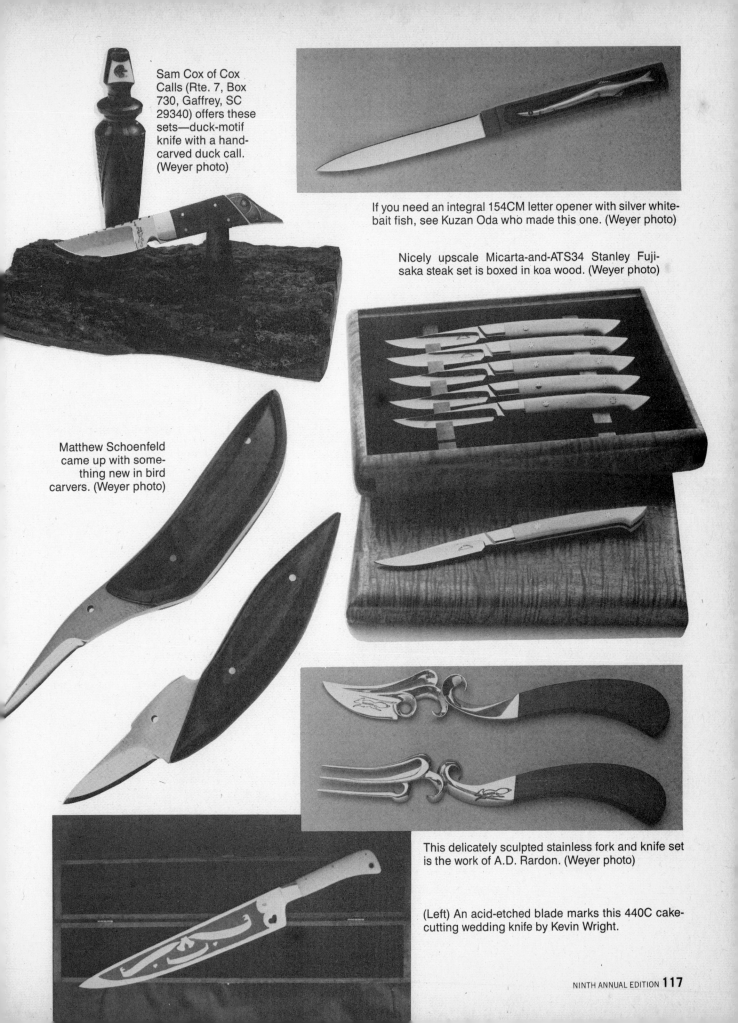

Sam Cox of Cox Calls (Rte. 7, Box 730, Gaffrey, SC 29340) offers these sets—duck-motif knife with a hand-carved duck call. (Weyer photo)

If you need an integral 154CM letter opener with silver whitebait fish, see Kuzan Oda who made this one. (Weyer photo)

Nicely upscale Micarta-and-ATS34 Stanley Fujisaka steak set is boxed in koa wood. (Weyer photo)

Matthew Schoenfeld came up with something new in bird carvers. (Weyer photo)

This delicately sculpted stainless fork and knife set is the work of A.D. Rardon. (Weyer photo)

(Left) An acid-etched blade marks this 440C cake-cutting wedding knife by Kevin Wright.

Earl Black's Green River skinner lays on an 1880s photo of his grandfather. (Rasmussen photo)

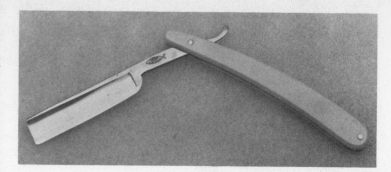

(Top and above) Shane Sloan's dark-handled razor can be locked open by that brass button on the tang; the Frank Lampson white-handled razor is conventional. (Sloan photo: Scadlock)

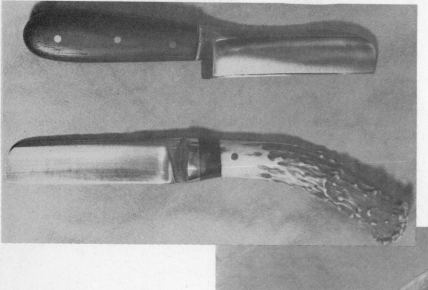

(Left and below) Roger Foust swears one of his buckskinner customers shaves with a Foust patch knife like one of these; he makes the small goat-horn-handled knives (and etches the age into the blades) too, and can fit a cap like a powderhorn if needed.

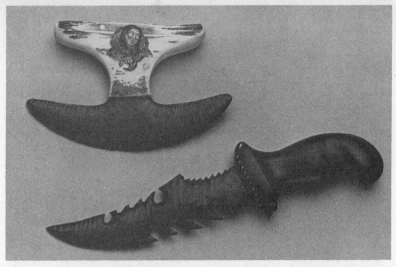

Still flaking, Errett Callahan can make ooloos, presentation pieces, really difficult shapes in obsidian. (Weyer photo)

What those teeth are for in this 15-inch blade Tom Enos hasn't said.

Norm Levine has put a real twist in this dagger blade. (Weyer photo)

Harold Corby has set up this nasty knife with choice of D-guards. (Weyer photo)

McEvoy shape rendered by Martin Kruse has some heavy bevels.

Larry Harley's Battle Bowie is on a photo of Harley and his dad and former live pig killed with the knife. (Long photo)

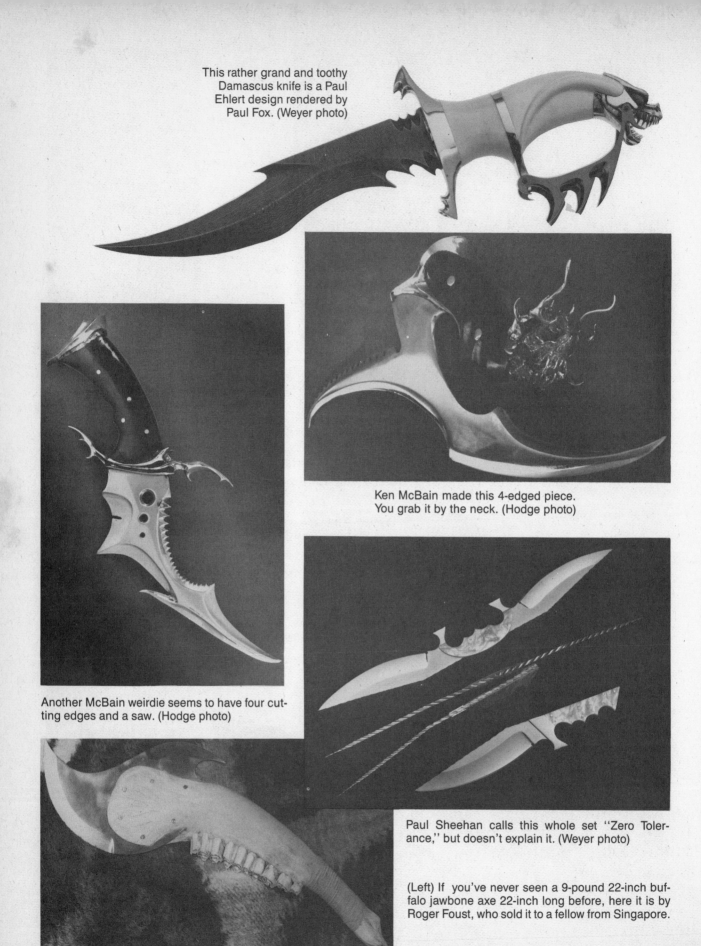

This rather grand and toothy Damascus knife is a Paul Ehlert design rendered by Paul Fox. (Weyer photo)

Ken McBain made this 4-edged piece. You grab it by the neck. (Hodge photo)

Another McBain weirdie seems to have four cutting edges and a saw. (Hodge photo)

Paul Sheehan calls this whole set "Zero Tolerance," but doesn't explain it. (Weyer photo)

(Left) If you've never seen a 9-pound 22-inch buffalo jawbone axe 22-inch long before, here it is by Roger Foust, who sold it to a fellow from Singapore.

STATE OF THE ART

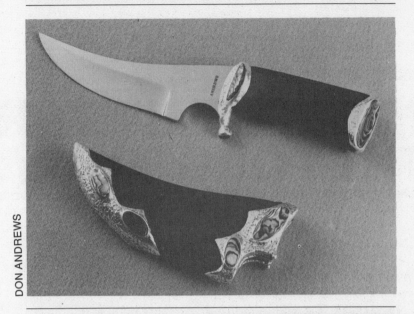

DON ANDREWS

We hope in this part of the book to provide some factual background for the decisions we think the readers will be making about
their own knives, knives they own and knives they hope to own.
The subject has become vast in the past 10 years. More people now
know more things about knives than ever before and that has the
inevitable result that more people will continue to find more new
things as time goes on. This is how some important parts of the
state of the art look now.

Ken Warner

**The Recent History
  of the Forged Blade
Differential Tempering
The Sad State of Knife Leather
Boyd & Father & Orion, Too
Damascus at the Crossroads
Engravers
Scrimshanders
Etching and Carving**

STATE OF THE ART
THE RECENT HISTORY OF THE FORGED BLADE

WHEN IT COMES to blades made of steel hit with hammers, the modern keeper of the flame, in more senses than one, was Randall. Randall-made blades have, with rare exceptions, all been forged. Bo Randall did not make much of the mystique of the bladesmith. He simply believed, then and now, that forging hot steel was a good way to make knives, and also a very efficient and inexpensive way to move metal.

From the beginning of World War II until now, there has stood Randall, metaphorically with hammer in hand, keeping the fires going and the anvils ringing. As a result, those who make knives the same way, those who are the core of, for one instance, the American Bladesmith Society, hold Randall in very high respect indeed. And one among those who accepted the flame and carried it farther than Randall was W.F. Moran, Jr.

Bill Moran was not alone, either. During World War II, a number of knifemakers labored, some of them very hard indeed, to provide sound edged weapons and tools for individual servicemen. Randall lasted through the war and made much the biggest thing of his knifemaking, but he had plenty of company early on. So, too, Bill Moran.

Indeed, it was not until the late '60s that there was much of an alternative for a knifemaker but to forge hot metal to make a knife. The availability of high carbon stainless steel, heat treatable to fairly high hardness and toughness, in small cutler quantities was probably responsible for what was seen at the time as a revolution. There were those who thought that the forged blade was going to remain in eclipse, perhaps to disappear. Randall was keeping on keeping on and some younger fellows also helped carry the torch, some of them on a very lonely basis.

There were, as it turned out, several things about the stock removal revolution, the smithless knives of the '70s, that made it unlikely that the forged blade was going to disappear.

First, of course, given iron with some carbon in it and a fire, you can have a knife. You cannot get a steel knife any other way. Now if the mill provides rolled and annealed bars which the knifemaker grinds to shape and then has heat-treated to get it hard, there is your steel and your fire. Hammer blows aside, the only real difference is who tends the fire.

Unwaveringly, from about 1960 or so until now, Bill Moran tended one fire or another, and so did many of his colleagues and compatriots, to the extent that they are now quite a numerous crew. Their American Bladesmith Society is an even more numerous crew, and has recently taken some serious steps to keep itself known in the world of crafts and the world of knives, of which more nearby.

It seems very likely to this reporter that the event which, more than any other recent event, made it inevitable that the forged-in-the-fire blade would come back strong, was the introduction on the national scene of pattern-welded cutlery steel, called "Damascus."

The guy who did that was—you are correct—W.F. Moran, Jr. Upon that introduction occurred an outstanding example of what is called the Bannister effect. The Bannister effect is named for Roger Bannister, who after decades and generations of people refusing to believe that a man could ever run a mile under 4 minutes,

The campus includes a multi-forge shop, class and study rooms — all it takes. The campus is in Arkansas, at Washington, where the legendary James Black once had his forge. At least 10 notable smiths are in Bill Moran's audience here. (Voyles photo)

did so. Within weeks, so did some other guys and now the sub-4-minute mile is a standard article at any up-scale track meet. Thus it was with Damascus steel for use in knives; given the idea, any competent smith could get it done. And if he couldn't, he could just call Bill Moran, who would tell him.

Damascus steel turned out to be that happy circumstance, possibly the happiest of circumstances for people who sell the stuff: Damascus gave the bladesmith something the other knifemakers didn't have. (Yes, after a while came Damascus bar stock, but it was not until after a while.)

Now, of course, there has been piled miracle upon miracle. People have written their names in Damascus patterns; other people are experimenting with the wonders of a variety of wire cables as a basic function; spurred no doubt by the interest in steel, other people are working on ways to make hard edges and soft backs and on and on and on.

It has been an interesting couple of decades for the forged blade. It went into relative obscurity, but it came out stronger than ever, and right now forged blades are very much leading the pack when it comes to art knives and high-priced collectibles.

And now, as you read this, there is a formal school of bladesmithing with its own campus and buildings, sponsored by the American Bladesmith Society and Texarkana College. It opened in 1988. During 1989, at least eight courses will be taught. (Write James Powell, Texarkana College, 2500 Robison Rd., Texarkana, TX 75501 for details.)

That is, many bladesmiths believe, splendid recognition of their craft. They are probably right. It surely is impressive.

That is not the rest of the story. It is, however, an overview of the recent history of the forged blade.

Ken Warner

With his dream solid, right before his eyes in fact, W.F. Moran, Jr. addresses a knifemaker multitude at opening ceremonies of the Texarkana College school of bladesmithing. (Voyles photo)

STATE OF THE ART
DIFFERENTIAL TEMPERING

KNIVES are tools. This means they get used and, in a world where knives are used as field implements, use often translates into what many makers and manufacturers call abuse. I don't condone abusing fine cutlery, but it does happen, so a good working knife should be able to stand up to a certain amount of abuse.

I believe the best way to accomplish such a knife is with a blade forged from high carbon steel and given a differential temper. The differential temper will greatly enhance the field performance and durability of any knife, whether forged or ground, regardless of the steel used.

Differential temper deals effectively with the dynamics of a blade in use. Different parts of the blade must stand up to punishment in different ways. In a properly tempered blade, there are three areas of different hardness. The edge must be hard enough to take and hold a good cutting edge. The spine should be tough—and therefore softer—so it can withstand shocks from hacking, chopping, or being pounded on if the knife is used for heavy splitting chores. Finally, the tang must be even less hard to allow a high degree of resiliency or springiness so as not to shear from the great stresses this area must withstand during chopping or prying.

Here's how it's done:

The primary requirement is a source of heat. You must have a way to get the steel hot. I use a coal forge. If you aren't a blacksmith and you decide to use a coal forge, your biggest hurdle will be learning to control the fire. If you're not ready to go out and get a forge, don't give up. Heat is heat, as long as there is enough of it and you can control it. An oxyacetylene torch will do the job if that's all you have. I know of one maker who got excellent results with a torch in a firebrick enclosure until he got a gas forge. He's now quite happy with the gas rig and so are several other knifemakers and bladesmiths I know. I suppose even one of them new-fangled electric furnaces would do the trick.

I take my blades to a 220-grit finish before hardening. This preparation is vital as deep scratches left from coarse grinding increase the chance of stress cracks when quenching hot steel.

Hardening is the process of heating the metal to critical temperature and quenching it. Heat the metal slowly, watching the colors change. Be especially patient when passing from black heat to dull red. Slow heat relieves the steel, minimizing the odds of cracks or warpage. This is the stage where any undue stress placed in the steel earlier will show up. Things like rapid localized heat buildup during grinding, cold straightening (a real no-no), plus things you have no control over such as uneven pressure or irregular cooling at the rolling mill can cause the blade to warp when the stress is relieved. In other words, if any of these conditions exist, the blade will warp as it reaches red heat. If this happens, take the piece out of the fire and straighten it while it's hot. Work quickly and get it back into the fire. If you heat-treat more than a few blades you'll have to deal with warping, so be aware and watch for it.

Continue to heat the blade, bringing the steel up to

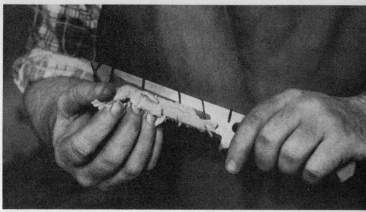

Clay on the hardened edge is Kruse's technique in its essence.

Fire is a requirement. Kruse uses his forge and charcoal — and long tongs.

The clayed and bright blade goes back in the fire for tempering.

The polished end product does not always show the technique.

Right out of the fire, these blades clearly show temper lines that tell what's hard, what's softer.

critical temperature. That's the cherry red you always hear about, called the decalescence point in technical language. With practice, you will be able to judge the color to determine this temperature by eye. There is, however, an easy way to check while you're learning. As the steel starts coming up to red heat, check it frequently with a magnet (hold the magnet with a pair of tongs). When the magnet no longer sticks, the piece has reached critical temperature. To achieve the desired results, you must harden the entire piece.

When it reaches decalescence, leave it in the fire for a few minutes; letting it soak in the heat to insure the temperature (and the hardening) reaches the center. If the steel doesn't reach critical temperature, it won't harden, but great care must be taken not to get it too hot or it will suffer grain growth which will greatly weaken it. Don't let the color reach bright orange.

Quenching completes this phase. I recommend oil. I use olive oil. The surface of the oil will, in all likelihood, flash when you immerse the hot steel. Get the piece down under the surface immediately; the flames will go out. Use long-handled tongs; with pliers you will find out why boiling oil was considered such an effective means of torture.

I've heard a lot of argument about the right way to put the blade in the tub, point down, edge up, or edge down. I go horizontally with the edge down, but I'm not convinced that there's any difference. There's also debate whether it's better to move the blade around or hold it still. I'm convinced moving it too much will cause warpage. Don't let the knife touch the sides or bottom of the quench tub. To do so will cause it to warp. Let the piece cool until you can hold it in your hand.

If everything went right, your blade will emerge straight, completely hard and pretty grungy from the burnt-on oil. Since you can't see the next set of temper colors run under all this crud, clean the piece to bright metal on the belt grinder.

You now can temper your blade, changing the molecular structure from "austenite" to "martensite." There is an art to controlling the process without a lot of high-tech gear. You will be watching for color changes in the steel to indicate temper.

The two factors which determine hardness are carbon content and temperature. If you know the carbon content of your steel, it is a simple matter to determine what temperature, as indicated by the color, will give you the hardness you want. Hotter is always softer.

And now we get to the differential hardening: the part you want the hardest is the thinnest and, therefore, heats faster. How do you get more heat into the thicker spine than the thin edge?

The ancient Japanese swordsmiths hardened and tempered their blades in one step by applying clay to the back of the blade to keep the heat from spreading

Long tongs and a magnet will tell when red hot steel is right for quenching.

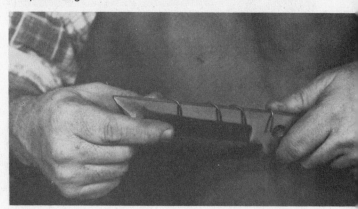

Certain little touches, like a modest wire armature to help hold the clay, are very useful.

After quenching, bright surfaces are required to permit viewing heat colors and this is how you do it.

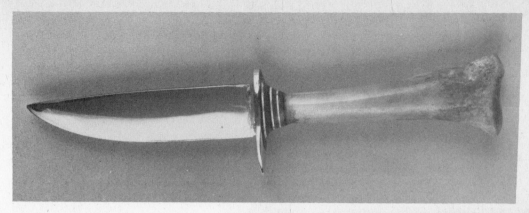

This little knife is tougher than it looks, Kruse believes, because it has a soft back to go with its hard edge. (Buckman & Marsh photo)

(Right) You can check finished hardnesses with a file.

through that portion of the steel. When they quenched, only the edge hardened, leaving the back tough. This gives good results with straight carbon steels. If you want to try this, I suggest you read the article on the samurai edge by Bob Engnath in *Knives '86*. He found this method only works with the 10-series steels such as 1060 and 1095. I believe he also had pretty good luck with W1 but I'm not sure. It does not work with more complex alloys.

You can modify the technique and it is then well-suited to any of the modern steels and gives better control than any other method I've tried. After hardening the blade uniformly, simply apply the tempering clay to the edge of the blade. As for finding tempering clay, well, almost all the old-time smiths had secret formulas, and the formula in Engnath's article works, and I've achieved acceptable results with a commercial product called Heat Fence, available at welding supply stores.

With the clay placed on the edge, heat the knife from the end of the tang. You can then watch the temper colors run the length of the knife. Let the tang draw to a sky blue for the springiness it needs. When the back of the blade (not covered by clay) turns purple or dark blue take the knife out of the fire and quench it again. When the clay comes off, it will reveal a deep bronze edge color and you have a perfectly tempered blade. With a file, you can feel the difference in the different areas of the knife.

There's no such thing as too thick when you put the clay on. Without enough, the edge will draw to the same color as the spine. If the clay was too thick, it will have stopped the heat from reaching the edge and this part won't have changed color at all. So, turn down your heat and put the blade back in the fire until you see the edge reach the proper shade of bronze. Now quench and your heat-treating is finished.

This knife will take more punishment than you can believe. Try it.

Martin Kruse

And as for checking keenness — how else but by shaving hair?

STATE OF THE ART
THE SAD STATE OF KNIFE LEATHER

YOU ARE at your first knife show and you have traveled some considerable distance, paid your entrance fee and are now perusing the tables. You don't know exactly what to expect, but are filled with enthusiasm and anticipation. Soon you are overwhelmed by the variety of blade shapes, the number of steel types—both high-tech and ancient Damascus forge-welded patterns. Handle materials range from exotic animal horn to space-age polymers. Designers offer possibilities from conservative 4-inch drop-point hunters to fantasies in steel.

It might seem, at first, that the current generation of knifemakers have covered all the ground, done their homework, busted their butts, and in general have things well under control. Look a little closer. Better yet, fall in love with a serendipitous knife—the perfect blade, handle, finish, and price—just what you have been searching for . . . still, you sense something missing.

You are an educated consumer; you even read the fine print on your electric bill. So you blurt out, "Does this knife come with some kind of a sheath?"

The knifemaker, an heretofore self-assured fellow of semi-mythic proportions, shrinks before your very eyes, takes on the demeanor of Daffy Duck, and reaches for a grocery bag under the table.

"Sure, one of these. You understand, I hate making sheaths. I just do it because customers expect it. I'm a knifemaker, not a leatherworker. Making knives is creative, I love it, but I hate making sheaths."

Mostly those sheaths show it, I'm sad to say.

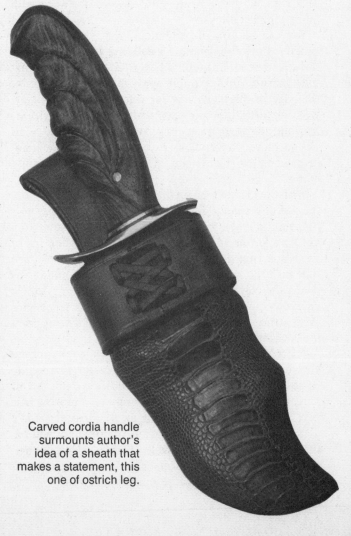

Carved cordia handle surmounts author's idea of a sheath that makes a statement, this one of ostrich leg.

Excluding, for the moment, the many excellent historical reproductions, most current sheath design falls into two general categories: Randallesque box jobs with or without stone pockets, but always it seems, with the retaining strap ready to be severed by the cutting edge of the blade; and Loveless-Morsethian puuko-derived pouches of an undeniable practicality, but not much romance, though sometimes made of black nylon.

Yes, romance is no small part of our interest in knives, I assure you. Ninety-nine point nine percent of the time the knife of your dreams is going to be seen by both you and everyone else in its damn sheath. Why, then should the aforementioned damn sheath not be given due aesthetic consideration by the knifemaker? I suspect that the answer lies in the simple fact that the vast majority of knifemakers came to the discipline via the avenue of metalworking through machine shop or forge. The craft of leatherworking, for most, is a secondary concern, dimly remembered from a junior high shop class of long ago.

A large part of the blame for this sorry state of affairs most surely also rests with collectors and connoisseurs who are themselves indifferent to the sheath as an integral part of the ensemble. It has been suggested to me by the Editor of this fine annual that a serious knife might have several sheaths for different occasions and/or uses. These might include:

The Full Dress Sheath

This sheath, made of the finest materials, would present the ensemble to the public in its most formal and beautiful aspect. The knife and its full dress sheath should be conceived as a whole (though not necessarily by the knife's maker) in order to present the piece as a unified statement. The "statement," of course, would depend on what the knife was about: elegance, forcefulness, ornament, fantasy, history, to name a few possibilities. Every knife-person should own at least one ensemble suitable for wearing to the opera.

(Left) Author ground the blade for this dagger, made the grips from mokume, then created a properly shaped cowhide sheath and covered it with the skin of an African frog. (Right) Wet-molding cowhide can also produce properly exotic shaping, as in these two dagger sheaths by Katz.

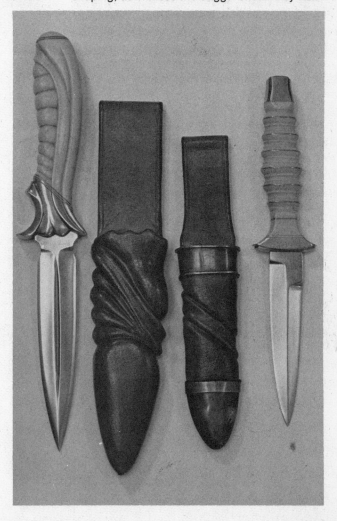

The Field Sheath

Safe carry and convenience—in that order—should govern the designer/maker here. Durable materials, safety straps that are out of harm's way when unsheathing the blade, comfortable carryability are other concerns. The vast majority of today's knife leather falls into this general category, and is derivative of one of the solutions to the problem postulated by the early masters—Randall and Loveless. The Randall box of WWII vintage uses a welt of leather around the blade to separate the back piece, which forms a belt-loop, from the sheath's front piece which usually has a covered pocket for a small and marginally useful sharpening stone. The blade is retained by a strap which passes over the guard and snaps to the sheath-front. This strap is in grave danger whenever the knife is being removed from or replaced in the sheath. As the strap has nowhere to go to get out of the way of the cutting edge, constant presence of mind in use is required of the owner. One of my solutions to the strap-cutting problem of the box sheath may be seen here.

The Loveless pattern of '60s vintage, I suspect, is derived from the Morseth design, which in turn was an evolution of the Finnish puuko sheath. An envelope of leather encloses the blade and some of the handle, although there is no agreement as to how much. The Finns solved the problem of the blade cutting through the stitching by sewing down the back side of the sheath and then wet-forming the leather to a snug fit around blade and hilt. Modern versions feature a plastic insert, much like the old Morseth sheath shown here.

Since the puuko knife had no protruding guard, the knife slid in and out smoothly. The sheath was suspended from the wearer's belt by a leather loop which allowed it to dangle harmlessly out of the way. The modern "pocket" sheath utilizes a seam down the edge side of its main piece, which folds over in the rear to form a belt loop, and along the blade's spine to form a pocket for both blade and part of the handle.

To prevent stitch cutting, a protective strip or "welt" separates the front and back so that the thread passes through three thicknesses of leather as in the Randall design. Most sheaths made today have incorporated this stitch-protecting welt or "cut strip" as some makers call it. Others, however, would prefer the term "anti-cut strip."

A tour of a Knifemaker's Guild show indicates the following breakdown of field sheaths:

Paramilitary knives invariably appear in box sheaths often accompanied by pockets containing compass, flashlight, knifesharpener, and inflatable dinghy and, more and more, these are being made out of synthetics. Nylon has been around in sheaths for some time, but Kydex, a semi-stiff, heat-formable plastic is a relative newcomer, and making serious inroads.

Hunting knives seem to be required by statute to reside in the simpler "pocket" sheaths which, when slipped onto the pants-belt, rest comfortably in the wearer's right-rear pocket. Comfortably, at least, until he or she sits down. Prolonged wearing of this style of knife sheath has been shown to put pressure on certain groups of nerves which may result in the wearer's development of a permanent and incurable rural southern dialect of speech.

The Concealment Sheath

While the blatant display of long knives dangling from belts is acceptable in the deep woods and on stage during the performance of certain Italian operas, most

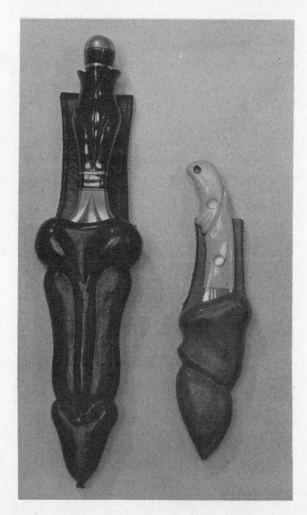

These two knives were actually two pair, made collaboratively with Tim Wright. The sheaths are the products of as much craft as the knives.

AUTHOR: *Professor Brian Katz is at least a semi-Renaissance man, a humorist and cartoonist and collector and teacher of photography with a Master of Science degree and a leatherworker who is an official Bachelor of Fine Arts.*   K.W.

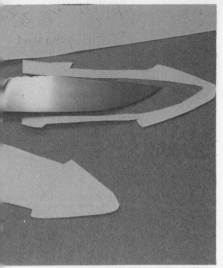

(Above) When exploring ways to sheath a Bowie creatively, books help. The sheath will be worn thrust through the belt, so the design should provide thick sections top and bottom.

Next is to make a set of patterns out of light card stock or heavy paper. The actual knife blade is used for reference to prevent a shock later on.

The paper pattern is made in two or three pieces and "assembled" several times. One measures twice and cuts once on leatherwork.

(Below) Trace the patterns onto the flesh side of the leather with a pen. An Exacto blade makes life bearable through this stage.

Leather cement (contact-cement sold in small tubes works fine) is applied to all of the surfaces which need to be glued together, but *nowhere else*. Then follow the glue manufacturer's directions.

With the pieces of leather glued together, carve the sheath to shape using whatever tools work. Rasps and files smooth out the curves. Small errors can be patched with Plastic Wood filler. Apply a generous coat of lacquer over the outside of the sheath and allow it to dry, then sand and repeat.

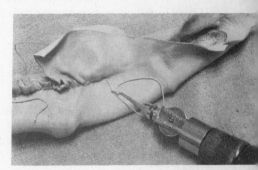

Very thin cow, goat, lizard, frog or sheepskin is selected. Only vegetable-tanned leathers will work when radical stretching and forming are required. I always make tests when using an unknown hide.

The stained and polished sheath is shown with the knife for which it was made. The sheath should be allowed to sit in a warm place for several days before use to allow thorough drying inside and out to prevent blade rusting.

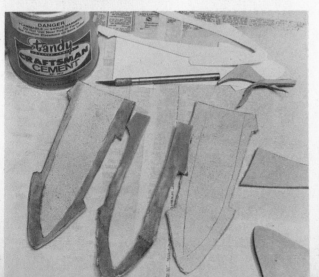

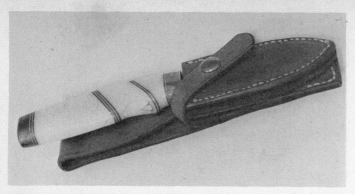

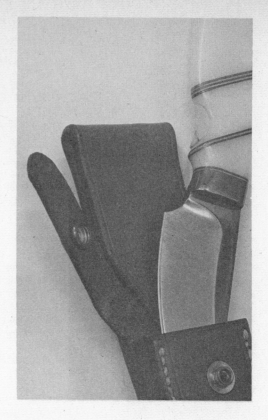

(Above and right) Usual box sheaths put the ever-present safety strap at constant hazard, but if it were arranged this way, one big objection to the box sheath would disappear. The strap here not only has a place to go, but does so easily and stays there until wanted.

of the nicer restaurants and beer joints in my part of town have been trying for years to get us to stop this behavior. A phenomenon that is often referred to as "The Social Contract" is responsible for two major changes in knife design since the Indian Wars.

First, and most obvious, is shorter knives. Again using a Guild show as an example, the 4-inch blade seems to be the most popular size for "hunting" as well as "boot" knives, and represents the vast majority of blades presently shown. Paramilitary or survival blades go a few inches longer, but rarely past 8 inches.

The second historical change is the development of low visibility or concealment sheaths. All of the subterfuges of firearms concealment have been adapted to knife sheath design in recent years: shoulder harnesses, ankle straps, etc. The all-time favorite in my collection is the Belt Buckle Knife—a clever device which has a serious 3-inch blade attached to a belt buckle which serves as its grip. The blade is secured within the belt, which acts as its sheath. Imagine this: you are approached on a dark street by a thug, you whip out your Belt Buckle Knife, and . . . your pants fall down around your ankles. Less favored by me are a few concealment sheaths that work.

The fraternity of knife lovers would be better served if leather-shy makers would adopt a policy either of reform or of abdication. That is, learn to love the sheath-making aspect of their craft or, if that proves to be out of the question, farm the work out to someone who will give the job the attention it deserves. An example of this sort of experimental collaboration is shown here where blades by Tim Wright of Chicago (a first rate sheathmaker himself), have been provided with furniture by the author.

Historically, this was the way it was done, and I am certain that there would be appreciation among collectors and enthusiasts for a long overdue renaissance of high-quality knife sheath making. The wonderful handmade knives of today far outshine their counterparts of yesterday, and it's time for their sheaths to catch up.

Brian Katz

The author's point of view is reinforced by his ability to practice what he preaches: The mokume patterns complement the shapes of the handle and the pattern in the skin complement the blade and the mokume. It is all of a piece.

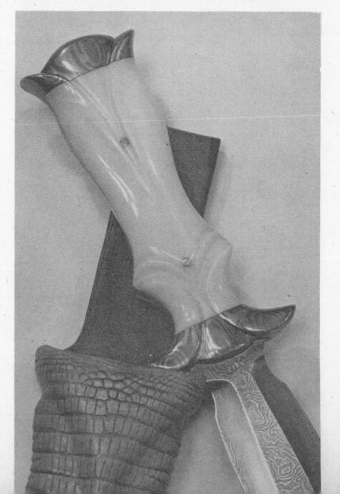

STATE OF THE ART
BOYD AND FATHER, AND ORION TOO

SOME knifemakers are sort of patent-oriented; most are not. Some of the inventive fellows make their marks — Paul Poehlmann of the Paul Knife for one, Bob Cargill differently for another. Others don't.

We're going to have a chance to see in the case of the knives you see here. Their patents are pending; their designs are set; all it takes now are customers.

Francis Boyd, who has patented square-axled locks, got together with Francis Boyd, Sr. to develop this one to be easier to make. They both think it will fly.

Del Reed is marketing the Orion Swing-Blade knife. He says it was invented by a hunter who hates dull knives. There are to be two models — one has identical clip blades; the other has a clip blade and a caper.

Ken Warner

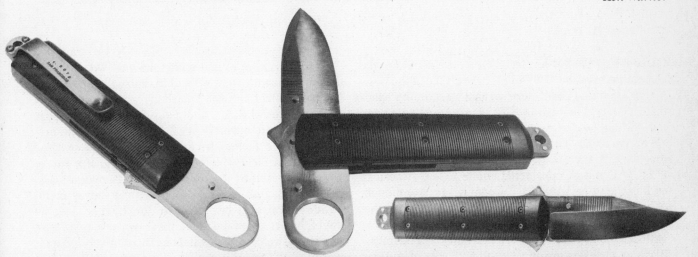

(Above) Francis Boyd and Father have developed this to-be-patented folder which they say is as strong as a straight knife, but folds. It is certainly handsome enough, regardless.

Del Reed's brand-new Orion Swing-Blade works by removing the handle surround, swinging the blade, and sliding the finger guard section back, where it latches under tension.

STATE OF THE ART
DAMASCUS AT THE CROSSROADS

QUICKER THAN anyone might have thought, the current price of the U.S. dollar has re-shaped the position of Damascus or pattern-welded steel on the hand-made cutlery market today. Things are simply not what they used to be.

Foreign sources are not nearly as important as once they were in the Damascus bar stock market, for one thing. All things considered, quite a few American smiths who 4 or 5 years ago would never have thought of creating bar stock for others to use have taken to that role very nicely. Any time an adept smith gets burnt out on forging blades or is in need of a quick and business-like check, he can get up on a roll with a forge and stay away, for a while, from all those picky details involved with putting handles on knives and making sheaths and dealing with one-at-a-time customers.

So there is a lot of that going on. The two who have done the most for what we will have to call commercial Damascus steel are Rob Charlton, who does business as Damascus-U.S.A., and Fain Edwards who does very little knife business at all anymore, but who created a whole factory to make a Damascus steel he called AmeriSteel which he turned over to Jim Parker who has combined it with an honest-to-goodness cutlery factory and makes Damascus steel knives there, besides furnishing bar stock to Tommy Lee and, no doubt, others. Between them, these two have made a lot of pattern-welded blades happen at relatively popular prices.

Meanwhile, in a hundred forges, all sorts of interesting Damascus patterns are happening. Some of them are pretty ingenious; some are just plain hard work.

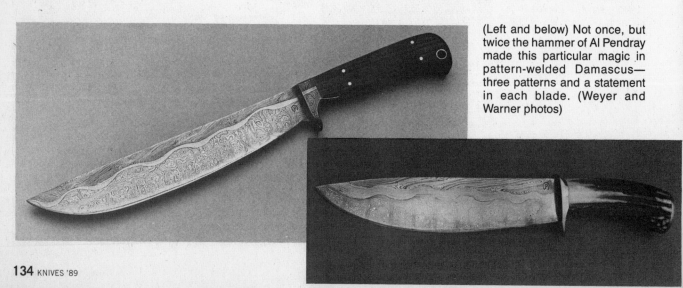

(Left and below) Not once, but twice the hammer of Al Pendray made this particular magic in pattern-welded Damascus—three patterns and a statement in each blade. (Weyer and Warner photos)

Sid Birt somewhat simplified his output recently. These four seem to be cable Damascus. (Weyer photo)

These are Dave Ber cable Damascus blades. (Scherrer photo)

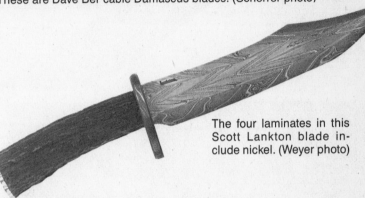

The four laminates in this Scott Lankton blade include nickel. (Weyer photo)

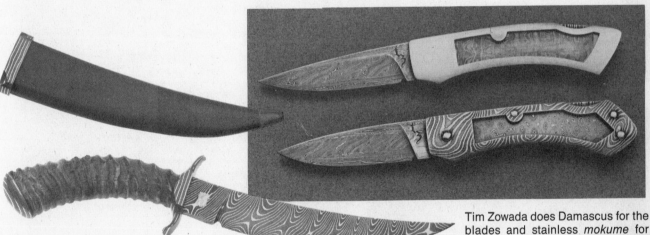

Tim Zowada does Damascus for the blades and stainless *mokume* for the handles here, calls these "picture frame folders." (Weyer photo)

(Above) Spring steel and nickel laminated make this striking curved dirk by Doc Hagen. (Weyer photo)

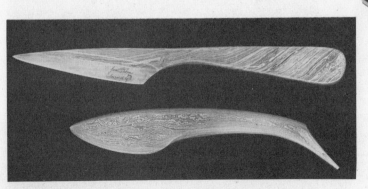

Two exercises in Damascus by Jim Batson: the straight knife is wrought iron with 01 steel; the other is L6 and low carbon steel.

This William Behnke big hunter has a *san mai* blade, cable Damascus over L6, and horn handle scales. (Weyer photo)

Cleston Sinyard says this mountain man Bowie blade is 440C Damascus steel. It's 11-inches long.

Chuck Stewart's little Duke interframe has a German stainless steel Damascus blade. (Weyer photo)

(Left) Robert Coogan made this tough-looking little knife with Shining Wave Damascus from Phil Baldwin.

(Below) These four working blades by Ed Lane are made in Parker-Edwards Damascus steel.

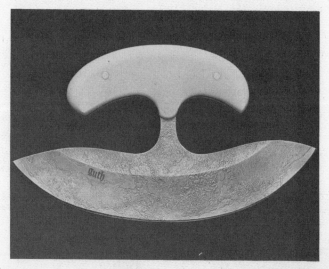

(Below) This ooloo blade is 440C. The surface treatment Kenneth Guth says, is called "Shini gaeru kawa."

(Above) Akihisa Kawasaki made this traditional carving knife of forged stainless steel. Fittings are nickel silver. (Weyer photo)

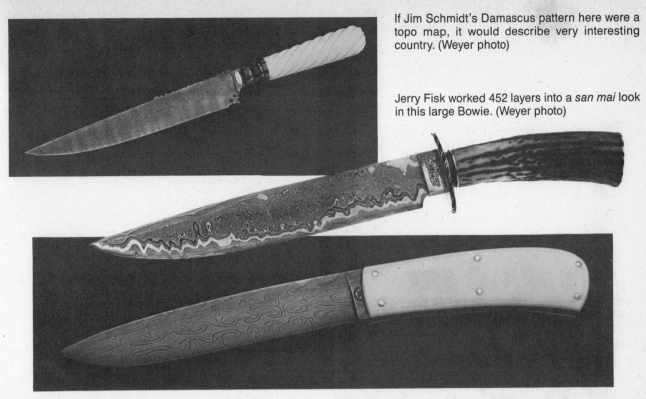

If Jim Schmidt's Damascus pattern here were a topo map, it would describe very interesting country. (Weyer photo)

Jerry Fisk worked 452 layers into a *san mai* look in this large Bowie. (Weyer photo)

(Above) This is four twisted bars with a spider bar on the top side, says Steve Schwarzer. (Weyer photo)

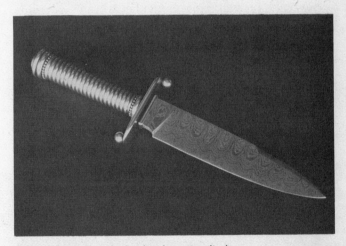

Tai Goo's blade here is simply meteorite iron and tool steel; the handle is simple sterling silver; the assembly is rich and complex.

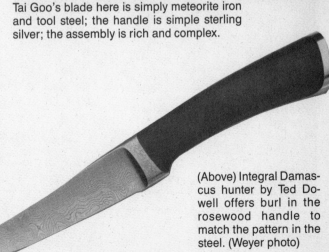

(Above) Integral Damascus hunter by Ted Dowell offers burl in the rosewood handle to match the pattern in the steel. (Weyer photo)

Among those who do the very difficult is Jerry Rados, who spends must of his time these days creating what might be called "perfected" Damascus patterns with tight little scrolls in almost geometrically precise layouts. Over on the ingenious side, there is Larry Pogreba, who buys Damascus shotgun barrels and uses the thick rear portions to provide a handsome and decorative *sanmai* layers around blades of forged tool steel.

(And what does Pogreba do with the rest of the shotgun barrels? Well, has found a jeweler who likes to make — believe it or not — Damascus rings by lining little slices of shotgun barrel with one or another more noble metals.)

Did we mention cable or welded wire Damascus? That's big stuff and getting bigger. And you'll see some stainless steel Damascus here and there.

Damascus steel has genuinely arrived as a commercial proposition outside of the far-flung Parker empire. The new knives of the Harley Owners Group are pattern-welded steel, a joint venture between Gil Hibben and Rob Charlton; the knives of the Safari Club International are pattern-welded, this time from Damascus-U.S.A. A considerable proliferation of other knifemakers are standardizing Damascus patterns — that is blade patterns — and making a series of knives.

So, once again now, Damascus is at a sort of crossroads. Everything is not coming up roses, but it is certainly coming up in patterns.

Ken Warner

STATE OF THE ART
ENGRAVERS

WE ARE getting some remarkable amalgamations these days in the application of engraving to knives. We see ambition and teamwork, and new business set-ups, and even new styles, some successful. There are, it seems, more knifemakers who engrave their own work, and a growing group of husband-wife teams, the lady doing the artwork, generally.

With all that happening, there's little wonder we are also seeing some very grandly executed knives alongside a very large number of well-covered pieces. Some

makers, obviously, have a considerable percentage of their output done up by engravers.

In part, we are seeing a cooperative effort wherein engravers do the work in advance of sale and share in the increase of value. A sound maker might send a $750 knife to an engraver who might do $750 worth of work on it. The two craftsmen share any advance over $1,500. This does not require so much trust as you might think because there are very few secrets about such things.

Ken Warner

This Centofante folder has become a memorial to its owners friend of 13 years thanks to Scott Pilkington's engraving. (Long photo)

A Steve Hoel coke bottle shape in nickel silver provides an engraver with a lot of scope and Steve Lindsay used it.

(Above) This Jess Horn folder is one of a marvelous set of four, each by a different engraver, commissioned by a New York collector. (Left) This is the Steve Lindsay-engraved knife.

High style engraving often meets high-tech cutlery when Patricia Walker engraves a Michael Walker knife.

Buster Warenski can engrave Warenski knives, but so can Julie Warenski, who did this one. (Weyer photo)

(Left) The team of knifemaker Wolfe Loerchner and engraver Martin Butler make quite a number of English-scrolled knives like this.

(Below) Integral Butch Beaver hunter here gets bolster and pommel engraving by Judy Beaver. (Weyer photo)

(Below) T.M. Dowell chose Ron Skaggs to engrave this integral folder. (Weyer photo)

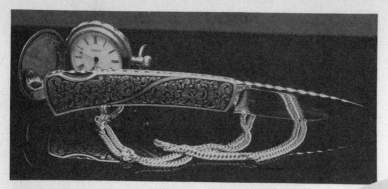

(Left) The full metal case of this Bill Cheatham knife got the full scroll treatment from Bruce Shaw.

(Below) Eric Meyer suggested this pattern to Mike Leach, who made the knives, and Joe Rundell engraved it. (Weyer photo)

(Above) Webster Wood's dress Bowie was engraved by himself. (Weyer photo)

(Right) Big scroll on a small Noel Wheeler knife is by Joe Kostelnik. (Weyer photo)

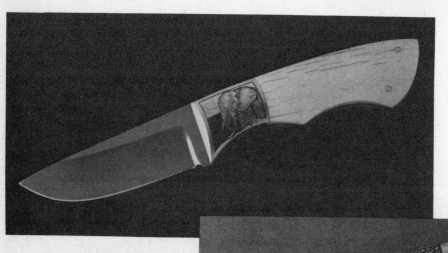

Style here is almost a signature for Dennis Brooker who put this tusker on an R.B. Johnson knife.

Ron Gaston's pearl folder is embellished with scroll by Louis Sanchez. (Weyer photo)

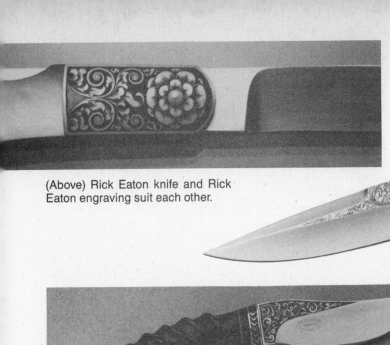

(Above) Rick Eaton knife and Rick Eaton engraving suit each other.

(Below) Steve Lawson signed this project, did it all. (Weyer photo)

This is a Richard Essegian production, *le tout ensemble.* (Weyer photo)

Beryl Driskill did the whole thing here. (Weyer photo)

Bob Conley engraved his own stainless steel bolsters here. (Weyer photo)

Jim Sornberger does his high style thing on this Sornberger folding dagger. (Weyer photo)

STATE OF THE ART
SCRIMSHAW

SCRIMMING, we have to remember, is mostly performed on surfaces people merely look at, whereas hereabouts we look only at scrimshaw on knife handles. Given their druthers, few scrimshanders would opt for knife handles. Big slices of whale or elephant tooth are a lot more fun.

Still, if someone will pay, scrimmers will scrim. And those who make and those who buy handmade knives are beginning—excuse this, please—to get a handle on scrimshaw. The use of the art form is more assured these days, and so, more and more, scrimshaw on knife handles appears to *belong* there.

A word about terminology: The art of drawing with scratches on the surfaces of natural materials like ivory is *scrimshaw.* Those who do this are called *scrimshanders.* Scrimshanders *scrim*—they do not *scrimshand*—and so most often call themselves *scrimmers* and sometimes call their art *scrimming.* Clear?

Ken Warner

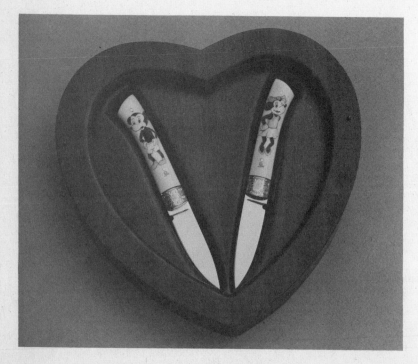

Joe McReynolds celebrated the Guild's arrival in Orlando and the Disney attractions by scrimming Mickey and Minnie on David Ree knives. (Weyer photo)

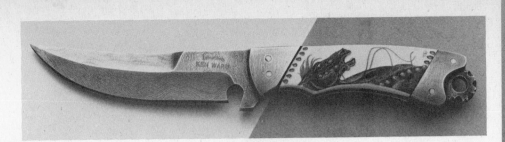

(Above) War horse by Tara Walker looks right at home on a Persian-style knife by Ken Ward. (Weyer photo)

Masterful eagle by Rick Fields is on mammoth ivory on a Lovestrand knife. (Weyer photo)

Dragon a wing and castle in color are by Linda Karst on a Bob Papp dagger. (Weyer photo)

Handsomely designed and placed Canada geese are by Charles Rece.

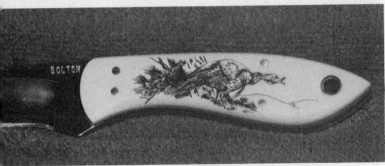

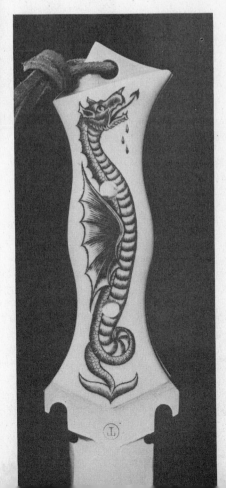

Gobbler on the make is on a Balton knife, scrimmed by Mike Ochonicky.

Cute pumas by Charles Hargraves, Sr. include mom and the kits.

This upright dragon's on a C.A. Jones knife.

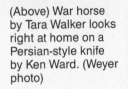

Joe McReynolds did this bearclawed warrior on a David Ree knife. (Weyer photo)

That's Quanah Parker on the ivory handle of one of Sean's folders says Carole McWilliams.

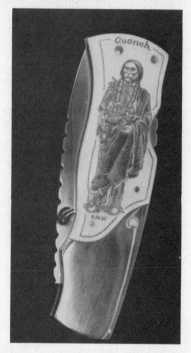

(Above and right) Bob Engnath and Charles Hargraves, Sr. both essayed the same Native American, working from the same photo, shown with the Hargraves scrim.

Dale Fisk did this handsome Indian with date on a Centofante folder.

CWM gets nicely scrimmed knives on Christmas and birthdays. The mountain men and Confederate heroes are scrimmed by Judy Bouchard.

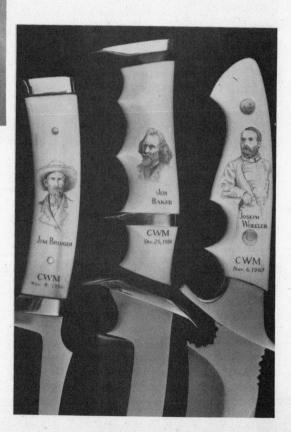

This warrior lady is into lions. John Ketner scrimmed her on a J.P. Miller dagger.

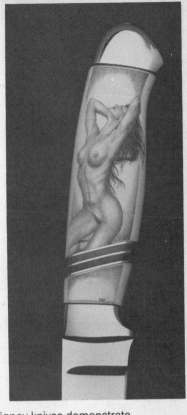

Rick Fields ladies on Gouker and Rigney knives demonstrate the scrimmer's fine sketching talent. (Weyer photos)

Charles Hargraves, Jr. brings us these women, wherever they are, from two different cultures.

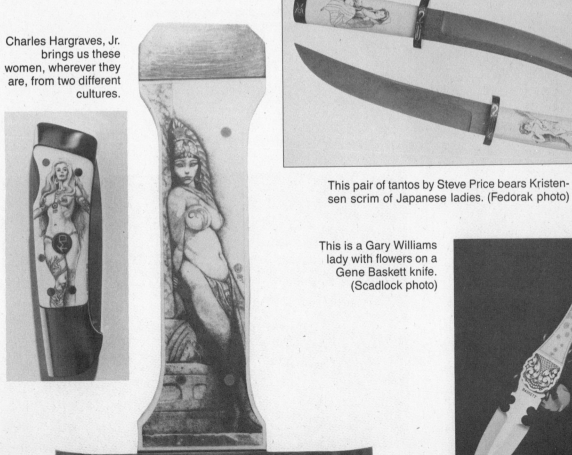

This pair of tantos by Steve Price bears Kristensen scrim of Japanese ladies. (Fedorak photo)

This is a Gary Williams lady with flowers on a Gene Baskett knife. (Scadlock photo)

STATE OF THE ART
ETCHING AND CARVING

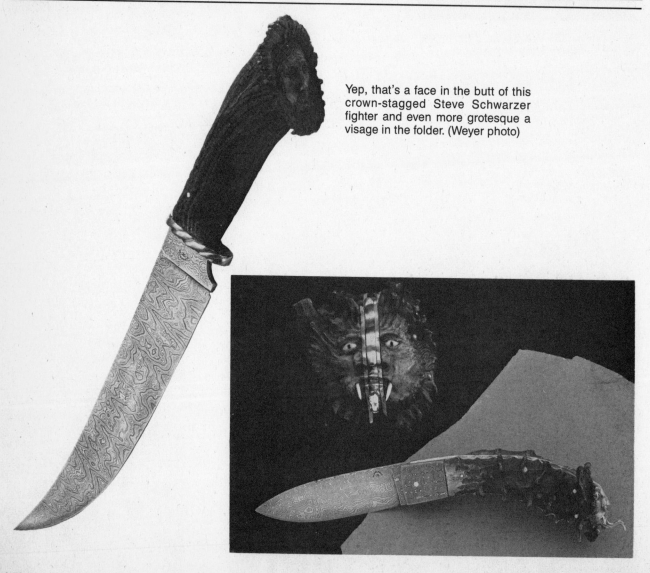

Yep, that's a face in the butt of this crown-stagged Steve Schwarzer fighter and even more grotesque a visage in the folder. (Weyer photo)

Dave Longworth did it all here — carved and wire-wrapped the ivory handle, inlaid some gold and etched the blade. (Scadlock photo)

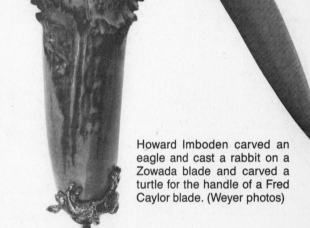

Howard Imboden carved an eagle and cast a rabbit on a Zowada blade and carved a turtle for the handle of a Fred Caylor blade. (Weyer photos)

(Below) For this Stanley Fujisaka personal design called Griffon, Bobby Tang provided the etching. (Weyer photo)

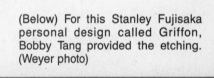

Jim Schmidt gets into grotesquerie now and again, but rarely more flamboyantly than on this all-out folder. (Weyer photo)

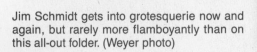

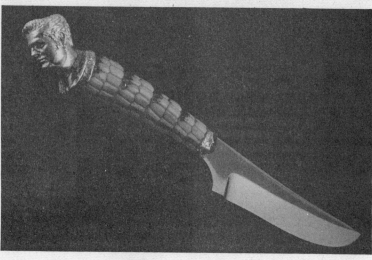

Yep, this odd Don Andrews knife has a man's head at the pommel and a handle wrapped with armadillo.

Jose C. deBraga provides a lady, a trident and a seahorse twice in ivory Micarta. (Weyer photo)

Norton hunter is haunted by Dennis Holland carving and embellished with Frank Clark scroll. (Weyer photo)

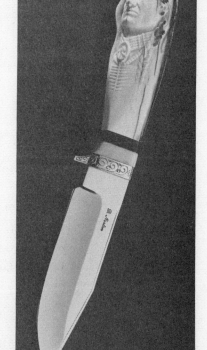

This Gary Little ramshead is sterling silver, the handle horn, the blade 840-layer Damascus. (Weyer photo)

Barr Quarton is still doing raptors, this one a peregrine head on a fighter in Damascus, fossil ivory and sterling silver.

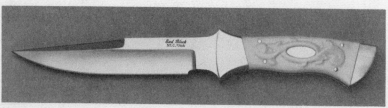

Earl Black made this knife and carved its ivory handle in relief. (Rasmussen photo)

MUELA

Here is background, both technical and historical, against which the reader can judge and consider commercial cutlery for his own use. Despite a natural tendency to market the tried and true, the factories try to meet new needs every year.

We'll look at the old standard patterns, too, sometimes. They are all knives, and these are the knives that sell in millions every year.

Ken Warner

Work Knives Today
Remington Repeater
Sabatier:
Forged Blades at $4 an Inch
SAK Now & Ever?
New Knives in Production

FACTORY TRENDS
WORK KNIVES TODAY

THE PURPOSE of any knife, of course, is to do cutting work, but that's not what we're talking about here. We are talking about those patterns of folding knives generally accepted by all of us as working patterns, patterns people work with, patterns working people choose to use.

There are several front-runners: The electrician's knife; the hawkbill pruning and linoleum knife; budding and grafting knives; florists' knives; and loads of really specialized blades. If any common patterns have stood the test of time, these certainly have. It is no trick at all to discover all but the electrician's knife in 19th century catalogs, printed before electricity was in general use. Indeed, in those catalogs you will find a great many more patterns then common and now virtually gone, but every one of them distinctly a work knife.

Apparently these patterns are not just stodgy old staples carried by the major companies as "open stock" and sold in the same places they've been selling for decades. No less an influence than Buck Knives is bringing out three new working patterns they call Guildmasters. They are definitely Buck's—all knife. They each have one standard Buck-style locking blade, and are done up with black checkered rubber handles and a finish suitable for their station in life—nothing fancy here.

With this advent of a pretty big name into a pretty old game we thought it a good time to round up some of the work knives of the other parties in the business, and you will find pictures in plenty nearby.

Ken Warner

Garden supply houses sell this unmarked (in English) Japanese trowel-weeder-root-cutter which is a *real* work knife. (Warner photo)

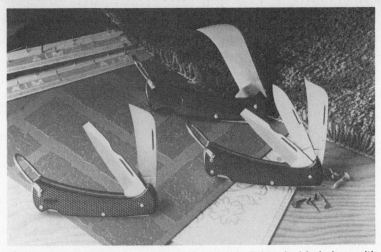

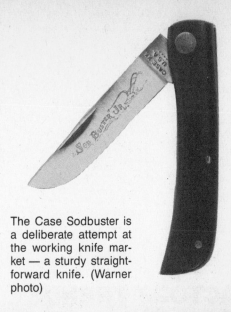

Buck's Guildmasters are sturdy, but relatively light, sizable knives with pretty easy actions.

The Case Sodbuster is a deliberate attempt at the working knife market — a sturdy straightforward knife. (Warner photo)

Colonial goes for the low end of the utility knife market with this 4-blader at $13 or so.

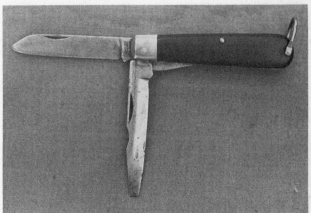

(Above) The TL-39 GI knife set a sort of standard for work knives. This one, by Camillus, has worked its way for a while. (Warner photo)

(Left) Three Colonial knives in the electrician series offer plain or stainless and a hawkbill option.

(Below) Classic Case styling surrounds this pruning hawkbill and hawkbill-equipped electrician's knife.

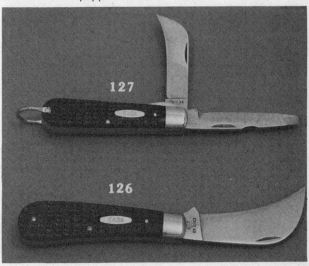

FACTORY TRENDS
REMINGTON REPEATER

IN CASE you have wondered what Remington is going to do next, here it is:

First, the new bullet pattern is the 1982 trapper design, but this time in cocobolo instead of Delrin bone. It's No. R-1128.

Then, they will have a neat gent's locker in Delrin bone with a 2¹/₈-inch pen or sharp drop-point blade. This one is built slim to be slim.

And the heavy design hit is in a deer hunter's 3⁵/₈-inch drop point fixed blade with a couple of interesting features beyond a slim handle in Delrin stag. The edge is a sweeping skinner edge, and the back is a bone-cutting saw. There's a finger-placement spot on the back,

just behind the point, and set into each side of the blade is a carbide dot—these together permit the user to choke way up on the point with some security, Remington says, for those fine cuts.

That's a pretty full program for somebody that isn't even in the knife business. Last year's introduction of four somewhat different hunter's knives together with a nifty small muskrat bullet pattern would have seemed enough for a while, but the people at Remington say this thing is going well and they are not going to let up on it right yet. It is already apparent that for collectors Remington has repeated itself. And to think—we were all here at the time.

Ken Warner

For 1989, Remington serves up this gent's locker with a 2¹/₈-inch blade.

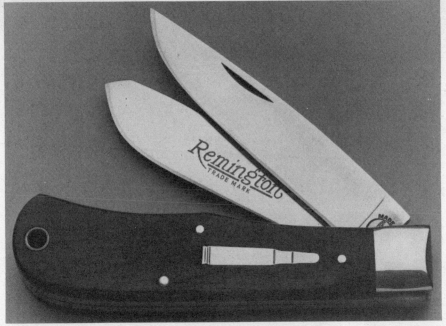

(Left) This great trapper pattern appeared in this new series in Delrin bone in 1982; for 1989, they have it again in cocobolo.

(Below) Remington's all-purpose deerhunter offers bone saw, good skinning sweep, and finger placement on the back and sides of the tip for fine cuts.

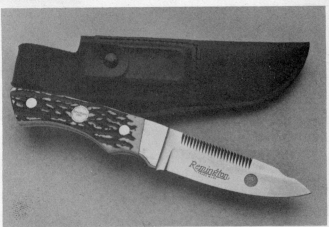

Outstanding replication of Remington bullets is this group in ivory and ATS34 by Bob Enders. (Weyer photo)

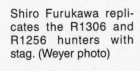

Shiro Furukawa replicates the R1306 and R1256 hunters with stag. (Weyer photo)

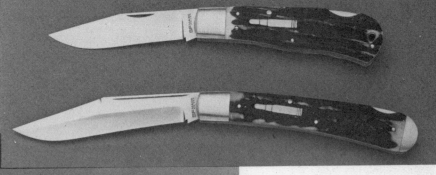

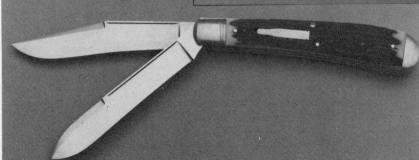

Seiichi Tasaki does the R-293 bullet in really grand grinding — 440C and stag are Remington. (Weyer photo)

FACTORY TRENDS
SABATIER: FORGED BLADES AT $4 AN INCH

Maybe the Trumpet Brand ain't what it was, but what's left ain't bad.

WHEN IT COMES to highway travel, the Warner family is proof against nearly everything except the need for toilet facilities, quarter-pounders with cheese, and gasoline, but we can be had. Sometimes it's an inescapable sight-see and here recently it was Sabatier.

When you travel by car from Orlando, Florida, north toward Almost Heaven, you spend some time in South Carolina. Indeed, it seems most of the trip is in South Carolina. And on one such trip, somewhere south of Columbia, no doubt on Route 26, there was this sign which read "Factory Outlet Sabatier." (No, it did not read "Sabatier Factory Outlet.")

As such places provide, there were several signs over a space of 20 or 30 miles and finally, having somewhat unusually made every other stop along the way that day, the Warners decided to investigate Sabatier as well. We were lucky to get out of there for under $200. We

bought only two knives, but another Warner was smitten by some most unusual cookware and the Warner plastic got a workout.

However, the knife part of it was well worth the price of admission. In the first place, they had one of those factory-furnished exhibits to show stages of manufacture of a forged knife—in this case they mean drop-forged, of course—and then they had a considerable array of Sabatier knives. Sabatier is the old, old, old name of France and indeed is almost a generic label for French chefs' knives, that triangular pattern of near universal usage in restaurant kitchens.

There are in fact two complete lines of Sabatier knives these days. One of them is pretty well the old line, plain carbon steel, forged and shaped by hand on a grindstone. You can be sure of that because you can pick up six different brand new knives and the naked

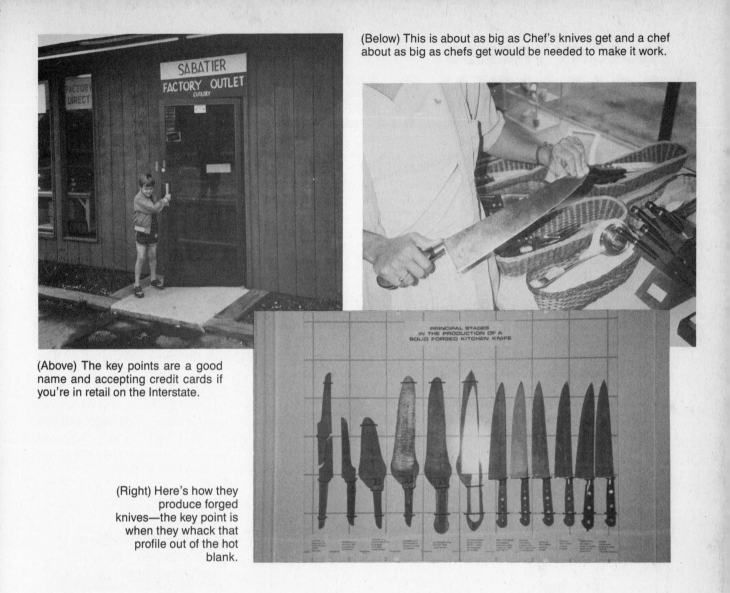

(Below) This is about as big as Chef's knives get and a chef about as big as chefs get would be needed to make it work.

(Above) The key points are a good name and accepting credit cards if you're in retail on the Interstate.

(Right) Here's how they produce forged knives—the key point is when they whack that profile out of the hot blank.

eye will gauge differences of as much as ¹/₁₆-inch among them in such things as blade width and bevel placements. The other line is a very robust stainless steel line in which, on this trip, the Warners did not dabble.

So, faced with several examples each of 30 or 40 patterns of forged blade, what would you do? The range, some very specialized fish knives and such apart, was from a 3-inch parer to a hearty 18-inch chef's knife. There were steak cutters and ham slicers and utility sizes and—oh—just a whole bunch of knives.

The prizes, for me, were those patterns calculated to take the best advantage of forging and handshaping, provided it was all done well. The choice settled, as I said, on two knives—a 4-inch triangular paring knife and a 12-inch pointed slicer. The short knife seems a pretty tough little dude, quite stiff and poky, and I believe it will work out just fine. The slicer—I picked and chose through six of them and discovered that even the Sabatier craftsmen will leave a little burn along the edge or at the point—is in prospect a marvelous knife. It is just one of those things one buys oneself when

taken unaware. For a slim 12-inch knife, it is stiff enough, and I like to think of the skill it took to start with that forging and grind it out cleanly, not as a part of a challenge, but simply as part of a work day.

I don't intend, incidentally, for these knives to be used in the kitchen, except upon a happenstance. Each is going to get a sheath suitable to its station in life and I am going to try to use them. I have long had the thought that an integrally forged, suitably shaped, carving knife might make a very nice companion. So now I'm going to find out.

A short trial out amongst the brambles produced cut brush. Obviously, there are chores beyond this slim and elegant knife, but those it will do, it will do very well. I like it.

I may also find out that thin edges and slimness pay off in dings and dints and other damage, but that's as it may be. The experiment is under way.

Oh, the $4 an inch? Well, I got 16 inches of blade for $64. I hadn't the least idea whether that was a low price, a fair price or I was had. A buddy says I was taken, but I don't care.

Ken Warner

FACTORY TRENDS
SAK NOW & EVER?

ANYONE MIGHT have thought of writing and publishing the *Swiss Army Knife Handbook,* but Kathyrn Kane actually did it. It would seem the first such handbook since the people making the Woodsman's Pal brush knife printed cute little handbooks for GIs in World War II.

So this is a real Swiss Army milestone, but not the last, and perhaps not the first. There is a Swiss Army Knife Society, and a *Swiss Army Knife Companion,* another book and foible of sorts, since it discusses handy tools *not* found on any Swiss Army knife. In lengthy discourse, by the way, the knife is referred to by its initials, which are SAK.

There are to be suspenders (with hangers for SAKs) and cloisonee pins, polo shirts and, naturally, coffee mugs, as well as Society-marked SAKs. This writer's favorites, if they come in XXL, are the T-shirts emblazoned with the unofficial motto "WHIP IT OUT!" The official motto is on the mugs and it's "SEMPER VERSATILIS," which is bound to lose a little in translation and by comparison.

The Swiss Army Knife Society — yes, it is known as SAKSOC — is to have a convention in early December, 1988, in San Diego. Any number of SAKish developments will be visible there, including, but not limited to, all SAK-related items mentioned here plus perhaps hoped-for contact with the most celebrated SAKist, MacGyver.

It all seems to be Kathryn Kane's fault, so we show you here a couple of pages of the book, and warn you it is published by something called Birdworks Publications of Mt. Lemmon and Thunder Roads in Oracle, AZ (85623) for $7.50 retail per copy. The lady swears it's a great gift.

Ken Warner

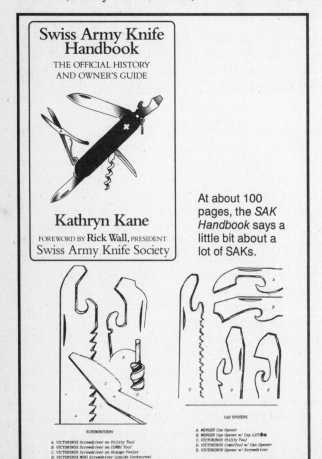

At about 100 pages, the *SAK Handbook* says a little bit about a lot of SAKs.

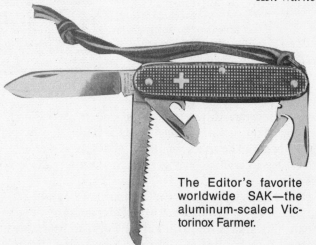

The Editor's favorite worldwide SAK—the aluminum-scaled Victorinox Farmer.

Jack and Yvonne Peterson of Nanaimo, B.C., make a mini-SAK.

NEW KNIVES IN PRODUCTION

A VERY small knife may be the most important new design of the 12 months past. It's the Boker Ceramic, a small gents' knife with a non-steel blade. Of it, Boker is able to say the blade material is second in hardness only to diamonds, abrasion and corrosion resistant, very light weight, durable at high pressure and high temperature.

The knife is made sharp and stays that way. One sample has shown no visible change, mark or stain in 90 days of intermittent use and carry. No doubt at present the material has its limitations, but this knife certainly functions and the Wright brothers didn't fly far at Kitty Hawk.

Big knives are big and getting bigger. Between the applied romance of high-hype movies and the innate appeal of cold steel, the sales appear to beckon. And down the other way, the low-priced folder is going great. Buck's little guys from last year in 8 or 10 colors ranging all the way to pink and purple and making the factory happy, so they're following on with new folders.

And the specialists are booming. Whether it's the fellow who just wants the would-be knife fighter business, or the guy offering the world's strongest knife, or the one who just wants all the skin diver business, they are all selling knives. So there are new knives in all those sorts of categories.

Look at them. These pictures *are* worth a lot of words.

Ken Warner

The made-in-USA Mamba from Blackjack Knives offers its own snaky shape and a full rolled Moran edge in high-carbon steel. (Fitzgerald photo)

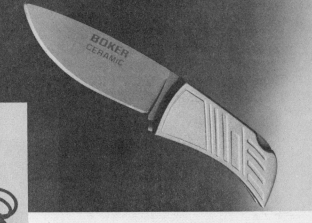

The blade of the first Boker Ceramic, Model 2030, is under 2-inch and the handle is titanium, so it is neither a big or heavy knife, however large its future.

ALCAS offers yet another patented cutlery system, this one a filleting knife at several lengths, lockable at each.

(Above right) More high style by Degen, Inc. in a many-model line of folders, most every one boldly colored, with high carbon blades Teflon-coated.

SOG Specialties is making a good thing—and several models—of belt and folding knives styled to match knives procured in the Far East for issue or sale in Vietnam.

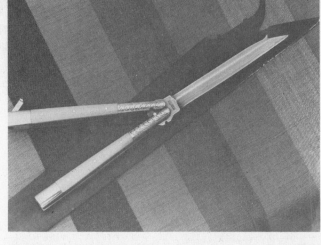

Somehow a *Kampilan* in *balisong* pattern makes sense. This one, with *san-mai* blade is from Cecil Quirino and Kris Cutlery and offers a 5-inch blade. (Quirino photo)

(Right) Interframe handles and leather linings class up this batch of new Bucks, all in gents' sizes.

(Below) The new Aitor Nova lockblades offer high-style, high-carbon stainless blades, and good looks. These two are about 4-inch long; there is another smaller. Handles are blue, with a red line.

(Right) Classy Continental hunting dagger from Muela is called the Brama, and is a no-fooling serious knife. (Weyer photo)

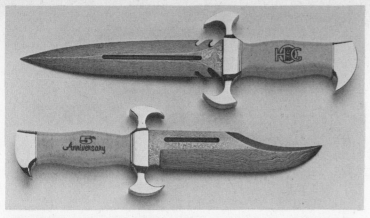

HOG stands for "Harley Owners Group" and for its 5th anniversary, that august body chose to offer its members these Gil Hibben/Damascus-USA collaborations. (Weyer photo)

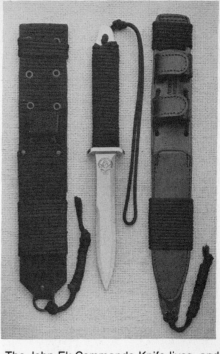

(Above) Over on the brute side, Frost Cutlery offers this monster Jack Crain knife from the movie *Predator*. (Weyer photo)

The John Ek Commando Knife lives, and in more and more variations as it progresses. This is one of the latest.

The fantasy sword potential is being met by such as this Glamdring from Museums Replicas, Inc.

(Below) Browning answers the hunter call for saws with this high-style folder.

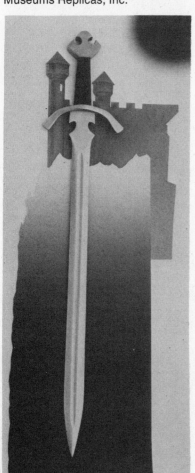

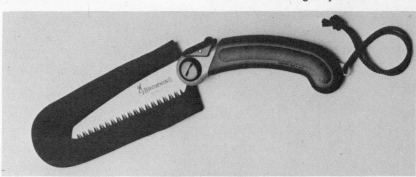

A.G. Russell's latest Knife Collector Club Knife is this American-pattern hunter made in Japan to Russell's high standards. (Weyer photo)

Safari Club International has offered club knives in Damascus lately. These are the 1988 and 1989 knives from Damascus-USA. (Weyer photo)

New Buck locking design comes first to market in this dress-up version.

Outdoor Edge Cutlery is pushing this minimum-bulk deerhunter's everything knife hard.

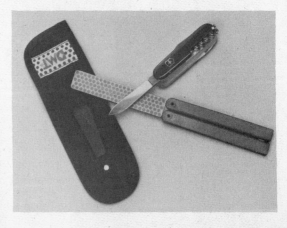

Lightweight tappers from Coleman-Western move the high-impact plastic high-tech approach one big step closer to traditional patterns.

(Below left) This Fold-A-Vee sharpener is from Lansky, offers two vees — one narrow, one broad.

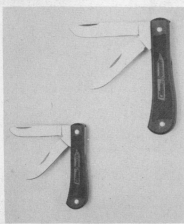

Dynatec has restyled the folding Swede saw so it packs as short as its blades.

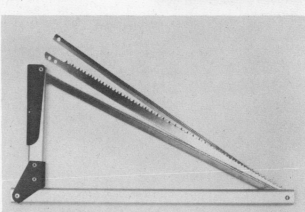

(Below) DMT's Diafold™ diamond whetstone will sharpen most any knife quickly, and the extended handle makes it safe to use.

(Below) Frederic Remington sculptures reproduced as scrimshaw in these sturdy Precise International folding hunters make these the American Heritage line.

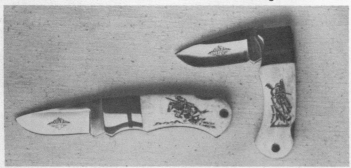

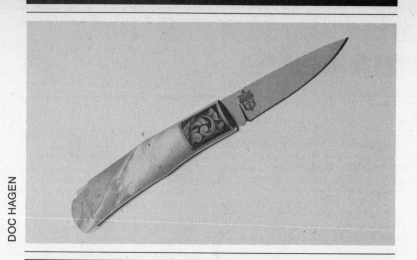

DOC HAGEN

The only reason a maker or a source in the United States is not listed somewhere in this section is that we didn't hear of him or it, or something went wrong. This is intended to be a complete directory for knive owners. If you know of someone who should be in this Directory and isn't, please write and tell us. If you are that someone, please write. We'll appreciate it.

This is not a catalog, so there will be incomplete entries, though not many. And with probably 1,000 or more entries, it will have omissions. Very often, that will be the result of error on the part of the omitted. We tried to give everyone a chance.

The Directory is divided into different lists. The biggest is a compilation of short profiles of custom knifemakers, followed by a state-by-state list of those same knifemakers, membership lists of professional knifemaker associations and then a photo index to previous editions. Then we list specialty cutlers; general cutlers, importers and foreign cutlers; sources for knifemaking supplies; mail-order houses that specialize in knives; knife services, which include scrimshanders, engravers, leatherworkers and several other categories; and finally, we list major organizations and publications. Those seem the most useful categories. We hope they work for you.

Ken Warner

Custom Knifemakers
Knifemakers State-by-State
Official Membership Lists
Photo Index
Specialty Cutlers
General Cutlers
Importers & Foreign Cutlers
Knifemaking Supplies
Mail-Order Sales
Knife Services
Organizations & Publications

Custom Knifemakers

This is probably the biggest list of currently working knifemakers in print. If someone is listed here, he or she makes knives.

Over the years we have published this list, some of those listed have stopped answering mail from us and we have begun to drop those listings. A list of those dropped is at the end of this section.

There are other lists worth consulting following this part of the Directory. Each knifemaker organization was asked, immediately before press-time for its current membership list. All names given are shown. There is an index to photos in previous editions. And there's a new state-by-state list.

A great many of the knifemakers in this Directory charge a fee to send catalogs. At a minimum, inquire by phone or with a self-addressed and stamped envelope, or send $1. Some charge $2 or $3 or more, then deduct that charge from a knife order.

WILLIAM M. ABBOTT, RR #2, Chandlerville, IL 62627/217-458-2325
Specialties: Plain and fancy fixed blade knives. **Patterns:** Hunters, fishing, utility, Bowies, and some art knives. **Technical:** Grinds D2, ATS34, 440C. Prefers natural handle materials. **Prices:** $50 to $500. **Remarks:** Full-time maker; first knife sold in 1984. Traditional archer. **Mark:** Name

A CUT ABOVE (See Phill Hartsfield)

ED ADDISON, 325 E. Pritchard St., Asheboro, NC 27203/919-625-1769
Specialties: Working straight knives in standard factory butcher patterns. **Patterns:** Kitchen, fish, and hunting knives; variety of woods offered. **Technical:** Grinds 01 steel, 440C; uses saw blades. **Prices:** $16 to $100. **Remarks:** Full-time maker; his first knife sold in 1961. **Mark:** Name, city, state

YOSHIHITO AIDA, 26-7, Narimasu 2-chome, Itabashi-ku, Tokyo 175, JAPAN/(03)-939-0052
Specialties: High-tech working straight and folding knives in own designs. **Patterns:** Tantos, Bowies, lockbacks, miniatures. **Technical:** Grinds 440C, ATS34; works in traditional Japanese fashion for some handles and sheaths. **Prices:** $170 to $500; some higher. **Remarks:** Full-time maker; sold first knife in 1978. **Mark:** Y. AIDA

ALASKA KNIFE & SERVICE CO. (See Thomas A. Trujillo)

DARREL ALEXANDER, Box 745, Big Piney, WY 83113/307-276-3734
Specialties: Straight working knives in traditional styles. **Patterns:** Hunters, boots, and fish knives. **Technical:** Grinds D2, 440C, and 154CM. **Prices:** $55 to $95; some $240. **Remarks:** Full-time maker; first knife sold in 1983. **Mark:** Name, city, and state

JOE ALLEN, RR #3, Box 182, Princeton, IN 47670/812-385-8010
Specialties: Hunting and outdoor knives. **Patterns:** Bowies, working hunters, daggers, and skinners. **Technical:** Grinds 440C. **Prices:** $80 to $150. **Remarks:** Part-time maker; first knife sold in 1976. **Mark:** Cable Joe Knives

MIKE "WHISKERS" ALLEN, Rt. 1 Box 1080, Malakoff, TX 75148/214-489-1026
Specialties: Folding and straight working knives. **Patterns:** Hunters, tantos, Bowies, swords, and miniatures. **Technical:** Forges to shape Damascus, and grinds 440C, and ATS34. **Prices:** $85 to $185; some $2,000. **Remarks:** Full-time maker; first knife sold in 1984. **Mark:** Whiskers and serial number

STEVE ALLEN, 200 Forbes St., Riverside, RI 02915/401-433-0235
Specialties: Working straight knives. **Patterns:** Hollow-handle survival knives, Bowies, camp and fish knives. **Technical:** Grinds 1095, 440C, and 154CM. **Prices:** $100 to $350; some $1,000. **Remarks:** Full-time maker; first knife sold in 1982. **Mark:** Running River

TIM (R.V.) ALVERSON, Box 92, Keno, OR 97627/503-884-9119
Specialties: Fancy working knives in custom designs. **Patterns:** Folding lockers, miniatures, boots, fighters, and hunters. **Technical:** Grinds 440C, 154CM; buys some Damascus. **Prices:** $80 to $150; some $400 and up. **Remarks:** Part-time maker; first knife sold in 1981. **Mark:** Rosebud or R.V.A.

A.W. AMOUREUX, 3210 Woodland Pk. Dr., Anchorage, AK 99517/907-248-4442
Specialties: Straight working knives for heavy duty. **Patterns:** Bowies, fighters, camp knives and hunters for Alaska use. **Technical:** Grinds 440C, ATS34, and 154CM. **Prices:** $80 to $2,000. **Remarks:** Part-time maker; first knife sold in 1974. **Mark:** ALSTAR

CHARLES B. ANDERSON, 5260 S. Landings Dr., Suite 1306, Ft. Myers, FL 33919/813-489-0286
Specialties: Straight high-tech working knives in own patterns. **Patterns:** Hunting, kitchen, and fish knives. **Technical:** Grinds 01, D2, 154CM and 440C. **Prices:** $95 to $500; exceptional knives to $1,000. **Remarks:** Part-time maker; first knife sold in 1980. **Mark:** Full name

EDWIN ANDERSON, 2050 Hillside Ave., New Hyde Park, NY 11040/516-488-7880
Specialties: Large hunters, fighters, and boot knives. **Patterns:** Standard classics. **Technical:** Grinds Stellite 6K, 01, and 125CM. **Prices:** $125 to $275; some to $750. **Remarks:** Part-time maker; first knife sold in 1977. **Mark:** Name over state

VIRGIL W. ANDERSON, 16318 S.E. Taggart, Portland, OR 97236/503-761-4053
Specialties: Straight working knives and fancy pieces of his own design. **Patterns:** Bowies, boots, hunters, and push knives; some with bottle opener in blade. **Technical:** Grinds D2, 154CM, and F8 Silvanite. **Prices:** $100 to $250; some $500. **Remarks:** Part-time maker; first knife sold in 1984. **Mark:** Anderson

DON ANDREWS, N. 5155 EZY St., Coeur D'Alene, ID 83814/208-765-8844
Specialties: Plain and fancy folders and straight knives. **Patterns:** Hunter with two butt caps; folder in a wrist rocket. **Technical:** Grinds D2, 440C, ATS34; does lost wax casting for guards and pommels. **Prices:** Moderate to upscale. **Remarks:** Full-time maker; first knife sold in 1983. **Mark:** Name

ANGEL SWORD (See D. Watson)

W.E. ANKROM, 14 Marquette Dr., Cody, WY 82414/307-587-3017
Specialties: Folding and straight knives in own designs; also period pieces and working knives. **Patterns:** Hunters, fighters, and boots. In folders: lockers, slip joints, two-blades, and interchangeables. **Technical:** Grinds ATS 34 and commercial Damascus. **Prices:** From $125 to $650. **Remarks:** Full-time maker; first knife sold in 1975. Offers some engraving. **Mark:** Name, city and state

WILLIAM J. ANTONIO, JR., P.O. Box 186, Rt. 299, Warwick, MD 21912/301-755-6789
Specialties: Fancy working straight knives in his own designs. **Patterns:** Hunting, survival, and fish knives. **Technical:** Grinds D2, 440C, and 154CM. **Prices:** $125 to $395; some to $900. **Remarks:** Part-time maker; first knife sold in 1978. **Mark:** Name, city, state

RAY APPLETON, Box 321, Byers, CO 80103/303-822-5866
Specialties: One-of-a-kind folding knives. **Patterns:** Uniquely personal—multi-locks and high-tech patterns. **Technical:** All parts machined or ground; likes D2. **Prices:** $500 up. **Remarks:** Spare-time maker; made first knife to sell in 1986. **Mark:** AP connected in arrowhead; dated

ARMAGEDDON FORGE (See Scott Lankton)

ARROW FORGE (See Walt Harless)

ASHLEY FORGE (See Hugh E. Bartrug)

ATHERN FORGE (See Athern (Al) Sanders)

DICK ATKINSON, 2524 S. 34th St., Decatur, IL 62521/217-429-6746
Specialties: Makes working folders and straight knives. Uses own designs; some are fancy. **Patterns:** Hunters, fighters, and boots. In folders: lockers in interframes. **Technical:** Grinds A2, 440C, and 154CM. **Prices:** $85 to $300; some exceptional knives. **Remarks:** Part-time maker; first knife sold in 1977. Likes filework. **Mark:** Name, city, state

directory/custom knifemakers

B.W. BAKER (See IMPORTERS)

RAY BAKER, P.O. Box 303, Sapulpa, OK 74067/918-224-8013
Specialties: Working high-tech straight knives. **Patterns:** Hunters, fighters, and boots, mostly own designs, but will make customer designs also. Custom-made scabbards for any knife. **Technical:** Grinds 440C and 1095 spring-steel or other steels of customer request. **Prices:** $40 to $135, some to $300. **Remarks:** Full-time maker; sold first knife in 1981. He scrimshaws some knives. **Mark:** R. BAKER

PHILLIP BALDWIN, P.O. Box 563, Snohomish, WA 98290/206-334-5569
Specialties: Elegant table cutlery; other exotics. **Patterns:** Contemporary and eclectic. Likes the challenge of axes and such. **Technical:** Forges W2, W1 and his own Damascus. **Prices:** From $300 to $500 to $2,500; some higher. **Remarks:** Full-time maker; first knife sold in 1973. **Mark:** Angular "B" marked with chisel

JIM BARBEE, Box 1173, Ft. Stockton, TX 79753/915-336-2882
Specialties: Texas-type hunter's knives. **Patterns:** Solid using patterns. **Technical:** Grinds 440C; likes stag and Micarta and ivory. **Prices:** $125 to $200; some to $500. **Remarks:** Full-time maker and heat-treater. Sold first knife in the '60s. **Mark:** Name and town

ROBERT E. BARBER, 1828 Franklin Dr., Charlottesville, VA 22901/804-295-4036
Specialties: Working straight knives, some fancy. **Patterns:** Hunters, skinners, fighters are his specialty. **Technical:** Grinds 440C, D2 and 154CM. **Prices:** $55 to $300. **Remarks:** Part-time maker; first knife sold in 1984. **Mark:** R.E.B. within rebel hat logo

NORMAN P. BARDSLEY, 197 Cottage St., Pawtucket, RI 02860/401-725-9132
Specialties: Straight working knives, some fancy. **Patterns:** Fighters, tantos, and boots. He does claws, minis, buckle, and push knives. **Technical:** Grinds D2 and 440C, and buys Damascus; offers Titanium nitriding coating process on blades. **Prices:** $150 to $350; some $1,500. **Remarks:** Full-time maker; offers scrimshaw and engraving; emphasizes carrying systems, plain or fancy. **Mark:** Name in script with logo

JOE W. BAREFOOT, P.O. Box 1248, Easley, SC 29641/803-843-2337
Specialties: Straight working knives in mirror finish and own designs. **Patterns:** Hunters, fighters and boots are standard; makes tantos and survival knives. **Technical:** Grinds D2, 440C and ATS34. **Prices:** $50 to $160; some to $500. **Remarks:** Part-time maker; first knife sold in 1980. Uses ivory and stag on customer request only. **Mark:** Barefoot print

KEN BARLOW, 3800 Rohner St., Fortuna, CA 95540/707-725-3106
Specialties: Straight and folding working knives, some fancy. **Patterns:** Hunters, Bowies, skinners, locking folders, and some boots. **Technical:** Grinds ATS34, 440C, and D2. Does his own heat-treat, engraving, and scrimshaw. Prefers mirror polish and hollow grinds. **Prices:** $90 to $150; some $500. **Remarks:** Part-time maker; first knife sold in 1980. **Mark:** Styled KB

GARY L. BARNES, 305 Church St., Box 138, New Windsor, MD 21776/301-635-6243
Specialties: High art and high-tech working knives in his own designs. Titanium and stainless folders popular for 2 years. **Patterns:** Hunters, Bowies, and daggers; in folders: lockers, slip joints, multi-blades, and one-of-a-kind creations. **Technical:** Forges mostly; makes his own Damascus; uses exotic handle materials, and creates unique locking mechanisms. **Prices:** $300 to $1,500; some to $8,000. **Remarks:** Full-time maker, an A.B.S. Master. First knife sold in 1976. Most knives are embellished. Believes strongly in sole authorship. **Mark:** Name or an ornate B with a dagger through it

BARR CUSTOM KNIVES (See Barr Quarton)

A.T. BARR, 54 Fox Circle, Denton, TX 76205/817-565-1580
Specialties: Full tang working knives. **Patterns:** Straight and folding knives in wide variety. **Technical:** Grinds A2, D2 and 440C. **Prices:** $75 to $325; some $1,000. **Remarks:** Part-time maker; first knife sold in 1979. **Mark:** Signature

JAMES J. BARRY, P.O. Box 1571, West Palm Beach, FL 33406/407-832-4197
Specialties: Straight high art and working knives in often unique personal designs of his own. **Patterns:** Hunters, daggers and fish knives predominate. **Technical:** Grinds 440C only. Prefers exotic materials for handles. **Prices:** $100 to $500; some to $4,000. **Remarks:** Part-time maker; first knife sold in 1975. Most knives embellished with filework or carving. Believes in sole authorship. **Mark:** JB as a brand

JOHN BARTLOW, 111 Orchard Rd., Box 568, Norris, TN 37828/615-494-9421
Specialties: Straight working knives, some fancy. **Patterns:** Makes hunters, fighters and survival knives; does some embellishing. **Technical:** Grinds and forges 01, 440C and ATS34; makes his own Damascus. **Prices:** $45 to $200; some $500. **Remarks.** Full-time maker, sold first knife in 1979. Field-tested knives as a guide and makes his knives for work. **Mark:** Last name

HUGH E. BARTRUG, 505 Rhodes St., Elizabeth, PA 15037/412-384-3476
Specialties: Offers straight and exotic folders; complete inlaid; prefers high art and period pieces. **Patterns:** Hunters, Bowies and daggers; in folders—hunters and traditional patterns. **Technical:** Forges laminated nickel and wrought iron; does grinding. Uses 01 steel. **Prices:** $210 to $2,500; some to $5,000. **Remarks:** Full-time maker; sold first knife in 1980. **Mark:** Ashley Forge or name

LEE GENE BASKETT, 240 Oakwood Dr., Elizabethtown, KY 42701/502-769-5816
Specialties: Fancy working knives and fantasy pieces, often set up in desk stands. **Patterns:** Fighters, Bowies, and survival knives, as well as folding lockers, butterflies, and traditional styles. **Technical:** Grinds 01, 440C, buys Damascus. **Prices:** $95 to $300; some $1,500. **Remarks:** Part-time maker; first knife sold 1980. File work provided on most knives; unique packaging of knives. **Mark:** BASKETT

JAMES BATSON, 171 Brentwood Lande, Madison, AL 35758/205-837-6160
Specialties: Working straight and folding knives, some art knives included. **Patterns:** Integral art knives, Bowies, boots, American-styled blades, and miniatures. **Technical:** Forges 01, L6, and his own Damascus. **Prices:** $150 to $1,800; some $2,500. **Remarks:** Part-time maker; first knife sold in 1978. **Mark:** Name, Artsmith with horse's head

PETER BAUCHOP, P.O. Box 68, Hunt Valley, MD 21030
Specialties: Straight working knives and period pieces. **Patterns:** Fighters, swords, and survival knives; some scrimshawed. **Technical:** Grinds 01, D2 and 440C. **Prices:** $100 to $350; some to $550. **Remarks:** Full-time maker; first knife sold in 1980. **Mark:** Bow and axe (BOW-CHOP)

BEAR CLAW (See B.R. Bryner)

BEAR PAW (See Pitt)

BEAR'S CUTLERY (See Carl Jensen)

CHARLES BEAR, 4042 Bones Rd., Sebastopol, CA 95472/707-829-9110
Specialties: High-tech fantasy working knives. **Patterns:** Swords, period belt knives. **Technical:** Forges stainless tool steels; makes stainless Damascus. **Prices:** $450 to $2,000. **Remarks:** Part-time maker; sold first knife in 1980. **Mark:** Stylized CB

GORDON H. BEATTY, Rt. 1, Box 79, Seneca, SC 29678/803-882-6278
Specialties: Working straight knives; some fancy. **Patterns:** Traditional patterns; hunters include a mini-skinner; letter openers. **Technical:** Grinds 440C, D2 and ATS34; makes knives one at a time. **Prices:** $45 to $200; some to $450. **Remarks:** Part-time maker; sold first knife in 1982. **Mark:** Name

DEVON BEAVER, Box 3067 New River Stage I, Phoenix, AZ 85029/602-465-7831
Specialties: Creates his own high art straight knives; does some working knives. Most knives are embellished. **Patterns:** Hunters, tantos and daggers are most usual work. **Technical:** Grinds 440C, 154CM and ATS34. **Prices:** $135 to $800; some very high. **Remarks:** Full-time maker. Judy Beaver helps with embellishment and is now making some straight art knives herself. First D. Beaver knife sold in 1979; first J. Beaver in 1984. **Mark:** Name, city, state in Old English type

P. F. BECK, 1504 Hagood Ave., Barnwell, SC 29812/803-259-5959
Specialties: Small working straight knives, especially for deer hunters. **Patterns:** Standard hunter and boot shapes; some experimental work. **Technical:** Flat grinds; mirror finishes. **Prices:** Low to medium. **Mark:** Name

FRANZ BECKER, Bruckbergstr. 23, 8261 Marktl/Inn, WEST GERMANY
Specialties: Stainless steel knives in working sizes. **Patterns:** Integral drop-point hunters and boot knives. **Technical:** Grinds stainless steels; likes natural materials for handles. **Prices:** Upscale. **Remarks:** New German maker. **Mark:** Name

MICHAEL R. BECKWITH, 48282 Donahue Dr., New Baltimore, MI 48047/313-949-2506
Specialties: Straight working knives; likes customer designs. **Patterns:** Hunters, fighters, and boots, but can provide axes, buckskinner and push knives. **Technical:**

directory/custom knifemakers

Grinds D2, 440C and 154CM. **Prices:** $80 to $200; some to $300. **Remarks:** Part-time maker; first knife sold in 1980. **Mark:** Last name

RAY BEERS, 8 Manorbrook Rd., Monkton, MD 21111/301-472-2229
Specialties: Straight working knives and a lot of fancy ones. **Patterns:** Fighters and tantos are his popular styles, but he makes everything. **Technical:** Grinds D2, 440C and 154CM. **Prices:** $65 to $300; some to $2,000. **Remarks:** Full-time maker; many patterns have a palm hunter handle. First knife sold in 1979. **Mark:** RB connected

WILLIAM BEHNKE, 3936 Wolcott Terr., West Bloomfield, MI 48033/313-363-8991
Specialties: Hunters and belt knives. **Patterns:** Traditional styling in moderate-size straight knives. **Technical:** Forges his own Damascus in several styles; likes brass and natural materials. **Prices:** NA. **Mark:** Name

FRANK BELL, 409 Town & Country Drive, Huntsville, AL 35806/205-837-2016
Specialties: Both folding and straight knives in period pieces and working knives. **Patterns:** Hunters, Bowies, and daggers; in folders, he makes lockers, slip joints in gents and hunter styles. **Technical:** Grinds 440C, 154CM and ATS34. Makes sheaths of ostrich leather. **Prices:** $100 to $175; some to $800. **Remarks:** Part-time maker; first knife sold in 1977. **Mark:** Bell shaped logo or last name

MICHAEL BELL, Rt. 1, Box 1217, Coquille, OR 97423
Specialties: Straight knives in standard patterns in period pieces and high art knives. **Patterns:** Tantos, daggers, and swords; some knives are engraved. **Technical:** Forges W2, 1095, and makes his own Damascus. Bell served an apprenticeship to a Japanese swordmaker. **Prices:** $1,000 to $6,000; some to $10,000. **Remarks:** Full-time maker; his first sold in 1972. His steel and handles are made in traditional Japanese style. **Mark:** KUNIMITSU or DRAGONFLY

GEORGE BENJAMIN, JR., The Leather Box, Mill Creek Mall, 1342 E. Vine St., Kissimmee, FL 32743/407-846-7259
Specialties: Fighters in various styles to include Persian, Moro, and military. **Patterns:** Daggers, skinners, and one-of-a-kind grinds. **Technical:** Grinds and forges 01, D2, ATS34, and Damascus. Favors Pakkawood and mirror finish. **Prices:** $150 to $600; some $1,200. **Remarks:** Co-worker Mike Schmid. **Mark:** Southern Pride Knives

DON BENSON, 2505 Jackson St. #112, Escalon, CA 95320/209-838-7921
Specialties: Straight working knives in his own designs. **Patterns:** Axes, Bowies, tantos, and hunters. **Technical:** Grinds 440C. **Prices:** $100 to $150; some $250. **Remarks:** Spare-time maker; first knife sold in 1980. **Mark:** BENSON

DAVE BER, P.O. Box 203, Nooksack, WA 98276/206-966-4243
Specialties: Working straight knives for the sportsman; camp knives. Welcomes customer designs. **Patterns:** Hunters, Bowies, kitchen and fish knives. **Technical:** Forges and grinds saw blade steel, welded wire Damascus, 01, L6, and 440C. **Prices:** $75 to $125; some to $300. **Remarks:** Full-time maker; first knife sold in 1985. **Mark:** Ber

LARRY BERZAS, 208 W. 26th St., Cut Off, LA 70345/504-693-3335
Specialties: Straight working knives in customer designs. **Patterns:** Gator skinners, Bowies, swords and tomahawks. **Technical:** Grinds L6; bolsters are gas-welded to blades. **Prices:** $85 to $175; some $500. **Remarks:** Part-time maker; first knife sold in 1979. **Mark:** Bear's behind logo; double red dots on handle

LEROY BESIC, 40881 Johnston Ave., Hemet, CA 92344/714-652-3384
Specialties: Straight working and high art knives. **Patterns:** Hunters, tantos, and daggers. Does one-of-a-kind pieces, too. **Technical:** Grinds 440C. All knives hand finished with solderless joints. **Prices:** $165 to $225; some $1,200. **Remarks:** Full-timer maker; his first knife sold in 1979. Offers embellishment. **Mark:** Name, city, and state

BEST FRIEND KNIVES (See John Phillips)

LARRY H. BEVERLY II, P.O. Box 6, Hartwood, VA 22471/703-752-4372
Specialties: Straight working knives, some folders. **Patterns:** Bowies, fighters, and drop-point hunters. Welcomes customer designs. **Technical:** Grinds 440C and A2. **Prices:** $55 to $250. **Remarks:** Part-time maker; first knife sold in 1986. **Mark:** LHB II

ROBERT F. BIRCH, P.O. Box 1901, Huntsville, TX 77340/409-291-1609
Specialties: Straight working knives. **Patterns:** Hunters, fighters and camp knives. **Technical:** Grinds 440C. Likes polished antler handles and pigskin sheaths. **Prices:** $90 to $300 and up. **Remarks:** Part-time maker; first knife sold in 1985. **Mark:** BIRCH

SID BIRT, RR3, Box 269A, Nashville, IN 47448/812-988-6502
Specialties: Grand straight and folding period pieces designed with a sure eye. **Patterns:** One-of-a-kind in all sizes, shapes and functions. **Technical:** Forges mostly; does some grinding, using W2, 1095 and his own Damascus. **Prices:** $600 to $2,500; some to $6,500. **Remarks:** Full-time maker; first knife sold in 1970. **Mark:** BIRT

EARL BLACK, 3466 South 700 East, Salt Lake City, UT 84106/801-466-8395
Specialties: Straight and folding high art knives and period pieces. **Patterns:** Boots, Bowies, and daggers; in folders: lockers and gents. **Technical:** Grinds 440C and 154CM. Buys some Damascus. **Prices:** $200 to $1,800; some to $2,500 and up. **Remarks:** Full-time maker; first knife sold in 1980. Some knives are scrimmed or engraved. **Mark:** Name, city, and state

BLACK OAK (See Sayen)

TOM BLACK, 921 Grecian NW, Albuquerque, NM 87107
Specialties: Belt knives, including big ones. **Patterns:** Traditional patterns, like Bowies. **Technical:** Grinds stainless steels. **Prices:** NA. **Remarks:** Part-time maker. **Mark:** Name

ANDREW E. BLACKTON, 12521 Fifth Isle, Bayonet Point, FL 33667/813-869-1406
Specialties: Straight and folding knives; some fancy knives. **Patterns:** Hunters, Bowies and daggers head the list. **Technical:** Grinds D2, 440C and 154 CM. **Prices:** $125 to $450; some to $2,000. **Remarks:** Full-time maker. Offers some knives with embellishment. **Mark:** State of Michigan outline with knife across it and "Blackton the Great Lakes Knifemaker"

WILLIAM E. BLAKLEY, II, Rt. 4, Box 106-B, Fredericksburg, VA 22405/703-775-3773
Specialties: Simple working knives. **Patterns:** Hunters and skinners; some Bowies and daggers. **Technical:** Grinds 440C; offers D2 and 01 on request. **Prices:** $75 to $300. **Remarks:** First knife sold in 1984. **Mark:** WEB II

ROY BLAUM, 319 N. Columbia St., Covington, LA 70433/504-893-1060
Specialties: Straight and folding working knives in his own designs; makes lightweight easy-open folders a lot. **Patterns:** Hunters, boots and fish knives. **Technical:** Grinds A2, D2, 154CM and ATS34. **Prices:** $75 to $200; some to $500. **Remarks:** Full-time maker; sold first knife in 1976. **Mark:** Signature engraved

GREGG BLOMBERG, Rt. 1, Box 1762, Lopez, WA 98261/206-468-2103
Specialties: Edged tools for carvers and sculptors. **Patterns:** Crooked knife; straight utilities; adzes. **Technical:** Forges and grinds W2, D2, 1095, and 440C. **Prices:** $40 to $125; some $300. **Remarks:** Full-time maker; first knife sold in 1978. Business name: Kestrel Tool. **Mark:** KESTREL with flying falcon logo

ALAN T. BLOOMER, Box 134, Maquon, IL 61458/309-875-3555
Specialties: Straight and folding working knives in his own designs. **Patterns:** Small hunters, slip joints and boots. **Technical:** Grinds 440C only. Offers filework. **Prices:** $65 to $200. **Remarks:** Spare-time maker; first knife sold in 1987. **Mark:** BLOOMER in block letters

L.H. BLOOMFIELD, P.O. Box 3588, Kingman, AZ 86402/602-757-8007
Specialties: Working straight knives, some fantasy pieces. Works largely with customer designs. **Patterns:** Hunters, boots, swords, survival and push knives. **Technical:** Grinds A2, 01, and 440A. **Prices:** $100 to $250; some $400. **Remarks:** Part-time maker; first knife sold in 1981. **Mark:** COYOTE KNIVES, city, state and date

CHUCK BLUM, 743 S. Brea Blvd. #10, Brea, CA 92621/714-529-0484
Specialties: Bowies, combat knives and fancy pieces. **Technical:** Mostly flat grinds 440C; all fittings stainless. **Prices:** $125 to $1,200. **Remarks:** Part-time maker; first knife sold in 1985. **Mark:** Blum with sailboat logo

RONALD A. BLUM, 28712 Colina Vista, Agoura Hills, CA 91301/818-889-1680
Specialites: Miniature knives only. Collectable one-of-a-kind straight knives. **Patterns:** Miniature swords, fantasy and historical replicas, some battle axes. **Technical:** Files and forges 1050, 440C, and bought Damascus. **Prices:** $90 to $200; some $300. **Remarks:** Part-time maker; first knife sold in 1988. **Mark:** Not presently

E.B. BOATNER (See Jimmy L. Fikes)

BOB-SKY (See Hajovsky)

directory/custom knifemakers

BRUCE BOCHMAN, Box 693, El Granada, CA 94018/415-728-5302
Specialties: Straight working knives in traditional patterns. **Patterns:** Bowies, hunters, fish and bird knives. **Technical:** Grinds 154CM, and ATS34; all knives hollow ground, and mirror finished. **Prices:** $140 to $250; some $750. **Remarks:** Part-time maker; first knife sold in 1977. **Mark:** BB

PHIL BOGUSZEWSKI, P.O. Box 99329, Tacoma, WA 98499/206-581-7096
Specialties: Folding working knives; some are fancy. Most are his design. **Patterns:** He makes folding lockers and slip joints and some minis. **Technical:** Grinds D2, 440C and 154CM; does filework. **Prices:** $150 to $600; exceptional knives $1,000. **Remarks:** Full-time maker; first knife sold in 1979. **Mark:** Name, city and state

BRUCE BOHRMANN, 29 Portland St., Yarmouth, ME 04096/207-846-3385
Specialties: Straight sports knives, designed for use. **Patterns:** Hunters, fish, camp and steak knives. **Technical:** Grinds 154CM; likes wood handles. **Prices:** All knives are $175. **Remarks:** Full-timer; sold first knife in 1976. **Mark:** Name, town and state

CHARLES B. BOLTON, P.O. Box 6, Jonesburg, MO 63351/314-488-5785
Specialties: Straight working knives in traditional patterns. **Patterns:** Hunters, skinners, tantos, boots and fighters. **Technical:** Grinds 440C, 154CM, and ATS34. **Prices:** $75 to $150; some $300. **Remarks:** Part-time maker; first knife sold in 1973. **Mark:** Bolton

BONE KNIFE CO., INC. (Owner: Charles Hipp), 4009 Ave. A, Lubbock, TX 79404/806-765-6812
Specialties: Working folding and straight knives in solid time-tested patterns. **Patterns:** Hunters to axes; fighters to miniatures; push knives to folding lockers. **Technical:** Grinds D2 and 440C. **Prices:** $125 to $500. **Remarks:** Owned and operated by Charles Hipp part-time. Old name. **Mark:** Bone

JEREMY BONNER, Rt. 5, Box 427A, Asheville, NC 28803
Specialties: Folding knives of his own design; some are working knives and some of those are fancy. **Patterns:** Unique style; done one-of-a-kind, but in series—pierced blades, carved handles, castings—as an artist. **Technical:** Forges and grinds 01 and Damascus. **Prices:** $200 to $500. **Remarks:** Part-timer; first knife sold in 1978. **Mark:** BONNER

TILTON and JAMES BOWEN, Rt. 1, Box 225A, Baker, WV 26801/304-897-6159
Specialties: Straight stout working knives. **Patterns:** Hunters, fighters and boots; also offers buckskinner and throwing knives. **Technical:** Grinds D2 and 4140. **Prices:** $65 to $150; some $275. **Remarks:** Full-time makers; first knives sold in 1982-1983. Sells wholesale to dealers. **Mark:** Initials of both and BOWEN BLADES, WV

FRANCIS BOYD, 2128 Market St., San Francisco, CA 94114/415-431-0520
Specialties: Folders and kitchen knives. **Patterns:** Push button locked sturdy folders; San Francisco style chefs knives. **Technical:** Forges and grinds; mostly uses high carbon steels. **Prices:** Moderate to heavy. **Remarks:** Designer. **Mark:** Name

DOUGLAS D. BRACK, 5274 Teton Lane, Ventura, CA 93003/805-642-7870
Specialties: Straight working knives in his own designs. **Patterns:** Heavy-duty skinners, fighters, and boots. **Technical:** Grinds 440C, buys Damascus, and ATS34. **Prices:** $65 to $165; some $300. **Remarks:** Part-time maker; first knife sold in 1984. **Mark:** "tat"

DENNIS BRADLEY, Rt. 3, Box 3815, Blairsville, GA 30512/404-745-4364
Specialties: Folding and straight working knives, some in high art style. **Patterns:** Hunters, boots and daggers; in folders: slip joints and two-blades. **Technical:** Grinds D2, 440C and bought Damascus. **Prices:** $75 to $200; some $750. **Remarks:** Part-time maker; first knife sold in 1973. **Mark:** BRADLEY KNIVES in double heart logo

EDWARD P. BRANDSEY, 406 St. Joseph Circle, Edgerton, WI 53534/608-884-4634
Specialties: Straight working knives, period pieces, and art knives. **Patterns:** Hunters, fighters, Bowies, and daggers; some buckskinner styles. **Technical:** Grinds ATS34, 440C and 01. **Prices:** $125 to $250; some $1,500. **Remarks:** Part-time maker; first sold knives in 1973. **Mark:** EB connected

LARRY BRANDSTETTER, 827 N. 25th, Paducah, KY 42001
Specialties: Bowie-era knives; some as working knives. **Patterns:** Old Sheffield Bowies and folders. **Technical:** Grinds 440. Likes ivory, stag, pearl. Casts handle parts when needed. **Prices:** $250 to $500; some to $950. **Remarks:** Spare-time maker; first knives sold in 1977. Not taking orders. **Mark:** L.D.B.

RALPH BRANNAN, RR #1, Box 342, West Frankfort, IL 62896/618-627-2450
Specialties: Working straight knives in his own designs. **Patterns:** Traditional using skinners, hunters, and utility knives. **Technical:** Grinds 1095, 440C, and bought Damascus. Filework available. **Prices:** $75 to $150; some $250. **Remarks:** Part-time maker; first knife sold in 1976. **Mark:** RB

ROBERT BRANTON, 4976 Seewee Rd., Awendaw, SC 29429/803-928-3624
Specialties: Straight working knives in his design or yours. **Patterns:** Hunters, fighters, and some miniatures. **Technical:** Grinds ATS34, D2, and A2. Offers hollow or flat grinds. **Prices:** $50 to $150. **Remarks:** Part-time maker; first knife sold in 1985. **Mark:** BRANTON

JIM BRAYTON, 713 Park St., Burkburnett, TX 76354/817-569-4726
Specialties: Working knives and period pieces, some fancy. **Patterns:** Bowies, hunters, fighters. **Technical:** Grinds ATS34, delivers it at 60 RC. **Prices:** $55 to $500. **Remarks:** Full-time maker; sold first knife in 1970. **Mark:** J.E.B, or name

DAN E. BRDLIK, 166 Campbell St. So., Prescott, WI 54021/715-262-5296
Specialties: Straight working knives; some fantasy pieces. **Patterns:** Fighters, boots and Bowies, especially utilitarian fighter designs. **Technical:** Grinds D2, 440C and 154CM. **Prices:** $65 to $250; some $500. **Remarks:** Full-time maker; first knife sold in 1983. **Mark:** DAN E. over stylized toothpick

WALTER J. BREND, 351 Pine Ave., Walterboro, SC 29488/803-538-8256
Specialties: Straight working knives; some fantasy types. **Patterns:** Fighters, Bowies and survival knives. Likes big knives, knives for military people. **Technical:** Grinds A2, D2 and ATS34. **Prices:** $150 to $500; some exceptional knives $3,500. **Remarks:** Full-time maker; first knife sold in 1980. **Mark:** Confederate flag

CLINT BRESHEARS, 2219 Belmont Lane, Redondo Beach, CA 90278/213-372-0739
Specialties: Straight and folding working knives. **Patterns:** Hunters, Bowies and survival knives. Folders are mostly hunters. **Technical:** Grinds 440C, 154CM and ATS34; prefers mirror finish. **Prices:** $125 to $175; some $300. **Remarks:** Part-time maker; first knife sold in 1978. **Mark:** CLINT KNIVES, city, state

WAYNE BREUER, 400 East Glenwood, Wasilla, AK 99687/907-373-2191
Specialties: Working straight knives, all fancy. **Patterns:** Hunters and camp and Bowie knives. Makes camp axes. **Technical:** Grinds L6, 440C, AEB-L and 154CM; likes wire inlay, scrimshaw, decorative filing. **Prices:** $60 to $150; some to $300. **Remarks:** Part-time maker; sold first knife in 1977. **Mark:** Signature

JACK BREWER, 2415 Brady Lane, Lafayette, IN 47905/317-474-1738
Specialties: Folding and straight period pieces and working knives. **Patterns:** Boots, Bowies and daggers; lockers and slip joints. Likes traditional types. **Technical:** Grinds A2, 01, L6; forges files. **Prices:** $18 to $125; some to $400. **Remarks:** Part-time maker; first knife sold in 1979. **Mark:** BREWER or JB connected

RICHARD A. BRIDWELL, Rt. 2, Milford Ch. Rd., Taylors, SC 29687/803-895-1715
Specialties: Working folding and straight knives. **Patterns:** Boot and fish knives, fighters and hunters; some folders. **Technical:** Grinds stainless steels and D2. **Prices:** $85 to $165; some $600. **Remarks:** Part-time maker; first knife sold in 1974. **Mark:** BRIDWELL logo

E.D. BRIGNARDELLO, Rt. 2, Box 152A, Beecher, IL 60401/312-946-6609
Specialties: Straight working knives; some display pieces. **Patterns:** Hunters, fighters, boots and Bowies. Also does some push knives. **Technical:** Grinds 440C, 154CM and ATS34; likes mirror finishes. **Prices:** $130 to $250; some to $500. **Remarks:** Part-time maker; first knife sold in 1978. **Mark:** Name and town

DAVID BROADWELL, P.O. Box 4314, Wichita Falls, TX 76308/817-692-1727
Specialties: Straight working knives, some fancy. **Patterns:** Hunters, fighters, tantos. **Technical:** Grinds 440C only; hand-finishes most. **Prices:** $150 to $600; some $2,200. **Remarks:** Part-time maker; first knife sold in 1982. Offers some embellished knives. **Mark:** BROADWELL-MADE, city and state

KENNETH L. BROCK, P.O. Box 375/207 N. Skinner Rd., Allenspark, CO 80510/303-747-2547
Specialties: Working full tang straight knives, folders and button-lock folders. **Patterns:** Hunters, survival knives, miniatures, and minis. **Technical:** Flat grinds D2; makes own sheaths. **Prices:** $50 to $250. **Remarks:** Part-time maker; sold first knife in 1978. **Mark:** BROCK with city, state and serial

BASKETT

S. ALLEN

C. ANDERSON

J. ALLEN

BALLEW

ABBOTT

E. BLACK

E. ANDERSON

BAREFOOT

T. BLACK

BLAKLEY

BAARDSEY

BATSON

BLACKTON

BOGUSZEWSKI

BRADFORD

DENNIS BROOKER, Rt. 1, Box 12A, Derby, IA 50068/515-533-2103
Specialties: Straight and folding fancy knives in his own designs. **Patterns:** Hunters, folders, and boots. **Technical:** Grinds and forges. Is a full-time engraver. **Prices:** Moderate to upscale. **Remarks:** Part-time maker. Takes no orders; sells only completed work. **Mark:** Name

MICHAEL BROOKS, 1108 W. 6th, Littlefield, TX 79339/806-385-4297
Specialties: Straight working knives to his own or customer designs. **Patterns:** Tantos, Bowies, hunters, skinners and boots. **Technical:** Grinds 440C, D2, and ATS34; offers wide variety of handle materials. **Prices:** $40 to $200. **Remarks:** Part-time maker; first knife sold in 1985. Business name: Weapons Shop. **Mark:** MB

STEVE R. BROOKS, Box 105, Big Timber, MT 59011/406-932-5114
Specialties: Straight and folding knives, some period pieces, some working knives. **Patterns:** Hunters, Bowies and camp knives; folding lockers. Offers axes, tomahawks and buckskinner knives; swords and stilettos. **Technical:** Forges 01 and his own Damascus. **Prices:** $100 to $350; some $1,000. **Remarks:** Full-time maker; first knife sold in 1982. Some knives come embellished. **Mark:** Lazy SB

THOMAS A. BROOME, P.O. Box 4294, Kenai, AK 99611/907-262-7812
Specialties: Traditional working knives; straight and folding. **Patterns:** Full range of straight knives with a few folders. **Technical:** Grinds D2, 440C, ATS34, and BG42. **Prices:** $75 to $175; some to $2,000. **Remarks:** Full-time maker; first knife sold in 1979. Business name Thom's Custom Knives. **Mark:** Full name, city, state in logo

MAX BROWER, 1721 Marshall St., Boone, IA 50036/515-432-2938
Patterns: Bowies, hunters, and boots. **Technical:** Grinds 440C, and 154CM. **Prices:** $80 to $350. **Remarks:** Spare-time maker; first knife sold in 1981. **Mark:** BROWER

DAVID B. BROWN, 922 D St., Fairbury, NE 68352/402-729-2358
Specialties: Folding and straight working knives; some are fancy. **Patterns:** Hunters, tantos and Bowies. In folding knives, makes lockers and butterflies. **Technical:** Grinds and forges W2, 440C and his own Damascus. Etches some. **Prices:** $85 to $750; some to $2,000. **Remarks:** Spare-time maker; first knife sold in 1979. **Mark:** D. B. Brown

E.H. BROWN, P.O. Box 1906, Eustis, FL 32727/904-669-1224
Specialties: Straight knives in standard patterns, generally period pieces and working styles. **Patterns:** Hunters, Bowies, survival and fish knives. **Technical:** Grinds D2 and 154CM. **Prices:** $250 to $350; some to $2,600. **Remarks:** Full-time maker; first knife sold in 1983. All knives are scrimmed. **Mark:** Name, city, state, and handmade

HAROLD E. BROWN, Rt. 7, Box 335, Arcadia, FL 33821/813-494-7514
Specialties: Straight working knives. **Patterns:** Hunters, boots, Bowies; knife and hatchet sets. **Technical:** Grinds D2, 440C and 154CM. **Prices:** $100 to $350; some to $1,000. **Remarks:** Part-time maker; first knife sold in 1976. Embellishment available. **Mark:** Name and town with logo

L.E. "RED" BROWN, 10709 Shelly Field Rd., Downey, CA 90247/ 213-923-2853
Specialties: Working straight knives. **Patterns:** Hunters, Bowies and survival knives made for heavy-duty use. **Technical:** Grinds 01 only. **Prices:** $125 to $900; some higher. **Remarks:** Full-time maker; started selling knives in 1941. Some knives are embellished. He's making a limited number of collectors knives—all numbered. **Mark:** Diamond B., autographed

PETER BROWN, 8 Myra Ave., Ryde NSW 2112, AUSTRALIA/02-807-3196
Specialties: Heavy-duty working knives. **Patterns:** Swords, fighters, tantos, hunting and fishing knives. **Technical:** Grinds 440C, 420 and ATS34; does own heat treating. Makes his own Damascus steel. Offers scrimshaw and engraving. **Prices:** $135 to $500; some to $800. **Remarks:** Spare-time maker; first knife sold in 1978. **Mark:** Interlacing PB

TED BROWN, 8609 Cavel, Downey, CA 90242/213-869-9945
Specialties: Working straight knives in traditional patterns. **Patterns:** Hunters, Bowies, fish knives. **Technical:** Grinds stainless steel; some integral work. **Prices:** $100 to $350; some to $500. **Remarks:** Part-time maker; first knife sold in 1982. **Mark:** Name, address in snake logo

RICK BROWNE, 1464 Gertrudita Ct., Upland, CA 91786/714-985-1728
Specialties: No heavy-duty knives. High-tech working straight knives in his own designs. **Patterns:** Hunters, fighters and daggers. **Technical:** Grinds D2, 440C and ATS34. **Prices:** $80 to $500; some $1,500. **Remarks:** Part-time maker; first knife sold in 1975. **Mark:** Name, city, state

C. LYLE BRUNCKHORST, Box 476, White Sulphur Springs, MT 59645/406-547-3897
Specialties: Working straight and folding knives, some fancy. **Patterns:** Functional hunters, backpacker knives. **Technical:** Grinds stainless steels; works for precision look. **Prices:** $100 to $300; some to $700. **Remarks:** Full-time maker; sold first knife in 1976. **Mark:** Name and serial

JACK and MORGAN BRYAN, 724 Highland Ave., Gardendale, AL 35071/205-631-3322
Specialties: Folding and straight working knives; some high-tech. **Patterns:** Hunters, survival and fish knives. In folders it's lockers—hunters and traditional patterns. **Technical:** Chip removal 01, D2 and 440C; use shop-made jigs and fixtures for some patterns. **Prices:** $50 to $150; exceptional knives $300. **Remarks:** Part-time maker; first knife sold in 1940. **Mark:** B in circle

BARRY R. BRYNER, 448 N. 1st Ave., Price, UT 84501/801-637-1343
Specialties: Folding and straight knives, most working knives. **Patterns:** Hunters, boots and kitchen knives. Folders include fighters and hunters. **Technical:** Grinds 440C. **Prices:** $90 to $150; some to $250. **Remarks:** Full-time maker; first knife sold in 1978. **Mark:** Name and town in logo

BILL BUCHMAN, 63312 South Rd., Bend, OR 97701/503-382-8851
Specialties: Straight working knives; some are high-tech. **Patterns:** Hunters, fighters and boots. Makes some saddle maker knives. **Technical:** Forges D2, 440C and Sandvik 15N20. Prefers 440C for saltwater; making his own Damascus. **Prices:** $75 to $150; some $225. **Remarks:** Part-time maker; first knife sold in 1982. **Mark:** BB or BUCHMAN

BILL BUCHNER, HC60, Box 35 B, Idleyld Park, OR 97447/503-498-2247
Specialties: Folding and straight working knives, many high art. **Patterns:** Folding lockers; slip-joints; forges his own patterns in whatever function required. **Technical:** Uses W1, L6 and his own Damascus. **Prices:** $100 to $600; some $2,000. **Remarks:** Full-time maker; started selling knives in 1978. Likes sculpturing and carving in Damascus. **Mark:** Signature

MARK A. BUCHOLZ, 10336 Ledoux, Eagle River, AK 99577
Specialties: Straight working knives in standard patterns, some fancy. **Patterns:** Hunters, fighters, and survival knives. **Technical:** Grinds 440C, 154CM, ATS34. **Prices:** $150 to $225; exceptional knives $1,250. **Remarks:** Full-time maker. **Mark:** Name, town and state in buffalo skull logo

DONALD M. BUCKBEE, 8704 Forest Ct., Warren, MI 48093/313-939-9676
Specialties: Straight working knives, some fancy. **Patterns:** The standards, folders, Bowies and tantos. **Technical:** Grinds D2, 440C, ATS34. Makes ultra-lights in hunter patterns. **Prices:** $100 to $250; some to $350. **Remarks:** Part-timer; sold first knife in 1984. **Mark:** Antlered bee—a buck bee

JIMMIE H. BUCKNER, P.O. Box 162, Putney, GA 31782/912-436-4182
Specialties: Straight high-tech working knives, locking folders, primarily his own design. Accepts customer designs, too. **Patterns:** Hunters, fighters and camp knives. **Technical:** Forges 01 and 1095; his own Damascus; heat-treats his own. **Prices:** $100 to $300; some $900. **Remarks:** Full-time maker; first knife sold in 1980. **Mark:** J spade B; also JS, a journeyman smith with ABS

JOHN BUGDEN, 106 So. 13th St., Murray, KY 42071/502-753-0305
Specialties: Straight working knives and period pieces. **Patterns:** Hunters, boots and survival knives. **Technical:** Grinds 01, 440C; buys Damascus. Likes filework. **Prices:** $55 to $85; some $200. **Remarks:** Full-time maker; sold first knife in 1975. **Mark:** J.W.B.

STEVE BUMPUS, 106 Bridle Ridge, Collinsville, IL 62234/618-345-8613
Specialties: Straight working knives in his own designs. **Patterns:** Hunters, bird and trout knives, and skinners. **Technical:** Grinds L6, 440C, and 154CM. **Prices:** $50 to $85; some $225. **Remarks:** Part-time maker; first knife sold in 1981. Makes hunters with gut hooks. **Marks:** Bumpus

PON BURGER, 12 Glenwood Ave., Woodlands, Bulawayo, ZIMBABWE (Africa)/48628
Specialties: Folding and straight working knives; high art with his own designs. **Patterns:** Fighters, locking folders of traditional styles, and buckles. **Technical:** Grinds D2; embellishes all knives made. **Prices:** $175 to $350; some $600. **Remarks:** Full-time maker; first knife sold in 1973. **Mark:** BURGER

directory/custom knifemakers

SKIP BURNETTE, 14 Wildwood Ct., Spartanburg, SC 29301/803-574-6768
Specialties: Straight high-tech working knives. **Patterns:** Hunters, fighters and camp knives. **Technical:** Grinds D2, 440C and ATS34. **Prices:** $65 to $125; some higher. **Remarks:** Spare-time maker; first knife sold in 1983. **Mark:** Name and town with pine trees

DAVE BURNS, 2825 SW 5 St., Boynton Beach, FL 33435/407-734-8806
Specialties: Working straight knives in his design or yours. **Patterns:** Hunters, boots, Bowies, and survival knives. **Technical:** Forges and grinds 01, L6, and 1095. **Prices:** $65 to $200; some $325. **Remarks:** Full-time maker; first knife sold in 1980. **Mark:** Burns and serial number

JOHN BUSFIELD, 153 Devonshire Circle, Roanoke Rapids, NC 27870/919-537-3949
Specialties: Investor grade folders; high-grade working straight knives. **Patterns:** Price-style interframe folders; one-of-a-kinds; drop-point hunters, skinners. **Technical:** Grinds 440C, 154CM and ATS34 very well. Does interframes and inlays; uses jade, agate, jasper. **Prices:** $400 to $550; exceptional knives to $1,000. (Prices for plain knives, before embellishment.) **Remarks:** Full-time maker; first knife sold 1979. **Mark:** Last name, & address

JERRY BUSSE, 11651 Co. Rd. 12, Wauseon, OH 43567/419-923-6471
Specialties: Working straight knives. **Patterns:** Heavy combat knives, and camp knives. **Technical:** Grinds D2, A2, ATS34, and 440C; hollow grinds most blades. **Prices:** $225 to $850; some $3,000. **Remarks:** Full-time maker; first knife sold in 1983. **Mark:** BUSSE in logo

GARY BUTLER, Unit 3/110 Harris St., Welshpool, Perth W.A. 6106, AUSTRALIA/Perth 361-2979
Specialties: Working straight and folding knives, some high-tech, in built-for-Australia design. **Patterns:** Translated standard U.S. patterns in mostly heavy knives. **Technical:** Grinds 440C. Likes bright finishes and hollow grinds. Uses titanium in some folders. **Prices:** $150 to $250 Australian. **Remarks:** Starting a Down Under Guild. **Mark:** Name, town, country

BUZZARD'S KNOB FORGE (See Jeff Hurst)

BARRY J. BYBEE, Rt. 1, Almo, KY 42020/502-759-1786
Specialties: Using straight knives. **Patterns:** Working hunters, skinners and Bowies. **Technical:** Grinds 440C. Likes stag and Micarta for handle materials. **Prices:** $85 to $300; some $400. **Remarks:** Part-time maker; first knife sold in 1968. **Mark:** Arrowhead logo with name, city and state inside

"BY GEORGE" (See George Englebretson)

CABLE JOE (See Joe Allen)

CADILLAC BLACKSMITHING (See Larry Pogreba)

BILL CALDWELL, Rt. 9, Box 170-S, West Monroe, LA 71291/318-323-3025
Specialties: Straight period pieces. **Patterns:** Fighters, Bowies and survival knives; tomahawks, razors and push knives. **Technical:** Forges with sledgehammer, uses no power hammer. **Prices:** $400 to $3,500; some to $10,000. **Remarks:** Full-time maker and self-styled blacksmith extraordinaire; first knife sold 1962. **Mark:** Wild Bill & Sons

ERRETT CALLAHAN, 2 Fredonia, Lynchburg, VA 24503/804-528-3444
Specialties: Obsidian knives. **Patterns:** Modern conceptions, as well as Stone Age replicas. **Technical:** Flakes and knaps to order. **Prices:** $90 and up. **Remarks:** Full-time maker; sold first flint blades in 1974. **Mark:** Unmarked

DICK CAMPBELL, 20000 Silver Ranch Rd., Conifer, CO 80433/303-697-0150
Specialties: Straight and folding fancy working knives; some period pieces. **Patterns:** Bowies and fighters, guts and miniatures. **Technical:** Grinds 440C. **Prices:** $130 to $750; some to $1,200. **Remarks:** Part-time maker; first knives sold in 1975. Prefers natural materials. **Mark:** Name

JOE CANDRELLA, 1219 Barness Dr., Warminster, PA 18974/215-675-0143
Specialties: Folding and straight working knives; some fancy. **Patterns:** Daggers, boots, Bowies, and locking folders. **Technical:** Grinds 440C and 154CM. **Prices:** $100 to $200; some to $1,000. **Remarks:** Part-time maker; first knife sold in 1985. Business name is Franjo. **Mark:** FRANJO with knife as J

DANIEL L. CANNADY, Box 301, Allendale, SC 29810/803-584-2813

Specialties: Straight working knives in traditional patterns. **Patterns:** Drop point hunters, Bowies, skinners. Fish knives with concave grind. **Technical:** Grinds D2, 440C, and ATS34. **Prices:** $65 to $100; some $150. **Remarks:** Part-time maker; first knife sold in 1980. **Mark:** CANNADY

RAYMOND W. CANNON, P.O. Box 871009, Wasilla, AK 99687/907-376-2510
Specialties: Fancy working knives in his own design. **Patterns:** Tantos, hunters, skinners, and utility knives. **Technical:** Forges and grinds 01, L6, 1095, and his own Damascus, and wire-welded Damascus. **Prices:** $65 to $95; some $225. **Remarks:** Part-time maker; first knife sold in 1984. **Mark:** CANNON-ALASKA

RONALD E. CANTER, 96 Bon Air Cir., Jackson, TN 38305/901-668-1780
Specialties: Traditional working knives in customer designs. **Patterns:** Beavertail skinners, Bowies, hand axes, and folding lockers. **Technical:** Grinds A1, 440C, and 154CM. **Prices:** $65 to $250; some $500 and up. **Remarks:** Spare-time maker; first knife sold in 1973. **Mark:** CCC intertwined

DON CANTINI, 3933 Claremont Pl., Weirton, WV 26062/304-748-4890
Specialties: Straight working and fancy knives. **Patterns:** Hunters, boots, daggers, minis and push knives. **Technical:** Grinds 440C and Damascus bars. **Prices:** $65 to $200; some to $800. **Remarks:** Part-time maker; first knife sold in 1976. **Mark:** Name, city, state in logo

BOB CARGILL, Route 1, Box 501-B, Oldfort, TN 37362/615-338-8418
Specialties: Largely folding working knives in his own designs. **Patterns:** Adaptations of traditional pocketknives in many styles. **Technical:** Grinds 1095, 440C, 440A and Damascus bars. **Prices:** $50 to $350; some $2,500. **Remarks:** Full-time maker; first knife sold in 1974. **Mark:** Cargill Knives or Cripple Creek

HAROLD J. "KIT" CARSON, 559 Congress Drive, Radcliff, KY 40160/502-351-9542
Specialties: Hard-working knives for military users; will make customer designs. **Patterns:** Fighters, folders, tantos, survival types. **Technical:** Grinds 440C, ATS34, and D2; likes 1/4-inch stock, integral guards; engraving offered. **Prices:** $100 to $300; some to $1,000. **Remarks:** Part-time maker; sold first knife in 1973. **Mark:** Name

FRED CARTER, 5219 Deer Creek Rd., Wichita Falls, TX 76302/817-723-4020
Specialties: High art investor-class straight knives; some working hunters and fighters. **Patterns:** Classical daggers, Bowies. **Technical:** Grinds a variety of steels. Uses no glue or solder. **Prices:** Generally upscale. **Remarks:** Full-time maker. Does his own engraving and inlay. Makes no folders. **Mark:** Signature in oval logo

DENNIS E. CASEY, 2758 Devonshire, Redwood City, CA 94063/415-365-2665
Specialties: Miniature straight knives in customer designs. **Patterns:** Various straight knives in miniature sizes. **Technical:** Grinds 440C, 154CM, and ATS34. **Prices:** $95 to $200; some $275. **Remarks:** Full-time maker; first knife sold in 1982. **Mark:** D.E. CASEY

DOUGLAS CASTEEL, Rt. 2, Box 237, Hillsboro, TN 37342/615-596-3142
Specialties: Fancy working knives in his own designs. **Patterns:** Boots, fighters, daggers, swords, locking folders, and miniatures. **Technical:** Grinds 440C, ATS34; makes his own wire-cable Damascus. All knives file-worked. **Prices:** $200 to $500; some $1,000. Swords $3,000. **Remarks:** Full-time maker; first knife sold in 1982. **Mark:** D. CASTEEL and year

CATTLE BARON LEATHER (See Tommy McKissack II)

TOM S. CELLUM, 9 Cude Cemetary Rd., Willis, TX 77378/409-856-5937
Specialties: Working straight knives in traditional styles. **Patterns:** Bowies, camp knives, hunters. **Technical:** Forges W2, 01, 5165; makes own Damascus; prefers natural handle materials. **Prices:** $85 to $150; some to $300. **Remarks:** Full-time maker; sold first knife in 1982. **Mark:** Name and J.S. from ABS

FRANK and MARK CENTOFANTE, P.O. Box 17587, Tampa, FL 33682-7587/813-961-0637
Specialties: Fancy folding working knives. **Patterns:** Locking folders and slip joints; and liner locks. **Technical:** Grinds 154CM and ATS34; high finishes. **Prices:** $200 to $550. **Remarks:** Full-time maker; first knife sold in 1968. Son Mark is co-worker. **Mark:** Name, city, state

JOHN A. CHAMBERLIN, 11535 Our Rd., Anchorage, AK 99516/907-346-1524
Specialties: Working knives in traditional style. **Patterns:** Hunters, tantos, large belt knives; some locking folders. **Technical:** Grinds ATS34, 440C, 154CM; uses some deluxe Alaskan materials, oosic and the like. **Prices:** $65 to $300; some higher.

Remarks: Full-time maker; first knife sold in 1984. **Mark:** Name in shield and dagger logo

ROBERT CHAMPION, 3710 Harmony, Amarillo, TX 79109/806-359-0450
Specialties: Traditional working knives, both straight and folding. **Patterns:** Hunters, locking and slip joint folders; some sub-hilt fighters. **Technical:** Grinds A2 and 440C, also D2. **Prices:** $200 to $600; some to $3,000. **Remarks:** Part-time maker; first knife sold in 1979. **Mark:** CHAMPION with dagger logo, city and state

MIKE CHAPMAN, 826 East 14th St., Houston, TX 77009/713-869-0581
Specialties: Using knives, mostly hunters. **Patterns:** Traditional styles, especially drop-points; some folders, fighters, camp knives. **Technical:** Grinds 440C and D2. **Prices:** Moderate. **Remarks:** Roy Etter is partner; full-time makers; sold first knives in 1975. **Mark:** Cherokee Knives

GORDON R. CHARD, 104 S. Holiday Lane, Iola, KS 66749/316-365-2311
Specialties: High-tech working straight knives. **Patterns:** Fighters, boots, daggers, Bowies and mini knives. **Technical:** Grinds D2, 440C, ATS34 and Vascowear. **Prices:** $75 to $1,000; some $2,000. **Remarks:** Part-time maker; first knife sold in 1983. **Mark:** Name, town and state in wheat logo

JOHN E. CHASE, P.O. Drawer H, Aledo, TX 76008/817-441-8331
Specialties: Straight high-tech working knives in standard designs. welcomes customer designs. **Patterns:** Hunters, fighters, daggers and Bowies. **Technical:** Grinds D2, 440C; does satin finishes, mostly. **Prices:** $125 and up. **Remarks:** Part-time maker; first knife sold in 1974. **Mark:** Last name in logo

BILL CHEATHAM, 2930 W. Marlette, Phoenix, AZ 85017/602-242-1497
Specialties: Straight working knives. **Patterns:** Hunters, fighters, boots and axes; also offers locking folders. **Technical:** Grinds 440C. **Prices:** $150 to $350; exceptional knives to $600. **Remarks:** Part-time maker; first knife sold in 1976. Still working after police work-related injury. **Mark:** Name, city state

DON E. CHEATHAM, 22 East 61st, Savannah, GA 31405/912-352-0075
Specialties: Working straight knives, some fancy. **Patterns:** Hunters, fighters and boots. **Technical:** Grinds D2, 440C and 154CM. **Prices:** $100 to $500; some to $1,000. **Remarks:** Full-time maker; first knife sold in 1983. **Mark:** D. CHEATHAM

CLIFF CHELQUIST, P.O. Box 91, Arroyo Grande, CA 93420/805-489-8095
Specialties: Highly polished sportsman's knives. **Patterns:** Bird knives to Bowies. Customer designs welcome. **Technical:** Grinds D2, 440C, and ATS34. **Prices:** $75 to $150; some $400. **Remarks:** Spare-time maker; first knife sold in 1983. **Mark:** C

CHEROKEE KNIVES (See Mike Chapman)

CISCO (See Chuck Syslo)

D.E. (LUCKY) CLARK, Box 314 Woodlawn St. RD #1, Mineral Point, PA 15942/814-322-4725
Specialties: Straight and folding working knives. **Patterns:** Making customer designs now, working from drawing. **Technical:** Grinds D2, 440C, 154CM. **Prices:** $100 to $200 and up. **Remarks:** Part-time maker; only making knives to customer's designs; sold first knife in 1975. **Mark:** Name on one side; "Lucky" on other

HOWARD CLARK, RR 1, Box 74, Runnells, IA 50237/515-966-2126
Specialties: Straight working knives of his own design; welcomes customer designs. **Patterns:** Hunters, skinners, Bowies, and fighters. **Technical:** Forges 5160, files, rasps, and his own Damascus. Uses no stainless steels or synthetic handle materials. **Prices:** $50 to $300. **Remarks:** Full-time maker; first knife sold in 1979. **Mark:** HC connected

J.D. CLAY, R.R. #1, Box 1655, Greenup, KY 41144/606-473-6769
Specialties: Straight and folding fancy working knives. **Patterns:** Hunters, boots, fish knives, and interchangeable blades. He also offers folding lockers and slip joints. **Technical:** Grinds 01, 440C. **Prices:** $55 to $270; some to $400. **Remarks:** Full-time maker; first knife sold in 1972. **Mark:** Name in small medallion in handle

WAYNE CLAY, Box 474B, Pelham, TN 37366/615-467-3472
Specialties: Both straight and folding working knives in standard patterns. **Patterns:** Hunters, fighters and kitchen knives. His folders include gents and hunter patterns. **Technical:** Grinds 154CM and ATS34. **Prices:** $125 to $250; some to $1,000. **Remarks:** Full-time maker; first knife sold in 1978. Highly finished functional working designs, made to complement fine firearms. **Mark:** Name

CLOUDY MT. IRON WORKS (See David Ber)

TERRY A. COHEN, 114 Barson St., Santa Cruz, CA 95060/408-429-9620
Specialties: Working straight and folding knives. **Patterns:** Bowies to boot knives and locking folders. Makes a mini-boot knife. **Technical:** Grinds stainless; hand rubs; tries for good balance. **Prices:** $85 to $150; some to $325. **Remarks:** Part-time maker; first knife sold in 1983. **Mark:** TERRY KNIVES, city and state etched

KEITH E. COLEMAN, 07 Jardin Rd., Los Lunas, NM 87031/505-864-0024
Specialties: Affordable collector-grade straight knives, some fantasy types. **Patterns:** Fighters, tantos, hunters, and swords. **Technical:** Grinds 440C, ATS34 and Damascus. Prefers specialty woods; does file work. **Prices:** $75 to $350; some to $1,200. **Remarks:** Full-time maker; first knife sold in 1980. **Mark:** Name, city and state

KEN COLEMAN, 45 Grand St., Brooklyn, NY 11211/718-963-0773
Specialties: One-of-a-kind knives of unorthodox nature—functional sculpture or creative tooling. **Patterns:** None. **Technical:** Grinds 01, 440C and ATS34. **Prices:** $160 to $340; some $480. **Remarks:** Spare-time maker; first knife sold in 1982. **Mark:** Signature

A.J. COLLINS, 1834 W. Burbank Blvd., Burbank, CA 91506/213-848-4905 (Home: 213-767-3467)
Specialties: Working dress knives. **Patterns:** Street survival knives; swords; axes—definitely personal patterns. **Technical:** Grinds 01, 440C, 154CM. **Prices:** $100 up. **Remarks:** Sold first knife 1972; does business as Kustom Krafted Knives—KKK; full-time maker. **Mark:** Name

LYNN M. COLLINS, 138 Berkley Dr., Elyria, OH 44035/216-366-7101
Specialties: Working straight knives. **Patterns:** Field knives, boots and fighters. **Technical:** Grinds D2, 154CM and 440C. **Prices:** $85 to $135; some more. **Remarks:** Spare-time maker; first knife sold in 1980. **Mark:** Initials, asterisks

CONKLIN MEADOWS FORGE (See Gary M. Little)

BOB CONLEY, Rt. #14, Box 467, Jonesboro, TN 37659/615-753-3302
Specialties: Folding and straight working knives. **Patterns:** Folding knives include lockers, two-blades, gents, hunters and traditional types. Straight knives are hunters, Bowies, daggers and miniatures. **Technical:** Grinds 440C, 154CM and ATS34. **Prices:** $150 to $350; some $600. **Remarks:** Full-time maker; first knife sold in 1979. **Mark:** Full name, city, state

C.T. CONN, JR., 206 Highland Ave., Attalla, AL 35954/205-538-7688
Specialties: Folding working knives, some fancy. **Patterns:** A full range of folding knives. **Technical:** Grinds 02, 440C and 154CM. **Prices:** $125 to $300; some to $600. **Remarks:** Part-time maker; first knife sold in 1982. **Mark:** Name

MICHAEL CONNOR, Box 502, Winters, TX 79567/915-754-5602
Specialties: Straight and folding high art knives. **Patterns:** From hunters to camp knives to folding lockers of the traditional types. **Technical:** Forges 01 and his own Damascus. **Prices:** $150 to $600; some to $2,500. **Remarks:** Spare-time maker; first knife sold in 1974. ABS Master smith. **Mark:** CONNOR M.S.

JEFFREY D. CONTI, 2495 John Carlson Rd. NE, Bremerton, WA 98310/206-692-2692
Specialties: Straight working knives in his design or yours. **Patterns:** Fighters and survival knives; hunters, camp knives and fish knives. **Technical:** Grinds D2, 154CM, and 01. **Prices:** $60 to $200. **Remarks:** Part-time maker; first knife sold in 1980. **Mark:** JC Knives

ROBERT COOGAN, Rt. 3, Box 430, Smithville, TN 37166/615-597-6801
Specialties: One-of-a-kind knives, Damascus steel. **Patterns:** Unique items like ooloo-style Appalachian herb knife. **Technical:** Forges 01 and 3 percent nickel mild steel. Makes his own Damascus. All knives hand-finished. **Prices:** $80 to $1,000; some higher. **Remarks:** Part-time maker; first knife sold in 1979. Not taking orders from Sept. '88 - July '89. **Mark:** RC

R.C. COOK, SR., 604 Phyllis, Conroe, TX 77303/409-756-6127
Specialties: Straight full-size and miniature knives, some fancy. **Patterns:** Traditional hunters, Bowies, hatchets; showcase miniatures. **Technical:** Grinds ATS34, 440C; does own heat-treat. **Prices:** $99 to $1,500 or more. **Remarks:** Sharpening expert, full-timer. **Mark:** Rams head with name

directory/custom knifemakers

GEORGE S. "STEVE" COPELAND, Star Route Box #36, Alpine, TN 38543/615-823-5214.
Specialties: Working straight and folding knives in traditional and fancy designs. **Patterns:** Wide range includes tomahawks, butterfly folders, camp knives, slip-joint folders. **Technical:** Grinds variety of steels. **Prices:** $60 to $350; can go over $1,000. **Remarks:** Part-time maker; first knife sold in 1979. **Mark:** Four-leaf clover, initials

CORBIN KNIVES (See Corbin Newcomb)

HAROLD CORBY, 1714 Brandonwood Dr., Johnson City, TN 37604/615-926-9781
Specialties: Straight and folding fancy working knives. **Patterns:** Hunters, fighters, Bowies and push knives, and traditional-type folders. **Technical:** Grinds 154CM, ATS34. Prefers natural materials. **Prices:** $100 to $600; some to $1,200. **Remarks:** Full-time maker; first knife sold in 1969. **Mark:** CORBY

JOSEPH G. CORDOVA, 1450 Lillie Drive, Bosque Farms, NM 87068/505-869-3912
Specialties: One of a kind designs; does some customer designs. **Patterns:** His fighter called the "Gladiator," hunters, boots, and cutlery. **Technical:** Forges 1095, 5160, and grinds ATS34, 440C, and 154CM. **Prices:** Moderate to upscale. **Remarks:** Full-time maker; first knife sold in 1955. **Mark:** Cordova made

JIM CORRADO, 2915 Cavitt Creek Rd., Glide, OR 97443/503-496-3951
Specialties: High-tech, high art folding knives. **Patterns:** Makes unusual and difficult pieces, following British and Continental historical design. **Technical:** Forges mostly L6, 154CM and his own Damascus. **Prices:** $200 to $500; some $3,000. **Remarks:** Full-time maker; first knife sold in 1974. **Mark:** Name, date and state with shield logo

DON CORWIN, 5064 Eber Rd., Monclove, OH 43542/419-877-5210
Specialties: Works to customer designs in folding knives. **Patterns:** Folders: 1 or 2 blades, slip joints, and lockers. **Technical:** Grinds 440C, ATS34, and 154CM. **Prices:** $60 to $150; some $500. **Remarks:** Part-time maker; first knife sold in 1987. **Mark:** Corwin, city and state within arrowhead logo

SCOTT COSTA, Rt. 2, Box 503, Spicewood, TX 78669/512-693-3431
Specialties: Straight working knives. **Patterns:** Hunters, survival, fishing and divers' knives. **Technical:** Grinds only D2. **Prices:** $65 to $350; some to $650. **Remarks:** Full-time maker; first knife sold in 1985. **Mark:** SC connected

JAMES I. COTTRILL, 1776 Ransburg Ave., Columbus, OH 43223/614-274-0020
Specialties: Working straight knives in his own designs. **Patterns:** Caters to the boating, wood-carving crowd, and makes utility-type knives. **Technical:** Grinds 01, D2, and 440C. Likes filework. **Prices:** $95 to $250; some to $500. **Remarks:** Full-time maker; first knife sold in 1977. **Mark:** Name, city, state, in oval logo

ELDON COURTNEY, 2718 Bullinger, Wichita, KS 67204/316-838-4053
Specialties: Straight working knives in his own designs. **Patterns:** Hunters and fighters, and one-of-a-kinds. **Technical:** Grinds and tempers L6, 440C and spring steel. **Prices:** $100 to $500; some to $1,500. **Remarks:** Full-time maker; first knife sold in 1977. **Mark:** Full name, city and state

GEORGE COUSINO, 22386 Beechwood Ct., Woodhaven, MI 48183/313-675-3284
Specialties: Straight working knives. **Patterns:** Hunters, Bowies, buckskinners and daggers. **Technical:** Grinds D2, 440C and 154CM. **Prices:** $85 to $125; some to $600. **Remarks:** Part-time maker; first knife sold in 1981. **Mark:** COUSINO

RAYMOND A. COVER, Rt. 1, Box 194, Mineral Point, MO 63660/314-749-3783
Specialties: Folding and straight knives in standard patterns, mainly working knives with high-tech materials. **Patterns:** Bowies and boots; two-bladed folders. **Technical:** Grinds D2, 440C and 154CM. **Prices:** $135 to $250; some to $400. **Remarks:** Part-time maker; first knife sold in 1974. **Mark:** Name

COLIN J. COX, 1609 Votaw Rd., Apopka, FL 32703/407-889-7887
Specialties: Folding and straight working knives and period pieces of his own design. **Patterns:** Hunters, fighters and survival shapes. Folding, two-blades, gents and hunters. **Technical:** Grinds D2, 440C, 154CM and ATS34. **Prices:** $125 to $750; some to $1,500. **Remarks:** Full-time maker; first knife sold in 1981. **Mark:** Full name, city and state

COYOTE KNIVES (See L.H. Bloomfield)

RICHARD C. CRAFT, 3045 Longwood Dr., Jackson, MS 39212/601-373-4046
Specialties: Fancy working knives. **Patterns:** Offers chopping knife and block for kitchen, bird knives, and steak knives with presentation case. **Technical:** Grinds 01, L6, and 440C. Cases made of cherry or mahogany. **Prices:** $65 to $275; some $600. **Remarks:** Full-time maker; first knife sold in 1985. **Mark:** CRAFT

JAMES H. CRAIG, 334 Novara, Manchester, MO 63021/314-391-8235
Specialties: Fancy straight working knives. **Patterns:** From hunters to swords to miniatures; some embellished. **Technical:** Grinds A2, D2 and 440C. **Prices:** $50 to $125; exceptional knives to $500. **Remarks:** Part-time maker; first knife sold in 1972. **Mark:** CRAIG

JACK W. CRAIN, Rt. 2 Box 221 F, Weatherford, TX 76086/817-599-6414
Specialties: Fancy period pieces of his own design in straight knives. **Patterns:** Bowies, daggers and survival knives; also limited edition commemorative Bowies. **Technical:** Forges and grinds D2, 440C and his own Damascus. **Prices:** $325 to $1,200; some to $4,000. **Remarks:** Full-time maker; first knife sold in 1969. **Mark:** Name with stylized crane

LARRY CRAWFORD, 1602 Brooks St., Rosenberg, TX 77471/713-341-5234
Specialties: Fancy straight and folding knives in traditional patterns. **Patterns:** Bowies, tantos, folders, interframes, and push knives. **Technical:** Forges 1095 and his own Damascus. **Prices:** $300 to $500; some to $800. **Remarks:** Part-time maker; sold first knife in 1983. **Mark:** CRAWFORD

PAT CRAWFORD, 205 N. Center, West Memphis, AR 72301/501-735-4632
Specialties: High-tech working folding and straight knives—self-defense and combat types. **Patterns:** Folding patent locks; interframes; fighters and boots. **Technical:** Grinds 01, 440C and 154CM. **Prices:** $35 to $500; some to $800. **Remarks:** Full-time maker; first knife sold in 1973. **Mark:** CRAWFORD

CRIPPLE CREEK (See Bob Cargill)

HAROLD CRISP, 3885 Bow St. N.E., Cleveland, TN 37312/615-476-8240
Specialties: Straight and folding fancy working knives. **Patterns:** Hunters to Bowies, tomahawks to miniatures. Folding lockers, both interframes and traditional styles. **Technical:** Grinds 01, D2 and 440C; also forges. **Prices:** $85 to $250; some $800. **Remarks:** Part-time maker; first knife sold in 1972. **Mark:** Initials or name

JACK CROCKFORD, 1859 Harts Mill Rd., Chamblee, GA 30341/404-457-4680
Specialties: Clean-lined working straight and folding knives, some period pieces. Works with customer design also. **Patterns:** Hunters and fish and camp knives; folders in traditional styles. **Technical:** Grinds A2, D2, ATS34 and 440C. **Prices:** $150 to $250; some to $300. **Remarks:** Part-time maker; first knife sold in 1975. **Mark:** Name

TIM CROSS, 743 Loma Vista Dr., Long Beach, CA 90813/213-435-5751
Specialties: Straight working knives, some fantasy. **Patterns:** Enjoys large knives, machetes, swords, hunters and daggers. **Technical:** Grinds ATS34, A2, and D2. **Prices:** $175 to $400; swords $1,500. **Remarks:** Spare-time maker; first knife sold in 1987. **Mark:** CROSS

ROBERT CROWDER, Box 1374, Thompson Falls, MT 59873/406-827-4754
Specialties: Customized working knives in traditional and original patterns. **Patterns:** Hunters, Bowies, fighters, fillets and folding knives. **Technical:** Grinds ATS34, 154CM, 440C, Vascowear and commercial Damascus. Filework on most knives. **Prices:** $80 to $225; some $600. **Remarks:** Part-time maker; first knife sold in 1985. **Mark:** Name, city and state in logo

JAMES L. CROWELL, H.C. 74, Box 368, Mtn. View, AR 72560/501-269-4215
Specialties: Fancy period pieces and working knives. Welcomes customer designs. **Patterns:** Straight knives from hunters to daggers, war hammers to tantos. Folding lockers and slip joints. **Technical:** Forges W2, 01 and his own Damascus. **Prices:** $400 to $1,000; some to $3,500. **Remarks:** Full-time maker; first knife sold in 1980. **Mark:** A shooting star. ABS Master Smith

JOHN CULPEPPER, 2102 Spencer Ave., Monroe, LA 71201/318-323-3636
Specialties: Working straight knives. **Patterns:** Hunters, Bowies and camp knives in heavy-duty patterns. **Technical:** Grinds 01, D2 and 440C; hollow grinds. **Prices:** $75 to $200; some $300. **Remarks:** Part-time maker; first knife sold in 1970. **Mark:** Pepper

R.J. CUMMING, American Embassy Copenhagen, APO New York, NY 09170
Specialties: Custom designs, especially for military personnel. **Patterns:** Hunters, fighters, Bowies and one-of-a-kind straight knives. Diver's tool knife. **Technical:** Grinds D2, 440C and 154CM. **Prices:** $100 to $450; some to $1,700. **Remarks:** Part-time maker presently in Foreign Service; first knife sold in 1978. **Mark:** CUMMING

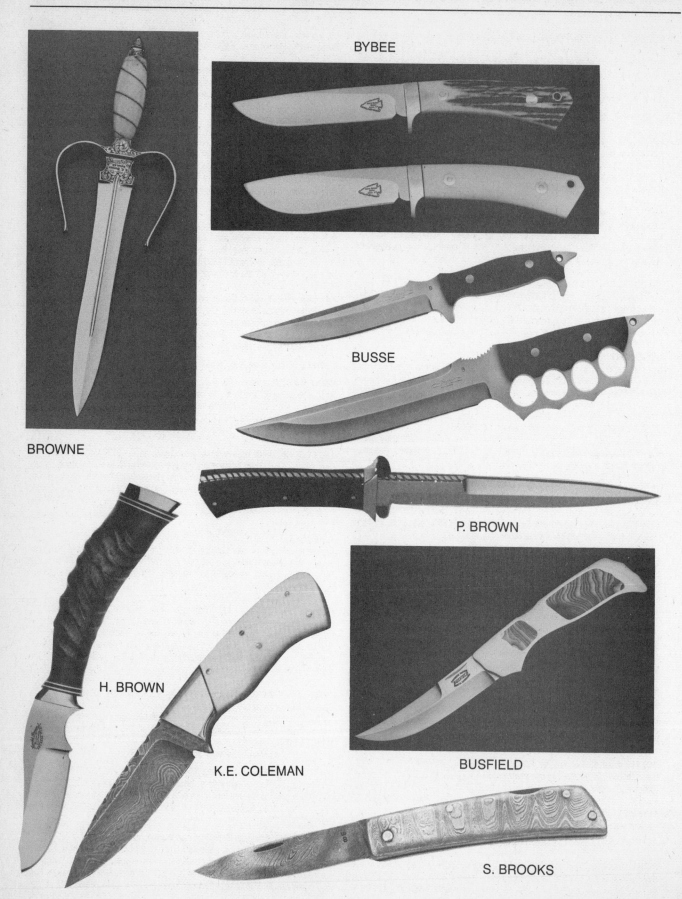

BYBEE

BUSSE

BROWNE

P. BROWN

H. BROWN

K.E. COLEMAN

BUSFIELD

S. BROOKS

directory/custom knifemakers

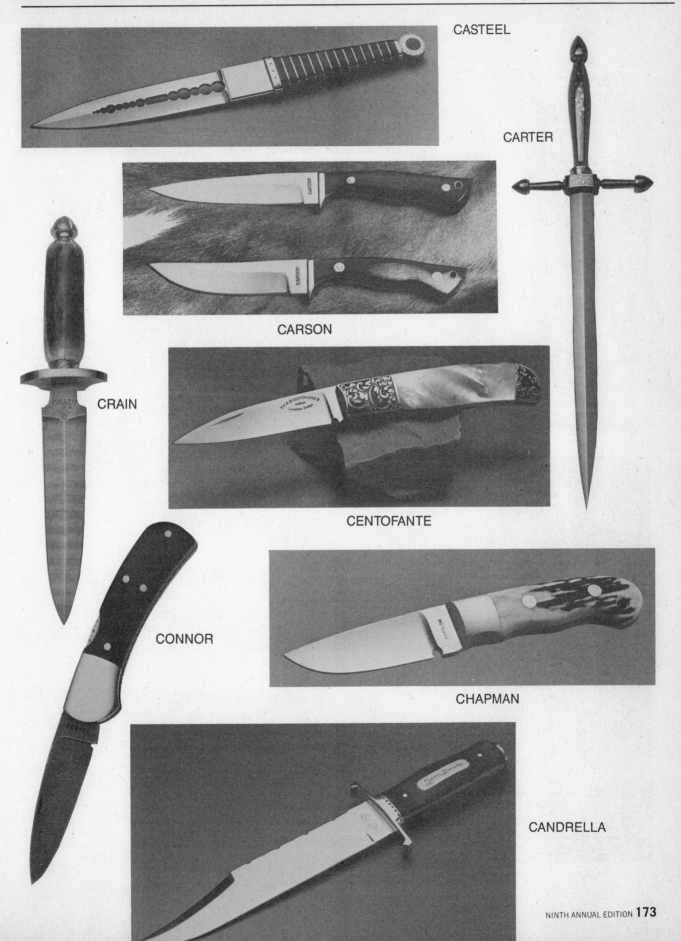

CASTEEL

CARTER

CARSON

CRAIN

CENTOFANTE

CONNOR

CHAPMAN

CANDRELLA

CROWELL

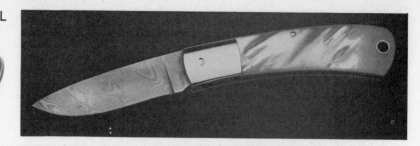

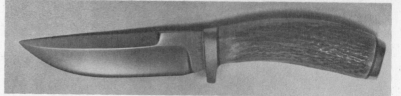

COURTNEY

L. CRAWFORD

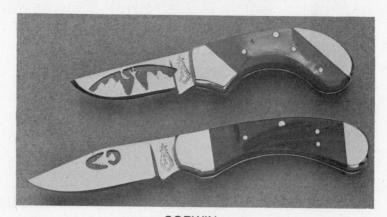

CORWIN

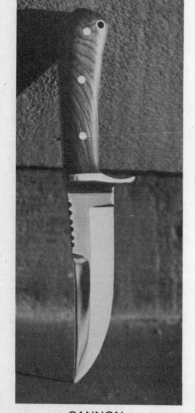

COX

CROWDER

CANNON

CRAFT

CUSTOM CUTLERY (See R. Von Boeckman)

THOMAS CUTE, RD 4, Rt. 90, Cortland, NY 13045/607-749-4055
Specialties: Straight working knives; will work to customer designs. **Patterns:** Bowies, skinners, camp knives, rifle sling knives. Does miniatures. **Technical:** Grinds 01, 440C, and 154CM. **Prices:** $100 to $300; some $500. **Remarks:** Full-time maker; first knife sold in 1974. **Mark:** Full name

CYPRESS BEND CUSTOM KNIVES (See W.B. Ellerbe)

DAN DAGGET, 1961 Meteor, Flagstaff, AZ 86001/602-774-7537
Specialties: High art straight knives; many embellished with inlays or gems. **Patterns:** Hunters, fighters, daggers. **Technical:** Grinds 440C and buys Damascus. **Prices:** $550 to $2,000; some to $4,000. **Remarks:** Part-time maker; first knife sold in 1973. **Mark:** Name

CRIS W. DAHL, Rt. 4, Box 558, Lake Geneva, WI 53147/414-248-2464
Specialties: Straight high-art working knives. **Patterns:** Hunters, fighters and push knives. **Technical:** Grinds 440C and imported stainless steel Damascus. **Prices:** $180 and $600; some to $3,000. **Remarks:** Full-time maker. **Mark:** Cris W. Dahl maker

G. E. DAILEY, 577 Lincoln St., Seekonk, MA 02771/617-336-5088
Specialties: Big working knives and period pieces. **Patterns:** Bowies and swords. **Technical:** Grinds 01 and 440C. Does leather wrapping. **Prices:** $150 to $1,500. **Remarks:** Part-time maker. Sold first knife in 1982. Likes broadswords. **Mark:** Signature

DAN D. (See D. Dennehy)

DAN E. (See D.E. Brdlik)

ALEX DANIELS, 1410 Colorado Ave., Lynn Haven, FL 32444/904-265-8449
Specialties: Working straight and folding knives; some period pieces; makes using knives. **Patterns:** Hunters, Bowies and fish knives. Folding lockers, slip joints in traditional types. **Technical:** Grinds D2, 440C and 154CM. **Prices:** $95 to $175; some to $500. **Remarks:** Full-time maker; first knife sold in 1963. **Mark:** Daniels

RICK DARBY, 4026 Shelbourne, Youngstown, OH 44511/216-793-3805
Specialties: Straight working knives. **Patterns:** Boots, fighters and hunters with mirror finish. **Technical:** Grinds 440C, 154CM and Stellite 6K. **Prices:** $85 to $125; some $160. **Remarks:** Part-time maker; first knife sold in 1974. **Mark:** R.J. DARBY

EDMUND DAVIDSON, Rt. 1 Box 319, Goshen, VA 24439/703-997-5651
Specialties: Working straight knives; some period style. **Patterns:** Heavy-duty skinners and camp knives. **Technical:** Grinds D2, ATS34, S-7; likes integral patterns. **Prices:** $75 to $150; some to $650. **Remarks:** Full-time maker; first knife sold in 1986. **Mark:** Name in deerhead or motorcycle logo

ROB DAVIDSON, 2419—25th St., Lubbock, TX 79411/806-762-1901
Specialties: Working folders and straight knives; some period pieces. **Patterns:** Battle axes to miniatures; daggers to swords; various types of folders. **Technical:** Grinds D2, 440C, and buys Damascus; keeps no patterns. **Prices:** $75 to $300; some to $1,000. **Remarks:** Full-time maker; first knife sold in 1982. **Mark:** Rocket logo

DAVIS BROTHERS KNIVES, 1209 Woodlawn Dr., Camden, SC 29020/803-432-3024
Specialties: Straight working knives. **Patterns:** Traditional; drop points; hunters and fish knives. **Technical:** Grind 440C, 154CM, ATS34; prefer full tang. **Prices:** $60 to $130; some to $200. **Remarks:** Part-timers; sold first knife in 1970. **Mark:** DAVIS

BARRY L. DAVIS, 1871 Pittsfield Rd., Castleton, NY 12033/518-477-5036
Specialties: Forged traditional and fancy straight knives and folders. **Patterns:** Daggers and Bowies; slip -joints and folders. **Technical:** Makes Damascus; uses only natural handle materials. **Prices:** $400 to $1,200; some to $2,500. **Remarks:** Part-time maker; sold first knife in 1980. **Mark:** B in a D

DIXIE DAVIS, Rt. 3, Clinton, SC 29325/803-833-4964
Specialties: Straight working knives; some fantasies. **Patterns:** Hunters, fighters and boots. **Technical:** Grinds 440C, 154CM and ATS34 with mirror finish. **Prices:** $85 to $140; some to $200. **Remarks:** Part-time maker; first knife sold in 1981. **Mark:** DIXIE

DON DAVIS, 3918 Ash Ave., Loveland, CO 80538/303-669-9016
Specialties: Straight working knives in traditional patterns. Welcomes customer designs. **Patterns:** Hunters, utility knives, skinners, and survival knives. **Technical:** Grinds 440C, ATS34. **Prices:** $75 to $250. **Remarks:** Full-time maker; first knife sold in 1985. **Mark:** Signature, city and state

JESSE W. DAVIS, 5810 Hwy. 301, Walls, MS 38680/601-781-0036
Specialties: Straight and folding working knives in traditional and customer designs. **Patterns:** Tantos, Bowies, locking folders, and hunters. **Technical:** Grinds D2, 440C, and bought Damascus. **Prices:** $100 to $200; some to $450. **Remarks:** Part-time maker; first knife sold in 1977. **Mark:** Name or initials

K.M. "TWIG" DAVIS, P.O. Box 267, Monroe, WA 98272/206-794-7274
Specialties: Fancy working straight knives. **Patterns:** Hunters, boots, fish knives, does some Bowies and daggers. **Technical:** Grinds D2, 440C and 154CM. **Prices:** $95 to $150; some to $400. **Remarks:** Part-time maker; first knife sold in 1979. **Mark:** Twig

SYD DAVIS, 1220 Courtney Dr., Richmond, TX 77469/713-342-2597
Specialties: Folding and straight working knives. **Patterns:** Folding lockers and slip-joints; some straight hunters and camp knives. **Technical:** Grinds D2 and 440C; forges his own Damascus. **Prices:** $100 to $250; some to $400. **Remarks:** Part-time maker; first knife sold in 1981. **Mark:** Name in script

TERRY DAVIS, Box 111, Sumpter, OR 97877/503-894-2307
Specialties: Folding working knives in traditional styles. **Patterns:** Lockers and slip-joints; some straight knives. Makes linerless Micarta folders with Vascowear. **Technical:** Grinds ATS34, Vascowear; likes flat grinds. **Prices:** $125 to $400; some to $1,000. **Remarks:** Full-time maker; sold first knife in 1985. **Mark:** Name in logo

VERNON M. DAVIS, 1226 LaClede, Waco, TX 76705/817-799-4478
Specialties: Working straight knives. **Patterns:** Bowies, bird knives, hunters, and skinners. **Technical:** Grinds 440C, 154CM, and D2. Sometimes grinds an esthetic grind line near choil. Prefers mirror polish and hollow grinds. **Prices:** $90 to $250; some $450. **Remarks:** Part-time maker; first knife sold in 1980. **Mark:** Davis and Waco inside outline of state

W.C. DAVIS, 2010 S. Madison, Raymore, MO 64083/816-331-4491
Specialties: Fancy working folding and straight knives. **Patterns:** Folding lockers and slip-joints; straight hunters, fighters and Bowies. **Technical:** Grinds 440C, A2, ATS34; **Prices:** $80 to $200; some to $1,000. **Remarks:** Full-time maker; first knife sold in 1972. **Mark:** W.C. DAVIS

DANE and BARRY DAWSON, Box 10, Marvel, CO 81329/303-588-2266
Specialties: Samurai swords, collector daggers, working knives, both straight and folding with non-glare finish. **Patterns:** Offers over 60 different models. **Technical:** Grinds 440C; does own heat-treat. **Prices:** $75 to $300; some to $1,000. **Remarks:** Full-time maker; first knife sold in 1975. **Mark:** DAWSON in print or script

HARVEY J. DEAN, Rt. 2, Box 137, Rockdale, TX 76567/512-446-3111
Specialties: Straight working knives, some fancy. **Patterns:** Hunters, Bowies, camp and combat knives. **Technical:** Forges W2, 01, and 5160. **Prices:** $100 to $500. **Remarks:** Part-time maker; first knife sold in 1981. **Mark:** Dean

RICHARD DEARHART, Rt. 1, Lula, GA 30554/404-869-3816
Specialties: Working straight knives, his designs and customer designs; some period styles. **Patterns:** Hunters, fighters, Bowies and buckskinner knives. **Technical:** Forges and grinds; uses A2, 01 and D2, some 440C. **Prices:** $75 to $200; some to $350. **Remarks:** Full-time maker; first knife sold in 1967. **Mark:** Dearhart

DEER (See D. Laughlin)

DEER CREEK FORGE (See Quarton)

ROBERT A. DEFEO, 12 Morningside Dr., Mays Landing, NJ 08330/609-625-3744
Specialties: Straight working knives and period pieces. **Patterns:** Hunters, fighters and Bowies. **Technical:** Grinds D2, 440C and ATS34. **Prices:** $100 to $300. **Remarks:** Part-time maker; first knife sold in 1982. **Mark:** DEFEO

WILLIAM G. DEFREEST, P.O. BOX 573, Barnwell, SC 29812/803-259-7883
Specialties: Straight and folding working knives. **Patterns:** Fighters, hunters and boots; makes some folding lockers and slip-joints. **Technical:** Grinds 440C, 154CM and ATS34; clean lines and mirror finishes. **Prices:** $100 to $700. **Remarks:** Full-time maker; first knife sold in 1974. **Mark:** GORDON

GORDON S. DEMPSEY, P.O. Box 7497, N. Kenai, AK 99635/907-776-8425
Specialties: Working straight and folding knives; some period pieces. **Patterns:** Hunters, Bowies and ooloos; harpoons. **Technical:** Forges 01 and 5160; makes Damascus. **Prices:** $80 to $250. **Remarks:** Full-time maker; first knife sold in 1974. **Mark:** Name, city, and state

DAN DENNEHY, 13321 Hwy. 160, Del Norte, CO 81132/303-657-2545
Specialties: Working fighting and military knives. **Patterns:** Full range of straight knives, tomahawks, buckle knives. **Technical:** Forges and grinds; uses A2, 01 and D2. **Prices:** $135 to $250; exceptional knives to $3,500. **Remarks:** Full-time maker; started selling knives in 1942. **Mark:** DAN-D, city, state and shamrock

DOUGLAS M. DENT, 1208 Chestnut St., So. Charleston, WV 25309/304-768-3308
Specialties: Sportsman's knives; working straight and folding models. **Patterns:** Hunters, boots and Bowies, interframe folders. **Technical:** Forges and grinds; uses D2, 440C, 154CM and plain tool steels. **Prices:** $70 to $300; exceptional knives to $800. **Remarks:** Full-time maker; started selling in 1969. **Mark:** DENT

LARRY DETLOFF, 130 Oxford Way, Santa Cruz, CA 95060/408-427-1554
Specialties: Large working folders. **Patterns:** Folders in a variety of blade shapes. **Technical:** Grinds 440C, 154CM and ATS34. **Prices:** Starting at $400. **Remarks:** Part-time maker; first knife sold 1970. **Mark:** DETLOFF

PHILLIP DETMER, Rt. 1 Box 149A, Breese, IL 62230/618-526-4834
Specialties: Working straight knives, some to customer design, some fancy. **Patterns:** Bowies and daggers, hunters. **Technical:** Grinds high carbon and high carbon stainless steels. **Prices:** $60 to $300. **Remarks:** Spare-time maker; sold first knife in 1977. **Mark:** Name

CLARENCE DeYONG, 5211 Maryland Ave., Racine, WI 53406/414-554-1760
Specialties: Straight working knives in traditional styles. **Patterns:** Bowies, fighters, hunters, and tantos, and steak knives. **Technical:** Grinds 440C, 01, and ATS34; does own scrimshaw. **Prices:** $65 to $110; some to $350. **Remarks:** Part-time maker; first knife sold in 1984; numbers knives. **Mark:** DeYong

D'HOLDER (See Holder)

DIAMOND "B" KNIFE CO. (See L.E. "Red" Brown)

JACK DIAS, P.O. Box 223, Palermo, CA 95968/916-533-9043
Specialties: Display knives; makes customer designs to order. **Patterns:** Wide variety of straight knives. **Technical:** Satin finishes standard; prefers natural materials. **Mark:** Name

JOSEPH M. DIGANGI, Box 225, Santa Cruz, NM 87567/505-753-6414
Specialties: Kitchen and table cutlery. **Patterns:** French chef knives; carving sets, steak knife sets; makes some camp knives and hunters. Holds patents and trademarks for kitchen cutlery set: "System II." **Technical:** Grinds 440C; buys Damascus. **Prices:** $150 to $450; some to $1,000. **Remarks:** Full-time maker; first knife sold in 1983. **Mark:** DiGangi

EARL E. DILLON, 8908 Stanwin Ave., Arleta, CA 91331
Specialties: Fancy folders and straight knives. **Patterns:** Contemporary interpretation of contemporary needs. **Technical:** Grinds 440C and AEB. **Prices:** $250 to $350; some over $500. **Remarks:** Part-time maker; sold first knife in 1984; collaboration with Chuck Stapel. **Mark:** STAPEL-DILLON

FRANK J. DILLUVIO, 13611 Joyce, Warren, MI 48093/313-775-1216
Specialties: Traditional working straight knives; some high-tech approaches. **Patterns:** Hunters, Bowies, fish knives. **Technical:** Grinds D2, 440C, CPM; works for precision fits—no solder. **Prices:** $75 to $350; some to $500. **Remarks:** Part-time maker; sold first knife in 1984. **Mark:** Circle FJD

SCOTT DINGMAN, 909 7th St., International Falls, MN 56649/218-283-2151
Specialties: Fancy working knives in his own designs. **Patterns:** Hunters, daggers, boots, and camp knives. **Technical:** Forges 01, L6, and D2. Provides lost wax casting and hard cast bronze. Prefers exotic woods and high mirror finishes. **Prices:** $150 to $225; some $500. **Remarks:** Full-time maker; first knife sold in 1983. **Mark:** DINGMAN

GREG DION, 3032 S. Jackson St., Oxnard, CA 93033/805-483-1781 (evenings)
Specialties: Working straight knives, some fancy. **Patterns:** Hunter specials, camp knives, Bowies, tantos and special boar knife. Welcomes special orders. **Technical:** Grinds ATS34, 154CM, 440C; can CNC mill handle shapes. **Prices:** $85 to $160; some to $400. **Remarks:** Part-time maker; first knife sold in 1985. **Mark:** Name

MALCOLM C. DION, 820 N. Fairview Ave., Goleta, CA 93117/805-967-6714
Specialties: Fancy working straight knives. Welcomes customer ideas. **Patterns:** Hunters, tantos, camp knives; some buckskinner models. **Technical:** Grinds 440C, 154CM and ATS34. **Prices:** $150 to $300; some to $800. **Remarks:** Full-time maker; first knife sold in 1984. **Mark:** MAL DION with cougar head.

LARRY DiTOMMASO, P.O. Box 12233, Longview, TX 75602/214-236-4285
Specialties: Handmade straight and folding knives. **Patterns:** Hunters and working knives, some fancy. No Bowies or fighters. **Technical:** Grinds all popular steels; prefers stainless. **Prices:** $45 and up. **Remarks:** Full-time maker; sold first knife in 1986. **Mark:** LD or LAD

DIXIE (See Dixie Davis)

ROBERT ORR DODGE, 1515 Braley St., Saginaw, MI 48602/517-790-3175
Specialties: Using straight knives in his design or yours. **Patterns:** Hunters, hatchets, fish and utility knives. **Technical:** Grinds ATS34, 440C, and A2. **Prices:** $60 to $300; some $850. **Remarks:** Full-time maker; first knife sold in 1976. **Mark:** DODGE

DOG KNIVES (See Dave Dugger)

JOHN DONAGHEY, P.O. Box 402021, Garland, TX 75046/214-272-7607
Specialties: Small working straight knives in personal designs; some camp knives. **Patterns:** Small Bowies and skinners; boots and fighters. **Technical:** Grinds 01, 440C and 154CM; likes exotic wood. **Prices:** $85 to $150; some to $300. **Remarks:** Spare-time maker; sold first knife 1981. **Mark:** JED

PATRICK DONOVAN, 1770 Hudson Dr., San Jose, CA 95124/408-267-9825
Specialties: Straight and folding working knives; period pieces. **Patterns:** Hunters, boots and daggers; lockers and slip-joints in folders. **Technical:** Grinds 440C. Does own embellishments. **Prices:** $75 to $475; some to $1,200. **Remarks:** Full-time maker; sold first knife 1980. **Mark:** PATRICK

MIKE DOOLITTLE, 13 Denise Ct., Novato, CA 94947/415-897-3246
Specialties: Working straight knives in standard patterns. **Patterns:** Hunters, and fish knives. **Technical:** Grinds 440C, 154CM, and ATS34. **Prices:** $90 to $200; some $300. **Remarks:** Part-time maker; first knife sold in 1981. **Mark:** Name, city, and state

DICK DOROUGH, Rt. 1, Box 210, Gadsden, AL 35901/205-442-5497
Specialties: Working knives—folders to Bowies. **Patterns:** Fancy interframe folders. **Technical:** Grinds 440C, D2. **Prices:** $150 to $375; some to $625. **Remarks:** Part-time maker. Sold first knife in 1968. **Mark:** Name

DALE DOUGLAS, 361 Mike Cooper Rd., Ponchatoula, LA 70454/504-345-6169
Specialties: Folding and straight working knives. **Patterns:** Folding lockers and slip-joints; hunters, boots and camp knives. **Technical:** Grinds D2, 440C and 154CM. **Prices:** $75 to $150; some to $350. **Remarks:** Spare-time maker; first knife sold in 1980. **Mark:** Name

DOVE KNIVES (See Steve Rollert)

T.M. DOWELL, 139 N.W. St. Helen's Pl., Bend, OR 97701/503-382-8924
Specialties: Integral construction in hunting knives, and period pieces. Famous "Funny" folders. **Patterns:** Hunters to sword canes; Price-style daggers to axes. **Technical:** Forges and grinds; uses D2, 440C and 154CM. Makes his own bright Damascus. **Prices:** $175 to $750; exceptional knives to $4,500. **Remarks:** Full-time maker; first knife sold in 1967. **Mark:** TMD logo

JAMES T. DOWNIE, R.R. #1, Thedford, Ont. NOM 2NO, CANADA/519-243-2290
Specialties: Serviceable straight knives; some period pieces; folders. **Patterns:** Hunters, Bowies, camp knives and miniatures. **Technical:** Grinds D2, 440C and 154CM. **Prices:** $90 to $300; some $500. **Remarks:** Part-time maker; first knife sold in 1978. **Mark:** J.T. DOWNIE

LARRY DOWNING, Route 1, Bremen, KY 42325/502-525-3523
Specialties: Working straight and folding knives. **Patterns:** From mini-knives to daggers; folding lockers to interframes. **Technical:** Grinds D2, 440C and 154CM. **Prices:** $90 to $350. **Remarks:** Part-time maker; first knife sold in 1979. **Mark:** Name in arrowhead

TOM DOWNING, 129 So. Bank St., Cortland, OH 44410/216-637-0623
Specialties: Straight working knives, period pieces. **Patterns:** Hunters, fighters and tantos. **Technical:** Grinds D2, 154CM and ATS34; prefers natural handle materials. **Prices:** $100 to $225; some to $700. **Remarks:** Part-time maker; first knife sold in 1979. **Mark:** T.W. Downing

JIM DOWNS, 35 Sunset Road, Londonderry, OH 45647/614-887-2099
Specialties: Straight working knives. **Patterns:** Hunting and utility knives, some boots. **Technical:** Grinds 440C. Does your design or his. Prefers stag, Micarta, and Pakkawood. **Prices:** $50 to $100. **Remarks:** Part-time maker; first knife sold in 1981. **Mark:** DOWNS

ROBERT LEE DOZIER, c/o A.G. Russell, 1705 Hwy. 471N, Springdale, AR 72764/501-751-7341
Specialties: Limited production fine knives. **Patterns:** Variety of collector-grade knives. **Technical:** Grinds 154CM. **Prices:** $400 and up. **Remarks:** Full-time maker; first knife sold in 1961. **Mark:** Name

DRAGON KNIVES (See Norman Levine)

BERYL DRISKILL, P.O. Box 187, Braggadocio, MO 63826/314-757-6262
Specialties: Fancy working knives. **Patterns:** Hunting knives, fighters, Bowies, boots, daggers, and lockback folders. **Technical:** Grinds 440C, ATS34, 154CM. **Prices:** $150 to $350; some to $4,000. **Remarks:** Part-time maker; first knife sold in 1984. **Mark:** Name

DUBBA (See Schulenberg)

DENNIS DUBLIN, 708 Stanley St., Box 986, Enderby, BC V0E 1V0, CANADA/604-838-6753
Specialties: Working straight and folding knives, plain or fancy. **Patterns:** Hunters and Bowies; locking hunters; combination knife/ axe. **Technical:** Grinds and forges high carbon steels. **Prices:** $100 to $400, and up. **Remarks:** Full-time maker; first knife sold in 1970. **Mark:** Name

BILL DUFF, P.O. Box 694, Virginia City, NV 89440/702-847-0566
Specialties: Straight and folding working knives. **Patterns:** Hunters and Bowies; folding lockers and interframes. **Technical:** Grinds D2, 440C and 154CM. **Prices:** $175 to $450; exceptional knives to $1,200. **Remarks:** Part-time maker; first knife sold in 1976. **Mark:** Name, city, state and date

ARTHUR J. DUFOUR, 8120 Dearmoun Rd., Anchorage, AK 99516/907-345-1701
Specialties: Working straight knives of traditional type. **Patterns:** Hunters, Bowies, camp and fish knives—grinds them very thin and pointed. **Technical:** Grinds 440C, ATS34, AEB-L. Tempers 57-58R, hollow grinds. **Prices:** $135; some to $250. **Remarks:** Part-time maker; first knife sold in 1970. **Mark:** Prospector logo

DAVE DUGGER, 2504 West 51, Westwood, KS 66205/913-831-2382
Specialties: Working straight knives and fantasy pieces. **Patterns:** Hunters, boots and daggers in one-of-a-kind styles. **Technical:** Grinds D2, 440C and 154CM. **Prices:** $75 to $350; some to $1,200. **Remarks:** Part-time maker; first knife sold in 1979; not accepting orders. **Mark:** DOG

LAWRENCE DUNGY, 10 Southmont Drive, Little Rock, AR 72209/501-568-2769
Specialties: Working straight knives. **Patterns:** Skinners, hunters, boots, bird and trout knives. Welcomes customer designs. **Technical:** Grinds 440C and high carbon steel. Prefers natural woods and mirror finishes. **Prices:** $65 to $150. **Remarks:** Part-time maker; first knife sold in 1983. **Mark:** Dungy Handcrafted

RICK DUNKERLEY, Box 114, Cameron, MT 59720/406-682-4508
Specialties: Working straight and folding knives. **Patterns:** Mainly hunters, some hatchets, fish knives, skinners, and miniatures. **Technical:** Grinds D2, 440C, 154CM, and ATS34. **Prices:** $65 to $130; some to $200. **Remarks:** Part-time maker; first knife sold in 1985. **Mark:** Full name, city, and state

MELVIN T. DUNN, 5830 N.W. Carlson Rd., Rossville, KS 66533/913-584-6856
Specialties: Folding and straight working knives. **Patterns:** Folding lockers and traditional styles along with straight hunters; fish and kitchen knives. **Technical:** Grinds D2 and 440C primarily; also A2, 154CM and Vascowear; likes latest materials; does own heat-treating. **Prices:** $60 to $500. **Remarks:** Full-time maker; first knife sold in 1972. **Mark:** DUNN in oval

JERRY T. DURAN, 442 Montclaire, S.E., Albuquerque, NM 87108/505-255-4255
Specialties: Working straight knives in his designs. **Patterns:** Hunters, skinners, capers, bird and trout knives, and fighters. **Technical:** Grinds 440C or others upon request. Favors Micarta handle materials. **Prices:** $75 to $225; some higher. **Remarks:** Influenced by Joe Cordova and Martin Gaigl. **Mark:** Initials in deer rack logo

FRED DURIO, 289 Gulino St., Opelousas, LA 70570/318-948-4831
Specialties: Straight working knives, some period pieces. **Patterns:** Bowies, camp knives, small hunters, some fancy period pieces, minis and miniatures. **Technical:** Grinds and forges 440C, W2, and 01. Offers filework, tapered tangs, and prefers exotic and natural materials. **Prices:** $50 to $150; some $500. **Remarks:** Part-time maker; first knife sold in 1986. **Mark:** DURIO or stylized initials

FRED DUVALL, Rt.8, Box 677, Benton, AR 72015/501-778-8368
Specialties: Folding and straight working knives. **Patterns:** Locking folders and slip-joints in traditional styles. Straight hunters, fighters and Bowies. **Technical:** Grinds A2, D2 and 440C. **Prices:** $75 to $150; some to $200. **Remarks:** Spare-time maker; first knife sold in 1981. **Mark:** DuVall

LARRY E. DUVALL, Rt. 3, Gallatin, MO 64640/816-663-2742
Specialties: Folding and straight fancy working knives. **Patterns:** Hunters to swords, minis to Bowies; makes lockers and butterflies. **Technical:** Grinds D2, 440C and 154CM. **Prices:** $150 to $350; exceptional knives to $2,000. **Remarks:** Part-time maker; first knife sold in 1980. **Mark:** Name and address in logo

EAGLE MOUNTAIN (See Al Krouse)

RUSSELL O. EASLER, JR., P.O. Box 301, Woodruff, SC 29388/803-476-7830
Specialties: Folding and straight working knives. **Patterns:** Hunters, tantos and boots. Locking folders and interframes. Some minis and miniatures. **Technical:** Grinds 440C, 154CM and ATS34. **Prices:** $85 to $250; some to $600. **Remarks:** Part-time maker; sold first knife in 1973. **Mark:** Name or name with bear logo

AL EATON, P.O. Box 43, Clayton, CA 94517/415-672-5351
Specialties: Fancy working straight knives. **Patterns:** Hunters, fighters and buckskinners; miniatures. **Technical:** Grinds 440C, 154CM and ATS34; does ivory and metal carving. **Prices:** $125 to $500; some to $2,000. **Remarks:** Part-time maker; first knife sold in 1981. **Mark:** Al Eaton, city and state

RICK EATON, 1847 Walnut Grove Ct., Oakley, CA 94561/415-625-4218
Specialties: His design or yours in fancy art knives. **Patterns:** Bowies, daggers, fighters, and boots. **Technical:** Grinds 440C, 154CM, and ATS34; does his own engraving. **Prices:** $150 to $1,000; some knives to $2,500. **Remarks:** Part-time maker; first knife sold in 1982. **Mark:** Rick Eaton

THOMAS W. EDWARDS, 6429 Camelback Rd., Phoenix, AZ 85033/602-846-7283
Specialties: One-of-a-kind miniatures only. Likes period pieces and fantasy types. **Patterns:** Anything goes. **Technical:** Grinds and forges; uses 01, 440C and purchased Damascus. **Prices:** $50 to $75; exceptional miniatures to $150. **Remarks:** Part-time maker; first piece sold in 1982. **Mark:** Name, city, state with scorpion

FAIN E. EDWARDS, 209 E. Mountain Ave., Jacksonville, AL 36265/205-435-4994
Specialties: Blacksmith-styled fancy working knives. **Patterns:** Bowies, patch and rifle knives; camp knives. **Technical:** Forges own Damascus; grinds D2. **Prices:** Full range. **Remarks:** Developed "Amensteel", but has sold it. **Mark:** Name with bleeding heart

JOEL ELLEFSON, 1233 Storymill Rd., Bozeman, MT 59715/406-587-5905
Specialties: Clean working straight knives, fancy daggers, and one-of-a-kind projects. **Patterns:** Hunters, daggers and some folders. **Technical:** Grinds A2, 440C and 154CM. Makes own mokume. **Prices:** $100 to $300; some to $700. **Remarks:** Part-time maker; first knife sold in 1978. **Mark:** Stylized E

W.B. ELLERBE, P.O. Box 712, Geneva, FL 32732/305-349-5818
Specialties: Fancy working straight knives. **Patterns:** Bowies to miniatures, tomahawks and buckskinners. **Technical:** Grinds 440C and ATS 34. **Prices:** $125 to $175; some to $800. **Remarks:** Part-time maker; first knife sold in 1971. **Mark:** Last name or initials

MARCUS ELLIOTT, 3 Bryn Maelgwyn, Llanrhos, Llandudno, Gwynedd, North Wales, Great Britain/0492-84352
Specialties: Fancy working knives; some period pieces. **Patterns:** Boots, and small hunters, "one offs." **Technical:** Grinds 01, 440C, and 12C27. **Prices:** $160 to $250. **Remarks:** Spare-time maker; first knife sold in 1981. Makes only a small number of knives each year. **Mark:** Last name

ERNEST R. EMERSON, 4166 W. 172nd St., Torrance, CA 90504/213-542-3050
Specialties: High-tech folders and practical fighting knives. **Patterns:** Fighters designed from practical, personal experience. Flolders with liner locks in M. Walker style. **Technical:** Grinds AEB-L, 440C, and ATS34. Makes folders with titanium fittings, liners, and locks. Standard is handrubbed satin finish. **Prices:** $350 to $550; some $1,200. **Remarks:** Full-time maker; first knife sold in 1983. **Mark:** E.R. Emerson

JIM ENCE, 145 So. 200 East, Richfield, UT 84701/801-896-6206
Specialties: High art period pieces. Always looking to do something new and different. **Patterns:** Mirror finished, crisp lined art knives in daggers and fighters. **Technical:** Grinds 440C, 154CM; buys Damascus. **Prices:** $300 to $900; exceptional knives to $4,000. **Remarks:** Full-time maker; first knife sold in 1977. **Mark:** Name, city, state

ROBERT ENDERS, 3028 White Rd., Cement City, MI 49233/517-529-9667
Specialties: Pocket knives and working straight knives. **Patterns:** Old traditional folders with natural materials. **Technical:** Grinds D2, 01, 440C and ATS34. **Prices:** $125 to $300; some to $1,200. **Remarks:** Full-time maker; first knife sold in 1981. **Mark:** Name in state map logo

VIRGIL ENGLAND, 629 W. 15th Ave., Anchorage, AK 99501/907-272-9340
Specialties: Edged weapons and equipage. **Patterns:** A variety of straight fighting knives, swords, lances and such. **Technical:** Grinds mostly stainless steels. **Prices:** Upscale. **Remarks:** A veteran knifemaker. **Mark:** Name

GEORGE ENGLEBRETSON, 1209 N.W. 49th St., Oklahoma City, OK 73118/405-840-4784
Specialties: Working straight knives and period pieces. **Patterns:** Hunters, Bowies, fish knives and axes—heavy-duty designs. **Technical:** Grinds D2, 440C and 154CM. **Prices:** $75 to $100; some to $150. **Remarks:** Full-time maker; first knife sold in 1967. **Mark:** "By George," name and city

BOB ENGNATH, 1217 B. Crescent Dr., Glendale, CA 91205/818-241-3629
Specialties: Replica antique tanto blades and complete knives and swords. **Patterns:** Traditional Japanese; makes some miniatures. **Technical:** Makes soft back-hard edge blades with temper line. **Prices:** $125 to $350; some to $600. **Remarks:** Full-time maker/grinder; first knife sold in 1972. **Mark:** KODAN in Japanese script

THOMAS M. ENOS, III, 12302 State Rd. 535, Orlando, FL 32819/407-239-6205
Specialties: Heavy-duty working knives; unusual knife designs. **Patterns:** Machetes, salt water sport knives, carvers and a variety of straight knives. **Technical:** Grinds 440C, D2, 154CM. **Prices:** $75 to $300. **Remarks:** Full-time maker; first knife sold in 1972. **Mark:** Name in knife logo and date

CURT ERICKSON, 449 Washington Blvd., Ogden, UT 84404/801-621-4437
Specialties: Daggers and large knives, integral construction. **Patterns:** Period pieces; some Bowies. **Technical:** Sculpts and carves components; grinds 440C and commercial Damascus steel. **Prices:** $240 to $1,500; some to $3,000. **Remarks:** Full-time maker; first knife sold in 1982. **Mark:** Name, state

L.M. ERICKSON, P.O. Box 132, Liberty, UT 84310/801-745-2026
Specialties: Period pieces and straight knives. **Patterns:** Bowies, fighters, boots and hunters. **Technical:** Grinds 440C, 154CM and purchased Damascus. **Prices:** $200 to $900; some to $1,900. **Remarks:** Full-time maker; first knife sold in 1981. **Mark:** Name, city, state

WALTER E. ERICKSON, 23883 Ada St., Warren, MI 48091/313-759-1105
Specialties: Unusual survival knives and high-tech working knives. **Patterns:** Butterflies, hunters, tantos and survival knives. **Technical:** Grinds 01, D2 and 440C. **Prices:** $90 to $200; some to $600. **Remarks:** Spare-time maker; first knife sold in 1981. **Mark:** ERIC or ERICKSON

RICHARD ESSEGIAN, 4219 E. Shields Ave., Fresno, CA 93726/209-222-7091
Specialties: Fancy working knives in his own designs. Some art knives. **Patterns:** Bowies mainly, some small hunters. **Technical:** Grinds A2, D2, 440C, and 154CM. Does his own engraving and inlay work. **Prices:** Starting at $600; some much more. **Remarks:** Part-time maker; first knife sold in 1986. **Mark:** Essegian, city and state

VINCENT K. EVANS, 556-B Kamani St., Honolulu, HI 96813/808-538-7288
Specialties: Period pieces and straight working knives. **Patterns:** Scottish patterns; clip point using knives. **Technical:** Forges and grinds ATS34, 440C, and 5160; his

own Damascus. **Prices:** $50 to $300; some to $500. **Remarks:** Full-time maker; first knife sold in 1983. **Mark:** Bronze filled double E with fish logo

JOHN H. EWING, Rt. 2, Box 301, Clinton, TN 37716/615-457-5757
Specialties: Straight working knives. **Patterns:** Using hunters, and fillet knives. **Technical:** Grinds 440C and ATS34. **Prices:** $50 to $200. **Remarks:** Part-time maker; first knife sold in 1985. **Mark:** J. EWING HANDMADE **THE FARM FORGE** (See Larry B. Wood)

MELVIN G. FASSIO, 2012 Rattlesnake Dr., Missoula, MT 59802/406-543-6160
Specialties: Working folders. **Patterns:** Folding lockers, hunters and traditional styles; in customer designs. **Technical:** Grinds 440C. **Prices:** $60 to $100, up to $200. **Remarks:** Part-time maker; first knife sold in 1975. **Mark:** Name and town, dove logo

HOWARD J. FAUCHEAUX, P.O. Box 206, Loreauville, LA 70552/318-229-6467
Specialties: Working straight and folding knives; some period pieces. **Patterns:** Locking folders in traditional styles; hunters, fighters and Bowies in straight knives with personal touches. **Technical:** Forges W2, 1095 and his own Damascus. **Prices:** $165 to $500; some to $1,500. **Remarks:** Spare-time maker; first knife sold in 1969. **Mark:** Last name

ALLAN FAULKNER, 6103 Park Ave., Marysville, CA 95901/916-743-1309
Specialties: Fancy straight and folding working knives. **Patterns:** Folding lockers of standard designs; also hunters, fighters and Bowies. **Technical:** Grinds D2, 440C and 154CM; prefers natural handle materials. **Prices:** $150 to $350; some to $1,500. **Remarks:** Part-time maker, first knife sold in 1978. **Mark:** Last name

STEPHEN J. FECAS, 117 Allee St., Clemson, SC 29631/803-654-6068
Specialties: Working straight and folding knives in standard patterns; some period pieces. **Patterns:** Hunters to claws, folding slip-joints to buckskinners. **Technical:** Grinds D2, 440C and 154CM; most knives hand-finished to 600 grit. **Prices:** $140 to $400; some to $750. **Remarks:** Full-time maker; first knife sold in 1977. **Mark:** FECAS

DON FERDINAND, P.O. Box 2790, San Rafael, CA 94941
Specialties: Working knives and period pieces. **Patterns:** Bowies and push knives; fish knives. **Technical:** Forges high carbon alloy steels—L6, D2; makes his own Damascus. **Prices:** $100 to $500. **Remarks:** Part-time maker since 1980; business name is Wyvern. **Mark:** df connected

JIM FERGUSON, P.O. Box 764, San Angelo, TX 76902/915-658-7287
Specialties: Straight and folding working knives. **Patterns:** General purpose belt knives, hardwood-handled puukos, hunters and folders. **Technical:** Grinds 440C, D2, and ATS34. **Remarks:** Full-time maker; first knife sold in 1987. **Mark:** J.E. FERGUSON

LEE FERGUSON, Rt. 2, Box 109, Hindsville, AR 72738/501-789-5748
Specialties: Straight and folding working knives, some are fancy pieces. **Patterns:** Hunters, daggers and swords; folding lockers and slip-joints. **Technical:** Grinds D2, 440C and ATS34; heat-treats his own work. **Prices:** $50 to $600; some to $4,000. **Remarks:** Part-time maker; first knife sold in 1977. **Mark:** Last name

WILLIAM V. FIELDER, 2715 Salem Bottom Rd., Westminster, MD 21157/301-848-1567
Specialties: Original designs in fancy working knives, both straight and folding. **Patterns:** Hunters, boots and daggers; folding lockers, both interframes and traditional. **Technical:** Forges W2, 01 and his own Damascus; likes wire inlay. **Prices:** $25 to $500; some to $1,000. **Remarks:** Full-time maker; first knife sold in 1982. **Mark:** FIELDER

JIMMY L. FIKES, P.O. Box 389, Orange, MA 01364/617-544-3049
Specialties: High art working knives; he calls some artifact knives. **Patterns:** From axes to buckskinners, camp knives to miniatures and tantos to tomahawks, but no folders. **Technical:** Forges W2, 01 and his own Damascus. **Prices:** $135 to $3,000; exceptional knives to $7,000. **Remarks:** Full-time maker. **Mark:** Clawed F

CLYDE E. FISCHER, P.O. Box 310, Nixon, TX 78140/512-582-1353
Specialties: Working knives for serious and professional hunters. **Patterns:** Heavy-duty hunters and survival blades; camp knives and buckskinner knives, too. **Technical:** Grinds and forges L6, 01 and his own Damascus. **Prices:** $100 to $250; some to $800. **Remarks:** Full-time maker; first started selling in 1957. **Mark:** Fish

THEO. (TED) FISHER, 8115 Modoc Lane, Montague, CA 96064/916-459-3804
Specialties: Moderate-priced working knives in carbon steel. **Patterns:** Hunters,

B.L. DAVIS

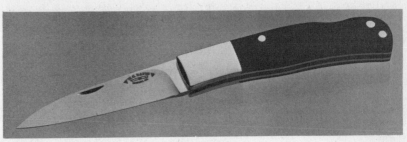

W.C. DAVIS

DILLUVIO

DOWNS

V.M. DAVIS

DETMER

DEAN

DIGANGI

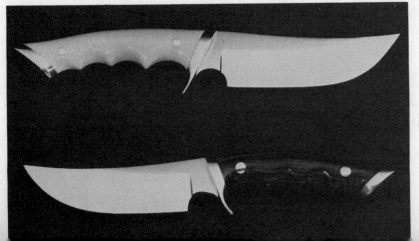

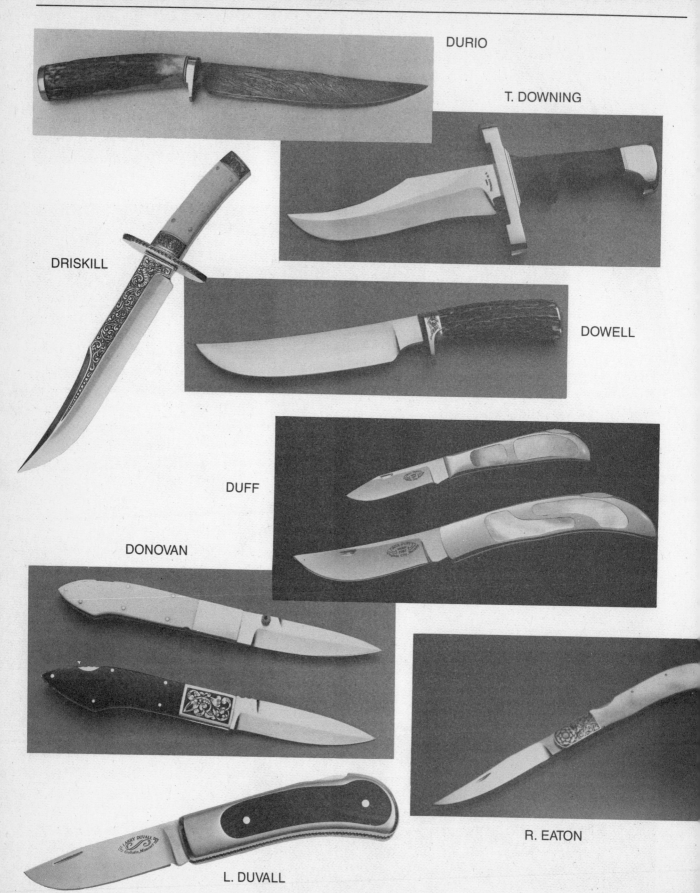

DURIO

T. DOWNING

DRISKILL

DOWELL

DUFF

DONOVAN

R. EATON

L. DUVALL

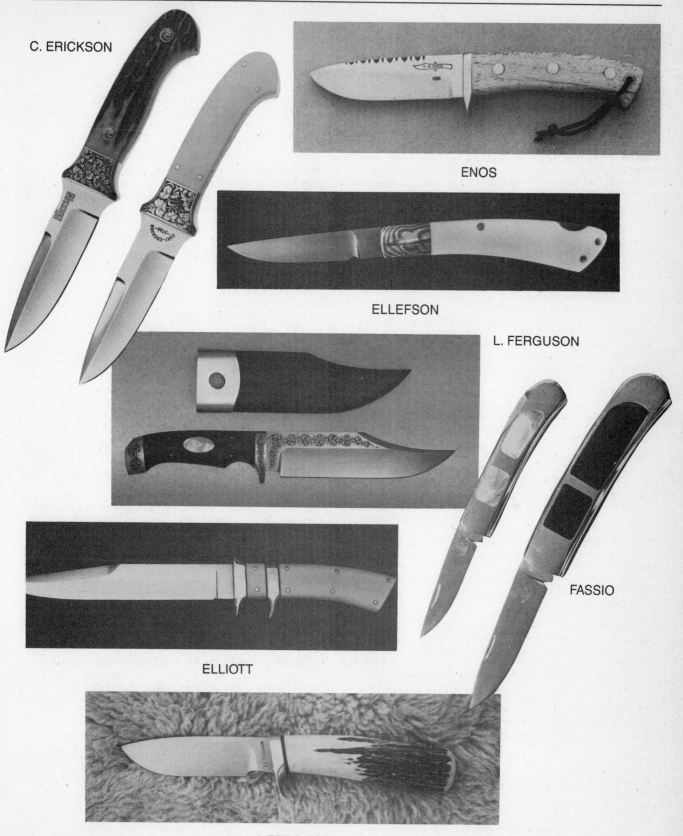

C. ERICKSON

ENOS

ELLEFSON

L. FERGUSON

FASSIO

ELLIOTT

J. FERGUSON

fighters, kitchen and buckskinner knives. **Technical:** Grinds ATS34, L6 and 440C. **Prices:** $65 to $100; exceptional knives to $300. **Remarks:** Full-time maker; first knife sold in 1981. **Mark:** Name in banner logo

JERRY FISK, Rt. 1, Box 41, Lockesburg, AR 71846/501-289-3240
Specialties: Working straight knives in traditional styles. **Patterns:** Bowies, fancy using hunters, camp knives. **Technical:** Forges 5160 and his own Damascus; does file work. **Prices:** $90 to $300; some to $800. **Remarks:** Full-time maker; first knife sold in 1980. Offers custom Bowies forged in restored James Black Smithy. **Mark:** Name

JIM FISTER, R. #1, Finchville, KY 40022/502-834-7841
Specialties: Straight and folding working knives. **Patterns:** Hunters, boots and buckskinners; fighters and daggers. **Technical:** Grinds and forges 01, 5160 and 440C; wire and regular Damascus. **Prices:** $100 to $250; some $700. **Remarks:** Part-time maker; first knife sold in 1982. **Mark:** Full name

DENNIS FITZGERALD, P.O. Box 12847, Fort Wayne, IN 46866-2847/219-447-1081
Specialties: Straight working knives. **Patterns:** Skinners, fighters, camp and utility knives. Also period pieces. **Technical:** Forges and grinds W2, 01, and cable-wire Damascus. **Prices:** $150 to $500. **Remarks:** Part-time maker; first knife sold in 1985. **Mark:** Name and circle logo

FLAMING A (See Dave Reed)

JOE FLOURNOY, Rt. 6, Box 233, El Dorado, AR 71730/501-863-7208
Specialties: Working straight and folding knives; some period pieces. **Patterns:** Hunters, fighters and buckskinners; straight knives. **Technical:** Forges using high carbon steel only. **Prices:** $100 to $350. **Remarks:** Part-time maker; first knife sold in 1977. **Mark:** Last name in script

BRUCE FLYNN, R #1, Box 234A, Middletown, IN 47356/317-779-4034
Specialties: Straight and some folding working knives. **Patterns:** Fighters, Bowies, daggers, skinners, and hunters. Offers some folders. **Technical:** Grinds 440C, 154CM, and D2. **Prices:** Moderate. **Remarks:** Full-time maker. **Mark:** B.C. FLYNN

DON FOGG (See Kemal)

ALLEN FORD, 3927 Plumcrest Rd., Smyrna, GA 30080/404-432-5061
Specialties: Art knives in his own designs. **Patterns:** Bowies, daggers and hunters. **Technical:** Hand finishes every knife. Does his own scrimshaw. **Mark:** A. FORD in script

PETE FORTHOFER, 711 Spokane Ave., Whitefish, MT 59937/406-862-2674
Specialties: Interframes with checkered wood inlays; working straight knives. **Patterns:** Both interframes and traditional patterns in folders; hunters, fighters and Bowies. **Technical:** Grinds D2, 440C, 154CM and ATS34. **Prices:** $165 to $500; some to $1,200. **Remarks:** Part-time maker; full-time gunsmith. First knife sold in 1979. **Mark:** Name and logo

AL FOSTER, St. Rt. HC 73, Box 117, Dogpatch, AR 72648/501-446-5137
Specialties: Straight working knives, and folders. **Patterns:** Bowies, hunters, lockback and slip-joint folders, and fish knives; likes trailing points and impala horn handles. **Technical:** Grinds D2, 440C, ATS34, and commercial Damascus. **Prices:** $65 to $250; some to $500. **Remarks:** Full-time maker; sold first knife in 1981. **Mark:** Scorpion logo and name

ROGER FOUST, 1925 Vernon Ave., Modesto, CA 95351
Specialties: Period pieces and fantasy styles. **Patterns:** Shifting to one-of-a-kinds. Welcomes customer designs. **Technical:** Grinds L6, 1095 and D2; also spring steel. **Prices:** $75 to $1,000. **Remarks:** Full-time maker; first knife sold in 1980. Now accepting orders. **Mark:** RF connected

ED A. FOWLER, Willow Bow Ranch, P.O. Box 1519, Riverton, WY 82501/307-856-9815
Specialties: Straight heavy-duty working knives. Makes knives to be used. **Patterns:** Hunters, Bowies, camp knives, skinners. **Technical:** Forges 5160 and his own Damascus; engraves all his knives; all handles are domestic sheep horn. **Prices:** $185 to $400; some to $700. **Remarks:** Spare-time maker; first knife sold in 1962. **Mark:** EAF connected

FOX VALLEY FORGE (See George W. Werth)

PAUL FOX, 80 Mineral Springs Mountain, Valdese, NC 28690/704-874-3400
Specialties: All-bolted construction, unusual one-of-a-kinds, but mostly folding knives. **Patterns:** High-tech folding fighters. Also makes straight daggers and fighters. **Technical:** Grinds 01, 154CM and purchased Damascus. **Prices:** $200 up to $6,000. **Remarks:** Full-time maker; first knife sold in 1977. **Mark:** Signature

HEINRICH H. FRANK, Box 984, Whitefish, MT 59937/406-862-2681
Specialties: High art investor-class folders; handmade and engraved personally. **Patterns:** Careful personal design in folding daggers, in hunter-size folders and gents knives. **Technical:** Grinds 07 and 01. **Prices:** $1,500 to $3,600; some to $12,000. **Remarks:** Full-time maker; first knife sold in 1965. **Mark:** Name, address and date

MIKE FRANKLIN, Rte. 41, Box M, Aberdeen, OH 45101/513-795-2571
Specialties: Small, lightweight hunters and boots. **Patterns:** Straight and folding knives, some period pieces. Does a variety of both, from his own designs. **Technical:** Grinds A2, 440C and ATS34; strives for fine design and execution in small working knives. **Prices:** $100 to $275; some to $750. **Remarks:** Full-time maker; first knife sold in 1973. **Mark:** Name

RON FRAZIER, 2107 Urbine Rd., Powhatan, VA 23139/804-794-8561
Specialties: Classy working knives in his own designs: some high-art straight knives. **Patterns:** Wide assortment of straight knives, including miniatures and push knives—does, he says, whatever he wants. **Technical:** Grinds 440C; offers satin, mirror or sand finishes. **Prices:** $85 to $700; some to $3,000. **Remarks:** Full-time maker; fist knife sold in 1976. **Mark:** Name in arch logo

ART F. FREEMAN, P.O Box 2545, Citrus Heights, CA 95611/916-725-5323
Specialties: Customer designs in working and some high art knives. **Patterns:** Hunters to Bowies; fighters to swords. **Technical:** Steels: 440C, ATS34, D2 and nickel/1095 Damascus. Customers requests; doesn't copy any design under 50 years old. **Prices:** $85 to $1,500 and up. **Remarks:** Full-time maker; first knife sold in 1979. **Mark:** A Freeman in script

JOHN FREEMAN, Box 541, Postal Station P, Tortonto, Ont. M5S 2T1, CANADA/416-971-7638
Specialties: Working straight knives. **Patterns:** Hunters, boots, fighters, and skinners. **Technical:** Grinds A2, 440C, and ATS34. Provides custom sheaths and rigging. **Prices:** $75 to $150; some $500. **Remarks:** Full-time maker; first knife sold in 1985. **Mark:** Freeman in script, CANADA

ALBERT J. FREILING, 3700 Niner Rd., Finksburg, MD 21048/301-795-2880
Specialties: Working straight and folding knives; some period pieces. **Patterns:** Boots, Bowies, survival knives, and tomahawks in 4130 and 440C; some locking folders and interframes; ball-bearing folders. **Technical:** Grinds 01, 440C and 154CM. **Prices:** $100 to $300; some to $500. **Remarks:** Part-time maker; first knife sold in 1966. **Mark:** AJF connected

WILLIAM R. FRESE, 5374 Fernbeach, St. Louis, MO 63128/314-849-3272
Specialties: Unusual blade designs coupled with exotic handles. **Patterns:** Hunters, skinners, and utility knives. Offers filework and scrimshaw. **Technical:** Grinds D2, 440C, and 01. Offers display stands. **Prices:** $50 to $150; miniatures range $25 to $35. **Remarks:** Part-time maker; first knife sold in 1985. **Mark:** FRESE

W. FREDERICK FREY, JR., 305 Walnut St., Milton, PA 17847/717-742-9576
Specialties: Working straight and folding knives, some fancy. **Patterns:** Wide range—boot knives to tomahawks. **Technical:** Grinds A2, 01 and D2; hand finishes only. **Prices:** $55 to $90; some to $600. **Remarks:** Spare-time maker; first knife sold in 1983. **Mark:** FREY in script

DENNIS E. FRIEDLY, 12 Cottontail Ln., Cody, WY 82414/307-527-6811
Specialties: Fancy working straight knives and daggers. **Patterns:** Hunters, fighters, boots, ooloos, axes, minis and miniatures. **Technical:** Grinds 440C, ATS34 and purchased Damascus; prefers hidden tang. **Prices:** $135 to $900; some to $2,500. **Remarks:** Full-time maker; first knife sold in 1972. **Mark:** Name, city and state

TED FRIZZELL, Rt. 2, Box 326, West Fork, AR 72774/501-839-3381
Specialties: Very heavy chopping and breaking tools at moderate prices. **Patterns:** Large hatchets to camp knives, using $3/8$" to $1/2$" bars of 5160 spring steel. **Technical:** Grinds 5160 almost exclusively, some L6. All hatchets come with 8-oz. leather head covers. **Prices:** $55 to $150; some $500. **Remarks:** Full-time maker; first knife sold in 1984. **Mark:** A boxed cross with circle in the middle

LARRY FUEGEN, RR 1, Box 279, Wiscasset, ME 04578/207-882-6391 **Specialties:** Folding and straight working knives; some fancy, even unusual. **Patterns:** Forged Scroll folders in crown stag; variety of classic straight blade knives. **Technical:** Forges W1, 5160, his own Damascus. Works in exotic leather; shoots for individuality. **Prices:** $200 to $700; some to $1,200. **Remarks:** Full-time maker; first knife sold in 1975. **Mark:** LF connected

YASUHIRO FUJIMOTO, 2-3-2 Shibyuya, Shibuya-ku, Tokyo 150, JAPAN/03-400-4573 **Specialties:** High art working folders of his own design. **Patterns:** Folding locker, slip-joints, patent locks; interframes and multi-blades. Also miniatures. **Technical:** Forges and grinds 440C, ATS34 and purchased Damascus. **Prices:** $100 to $700; some $10,000. **Remarks:** Full-time maker; first knife sold in 1949. **Mark:** Y. FUJIMOTO

STANLEY FUJISAKA, 45-004 Holowai St., Kaneohe, HI 96744/808-247-0017 **Specialties:** Fancy working straight knives. **Patterns:** Hunters and boots and personal knives, and folding knives. **Technical:** Grinds 440C, 154CM, and ATS34; clean lines, inlays. **Prices:** $150 to $1,200; some $600. **Remarks:** Full-time maker; first knife sold in 1984. **Mark:** Name, city and state

TAK FUKUTA, 38-Umeagae-cho, Seki-City, Gifu-Pref, JAPAN/0575-22-0264 **Specialties:** Benchmade fancy straight and folding knives. **Patterns:** Folders in Sheffield-style. Bowies, and fighters. **Technical:** Grinds bought Damascus. **Prices:** $300 and higher. **Remarks:** Full-time maker. **Mark:** Name in knife logo

JIM FULLER, P.O. Box 51, Burnwell, AL 35038/205-648-2083 **Specialties:** Working straight knives—lightweight and low cost. **Patterns:** Hunters, fighters and Bowies; straight and folding knives; utility knives. **Technical:** Grinds A2, 01, but mostly 440C. **Prices:** $60 to $150; some to $1,000. **Remarks:** Full-time maker; first knife sold in 1983. **Mark:** Jim Fuller

JOHN W. FULLER, 6156 Ridge Way, Douglasville, GA 30135/404-942-1155 **Specialties:** Fancy working straight and folding knives in standard patterns. **Patterns:** Folding gents and hunting knives; straight hunters and fighters. **Technical:** Grinds D2, 440C and purchased Damascus. **Prices:** $75 to $300. **Remarks:** Part-time maker; first knife sold in 1978. **Mark:** Name, city, state

W.T. FULLER, JR., 400 S. 8th St., East Gadsden, AL 35903/205-546-8114 **Specialties:** Working folding knives. **Patterns:** Folding lockers, two-blades, fighters, hunters and traditional knives. **Technical:** Grinds D2 and 440C; does it all with one hand. **Prices:** $175 to $250; some to $600. **Remarks:** Part-time maker; first knife sold in 1975. **Mark:** One-Hander and name in hand logo

JOE FUNDERBURG, 1255 Bay Oaks Dr., Los Osos, CA 93402/805-528-2317 **Specialties:** Working straight knives; some period pieces. **Patterns:** Fighters, boots, daggers and push knives. **Technical:** Grinds D5, 440C and 154CM. **Prices:** $90 to $150; some to $1,000. **Remarks:** Spare-time maker; first knife sold in 1965. **Mark:** JF connected

SHIRO FURUKAWA, 4-7-7 Sakuragaoka, Tama-shi, Tokyo 206, JAPAN/0423-71-8263 **Specialties:** Both straight and folding working knives; some are high art. **Patterns:** His own designs especially for the outdoor life. **Technical:** Grinds D2, 440C and 154CM. **Prices:** $200 to $2,300; some to $5,000. **Remarks:** Full-time maker; first knife sold in 1977. **Mark:** SF MADE KNIVES

FRANK GAMBLE, P.O. Box 2243, Gilroy, CA 95021-2243/408-847-5067 **Specialties:** Scagel replicas; fancy working knives; some fantasy pieces. **Patterns:** Wide range of straight and folding knives; razors and miniatures. **Technical:** Grinds and forges; uses 440C; 154CM and ATS34 and buys Damascus; all knives hand-finished. **Prices:** $150 to $750; some to $2,000. **Remarks:** Full-time maker; first knife sold in 1978. **Mark:** Name

WILLIAM O. GARNER, JR., 2803 East DeSoto St., Pensacola, FL 32503/904-438-2009 **Specialties:** Working straight knives; some fancy pieces. **Patterns:** Hunters, Bowies, fighters, double-edged daggers, kitchen and fish knives. **Technical:** Grinds 440C, 154CM and ATS34, D2 and 01 steels; all knives have heavy spines and sharp lines. **Prices:** $85 to $300. **Remarks:** Full-time maker; first knife sold in 1985. **Mark:** William Garner in oval logo or Garner

M.D. GARTMAN, Rt. 3, Box 13, Gatesville, TX 76528/817-865-6090 **Specialties:** Folding and straight working knives in standard patterns. **Patterns:** A large variety of folders, up to 5-bladed styles; some Bowies and miniatures. **Technical:** Grinds D2, 01, and 440C; likes unusual natural handles, swordfish bill for one. **Prices:** $85 to $135. **Remarks:** Part-time maker; first knife sold in 1982. **Mark:** GARTMAN inside arrowhead logo

RON GASTON, 330 Gaston Dr., Woodruff, SC 29388/803-439-4766 **Specialties:** Working period pieces. **Patterns:** Hunters, fighters, tantos, boots and a variety of other straight knives; single blade slip-joint folders. **Technical:** Grinds 440C, 154CM and ATS34. Hand-rubbed satin finish is standard **Prices:** $100 to $350; some to $1,000. **Remarks:** Full-time maker; first knife sold in 1980. **Mark:** Name

LINDEN L. GAUDETTE, 5 Hitchcock Rd., Wilbraham, MA 01095/413-596-4896 **Specialties:** Traditional working knives in standard patterns. **Patterns:** Broad-bladed hunters, Bowies, and camp knives, some locking folders. **Technical:** Grinds ATS34, 440C, and 154CM. **Prices:** $135 to $350; some higher. **Remarks:** Full-time maker; first knife sold in 1975. **Mark:** Last name in Gothic logo; used to be LG in circle

CLAY GAULT, Rt. 1, Box 287, Lexington, TX 78947/512-273-2873 **Specialties:** Straight and folding hunting knives. **Patterns:** Classic drop-points, other traditional styles in folders. **Technical:** Grinds Vascowear only; natural materials carefully chosen and hand-finished. **Prices:** $225 to $325; some to $500. **Remarks:** Full-time maker; first knives sold in 1970. **Mark:** Name or name with cattle brand

GARY R. GEISLER, P.O. Box 294, Clarksville, OH 45113/513-289-2469 **Specialties:** Traditional working straight knives. **Patterns:** English-styled Bowies, drop-point hunters, fighters, and daggers. **Technical:** Grinds A2, 440C and M2. Prefers flat grinds and mirror finishes. **Prices:** $45 to $75; some $150. **Remarks:** Part-time maker; first knife sold in 1982. **Mark:** G.R. Geisler maker in script

ROY E. GENGE, P.O. Box 57, Eastlake, CO 80614/303-451-7991 **Specialties:** High-tech working knives. **Patterns:** Bowies, hatchets, hunters, survival knives, buckskinners, kukris and others. **Technical:** Grinds and forges L6, S7, W1, W2, 01, Vascowear, 154CM, ATS34 and bought Damascus. **Prices:** $50 to $500; embellished is higher. **Remarks:** Part-time maker; first knife sold in 1968. **Mark:** Name, city, state

HARRY GEORGE, 3137 Old Camp Long Rd., Aiken, SC 29801/803-649-1963 **Specialties:** Working straight knives in his design. Welcomes customer designs. **Patterns:** Hunters, skinners, and utility knives. **Technical:** Grinds ATS34 or 154CM. Prefers natural handle materials, hollow grinds and mirror finishes. **Prices:** Moderate. **Remarks:** Part-time maker; first knife sold in 1985. Trained under George Herron. **Mark:** Name, city and state

TOM GEORGE, P.O. Box 1298, Magalia, CA 95954/916-873-3306 **Specialties:** Specializing in large Bowies and display knives. **Patterns:** Hunters, Bowies, daggers and buckskinners. **Technical:** Uses D2, 440C and 154CM. **Prices:** $175 to $1,200; some to $3,000. **Remarks:** Part-time maker; first knife sold in 1981. **Mark:** Name

RANDALL GILBREATH, P.O. Box 195, Dora, AL 35062/205-648-3902 **Specialties:** Fancy working knives; some one-of-a-kind knives. **Patterns:** Fighters, hunters, Bowies and miniatures. Locking folders in fighter and hunter patterns. **Technical:** Grinds A2, 01 and 440C; satin finishes. **Prices:** $100 to $150; some to $1,300. **Remarks:** Part-time maker; first knife sold in 1979. **Mark:** Name in a ribbon

E.E. "DICK" GILLENWATER, 921 Dougherty Rd., Aiken, SC 29801/803-649-6787 **Specialties:** Working straight sportsmen's knives. **Patterns:** Boot knives, hunters, fillet and steak knives. **Technical:** Grinds 154CM and ATS34. **Prices:** $75 to $400; some to $600. **Remarks:** Part-time maker; first knife sold in 1979. **Mark:** Signature

JON GILMORE, 849 University Place, St. Louis, MO 63132 **Specialties:** Simple straight knife designs, using natural materials. **Patterns:** Working knives and hunters under 5 inches. **Technical:** Forges W1, 1095 and his own Damascus. **Prices:** $85 to $150; some to $250. **Remarks:** Spare-time maker. Currently only making the smaller-range knives. First knife sold in 1983. **Mark:** Initials form a logo

KEN GLASER, Rt. #1, Box 148, Purdy, MO 65734/417-442-3371 **Specialties:** Straight working knives in standard patterns. **Patterns:** Hunters, including buckles and mini knives. **Technical:** Grinds 01, D2 and 440C; prefers hollow

directory/custom knifemakers

grinds; likes file work. **Prices:** $75 to $125; some $250. **Remarks:** Full-time maker; first knife sold in 1983. **Mark:** Initials, KAG

RON GLOVER, P.O. Box 44132, Cincinnati, OH 45244/513-398-7857
Specialties: High-tech working knives, folding and straight. **Patterns:** Hunters to Bowies; has some interchangeable blade models; unique locking mechanisms. **Technical:** Grinds 440C, 154CM; buys Damascus. **Prices:** $70 to $500; some to $800. **Remarks:** Part-time maker; first knife sold in 1981. **Mark:** Name in script

WAYNE GODDARD, 473 Durham Ave., Eugene, OR 97404/503-689-8098
Specialties: Two-year backlog; accepting custom work only. **Patterns:** Camp knives to miniatures; makes heavy-duty traditional types; large display folders. **Technical:** Forges and grinds; uses D2, 154CM and his own Damascus, both pattern-welded and welded cable. **Prices:** $75 to $400; some up to $1,500. **Remarks:** Full-time maker; first knife sold in 1963. **Mark:** Blocked initials on forged blades; regular capital initials on stock removal

PAUL S. GOERTZ, 201 Union Ave. S.E., #207, Renton, WA 98056/206-228-9501
Specialties: Straight working knives. **Patterns:** Hunters, skinners, camp, bird and fish knives. Does some Bowies and fighters. **Technical:** Grinds 440C, ATS34, and 154CM. **Prices:** $50 to $175; some $450. **Remarks:** Full-time maker; first knife sold in 1985. **Mark:** Signature

DARREL W. GOFF, 5725 Newholme Ave., Baltimore, MD 21206/301-488-2230
Specialties: Fancy working fixed and folding knives. **Patterns:** Hunters, Bowies, skinners, bird and fish knives. **Technical:** Grinds Swedish high carbon steel, ATS34, 440C. Forges W1, and bar stock Damascus. Does own scrimshaw. **Prices:** $50 to $600; some $1,500. **Remarks:** Part-time maker; first knife sold in 1982. **Mark:** Lightning bolt, GOFF, and serial #

JIM GOFOURTH, 3776 Aliso Cyn. Rd., Santa Paula, CA 93060/805-659-3814
Specialties: Period pieces and working knives. **Patterns:** Bowies, folding lockers, patent lockers and others. **Technical:** Grinds A2 and 154CM. **Prices:** Moderate. **Remarks:** Spare-time maker. **Mark:** JG interconnected

T.S. GOLDENBERG, P.O. Box 963, Herndon, VA 22070
Specialties: Working straight knives and period pieces to customer order. **Patterns:** Hunters, boots, Bowies and tomahawks, axes. **Technical:** Grinds A2, 01 and 440C. **Prices:** $90 to $175; some to $350. **Remarks:** Part-time maker; first knife sold in 1975. **Mark:** Surname in mountain; some with TEDDYHAWK

ROBIN GOLDING, 14911 E. Hwy. 120, Ripon, CA 95366/209-599-4677
Specialties: Working straight knives in his own designs. **Patterns:** Survival knives, Bowie extractions, camp and divers knives, and skinners. **Technical:** Grinds 440C, 154CM, and ATS34. **Prices:** $75 to $250; some $600. **Remarks:** Full-time maker; first knife sold in 1985. **Mark:** GOLDING stylized and USA

WARREN L. GOLTZ, 802 E. 4th Ave., Ada, MN 56510/218-784-7721
Specialties: Fancy working knives in standard patterns. **Patterns:** Hunters, fighters and Bowies; camp knives. **Technical:** Grinds 440C and ATS34. **Prices:** $95 to $450; some to $850. **Remarks:** Full-time maker; first knife sold in 1984. **Mark:** Goltz

GOMER (See Gomer G. Jones)

GENE GONZALEZ, JR., P.O. Box 33, Roma, TX 78584/512-849-2642
Specialties: High-tech interframe folders, and traditional patterns. **Patterns:** Interframe folders, hunters, skinners, Bowies, and miniatures. **Technical:** Grinds 440C, and D2. Hollow grinds only. **Prices:** $95 to $295; some $525. **Remarks:** Part-time maker; first knife sold in 1986. **Mark:** G.G. maker

TAI GOO, 506 W. First St., Tempe, AZ 85281/602-894-2763
Specialties: High art and fantasy knives; some working knives. **Patterns:** Fighters, daggers, Bowies and buckskinners. **Technical:** Forges and grinds; uses A6, 440C and his own Damascus. Uses iron meteorites in Damascus. **Prices:** $350 to $1,800; some $10,000. **Remarks:** Full-time maker; first knife sold in 1978. **Mark:** Chiseled signature; mark in spacer and tang

BUTCH GOODWIN, 1345 Foothill Dr., Vista, CA 92084/619-758-4237
Specialties: Period pieces and working knives. **Patterns:** Integral Damascus fighters, Bowies; makes swords, miniatures, and large display folders. **Technical:** Forges L6, 1095, welded wire Damascus, pattern-welded Damascus. **Prices:** $100 to $350; some to $1,000. **Remarks:** Spare-time maker; first knife sold in 1983. **Mark:** Anvil G

GORDON (See De Freest)

DANTE GOTTAGE, 21700 Evergreen, St. Clair Shores, MI 48082/313-293-6615
Specialties: Custom working knives—your pattern or mine. **Patterns:** Skinners large or small, fighters, Bowies, fillet knives and miniatures. **Technical:** Grinds 01, 440C and 154CM. **Prices:** $100 to $400; some to $500. **Remarks:** Part-time maker; first knife sold in 1975. **Mark:** Gottage Custom Knives

JUDY GOTTAGE, 21700 Evergreen, St. Clair Shores, MI 48082/313-293-6615
Specialties: Folding and straight knives in her own design and traditional patterns. **Patterns:** Integral and interframe folders in many styles; some fish knives. **Technical:** Grinds 440C, 154CM and commercial Damascus. **Prices:** $175 to $600; some to $2,500. **Remarks:** Full-time maker; first knife sold in 1980. **Mark:** Judy Gottage, also Judy on small knives

GREGORY J. GOTTSCHALK, 12 First St. (Ft. Pitt), Carnegie, PA 15106/412-279-6692
Specialties: Fancy working straight and folding knives in customer designs. **Patterns:** Hunters to tantos, folding lockers to mini knives; most are mirror finished. **Technical:** Grinds 440C, 154CM and purchased Damascus. **Prices:** $60 to $400; some to $2,000. **Remarks:** Part-time maker; first knife sold in 1977. **Mark:** Full name in crescent

GARY B. GOUKER, P.O. Box 955, Sitka, AK 99835/907-747-3476
Specialties: Hunting knives for hard use. **Patterns:** Skinners, semi-skinners, and such. **Technical:** Likes natural material, inlays, stainless steel. **Prices:** Moderate. **Remarks:** New Alaskan maker. **Mark:** Name

WILLIAM R. GRANQUIST, 5 Paul St., Bristol, CT 06010/203-582-4012
Specialties: Working straight knives and period pieces. **Patterns:** Hunters, fighters, boots and Bowies. **Technical:** Grinds A2, D2 and 440C. **Prices:** $75 to $125; some to $300. **Remarks:** Part-time maker; first knife sold in 1978. **Mark:** GRANQUIST

GORDON S. GREBE, 3605 Arctic #1109, Anchorage, AK 99503/907-243-2525
Specialties: Working straight knives and folders; some fancy. **Patterns:** Does tantos, Bowies, boot knife-fighter sets, locking folders. **Technical:** Grinds stainless steels; likes $1/4$-inch stock and glass-bead finishes. **Prices:** $75 to $250; some to $2,000. **Remarks:** Full-time producer; sold first knife in 1968. **Mark:** GSG in lightning logo

JOHN GRECO, Rt. 6, Box 55, Bay St. Louis, MS 39520/NA
Specialties: Kitchen and outdoor use cutlery, to short swords in his own designs. **Patterns:** Mostly kitchen knives, fillets, oyster, and camp knives, Bowies, and short swords. **Technical:** Grinds 440C, and ATS34, others if requested. Hollow-ground, guardless, and full tangs are his preference. **Prices:** $35 to $85; some over $200. **Remarks:** Full-time maker; first knife sold in 1986. **Mark:** GRECO

L.G. GREEN, 4301 W. 63rd, Prairie Village, KS 66208/913-432-6950
Specialties: Working straight and folding knives; some period pieces. **Patterns:** Folding lockers and interframes; makes hunters, tantos and daggers in straight knives; and mini knives. **Technical:** Grinds D2, 154CM and ATS34; has special sheaths. **Prices:** $140 to $275; some to $700. **Remarks:** Part-time maker; first knife sold in 1979. **Mark:** L.G.

ROGER M. GREEN, 3412 Co. Rd. 1022, Joshua, TX 76058/817-641-5057
Specialties: Straight working and some fancy knives in traditional designs. **Patterns:** Hunters, boots, Bowies and daggers. **Technical:** Grinds 440C and D2; prefers flat grinds; does his own scrimshaw. **Prices:** $85 to $150; some to $500. **Remarks:** Spare-time maker; first knife sold in 1984. **Mark:** R.M. GREEN

WILLIAM (Bill) GREEN, P.O. Box 168, Rosanna, Vic. 3084, AUSTRALIA/03-459-1529
Specialties: Traditional and high-tech straight and folding knives. **Patterns:** Japanese influenced designs, hunters, Bowies, folders, and miniatures. **Technical:** Forges 01, D2, and his own Damascus. Does his own lost wax castings for bolsters and pommels. **Prices:** $400 to $750; some $1,200. **Remarks:** Full-time maker; likes natural handle materials, gems, silver and gold. **Mark:** W.W.G.

MICHAEL GREGORY, 211 Calhoun Rd., Belton, SC 29627/803-338-8898
Specialties: Working folding and straight knives. **Patterns:** Hunters, tantos, folding locker and slip-joints, boots and fighters. **Technical:** Grinds 440C, 154CM and ATS34; mirror finishes. **Prices:** $85 to $140; some to $500. **Remarks:** Full-time maker; first knife sold in 1980. **Mark:** Name, town in logo

directory/custom knifemakers

ROGER GRENIER, 4595 Montee Saint Hubert, Saint Hubert, P. Que. J3Y1V3, CANADA/514-676-7128
Specialties: Working straight knives. **Patterns:** Heavy-duty Bowies, fighters, hunters; swords and miniatures. **Technical:** Grinds 01, D2 and 440C. **Prices:** $70 to $225; some to $800. **Remarks:** Full-time maker; first knife sold in 1981. **Mark:** GRENIER in logo

HOWARD A. GRIFFIN, JR., 14299 S.W. 31st Ct., Davie, FL 33330/305-474-5406
Specialties: Straight and folding working knives. **Patterns:** Hunters, Bowies, locking folders; especially likes his own pushbutton lock design. **Technical:** Grinds 440C. **Prices:** $100 to $200; some to $500. **Remarks:** Part-time maker; first knife sold in 1983. **Mark:** HAG

RENDON and MARK GRIFFIN, 9706 Cedardale, Houston, TX 77055/713-468-0436
Specialties: Working folding knives of their own designs. **Patterns:** Standard lockers and slip-joints. **Technical:** Grind and forge; use 440C, 154CM, and their own Damascus. **Prices:** $185 to $300; some to $800. **Remarks:** Part-time makers; Rendon first knife sold in 1966; Mark's in 1974. **Mark:** Griffin in griffon logo

BEN GRIGSBY, 80 King George St., Batesville, AR 72501/501-251-1367
Specialties: Working knives and period pieces. **Patterns:** Hunters, buckskinners, Bowies and daggers. **Technical:** Grinds 01, D2 and 440C. **Prices:** $65 to $175; some to $300. **Remarks:** Spare-time maker; first knife sold in 1976. **Mark:** GRIGSBY

JOHN D. (Butch) GRIGSBY, 5320 Circle Rd., Corryton, TN 37721/615-933-7802
Specialties: Miniature knife pins. **Patterns:** All patterns of using knives, including folding lockers, all in miniatures. **Technical:** Grinds 304 stainless and 440C. **Prices:** $10 to $100. **Remarks:** Part-time maker. **Mark:** Name

GRIZZLY FORGE (See Charles Bear)

W.W. GROSS, 325 Sherbrook Dr., High Point, NC 27260
Specialties: Working knives. **Patterns:** Hunters, boots, fighters. **Technical:** Grinds. **Prices:** Moderate. **Remarks:** Full-time maker. **Mark:** Name

STEWART GROSSMAN, 747 Main St. #1, Clinton, MA 01510/508-368-0060
Specialties: Makes mostly miniatures, but also makes regular-sized knives. **Patterns:** One-of-a-kind miniatures—jewelry, replicas—and wire-wrapped figures with miniatures. **Technical:** Grinds and forges 01, 440C, and buys Damascus. Uses gemstones and exotic materials. **Prices:** $30 to $100; some $300. **Remarks:** Full-time maker; first knife sold in 1985. **Mark:** G1

JACK GUESS, 12 N. Rockford, Tulsa, OK 74120/918-584-3876
Specialties: Straight and folding working knives. **Patterns:** Hunters, utility knives, folders, and boots. **Technical:** Grinds 440C, ATS34, and 01. **Prices:** $75 to $125; some $250. **Remarks:** Part-time maker; first knife sold in 1972. **Mark:** J. Guess

MELVIN H. GURGANUS, Star Rt., Box 50-A, Colerain, NC 27924/919-356-4831
Specialties: Fancy working knives and period pieces. **Patterns:** Belt knives, folders, short swords, throwing knives, Bowies, and same miniatures. **Technical:** Forges and grinds A2, D2 and ATS34. Wife Carol does scrimshaw. He does own heat-treat, carving and lost wax carving. **Prices:** $65 to $170; some $400. **Remarks:** Part-time maker; first knife sold in 1983. **Mark:** M. Gurganus

KENNETH GUTH, 8 S. Michigan, 32nd Floor, Chicago, IL 60603/312-346-1760
Specialties: One-of-a-kind ornate straight and folding knives. **Patterns:** Flemish, Japanese and African-styled knives. **Technical:** Forges and grinds high carbon and 440C. Does brass and steel laminations, goldsmithing. **Prices:** Upscale. **Remarks:** Full-time goldsmith and knifemaker. **Mark:** Guth

GEORGE B. GUTHRIE, Rt. 3 Box 432, Bessemer City, NC 28016/704-629-3031
Specialties: Working knives—his design or yours. **Patterns:** Hunters, boots, fighters, locking folders, and slip-joints in traditional styles. **Technical:** Grinds D2, 440C and 154CM. **Prices:** $85 to $300; some to $450. **Remarks:** Part-time maker; first knife sold in 1978. **Mark:** Name in state

BOB GWOZDZ, 71 Starr Ln., Attleboro, MA 02703/617-226-7475
Specialties: Fancy working straight knives. **Patterns:** Fighters, tantos and hunters. **Technical:** Grinds 440C. **Prices:** $125 to $300; some to $500. **Remarks:** Part-time maker; first knife sold in 1983. **Mark:** Name and serial number

H&W KNIVES, 752 Spencerfield Rd., Pace, FL 32570/904-949-4559

Specialties: Outdoorsmen's knives. **Patterns:** Traditional styles in belt knives. **Technical:** Hollow-grind ATS34 and 440C; likes Micarta. **Prices:** Moderate. **Remarks:** This is a partnership of Frank H. Johnston, Jr. and Floyd W. Sharp III. **Mark:** H&W

PHILIP L. HAGEN, P.O. Box 58, Pelican Rapids, MN 56572/218-863-8503
Specialties: High-tech working straight and folding knives. **Patterns:** A wide variety of folders; makes defense-related straight knives. **Technical:** Forges and grinds; uses 440C, his own Damascus, others like Uddeholm UHB. **Prices:** $100 to $800; some to $3,000. **Remarks:** Part-time maker, first knife sold in 1975. **Mark:** DOC HAGEN in shield, knife, banner logo

GEORGE S. HAGGERTY, 414 Hammertown Road, Monroe, CT 06468/203-261-4626
Specialties: Working folding and straight knives. **Patterns:** Hunters, claws, camp and fish knives, and locking folders. **Technical:** Forges and grinds; uses W2, 440C and 154CM. **Prices:** $85 to $150. **Remarks:** Part-time maker; first knife sold in 1981; has taken over Anderson Cutlery, which is now Discount Steel and Handle. **Mark:** GSH

ROBERT J. HAJOVSKY, P.O. Box 21, Scotland, TX 76379/817-541-2219
Specialties: Working straight knives. **Patterns:** Fighters, tantos, daggers—all as heavy-duty knives. **Technical:** Grinds 440C, 154CM and ATS34. **Prices:** $150 to $500. **Remarks:** Part-time maker; first knife sold in 1973. **Mark:** Bob-Sky Knives or name, city, state

JIM HAMMOND, P.O. Box 486, Arab, AL 35016/205-586-4151
Specialties: High-tech working straight knives. **Patterns:** Hunters in several patterns, fighters and boots. **Technical:** Grinds 440C and 154CM, very carefully. **Prices:** $200 to $975; some to $8,500. **Remarks:** Full-time maker; first knife sold in 1977. **Mark:** Full name, city, state in shield logo

HANGAS & SONS (See Ruana Knife Works)

ROBERT W. HANSEN, R.R. 2, Box 88, Cambridge, MN 55008/612-689-3242
Specialties: Straight and folding working knives. **Patterns:** From hunters to minis, camp knives to miniatures. Also makes folding lockers, slip joints in traditional styles. **Technical:** Grinds 01, 440C and 154CM; likes filework. **Prices:** $60 to $100; some to $550. **Remarks:** Part-time maker; first knife sold in 1983. **Mark:** Fish with H inside

HARBINGER (See Jimmy L. Fikes)

FRANK L. HARGIS, 321 S. Elm St., Flora, IL 62839/618-662-8281
Specialties: Fancy working knives. **Patterns:** Hunters, fighters, locking folders and Bowies. **Technical:** Grinds 440C, 154CM and ATS34; does filework. **Prices:** $90 to $1,000; some to $5,000. **Remarks:** Full-time maker; first knife sold in 1980. **Mark:** Name in logo

WALT HARLESS, P.O. Box 5913, Lake Worth, FL 33466-5913/407-964-3325
Specialties: Working straight knives in traditional style. **Patterns:** Hunters, utility and combat knives, historical reproductions, and smaller scaled models for ladies. Limited editions. **Technical:** Grinds ATS34 and 440C; offers bone handles. **Prices:** $65 to $250; some to $500. **Remarks:** Full-time maker; sold first knife in 1978. **Mark:** A with arrow

LARRY W. HARLEY, Route 3, 348 Deerfield Dr., Bristol, TN 37620/615-878-5368
Specialties: Period pieces and working knives. **Patterns:** Full range of straight knives, tomahawks, razors, buckskinners and hog spears. **Technical:** Forges and grinds; uses D2, 154CM and his own Damascus. All knives come very sharp. **Prices:** $50 to $500; some to $1,500. **Remarks:** Full-time maker; first knife sold in 1983; father is co-worker. **Mark:** Name, city and state in pine logo

JAY HARMON, 462 Victoria Rd., Woodstock, GA 30188/404-928-2734
Specialties: Straight working knives. **Patterns:** Bowies, daggers, fighters, boots, camp and fish knives, and folders. **Technical:** Grinds 440C, ATS34, D2, and 01. Buys Damascus; does his own heat-treat. **Prices:** $85 to $500. **Remarks:** Part-time maker; first knife sold in 1984. **Mark:** J. HARMON

MIKE HARRINGTON, 408 S. Cedar, Abilene, KS 67410/913-263-3278
Specialties: Working straight knives. **Patterns:** Hunters, tantos and Bowies. **Technical:** Forges and grinds; uses 01, 440C, ATS34 and 154CM. **Prices:** $65 to $100; some $160. **Remarks:** Spare-time maker; first knife sold in 1981. **Mark:** MH connected

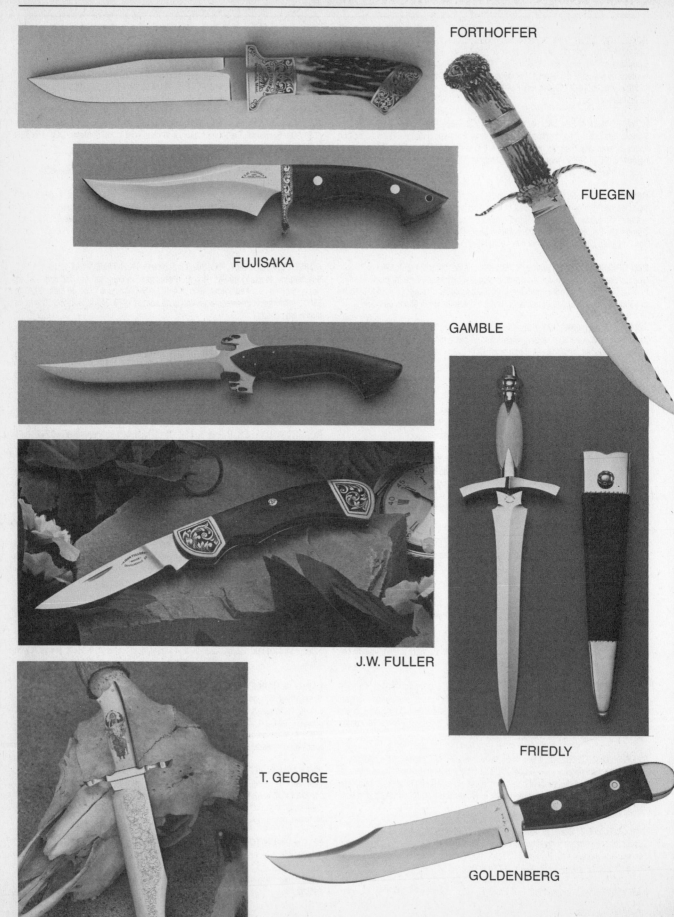

FORTHOFFER

FUEGEN

FUJISAKA

GAMBLE

J.W. FULLER

FRIEDLY

T. GEORGE

GOLDENBERG

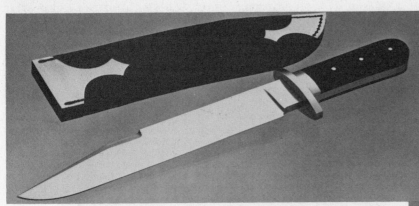

GLOVER

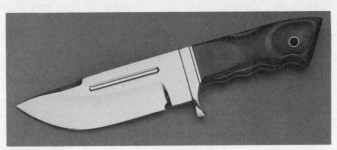

GOTTAGE

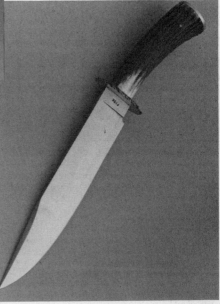

FISK

R.M. GREEN

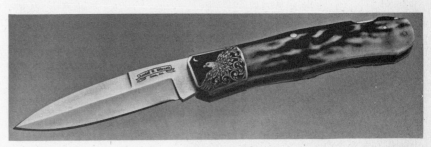

GILBREATH

W. GREEN

GOERTZ

directory/custom knifemakers

RALPH DEWEY HARRIS, P.O. Box 597, Grovetown, GA 30813/404-860-8719
Specialties: Interframe locking folders, straight working knives; some wall hangers. **Patterns:** Folding hunters, fighters, and pocket knives. Straight knives from boots to Bowies, hunters to fighters, tantos to utility knives. **Technical:** Grinds 440C, D2, and some commercial Damascus. **Prices:** $80 to $500; some $800. **Remarks:** Full-time maker; first knife sold in 1978. **Mark:** HARRIS, or name and city

WILLIAM W. HARSEY, 82710 N. Howe Ln., Creswell, OR 97426/503-895-4941
Specialties: High-tech kitchen and outdoor knives. **Patterns:** Folding hunters, as well as trout and bird folders. Makes straight hunters, camp knives, and axes. **Technical:** Grinds, etches. **Prices:** $125 to $300; some up to $1,500. Folders start at $350. **Remarks:** Full-time maker; first knife sold in 1979. **Mark:** Full name, state, U.S.A.

ARLAN (LANNY) HARTMAN, 340 Ruddiman, N. Muskegon, MI 49445/616-744-3635
Specialties: Working straight knives. **Patterns:** Ultra-light drop point hunters, Bowies, and boots. **Technical:** Grinds D2 for working knives and 440C for display knives; flat grinds only. **Prices:** $100 to $150; some $400. **Remarks:** Part-time maker; first knife sold in 1982. **Mark:** HARTMAN

PHILL HARTSFIELD, 13095 Brookhurst St., Garden Grove, CA 92643/714-636-7633
Specialties: Working and heavy-duty straight knives. **Patterns:** Fighters, swords and survival knives, most in Japanese profile. **Technical:** Grinds A2 and M2. Believes in sole authorship. **Prices:** $150 to $5,000. **Remarks:** Full-time maker; first knife sold about 1966. **Mark:** Initials, chiseled character

HARVEY MOUNTAIN KNIVES (See H. F. Wahlers)

MAX HARVEY, 14 Bass Rd., Bull Creek, Perth, 6155, WESTERN AUSTRALIA/09-332-7585
Specialties: Working straight knives, period and traditional, in heavy-duty weight. **Patterns:** Hunters, daggers, Bowies, tantos. **Technical:** Grinds 440C, 154CM, ATS34 and Damascus. **Prices:** $220 to $450; some to $1,500. **Remarks:** Part-time maker; first knife sold in 1981. **Mark:** M.C. HARVEY

HASTINGS (See Dwayne Parrish)

RADE HAWKINS, P.O. Box 400, Red Oak, GA 30272/404-964-1177
Specialties: Working knives to customer order. **Patterns:** Hunters, boots and camp knives; makes traditional folders. **Technical:** Grinds 154CM; 440C and D2. **Prices:** $140 to $400; some $1,200. **Remarks:** Part-time maker; first knife sold in 1972. **Mark:** Rade Hawkins, city, state, and zip code

CHAP HAYNES, R.R. #4, Tatamagouche, NS B0K 1V0, CANADA
Specialties: Working straight knives of his own designs. **Patterns:** Hunters, Bowies, tomahawks, swords, miniatures. **Technical:** Forges 01, his own Damascus, and laminates pure iron and nickel 200. **Prices:** $200 to $450; some to $1,500. **Remarks:** Part-time maker; first knife sold in 1985. **Mark:** Smith at anvil logo with HAYNES GREAT BLADES

WALTER F. HEDGECOCK, III, Box 175, Glen Daniel, WV 25844/304-934-6383
Specialties: Straight working knives in his design or yours. **Patterns:** Hunters, buckskinners, axes and tomahawks. **Technical:** Forges his own Damascus. **Prices:** $200 average. **Remarks:** Full-time maker; been smithing for 8 years. **Mark:** W.F.H. occasionally; SAXON FORGE

DON HEDRICK, 131 Beechwood Hills, Newport News, VA 23602/804-877-8100
Specialties: Working straight knives; period pieces and fantasy knives. **Patterns:** Hunters, boots, Bowies and miniatures. **Technical:** Grinds 440C and purchased Damascus. **Prices:** $150 to $550; some to $1,200. **Remarks:** Part-time maker; first knife sold in 1982. **Mark:** D. HEDRICK in oval logo

LOU HEGEDUS, JR., P.O. Box 441, Cave Spring, GA 30124
Specialties: Working straight and folding knives to customer order. **Patterns:** Full range of straight knives, folding lockers and slip joints. **Technical:** Grinds and forges; uses D2, 440C and his own Damascus. **Prices:** $75 to $250; some to $800. **Remarks:** Full-time maker; first knife sold in 1966. **Mark:** HEGEDUS

J. L. HEGWALD, 1106 Charles, Humboldt, KS 66748/316-473-3523
Specialties: Working straight knives, some fancy. **Patterns:** Makes Bowies, miniatures as well. **Technical:** Forges or grinds; uses 01, L6, 440C; mixes materials in handles. **Prices:** $35 to $200; some higher. **Remarks:** Part-time maker; first knife sold in 1983. **Mark:** JL

JOEL HEGWOOD, Rt. 4, Box 229, Summerville, GA 30747/404-397-8187
Specialties: High-tech working knives of his own design. **Patterns:** Hunters, boots and survival knives; locking folders, slip joints and interframes. **Technical:** Grinds A2, 01 and D2; uses 7075 aluminum in lightweight folder frames. **Prices:** $65 to $125; some to $200. **Remarks:** Part-time maker; first knife sold in 1979. **Mark:** Last name

RICHARD KARL HEHN, Karlsruhe Str. 7, D-7517 Waldbronn 1, WEST GERMANY/(07243) 61922
Specialties: High-tech working knives. **Patterns:** Hunters, fighters, Bowies, and locking folders. **Technical:** Grinds and forges 440C, CPM, and his own stainless Damascus; high-tech polishing for all steels; clean grinds; deluxe natural handles. **Prices:** $350 to $4,000; some $9,000. **Remarks:** Full-time maker; first knife sold in 1963. Has partner. **Mark:** Runic H in logo

RON HEMBROOK, P.O. Box 153, Neosho, WI 53059/414-625-3607
Specialties: Period pieces and straight working knives. **Patterns:** Hunters, buckskinners, tomahawks, fighters and Bowies. **Technical:** Grinds 01 and D2, and bought Damascus. **Prices:** $60 to $100; some to $350. **Remarks:** Part-time maker; first knife sold in 1970. **Mark:** Name with serial number

LORENZO "LARRY" HENDRICKS, 9919 E. Apache Trail, Mesa, AZ 85207/602-986-9252
Specialties: The Kangaroo design, U.S. patent—a small knife piggybacked in larger knife. **Patterns:** All sizes, boots, fighters, daggers, Bowies, and working type designs. **Technical:** Grinds 440C; Damascus, does own engraving; sculptured gold figures for inlays and overlays; also designs in straight knives. **Prices:** $550 to $1,600; some to $6,000. **Remarks:** Full-time maker; first knife sold in 1943. **Mark:** Name, town and state

E.J. (Jay) HENDRICKSON, 4204 Ballenger Creek Pike, Frederick, MD 21701/301-663-6923
Specialties: Working straight knives. **Patterns:** Bowies, hunters, camp knives, fighters in the Moran styles. **Technical:** Forges W2, 01, 1095, 5160; makes Damascus; does a lot of wire inlay. **Prices:** $250 to $2,500. **Remarks:** Full-time maker; first knife sold in 1975. **Mark:** Name

D.E. HENRY, Star Route, Old Gulch Road, Mountain Ranch, CA 95246/209-754-4537
Specialties: Investor-class knives in standard patterns—premier maker of Sheffield-type Bowies. **Patterns:** Bowies of course, but also folding lockers, patent locks and push knives, even hunters. **Technical:** Grinds D2, D3 and 440C; finishes to immaculate line and grinds. **Prices:** $2,200 and up. **Remarks:** Full-time maker; first knife sold in 1955. **Mark:** Name in Roman or Gothic lettering

PETER HENRY & SON, 332 Nine Mile Ride, Wokingham, Berkshire RG11 3NJ, ENGLAND/0734-734475
Specialties: Period pieces and working straight knives; will work to customer order. **Patterns:** Hunters to push knives, survival knives to boots; Sheffield-style a mainstay. **Technical:** Grind 01 and 154CM; make "faithful copies of Bowies, Scottish dirks and sgian dubhs." **Prices:** £42 to £155. **Remarks:** Full-time maker; first knife sold in 1974. **Mark:** P. Henry & Son

WAYNE HENSLEY, P.O. Box 904, Conyers, GA 30207/404-483-8938
Specialties: Period pieces and fancy working knives. **Patterns:** Boots to Bowies, folding lockers to miniatures. Large variety of straight knives. **Technical:** Grinds D2, 440C, 154CM and commerical Damascus. **Prices:** $50 to $150; some to $800. **Remarks:** Part-time maker; first knife sold in 1974. **Mark:** Hensley

TIM HERMAN, 7721 Foster, Overland Park, KS 66204/913-649-3860
Specialties: Exceptionally ornate knives and period pieces in his own designs. **Patterns:** Boots, Bowies, daggers and push knives; high quality folders and interframes. **Technical:** Grinds D2, 440C, ATS34 and 154CM. Intricate handle designs, gold inlays; all knives fully embellished. **Prices:** $300 to $1,750; some to $3,000. **Remarks:** Part-time maker; first knife sold in 1978. **Mark:** Etched signature

WM. R. "BILL" HERNDON, 32520 Michigan Ave., Acton, CA 93510/805-269-5860
Specialties: Working and fancy straight knives, some collector knives. **Patterns:** Hunters, tantos, buckskinners, and miniatures. **Technical:** Grinds D2, 01, 440C, 154CM. **Prices:** $90 to $200 and up. **Remarks:** Part-time maker; first knife sold in 1981. **Mark:** Signature or last name

GEORGE HERRON, Rt. 1, Box 24, Springfield, SC 29146/803-258-3914
Specialties: High-tech working straight knives; some folders. **Patterns:** Hunters,

directory/custom knifemakers

fighters, boots in personal style. **Technical:** Grinds 154CM, ATS34; builds knives to be used. **Prices:** $75 to $500; some $750. **Remarks:** Full-time maker; first knife sold in 1963. **Mark:** HERRON in script

DON HETHCOAT, Box 1764, Clovis, NM 88101/505-762-5721
Specialties: Straight working and folding knives. **Patterns:** Hunters, axes, fish knives, buckskinners and boots, and locking folders. **Technical:** Grinds D2, 440C and 154CM. **Prices:** $80 to $250; some $500. **Remarks:** Part-time maker; first knife sold in 1969. **Mark:** HETHCOAT, zip code and state

THOMAS S. HETMANSKI, 1107 William St., Trenton, NJ 08610/609-989-9371
Specialties: Working knives; some fantasy pieces. **Patterns:** Folding lockers and interframes; straight hunters, boots, fish knives, and miniatures. **Technical:** Grinds A2, 440C and commercial Damascus. **Prices:** $135 to $300; some to $400. **Remarks:** Part-time maker; first knife sold in 1982. **Mark:** Initials in monogram

DARYL HIBBEN, P.O. Box 2287, Pocatello, ID 83206/208-238-1593
Specialties: Working straight knives, some fancy. **Patterns:** Simple hunters; complex fighters; Bowies and swords. **Technical:** Grinds 440C, 154CM; prefers hollow grind. **Prices:** $140 to $450; some to $3,000. **Remarks:** Full-time maker; first knife sold in 1979. **Mark:** Signature

GIL HIBBEN, P.O. Box 42413, Louisville, KY 40224/502-499-9097
Specialties: Working knives and fantasy pieces, made to customer order. **Patterns:** Full range of straight knives, including swords, axes, and miniatures. Does some locking folders. Maker and designer of Rambo III knife. **Technical:** Grinds D2, 440C and 154CM. (Makes any kind of knife, welcomes one-of-a-kind designs.) **Prices:** $300 to $2,000; some $10,000. **Remarks:** Full-time maker; first knife sold in 1957. **Mark:** Name, city and state, or signature

VERNON W. HICKS, Rte. 1, Box 387, Bauxite, AR 72011/501-557-2813
Specialties: Working knives; some fancy pieces. **Patterns:** Folding lockers, slip joints in traditional styles; straight hunters, boots and Bowies. **Technical:** Grinds D2, 440C and 154CM. **Prices:** $75 to $300. **Remarks:** Spare-time maker; first knife sold in 1974. **Mark:** HICKS

TOM HIGH, 5474 S. 112.8 Rd., Alamoso, CO 81101/719-589-2108
Specialties: Hunter's knives, some fancy. **Patterns:** Drop-points in several shapes; some semi-skinners. Knives designed by and for top outfitters and guides. **Technical:** Grinds ATS34, unless other steel requested; likes hollowgrinds, mirror finishes; prefers scrimmable handles. **Prices:** $55 to $130; some to $350. **Remarks:** Full-time maker; first knife sold in 1965. Capable scrimshander; bowhunter. **Mark:** T and H connected

TOM HILKER, 4884 Harmony Lane, Santa Maria, CA 93455/805-937-5001
Specialties: Traditional straight and folding working knives. **Patterns:** Folding skinner in two sizes; Bowies, fork and knife sets, camp knives, and interchangeables. **Technical:** Grinds D2, 440C, and ATS34. Does own heat-treating. **Prices:** $50 to $350; some $400. **Remarks:** Full-time maker; first knife sold in 1983. **Mark:** HILKER

HOWARD E. HILL, Jette Lake, Polson, MT 59860/406-883-3405
Specialties: Working knives in personal designs, especially folders, fantasy pieces. **Patterns:** Locking folders, interframes; straight hunters and fighters. **Technical:** Grinds W2, 440C and 154CM; standard folder has grease ring joint. **Prices:** $100 to $300; some exceptional knives $5,000. **Remarks:** Part-time maker; first knife sold in 1981. **Mark:** Persuader

RICK HILL, 576 Clover Dr., Edwardsville IL, 62025/618-656-6850
Specialties: Working knives and period pieces; will fabricate to order. **Patterns:** Hunters, locking folders, fighters and daggers. **Technical:** Grinds D2, 440C and 154CM. **Prices:** $75 to $300; some to $1,500. **Remarks:** Part-time maker; first knife sold in 1983. Welcomes customer designs. **Mark:** Full name in hill shape logo

R. HINSON and SON, 2419 Edgewood Rd., Columbus, GA 31906/404-327-6801
Specialties: Straight and folding working knives. **Patterns:** Folding lockers and combat knives. **Technical:** Grinds 440C and bought Damascus. **Prices:** $100 to $350. **Remarks:** Part-time maker; first knife sold in 1983. Bob, his son, is co-worker. **Mark:** R. HINSON AND SON

HARUMI HIRAYAMA, 4-5-13, Kitamachi, Warabi City, Saitama Pref., JAPAN #335/0484-43-2248
Specialties: High-tech working knives of her own design. **Patterns:** Folding lockers, interframes and straight gents knives. **Technical:** Grinds 440C or equivalent; uses natural handle materials and gold. **Prices:** $200 to $1,200; some to $5,000. **Remarks:** Part-time maker; first knife sold in 1985. **Mark:** H. Harumi

HOWARD HITCHMOUGH, 3 Highland Lodge, Fox Hill, London SE 19 2UJ, ENGLAND/01-653-6166
Specialties: Fancy working knives. **Patterns:** Fighters, boots and hunters, also folding lockers in traditional patterns. **Technical:** Grinds D2, Sandvik 12C27, and others. Prefers handrubbed finishes and natural handle materials. **Prices:** $200 to $400; some to $800. **Remarks:** Full-time maker; first knife sold in 1967. **Mark:** HITCHMOUGH, LONDON, ENGLAND

J.B. HODGE, 1100 Woodmont Ave. SE, Huntsville, AL 35801/205-536-8388
Specialties: Fancy folding working knives. **Patterns:** Lockers, slip joints, two-blades, fighters and traditional patterns. **Technical:** Grinds D2, 154CM and ATS34. Uses his own front lock on his folders. **Prices:** $150 to $300; some to $750. **Remarks:** Part-time maker; first knife sold in 1978. **Mark:** Name, city and state

JOHN HODGE, III, 422 S. 15th St., Palatka, FL 32077/904-328-3897
Specialties: Fancy folding and straight working knives. **Patterns:** Camp knives, boots, hunters and buckles. Makes folding lockers, slip joints and gents patterns. **Technical:** Forges 01, D1 and makes his own "Southern-style" Damascus. **Prices:** $200 to $600; some to $1,000. **Remarks:** Part-time maker; first knife sold in 1981. **Mark:** JH3 in logo

RICHARD J. HODGSON, 9081 Tahoe Lane, Boulder, CO 80301/303-666-9460
Specialties: Straight and folding knives in traditional styles. **Patterns:** High tech knives in various patterns. **Technical:** Grinds 440C, AEB-L, and CPM. **Prices:** $850 to $2,200. **Remarks:** Part-time maker. **Mark:** None

STEVE HOEL, P.O. Box 283, Pine, AZ 85544/602-476-4278
Specialties: Investor-class folders and period pieces in his own designs. **Patterns:** Folding interframes, both lockers and slip joints; straight Bowies, boots and daggers. **Technical:** Grinds 154CM, ATS34, and commercial Damascus. **Prices:** $450 to $750; some to $7,500. **Remarks:** Full-time maker of quality knives. **Mark:** SH logo with name and address

KEVIN L. HOFFMAN, 3361 Calcutta Ave., Orlando, FL 32817/407-678-3124
Specialties: High-tech working knives. **Patterns:** Fighters, tantos, claws, survival and push knives. **Technical:** Grinds 01, 440C and 154CM. Tantos with polished temper line and sandblasted finish. **Prices:** $100 to $300; some to $500. **Remarks:** Full-time maker; first knife sold in 1981. **Mark:** KLH

D'ALTON HOLDER, 3200 N. Carlton, Farmington, NM 87401/505-326-0611
Specialties: Deluxe working knives and high art hunters. **Patterns:** "My" knife is drop-point hunter most-sold, but makes fighters, Bowies, miniatures and locking folders. **Technical:** Grinds 440C and 154CM; uses amber and other materials in combination on stick tangs. **Prices:** $150 to $350; some to $1,000. **Remarks:** Full-time maker; first knife sold in 1970. **Mark:** D'HOLDER, city and state

DALE J. HOLLAND, 204 N.E. 82nd St., Kansas City, MO 64118/816-436-1493
Specialties: Fancy high-tech knives. **Patterns:** Locking folders, patent locks, and interframes. **Technical:** Grinds 440C, 154CM and ATS34. **Prices:** $120 to $350; some to $450. **Remarks:** Part-time maker; first knife sold in 1980. **Mark:** DJH

PAUL HOLLOWAY, 714 Burksdale Rd., Norfolk, VA 23518/804-588-7071
Specialties: Working straight and folding knives; will work to customer order. **Patterns:** Both lockers and slip joints; fighters and boots in straight knives; fish and push knives, from swords to miniatures. **Technical:** Grinds A2, D2, 154CM, 440C and ATS34. **Prices:** $95 to $230; some to $700. **Remarks:** Part-time maker; first knife sold in 1981. **Mark:** Holloway or name and city in logo

JESS HORN, 2850 Goodwater Ave., Redding, CA 96002/916-221-3681
Specialties: Investor-class working folders; some period pieces; famously collectible. **Patterns:** High-tech design and finish in locking folders; now offers traditional slip joints. **Technical:** Grinds 440C, 154CM and commercial Damascus. **Prices:** $400 to $700. **Remarks:** Full-time maker; first knife sold in 1968. **Mark:** Full name or Horn

GLEN HORNBY, P.O. Box 444, Glendale, CA 91209/818-244-1354
Specialties: Fancy working knives. **Patterns:** Bowies, fighters, hunters mainly. **Technical:** Grinds ATS34, 154CM and 440C; likes big horn sheep handles. **Prices:** $95 to $175; some to $900. **Remarks:** Part-time maker. **Mark:** Script name under sheep horns

directory/custom knifemakers

HOUSE OF KOGATANA (See Stewart G. Rowe)

DURVYN M. HOWARD, Rt. 5, Box 77, Gadsden, AL 35903/205-492-5720
Specialties: Collectable upscale folders in working designs. **Patterns:** Folding lockers, gents, hunters, fighters, gent's dinner set—but folders only right now. **Technical:** Grinds 440C, satin finish, natural handle materials; clean execution. **Prices:** $500 to $1,200; some to $2,500. **Remarks:** Full-time maker; now accepting orders. **Mark:** HOWARD etched on tang

JOHN C. HOWSER, Rt. 9, Box 579, Bell Ln., Frankfort, KY 40601/502-875-3678
Specialties: Practical working knives. **Patterns:** Hunters and fighters and folding lockblades. **Technical:** Grinds D2, 440C and 154CM; clean crisp lines and mirror surface; natural materials. **Prices:** $85 to $125; some to $200. **Remarks:** Part-time maker; first knife sold in 1974. **Mark:** Signature

JIM HRISOULAS, 15258 Lakeside, Sylmar, CA 91342/818-362-5339
Specialties: Period pieces and straight working knives. **Patterns:** Swords, Bowies, tomahawks, daggers and sgian dubhs. **Technical:** Forges (only) 01, 1095, 5160, and makes his own Damascus. **Prices:** $85 to $175; some exceed $600. **Remarks:** Full-time maker; first knife sold in 1973. **Mark:** 8R in heart logo

ARTHUR J. HUBBARD, 574 Cutlers Farm Road, Monroe, CT 06468/203-268-3998
Specialties: Fancy working knives, his design or yours. **Patterns:** Hunters, fighters, boots, wood carving knives; folding lockers in traditional styles. **Technical:** Grinds and forges; uses W2, 440C and 154CM. **Prices:** $65 to $350; some to $1,000. **Remarks:** Full-time maker; first knife sold in 1976. **Mark:** Name, city and state

C. ROBBIN HUDSON, Rt. 1, Box 128B, Rock Hall, MD 21661/301-639-7273
Specialties: High art forged working knives. **Patterns:** Hunters, Bowies, fighters and kitchen knives. **Technical:** Forges W2, 01 and his own Damascus; makes knives one at a time; ABS Master. **Prices:** $300 to $700; some to $5,000. **Remarks:** Full-time maker; first knife sold in 1970. **Mark:** Hudson and MS

ROBERT HUDSON, 3802 Black Cricket Ct., Humble, TX 77396/713-454-7207
Specialties: Working straight knives in his own designs. **Patterns:** Bowies, hunters, skinners, fighters, and utility knives. **Technical:** Grinds D2, 440C, 154CM, and bought Damascus. **Prices:** $85 to $350; some $1,500. **Remarks:** Part-time maker; first knife sold in 1980. **Mark:** Full name, handmade, city, and state

CHUBBY HUESKE, 4808 Tamarisk Dr., Bellaire, TX 77401/713-667-0344
Specialties: Working knives, fancy and plain, with the hand of the maker easy to see. **Patterns:** Hunters, boots, fighters; folding lockers, slip joints and gents. **Technical:** Grinds D2. **Prices:** $100 to $225; some to $650. **Remarks:** Part-time maker every day; now making some specials like sesquicentennial Sam Houston and Yellow Rose knives; first knife sold in 1968. **Mark:** Name and Texas logo

STEVE HUEY, 27645 Snyder Rd. #38, Junction City, OR 97448/503-689-8362
Specialties: Straight working knives, some one of a kind. **Patterns:** Hunters, fighters, fish knives and kitchen cutlery. **Technical:** Hollow or flat grinds 1095, L6, 440C, D2 and ATS34. **Prices:** $75 to $600. **Remarks:** Part-time maker; first knife sold in 1981. **Mark:** HUEY in rectangle

DAN HUGHES, 13743 Persimmon Blvd., West Palm Beach, FL 33411/407-798-2241
Specialties: Straight working knives. **Patterns:** Hunters, fighters, fillet knives. Customer designs. **Technical:** Grinds 440C and ATS34. **Prices:** $55 to $175; some to $300. **Remarks:** Part-time maker; first knife sold in 1984. **Mark:** Initials

DARYLE HUGHES, 10979 Leonard, Nunica, MI 49448/616-837-6623
Specialties: Working knives. **Patterns:** Buckskinners, hunters, camp knives, kitchen and fish knives. **Technical:** Grinds and forges; uses W2, 01 and D2. **Prices:** $40 to $100; some to $400. **Remarks:** Part-time maker, first knife sold in 1979. **Mark:** Name and town in logo

ED HUGHES, 280^1/2 Holly Lane, Grand Junction, CO 81503/303-243-8547
Specialties: Working and miniature knives in traditional modes. **Patterns:** Bowies, push knives; has a pocketable straight knife he likes. **Technical:** Grinds stainless steels. **Prices:** $75 to $250; some to $600. **Remarks:** Full-time maker; sold first knife in 1978. **Mark:** Name or initials

LAWRENCE HUGHES, 207 W. Crestway, Plainview, TX 79072/806-293-5406
Specialties: Working and display knives. **Patterns:** Bowies, daggers, hunters, buckskinners and push knives. **Technical:** Grinds D2, 440C and 154CM. **Prices:** $50 to

$125; some to $2,000. **Remarks:** Part-time maker; first knife sold in 1979. **Mark:** Name with buffalo skull in center

MICHAEL J. HULL, 1330 Hermits Circle, Cottonwood, AZ 86326/602-634-2871
Specialties: Working knives and period pieces. **Patterns:** Fighters, Bowies and camp knives especially, but does Mediterranean and boots. **Technical:** Grinds 440C, ATS34 and D2. **Prices:** $75 to $275; some to $700. **Remarks:** Full-time maker; first knife sold in 1983. **Mark:** Name, city, state

ROY HUMENICK, P.O. Box 414, Rescue, CA 95672/916-677-2778
Specialties: Working knives in his own style. **Patterns:** Hunters and fighters, as well as other original designs. **Technical:** Forges and grinds. Uses stainless; makes Damascus. **Prices:** $125 to $250; some to $600. **Remarks:** Part-time maker; first knife sold in 1984. **Mark:** Name

ROBERT E. HUNNICUTT, 2636 Magnolia Way, Forest Grove, OR 97116/503-357-3950
Specialties: Working knvies and period pieces. **Patterns:** Fighters, boots and Bowies; also miniatures. **Technical:** Grinds D2 and 440C; prefers his rebated flat grind to standard designs. **Prices:** $150 to $400. **Remarks:** Full-time maker; first knife sold in 1979. **Mark:** Name plus production number

JEFF HURST, Rt. 1, Box 22-A, Rutledge, TN 37861/615-828-3909
Specialties: Straight working knives forged in his own designs. **Patterns:** Tomahawks, hunters, boots, and fighters. **Technical:** Forges W2, 01, and his own Damascus. **Prices:** $175 to $350; some $500. **Remarks:** Full-time maker; first knife sold in 1984. Marks partnered knives—with Newman L. Smith, handle artisan—SH in script. **Mark:** HURST

HOWARD L. IMBODEN, II, 4216 Barth Lane, Kettering, OH 45429/513-293-1552
Specialties: Unique one-of-a-kind art knives, each with hand-carved handles. **Technical:** Grinds bought Damascus. Does his own lost wax casting. **Prices:** $95 to $3,000. **Remarks:** Part-time maker; first knife sold in 1986. **Mark:** Name

BILLY MACE IMEL, 1616 Bundy Ave., New Castle, IN 47362/317-529-1651
Specialties: High art working knives, period pieces and personal cutlery. **Patterns:** Daggers, fighters, hunters; folding lockers and slip joints with interframes; folding hunters. **Technical:** Grinds and forges D2, 440C and 154CM. **Prices:** $200 to $2,000; some to $4,000. **Remarks:** Part-time maker; first knife sold in 1973. **Mark:** Name in monogram

THE IRON DUCKLING (See John Sloan)

JACK KNIVES (See Jack Shedenhelm)

JIM JACKS, P.O. Box 2782, Covina, CA 91722/818-331-5665
Specialties: Straight working knives in traditional patterns. **Patterns:** Tantos, Bowies, fish and camp knives, even miniatures. **Technical:** Grinds Stellite 6K, 440C and 154CM. **Prices:** $100 to $250; some to $650. **Remarks:** Spare-time maker; first knife sold in 1980. **Mark:** JJ in diamond logo

JAGED (See Gregory H. Smith)

GERRY JEAN, 25B Cliffside Drive, Manchester, CT 06040/203-649-6449
Specialties: Working knives. **Patterns:** Folding lockers and butterflies. Straight hunters, survival and camp knives, some miniatures. **Technical:** Grinds A2, 440C and 154CM. Handle slabs applied in unique tongue-and-groove method. **Prices:** $125 to $250; some $450. **Remarks:** Spare-time maker; first knife sold in 1973. **Mark:** GJ and serial number

CARL A. JENSEN, JR., R.R. #3, Box 74, Blair, NE 68008/402-426-3353
Specialties: Working knives and period pieces. **Patterns:** Hunters mainly, and fighters, boots and Bowies. Customer design. **Technical:** Grinds D2, 01 and 440C; does own heat treating. **Prices:** $35 to $200 and up. **Remarks:** Part-time maker; first knife sold in 1980. **Mark:** Bear's Cutlery

STEVE JERNIGAN, 298 Tunnel Rd., Milton, FL 32571/904-994-0802
Specialties: Fancy working knives; some one-of-a-kind knives. **Patterns:** Daggers and hunters; folding lockers and slip joints. **Technical:** Grinds D2, ATS34 and 440C. Uses "Italian Smalti" glass tiles for his unique mosaic handles. **Prices:** $150 to $350; some to $4,000. **Remarks:** Part-time maker; first knife sold in 1982. Not taking orders for folders. **Mark:** JERNIGAN

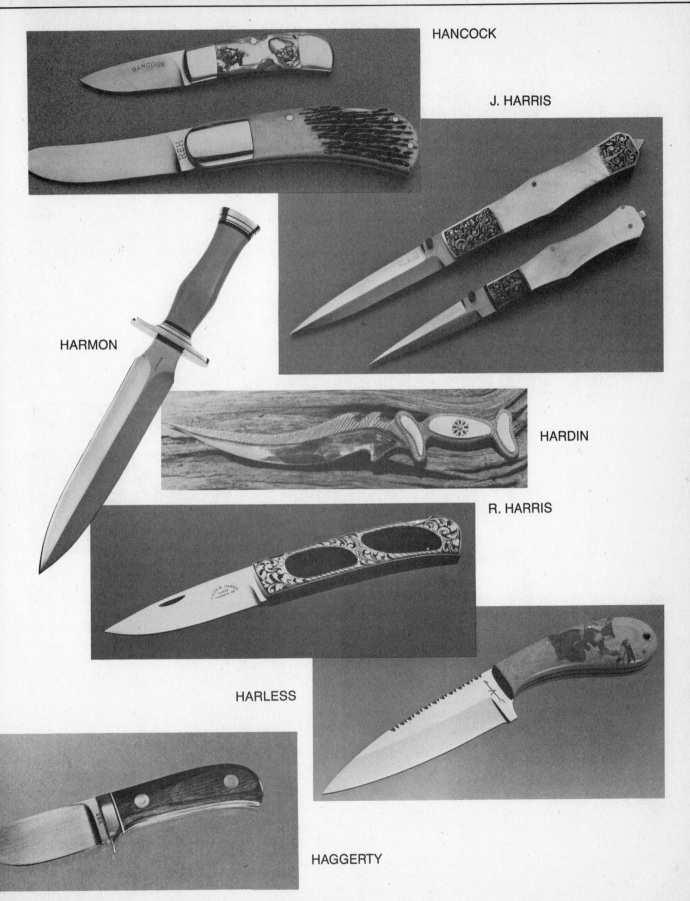

HANCOCK

J. HARRIS

HARMON

HARDIN

R. HARRIS

HARLESS

HAGGERTY

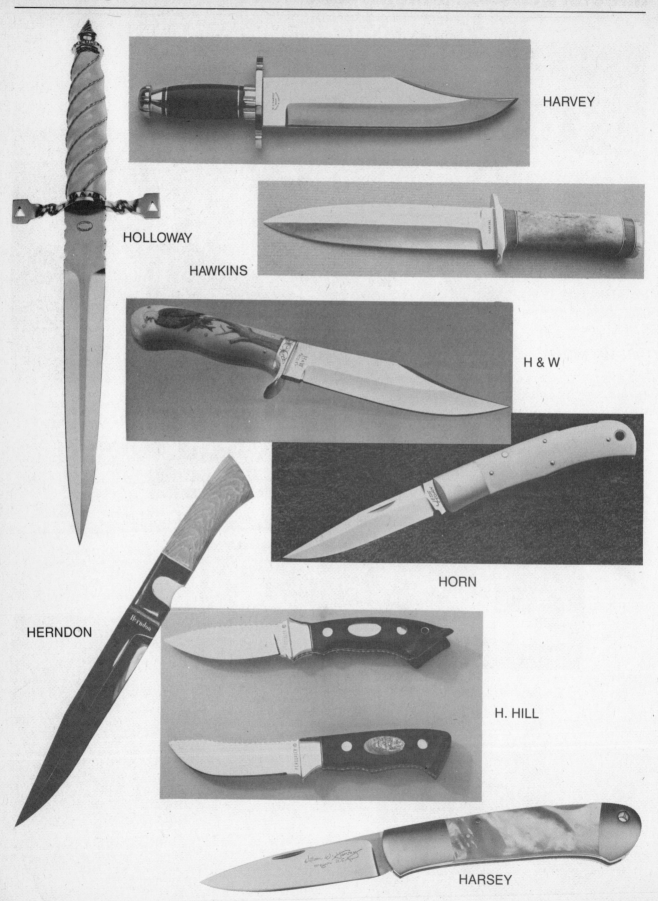

HARVEY

HOLLOWAY

HAWKINS

H & W

HORN

HERNDON

H. HILL

HARSEY

directory/custom knifemakers

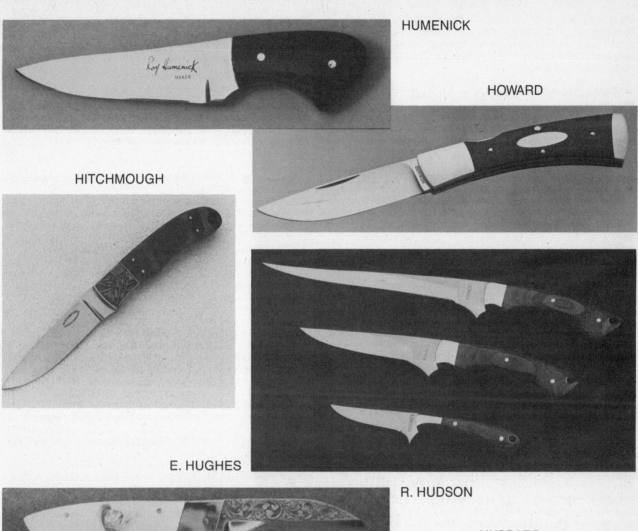

HUMENICK

HOWARD

HITCHMOUGH

E. HUGHES

R. HUDSON

HUBBARD

JACKS

IMEL

directory/custom knifemakers

SID JIRIK, 11301 Patro St., Anchorage, AK 99516/907-346-2661
Specialties: Straight working knives. **Patterns:** Hunters, fighters and survival knives; distinctive variations on the standard themes. **Technical:** Grinds A2, D2 and 154CM; mirror finishes. **Prices:** $90 to $150; some to $1,000. **Remarks:** Full-time maker. **Mark:** Full name, city, state

JACQUES JOBIN, 46 St. Dominique, Lauzon, PQ G6V 2M7, CANADA/418-833-0283
Specialties: Fancy working straight knives. **Patterns:** Hunters, fighters, skinners, and some art knives. **Technical:** Grinds 440C, and ATS34. Likes native snakewood. Does own heat-treating. **Prices:** $90 to $250. **Remarks:** Part-time maker; first knife sold in 1986. **Mark:** Signature and serial #

BRAD JOHNSON, 3477 Running Deer Dr., El Paso, TX 79936/915-595-1035
Specialties: Traditional working straight knives. **Patterns:** For hunters and out-doorsmen; has capers and deep-bellied skinners. **Technical:** Grinds stainless steels; uses pins and not solder to install bolsters, etc. **Prices:** $50 to $150; some to $250. **Remarks:** Part-time maker; first knife sold in 1985; serving officer, U.S. Army. **Mark:** BNJ

C.E. "GENE" JOHNSON, 5648 Redwood Ave., Portage, IN 46368/219-762-5461
Specialties: Heavy-duty working knives of his own design. **Patterns:** Hunters, Bowies, survival knives and axes; locking folders. **Technical:** Grinds D2 and 440C; A18. **Prices:** $80 to $750; some to $1,000. **Remarks:** Part-time maker; first knife sold in 1975. **Mark:** Gene

GORDEN W. JOHNSON, 5426 Sweetbriar, Houston, TX 77017/713-645-8990
Specialties: Working knives and period pieces. **Patterns:** Hunters, boots and Bowies. **Technical:** Grinds 440C; all knives flat grind; most knives have narrow tang. **Prices:** $60 to $90; some to $300. **Remarks:** Full-time maker; first knife sold in 1974. **Mark:** Name, city, state

HAROLD "HARRY" C. JOHNSON, 1014 Lafayette Rd., Chickamauga, GA 30707/404-375-2321
Specialties: Working straight knives in "time-tested patterns and styles." **Patterns:** Mostly hunters, fighters and boots. **Technical:** Grinds 01, 440C, 154CM and commercial Damascus; keeps 50 woods in stock. **Prices:** $60 to $200; some $1,000. **Remarks:** Part-time maker; first knife sold in 1973; full-time gunsmith with retail store. **Mark:** H. JOHNSON, city, state in oval logo

RONALD B. JOHNSON, Box 11, Clearwater, MN 55320/612-558-6128
Specialties: Fancy working knives. **Patterns:** Hunters, fighters and folding lockers, all in traditional styles. **Technical:** Grinds 440C, 154CM, 1095 steel and ATS34; uses no plastic; prefers natural materials. **Prices:** $90 to $250; some to $850. **Remarks:** Full-time maker; first knife sold in 1973. Currently not taking custom orders. **Mark:** Signature; R.B. JOHNSON

RUFFIN JOHNSON, 215 LaFonda Dr., Houston, TX 77060/713-448-4407
Specialties: Working straight and folding knives. **Patterns:** Hunters, fighters and Bowies; folding lockers and slip joints. **Technical:** Grinds 440C and 154CM; hidden tangs and fancy handles. **Prices:** $165 to $325; some to $1,095. **Remarks:** Full-time maker; first knife sold in 1972. **Mark:** Wolf head logo and signature

RYAN M. JOHNSON, P.O. Box 267, Hixson, TX 37343/615-842-9323
Specialties: Straight working knives in traditional patterns. **Patterns:** Bowies, stilettos, hunters, and fighters. **Technical:** Forges 1095, 01, his own Damascus; also sells Damascus blanks to knifemakers. **Prices:** $20 to $500; some $700. **Remarks:** Full-time maker; first knife sold in 1986. **Mark:** RMJ or RMJ Forge

STEVE R. JOHNSON, P.O. Box 5, 554 S. 500 E., Manti, UT 84642/801-835-7941
Specialties: Investor class working knives. **Patterns:** Hunters, fighters and boots in clean-lined contemporary patterns. **Technical:** Grinds ATS34, 154CM and 440C; buys Damascus. **Prices:** $225 to $1,000; some to $2,000. **Remarks:** Full-time maker; first knife sold in 1972. **Mark:** Name, city, state

W.C. "BILL" JOHNSON, 2242 N.W. 5th St., Okeechobee, FL 34972/813-467-4427
Specialties: Fancy working knives to order. **Patterns:** Hunters, fighters, tantos and push knives. He also makes folding lockers and slip joints. **Technical:** Grinds 440C, ATS34 and 154CM. **Prices:** $125 to $185; some to $500. **Remarks:** Full-time maker; first knife sold in 1979. **Mark:** W. C. Johnson

CHARLES JOKERST, 9312 Spaulding, Omaha, NE 68134/402-571-2536

Specialties: Working knives in standard patterns. **Patterns:** Hunters, fighters and Bowies; slip-joints, and miniatures. **Technical:** Grinds 440C, ATS34 and buys Damascus. **Prices:** $50 to $100; some $140. **Remarks:** Spare-time maker, first knife sold in 1984. **Mark:** Name and town

JONES CUSTOM KNIVES (See John Jones)

BOB JONES, 6219 Aztec N.E., Albuquerque, NM 87110/505-881-4472
Specialties: Fancy working knives of his own design. **Patterns:** Mountainman/buck-skinner types; folding lockers and slip joints. **Technical:** Grinds A2, 01, 1095 and commercial Damascus; uses no stainless steel. **Prices:** $75 to $300; some to $1,000. **Remarks:** Full-time maker; first knife sold in 1960. **Mark:** BJ on fixed blades; BJ en-circled on folders

CHARLES ANTHONY JONES, 36 Broadgate Close, Bellaire Barnstaple, No. Devon E31 4AL, ENGLAND/0271-75328
Specialties: Working straight knives. **Patterns:** Simple hunters, fighters and utility knives. **Technical:** Grinds 01 and D2; file work offered. **Prices:** $100 to $300; engraving higher. **Remarks:** Spare-time maker; sold first knife in 1987. **Mark:** Circle T

CURTIS J. JONES, 39909 176th St. E., Palmdale, CA 93550/805-264-2753
Specialties: Straight working, and traditional-styled knives. **Patterns:** Bowies, hunters, boots and miniatures. **Technical:** Grinds A2, 440C, and D2. Uses no solder, heat-treats his own. Custom sheaths—hand-tooled and stitched. **Prices:** $150 to $700; some $1,200. **Remarks:** Part-time maker; first knife sold in 1975. **Mark:** Stylized initials on either side of three triangles interconnected

ENOCH JONES, 4132 Novar Dr., Chantilly, VA 22021/703-378-0584
Specialties: Fancy straight working knives. **Patterns:** Hunters, fighters, boots and Bowies. **Technical:** Forges and grinds W2, 440C and commercial Damascus. **Prices:** $100 to $350; some to $1,000. **Remarks:** Part-time maker; first knife sold in 1982. **Mark:** ENOCH

GOMER G. JONES, 13313 E. 13th, Tulsa, OK 74108/918-437-3042
Specialties: Working straight knives in his own designs. **Patterns:** Bowies, hunters, utilities, and small using knives. **Technical:** Grinds 440C, 154CM, and ATS34. **Prices:** $100 to $300; some $400. **Remarks:** Knives tested by cowboys. **Mark:** Gomer

JOHN JONES, 12 Sea Breeze Rd. Manly, Brisbane 4179, AUSTRALIA/07-393-3390
Specialties: Straight and folding knives. **Patterns:** Makes working hunters, folding lockbacks and fancy daggers and miniatures. **Technical:** Grinds 440C, 01 and L6. **Prices:** $100 to $500; some $1,200. **Remarks:** Part-time maker; first knife sold in 1986. **Mark:** Jones Custom in script

JUDY (See J. Gottage)

JOSEPH F. KEESLAR, R #1, Box 252, Almo, KY 42020/502-753-7919
Specialties: Forged blades in traditional styles. **Patterns:** Period pieces—rifle knives, hunters, daggers. Forges small working knives from files. **Technical:** Forges 01-5160, his own Damascus, and carbon files. **Prices:** $100 to $1,500; some over $2,000. **Remarks:** Full-time maker; first knife sold in 1976. **Mark:** KEESLAR with hammer/anvil logo and J.S. (Journeyman Smith with ABS)

WILLIAM L. KEETON, Route 2, Box 20, Laconia, IN 47135/812-969-2836
Specialties: Plain and fancy working knives. **Patterns:** Hunters and fighters; folding lockers, and slip joints too. Names patterns for Derby winners. **Technical:** Grinds D2, 440C and 154CM; likes mirror finish. **Prices:** $75 to $475; some to $5,000. **Remarks:** Full-time maker; first knife sold in 1971. **Mark:** Logo of key

KELGIN KNIVES (See Ken Largin)

GARY KELLEY, 17485 S.W. Pheasant Lane, Aloha, OR 97006/503-649-7867
Specialties: Only miniature knives in exotic materials and designs. **Patterns:** Mostly miniature period pieces and fancy art knives. **Technical:** Forges and heat-treats 440C, purchased Damascus. **Prices:** $45 to $1,000. **Remarks:** Part-time maker; first knife sold in 1969. **Mark:** Kelley in gold inlay

LANCE KELLY, 1824 Royal Palm Dr., Edgewater, FL 32032/904-423-4933
Specialties: Engraved folding and straight knives in the investor class. **Patterns:** Distinctly Kelly style in contemporary outlines. **Technical:** Grinds 01, D2 and 440C; engraves scroll in many patterns; inlays gold and silver. **Prices:** $600 to $3,500. **Remarks:** Full-time engraver/knifemaker; first knife sold in 1975. **Mark:** KELLY

KEMAL (Don Fogg and Murad Sayen), P.O. Box 127, Bryant Pond, ME 04219/207-665-2438
Specialties: High art straight knives; investor class one-of-a-kinds. **Patterns:** Fighters, daggers and tantos. **Technical:** Forges own Damascus. **Prices:** $3,500 to $6,500; some to $9,000. **Remarks:** Full-time makers; first knife sold in 1977. Fogg does blades; Sayen the handles and furniture. Not accepting orders. **Mark:** KEMAL and date.

BILL KENNEDY, JR., P.O. Box 850431, Yukon, OK 73085/405-354-9150
Specialties: Straight working knives. **Patterns:** Hunters, fighters, minis and fish knives. **Technical:** Grinds D2, 440C and 154CM. **Prices:** $80 to $250; some to $1,000. **Remarks:** Part-time maker; first knife sold in 1980. **Mark:** KENNEDY and year made

J.C. KENNELLEY, Box 145, Leon, KS 67074/316-745-3797
Specialties: Working straight knives; some fantasy pieces. **Patterns:** Hunters, fighters, skinners and fillet knives. **Technical:** Grinds D2 and 440C. **Prices:** $75 to $200; some to $500. **Remarks:** Part-time maker; first knife sold in 1982. **Mark:** Name logo

RALPH A. KESSLER, P.O. Box 202, Gary Goff Rd., Elgin, SC 29045/803-438-5360
Specialties: Working knives in standard patterns. **Patterns:** Hunters, fighters, kitchen knives. **Technical:** Grinds 154CM, D2 and ATS34; some scrimshaw. **Prices:** $75 to $200; some to $400. **Remarks:** Full-time maker; first knife sold in 1982. **Mark:** Name or name with logo

KESTREL TOOL (See Gregg Blomberg)

JOT SINGH KHALSA, 368 Village St., Millis, MA 02054/508-376-8162
Specialties: High art knives in traditional patterns. **Patterns:** Contemporary and traditional styles. **Technical:** Grinds and forges; uses W2, 440C and his own Damascus. **Prices:** $140; some considerably more. **Remarks:** Full-time maker; first knife sold in 1978. **Mark:** Crossed blade logo and name

SHIVA KI, 5222 Ritterman Ave., Baton Rouge, LA 70805/504-356-7274
Specialties: Fancy working straight and folding knives; welcomes customer designs. **Patterns:** Emphasis on defense styles in personal knives. Makes martial arts weapons. **Technical:** Forges and grinds; makes his own Damasucus; prefers natural handle materials. **Prices:** $135 to $850; some $1,800. **Remarks:** Full-time maker; first knife sold 1981. **Mark:** Name with logo

KEITH KILBY, Foxwood Forge, Foxwood Rt. 4, Jefferson, GA 30549/404-887-4686
Specialties: Plain and fancy working knives in traditional patterns. **Patterns:** Mostly hunters, some Bowies and daggers. **Technical:** Forges 01, 5160, W1, L6 and his own Damascus. **Prices:** $30 to $3,000. **Remarks:** Part-time maker; ABS member; first knife sold in 1974. **Mark:** Name or knife logo

BILL KING, 14830 Shaw Road, Tampa, FL 33625/813-961-3455
Specialties: Fancy working knives; folding lockers in many varieties. **Patterns:** "Stud opener" is his specialty in folding knives. **Technical:** Grinds 440C, 154CM, ATS34 and bought Damascus. **Prices:** $135 to $250; some to $500. **Remarks:** Part-time maker; first knife sold in 1976. **Mark:** Name in crown

JOE KIOUS, Rt. 2, Box 232, Alamo, TX 78516/512-787-3178
Specialties: Fancy working knives in good contemporary styling. **Patterns:** Hunters, fighters, Bowies and miniatures; folders in traditional styles. **Technical:** Grinds D2, 440C and 154CM. **Prices:** $130 to $600; some to $5,000. **Remarks:** Full-time maker; first knife sold in 1969. **Mark:** KIOUS, city and state

JERRY KITSMILLER, 62435 Gerry Rd., Montrose, CO 81401/303-249-4290
Specialties: Straight working knives in traditional patterns. **Patterns:** Hunters, boots and locking folders. **Technical:** Grinds D2, 440C and 154CM. **Prices:** $75 to $200; some to $300. **Remarks:** Spare-time maker; first knife sold in 1984. **Mark:** J&S Knives

K.K.K. CO. (See A.J. Collins)

W.K. KNEUBUHLER (See David Votaw)

THE KNIFE GALLERY (See Vernon M. Davis)

TERRY KNIPSCHIELD, 808 12th Ave. N.E., Rochester, MN 55904/507-288-7829
Specialties: Working straight knives in traditional patterns. **Patterns:** Fillet knives

mostly, Bowies, hunters, and utility knives. **Technical:** Grinds 440C and ATS34. **Prices:** $55 to $125; some $250. **Remarks:** Part-time maker; first knife sold in 1986. **Mark:** KNIP in Old English with shield logo

KODAN (See B. Engnath)

ROBERT KOLITZ, W9342 Canary Rd., Beaver Dam, WI 53916/414-887-1287
Specialties: Working straight knives. **Patterns:** Hunters, boots and Bowies. **Technical:** Grinds 01 and 440C. **Prices:** $35 to $80; some to $400. **Remarks:** Spare-time maker; first knife sold in 1979. **Mark:** K

CHRIS KORMANIK, 510 Highland Ave., Athens, GA 30606/404-548-2430
Specialties: Straight working knives. **Patterns:** Hunters, skinners, boots and utility knives in your design or his. **Technical:** Grinds A2, D2, ATS34 and 01. **Prices:** $60 to $120. **Remarks:** Part-time maker; first knife sold in 1987. **Mark:** KORMANIK

GEORGE KOUTSOPOULOS, 41491 Biggs Rd., La Grange, OH 44050/216-355-4949
Specialties: Heavy-duty working straight and folding knives. **Patterns:** Traditional hunters and skinners, lockbacks. **Technical:** Grinds 440C, 154CM, ATS34. **Prices:** $75 to $275; some higher. **Remarks:** Spare-time maker; first knife sold in 1976. **Mark:** GEK in diamond logo

MICHAEL T. KOVAL, 822 Busch Ct., Columbus, OH 43229/614-888-6486
Specialties: Period pieces and straight working knifes of his own design. **Patterns:** Bowies, boots and daggers. **Technical:** Grinds D2, 440C and 154CM. **Prices:** $95 to $195; some $495. **Remarks:** Full-time knifemaker supply house, spare-time knifemaker. **Mark:** KOVAL

EUGENE KOVAR, 2626 W. 98th St., Evergreen Park, IL 60642/312-636-3724
Specialties: One-of-a-kind miniature knives only. **Patterns:** Miniature knives from the fancy to fantasy; also makes knife pendants and tie tacks. **Technical:** Files and grinds nails, nickel silver, and sterling silver. **Prices:** $5 to $35; some up to $100. **Remarks:** Spare-time maker; first knife sold in 1987. **Mark:** GK connected

STEVE KRAFT, 315 S.E. 6th, Abilene, KS 67410/913-263-2198
Specialties: Working knives in traditional style. **Patterns:** Hunters, boot knives, fighters, and tantos. **Technical:** Grinds 01, L6, ATS34. **Prices:** Starting at $90. **Remarks:** Part-time maker; sold first knife in 1984. **Mark:** SJK

TERRY L. KRANNING, 1900 West Quinn, #153, Pocatello, ID 83202/208-237-9047
Specialties: Miniature working and fantasy knives of his own design. **Patterns:** Miniature and some mini straight knives including razors, tomahawks, hunters, Bowies and fighters. **Technical:** Grinds 1095, 440C, purchased Damascus and nickel silver. Uses exotic materials, like meteorite. Makes cases for miniature sets made of brass or silver. **Prices:** $20 to $100; some to $250. **Remarks:** Part-time maker; first knife sold in 1978. **Mark:** K or TLK in eagle head logo

DONALD L. KREIBICH, 6082 Boyd Ct., San Jose, CA 95123/408-225-4719
Specialties: Straight working knives in standard patterns. **Patterns:** Bowies, boots and daggers; camp and fish knives in using finish. **Technical:** Grinds 440C, 154CM and ATS34; likes integrals. **Prices:** $100 to $200; some to $500. **Remarks:** Part-time maker; first knife sold in 1980. **Mark:** D.L. KREIBICH

JAMES J. KREIMER, Rt. 2, Box 280, Milan, IN 47031/812-654-2327
Specialties: Period pieces and working knives. **Patterns:** Hunters, fighters, tomahawks, buckskinners and camp knives. **Technical:** Forges 1095 and his own Damascus, and files. **Prices:** $35 to $200. **Remarks:** Part-time maker; first knife sold in 1978. **Mark:** JK connected

RAYMOND L. KREMZNER, 6620 Bonnie Ridge Dr., Baltimore, MD 21209-1940/301-653-2657
Specialties: Working straight knives in traditional styles, some fancy. **Patterns:** Hunters, fighters, Bowies and camp knives. **Technical:** Forges 5160, 9260, W2 and his own Damascus. **Prices:** $125 to $500. **Remarks:** Part-time maker; apprenticed to W.V. Fielder; sold first knife in 1987. **Mark:** Last name

D.F. KRESSLER, Lochhauser Strasse 86, 8039 Puchheim, WEST GERMANY/08142-30907
Specialties: High-tech working knives. **Patterns:** Hunters, fighters, daggers; follows Loveless style. **Technical:** Grinds new state-of-the-art steels; prefers natural handle materials. **Prices:** Upscale. **Mark:** Name in logo

directory/custom knifemakers

PHILIP W. KRETSINGER, JR., Rt. #1, Box 158, Boonsboro, MD 21713/301-432-6771
Specialties: Period pieces in traditional and fancy styles. **Patterns:** Hunters, Bowies, camp knives, daggers, carvers, fighters. **Technical:** Forges W2 and 1095 and his own Damascus. **Prices:** $100 to $500; some to $1,500. **Remarks:** Full-time production. Strict attention to balance and temper. **Mark:** Name, city and state

AL KROUSE, 1903 Treble Drive #4A, Humble, TX 77338/713-446-5503
Specialties: Straight working knives in traditional patterns. **Patterns:** Bowies, hunters, skinners, and fish knives; some miniatures. **Technical:** Grinds 01, 440C and 154CM. Does own heat-treating and embellishments. **Prices:** $90 to $275; some to $750. **Remarks:** Full-time maker; first knife sold in 1981. **Mark:** KROUSE

MARTIN KRUSE, P.O. Box 487, Reseda, CA 91335/818-713-0172
Specialties: Period pieces, fighters and straight working knives. **Patterns:** Full line of straight knives, swords, fighters, axes, tomahawks, razors, claws, and push knives. **Technical:** Grinds and forges 01, 1095, 5160 and Damascus; differential tempering. **Prices:** $85 to $700; some to $2,000. **Remarks:** Full-time maker; first knife sold in 1964. **Mark:** Initials

HANK KUBAIKO, Box 521485, Big Lake, AK 99652
Specialties: Working straight and folding knives. **Patterns:** Bowies, fighters, fish knives, kitchen cutlery, lockers, and slip-joints, camp knives, axes and miniatures. **Technical:** Grinds 440C, ATS34, AEB-L and D2. Worked under Joe Cordova. **Prices:** Moderate. **Remarks:** Part-time maker in summer, full-time in winter; first knife sold in 1982. **Mark:** Alaskan Maid and Name in logo

KUNI MITSU (See Michael Bell)

JIM KUYKENDALL, P.O. Box 539, Tulare, CA 93275/209-686-6130
Specialties: Fancy working knives. **Patterns:** Straight hunters, Bowies, buckskinners; developing full line in Japanese style. **Technical:** Grinds and forges A2, ATS34 and 440C. **Prices:** $75 to $240; some to $900. **Remarks:** Full-time maker; first knife sold in 1982. **Mark:** Name

JIM LADD, 1120 Helen, Deer Park, TX 77536/713-479-7286
Specialties: Period pieces and working knives. **Patterns:** Hunters, boots, Bowies and some other straight knives. **Technical:** Grinds D2, 440C and 154CM. **Prices:** $125 to $225; some to $550. **Remarks:** Part-time maker; first knife sold in 1965. **Mark:** J.S. Ladd

JIMMIE L. LADD, 1120 Helen, Deer Park, TX 77536/713-479-7186
Specialties: Working straight knives. **Patterns:** Hunters, skinners, and utility knives. **Technical:** Grinds 440C, and D2. **Prices:** $75 to $225. **Remarks:** First knife sold at the age of 13, he's now 22. **Mark:** Name

TONY LAINSON, 114 Park Ave., Council Bluffs, IA 51503/712-322-5222
Specialties: Straight working knives, folding lockers, tantos and short swords. **Technical:** Grinds ATS34, and 440C. Prefers mirror finishes and Micarta and pakkawood as handle materials. **Prices:** $32 to $280; some to $450. **Remarks:** Part-time maker; first knife sold in 1987. **Mark:** Name and state

RON LAKE, 3360 Bendix Ave., Eugene, OR 97401/503-484-2683
Specialties: High-tech working knives; inventor of the modern interframe folder. **Patterns:** Hunters, boots, other small straight knives; folding lockers. **Technical:** Grinds 154CM and ATS34; fine workmanship. Patented interframe with special lock release tab. **Prices:** $900 to $1,200; some to $4,000. **Remarks:** Full-time maker; first knife sold in 1968. **Mark:** LAKE

FRANK G. LAMPSON, 2052 I Rd., Fruita, CO 81521/303-858-7292
Specialties: Fancy working folders. **Patterns:** Full range of using designs, both straight and folding; some Bowies, and art knives. **Technical:** Grinds A2, 440C and 154CM. **Prices:** $80 to $280; some to $2,500. **Remarks:** Full-time maker; first knife sold in 1971. **Mark:** Name in fish logo

ED LANE, 440 N. Topping, Kansas City, MO 64123/816-241-3217
Specialties: Fancy working knives to order. **Patterns:** Buckskinners, hunters, fighters, tantos, fish knives, and working folders. **Technical:** Grinds 440C, 154CM, ATS34 and commercial Damascus; prefers knives very sharp. **Prices:** $65 to $350; some to $1,000. **Remarks:** Full-time maker; first knife sold in 1982. **Mark:** Signature

JERRY I. LANE, 1529 Stafford, Carbondale, IL 62901/618-549-2087

Specialties: Working straight knives. **Patterns:** Hunters, Bowies; does some tomahawks and buckle knives. **Technical:** Grinds 440C, 154CM and 01; makes knives to be used. **Prices:** $125 to $450; some to $3,000. **Remarks:** Full-time maker; first knife sold in 1970. **Mark:** J.I. LANE

GENE H. LANGLEY, Rt. 1, Box 426, Florence, SC 29501/803-669-3150
Specialties: Working knives in standard patterns. **Patterns:** Hunters, boots, fighters, folding lockers and slip joints. **Technical:** Grinds 440C, 154CM and ATS34. **Prices:** $70 to $165; some $475. **Remarks:** Spare-time maker; first knife sold in 1979. **Mark:** Name or Name, city and state

MICK LANGLEY, Box 2313, Qualicum Beach, B.C. V0R 2T0, CANADA/604-752-5856
Specialties: Period pieces and working knives. **Patterns:** Fighters, tantos, boots, minis and miniatures; some folding lockers. **Technical:** Forges W2, 01 and his own Damascus. **Prices:** $150 to $1,000; some to $2,500. **Remarks:** Full-time maker; first knife sold in 1977. **Mark:** LANGLEY with M.S. (for ABS Master Smith)

SCOTT LANKTON, 8065 Jackson Rd., Ann Arbor, MI 48103/313-426-3735
Specialties: Krisses, Viking swords, the non-standard forged blade. **Patterns:** Generally one-of-a-kind in series; cloisoneé enameled handles were one such. **Technical:** Forges W2, L6 and his own Damascus. **Prices:** $300 to $900; some to $4,000. **Remarks:** Part-time maker, full-time smith; first knife sold in 1976. **Mark:** LANKTON logo

CHARLES LAPEN, 40 North St., Ware, MA 01082/413-967-7974
Specialties: Fancy straight working knives. **Patterns:** Camp knives, Japanese-style swords, and wood working tools. **Technical:** Forges 1075, 9260, and his own Damascus. Favors narrow Japanese tangs. **Prices:** $200 to $400; some to $2,000. **Remarks:** Full-time maker; first knife sold in 1972. **Mark:** LAPEN

BRETT LAPLANTE, 301 Coral Circle, Richardson, TX 75081/214-783-9201
Specialties: Working straight and folding knives. **Patterns:** Survival knives, Bowies, skinners, hunters, and folders. **Technical:** Grinds D2, and 440C. Does own heat-treat. Welcomes customer designs. **Prices:** $55 to $190. **Remarks:** Part-time maker; first knife sold in 1987. **Mark:** Laplante in Canadian maple leaf logo

KEN LARGIN, 110 W. Pearl, Batesville, IN 47006/812-934-5938
Specialties: Working knives in standard patterns, some at low prices. **Patterns:** Hunters, tantos, swords, hatchets and folding butterflies. **Technical:** Grinds 01, 440C and buys Damascus; does filework. **Prices:** $49 to $150; some to $500. **Remarks:** Full-time maker; first knife sold in 1980. **Mark:** KELGIN or name

ED LARY, 651 Rangeline Rd., Mosinee, WI 54455/715-693-3940
Specialties: Fancy working straight and folding knives; period pieces. **Patterns:** Hunters, buckskinners, folding lockers, in his own design. **Technical:** Grinds A2, D2, 440C, and 154CM. Likes filework. **Prices:** $125 to $500. **Remarks:** Part-time maker; first knife sold in 1974. **Mark:** Name in script

DON LAUGHLIN, 190 Laughlin Dr., Vidor, TX 77662/409-769-3390
Specialties: Working knives of his design. **Patterns:** Hunters, fighters, Bowies, folding lockers and two-blades. **Technical:** Grinds D2, 440C and 154CM. **Prices:** $75 to $200; some to $350. **Remarks:** Full-time maker; first knife sold in 1973. **Mark:** DEER or full name

STEPHEN M. LAWSON, 2638 Baker Rd., Placerville, CA 95667/916-626-1782
Specialties: Fancy working knives in his design or yours. **Patterns:** Cleavers, Bowies, fish and push knives; locking folders. **Technical:** Grinds 440C, 154CM and ATS34; engraves his own knives. **Prices:** $160 to $1,500; some to $2,500. **Remarks:** Full-time maker; first knife sold in 1978. **Mark:** S. LAWSON

L.J. LAY, 602 Mimosa Dr., Burkburnett, TX 76354/817-569-1329
Specialties: Working straight knives in traditional patterns, some period style. **Patterns:** Drop point hunters, some Bowies and fighters. **Technical:** Grinds ATS34 to mirror finish; likes linen Micarta. **Prices:** Moderate. **Remarks:** Part-time maker; sold first knife in 1985. **Mark:** Name and serial

MIKE J. LEACH, 5377 W. Grand Blanc Rd., Swartz Creek, MI 48473/313-655-4850
Specialties: Fancy working knives. **Patterns:** Hunters, fighters, Bowies, heavy-duty knives. Does slip joint folders and integral straight patterns. **Technical:** Grinds D2, 440C, 154CM; buys Damascus. **Prices:** $120 to $600; some to $2,500. **Remarks:** Part-time maker; first knife sold in 1952. **Mark:** LEACH

PAUL M. LeBATARD, 14700 Old River Rd., Vancleave, MS 39564/601-826-4137 **Specialties:** Sound working knives, some fancy. **Patterns:** Utility hunters, small game and fish knives, Bowies, survival and boot knives, camp and kitchen cutlery. **Technical:** Grinds D2, 440C, and ATS34. **Prices:** $50 to $250; some to $350. **Remarks:** Part-time maker; first knife sold in 1974. **Mark:** LEBATARD

HEINZ LEBER, Box 446, Hudson Hope, BC VOC 1V0, CANADA/604-783-5304 **Specialties:** Working straight and folding knives for use. **Patterns:** Personal hunter designs, kitchen knives, work knives for trappers. **Technical:** Grinds M2; uses some L6 and 01; likes moose antler for handles. **Prices:** $125 to $200; some to $500. **Remarks:** Full-time maker; sold first knife in 1975. **Mark:** HL connected

BRACY R. LEDFORD, 1917 Northgate St., Indianapolis, IN 46208/317-253-9740 **Specialties:** Working knives and some fantasy knives. **Patterns:** Bowies, locking folders and hunters. **Technical:** Files and sandpapers A2, D2, and 440C; no power tools used—all done by hand. **Prices:** $125 to $350; some to $500. **Remarks:** Part-time maker; first knife sold in 1983. **Mark:** B.R. LEDFORD

TOMMY LEE, Rt. 2, Box 392, Gaffney, SC 29340/803-489-6699 **Specialties:** Period pieces and working knives. **Patterns:** Fighters, boots, daggers and axes; folding lockers, slip joints in traditional styles. **Technical:** Forges and grinds; uses 440C, ATS34 and his own and commercial Damascus. **Prices:** $150 to $300; some to $1,500. **Remarks:** Full-time maker; first knife sold in 1974. **Mark:** LEE

NICK LEONE, 9 Georgetown, Pontoon Beach, IL 62040/618-797-1179 **Specialties:** Working straight knives. **Patterns:** Bowies, skinners, hunters, miniatures, and kitchen cutlery. **Technical:** Forges 5160 and 01. **Prices:** $25 to $200. **Remarks:** Part-time maker; first knife sold in 1987. **Mark:** LEONE or NL on miniatures

BILL LEVENGOOD, 15011 Otto Rd., Tampa, FL 33624/813-961-5688 **Specialties:** Straight and folding working knives. **Patterns:** Hunters, bird and trout, kitchen, and fillet knives. **Technical:** Grinds ATS34, 440C, and D2. **Prices:** $65 to $500. **Remarks:** Full-time maker; first knife sold in 1983. **Mark:** Levengood or BL

BOB LEVINE, 3201 Iowa Drive, Anchorage, AK 99517/907-243-3878 **Specialties:** Working straight knives in traditional styles. **Patterns:** Full range of hunters, fighters, Bowies, tantos; makes all as miniatures as well. **Technical:** Grinds 440C, AEB-L, and ATS34; works backs. **Prices:** $85 to $135; some to $300. **Remarks:** Full-time maker; sold first knife in 1984. **Mark:** Name in logo

NORMAN LEVINE, Spring Valley Lake #7707, Victorville, CA 92392/619-245-1661 **Specialties:** Fancy art knives. **Patterns:** Hunters, boots, daggers, folding lockers and slip joints in gents and hunter patterns. **Technical:** Grinds 440C, 154CM, ATS34; provides ball bearing pivot in folders. **Prices:** $85 to $200; some to $1,500. **Remarks:** Full-time maker; first knife sold in 1974. **Mark:** Dragon on shield, with name

RON LEWIS, Box S-365, Edgewood, NM 87015/505-281-8343 **Specialties:** Classic design straight knives. **Patterns:** Bowies, skinners, buckskinners, and utility knives. **Technical:** Grinds 1095, 1084, and 440C. Welcomes customer designs. **Prices:** $75 to $300. **Remarks:** Full-time maker; first knife sold in 1987. **Mark:** Name or logo with serial #

TOM R. LEWIS, 1613 Standpipe Rd., Carlsbad, NM 88220/505-885-3616 **Specialties:** Traditional working straight knives. **Patterns:** Outdoors knives and tantos and Bowies. **Technical:** Grinds and forges; offers 440C and ATS34 and welded wire Damascus. **Prices:** $60 to $175; some to $300. **Remarks:** Part-time maker; sold first knife in 1980. **Mark:** TRL

STEVE LIKARICH, 2780 Randolph Ave., Carmichael, CA 95608/916-481-5326 **Specialties:** Traditional designs in straight knives. **Patterns:** Likes oriental designs, such as tantos and Persian curves. **Technical:** Grinds stainless steels; likes high polishes and filework. **Prices:** NA. **Remarks:** New maker; working part-time. **Mark:** Name

LIL BEAR KNIVES (See Larry Berzas)

JIMMY (JAMES B.) LILE, Rt. 6, Box 27, Russellville, AR 72801/501-968-2011 **Specialties:** Creator of the original *First Blood* and *Rambo* survival knives. Makes fancy working knives. **Patterns:** Bowies and full line of straight knives and his own pattern in button-locking folders. **Technical:** Grinds D2 and 440C. **Prices:** $125 to $800; some "unlimited." **Remarks:** Full-time maker; first knife sold in 1944. **Mark:** Lile

CHRIS A. LINDSAY, 16237 Dyke Rd., La Pine, OR 97739/503-536-2386 **Specialties:** Working knives in standard patterns. **Patterns:** Hunters, kitchen and camp knives. **Technical:** Grinds D2, 440C and 154CM; brushed finishes, tapered tangs, hollow or flat ground. **Prices:** $65 to $130. **Remarks:** Part-time maker; first knife sold in 1980. **Mark:** Lindsay

GARY M. LITTLE, HC84 Box 10301, Broadbent, OR 97414-9801/503-572-2656 **Specialties:** Fancy working knives to order. **Patterns:** Hunters, tantos, Bowies, axes and buckskinners; folding lockers and interframes. **Technical:** Forges and grinds 01, L6, 1095 and makes his own Damascus; bronze fittings. **Prices:** $85 to $300; some to $2,500. **Remarks:** Full-time maker; first knife sold in 1979. **Mark:** Name, city and state

STERLING LOCKETT, 527 E. Amherst Dr., Burbank, CA 91504/818-846-5799 **Specialties:** Customer designs in working straight and folding knives. **Patterns:** Hunters and fighters. **Technical:** Grinds. **Prices:** Moderate. **Remarks:** Spare-time maker. **Mark:** Name, city with hearts

WOLFGANG LOERCHNER, P.O. Box 255, Bayfield, Ont. N0M 1G0, CANADA/519-565-2196 **Specialties:** Straight traditional knives, some fancy. **Patterns:** Bowies, swords, hunters, bird knives and miniatures; folding lockers and interframes; making elaborate daggers as well. **Technical:** Grinds D2, 440C, and 154CM; all knives hand-filed and flat ground. **Prices:** $150 to $600; some to $3,000. **Remarks:** Part-time maker; first knife sold in 1983. **Mark:** WOLFE

BOB LOFLIN, Rt. 7, Box 199A, Fayetteville, AR 72701/501-521-4907 **Specialties:** Fancy working knives in his own designs. **Patterns:** Hunters, fighters and camp knives; locking folders. **Technical:** Grinds D2, 440C and ATS34. **Prices:** $75 to $250; some to $700. **Remarks:** Part-time maker; first knife sold in 1983. **Mark:** Name

LONESOME PINE (See Larry W. Harley)

DAVE LONGWORTH, 151 McMurchy, Bethel, OH 45106/513-734-7719 **Specialties:** High-tech working knives in clean designs. **Patterns:** Folding lockers, hunters, fighters, and elaborate daggers. **Technical:** Grinds 01, 440C and buys Damascus. **Prices:** $125 to $600; some upscale. **Remarks:** Full-time maker; first knife sold in 1980. **Mark:** Longworth

ED LOVE, 125 Carriage Trace Dr., Stockbridge, GA 30281/404-389-3544 **Specialties:** Fancy working knives in standard patterns, and occasional custom designs. **Patterns:** Hunters, Bowies and fish knives. **Technical:** Grinds ATS34. **Prices:** $75 to $140; some to $250. **Remarks:** Part-time maker; first knife sold in 1980. **Mark:** Name in oval logo

R.W. LOVELESS, P.O. Box 7836, Arlington Sta., Riverside, CA 92503/714-689-7800 **Specialties:** Master designer of working knives, fighters and hunters. **Patterns:** Hunters, fighters and boots in the contemporary line he originated. **Technical:** Grinds 154CM and ATS34. **Prices:** $500 to $1,850; some to $3,000. **Remarks:** Full-time maker; still working on orders. **Mark:** Name in logo

SCHUYLER LOVESTRAND, 325 Rolfe Dr., Apopka, FL 32703/407-886-0494 **Specialties:** Fancy working straight knives; welcomes designs from customers. **Patterns:** Hunters, fighters, Bowies and fish knives. **Technical:** Grinds 440C, ATS34 and commercial Damascus. **Prices:** Under $100 to $400; some higher. **Remarks:** Part-time maker; first knife sold in 1982. **Mark:** Name, city and state in logo

MIKE LOVETT, 3219E Rancier, Killeen, TX 76543/817-690-1122 **Specialties:** High-tech straight and folding knives for the hunter and soldier. **Patterns:** Bowies, fighters, small hunters, boots, folders for gents and ladies. **Technical:** Grinds D2 to mirror finish, 440C, ATS34, Vascowear and several types of Damascus. **Prices:** $100 to $500; some to $2,500. **Remarks:** Full-time maker; sold first knife in 1975. **Mark:** A chess knight with name

BILL LUCKETT, 10 Amantes Lane, Weatherford, TX 76086/ 817-599-4629 **Specialties:** Uniquely patterned robust straight knives. **Patterns:** Fighters, Bowies and tantos; making hunters now. **Technical:** Grinds 440C, 154CM and commercial Damascus; heavy knives, deep grinding, attention-getting work. **Prices:** $350 to $750; some to $2,000. **Remarks:** Part-time maker; first knife sold in 1975. **Mark:** Last name over Bowie logo

RONALD LUI, 4042 Harding Ave., Honolulu, HI 96816/808-734-7746
Specialties: Working straight knives in traditional styles. **Patterns:** Hunters, boots. **Technical:** Grinds 440C, and ATS34. **Prices:** $75 to $200. **Remarks:** Spare-time maker; first knife sold in 1988. **Mark:** RML connected

ROBERT W. LUM, 901 Travis Ave., Eugene, OR 97404/503-688-2737
Specialties: High art working knives of his own design. **Patterns:** Hunters, fighters and tantos. **Technical:** Grinds 440C, 154CM and ATS34; plans to forge soon. **Prices:** $175 to $500; some to $800. **Remarks:** Full-time maker; first knife sold in 1976. **Mark:** Chop with Lum underneath

JAN-AKE LUNDSTROM, Mastmostigen 8, 66010 Dals-Langed, SWEDEN/0611-41259
Specialties: Viking swords, axes and knives in cooperation with handlemakers. **Patterns:** All traditional styles, especially swords and inlaid blades. **Technical:** Forges his own Damascus and laminated steel. **Prices:** $200 to $1,000. **Remarks:** Sold first knife in 1985; works full-time; collaborates with museums. **Mark:** Runic

ROBERT LUTES, 24878 U.S.6 (R.R. 1), Nappanee, IN 46550/219-773-4773
Specialties: Straight working knives—his design and standard patterns. **Patterns:** Hunters, fighters, boots and axes. **Technical:** Grinds 440C, and bought Damascus. **Prices:** $50 to $1,500. **Remarks:** Part-time maker; first knife sold in 1980. Offers knives with stone handles. **Mark:** Lutes

ERNEST L. LYLE, III, 4501 Meadowbrook Ave., Orlando, FL 32808/407-299-7227
Specialties: Fancy period pieces in standard patterns. **Patterns:** Arabian/Persian influenced fighters, Bowies and Roman short swords. Offers minis and miniatures, too. **Technical:** Grinds D2, 440C and 154CM. **Prices:** $110 to $500; some to $2,100. **Remarks:** Part-time maker; first knife sold in 1972. **Mark:** LYLE

BRIAN LYTTLE, Box 1180, High River, AB T0L IB0, CANADA/403-558-3638
Specialties: Fancy straight and folding working knives, some art knives. **Patterns:** Hunters, Bowies, Persian fighters, camp knives, lockbacks, and miniatures. **Technical:** Forges his own Damascus; offers scrimshaw and forged jewelry to Damascus spurs. **Prices:** $175 to $800; some $2,000. **Remarks:** Full-time maker; first knife sold in 1983. **Mark:** BL chiseled into the handle

MW KNIVES (See Mark Wahlster)

M. W. KNIVES (See Mike Wesolowski)

KENNETH C. MacBAIN, 30 Briarwood Ave., Norwood, NJ 07648/201-768-0652
Specialties: Straight and folding fantasy knives, some high tech. **Patterns:** Swords, knife-rings, push daggers, and some miniatures. **Technical:** Forges and grinds A2, W2, and 01. **Prices:** $200 to $500; some $2,500. **Remarks:** Part-time maker; first knife sold in 1986. **Mark:** KCM

MIKE MACRI, Box 222, Churchill, MB R0B 0E0, CANADA/204-675-2195
Specialties: Straight working knives in traditional patterns. **Patterns:** Arctic survival knives, tantos, Bowies, camp knives and locking folders. **Technical:** Grinds 440C, ATS34 and bought Damascus. Full-tapered tangs and hollow grinds. **Prices:** $100 to $500; some to $2,000. **Remarks:** Full-time maker; first knife sold in 1982. **Mark:** MACRI

MADRONA KNIVES (See Adrienne Rice)

JACK MADSEN, 3311 Northwest Dr., Wichita Falls, TX 76305/817-322-4112
Specialties: Working straight knives in traditional patterns. **Patterns:** Bowies, hunters, swords, tomahawks and heavy-duty camp knives. **Technical:** Forges W2, 01 and his own Damascus. **Prices:** $85 to $350; some to $1,000. **Remarks:** Full-time maker; first knife sold in 1975. **Mark:** Name and city

PETER A. MAESTRI, Rt. 1, Box 111, Spring Green, WI 53588/608-546-4481
Specialties: Straight working knives in traditional styles. **Patterns:** Camping and fishing knives, utility green-river styled. **Technical:** Grinds 440C, 154CM and 440A; professional cutler service to professional cutters. **Prices:** $5 to $25; some $150. **Remarks:** Full-time maker; first knife sold in 1981. **Mark:** CARISOLO or signature

JEFFREY G. MALITZKE, 4804 Lovers Lane, Wichita Falls, TX 76310/817-692-2604
Specialties: Straight knives. **Patterns:** Standard and traditional. **Technical:** Forges his own Damascus in precise patterns. **Mark:** Name

KENNETH MANEKER, R.R. 2, Galiano Island, B.C. V0N 1P0, CANADA/604-539-2084

Specialties: Period pieces and straight working knives. **Patterns:** Camp knives and hunters; French chef knives. **Technical:** Grinds 440C, 154CM and Vascowear. **Prices:** $50 to $200; some to $300. **Remarks:** Part-time maker; first knife sold in 1981. Water Mountain Knives label. **Mark:** Japanese Kanji, KM connected plus glyph

DAN MARAGNI, R.D. 1, Box 106, Georgetown, NY 13072/315-662-7490
Specialties: Heavy-duty working knives; some are investor class. **Patterns:** Hunters, fighters and camp knives; some Scottish types. **Technical:** Forges W2 and his own Damascus; gives toughness and edge holding a high priority. **Prices:** $125 to $500; some to $1,000. **Remarks:** Full-time maker; ABS Master; first knife sold in 1975. **Mark:** Celtic DM in circle

TOM MARINGER, 2306 S. Powell St., Springdale, AR 72764/501-751-9220
Specialties: High-tech and fantasy straight knives to order. Investor class work. **Patterns:** Swords, axes, daggers; state-of-the-art fighters; wire wrapped handles; Kydex sheaths. **Technical:** Grinds 01, D2 and 154CM; forges some. **Prices:** $350 to $3,000; some to $10,000. **Remarks:** Full-time maker; first knife sold 1975. **Mark:** Full name, serial number and year

CHRIS MARKS, Rt. 2 Box 879-R, Breaux Bridge, LA 70517/318-332-3930
Specialties: Traditional working knives; some period pieces. **Patterns:** Full range of straight knives, all the way to tomahawks. **Technical:** Forges W2, 1095 and his own Damascus. **Prices:** $165 to $400; some to $1,500. **Remarks:** Full-time maker; sold first knife in 1980. **Mark:** Name in anvil logo

GLENN MARSHALL, P.O. Box 1099 (305 Hofmann St.), Mason, TX 76856/915-347-6207
Specialties: Period pieces and working knives to order. **Patterns:** Straight and folding hunters, fighters and camp knives. **Technical:** Grinds and forges; uses 01, D2 and 440C. **Prices:** $90 to $150; some to $450. **Remarks:** Full-time maker; first knife sold in 1932. **Mark:** G. MARSHALL, city and state with anvil logo

PETER MARZITELLI, 14143 110A Ave., Surrey, BC V3R 2B2, CANADA/604-581-6759
Specialties: Straight working knives in traditional patterns. **Patterns:** Hunters, tantos, camp, kitchen and fish knives. **Technical:** Grinds 154CM. **Prices:** $100 to $350. **Remarks:** Part-time maker; first knife sold in 1984. **Mark:** Circular logo reads "Marz"

MASA.T (See Masao Takahashi)

BILL MASON, 1114 St. Louis, #33, Excelsior Springs, MO 64024/816-637-7335
Specialties: Combat knives; some folders. **Patterns:** Designs fighters to suit techniques in book Cold Steel. **Technical:** Grinds 01, 440C and ATS34. **Prices:** $115 to $250; some to $350. **Remarks:** Spare-time maker; first knife sold in 1979. **Mark:** BM connected

MAX'S GUNSHOP (See Max Mitchell)

LYNN MAXFIELD, 382 Colonial Ave., Layton, UT 84041/801-544-4176
Specialties: Working knives, some fancy. **Patterns:** Hunters, survival and fish knives; some folding lockers. **Technical:** Grinds D2, 440C and 154CM. **Prices:** $90 to $250; some to $600. **Remarks:** Full-time maker; first knife sold in 1979. **Mark:** Name, city and state

JAMES E. MAY, Rt. 2, Box 191, Auxvasse, MO 65231/314-386-2910
Specialties: Working knives in his own designs. **Patterns:** Hunters, Bowies, fighters, boots, and folders. **Technical:** Grinds D2 and 440C. **Prices:** $45 to $250; some to $350. **Remarks:** Spare-time maker; first knife sold in 1978. **Mark:** J in diamond

LARRY JOE MAYNARD, Box 85, Helen, WV 25853/304-774-0134
Specialties: Fancy and fantasy straight knives. **Patterns:** Big knives; makes a Bowie with full false edge, and fighting knives. **Technical:** Grinds standard steels. **Prices:** $350 to $500; some to $1,000. **Remarks:** Full-time maker; sold first knife in 1986. **Mark:** J.K.

TOM MAYO, JR., 67-177 Kanoulu St., Waialua, HI 96791/808-637-6560
Specialties: Straight working knives. **Patterns:** Hunters, fighters, boots, locking folders and miniatures. **Technical:** Grinds D2, 440C and ATS34. **Prices:** $125 to $250; some to $500. **Remarks:** Part-time maker; first knife sold in 1983. **Mark:** Volcano logo with name and state

OSCAR L. MAYVILLE, 5660 Cooper Rd., Indianapolis, IN 46208/317-298-4912
Specialties: Period pieces and straight working knives. **Patterns:** Kitchen cutlery,

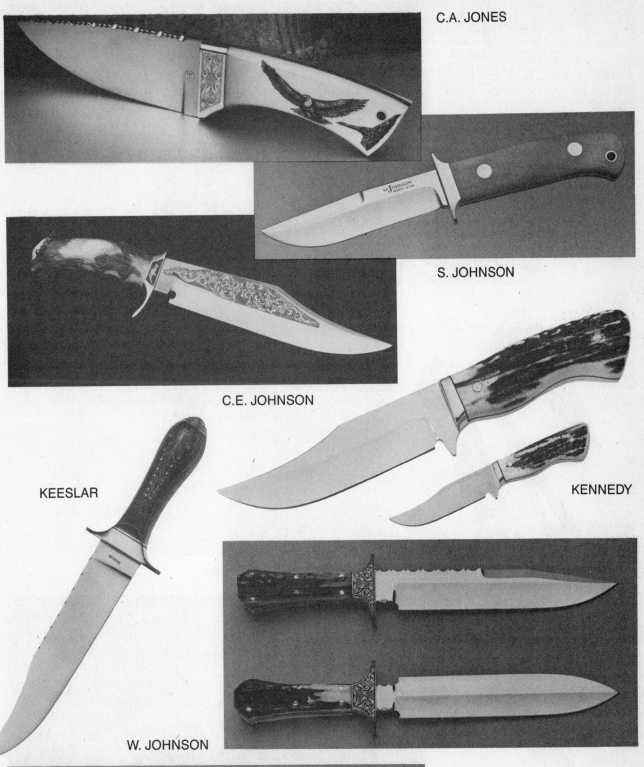

C.A. JONES

S. JOHNSON

C.E. JOHNSON

KEESLAR

KENNEDY

W. JOHNSON

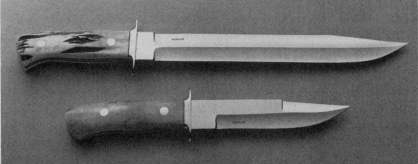

KESSLER

KNIPSCHIELD

LARGIN

LANGLEY

KITZMILLER

LAPEN

KI

LARY

LAMPSON

N. LEVINE

LITTLE

R. LEWIS

LILE

LUI

LOERCHNER

LOVESTRAND

Bowies, camp knives and hunters. **Technical:** Grinds A2, 01, and 440C. **Prices:** $50 to $350; some to $500. **Remarks:** Part-time maker; first knife sold in 1984. **Mark:** Initials over knife logo

HARVEY McBURNETTE, P.O. Box 227, Eagle Nest, NM 87718/505-377-6254
Specialties: Fancy working folders; some in customer designs. **Patterns:** Front-locking folders; traditional straight knives. **Technical:** Grinds D2, 440C and 154CM; engraves his own. **Prices:** $200 to $400; some to $1,200. **Remarks:** Full-time maker; first knife sold in 1972. **Mark:** McBURNETTE, city and state

JOHN McCARLEY, 1710 Keysville Rd. So., Keymar, MD 21757/301-775-2464
Specialties: Period pieces and working straight knives. **Patterns:** Hunters, Bowies, camp knives, miniatures; also throwing knives. **Technical:** Forges W2, 01, and his own Damascus. **Prices:** $150 to $300; some to $1,000. **Remarks:** Part-time maker; first knife sold in 1977. **Mark:** J.M. in script

HARRY McCARTY, 1121 Brough Ave., Hamilton, OH 45015/513-868-2290
Specialties: Period pieces and straight working knives. **Patterns:** Bowies, camp knives, daggers and buckskinner designs. **Technical:** Grinds and forges; uses 01 and D2. **Prices:** $75 to $350; some to $600. **Remarks:** Part-time maker; first knife sold in 1977. **Mark:** Name or initials

ZOLLAN McCARTY, 101 1/2 Ave. E, Thomaston, GA 30286/404-647-6869
Specialties: Period pieces and working knives. **Patterns:** Wide variety of straight and folding knives; Scagel replicas; gut hook hatchets. **Technical:** Forges and grinds; uses 440C, 154CM and ATS34. **Prices:** $110 to $600. **Remarks:** Full-time maker; first knife sold in 1971. **Mark:** Z. McCARTY

CHARLES R. McCONNELL, 158 Genteel Ridge, Wellsburg, WV 26070/304-737-2015
Specialties: Straight working knives. **Patterns:** Hunters, Bowies, daggers, minis and push knives. **Technical:** Grinds 440C and 154CM; likes full tangs. **Prices:** $65 to $325; some to $800. **Remarks:** Part-time maker; first knife sold in 1977. **Mark:** Name

LOYD A. McCONNELL, JR., P.O. Box 7162, Odessa, TX 79760/915-366-9674
Specialties: Working straight and folding knives; some fancy. **Patterns:** Hunters, boots, Bowies, folding lockers and slip joints. Makes black-finish specials. **Technical:** Grinds A2, 154CM and commercial Damascus. **Prices:** $125 to $2,500; some to $4,000. **Remarks:** Part-time maker; first knife sold in 1978. **Mark:** Name, city and state in cactus logo

V. J. McCRACKIN and SON, 3720 Hess Rd., House Springs, MO 63051/314-376-4242
Specialties: Straight working knives in traditional patterns. **Patterns:** Hunters, Bowies, camp knives and tomahawks. **Technical:** Forges L6, 5160, and his own Damascus. **Prices:** $50 to $150; some $400. **Remarks:** Part-time maker; first knife sold in 1983. Son Kevin helps make the knives. **Mark:** McCRACKIN

LARRY E. McCULLOUGH, Route 4, Box 556, Mocksville, NC 27028/704-634-5632
Specialties: Straight working knives. **Patterns:** Hunters, boots, Bowies and push knives. **Technical:** Grinds D2, 440C and 154CM; scrims. **Prices:** $60 to $250; some to $500. **Remarks:** Spare-time maker; first knife sold in 1978. **Mark:** McCullough

DAVE McDEARMONT, 1618 Parkside Trail, Lewisville, TX 7567/214-436-4335
Specialties: High-tech working knives. **Patterns:** Hunters, buckskinners, fighters and boots. **Technical:** Grinds 440C; full tangs, mirror finishes. **Prices:** $125 to $300; some to $800. **Remarks:** Part-time maker; first knife sold in 1981. **Mark:** Name

KEN McFALL, P.O. Box 458, Lakeside, AZ 85929/602-537-2026
Specialties: Fancy working straight knives. **Patterns:** Daggers, boots, tantos, Bowies; some miniatures. **Technical:** Grinds D2, 154CM, and ATS34; does gold and silver inlay. **Prices:** $125 to $500; some $800. **Remarks:** Part-time maker; first knife sold in 1984. **Mark:** Name, city, and state

JOHN McGILL, P.O. Box 302, Blairsville, GA 30512/404-745-4686
Specialties: Working knives. **Patterns:** Traditional patterns; likes camp knives. **Technical:** Forges L6 and 9260; makes Damascus. **Prices:** $50 to $250; some to $500. **Remarks:** Full-time maker; first knife sold in 1982. **Mark:** XYLO

JIM McGOVERN, 31 Scenic Dr., Oak Ridge, NJ 07438/201-697-4558
Specialties: Working straight knives. **Patterns:** Hunters and boots. **Technical:**

Grinds 440C, ATS34, in full tapered tang and hollow grind. **Prices:** $95 to $195; some to $400. **Remarks:** Part-time maker; sold first knife in 1985. **Mark:** Name

FRANK E. McGOWAN, 12629 Howard Lodge Dr., Sykesville, MD 21784/301-489-4323
Specialties: Customer designs, in fancy working knives. **Patterns:** Survivor knives, fighters, fish knives and hunters. **Technical:** Grinds 01, 440C, and ATS34. **Prices:** $75 to $300; some $500. **Remarks:** Full-time maker; first knife sold in 1986. **Mark:** McGowan

TOMMY McKISSACK II, P.O. Box 991, Sonora, TX 76950/915-387-3253
Specialties: Working knives, some fancy, most heavy-duty. **Patterns:** From swords to folders in his own designs, or yours. **Technical:** Grinds D2, 154CM, ATS34, Vascowear; is commercial heat-treater. **Prices:** $65 to $700; some to $2,100. **Remarks:** Full-time maker; first knife sold in 1980. **Mark:** Name, town and state

THOMAS McLANE, 7 Tucson Terrace, Tucson, AZ 83745/602-623-6895
Specialties: Period pieces and display-class working knives. **Patterns:** Traditional tantos, daggers, swords and razors; folding lockers, interframes, two-blades. **Technical:** Forges 01, 1095 and his own Damascus. Uses old metalworking techniques, especially Japanese. **Prices:** $300 to $2,000; some to $8,000. **Remarks:** Full-time maker; first knife sold in 1979. **Mark:** Initials in a logo

JAMES McLEOD, 941 Thermalito Ave., Oroville, CA 95965/916-533-3539
Specialties: Scottish period pieces and working knives. **Patterns:** Dirks and sgian dubhs; buckskinners, boots and daggers. **Technical:** Grinds, and files, A2, 154CM, ATS34; hand-sanded finishes; full or tapered tangs. **Prices:** $200 to $500; some to $2,500. **Remarks:** Spare-time maker; first knife sold in 1983; a McLeod clansman, their motto "HOLD FAST." Average production, 20 knives per year. **Mark:** Name and clan badge

SEAN McWILLIAMS, 4334 C.R. 509, Bayfield, CO 81122/303-884-9854
Specialties: Forged stainless fighters, folders, period pieces and working knives. **Patterns:** Fighters, buckskinners blades, swords, Bowies and daggers; folding lockers. **Technical:** Forges only; uses CPM-T-440V, 01, 440C, ATS34 and his own Damascus; all knives individually tempered. **Prices:** $180 to $500; some to $1,500. **Remarks:** Full-time maker; first knife sold in 1979. **Mark:** Stylized bear paw

RICHARD (Rick) MECCHI, 6504 Fair Ave., North Hollywood, CA 91606/818-980-8321
Specialties: Working straight knives, some fancy. **Patterns:** Hunters, daggers, Bowies, and fillets. **Technical:** Grinds 440C, ATS34, and 154CM. Exotic handle materials offered. **Prices:** $70 to $800. **Remarks:** Part-time maker; first knife sold in 1982. **Mark:** R. Mecchi maker

DARYL MEIER, R.R. 4, Carbondale, IL 62901/618-549-3234
Specialties: Damascus steel; buckskinner blades; swords. **Patterns:** Provides blades in collaboration; makes bars and forged blades for sale; makes production and high art tomahawks. **Technical:** Forges his own Damascus W1 and A203E; W1 and Nickel 200. **Prices:** $250 to $450; some to $6,000. **Remarks:** Full-time smith and researcher since 1974; first knife sold in 1974. **Mark:** Name or circle/arrow symbol or SHAWNEE

HARRY E. MENDENHALL, 1848 Everglades Dr., Milpitas, CA 95035/408-263-0677
Specialties: Working straight knives. **Patterns:** Hunters, boots, buckskinners, and push knives. **Technical:** Grinds 440C, 154CM, and ATS34; engraving and scrimshaw available. **Prices:** $65 to $150; some $1,000. **Remarks:** Full-time maker; first knife sold in 1970. Business name is Thunderbird. **Mark:** Thunderbird with logo, or signature

TED MERCHANT, 7 Old Garrett Ct., White Hall, MD 21161/301-343-0380
Specialties: Working knives in traditional and period styles. **Patterns:** Makes using knives for hunters; some Bowies and camp knives. **Technical:** Forges W2 and 5160. **Prices:** $150 to $450; some to $600. **Remarks:** Full-time maker; sold first knife in 1985. **Mark:** Name

ROBERT L. MERZ III, 20219 Prince Creek Dr., Katy, TX 77450/713-492-7337
Specialties: Straight working knives, some fancy. **Patterns:** Hunters, skinners, fighters, folders and camp knives. Own designs. **Technical:** Grinds 440C, D2, 01, ATS34, and commercial Damascus. **Prices:** $70 to $200; some to $550. **Remarks:** Part-time maker; sold first knife in 1974. **Mark:** MERZ and serial number

directory/custom knifemakers

CHRIS MILLER, JR., 3959 U.S. 27 South, Sebring, FL 33870/813-382-4402 **Specialties:** Fancy working straight knives. **Patterns:** Swords and large knives of all kinds, and a variety of working knives. **Technical:** Grinds D2, 440C, 154CM. **Prices:** $100 to $500. **Remarks:** Full-time maker; first knife sold in 1976. **Mark:** M on the blade

HANFORD J. MILLER, 5105 S. LeMaster Rd., Evergreen CO 80439/303-674-5263 **Specialties:** Period pieces and working knives in Moran style. **Patterns:** Bowies, fighters, camp knives and other large straight knives. **Technical:** Forges W2, 1095, 5160 and his own Damascus; differential tempers; wire inlay. **Prices:** $250 to $750; some to $1,500. **Remarks:** Part-time maker; first knife sold in 1968. **Mark:** Initials; name within Bowie logo

JAMES P. MILLER, 9024 Goeller Rd., R.R. 2, Fairbank, IA 50629/319-635-2294 **Specialties:** Period pieces and working knives. **Patterns:** Hunters, Bowies, camp knives and folding lockers. **Technical:** Forges and grinds; uses 1095, 440C, 5160 and his own Damascus. **Prices:** $75 to $350; some to $1,000. **Remarks:** Part-time maker; first knife sold in 1970. **Mark:** J. P. MILLER

R.D. MILLER, 10526 Estate Lane, Dallas, TX 75238/214-348-3496 **Specialties:** One-of-a-kind collector-type knives. **Patterns:** Boots, hunters, Bowies, camp and utility knives, fish and bird knives, and miniatures. **Technical:** Grinds a variety of steel to include 01, D2, 440C, 154CM and 1095. **Prices:** $65 to $300; some to $900. **Remarks:** Full-time maker; first knife sold in 1984. **Mark:** R.D. Custom Knives with date or with bow and arrow logo

RONALD T. MILLER, 12922 127th Ave. N., Largo, FL 33544/813-595-0378 (after 5 PM) **Specialties:** Straight working knives in traditional patterns. **Patterns:** Combat and camp knives, tantos, and kitchen cutlery; fillet knives; locking folders and butterflies. **Technical:** Grinds D2, 440C and ATS34; offers brass inlays and scrimshaw. Does own leatherwork. **Prices:** $35 to $125; some to $400. **Remarks:** Part-time maker; first knife sold in 1984. **Mark:** Name, city and state in palm tree logo

TED MILLER, P.O. Box 6328, Santa Fe, NM 87502/505-984-0338 **Specialties:** Carved antler display knives. **Patterns:** Hunters, swords, tomahawks and miniatures of his own designs. **Technical:** Grinds 440C. **Prices:** $110 to $350; some average $900. **Remarks:** Full-time maker; first knife sold in 1971. **Mark:** Initials and serial number

TERRY MILLER, 450 S. 1st, Seward, NE 68434/402-643-4726 **Specialties:** Working knives, some fancy. **Patterns:** Hunters, fighters, Bowies and folders; slip joints and locking. **Technical:** Grinds 440C. **Prices:** $90 to $145; some higher. **Remarks:** Full-time maker; first knife sold in 1978. **Mark:** Stylized name in knife logo

ANDY MILLS, 414 E. Schubert, Fredericksburg, TX 78624/512-997-8167 **Specialties:** Working straight and folding knives. **Patterns:** Hunter patterns, including folders. **Technical:** Grinds 440C, D2, A2, and 154CM. Does all—leatherwork, fabrication, heat treating. **Prices:** Moderate. **Remarks:** A Jim Barbee associate; full-time since 1984; sold first knife in 1980. **Mark:** Name

LOUIS G. MILLS (YASUTOMO), 9450 Water Rd., Ann Arbor, MI 48103/313-668-1839 **Specialties:** High art period pieces in Japanese mode. **Patterns:** Traditional tantos, daggers and swords. **Technical:** Makes own steel from iron; his own Damascus in traditional Japanese techniques. **Prices:** $900 to $2,000; some to $8,000. **Remarks:** Spare-time maker in partnership with Jim Kelso. **Mark:** Yasutomo in Japanese Kanji

MINERAL MTN. HATCHET WORKS (See Ted Frizzell)

JAMES A. MITCHELL, 1355 Autumnridge Dr., Columbus, GA 31904/404-322-8511 **Specialties:** Fancy working knives. Sells knives in sets. **Patterns:** Hunters, fighters, Bowies and folding lockers. **Technical:** Grinds D2, 440C and commercial Damascus. **Prices:** $100 to $400; some to $900. **Remarks:** Part-time maker; first knife sold in 1976. **Mark:** Signature and city

MAX and DEAN MITCHELL, 997 V.F.W. Road, Leesville, LA 71446/318-239-6416 **Specialties:** Period pieces and working knives. **Patterns:** Hunters, axes, tomahawks, buckskinners; makes hatchet-knife sets. **Technical:** Grinds 01, D2 and 440C. **Prices:** $120 to $200; some to $1,000. **Remarks:** Part-time makers; first knife sold in 1976. **Mark:** Max or Dean in oval logo

HARALD MOELLER, RR 3, Thornton, Ontario L0L 2N0, CANADA/705-424-6088 **Specialties:** Classy working straight knives. **Patterns:** Viper throwing knives. Has four new series: Crest, Canadian Hunter, Viper, and Bearclaw survival series. **Technical:** Grinds; mirror and sandblasted finishes in combination. **Prices:** $80 to $10,000. **Mark:** Name in logo

DELMAR R. MONTEGNA, P.O. Box 6261, Sheridan, WY 82801/307-672-2816 **Specialties:** Fancy working knives. **Patterns:** Hunters, boots and Bowies, as well as folding lockers. **Technical:** Grinds D2, 440C and 154CM; some knives embellished. **Prices:** $65 to $165. **Remarks:** Full-time maker. **Mark:** DELMAR Knives

CLAUDE MONTJOY, R.R. 2, Box 470C, Clinton, SC 29325/803-697-6160 **Specialties:** Fancy working knives. **Patterns:** Hunters, boots, fighters, folding lockers, slip joints and interframes. **Technical:** Grinds 440C, 154CM and ATS34; does filework. **Prices:** $75 to $125; some to $1,000. **Remarks:** Part-time maker; first knife sold in 1982. **Mark:** Montjoy

KEITH MOORBY, 63 Cawdor Rd., Sheffield, South Yorkshire S22EP, ENGLAND/0742-651400 **Specialties:** Working knives, many in Sheffield style. **Patterns:** Lockback folders, boots and daggers. **Technical:** Grinds and forges; prefers Damascus, SF67, D2 and 01; mirror finishes, except Damascus. **Mark:** Full name and address

JAMES B. MOORE, 1707 N. Gillis, Ft. Stockton, TX 79735/915-336-2113 **Specialties:** Straight and folding working knives. **Patterns:** Hunters, Bowies, tomahawks, folding lockers and camp knives. **Technical:** Grinds D2, 440C and 154CM. **Prices:** $85 to $135; some to $500. **Remarks:** Full-time maker; first knife sold in 1977. **Mark:** Name, town and state

TOM W. MOORE, JR., Rt. 7, Reece Church Rd., Columbia, TN 38401/615-381-2377 **Specialties:** Traditional straight working knives—his design or yours. **Patterns:** Bowies, tantos, hunters and fighters. **Technical:** Grinds 01, D2, and 440C. **Prices:** $50 to $320; some to $400. **Remarks:** Part-time maker; first knife sold in 1984. **Mark:** Rabbit Hill Custom Knives with signature

WM. F. MORAN, JR., P.O. Box 68, Braddock Heights, MD 21714/301-371-7543 **Specialties:** High art working knives of his own very well-known design. **Patterns:** Fighters, camp knives, Bowies, daggers, axes, tomahawks, push knives and miniatures. **Technical:** Forges W2, 5160 and his own Damascus; puts silver wire inlay on most handles; uses natural handle materials exclusively. **Prices:** $400 to $7,500; some to $9,000. **Remarks:** Full-time maker. ABS Master. **Mark:** W.F. MORAN M.S.

EMIL MORGAN, 2690 Calle Limonero, Thousand Oaks, CA 91360/805-492-6830 **Specialties:** Straight and folding working knives in his design or customers'. **Patterns:** Bowies, skinners, locking folders and fish knives. **Technical:** Forges and grinds L6, 1095 and 440C; makes horizontal sheaths. **Prices:** $90 to $225; some $500. **Remarks:** Part-time maker; first knife sold in 1980. **Mark:** Name and town

JEFF MORGAN, 9200 Arnaz Way, Santee, CA 92071/619-448-8430 **Specialties:** Fancy working straight knives. **Patterns:** Hunters, fighters, boots, miniatures and push knives. **Technical:** Grinds D2, 440C and 154CM; likes exotic handles. **Prices:** $65 to $140; some to $500. **Remarks:** Full-time maker; first knife sold in 1977. **Mark:** JM connected

JUSTIN MORGAN, 2690 Calle Limonero, Thousand Oaks, CA 91360/805-492-6830 **Specialties:** Working straight knives. **Patterns:** Hunters, boots and utility knives. **Technical:** Grinds 440C, 154CM and ATS34; mirror finishes. **Prices:** $85 to $200; some to $250. **Remarks:** Spare-time maker; first knife sold in 1983. **Mark:** Name in script

TOM MORGAN, 14689 Ellett Rd., Beloit, OH 44609/216-537-2023 **Specialties:** Period pieces and straight working knives. **Patterns:** Hunters, boots, daggers, presentation tomahawks. **Technical:** Grinds 01, 440C and 154CM. **Prices:** $45 to $125; some to $225. **Remarks:** Part-time maker; first knife sold in 1977. **Mark:** Morgan, date and steel

TOM MORLAN, 30635 S. Palm, Hemet, CA 92343/714-658-4113 **Specialties:** Fancy working knives in customer designs. **Patterns:** Bowies, tantos, fish knives, and locking folders. **Technical:** Grinds 440C, 154CM and ATS34. **Prices:** $75 to $250; some to $3,000. **Remarks:** Full-time maker; first knife sold in 1979. **Mark:** TM connected

C.H. MORRIS, 828 Meadow Dr., Atmore, AL 36502/205-368-2089 **Specialties:** Specializing in liner-lock folding knives. **Patterns:** Liner-lock folders; new interframe liner-lock. **Technical:** Grinds 440C. **Prices:** $600 and up. **Remarks:** Full-time maker; first knife sold in 1973. **Mark:** C.H. Morris

MORSETH SPORTS EQUIP. CO. (See A.G. Russell)

GARY E. MOSSER, 15605 - 204th Ave. S.E., Renton, WA 98056/206-226-8949 **Specialties:** Working straight knives, some fancy. **Patterns:** Hunter types; some Bowies, camp knives, hatchets. **Technical:** Grinds stainless alloy steels; likes leather and concave grind. **Prices:** $75 to $150; some $250 and up. **Remarks:** Full-time maker; sold first knife in 1976. **Mark:** Name

MOUNTAIN FORGE (See Bill Buchman)

RUSS MOYER, P.O. Box 2409, Havre, MT 59501/406-265-5116 **Specialties:** Working knives to order. **Patterns:** Hunters, Bowies, survival knives; folding lockers, too. **Technical:** Forges W2, 01 and D2. **Prices:** $150 to $350 average. **Remarks:** Part-time maker; first knife sold in 1976. **Mark:** RAM in logo

STEVE MULLIN, 500 W. Center Valley Rd., Sandpoint, ID 83864/208-263-7492 **Specialties:** Contemporary and period working knives. **Patterns:** Full range of folders, hunters, Bowies. Some buckskinner designs. **Technical:** Grinds and forges; uses 01, D2, 154CM and his own Damascus. **Prices:** $75 to $500; some to $1,200. **Remarks:** Full-time maker; first knife sold in 1975. **Mark:** Full name, city and state

PAUL MUNRO, RFD 1, Box 32, Franklin, ME 04634 **Specialties:** Working straight knives; some fancy pieces. **Patterns:** Standard hunters, fighters and daggers. **Technical:** Grinds 01, L6 and ATS34; offers Maine deer antler for handles. **Prices:** $70 to $125; some to $250. **Remarks:** Part-time maker; first knife sold in 1980. **Mark:** Munro clan badge

DAVE MURPHY, P.O. Box 256, Gresham, OR 97030/503-665-8634 **Specialties:** Fancy working knives in his own designs. **Patterns:** Hunters, fighters, boots. **Technical:** Grinds F-8 Silvanite and 154CM; likes narrow tangs, composite handles. **Prices:** $95 to $450; some to $3,900. **Remarks:** Full-time maker; first knife sold in 1940. Presently not taking orders. **Mark:** Name, city and state

MEL MYERS, 611 Elmwood Drive, Spencer, IA 51301/712-262-3383 **Specialties:** Working hunters. **Patterns:** Hunters and small utilitarian knives. **Technical:** Uses 440C and no power tools except polisher. **Prices:** $75 to $150. **Remarks:** Spare-time maker; first knife sold in 1982. **Mark:** Signature

PAUL MYERS, 128 12th St., Wood River, IL 62095/618-254-2714 **Specialties:** Fancy working straight and folding knives. **Patterns:** Full range of folders, straight hunters, Bowies; tie tacks; knife and fork sets. **Technical:** Grinds D2, 440C and 154CM. **Prices:** $100 to $350; some to $3,000. **Remarks:** Full-time maker; first knife sold in 1974. **Mark:** P.M. with setting sun on front; name and number on back

WOODY NAIFEH, Rt. 13, Box 380, Tulsa, OK 74107/918-224-3943 **Specialties:** Working folding knives of his own design. **Patterns:** Folding patent lockers. **Technical:** Grinds 440C and Uddeholm "AEBL" stainless. **Prices:** $80 to $175. **Remarks:** Part-time maker, first knife sold in 1969. **Mark:** NAIFEH

JERRY C. NEAL, P.O. Box 1092, Banner Elk, NC 28604/304-727-2545 **Specialties:** Fancy working straight and folding knives. **Patterns:** From hunters to axes; folding lockers to slip joints, tomahawks to claws, even miniatures. **Technical:** Grinds 01, D2, 440C and 154CM; does some chip finish like Indian Flint knives. **Prices:** $40 to $350; some to $1,500. **Remarks:** Full-time maker; first knife sold in 1970. **Mark:** J. NEAL

BUD NEALY, 822 Thomas St., Stroudsburg, PA 18360/717-421-4040 **Specialties:** Working knives of his own design. **Patterns:** Hunters, tantos, kitchen ware and boots; carving sets. **Technical:** Forges and grinds W1, A203E, 440C, ATS34, and makes Damascus; mirror finishes; sharpens knives with "Moran edge." **Prices:** $75 to $300; some to $1,200. **Remarks:** Full-time maker; first knife sold in 1980. **Mark:** Name, city and state

IVAN F. (Frank) NEALEY, c/o Rocky Bar Stage, Anderson Dam Rd., Box 11, Mt. Home, ID 83647/208-587-4060 **Specialties:** Straight working knives in traditional patterns. **Patterns:** Hunters, skin-

ners, and utility knives. **Technical:** Grinds D2, 440C, and 154CM. **Prices:** $80 to $125. **Remarks:** Part-time maker; first knife sold in 1975. **Mark:** Name

VAUGHN NEELEY (See Timberline Knives)

ROGER S. NELSON, Box 294, Central Village, CT 06332/203-774-6749 **Specialties:** Working knives to order. **Patterns:** Hunters, fighters, camp knives, folding lockers, butterflies. **Technical:** Grinds D2, 440C and 154CM. **Prices:** $90 to $140; some to $250. **Remarks:** Spare-time maker; first knife sold in 1975. **Mark:** R. NELSON

CORBIN NEWCOMB, 628 Woodland Ave., Moberly, MO 65270/816-263-4639 **Specialties:** Period pieces and working straight knives. **Patterns:** Hunters, axes, Bowies, buckskinner blades and boots. **Technical:** Hollow grinds D2, 440C and 154CM; prefers natural handle materials. **Prices:** $85 to $130; some to $350. **Remarks:** Full-time maker; first knife sold in 1982. **Mark:** CORBIN and serial number

CHARLIE NIBARGER, 4908 E. 15th St., Tulsa, OK 74112/918-749-8042 **Specialties:** Straight working knives in traditional styles. **Patterns:** Hunters, fighters, and utility knives. **Technical:** Grinds 440C, ATS34, and D2. **Prices:** $90 to $150. **Remarks:** Full-time maker; first knife sold in 1983. **Mark:** NIBARGER

R. KENT NICHOLSON, 615 Hollen Rd., Baltimore, MD 21212/301-323-6925 **Specialties:** Large using knives. **Patterns:** Bowies, camp knives, in the Moran style. **Technical:** Forges W2, 9260, 5160; makes Damascus. **Prices:** $295 to $995. **Remarks:** Part-time maker; first knife sold in 1984. **Mark:** Name; Journeyman Smith with ABS.

NIMO FORGE (See Cleston S. Sinyard)

FRANK NIRO, Box 552, Mackenzie, BC V0J 2C0, CANADA/604-997-6975 **Specialties:** Comfortable working straight knives. **Patterns:** Hunters, Bowies, camp and kitchen knives; some axes. **Technical:** Grinds L6, 440C; likes flat grind. **Prices:** $40 to $135; some to $175. **Remarks:** Part-time maker; first knife sold in 1983. **Mark:** NIRO

MELVIN S. NISHIUCHI, 45-006 Waikalua Rd., Kaneohe, HI 96744/808-235-1105 **Specialties:** Period pieces and straight working knives. **Patterns:** Chinese and Japanese-style blades, Bowies. **Technical:** Grinds 5160, ATS34, and 440C; edge hardens carbon steels. **Prices:** $135 to $350; some $1,000. **Remarks:** Full-time maker; first knife sold in 1985. **Mark:** O, some with mark and HAWAII

R.D. and GEORGE NOLEN, Box 2895, Estes Park, CO 80517/303-586-5814 **Specialties:** Working knives; many display pieces. **Patterns:** Wide variety of straight knives, folding lockers, butterflies and buckles. **Technical:** Grind D2, 440C and 154CM; filework on many knives; exotic handles nearly normal. **Prices:** $100 to $800; some very high. **Remarks:** Full-time makers; first knife sold in 1968. **Mark:** NK in oval logo

MIKE NORRIS, 2115 Charlotte Rd., Albemarle, NC 28001/704-982-8445 **Specialties:** Working straight knives in traditional patterns. **Patterns:** Bowies, fighters, hunters, and locking folders. **Technical:** Grinds 154CM, and ATS34. **Prices:** $75 to $300; some $600. **Remarks:** Full-time maker; first knife sold in 1982. **Mark:** Norris

NORTH and PRATER, Rt. 3, Box 1240, Chickamauga, GA 30707/404-931-2617 **Specialties:** Stag-handled belt knives. **Patterns:** Traditional patterns in large and small narrow-tang construction. **Technical:** They grind 01, and heat-treat it themselves. **Prices:** $100 to $225. **Remarks:** Partnership of David North and Mike Prater; sold first knives in 1980. **Mark:** Names, date, serial #

DON NORTON, 3206 Aspen Dr., Farmington, NM 87401/505-327-3604 **Specialties:** Fancy and plain fixed blades. **Patterns:** Hunters, small Bowies, tantos, bootknives, fillets. **Technical:** Prefers 440C, Micarta, exotic woods and other natural handle material. Hollow ground except fillet knives. **Prices:** $85 to $1,000. Average is $200. **Remarks:** Full-time maker since 1986; first knife sold in 1980. **Mark:** D. Norton in script

EARL NYMEYER, 2802 N. Fowler, Hobbs, NM 88240/505-392-2164 **Specialties:** Straight working knives in his own designs. **Patterns:** Variations on the tanto design, fighters, and hunters. **Technical:** Grinds knives, prefers hollow grinds and filework. **Prices:** $55 to $95; some $125. **Remarks:** Spare-time maker; first knife sold in 1983. **Mark:** ERN or E. NYMEYER

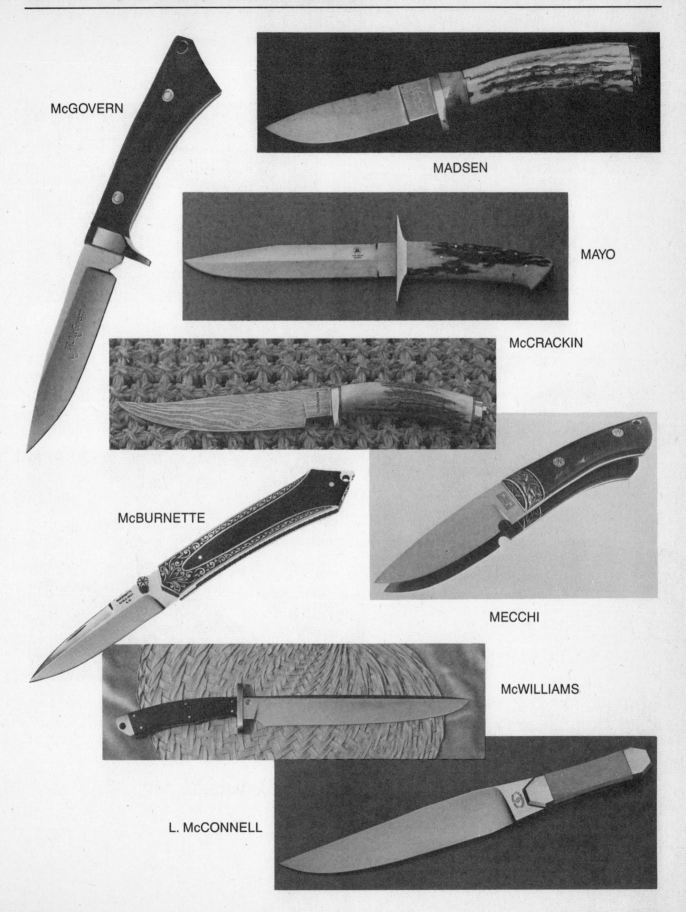

McGOVERN

MADSEN

MAYO

McCRACKIN

McBURNETTE

MECCHI

McWILLIAMS

L. McCONNELL

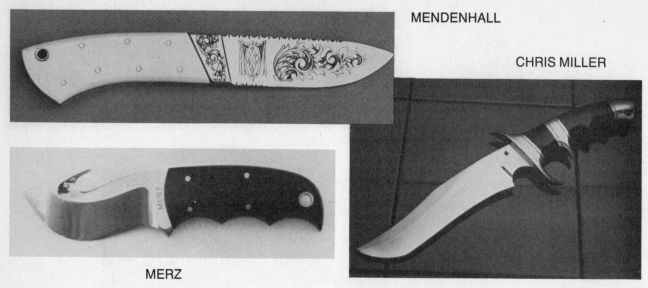

MENDENHALL

CHRIS MILLER

MERZ

MOSSER

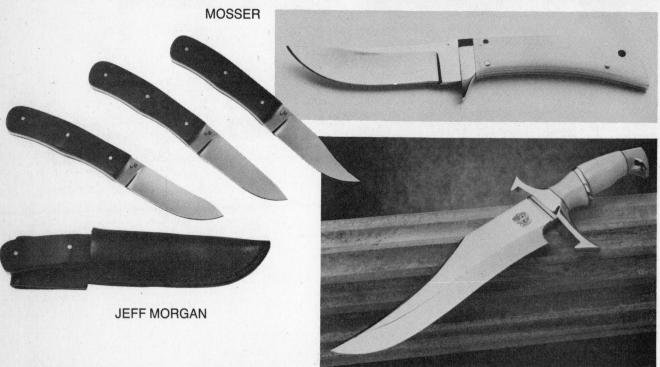

JEFF MORGAN

MOELLER

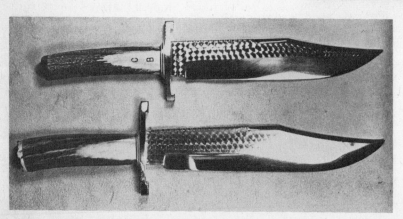

M. MITCHELL

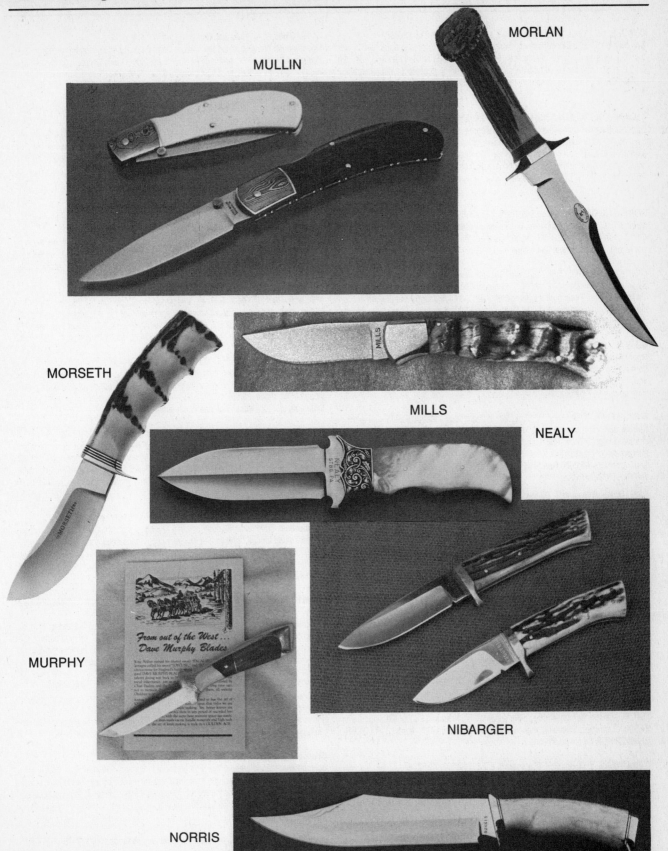

MORLAN

MULLIN

MORSETH

MILLS

NEALY

MURPHY

NIBARGER

NORRIS

CHARLES F. OCHS, 124 Emerald Lane, Largo, FL 34641/813-536-3827
Specialties: Period pieces and working knives. **Patterns:** Hunters, fighters, Bowies, buckskinners and razors. **Technical:** Forges 01, 1095, SAE 5160 and his own Damascus; stag handles standard. **Prices:** $100 to $600; some to $1,000. **Remarks:** Full-time maker; first knife sold in 1978. **Mark:** OX Forge; Journeyman Smith with ABS.

KUZAN ODA, P.O. Box 2213, Hailey, ID 83333/208-823-4638
Specialties: High-tech in Japanese fashion; contemporary working knives. **Patterns:** Swords, fighters, hunters, spears and folding lockers. **Technical:** Forges and grinds; uses 154CM and Tamahagane, and his own Damascus; offers traditional and authentic Japanese sword-smithing and polishing. **Prices:** $200 to $600; some to $5,000. **Remarks:** Full-time maker; first knife sold in 1957. Not taking orders. **Mark:** KUZAN, variously

ROBERT G. OGG, Rt. 1, Box 345, Paris, AR 72855/501-963-2767
Specialties: Plain and fancy working knives. **Patterns:** Folding slip joints. **Technical:** Grinds 440C, Sandvik 15LM and commercial Damascus. **Prices:** $60 to $85; some to $115. **Remarks:** Spare-time maker; first knife sold in 1964. **Mark:** Name

GORDON O'LEARY, 2566 Hearthside Dr., Ypsilanti, MI 48198/313-484-1230
Specialties: Period pieces and working straight knives. **Patterns:** Hunters, Bowies, boots and minis. **Technical:** Hollow grinds 440C; does full tangs and prefers natural handle materials. **Prices:** $100 to $200; some $300. **Remarks:** Spare-time maker; first knife sold in 1980. **Mark:** O'LEARY in script

MILFORD OLIVER, 3832 W. Desert Park Lane, Phoenix, AZ 85021/602-841-7038
Specialties: High-tech working knives. **Patterns:** Frontlock folders, slip joints, interframes; straight hunters, Bowies and camp knives. **Technical:** Grinds 440C, 154CM and ATS34. **Prices:** $225 to $450; some to $600. **Remarks:** Full-time maker; first knife sold in 1977. **Mark:** M.J. Oliver in logo

WAYNE C. OLSON, 11655 W. 35th Ave., Wheat Ridge, CO 80033/303-420-3415
Specialties: High-tech working knives. **Patterns:** Hunters to folding lockers; some integral designs. **Technical:** Grinds 440C, 154CM and ATS34; hand finish is standard; precision-fits stainless steel fittings—no solder, no nickel silver. **Prices:** $275 to $600; some to $3,000. **Remarks:** Full-time maker; first knife sold in 1979. **Mark:** WAYNE OLSON maker

ONE HANDER (See W.T. Fuller, Jr.)

WARREN OSBORNE, 803 Ellis St., Waxahachie, TX 75165/214-937-0899
Specialties: Working knives and fancy pieces. **Patterns:** Folders, miniatures, bolstered and interframes, conventional, front and back locks; some slips; some high art pieces. **Technical:** Grinds D2, 440C and 154CM; does serrated bolsters. **Prices:** $175 to $285; some to $2,000. **Remarks:** Full-time maker; first knife sold in 1980. **Mark:** OSBORNE in boomerang logo

ANTHONY (Tony) L. OUTLAW, 1131 E. 24th Plaza, Panama City, FL 32405/904-769-7754
Specialties: Traditional straight knives in working styles. **Patterns:** Makes tantos, Bowies, camp knives—a full range. **Technical:** Grinds A2, W2, 01, L6, 1095 and stainless steels to mirror finish. **Prices:** $85 to $175; some to $300. **Remarks:** Part-time maker; sold first knife in 1984. **Mark:** OUTLAW

T.R. OVEREYNDER, 1800 S. Davis Dr., Arlington, TX 76013/817-277-4812
Specialties: Highly finished working knives. **Patterns:** Fighters, Bowies, daggers, folding lockers, slip joints and interframe folders. **Technical:** Grinds D2, 440C and 154CM. Making titanium-frame folder since 1977. **Prices:** $250 to $700; some to $4,500. **Remarks:** Part-time maker; first knife sold in 1977. **Mark:** T.R. OVEREYNDER KNIVES, city and state

DAN OWENS, P.O. Box 284, Blacksburg, SC 29702/803-839-2287
Specialties: Traditional straight and folding knives, some fancy. **Patterns:** Fighters, Bowies, daggers, hunters, and utility knives. **Technical:** Grinds 440C, ATS34, and Damascus. Offers mirror or satin finishes. **Prices:** $75 to $150; some $400. **Remarks:** Full-time maker; first knife sold in 1985. **Mark:** D. Arvel

DANNY OWENS, P.O, Box 284, Blacksburg, SC 29702/803-839-2287
Specialties: Traditional folders and straight knives, some fancy. **Patterns:** Full-sized and miniatures in hunter patterns. **Technical:** Grinds stainless steels and Damascus bars. **Prices:** $75 to $150; some to $400. **Remarks:** Full-time maker; sold first knife in 1982. **Mark:** DANO

JOHN OWENS, 6513 E. Lookout Dr., Parker, CO 80134
Specialties: Working straight knives in contemporary design; some period pieces. **Patterns:** Hunters, Bowies and camp knives. **Technical:** Grinds and forges; uses 440C and 154CM. **Prices:** $125; some to $350. **Remarks:** Spare-time maker. **Mark:** OWENS

OX FORGE (See Charles F. Ochs)

LOWELL R. OYSTER, RFD #1, Box 432, Kenduskeag, ME 04450/207-884-8663
Specialties: Working knives in his design or to customer order. **Patterns:** Hunters, minis, camp and fish knives; folding slip joints. **Technical:** Grinds 01; does own heat-treat. **Prices:** $35 to $125; some to $300. **Remarks:** Full-time maker; first knife sold in 1981. **Mark:** A clamshell

PACK RIVER KNIFE CO. (See Steve Mullin)

LARRY PAGE, 165 Rolling Rock Rd., Aiken, SC 29801/803-648-0001
Specialties: Period pieces and working knives in his own design. **Patterns:** Hunters, boots, fighters and mini knives. **Technical:** Grinds 154CM and ATS34. **Prices:** $75 to $150; some $250. **Remarks:** Part-time maker; first knife sold in 1983. **Mark:** Name, city, state, in oval

PHILIP R. PANKIEWICZ, RFD #1, Waterman Rd., Lebanon, CT 06249
Specialties: Working straight knives. **Patterns:** Hunters, daggers, minis and fish knives. **Technical:** Grinds D2, 440C and 154CM. **Prices:** $60 to $125; some $250. **Remarks:** Spare-time maker; first knife sold in 1975. **Mark:** P in star

ROBERT "BOB" PAPP, P.O. Box 246, Elyria, OH 44036/216-458-8565
Specialties: High-tech working straight knives; some display knives. **Patterns:** Hunters, fighters, minis and boots; integral designs in all. **Technical:** Grinds D2, 440C and 154CM. **Prices:** $135 to $500; some to $2,500. **Remarks:** Full-time maker; first knife sold in 1964. **Mark:** Full name, city and state

MELVIN M. PARDUE, Rt. 1, Box 130, Repton, AL 36475/205-248-2686
Specialties: Fancy folding and straight knives. **Patterns:** Locking folders, large and small; makes folding tantos and krisses, too. Fighters, tantos and boots in straight patterns. Likes coffin handles. **Technical:** Grinds D2, 440C and 154CM; also UHB-A-EBL. **Prices:** $140 to $350. **Remarks:** Full-time maker; first knife sold in 1974. **Mark:** PARDUE

DWAYNE PARRISH, P.O. Box 181, Palestine, TX 75801/214-729-7319
Specialties: Traditional working straight knives. **Patterns:** Don Hastings hunters, Bowies, camp knives, fighters. **Technical:** Forges Damascus and 5160. **Prices:** $190 to $475; some to $650. **Remarks:** Full-time maker; sold first knife in 1984; has taken over for the late great Don Hastings. **Mark:** PARRISH one side; HASTINGS KNIFE WORKS the other.

ROBERT PARRISH, 1922 Spartanburg Hwy., Hendersonville, NC 28739/704-692-3466
Specialties: Heavy-duty working knives in his design or yours. **Patterns:** Survival and duty knives; hunters, fighters. **Technical:** Grinds 440C, D2, 01 and commercial Damascus. **Prices:** $200 to $300; some to $6,000. **Remarks:** Full-time maker; first knife sold in 1970. **Mark:** RP connected; sometimes with city and state

LLOYD D. PATE, 219 Cottontail Ln., Georgetown, TX 78626/512-863-7805
Specialties: Traditional working straight knives. **Patterns:** Hunters, fighters, Bowies and folders, makes a special lady's knife. **Technical:** Grinds D2 and 440C; hollow-grinds and mirror-finishes. **Prices:** $85 to $165; some to $350. **Remarks:** Part-time maker; sold first knife in 1983. **Mark:** Name, city, state in semi-circle logo

CHUCK PATRICK, Rt. #1, Brasstown, NC 28902/704-837-7627
Specialties: Period pieces and high art knives. Has serious interest in martial arts. **Patterns:** Hunters, camp knives, tomahawks; all pre-1860 styles. **Technical:** Forges 5160, his own cable and Damascus; forges all hardware. **Prices:** $100 to $500 and up. **Remarks:** Full-timer who sold first knife in 1980. **Mark:** CP connected; knife; or eagle

HILL EVERETT PEARCE, III, Box 72, Gurley, AL 35748/205-776-3965
Specialties: High-art period pieces in his own design. **Patterns:** Folding lockers; straight Bowies, daggers and fighters. **Technical:** Forges W2, 01 and his own Damascus; does filework on all knives. **Prices:** $300 to over $600. **Remarks:** Full-time maker; first knife sold in 1982. Striving for sole authorship. **Mark:** Small script P

directory/custom knifemakers

W.D. PEASE, Rt. 2 Box 13, Ewing, KY 41039/606-267-2304
Specialties: Display-quality working knives, folders and straight. **Patterns:** Fighters, tantos and boots; folding lockers and interframes. **Technical:** Grinds 440C, 154CM and commercial Damascus; has his own side release lock system. **Prices:** $300 to $500; some to $1,500. **Remarks:** Full-time maker; first knife sold in 1970. **Mark:** W.D. PEASE

LLOYD PENDLETON, 2116 Broadmore Ave., San Pablo, CA 94806/415-724-6104
Specialties: Contemporary working knives in standard patterns. **Patterns:** Hunters, fighters and boots. **Technical:** Grinds 154CM and ATS34; mirror finishes. **Prices:** $180 to $400; some to $1,300. **Remarks:** Full-time maker; first knife sold in 1973. **Mark:** L Pendleton logo, with city and state

ALFRED H. PENDRAY, Rt. 2, Box 1950, Williston, FL 32696/904-528-6124
Specialties: Period pieces and working knives. **Patterns:** Straight and folding fighters hunters. Also offers axes, camp knives and tomahawks. **Technical:** Forges Wootz steel; makes his own Damascus; does some traditional knives from old files and rasps. **Prices:** $125 to $1,000; some to $3,500. **Remarks:** Part-time maker; first knife sold in 1954. **Mark:** P in horseshoe logo

STEPHAN PEPIOT, P.O. Box 41, Lancaster Park, (Edmonton) AB T0A 2H0, CANADA
Specialties: Working straight knives in standard patterns. **Patterns:** Hunters and camp knives. **Technical:** Grinds 440C, and industrial hacksaw blades. **Prices:** $75 to $125. **Remarks:** Spare-time maker; first knife sold in 1982. **Mark:** PEP

PEPPER KNIVES (See J. Culpepper)

PERSUADER (See Howard Hill)

DAN L. PETERSEN, 327 N. Rim, Billings, MT 59102/406-252-5135
Specialties: Period pieces and straight working knives. **Patterns:** Hunters, Bowies, boots, fighters; does Persian/Northern India styles in Damascus steel. **Technical:** Forges W2, 5160 and his own Damascus. **Prices:** $125 to $400; some to $1,000. **Remarks:** Full-time maker; first knife sold in 1978. **Mark:** Stylized initials, DLP; JS for Journeyman Smith with the ABS

ELDON G. PETERSON, 260 Haugen Hts. Rd., Whitefish, MT 59937/406-862-2204
Specialties: Fancy working knives. **Patterns:** Folding lockers, interframes, and bolster lockers, two-blades and both straight and folding hunters. **Technical:** Grinds D2, 01, 440C and ATS34; uses no tracing mill for interframes—all done by hand. Offers engraving. **Prices:** $285 to $500; some $1,500. **Remarks:** Full-time maker; first knife sold in 1974. **Mark:** Name, city and state

JACK PETERSON, 532 Duke St., Nanaimo, BC V9R 1K1, CANADA/604-753-0107
Specialties: Makes miniature folders. **Patterns:** Locking designs at 1 5/16-inch open; makes two-blade patterns, too. Also 8-bladed Swiss Army 1 1/4-inch closed. **Technical:** Grinds 1095 and 440C; makes cap and spring one piece and bolster and liner one-piece; uses front cam release. **Prices:** $100 to $300. **Remarks:** Part-timer; sold first knife in 1976. **Mark:** JVP

JOHN PHILLIPS, 31 Parker Way, Santa Barbara, CA 93101/805-963-0499
Specialties: Traditional working knives; straight or folding. **Patterns:** Usual straight knives; both locking and slip-joint folders, including interframes in aluminum or titanium. **Technical:** Grinds D2, 154CM, ATS34. **Prices:** $75 to $250; some to $450. **Remarks:** Part-time maker; sold first knife in 1986. **Mark:** Name in dog head logo

RANDY PHILLIPS, P.O. Box 792, Bloomington, CA 92316/714-875-8105
Specialties: Does some hunters; mostly collector-grade boots and high artpieces (daggers). **Technical:** Grinds D2, 440C and 154CM; embellishes some. **Prices:** $100 and up. **Remarks:** Part-time maker; first knife sold in 1981. **Mark:** Name, city and state in eagle head

PHOENIX BLADES (See Darrel W. Goff)

HAROLD L. PIERCE, 7150 Bronner Circle #10, Louisville, KY 40218/502-499-6615
Specialties: Working straight knives, some fancy. **Patterns:** Big fighters and Bowies. **Technical:** Grinds D2, 440C, 154CM; likes sub-hilts. **Prices:** $150 to $450; some to $1,200. **Remarks:** Full-time production; sold first knife in 1982. Police officer background **Mark:** Name

DAVID PITT, P.O. Box 7653, Klamath Falls, OR 97602/503-883-3430

Specialties: Working knives. **Patterns:** Straight knives for deer and elk hunters, including hatchets and cleavers. Small guthook hunters and capers big sellers. **Technical:** Grinds A2, 440C and 154CM. **Prices:** $100 to $200; some to $450. **Remarks:** Full-time maker; first knife sold in 1972. **Mark:** Bear Paw with name

LEON PITTMAN, Rt. 2, Box 2097, Pendergrass, GA 30567/404-654-2597
Specialties: Working folders, some very dressy. **Patterns:** Patent folding lockers and slip joints, interframes, two-blades and gents. **Technical:** Grinds D2, 440C and 154CM. **Prices:** $125 to $500; some $1,000 **Remarks:** Part-time maker; first knife sold in 1973. **Mark:** "Worm" and full name

JAMES POAG, RR 1, Box 213, New Harmony, IN 47631/812-682-3226
Specialties: Working knives and period pieces, straight or folding. **Patterns:** Does Bowies and camp knives, lockers and slip joints. **Technical:** Grinds and forges stainless steels and others; provides serious leather; offers own embellishments. **Prices:** $65 to $1,2000. **Remarks:** Full-time maker; sold first knife in 1967. **Mark:** Name

LARRY POGREBA, Box 861, Lyons, CO 80540/303-823-6691
Specialties: Working straight knives. **Patterns:** Hunters and fighters, tomahawks and axes, camp knives; pole arms. **Technical:** Forges and grinds W2, 154CM, and his own Damascus. **Prices:** $150 to $350; some to $1,000. **Remarks:** Full-time maker; first knife sold in 1976. **Mark:** Rocking Lazy LP brand

CLIFTON POLK, 3526 Eller St., Ft. Smith, AR 72904/501-782-1396
Specialties: Fancy working folders and straight knives. **Patterns:** Folding lockers, slip joints, and two-blades; straight hunters, Bowies, hatchets and kitchen cutlery. **Technical:** Grinds 440C and forges D2, ATS34 and his own Damascus. **Prices:** $100 to $300; some to $3,000. **Remarks:** Full-time maker; accepts mail for son Rusty. **Mark:** Name

RUSTY POLK (See Clifton Polk)

AL POLKOWSKI, 8 Cathy Ct., Chester, NJ 07930/201-879-6030
Specialties: Working straight knives in your design or his. **Patterns:** Bowies, hunters and boots. **Technical:** Grinds D2, 440C, and ATS34. Prefers flat grinds and hand-rubbed satin finishes. Embellishments and leather sheaths in house. **Prices:** $75 to $300; some $600. **Remarks:** Part-time maker; first knife sold in 1985. **Mark:** AL POLKOWSKI HANDMADE

JAMES L. POPLIN, Rt.2, Box 191A, Washington, GA 30673/404-678-2729
Specialties: Contemporary patterns for hunters. **Patterns:** Hunters, a few boots. **Technical:** Very clean work, deep hollow grinds. **Prices:** Reasonable. **Mark:** POP

JAMES E. PORTER, P.O. Box 2583, Bloomington, IN 47402/812-859-4302
Specialties: Straight knives as period pieces or working blades. **Patterns:** Outdoors knives; some Bowies and miniatures **Technical:** Forges 01 and 1095; makes pattern-welded Damascus; likes integral pommels. **Prices:** $50 to $175; some to $375. **Remarks:** Part-time maker; sold first knife in 1986. **Mark:** JP connected

ALVIN POSTON, 1813 Old Colony Rd., Columbia, SC 29209/803-776-2589
Specialties: Straight working knives. **Patterns:** Hunters, Bowies and fish knives; some miniatures. **Technical:** Grinds 154CM and ATS34. **Prices:** $80 to $125; some to $250. **Remarks:** Part-time maker; first knife sold in 1979. **Mark:** POSTON

ROBERT PREUSS, P.O. Box 65, Cedar, MN 55011
Specialties: Straight working knives in traditional patterns. **Patterns:** Bowies, swords, hunters, and fish knives. **Technical:** Grinds 440C, 440A, and 154CM. **Prices:** $65 to $135; some to $500. **Remarks:** Full-time maker; first knife sold in 1982. Business name is Sharp Custom Knives. **Mark:** RP connected

JERRY L. PRICE, P.O. Box 782, Springdale, AR 72764
Specialties: Straight working knives in standard patterns. **Patterns:** Fighters, boots and Bowies. **Technical:** Grinds A2, 440C and 154CM; offers Kydex sheaths, matte black oxide finish on fighters. **Prices:** $60 to $200; some to $400. **Remarks:** Full-time maker; first knife sold in 1975. **Mark:** J. PRICE

JOEL HIRAM PRICE, Rt. 1, Box 3067, Palatka, FL 32077/904-325-5621
Specialties: Working straight knives to customer order. **Patterns:** Wide variety of straight knives, all with filework. **Technical:** Forges and grinds W2, 01, D2 and 440C – customer choice. Buys Damascus, too. **Prices:** $50 to $250; some over $750. **Remarks:** Full-time maker; first knife sold in 1984. **Mark:** HIRAM Knives in script

STEVE PRICE, 899 Ida Lane, Kamloops, BC V2B 6V2, CANADA/604-579-8932
Specialties: Working knives and fantasy pieces—your design or his. **Patterns:** Hunters, axes, tantos, survival knives, folding lockers and some miniatures. **Technical:** Grinds D2, 440C and ATS34. **Prices:** $90 to $350; some to $1,200. **Remarks:** Full-time maker; first knife sold in 1982. **Mark:** S. PRICE

RON PRITCHARD, 613 Crawford Ave., Dixon, IL 61021/815-284-6005
Specialties: Plain or fancy working knives. **Patterns:** Wide variety of straight knives, locking folders, interframes and miniatures. **Technical:** Grinds 440C, 154CM and commercial Damascus. **Prices:** $100 to $200; some to $1,500. **Remarks:** Part-time maker; first knife sold in 1979. **Mark:** Name and town

JOSEPH D. PROVENZANO, 3024 Ivy Place, Chalmette, LA 70043/504-279-3154
Specialties: Straight working knives in traditional patterns. **Patterns:** Hunters with hollow grinds, Bowies, camp and fish knives. **Technical:** Grinds ATS34, 440C, and 154CM. **Prices:** $60 to $300; some $500. **Remarks:** Part-time maker; first knife sold in 1980. **Mark:** Joe-Pro

JIM PUGH, P.O. Box 711, Azle, TX 76020/817-444-2679
Specialties: High art knives in working styles of his own designs. **Patterns:** Hunters, Bowies and fighters; some commemoratives; designs animal heads for buttcaps and paws or claws for guards. **Technical:** Grinds 440C, ASP23, ASP60; casts guards in bronze, silver or gold, all finish-engraved by hand. **Prices:** $500 to $5,500; some to $20,000. **Remarks:** Full-time maker; first knife sold in 1970. **Mark:** Pugh

MARTIN PULLEN, 813 Broken Bow WHH, Granbury, TX 76048/817-573-1784
Specialties: Period pieces and straight working knives. **Patterns:** Fighters, Bowies and daggers; folding lockers. **Technical:** Grinds D2, 440C and 154CM. **Prices:** $100 to $300; some to $600. **Remarks:** Spare-time maker; first knife sold in 1978. **Mark:** PULLEN

MORRIS C. PULLIAM, Rt. 7, Box 272, Shelbyville, KY 40065/502-633-2261
Specialties: Period pieces and working knives. **Patterns:** Hunters, tomahawks and buckskinner knives, and Bowies; makes folding slip joints in old patterns. **Technical:** Forges 5160 and wire Damascus. Also wire and barn nails mixed. **Prices:** $165 to $475; some higher. **Remarks:** Full-time maker; first knife sold in 1974. **Mark:** PULLIAM or P

AARON PURSLEY, Box 1037, Big Sandy, MT 59520/406-378-3200
Specialties: Fancy working knives. **Patterns:** Folding lockers, straight hunters and daggers in individual style. Also makes personal wedding knives and letter openers. **Technical:** Grinds 01 and 440C; all knives are engraved by Pursley. **Prices:** $300 to $600; some to $1,500. **Remarks:** Full-time maker; first knife sold in 1975. **Mark:** AP connected, with year

BARR QUARTON, P.O. Box 2211, Hailey, ID 83333/208-788-2529
Specialties: Plain and fancy working knives and period pieces. **Patterns:** Hunters, tantos and swords. **Technical** Grinds and forges; uses 154CM, ATS34 and his own Damascus. **Prices:** $180 to $450; some to $3,500. **Remarks:** Full-time maker; first knife sold in 1978. **Mark:** Barr with bear logo

WARNER QUENTON, P.O. Box 607, Petersworn, WV 24963
Specialties: Small using knives in high-tech style. **Patterns:** Personal designs exclusively, non-traditional. **Technical:** Grinds stainless steel only; prefers bevel edges. **Prices:** $25 to $200. **Remarks:** Spare-time maker; sold first knife in 1985. **Mark:** WQ

GEORGE QUINN, P.O. Box 692, Julian, CA 92036/619-765-1415
Specialties: Contemporary daggers; integral designs. **Patterns:** Hunters, fighters and daggers. **Technical** Grinds mostly 440C, some 154CM and ATS34; elaborate filework; all knives scrimmed or engraved by Mrs. Quinn. **Prices:** $100 to $600; some to $1,500. **Remarks:** Full-time maker; first knife sold in 1982. **Mark:** QUINN in script

RP KNIVES (See Robert Parrish)

JERRY F. RADOS, Rt 1, Box 516, Grant Park, IL 60940/815-472-3350
Specialties: Deluxe knives in period designs. **Patterns:** Hunters, fighters, locking folders, daggers and camp knives. **Technical:** Forges and grinds; uses 01, L6 and his own Damascus. Makes own pattern-welded Turkish Damascus. Sells own Damascus commercially. **Prices:** $300 to $1,550; some to $5,000. **Remarks:** Full-time maker; first knife sold in 1981. **Mark:** JR connected; sometimes in diamond logo

RICHARD RAINVILLE, 126 Cockle Hill Rd., Salem, CT 06415/203-859-2776
Specialties: Traditional working straight knives. **Patterns:** Outdoors knives, including fish knives. **Technical:** Grinds 01, L6, D2; heat treats; custom-fits handles. **Prices:** $85 to $165; some to $250. **Remarks:** Part-time maker; sold first knife in 1982. **Mark:** RJR

MARSHALL F. RAMEY, P.O. Box 2589, West Helena, AR 72390/501-572-1831
Specialties: Working knives of traditional types. **Patterns:** Designs military combat knives; makes butterfly folders, camp knives, miniatures. **Technical:** Grinds D2 and 440C. **Prices:** $100 to $200; some to $300. **Remarks:** Full-time maker; sold first knife in 1978. **Mark:** Name with Ram's head

RANDALL MADE KNIVES, P.O. Box 1988, Orlando, FL 32802/407-855-8075
Specialties: Straight working knives; a standard. **Patterns:** Hunters, fighters and Bowies. **Technical:** Forges and grinds 01 and 440B. **Prices:** $65 to $250; some to $450. **Remarks:** Full-time maker; first knife sold in 1937; leader in the field. **Mark:** Randall, city, state in scimitar logo

STEVEN J. RAPP, 3437 Crestfield Dr., Salt Lake City, UT 84119/801-966-5595
Specialties: Period pieces and fancy hunter straight knives. **Patterns:** Gold Rush era cutlery. **Technical:** Grinds 440C and Damascus bars. **Prices:** $125 to $300; some to $1,000. **Remarks:** Part-time maker; sold first knife in 1981. **Mark:** Name and state

RICHARD RAPPAZZO, 217 Troy-Schenectady Rd., Latham, NY 12110/518-783-6843
Specialties: Locking Damascus folders and straight knives. **Patterns:** Folders, dirks, fighters and tantos in original and traditional designs. **Technical:** Hand forges all blades, specializing in Damascus; uses only natural handle material. **Prices:** $250 to $800. **Remarks:** Full-time maker; sold first knife in 1985. **Mark:** Name, date, serial

A.D. RARDON, Rt. 1, Box 79, Polo, MO 64671/816-354-2330
Specialties: Working knives; some fancy. **Patterns:** Hunters, buckskinners, Bowies and daggers; some folders. **Technical:** Grinds 01, D2 and 440C, some ATS34. **Prices:** $100 to $500; some to $1,000. **Remarks:** Part-time maker; first knife sold in 1954. **Mark:** Name, address in fox logo

MICHAEL RAY, 533 W. 36th North, Wichita, KS 67204/316-838-4844
Specialties: High-tech working straight and folding knives. **Patterns:** Hunters, fighters and survival knives; gents and hunters in folders. **Technical:** Grinds A2, 440C and ATS34. **Prices:** $80 to $350; some to $500. **Remarks:** Part-time maker. **Mark:** RAY, city and state

CHARLES V. RECE, P.O. Box 574, Troy, NC 27371/704-982-2572
Specialties: Engraved straight knives. **Patterns:** Tantos and Bowies. **Technical:** Grinds ATS34 primarily. **Prices:** Starting at $150. **Remarks:** Spare-time maker; sold first knife in 1986. **Mark:** Timber rattler (engraved)

BILL REDDIEX, 27 Galway Ave., Palmerston North, NEW ZEALAND/64-63-70383
Specialties: Using and collector-grade straight knives. **Patterns:** Traditional-styled Bowies and drop point hunters. **Technical:** Grinds 440C, D2, and 01; offers variety of grinds and finishes. **Prices:** $130 to $750. **Remarks:** Part-time maker; first knife sold in 1980. **Mark:** Reddiex NZ around kiwi bird logo

DAVID REE, 816 Main St., Van Buren, AR 72956/501-474-3198
Specialties: Fancy working knives. **Patterns:** Hunters, folding lockers and boots. **Technical:** Grinds 01, D2 and 440C; prefers exotic and unusual handle materials. **Prices:** $90 to $250; some to $600. **Remarks:** Full-time maker; first knife sold in 1982. **Mark:** REE

DAVE REED, Box 132, Brimfield, MA 01010/413-245-3661
Specialties: Period pieces and traditional styles. **Patterns:** Bowies, swords, hunters, camp and utility knives. **Technical:** Forges 1075, 9260, and his own Damascus. Makes one sword measuring 50"x15"—a collaboration with Charlie Lapen. **Prices:** $150 to $1,500. **Remarks:** Full-time maker; first knife sold in 1970. **Mark:** DR

DEL REED, 13765 S.W. Parkway, Beaverton, OR 97005
Specialties: Unusual configurations. **Patterns:** Swing-blade knives. **Technical:** Grinds stainless. **Prices:** $100 to $125. **Remarks:** New maker; first knife sold in 1988. **Mark:** ORION

CHRIS REEVE, 6 Patricia Rd., Chelmsfordville, Gillitts 3610, SOUTH AFRICA/031-743158

directory/custom knifemakers

Specialties: Straight working knives in his own designs. **Patterns:** Hollow-handle integral survival and combat knives; lightweight backpackers and bird and trout knives. **Technical:** Grinds, mills and bores D2. **Prices:** $150 to $259. **Remarks:** Full-time maker; first knife sold in 1984. **Mark:** CR connected

WINFRED M. REEVES, P.O. Box 300, West Union, SC 29696/803-638-6121
Specialties: Working straight knives; some elaborate pieces. **Patterns:** Hunters, tantos, fish knives. **Technical:** Grinds D2, 440C and ATS34. No solder joints, no buffer unless requested.**Prices:** $75 to $150; some to $300. **Remarks:** Part-time maker; first knife sold in 1975. **Mark:** Reeves, Walhalla, S.C.

BILL REH, 4610 South Ave. W., Missoula, MT 59801/406-721-2883
Specialties: Straight working knives; some to order. **Patterns:** Hunters, boots, daggers. **Technical:** Grinds D2, 440C and buys Damascus; does his own scrimshaw. **Prices:** $70 to $140; some to $250. **Remarks:** Full-time maker; first knife sold in 1982. **Mark:** REH in sun ray logo

TERRY LEE RENNER, P.O. Box 575, Estes Park, CO 80517/303-586-8951
Specialties: Fancy working straight and folding knives. **Patterns:** Has "star-lock" button lock for his folders. Also offers hunters, game sets, fillets, and miniatures. **Technical:** Grinds 440C, D2, or 01. Does own scrimshaw or deep-relief carving. **Prices:** $95 to $450; some higher. **Remarks:** Full-time maker; first knife sold in 1975. Business name is: Firepoint Knives. **Mark:** Name

DAVE REYNOLDS, 4519 26th Loop S.E., Lacey, WA 98503/206-491-2526
Specialties: Working straight knives in his own designs. **Patterns:** Swords, Bowies, kitchen and utility knives. **Technical:** Grinds and forges L6, 1095, and 440C. Does own heat-treating. **Prices:** $50 to $85; some $175. **Remarks:** Full-time maker; first knife sold in 1980. **Mark:** Terra-Gladius over oval with mountains and sword logo

JOHN C. REYNOLDS, Box 119, Mica Court, Gillette, WY 82716/307-682-6076
Specialties: Working knives, some fancy. **Patterns:** Hunters, Bowies, tomahawks and buckskinners; some folders. **Technical:** Grinds D2, 440C and commerical Damascus; scrims his own. **Prices:** $75 to $320; some to $500. **Remarks:** Spare-time maker; first knife sold in 1969. **Mark:** REYNOLDS

DAVID RHEA, Rt. 1, Box 272, Lynnville, TN 38472/615-363-5993
Specialties: High art and fantasy knives. **Patterns:** Fighters, Bowies, survival knives; folding lockers. **Technical:** Grinds and forges; uses D2, 440C and 154CM; makes bronze or silver blades for custom orders; does all embellishing himself. **Prices:** $45 to $300; some to $1,000. **Remarks:** Full-time maker; first knife sold in 1982. **Mark:** D. RHEA, year in circle

DOUGLAS RIAL, Rt. 2, Box 117A, Greenfield, TN 38230/901-235-3994
Specialties: Period pieces and working knives, some to order. **Patterns:** Hunters, fighters, boots, folding lockers, slip joints and miniatures. **Technical:** Grinds D2, 440C and 154CM. **Prices:** $60 to $100; some to $250. **Remarks:** Spare-time maker; first knife sold in 1978. **Mark:** Name and hometown

ADRIENNE RICE, Rt. 1, Box 1744, Lopez Island, WA 98261/206-468-2522
Specialties: Straight knives, either working or fantasy. **Patterns:** Hunters and daggers, women's knives; "power objects" and ceremonial knives. **Technical:** Forges and grinds 01, D2, 440C; also works in bronze. **Prices:** $90 to $150; some to $650. **Remarks:** Full-time production; sold first knife in 1981. **Mark:** AR connected in Madrona logo with date

DAVE RICKE, 1209 Adams, West Bend, WI 53095/414-334-5739
Specialties: Period pieces and working knives. **Patterns:** Hunters, boots, Bowies; folding lockers and slip joints. **Technical:** Grinds A2, 440C and 154CM. **Prices:** $75 to $260; some to $500. **Remarks:** Part-time maker; first knife sold in 1976. **Mark:** RICKE

WILLIE RIGNEY, R.R. 3, Box 404, Shelbyville, IN 46176/317-398-4151
Specialties: High-style period pieces and fancy working knives. **Patterns:** Fighters, boots, daggers and push knives. **Technical:** Grinds 440C and 154CM; most knives with embellished surfaces. **Prices:** $150 to $1,500; some to $10,000. **Remarks:** Full-time maker; first knife sold in 1978. **Mark:** W. RIGNEY

THE RINGING CIRCLE (See Dennis M. Fitzgerald)

RIO VERDE BLADES (See V.E. Harrison)

DEAN ROATH, 3050 Winnipeg Dr., Baton Rouge, LA 70819/504-272-5562

Specialties: Classic styling in working straight knives. **Patterns:** Hunters, fighters and camp knives. **Technical:** Grinds 440C and ATS34; clean lines and profiles. **Prices:** $150 to $400; some to $1,500. **Remarks:** Part-time maker; first knife sold in 1978. **Mark:** Name, city and state

HOWARD P. ROBBINS, 875 Rams Horn Rd.—Moraine Rt., Estes Park, CO 80517/303-586-8755
Specialties: Working knives; some fancy. **Patterns:** Hunters, fish knives and folders. **Technical:** Grinds 440C and ATS34. **Prices:** $75 to $200; some to $500. **Remarks:** Full-time maker; first knife sold in 1982. **Mark:** Name, city and state

RON ROBERTSON, 6708 Lunar Dr., Anchorage, AK 99504/907-338-3686
Specialties: Working straight knives of traditional type. **Patterns:** Hunters, tantos, Bowies, camp and fish knives. **Technical:** Grinds 440C and ATS34; likes some guardless designs. **Prices:** $120 to $250; some to $400. **Remarks:** Part-time maker; sold first knife in 1983. **Mark:** Talon in eagle logo

MICHAEL R. ROCHFORD, Trollhaugen Ski Area, P.O. Box 607, Dresser, WI 54009/715-755-3520
Specialties: Straight working knives in standard patterns. **Patterns:** Bowies, fishing and camp knives, miniatures. **Technical:** Grinds and forges W2, 440C, 154CM and his own Damascus. **Prices:** $80 to $400; some to $800. **Remarks:** Full-time maker; first knife sold in 1984. **Mark:** Name

ROCKET (See Rob Davidson)

FRED D. ROE, Jr., 4005 Granada Dr., Huntsville, AL 35802/205-881-6847
Specialties: Period pieces and highly finished working knives of his own designs. **Patterns:** Hunters, fighters and survival knives; folding lockers; specialty designs like divers' knives. **Technical:** Grinds D2, 154CM and ATS34; field-tests his own blades. **Prices:** $125 to $250; some to $700. **Remarks:** Part-time maker; first knife sold in 1980. **Mark:** ROE

ROBERT P. ROGERS, JR., 3979 South Main St., Acworth, GA 30101/404-974-9982
Specialties: Working knives in traditional modes. **Patterns:** Hunter types; has a 4-inch trailing point he likes. **Technical:** Grinds D2, 154CM, ATS34; likes ironwood and ivory Micarta. **Prices:** $65 to $85; some to $125. **Remarks:** Spare-time maker; sold first knife in 1975. **mark:** Name

FRED ROHN, W7615 Clemetson Rd., Coeur d'Alene, ID 83814/208-667-0774
Specialties: Straight working knives, some unusual. **Patterns:** Hunters, fighters, a unique Bowie design, and folding lockers. **Technical:** Grinds 440C and 154CM; stainless steel pins, bolsters and guards on all knives. **Prices:** $65 to $200; some over $450. **Remarks:** Part-time maker. **Mark:** Name in logo and each knife with serial number.

STEVE ROLLERT, P.O. Box 65, Keenesburg, CO 80643/303-732-4858
Specialties: Highly finished affordable working knives. **Patterns:** Full range of straight knives, including kitchen cutlery; also folding lockers and slip joints. **Technical:** Forges and grinds W2, 1095, 440C and his own Damascus. **Prices:** $75 to $250; some to $2,000. **Remarks:** Full-time maker; first knife sold in 1980; Dove Knives label. **Mark:** Rollert in script

MARK H. ROPER, Jr., 206 Plymouth Rd., Martinez, GA 30907/404-863-2972
Specialties: Working knives and some fantasy pieces. **Patterns:** Hunters, fighters and boots, also folding lockers. **Technical:** Grinds 440C, 154CM and ATS34. **Prices:** $90 to $350; some to $600. **Remarks:** Part-time maker; first knife sold in 1980. **Mark:** Name in arc

ALEX ROSE, 3624 Spring Valley Dr., New Port Richey, FL 34655/813-376-5059
Specialties: Miniatures of a wide variety. **Patterns:** Miniature tantos, Bowies, Mid-East styles, and push knives. **Technical:** Grinds 440C, 154CM, and bought Damascus; carving, scrimshaw and inlay on handles. **Prices:** $75 to $125; some $350. **Remarks:** Spare-time maker; first knife sold in 1981. **Mark:** Name with rose logo

TIM ROSS, 3329 Oliver Rd., RR #17, Thunder Bay, ON P7B 6C2, CANADA/807-935-2667
Specialties: Fancy working knives in his own designs. **Patterns:** Fish and hunting knives in his own designs. **Technical:** Grinds and forges D2, Stellite 6K, 440C, and his own Damascus. Prefers natural materials only. Wife Katherine does scrimshaw. **Prices:** $100 to $350; some to $1,500. **Remarks:** Part-time maker; first knife sold in 1975. Has supply of bear claws and moose antlers for trade. **Mark:** ROSS stamped on tang

S. PRICE

OVEREYNDER

OSBORNE

PARDUE

RAPPAZZO

PEASE

PENDRAY

PORTER

RIGNEY

RADOS

DAVE REED

RAPP

ROE

PETERSON

PIERCE

RICHARD A. ROTELLA, 7022 Stephenson Ave., Niagara Falls, NY 14304/716-283-0591
Specialties: True working knives in his designs; welcomes custom work. **Patterns:** Various types of fishing, utility and hunting knives. **Technical:** Grinds D2, 440C, and ATS34. Prefers handrubbed and mirror finishes. **Prices:** $50 to $85; some to $300. **Remarks:** Part-time maker; first knife sold in 1977. **Mark:** Name and city in stylized waterfall logo

STEWART G. ROWE, 56 Baildon St., Kangaroo Point, Bris. 4169, AUSTRALIA/393-1192
Specialties: Period pieces and fancy working knives in traditional patterns and his own. **Patterns:** Traditional Japanese tantos, daggers, working knives and swords. **Technical:** Forges W1 and 2, D2, and a variety of alloy steels, and pattern welded Damascus. **Prices:** $125 to $3,000. **Remarks:** Full-time maker; sold first knife in 1981. **Mark:** Kogatana

B.M. " RED" ROYAL, P.O. Box 934, Helen, GA 30545/404-878-3227
Specialties: A former charter captain designs his own salt water and game straight knives. **Patterns:** Fillets, hunters; bait and sailor's rigging knife, complete with marlin spike. Does a few survival/combat knives. **Technical:** Grinds 440C, A2, D2, and ATS34. **Prices:** $100 to $250; some to $400. **Remarks:** Full-time maker; first knife sold in 1976. **Mark:** R.R. in diagonal line

RUANA KNIFE WORKS, Box 520, Bonner, MT 59823/406-258-5368
Specialties: Working knives and period pieces in their unique style. **Patterns:** Full range of straight knives, mostly as Rudy made them. **Technical:** Forges 5160 chrome alloy for Bowies and 1095. **Prices:** $60 to $240; some over $300. **Remarks:** Full-time maker; first Ruana knife sold in 1938; Victor N. Hangas now in charge; no quality change in fine knives. **Mark:** Name

JAMES A. RUBLEY, R.R. 3, Box 682, Angola, IN 46703/219-833-1255
Specialties: Civil War work. Knives and collectables for buckskinners, re-inactment groups, and collectors. **Patterns:** Anything authentic, barring folders—dirks, Bowies, rifle knives and smaller pieces. **Technical:** Iron fittings, natural materials; forges files and buggy seat springs; does it the old ways. **Prices:** $175 and higher; some to $2,500. **Remarks:** Museum consultant and two decades a blacksmith. **Mark:** Lightning bolt

RUNNING RIVER KNIVES (See Steve Allen)

A.G. RUSSELL, 1705 Hwy. 471 N., Springdale, AR 72764/501-751-7341
Specialties: Morseth Knives; contemporary working knives. **Patterns:** Hunters, Bowies, personal utility knives in Morseth line; drop-points and boots in Russell line. **Technical:** Morseth laminated blades; modern stainless in Russell name; classic shapes. **Prices:** Moderate. **Remarks:** Old name still at work. **Mark:** MORSETH or A.G. RUSSELL

CHARLES C. RUST, P.O. Box 374, Palermo, CA 95968/916-533-9389
Specialties: Period pieces and working knives, some fancy. **Patterns:** Hunters, Bowies, buckskinners, sets. **Technical:** All handwork; low production **Prices:** $125 to $2,000; some to $3,500; no orders. **Remarks:** Full-time maker; first knife sold in 1972. **Mark:** Rustway in logo

RUSTWAY (See Charles C. Rust)

SF MADE KNIVES (See Shiro Furukawa)

SUZANNE ST. AMOUR, Oldstore House R.R. 1, Hillsburgh, Ont. N0B 1Z0, CANADA/519-855-6494
Specialties: Fine art and fantasy; fancy working knives. **Patterns:** Knives as art, hunters, kitchen cutlery and camp knives. **Technical:** Grinds D2, 440C and 154CM; embellishes most knives; trained as a jeweler. **Prices:** $85 to $500; some to $1,000. **Remarks:** Full-time maker. **Mark:** St. Amour in script

SALAMANDER ARMOURY (See Jim Hrisoulas)

JOHN D. SALLEY, 3965 Frederick-Ginghamsburg Rd., Tipp City, OH 45371/513-698-4588
Specialties: Fancy working knives. **Patterns:** Hunters, survival knives and butterfly folding knives; some swords. **Technical:** Grinds D2, 440C; buys Damascus. **Prices:** $75 to $500; some to $3,000. **Remarks:** Part-time maker; first knife sold in 1979. **Mark:** J. Salley

BOB SALPAS, P.O. Box 117, Homewood, CA 95718/916-525-6833
Specialties: Fancy working straight knives. **Patterns:** Hunters, Bowies, tantos, push knives and miniatures. **Technical:** Grinds 440C, ATS34 and AEB-L. **Prices:** $100 to $160; some $450. **Remarks:** Full-time maker; first knife sold in 1981. **Mark:** SALPAS

SAM ENTERPRISES (See George Cooper)

LYNN SAMPSON, Rt. 2, Box 283, Jonesboro, TN 37659/615-753-2090
Specialties: Highly finished working knives, mostly folders. **Patterns:** Folding lockers, slip-joints, interframes and two-blades, all with extensive filework. **Technical:** Grinds D2, 440C and ATS34. **Prices:** $200 to $400 and higher. **Remarks:** Full-time maker; first knife sold in 1982. **Mark:** Name and town in logo

JOSEPH D. SAMS, 5108 Juliandra Ave., El Paso, TX 79924/915-755-0681
Specialties: Heavy-duty straight knives, some fancy. **Patterns:** Hunters, fighters, boots. **Technical:** Grinds D2, 440C, ATS34, 154CM, and Damascus on request. **Prices:** $50 to $1,000. **Remarks:** Part-time maker; first knife sold in 1978. **Mark:** Name.

JODY SAMSON, 1834 W. Burbank Blvd., Burbank, CA 91506/818-843-4006
Specialties: Straight knives, some fancy, some fantasy—his design or yours. **Patterns:** Hunters, Bowies, swords, axes and camp knives. Does movie props. **Technical:** Grinds 5160, 440C and bought Damascus. **Prices:** $200 to $800; some to $4,500. **Remarks:** Full-time maker; first knife sold in 1970. **Mark:** Lion logo with name

ATHERN (AL) SANDERS, 3850 72 Ave. N.E., Norman, OK 73071/405-364-8660
Specialties: Working straight knives in your design or his. **Patterns:** Hunters, fighters, boots, Bowies, and daggers. **Technical:** Forges his own Damascus, 01, W1, and 109S. He grinds ATS34. **Prices:** $85 to $500. **Remarks:** Full-time maker; first knife sold in 1985. **Mark:** Name, city, state in banner logo with date, or Athern Forge

BILL SANDERS (See Timberline Knives)

MICHAEL M. SANDERS, P.O. Box 1106, Ponchatoula, LA 70454/504-294-3601
Specialties: Working straight knives; some deluxe. **Patterns:** Hunters, fighters, Bowies, daggers and large folders. **Technical:** Grinds 01, D2, 440C, ATS34 and Damascus. **Prices:** $75 to $650; some higher. **Remarks:** Part-time maker; first knife sold in 1967. **Mark:** Name and state

SCOTT SAWBY, 500 W. Center Valley Rd., Sand Point, ID 83864/208-263-4171
Specialties: High-tech working folders. **Patterns:** Folding lockers, patent locking systems and interframes. **Technical:** Grinds D2, 440C, 154CM and ATS34. **Prices:** $250 to $350; some to $500. **Remarks:** Full-time maker; first knife sold in 1974. **Mark:** SAWBY, city and state

MURAD SAYEN (See Kemal)

WILL SCARROW, P.O. Box 33, El Cerrito, CA 94804-1133/415-236-3742
Specialties: Working straight knives in traditional patterns or customer designs. **Patterns:** Hunters, skinners, swords and Bowies. Will attempt any design. **Technical:** Grinds and forges; uses W1, W2, 5160, 1095, 440C, ABE-L, and ATS34; other steels on request; file-works some. **Prices:** $85 to $300; some to $800. **Remarks:** Part-time maker; first knife sold in 1983. **Mark:** SC with arrow logo and date

MAGGIE SCHEID, P.O. Box 8059, W. Webster, NY 14580/716-671-8137
Specialties: Straight and simple working knives. **Patterns:** Kitchen and utility knives; some miniatures. **Technical:** Forges 5160 high carbon steel. **Prices:** $100 to $200. **Remarks:** Part-time smith; sold first knife in 1986. **Mark:** Full name

GEORGE B. SCHEPERS, Box 83, Chapman, NE 68827/308-986-2444
Specialties: Fancy period pieces in his own designs. **Patterns:** Bowies, swords, tomahawks; also folding lockers and miniatures. **Technical:** Grinds W1, W2 and his own Damascus; etches some knives. **Prices:** $125 to $600; some more. **Remarks:** Full-time maker; first knife sold in 1981. **Mark:** Schep

JAMES A. SCHMIDT, R.D. 3, Eastern Ave., Ballston Lake, NY 12019/518-882-9322
Specialties: High art Damascus in folders and collector-quality period pieces—sole authorship. **Patterns:** Schmidt patterns in folders; variety of investor-class straight knives. **Technical:** Forges W2 and his own Damascus; elaborate file work and etching, and exotic handle materials. **Prices:** $900 to $2,200; some to $5,000. **Remarks:** Full-time maker; first knife sold in 1975; an ABS Master. **Mark:** SCHMIDT

HERMAN J. SCHNEIDER, 24296 Via Aquara, Laguna Niguel, CA 92677/714-495-4589
Specialties: Investor-class straight knives and fantasies. **Patterns:** Hunters, daggers, fighters and push knives, all personal designs, fully finished. **Technical:** Grinds

and forges; uses 154CM, ATS34 and his own Damascus; exotic materials, even rare and expensive materials, a specialty. **Prices:** $800 to $5,000; some to $12,000. **Remarks:** Full-time maker; first knife sold in 1972. **Mark:** H.J. Schneider

MATTHEW A. SCHOENFELD, RR #1, Galiano Island, B.C. V0N 1P0, CANADA/604-539-2806
Specialties: Working knives in distinctly personal style. **Patterns:** All his own in kitchen cutlerly, camp knives, hunters, even swords. **Technical:** Grinds 440C, ATS34; buys Damascus. **Prices:** $85 to $200; some to $500 and up. **Remarks:** Full-time maker; first knife sold in 1978. **Mark:** Signature, Galiano Is. B.C., and date

KARL SCHRÖEN, 4042 Bones Rd., Sebastopol, CA 95472/707-823-4057
Specialties: User knives made to fit and work as an extension of the hand. **Patterns:** Skene Dhus, carving sets, wood-carving knives; original fish designs, and kitchen knives. **Technical:** Forges A2, Bg42, ATS34, and D2. **Prices:** $200 to $600; some to $3,700. **Remarks:** Full-time maker; first knife sold in 1968. Author of *The Hand Forged Knife*. **Mark:** Schroen

STEPHEN SCHWARZER, 2119 Westover Dr., Palatka, FL 32077/904-328-3316
Specialties: Fancy forged working knives. **Patterns:** Hunters, fighters, folding lockers, axes and buckskinners—all personally expressed. **Technical:** Forges W2, 01, Wootz steel and his own Damascus; all knives have carving or filework. **Prices:** $800 to $1,800; some $6,000. **Remarks:** Full-time maker; first knife sold in 1976; ABS Master. **Mark:** Name over anvil

WINSTON SCOTT, Rt. 2, Box 62, Huddleston, VA 24104/703-297-6130
Specialties: Working knives. **Patterns:** Hunters, fighters, tantos and mini knives. **Technical:** Grinds D2, 440C and 154CM; likes full tangs, natural materials, sterling silver guards. **Prices:** $100 to $150; some to $200. **Remarks:** Part-time maker; first knife sold in 1984. **Mark:** *SCOTT*

HARALD SELLEVOLD, S.Kleivesmau:2, 5023 Dreggen, NORWAY/05-310682
Specialties: Norwegian styles; collaboration with other Norse craftsmen. **Patterns:** Distinctive ferrules and other mild modifications of traditional patterns. **Technical:** Grinds 440C, 12C27; buys Damascus blades. **Prices:** $100 to $350; some $1,000. **Remarks:** Full-time maker; first knife sold in 1980. **Mark:** Horseshoe S

JIM SERVEN, 6153 Third St., Mayville, MI 48744/517-843-6539
Specialties: Highly finished unique folders. **Patterns:** Most known for his fancy working folders; does axes, miniatures and razors, but not many straight knives. **Technical:** Grinds 440C; forges his own Damascus. **Prices:** $150 to $800; some to $1,500. **Remarks:** Full-time maker; first knife sold in 1971. **Mark:** Name in map logo

SHADOWMAKER (See E.E. Urstadt)

ROBERT G. SHARP, 17540 St. Francis Blvd., Anoka, MN 55303/612-753-2858
Specialties: Working straight knives. **Patterns:** Hunters, Bowies, daggers and push knives; some axes. **Technical:** Grinds 440C and 154CM. **Prices:** $75 to $175; some to $450. **Remarks:** Full-time maker; first knife sold in 1978. **Mark:** Signature

PHILIP S. SHARPE, 483 Landmark Way S.W., Austell, GA 30001/404-944-9276
Specialties: Knives from 1770 to present; etched and stained to appear old and used. **Patterns:** Hunters, rifleman's knives, skinners and daggers. **Technical:** Grinds D2. **Prices:** $70 to $250. **Remarks:** Part-time maker; first knife sold in 1978; known as "Pasquinel;" sells mainly at rendezvous. **Mark:** Fancy P with two dots

ROBERT A. SHEARER, 2121 Avenue T, Huntsville, TX 77340/409-295-0779
Specialties: Working straight knives in traditional patterns. **Patterns:** Fighters, survival knives, and Bowies. **Technical:** Grinds 440C, and 154CM. **Prices:** $50 to $250; some $400. **Remarks:** Part-time maker; first knife sold in 1972. **Mark:** SHEARER

PAUL P. SHEEHAN, P.O. Box 90, Sandwich, MA 02563/508-888-5114
Specialties: Working straight knives in his design, but welcomes customer designs. **Patterns:** Bowies, kukris, sub-hilts and gents utility knives; tantos and fantasy knives. **Technical:** Hollow grinds 440C and bought Damascus; prefers natural materials. Filework and full tang are standard. **Prices:** $150 to $350; some $600. **Remarks:** Part-time maker; first knife sold in 1987. **Mark:** Full name, city and state

SCOTT SHOEMAKER, 316 S. Main St., Miamisburg, OH 45342/513-859-1935
Specialties: Twisted wire-wrapped handles on swords, fighters, and fantasy blades. **Patterns:** Bowies, boots, one-of-a-kinds in your design or his. **Technical:** Grinds A6 and ATS34; buys Damascus. Hand satin finish is standard. **Prices:** $100 to $300;

swords to $2,000. **Remarks:** Part-time maker; first knife sold in 1984. **Mark:** Angel wings with an S, or Shoemaker

RICK SHUFORD, 431 Hillcrest Dr., Statesville, NC 28677/704-873-0633
Specialties: Fancy working knives in customer design. **Patterns:** Hunters, buckskinners, camp and fish knives, and miniatures. **Technical:** Grinds and forges; uses 01, D2 and 440C. **Prices:** $100 to $250; some to $400. **Remarks:** Part-time maker; first knife sold in 1981. **Mark:** SHUFORD and 3 dots

CORBET R. SIGMAN, Rte. 1, Box 212-A, Liberty, WV 25124/304-586-9131
Specialties: Collectible working straight knives, highly evolved. **Patterns:** Hunters, fighters, boots, camp knives and exotics like sgian dubhs—distinctly Sigman lines. **Technical:** Grinds D2, 154CM, plain carbon tool steel and ATS34; fine craftsmanship, clean lines. **Prices:** $60 to $800; some to $4,000. **Remarks:** Full-time maker; first knife sold in 1970. **Mark:** Name or initials

JAMES P. SIGMAN, 52474 Johnson Rd., Three Rivers, MI 49093/616-279-2508
Specialties: High tech working knives of his own design. **Patterns:** Daggers, hunters, fighters, and folders. **Technical:** Forges and grinds L6, 01, W2, and his own Damascus. **Prices:** $125 to $300. **Remarks:** Full-time maker; first knife sold in 1982. **Mark:** J. Sigman or SIG

KURT BARNES SIMMONDS, 1 Yeats St., Castlemaine, Vic. 3450, AUSTRALIA/054-724387
Specialties: Fancy period pieces, straight and folding knives. **Patterns:** Art daggers, traditional Bowies, fancy folders, and miniatures. **Technical:** Grinds ATS34, D2, 440C, and offers filework, chisel work and inlays. **Prices:** $100 to $375; some to $1,000. **Remarks:** Full-time maker; first knife sold in 1983. **Mark:** K.B.S., address within Southern Cross motif

ROB SIMONICH, P.O. Box 278, Clancy, MT 59634/406-933-8274
Specialties: Working knives in standard patterns. **Patterns:** Hunters, combat knives, Bowies, and small fancy knives. **Technical:** Grinds D2, ATS34, and 440C; filework on most knives. **Prices:** $50 to $250; some $600. **Remarks:** Full-time maker; first knife sold in 1984. **Mark:** Simonich in buffalo logo

BILL SIMONS, P.O. Box 311, Highland City, FL 33846/813-646-3783
Specialties: Working folding knives. **Patterns:** Folding lockers, slip joints in hunters; some straight camp knives. **Technical:** Grinds D2, 440C and ATS34. **Prices:** $50 to $300. **Remarks:** Full-time maker; first knife sold in 1970. **Mark:** Simons, city and state

BOB SIMS, P.O. Box 772, Meridian, TX 76665/817-435-6240
Specialties: Working straight and folding knives in traditional patterns. **Patterns:** Enjoys locking folders and multi-bladed folding knives. Also offers hunters and boot straight knives. **Technical:** Grinds L6, D2, and 440C. Does file work on some knives. **Prices:** $85 to $175; some over $300. **Remarks:** Spare-time maker; first knife sold in 1978. **Mark:** The division sign

CLESTON S. SINYARD, 27522 Burkhardt Dr., Elberta, AL 36530/205-986-7984
Specialties: Working straight knives in his designs. **Patterns:** Hunters, buckskinner knives, Bowies, daggers and fighters. **Technical:** Now making Damascus from 440C, stainless steels, D2, and regular high carbon steel. Prices increase with his new Damascus; forges "forefinger pad" into hunters and skinners. **Prices:** In Damascus: $450 to $1,500; some to $2,500. **Remarks:** Full-time maker; first knife sold in 1980. **Mark:** SINYARD. U.S.A. in anvil

JIM SISKA, 6 Highland Ave., Westfield, MA 01085/413-568-9787
Specialties: Traditional types of working knives, straight or folding. **Patterns:** Hunters, folders, fighters, Bowies and one-of-a-kind pieces. **Technical:** Grinds D2, 154CM, ATS34; likes ivory and stag. Also buys Damascus. **Prices:** $165 to $300; some much higher. **Remarks:** Part-time maker; sold first knife in 1983. **Mark:** Name

SAMUEL SKIRCHAK, JR., RD #1, Lisbon Rd., Midland, PA 15059/412-495-3948
Specialties: Straight and folding working knives in traditional types. **Patterns:** Full range of standard and survival knives; does miniatures. **Technical:** Grinds 01, 440C and 154CM; will try customer designs. **Prices:** $75 to $300; some to $600. **Remarks:** Part-time maker; sold first knife in 1983. **Mark:** Name

FRED SLEE, 9 John St., Morganville, NJ 07751/201-591-9047
Specialties: Straight working knives; some fancy. **Patterns:** Hunters, fighters, boots, and push knives; welcomes customer designs. **Technical:** Grinds D2, 440C and 154CM. **Prices:** $90 to $250; some to $600. **Remarks:** Part-time maker; first knife sold in 1980. **Mark:** SLEE

JOHN SLOAN, P.O. Box 486, Foxboro, MA 02035
Specialties: Affordable working knives of his own design; some whimsical. **Patterns:** Hunters, fighters and kitchen cutlery. **Technical:** Forges 01, D2 and his own Damascus. **Prices:** $20 to $40; some to $300. **Remarks:** Full-time maker; first knife sold in 1978. **Mark:** Iron duckling

SHANE SLOAN, Rt. 1, Box 17, Newcastle, TX 76372/817-846-3290
Specialties: Working straight and folding knives, some fancy. **Patterns:** Does tantos, Bowies, lockers, slip-joints; makes fancy fighters and period pieces. **Technical:** Grinds D2, 440C, and ATS34; tempers 440Cs to be tough; mixes mirror and satin finishes. **Prices:** $125; some higher. **Remarks:** Full-time maker; sold first knife in 1985. **Mark:** Name in logo with eagle

ED SMALL, Rt. 1, Box 178-A, Keyser, WV 26726/304-298-4254
Specialties: Period pieces and working knives of his own designs. **Patterns:** Hunters, daggers, buckskinners and camp knives; likes one-of-a-kinds. **Technical:** Forges and grinds W2, L6, and his own Damascus. Uses no solder joint at guard or spacing material. **Prices:** $150 to $600. **Remarks:** Part-time maker; first knife sold in 1978. Business name is Iron Mountain Forge Works. **Mark:** Script ES connected

JIM SMALL, P.O. Box 67, Madison, GA 30650/404-342-4707
Specialties: Fancy working knives in his design or yours. **Patterns:** Bowies, camp and fish knives, hunters and locking folders. **Technical:** Grinds D2, 440C, 154CM and ATS34; offers engraving on his knives or others. **Prices:** $75 to $185; some to $1,000. **Remarks:** Full-time maker; first knife sold in 1970. **Mark:** SMALL

DAVID LYNN SMITH, 1773 E. 4500 South, Vernal, UT 84078/801-789-5130
Specialties: Working straight knives in traditional styles. **Patterns:** All steel wallet knives; fighters, Bowies and camp knives in modern treatment. **Technical:** Textured finish ATS34 and 154CM. **Prices:** $50 to $200; some to $300. **Remarks:** Part-time maker; first knife sold in 1983. **Mark:** D. LYN

GLENN L. SMITH, 630 E. 39 St., Hialeah, FL 33013/305-691-2656
Specialties: Working straight and folding knives. **Patterns:** Small folders with engraved bolsters; utility straight knives. **Technical:** Grinds 01, 440C, and 154CM. **Prices:** $90 to $135; some to $500. **Remarks:** Full-time maker; first knife sold in 1970. **Mark:** G.L. Smith, maker

GREGORY H. SMITH, 8607 Coddington Ct., Louisville, KY 40299/502-491-7439
Specialties: Traditional straight working knives; some fantasy knives; likes customer design work. **Patterns:** Fighters and modified Bowies; some camp knives and swords. **Technical:** Grinds 01, 440C, commercial Damascus bars. **Prices:** $55 to $300. **Remarks:** Part-time maker; sold first knife in 1985. **Mark:** JAGED, plus signature

HARRY R. SMITH, 2105 So. 27th Ave., Missoula, MT 59801/406-549-5940
Specialties: Working knives, some fancy. **Patterns:** Hunters, Bowies, folding lockers; some swords and axes. **Technical:** Forges and grinds 01, D2, and 154CM. **Prices:** $75 to $135; some $650. **Remarks:** Part-time maker; first knife sold in 1941. **Mark:** H. SMITH

JAMES B. "RED" SMITH, Jr., Rt. 2, Box 199, Morven, GA 31638/912-775-2844
Specialties: Folding and straight working knives. **Patterns:** Hunters, camp knives, machetes, and folding lockers. **Technical:** Grinds ATS34, 440C, and D2. **Prices:** $90 to $150; some $250. **Remarks:** Full-time maker; first knife sold in 1985. **Mark:** GA RED in cowboy hat

JOHN M. SMITH, RR 6, Box 52, Centralia, IL 62801/618-249-6444
Specialties: Working straight knives, some fancy. **Patterns:** Bowies, in contemporary and self-defense styles; hunters, skinners, and boots. **Technical:** Forges W2, medium carbon spring steel, cable, and Damascus. Flat ground preferred. **Prices:** $100 to $295; some to $1,000. **Remarks:** Full-time maker; first knife sold in 1980. **Mark:** Etched signature

NEWMAN L. SMITH, Rt. 1, Box 119A, Glades Rd., Gatlinburg, TN 37738/615-428-0811 (evenings)
Specialties: Working knives, some fancy, both straight and folding. **Patterns:** Hunters and slip-joint folders; some miniatures. **Technical:** Grinds 01 and 440C; makes extra-fancy sheaths. **Prices:** $85 to $450; some to $800. **Remarks:** Full-time production; sold first knife in 1984. Partners part-time to handle Damascus blades by Jeff Hurst and marks these SH connected. **Mark:** NLS

RALPH L. SMITH, P.O. Box 395, Greer, SC 29652/803-877-7580

Specialties: Affordable working knives. **Patterns:** Hunters, fighters, boots, folding lockers; some axes and push knives. **Technical:** Grinds 440C, 154CM and ATS34. **Prices:** $100 to $225; some to $500. **Remarks:** Part-time maker; first knife sold in 1971. **Mark:** Smith in map logo

W.F. "RED" SMITH, P.O. Box 6, Gatlinburg, TN 37738/615-436-3520
Specialties: Straight working knives; some fancy. **Patterns:** Hunters, fighters, daggers, tomahawks. Some commemorative series. **Technical:** Grinds and forges; offers 440C and his own Damascus. **Prices:** $150 to $600; some to $3,500. **Remarks:** Full-time maker; first knife sold in 1975. **Mark:** RED SMITH

JERRY L. SNELL, 235 Woodsong Dr., Fayetteville, GA 30214/404-461-0586
Specialties: Working straight knives in traditional patterns. **Patterns:** Hunters, skinners, and working utility knives. **Technical:** Grinds 440C, ATS34, and buys Damascus. **Prices:** Moderate to upscale. **Remarks:** Part-time maker. **Mark:** SNELL

W.J. SONNEVILLE, 1050 Chalet Dr. W., Mobile, AL 36608/205-342-5447
Specialties: Working straight knives. **Patterns:** Hunters, fighters, Bowies in heavy duty styles. **Technical:** Grinds and forges; uses 1095 and 440C. **Prices:** $130 to $250; some $750. **Remarks:** Full-time maker; first knife sold in 1965. **Mark:** SONNEVILLE, city and state

G. DOUGLAS SONTHEIMER, 1705 Chester Mill Road, Silver Spring, MD 20906/301-924-3657
Specialties: Working straight knives to his own images. **Patterns:** Fighters, backpackers, claws, straight edges. **Technical:** Grinds. **Price:** $275 to $900; some to $1,500. **Remarks:** Spare-time maker; sold first knife in 1976. **Mark:** LORD

JIM SORNBERGER, 25126 Overland Dr., Volcano CA 95689
Specialties: Collectible straight knives, highly finished. **Patterns:** Fighters, daggers, Bowies; some folding lockers and miniatures; some hunters. **Technical:** Grinds 440C, 154CM and ATS34; does his own engraving, carving and other embellishment. **Prices:** $500 to $1,500; some to $3,500. **Remarks:** Full-time maker; first knife sold in 1970. **Mark:** SORNBERGER U.S.A.

BERNARD SPARKS, Box 73, Dingle, ID 83233/208-847-1883
Specialties: Original designs in straight and folding working knives. **Patterns:** Hunters, fighters, folding lockers, camp knives and miniatures. **Technical:** Grinds and forges; offers 440C, 154CM, Vascowear and his own Damascus. **Prices:** $100 to $500; some to $1,000. **Remarks:** Full-time maker; first knife sold in 1966. **Mark:** SPARKS

JOHN E. SPENCER, Box 582-B—Star Rt., Harper, TX 78631/512-864-4216
Specialties: Straight working knives. **Patterns:** Hunters, fighters and survival knives; locking folders; some axes. **Technical:** Grinds 01, D2 and 440C; commercial Damascus. **Prices:** $60 to $300; some $500. **Remarks:** Full-time maker; first knife sold in 1982. **Mark:** SPENCER

RICHARD SPINALE, 3415 Oakdale Ave., Lorain, OH 44055/216-246-5344
Specialties: High art working knives of individual designs. **Patterns:** Hunters, fighters, daggers and folding lockers. **Technical:** Grinds 440C and 07; all knives are engraved by this maker; offers gold bolsters, other deluxe treatments. **Prices:** $125 to $800; some to $2,000. **Remarks:** Spare-time maker; first knife sold in 1976. **Mark:** Name, address, year and model number

JEFFERSON SPIVEY, P.O. Box 60584, Oklahoma City, OK 73146/405-282-1802
Specialties: Heavy-duty straight knives. **Patterns:** Personal designs only; his horseman's Sabertooth at first, now similar profiles in a couple of sizes. **Technical:** Grinds chrome-moly steel. **Prices:** $225 up. **Remarks:** Sold first knives in 1977; is a famous long-distance rider. **Mark:** Varies, but includes name and patent number.

RICHARD STAFFORD, 104 Marcia Ct., Warner Robins, GA 31088/912-923-6372
Specialties: Working knives, some fancy. **Patterns:** Hunters, fighters, tantos and mini knives. **Technical:** Grinds D2, 440C and 154CM; favors bolsters and satin finishes. **Prices:** $75 to $250; some to $600. **Remarks:** Full-time maker; first knife sold in 1983. **Mark:** STAFFORD

JOHN STAHL, 2049 Windsor Rd., Baldwin, NY 11510/516-223-5007
Specialties: Makes miniature knives only. **Patterns:** Offers own scrimshaw. **Prices:** Moderate.

HARRY L. STALTER, 2509 N. Trivoli Rd., Trivoli, IL 61569/309-362-2306

Specialties: Working knives; some period pieces. **Patterns:** Hunters, fighters and Bowies; locking folders; rifle stock handle models. **Technical:** Grinds 440C, D2, 154CM and ATS34. Now making 45 styles of miniatures. **Prices:** $80 to $300. **Remarks:** Full-time maker; first knife sold in 1980. **Mark:** STALTER

CHUCK STAPEL, Box 1617, Glendale, CA 91209/213-66-KNIFE
Specialties: Original approaches to working knife design. **Patterns:** A full range of straight knives, individually patterned—tantos, hunters, folders, utility knives. **Technical:** Grinds D2, 440C, AEB-L. **Prices:** $150 to $3,000. **Remarks:** Full-time maker; first knife sold in 1974. **Mark:** STAPEL

CRAIG STAPEL, Box 1617, Glendale, CA 91209/213-668-2669
Specialties: Working knives. **Patterns:** Hunters, tantos, fish knives. **Technical:** Grinds 440C and AEB-L. **Prices:** $80 to $100; some $150. **Remarks:** Spare-time maker; first knife sold in 1981. **Mark:** C.C. STAPEL

RANDY STEFANI, 2393 Mayfield Ave., Montrose, CA 91020/818-957-4204
Specialties: Working straight knives in traditional models. **Patterns:** Hunters, fighters, tantos, Bowies; makes small utility knives. **Technical:** Grinds 440C, 154CM, ATS34. **Prices:** $75 to $250; some to $500. **Remarks:** Part-time maker; sold first knife in 1983. **Mark:** Last name

KEITH STEGALL, 3206 Woodland Pk. Dr., Anchorage, AK 99517/907-243-2001
Specialties: Straight knives in traditional working styles. **Patterns:** Most patterns. **Technical:** Grinds 440C, 154CM; tries for clean lines, good detail. **Prices:** $100 to $300. **Remarks:** Spare-time maker; sold first knife in 1987. **Mark:** Name, state, with anchor

AL STEINBERG, 2499 Trenton Dr., San Bruno, CA 94066/415-583-8281
Specialties: Fancy straight working knives in customer designs. **Patterns:** Hunters, Bowies, fish and camp knives; some push knives. **Technical:** Grinds 01, 440C and 154CM. **Prices:** $60 to $125; some to $300. **Remarks:** Full-time maker; first knife sold in 1972. **Mark:** Signature, city and state

KELLY LEE STEPHENS, 4235 78th Ln. N., St. Petersburg, FL 33709
Specialties: Working knives and period pieces, some fancy. **Patterns:** Straight and folding hunters; centerline Bowies; some swords. **Technical:** Grinds stainless steels. **Mark:** Name

STEVES KNIVES (See Steve Davenport)

CHARLES (CHUCK) STEWART, P.O. Box 514, 2996 Walmsley Circle, Lake Orion, MI 48035/313-391-2289
Specialties: Working knives, personally designed. **Patterns:** Makes exotic opening mechanisms for his designs of folders; personally designed and patented release locks; also straight knives, some fancy. **Technical:** Forges and grinds 440C, 154CM and ATS34; offers finishes from gold to blueing. **Prices:** $200 to $800; some to $9,500. **Remarks:** Full-time maker; first knife sold in 1968. **Mark:** Stylized initials

DOUGLAS STICE, 507 Inwood Dr., Norman, OK 73072/405-360-3957
Specialties: Working straight knives. **Patterns:** Hunters, Bowies, fighters, tantos, and fish knives. **Technical:** Grinds 440C and D2. **Prices:** $50 to $150; some to $225. **Remarks:** Part-time maker; first knife sold in 1985. **Mark:** Name

KAY STITES, 4931 Rands Rd., Bloomfield Hills, MI 48013/313-251-7336
Specialties: Working straight knives in traditional patterns. **Patterns:** Hunters and fish knives. **Technical:** Grinds D2, 01, and 440C. **Prices:** $75 to $225; some to $500. **Remarks:** Spare-time maker; first knife sold in 1986. **Mark:** Stites

W.B. "BILL" STODDART, 917 Smiley, Forest Park, OH 45240/513-851-1543
Specialties: Sportsmen's working knives. **Patterns:** Hunters, camp and fish knives; folding lockers in traditional styles. **Technical:** Grinds A2, 440C and ATS34; makes sheaths to match handle material. **Prices:** $80 to $150; some $400. **Remarks:** Full-time maker; first knife sold in 1976. **Mark:** Name, city and state

G.W. STONE and JIM ERICKSON, 610 No. Glenville Dr., Richardson, TX 75081/214-231-0970
Specialties: Working knives in standard patterns built for heavy duty. **Patterns:** Hunters, fighters and kitchen cutlery and locking folders. **Technical:** Grinds D2, 440C, and ASP-23. **Prices:** $100 to $300; some to $600. **Remarks:** Veteran full-time maker; first knife sold in 1964. **Mark:** Name

JOHNNY STOUT, 1514 Devin, Braunfels, TX 78130/512-629-1011
Specialties: Working knives, some fancy. **Patterns:** Hunters, Bowies, fishing knives and folding lockers. **Technical:** Grinds D2, 440C and ATS34; satin and mirror finishes; uses local woods for handles—mesquite, cat claw, cedar. **Prices:** $100 to $250; some to $1,500. **Remarks:** Part-time maker; first knife sold in 1983. **Mark:** Name, and city in logo; serial number

SCOTT STRONG, 2138 Oxmoor Dr., Beaver Creek, OH 45431/513-426-9290
Specialties: Working knives, some deluxe. **Patterns:** Hunters, fighters, survival knives. **Technical:** Forges and grinds 01, D2, 440C; offers hollow grinds and variety of finishes, some bead blasted. **Prices:** $40 to $250; some $500. **Remarks:** Spare-time maker; first knife sold in 1983. **Mark:** STRONG KNIVES

GEORGE STUMPFF, JR., P.O. Box 2, Glorieta, NM 87535/505-757-6036
Specialties: Traditional working straight and folding knives, some fancy. **Patterns:** Skinners and hunters; lockers and slip-joints in the old style. Does fancy pin and file work. **Technical:** Grinds A2, 01, ATS34; triple flat-grinds some blades. **Prices:** $70 to $250; some to $500. **Remarks:** Full-time production; sold first knife in 1975. **Mark:** GWS MAKER in logo

HARLAN SUEDMEIER, RFD2, Nebraska City, NE 68410/402-873-4372
Specialties: Working straight knives. **Patterns:** Hunters, fighters and Bowies. **Technical:** Grinds A2, D2 and 440C. **Prices:** $65 to $300; some to $750. **Remarks:** Part-time maker; first knife sold in 1982. **Mark:** H. Suedmeier

ROD SWAIN, 1020 Avon Place, South Pasadena, CA 91030/818-799-7666
Specialties: Working straight knives, some fancy. **Patterns:** Outdoors patterns, and Bowies and push knives; likes his utility drop-point. **Technical:** Grinds 01, 440C, AEB-L; takes on some customer designs. **Prices:** $60 to $200; some to $400. **Remarks:** Part-time maker; sold first knife in 1981. **Mark:** Last name in logo

CHUCK SYSLO, 3418 South 116 Ave., Omaha, NE 68144/402-333-0647
Specialties: High-tech working straight knives. **Patterns:** Hunters, daggers, survival knives; some folding lockers. **Technical:** Grinds D2, 440C and 154CM; hand polishes only; flat ground only. **Prices:** $175 to $375; some to $1,000. **Remarks:** Part-time maker; first knife sold in 1978. **Mark:** CISCO in logo

ANTONIO J. TAGLIENTI, P.O. Box 221, Darlington, PA 16115/412-846-5259
Specialties: Straight working knives in traditional style. **Patterns:** Hunters—likes forefinger radius; also makes Bowies, tantos, camp knives. **Technical:** Grinds D2, 440C, 154CM; does full tangs only; fancy filework on most knives. **Prices:** $85 to $200; some to $350. **Remarks:** Part-time maker; sold first knife in 1985. **Mark:** Last name

MASAO TAKAHASHI, Umemoto-so, 2-28 Chihaya-cho, Toshima-Ku, Tokyo 171, JAPAN/03-959-6087
Specialties: Highly finished working knives. **Patterns:** Hunters, fishing knives and miniatures. **Technical:** Grinds ATS34. **Prices:** $80 to $145; some to $300. **Remarks:** Part-time maker; first knife sold in 1982. **Mark:** M. TAKAHASHI

TALON KNIVES (See Ron Robertson)

MICHAEL TAMBOLI, 12447 N. 49 Ave., Glendale, AZ 85304/602-978-4308
Specialties: Miniatures, some full size. **Patterns:** Full range of miniature hunting knives to fantasy art. **Technical:** Grinds 01, 440C and Damascus bars; heat-treats blades on request only. **Prices:** $35 to $100; some to $500. **Remarks:** Part-time maker; sold first knife in 1978. **Mark:** MT or Tamboli, city and state

SEIICHI TASAKI, 2-17-8, Shiba-Tsukahara, Kawaguchi-City, Saitama 332, JAPAN/0482-61-0517
Specialties: Does high-tech and traditional folding and straight knives. **Patterns:** Full range of types—hunters, miniatures, interframe folders, and more. **Technical:** Grinds and forges; uses 440C and carbon steel. **Prices:** $230 to $850; some to $5,000. **Remarks:** Full-time maker; sold first knife in 1984. **Mark:** ST connected

"tat" (See Douglas D. Brack)

C. GRAY TAYLOR, 137 Lana View Dr., Kingsport, TN 37664/615-288-5969
Specialties: Period pieces and high art display knives. **Patterns:** Fighters, Bowies, daggers, folding lockers, and interframes. **Technical:** Grinds 440C, 154CM and ATS34. **Prices:** $200 to $3,000; some to $7,000. **Remarks:** Part-time maker; first knife sold in 1975. **Mark:** Name, city and state

DAVID TAYLOR, 137 Lana View Dr., Kingsport, TN 37664/615-288-5969
Specialties: High-tech working knives. **Patterns:** Hunters, fighters, boots and locking folders. **Technical:** Grinds 440C, 154CM and ATS34. **Prices:** $80 to $200; some to $750. **Remarks:** Part-time maker; first knife sold in 1981. Now serving in the armed forces full time; not taking any orders. **Mark:** Name, city state

MICKEY TEDDER, Rt. 2, Box 22, Conover, NC 28613/704-464-9002
Specialties: Working folders. **Patterns:** Lockers in hunter, fighter and boot designs. **Technical:** Grinds D2, 440C and 154CM; makes gold miniatures as jewelry. **Prices:** $150 to $300; some to $1,500. **Remarks:** Part-time maker. **Mark:** TEDDER

LOU TEICHMOELLER, P.O.B. 282, Dolores, CO 81323
Specialties: Working knives, straight and folding. **Patterns:** Hunters, fighters, boots and slip-joint pocketknives. **Technical:** Forges W2, 1025, 5160, and his own Damascus. **Prices:** $75 to $150; some to $250. **Remarks:** Spare-time maker; first knife sold in 1976. **Mark:** TEICHMOELLER

TERRA-GLADIUS KNIVES (See Dave Reynolds)

STEPHEN TERRILL, 21363 Rd. 196, Lindsay, CA 93247/209-562-4395
Specialties: Deluxe working straight and folding knives. **Patterns:** Fighters, tantos, boots, folding lockers and axes. Oriental patterns done in traditional manner. **Technical:** Forges 440C, 1084, and his own Damascus; clean lines. **Prices:** $80 to $550; some to $4,000. **Remarks:** Part-time maker; first knife sold in 1972. **Mark:** Name, city, state in logo

ROBERT TERZUOLA, Route 6, Box 83A, Santa Fe, NM 87501/505-473-1002
Specialties: Period pieces and working knives in his own designs. **Patterns:** Hunters, fighters and tantos—high-tech style and substance in mostly defense knives. **Technical:** Grinds D2, offers titanium handles for his sidelock folders; working knives with Kydex sheath. **Prices:** $175 to $300; some to $3,000. **Remarks:** Full-time maker; first knife sold in 1980. **Mark:** Mayan dragon head and name, city and state

LEON THOMPSON, 1735 Leon Drive, Forest Grove, OR 97116/503-357-2573
Specialties: Period pieces and working knives. **Patterns:** Hunters, Bowies, locking folders, fishing knives and miniatures. **Technical:** Grinds D2, 440C and 154CM. **Prices:** $125 to $250; some to $600. **Remarks:** Part-time maker; first knife sold in 1976. **Mark:** L.J. THOMPSON, city and state

MICHAEL W. THOUROT, T814RR1, RD 11, Napoleon, OH 43545/419-533-6832
Specialties: Working straight knives in customer designs. **Patterns:** Fish and fillet knives; Bowies, tantos and hunters. **Technical:** Grinds 01, D2, and 440C. **Prices:** $200 to $325; some to $1,500. **Remarks:** Part-time maker; first knife sold in 1969. **Mark:** MWT

ED THUESEN, 10649 Haddington, Suite 190, Houston, TX 77043/713-461-8632
Specialties: Working straight knives. **Patterns:** Hunters, fighters and survival knives. **Technical:** Grinds D2, 440C, ATS34 and Vascowear. **Prices:** $85 to $250; some to $600. **Remarks:** Full-time maker; first knife sold in 1979; runs knifemaker supply business. **Mark:** THUESEN

KEVIN THUESEN, 10649 Haddington, Suite 190, Houston, TX 77043/713-461-8632
Specialties: Working straight knives. **Patterns:** Hunters, including upswept skinners; also makes custom walking sticks. **Technical:** Grinds D2, 440C, 154CM and ATS34. **Prices:** $85 to $125; some to $200. **Remarks:** Part-time maker; sold first knife in 1985. **Mark:** KAT on slant

THUNDERBOLT ARTISANS (See Thomas N. Hilker)

TIMBERLINE KNIVES, P.O. Box 36, Mancos, CO 81328/303-533-7006
Specialties: High-tech straight and folding working knives. **Patterns:** Survival knives in complete systems; stag hunters—high-tech approaches; locking folders and interframes. **Technical:** Grinds 440C, D2, and 154CM. **Prices:** Moderate. **Remarks:** Full-time makers. Partnership of V. Neeley and W. Sanders since 1982. **Mark:** Timberline

THE TINKER (See Jim Ladd)

CAROLYN D. TINKER, P.O. Box 5123, Whittier, CA 90607/213-696-9202
Specialties: Working straight knives in her own designs. **Patterns:** Hunters, kitchen and fish knives; small tools. **Technical:** Grinds D2, 440C and 154CM. **Prices:** $85 to $125. **Remarks:** Full-time maker; first knife sold in 1974. **Mark:** Name and city in logo

TKM (TENNESSEE KNIFE MAKER) (See W.C. Ward)

DANIEL TOKAR, Box 1776, Shepherdstown, WV 25443
Specialties: Period pieces and working knives. **Patterns:** Hunters, camp knives, buckskinner blades; also axes, swords and battle gear. **Technical:** Forges L6, 1095 and his own Damascus. Makes mokume, Japanese alloys and bronze daggers; restores old edged weapons. **Prices:** $125 to $400; some to $1,500. **Remarks:** Part-time maker; first knife sold in 1979. **Mark:** Arrow over rune and date

P.J. TOMES, P.O. Box 37268, Jacksonville, FL 32236/904-786-1731
Specialties: Period pieces and plain and fancy working knives. **Patterns:** Boots, daggers, Bowies; locking lockers; simple lightweight hunters and household cutlery. **Technical:** Grinds and forges; uses D2, ATS34 and his own Damascus. **Prices:** $75 to $500; some to $2,000. **Remarks:** Full-time maker. **Mark:** TOMES

DAN TOMPKINS, 310 N. Second St., Peotone, IL 60468/312-258-3620
Specialties: Working knives, some deluxe. **Patterns:** Hunters, boots, daggers and push knives. **Technical:** Grinds D2, 440C and 154CM; buys Damascus. **Prices:** $85 to $150; some to $400. **Remarks:** Part-time maker; first knife sold in 1975. **Mark:** TOMPKINS, city and state

DWIGHT L. TOWELL, Rt. 1, Box 66, Midvale, ID 83645/208-355-2419
Specialties: Solid and elegant working, and art-type knives. **Patterns:** Hunters, Bowies, daggers; folders in several weights. **Technical:** Grinds 154CM; some knives engraved. **Prices:** $250 to $800; some over $3,500. **Remarks:** Part-time maker; first knife sold in 1970. **Mark:** TOWELL

R.W. TRABBIC, 4550 N. Haven, Toledo, OH 43612/419-478-9578
Specialties: Working knives. **Patterns:** Hunters, Bowies; locking hunters and springbacks in standard patterns. **Technical:** Grinds D2, 440C and 154CM. **Prices:** $80 to $250. **Remarks:** Part-time maker; first knife sold in 1973. **Mark:** R. W. TRABBIC

TERRY A. TREUTEL, P.O. Box 187, Hamilton, MT 59840/406-363-4142
Specialties: Working straight knives in his designs and traditional patterns. **Patterns:** Hunters, skinners, camp and fish knives; roached back short hunters. **Technical:** Grinds D2, 154CM, and 440C on request basis; does own heat-treating. **Prices:** $107 to $180; some $450. **Remarks:** Full-time maker; first knife sold in 1983. **Mark:** Name

BARRY TRINDLE, RR #1, Box 63, Earlham, IA 50072/515-462-1237
Specialties: Engraved folding knives. **Patterns:** Folders in his own designs; will consider customer designs. **Technical:** 440 only. Heat-treats and offers engraving in house. Natural handle materials only. **Prices:** Starts at $350. **Mark:** Name inside oak leaf

TRO KNIVES (See Overeynder)

THOMAS A. TRUJILLO, 2905 Arctic Blvd., Anchorage, AK 99503/907-563-2738
Specialties: Working knives. **Patterns:** Hunters, Bowies, daggers, folding lockers. **Technical:** Grinds 01, ATS34, and commercial Damascus. **Prices:** $150 to $900; some to $6,000. **Remarks:** Full-time maker; first knife sold in 1976. **Mark:** Alaska Knife and/or Thomas Anthony

JON J. TSOULAS, 1 Home St., Peabody, MA 01960/617-532-3163
Specialties: Fancy straightworking knives of his own design. **Patterns:** Hunters, fighters, and Bowies. **Technical:** Grinds D2, 440C, and 154CM; high polish grinds, and likes wood handles. **Prices:** $75 to $225; some $450. **Remarks:** Part-time maker; first knife sold in 1984. **Mark:** TSOULAS

JIM TURECEK, 360 Long Hill Ave., Shelton, CT 06484/203-734-8406
Specialties: Unique straight and folding knives of his own designs. **Patterns:** Trout and bird knives with split bamboo handles; hunters, skinners, Bowies and folders. **Technical:** Grinds 440C, D2, and 154CM. **Prices:** $80 to $300; some over $600. **Remarks:** Full-time maker; first knife sold in 1983. Teaches fly fishing and tying. **Mark:** T in script or name

RALPH A. TURNBULL, 5722 Newburg Rd., Rockford, IL 61108/815-398-3799
Specialties: Plain or fancy working knives. **Patterns:** Hunters, fighters, boots, folders and Bowies. **Technical:** Grinds ATS34, 440C, 154CM, CPM and others; Damascus; does wood into wood inlay handles. **Prices:** $100 to $300; some to $2,000. **Remarks:** Full-time maker; first knife sold in 1973. **Mark:** Signature or initials in circle used on Damascus

TWIG (See K.M. Davis)

E.W. URSTADT, Rt. 4, Box 296, Deer Park, MD 21550/301-387-9616

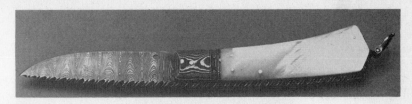

SCHMIDT

SCHWARZER

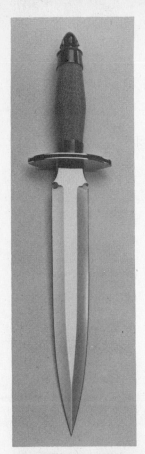

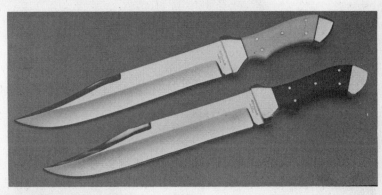

SHEEHAN

SALLEY

SINYARD

SIMMONDS

SHOEMAKER

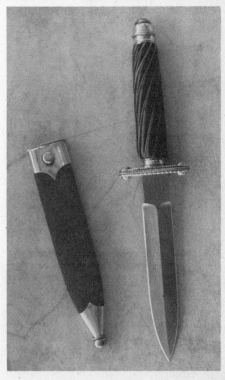

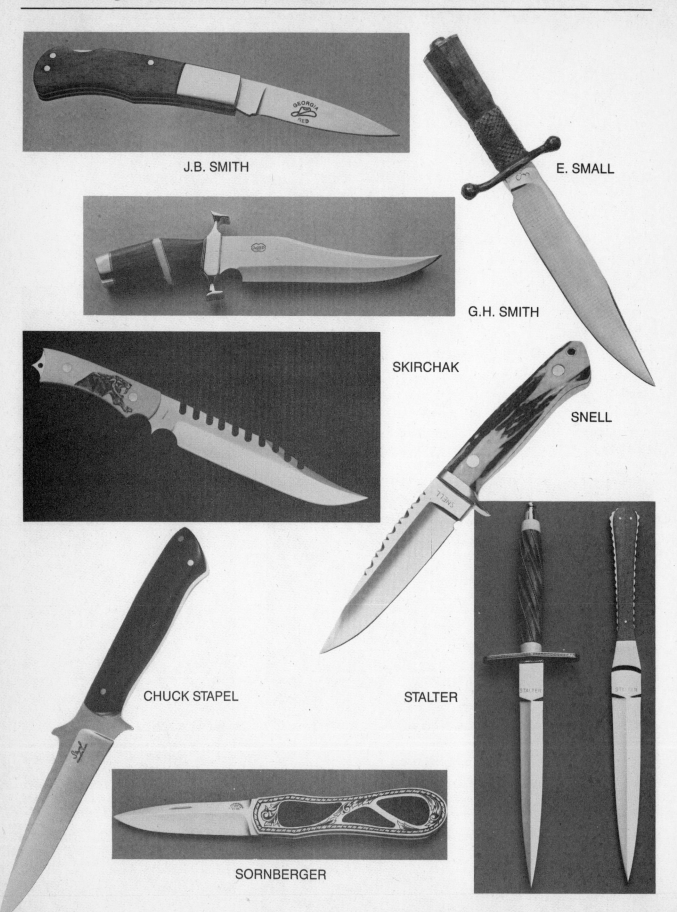

J.B. SMITH

E. SMALL

G.H. SMITH

SKIRCHAK

SNELL

CHUCK STAPEL

STALTER

SORNBERGER

STEINBERG

STRONG

TURNBULL

TOMES

TOWELL

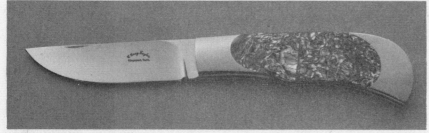

C. TAYLOR

directory/custom knifemakers

Specialties: From practical to fantasy straight knives and swords. **Patterns:** One-of-a-kind period pieces, fighters, boots, even wood-carving tools. **Technical:** Forges A2, and 154CM. Enjoys doing his own embellishments. **Prices:** $50 to $5,000. **Remarks:** Full-time maker; first knife sold in 1971. **Mark:** Shadowmaker in script

UWHARRIE RATTLER KNIVES (See Charles V. Rece)

WAYNE VALACHOVIC, RFD #1 Box 215B, Dept. K89, Hillsboro, NH 03244/603-464-5773
Specialties: Damascus folders in unique designs with Persian influence. **Patterns:** Persian-influenced fighters, a number of robust folding designs; camp knives. **Technical:** Forges own Damascus; most knives have filework. **Prices:** $125 and up. **Remarks:** Full-time maker. **Mark:** V with cross; ABS Master Smith

A. DANIEL VALOIS, 4299 Hawthorne Rd., Walnutport, PA 18088/215-767-0213
Specialties: Big knives for rough duty. Lockback folders in all sizes. **Patterns:** Fighters in survival packs; sturdy working knives; belt buckle knives; military styling. **Technical:** Forges and grinds A2, 01 and 440C; likes full tangs. **Prices:** $65 to $240; some to $600. **Remarks:** Full-time maker; first knife sold in 1969. **Mark:** Initials, anvil logo

FRANS VAN ELDIK, Ho Flaan 3, 3632 BT Loenen, NETHERLANDS/02943-3095
Specialties: Fancy working knives in his own designs. **Patterns:** Hunters, fighters, boots. **Technical:** Grinds and forges; uses D2, 154CM, ATS34 and Damascus from Germany. **Prices:** $225 to $1,750; some to $2,500. **Remarks:** Spare-time maker; first knife sold in 1979. **Mark:** Lion with F.V.E. Amsterdam

MICHAEL VEIT, Rt. 1, 3070 E. Fifth Rd., LaSalle, IL 61301/815-223-3538
Specialties: Period pieces and fancy straight knives. **Patterns:** Fighters, Bowies and daggers. **Technical:** Forges his own Turkish Damascus, 01 and L6. All hidden tang knives have complete disassembly. **Prices:** $200 to $650; some to $1,200. **Remarks:** Full-time maker; first knife sold in 1985. **Mark:** Name in script

H.J. VIELE, 88 Lexington Ave., Westwood, NJ 07675/201-666-2906
Specialties: Clean design in folding knives of distinctive shapes. **Patterns:** High-tech folders. **Technical:** Grinds 440C, ATS34. **Prices:** $500 and up. **Remarks:** Part-time maker; first knife sold in 1973. **Mark:** VIELE with Japanese crane

R. VON BOECKMAN, P.O. Box 40506, Memphis, TN 38174/800-727-0201
Specialties: Professional tools for police and military. One-of-a-kind designs. **Patterns:** Hunters, skinners, and high-grade functional designs for military. **Technical:** Grinds stainless steels. **Prices:** $90 to $150; some $250. **Remarks:** Full-time maker; first knife sold in 1987. **Mark:** Pyramid logo with RA inside

BEN VOSS, P.O. Box 3654, Davenport, IA 52808/319-322-2895
Specialties: Fancy workable knives in his own designs. **Patterns:** Sub-hilt fighters, hunters, boots, and folders. **Technical:** Grinds 440C, 154CM, and D2. Has good proportions. **Prices:** $60 to $200; some to $400. **Remarks:** Full-time maker; first knife sold in 1986. **Mark:** Name, city and state

DAVID P. VOTAW, Box 327, Pioneer, OH 43554/419-737-2774
Specialties: Period pieces as working knives. **Patterns:** Hunters, Bowies, camp knives, buckskinners, tomahawks to W-K's traditional standards. **Technical:** Grinds 01 and D2. **Prices:** $75 to $200; some to $500. **Remarks:** Part-time maker; took over for the late Walter Kneubuehler. **Mark:** WK with V inside anvil

FRANK VOUGHT, JR., 115 Monticello Dr., Hammond, LA 70401/504-345-0278
Specialties: Distinctive working knives, and embellished collectables. **Patterns:** Bowies, hunters, survival knives; daggers and swords; folding lockers. **Technical:** Grinds and forges; offers D2, 440C, and ATS34; has new "field grade" Outfitter line. **Prices:** $50 to $1,500; some $15,000. **Remarks:** Full-time maker; first knife sold in 1973. **Mark:** Signature with fleur-de-lis, or Outfitter

ROBERT "BOB" VUNK, 4408 Buckeye Ct., Orlando, FL 32804/305-628-3970
Specialties: Working knives, some fancy or period pieces. **Patterns:** Tantos in many flavors; some swords and camp knives. **Technical:** Grinds 01, 440C, ATS34; provides mountings, cases, stands. **Prices:** $35 to $500; some to $1,000. **Remarks:** Part-time maker; sold first knife in 1985. **Mark:** RV and date

JAMES M. WADE, Rt. 1, Moss Road, Box 56, Wade, NC 28395/919-483-3548
Specialties: Straight working knives. **Patterns:** Hunters, boots, fillets, push knives and miniatures. **Technical:** Grinds D2, 440C, 154CM and ATS34. **Prices:** $100 to

$450; some to $1,000. **Remarks:** Spare-time maker; first knife sold in 1982. **Mark:** Name and serial number

JOHN K. WAGAMAN, 903 Arsenal Ave., Fayetteville, NC 28305/919-485-7860
Specialties: Fancy working knives. **Patterns:** Bowies, miniatures, hunters, fighters, boots. **Technical:** Grinds D2, 440C and 154CM, and bought Damascus; inlays mother-of-pearl. **Prices:** $80 to $340; some to $800. **Remarks:** Part-time maker; first knife sold in 1975. **Mark:** WAGAMAN

HERMAN F. WAHLERS, Star Route Box 1, Austerlitz, NY 12017/518-392-3570
Specialties: Straight working knives of his own design. **Patterns:** Bowies, hunters and camp knives; favors clip-point for general use. **Technical:** Grinds D2 and 440C. **Prices:** $75 to $200; some $400. **Remarks:** Full-time maker; first knife sold in 1983. **Mark:** H.W. or Herman F. Wahlers, maker

MARK DAVID WAHLSTER, 1404 No. Second St., Silverton, OR 97381/503-873-3775
Specialties: Working knives and period pieces. **Patterns:** Folders in antique factory patterns. High-tech folders in hunting styles; offers combat-styled knives also. **Technical:** Grinds and forges; offers 01, L6, 440C, ATS34 and buys D2. **Prices:** $55 to $400. **Remarks:** Full-time maker; first knife sold in 1981. **Mark:** Name, city and state, or Wahlster

MARK WALDROP, P.O. Box 129, Lady Lake, FL 32659/904-821-2530
Specialties: Period pieces and working knives. **Patterns:** Folding lockers, hunters, Bowies and daggers. **Technical:** Forges A2, 01 and his own Damascus; forges ribbed blades. Engraving done by maker. **Prices:** Moderate to upscale. **Remarks:** Part-time maker; first knife sold in 1978. **Mark:** WALDROP

GEORGE A. WALKER, Star Route, Alpine, WY 83128/307-883-2372
Specialties: Deluxe working knives in partnership. **Patterns:** Hunters, boots, fighters, Bowies and folders. **Technical:** Forges own Damascus and cable; engraving, scrimshaw, and sheaths all in house. **Prices:** $125 to $750; some to $1,000. **Remarks:** Full-time maker; first knife sold in 1979. **Mark:** Name, city and state

JOHN W. WALKER, Rt. 2, Box 376, Bon Aqua, TN 37025/615-670-4754
Specialties: Working straight knives in standard patterns. **Patterns:** Hunters, boots, push knives and miniatures. **Technical:** Grinds 440C, 154CM and ATS34. **Prices:** $85 to $200; some to $450. **Remarks:** Full-time maker; first knife sold in 1982. **Mark:** Hohenzollern Eagle below name

MICHAEL L. WALKER, Box 2343, Taos, NM 87571/505-758-0233
Specialties: High-tech folders of original design and execution. **Patterns:** Folding lockers, patent locks, interframes—engraved, scrimmed, anodized in titanium colors, furnished with rich materials. **Technical:** Grinds AEB-L, 6K, commercial Damascus; most knives a team effort with Patricia Walker. **Prices:** $475 to $1,800; some to $4,500. **Remarks:** Full-time maker; first knife sold in 1980. **Mark:** Walker's Lockers by M.L. Walker, or initials

A.F. WALTERS, 609 E. 20th St., Tifton, GA 31794/912-382-1282
Specialties: Working knives; some to order. **Patterns:** Folding lockers; fixed hunters, fish and survival knives. **Technical:** Grinds D2, 154CM and 13C26. **Prices:** $100 and up. **Remarks:** Part-time maker. Label: "The jewel knife." **Mark:** J in diamond and knife logo

KEN WARD, 3401 Becerra Wy., Sacramento, CA 95821/916-482-9650
Specialties: Working knives, some to custom design. **Patterns:** Hunters, folding and fixed; axes, Bowies, buckskinners and miniatures. **Technical:** Grinds 440C, 154CM and ATS34. **Prices:** $85 to $180; some to $800. **Remarks:** Full-time maker; first knife sold in 1977. **Mark:** Name, city and state in oval logo

W.C. WARD, Rte. 6, Lynn Rd, Box 184-B, Clinton, TN 37716/615-457-3568
Specialties: Straight working knives, and some period pieces. **Patterns:** Hunters, Bowies, swords and kitchen cutlery. **Technical:** Grinds 01. **Prices:** $85 to $150; some $500. **Remarks:** Part-time maker; first knife sold in 1969; styled the Tennessee Knife Maker. **Mark:** TKM

DAVE WARDMAN, 9910 U.S.-23, Ossineke, MI 49766/517-471-2090
Specialties: Straight working knives to order. **Patterns:** Hunters, minis, boots and survival knives. **Technical:** Hollow grinds D2, 440C and 154CM. **Prices:** $55 to $150. **Remarks:** Spare-time maker; first knife sold in 1977. **Mark:** Wardman

BUSTER WARENSKI, P.O. Box 214, Richfield, UT 84701/801-896-5319
Specialties: Investor-class design and execution in straight knives. **Patterns:** Daggers, swords, fighters and Bowies. **Technical:** Grinds; does own engraving and inlays; surface treatments. **Prices:** Upscale. **Remarks:** Full-time maker. Not taking orders. **Mark:** Buster or Warenski

AL WARREN, P.O. Box 332, Porterville, CA 93258/209-784-5855
Specialties: Straight working knives, some quite fancy. **Patterns:** Hunter patterns, some Bowies; incorporates intact fossil ivory artifacts. **Technical:** Grinds D2, 440C and F8 (a high carbon, high tungsten steel); laminates $^3/_{32}$-inch ivory over ebony or koa; brass-wraps all full tangs. **Prices:** $195 to $850; some to $1,500. **Remarks:** Full-time maker; sold first knife in 1978. **Mark:** NAME, serial

DALE WARTHER, 164 West St., Box 265, Bolivar, OH 44612/216-343-7513
Specialties: Period pieces and working knives. **Patterns:** Kitchen cutlery, daggers, hunters and some folders. **Technical:** Grinds and forges; uses 01, D2 and 440C. **Prices:** $100 to $350; some to $5,000. **Remarks:** Full-time maker; first knife sold in 1967. Taking orders only at shows or personal interviews at shop. **Mark:** WARTHER ORIGINALS

STANLEY WARZOCHA, 32540 Wareham Dr., Warren, MI 48092/313-939-9344
Specialties: Straight working knives; some period pieces. **Patterns:** Hunters, buckskinners; fighters and fish knives. **Technical:** Grinds 01, 440C and 154CM. **Prices:** $80 to $140; some to $300. **Remarks:** Spare-time maker; first knife sold in 1978. **Mark:** WARZOCHA

WATER MOUNTAIN KNIVES (See Kenneth Maneker)

DANIEL and BILL WATSON, 350 Jennifer Ln., Driftwood, TX 78619/512-847-9679
Specialties: Fancy working knives and swords. **Patterns:** Hunters, daggers and swords. **Technical:** Hand forges 1080, 5160, and their own Damascus and cable; European and Japanese temper; uses leaf springs, too. **Prices:** $90 to $4,000; swords to $10,000. **Remarks:** Full-time maker; Daniel sold his first knife in 1979. Bill sold his in 1982. **Mark:** "Angel Sword" or A.S.

FREDDIE WATT, III, P.O. Box 1372, Big Spring, TX 79721/915-263-6629
Specialties: Straight and folding working knives; some fancy. **Patterns:** Hunters, fighters, Bowies; some folders. **Technical:** Grinds D2, 440C and ATS34; likes mirror finishes. **Prices:** $150 to $220; some to $500. **Remarks:** Full-time maker; first knife sold in 1979. **Mark:** WATT, city, state

WALLY WATTS, Rt. 1, Box 81, Gatesville, TX 76528/817-487-2866
Specialties: Folders only in traditional and unique personal patterns. **Patterns:** Folders; single-blade gents, and various blade shapes. **Technical:** Grinds 440C, D2, and ATS34. **Prices:** $85 to $165; some $200. **Remarks:** Full-time maker; first knife sold in 1986. **Mark:** WATTS

FRED E. WEBER, 517 Tappan St., Forked River, NJ 08731/609-693-0452
Specialties: Working knives in standard patterns. **Patterns:** Hunters, fighters, Bowies, boots and daggers; various-sized fillets. **Technical:** Grinds D2, 154CM and 440V. **Prices:** $110 to $250; some $500. **Remarks:** Full-time maker; first knife sold in 1973. **Mark:** F.E. WEBER

DEL WEDDLE, Jr., Box 10, Stewartsville, MO 64490/816-669-3478
Specialties: Working knives; some period pieces. **Patterns:** Hunters, fighters, folding lockers; makes push knives. **Technical:** Grinds D2 and 440C; can provide precious metals and set gems. **Prices:** $80 to $250; some to $2,000. **Remarks:** Full-time maker; first knife sold in 1972. **Mark:** Signature with last name and date

RUDY WEHNER, 2713 Riverbend Dr., Violet, LA 70092/504-682-3168
Specialties: Working straight knives in traditional patterns. **Patterns:** Full-size to miniature Bowies of various styles, skinners, camp knives. **Technical:** Grinds D2, 440C, and 154CM. **Prices:** $60 to $125; some up to $450. **Remarks:** Part-time maker; first knife sold in 1975. **Mark:** Full name, city and state

J. REESE WEILAND, JR., 14919 Nebraska Ave., Tampa, FL 33612/813-971-5378 (M-F 7:30-5:00)
Specialties: Straight and folding working knives of traditional types. **Patterns:** Hunters, tantos, Bowies, butterflies, some swords; distinctive bird-shaped handle on some models. **Technical:** Grinds 440C, ATS34 and Damascus bars. **Prices:** $100 to $250; some higher. **Remarks:** Full-time production; sold first knife in 1983. **Mark:** RW slant

DONALD E. WEILER, P.O. Box 1576, Yuma, AZ 85364/602-782-1159
Specialties: Period pieces and straight working knives. **Patterns:** Dirks, daggers, fighters, survival knives; scramasax; likes Norse designs. Reforges bought Damascus. **Technical:** Grinds and forges; uses 01, A2, 5160, W1 and D2. **Prices:** $60 to $200; some to $750. **Remarks:** Part-time maker; first knife sold in 1952. **Mark:** WEILER, YUMA

GEROME W. WEINAND, Box 385, Lolo, MT 59847/406-273-6553
Specialties: Straight working knives. **Patterns:** Bowies, fish and camp knives; large special hunters. **Technical:** Grinds 01, 440C, and L6. Does own heat-treating. **Prices:** $25 to $50; some $250. **Remarks:** Full-time maker; first knife sold in 1982. **Mark:** Name, city and state

CHARLES L. WEISS, 18847 N. 13th Ave., Phoenix, AZ 85027/602-869-0425
Specialties: Deluxe period pieces; high art straight knives. **Patterns:** Daggers, fighters, boots, push knives and miniatures. **Technical:** Grinds 440C, 154CM and ATS34. **Prices:** $300 to $1,200; some to $2,000. **Remarks:** Full-time maker; first knife sold in 1975. **Mark:** Name and town

WILLIAM H. WELCH, 5226 Buell Drive, Fort Wayne, IN 46807/219-745-0411
Specialties: Working knives and deluxe period pieces. **Patterns:** Hunters, tantos, Bowies, locking folders and spears. **Technical:** Grinds A2, D2 and 440C. **Prices:** $80 to $400; some to $1,000. **Remarks:** Part-time maker; first knife sold in 1976. **Mark:** WELCH

GEORGE W. WERTH, 9010 Cary Rd., Cary, IL 60013/312-639-9308
Specialties: Period pieces, some fancy. **Patterns:** Straight knives in fighters, daggers, Bowies. **Technical:** Forges and grinds 01, 1095 and his own Damascus, including mosaic patterns. **Prices:** $200 to $650; some much more. **Remarks:** Full-time production. **Mark:** Name in logo or GWW connected

CODY WESCOTT, 5610 Hanger Lake Ln., Las Cruces, NM 88001/505-382-5008
Specialties: Fancy working knives. **Patterns:** Hunters, buckskinners, Bowies, fighters and folders. **Technical:** Hollow grinds and forges; offers D2, 440C and commercial Damascus; all knives extensively fileworked. **Prices:** $50 to $240; some to $700. **Remarks:** Full-time maker; first knife sold in 1982. **Mark:** C. WESCOTT

JIM WESCOTT, 4225 Elks Dr., Las Cruces, NM 88005/505-526-8926
Specialties: Working knives. **Patterns:** Bowies, hunters and locking folders. **Technical:** Grinds D2 and 440C. **Prices:** $90 to $170; some to $300. **Remarks:** Part-time maker; first knife sold in 1982. **Mark:** Wescott

MIKE WESOLOWSKI, 902-A Lohrman Lane, Petaluma, CA 94952/707-762-7564
Specialties: Working knives; display Bowies. **Patterns:** Hunters, utility and using knives, and miniatures. **Technical:** Flat grinds; finger placement choils. Uses D2, 440C, and 154CM. **Prices:** $90 to $200; some $500. **Remarks:** Part-time maker; first knife sold in 1973. **Mark:** M.W., city and state in knife logo

WHISKERS (See Mike Allen)

GENE E. WHITE, 5415 Taney Ave., Alexandria, VA 22304/703-751-1833
Specialties: Working knives; period pieces to order. **Patterns:** Simple guardless hunters and utility knives; makes fighters to order. **Technical:** Grinds; uses stainless steels. **Prices:** $60 to $150; some to $300. **Remarks:** Part-time maker; first knife sold in 1971. **Mark:** Last name

ROBERT J. "BOB" WHITE, RR 1, Gilson, IL 61436/309-289-4487
Specialties: Working knives; some quite deluxe. **Patterns:** Bird and trout knives, hunters, survival knives and folding lockers. **Technical:** Grinds and forges A2, D2 and 440C; commercial Damascus. Does own heat-treating. **Prices:** $95 to $185; some to $600. **Remarks:** Full-time maker; first knife sold in 1976. **Mark:** White in script

ROBERT J. "BUTCH" WHITE, JR., R.R. 1, Gilson, IL 61436/309-289-4487
Specialties: Fixed and folding working knives. **Patterns:** Hunters, fighters and boots and Damascus miniatures. **Technical:** Grinds and forges; offers D2, 440C and his own Damascus. **Prices:** $100 to $500. **Remarks:** Full-time maker; first knife sold in 1980. **Mark:** WHITE in block letters; a block W on miniatures

WHITEFISH SPORTSMAN (See Pete Forthofer)

JAMES D. WHITEHEAD, P.O. Box 540, Durham, CA 95938/916-894-3938
Specialties: Highly detailed straight and folding miniatures. **Patterns:** Traditional and fancy. **Technical:** Forges and grinds 01 and bought Damascus. **Prices:** $150 to $500, some higher. **Remarks:** Part-time maker; first knife sold in 1985. **Mark:** JDW

directory/custom knifemakers

JIM WHITMAN, HC80, Box 5387, Chugiak, AK 99567/907-688-4575
Specialties: Working straight knives and some art pieces. **Patterns:** Hunters, especially skinners, Bowies, camp knives; working fighters. **Technical:** Grinds 440C, ABL-SWD in "semi-flat" grind for good edge-holding. Likes to use natural and native handle materials. **Prices:** $85 to $350; some higher. **Remarks:** Part-time maker; sold first knife in 1983. **Mark:** Name, city, state

EARL T. WHITMIRE, 725 Colonial Dr., Rock Hill, SC 29730/803-324-8384
Specialties: Working straight knives, some to order. **Patterns:** Hunters, fighters, fish knives; some fantasy pieces. **Technical:** Grinds D2, 440C and 154CM. **Prices:** $40 to $200; some to $250. **Remarks:** Full-time maker; first knife sold in 1967. **Mark:** Name, city, state in oval logo

ROBERT E. WHITTAKER, P.O. Box 204, Mill Creek, PA 17060/717-643-5676
Specialties: Using straight knives. **Patterns:** Hunters, skinners and Bowies. **Technical:** Grinds 01, A2 and D2. Likes filework. **Prices:** $35 to $100. **Remarks:** Full-time maker; first knife sold in 1980. **Mark:** W or REW in circle logo

KEN J. WHITWORTH, 41667 Tetley Ave., Sterling Heights, MI 48078/313-739-5720
Specialties: Straight and folding working knives. **Patterns:** Locking folders, slip joints, and boot knives. **Technical:** Grinds 440C, 154CM and D2. **Prices:** $100 to $225; some to $450. **Remarks:** Part-time maker; first knife sold in 1976. **Mark:** WHITWORTH

HORACE WIGGINS, 203 Herndon, Box 152, Mansfield, LA 71502/318-872-4471 (evenings)
Specialties: Fancy working knives. **Patterns:** Hunters, fixed and folding. **Technical:** Grinds 01, D2 and 440C. **Prices:** $90 to $275. **Remarks:** Part-time maker; first knife sold in 1970. **Mark:** Name, city, state in diamond logo

JAMES C. WIGGINS, 1540 W. Pleasant Rd., Hammond, LA 70403/504-345-0454
Specialties: Folding and straight working knives in standard patterns: **Patterns:** Hunters, camp knives and locking folders. **Technical:** Grinds D2, 440C and 154CM. **Prices:** $75 to $150; some to $600. **Remarks:** Part-time maker; first knife sold in 1981. **Mark:** Full name

WILD BILL & SONS (See Bill Caldwell)

GERI L. WILLEY, Rt. 1, Box 235-B, Greenwood, DE 19950/302-349-4070
Specialties: Straight working knives of her own design. **Patterns:** Hunters. **Technical:** Grinds 440C. **Prices:** $45 to $75; some $90. **Remarks:** Spare-time maker; daughter of W.G. Willey. Has worked in his shop for five years. **Mark:** Willey in diamond logo

W.G. WILLEY, R.D. 1, Box 235-B, Greenwood, DE 19950/302-349-4070
Specialties: Fancy working straight knives. **Patterns:** Small game knives, Bowies and throwing knives. **Technical:** Grinds 440C and 154CM. **Prices:** $225 to $600; some to $1,500. **Remarks:** Part-time maker; first knife sold in 1975. Has retail store. **Mark:** WILLEY inside map logo

SHERMAN A. WILLIAMS, 1709 Wallace St., Simi Valley, CA 93065/805-583-3821
Specialties: Straight working knives in standard patterns. **Patterns:** Hunters, boots, utility knives, also unusual trail knives. **Technical:** Grinds and forges; uses ATS34, 1095, DA and A2. **Prices:** $45 to $250. **Remarks:** Part-time maker; first knife sold in 1983. **Mark:** SHERMAN in crow logo

THE WILLOW FORGE (See Daniel Tokar)

WILSONHAWK (See James G. Wilson)

JAMES G. WILSON, Moraine Rt. UC 2004, Estes Park, CO 80517/303-586-3944
Specialties: The Bronze Age first; the 20th century second. **Patterns:** Bronze knives and swords and battle axes. Bowies and boots. **Technical:** Casts bronze; grinds D2, 440C and 154CM. **Prices:** $65 to $250; some to $1,200. **Remarks:** Part-time maker; first knife sold in 1975. **Mark:** WilsonHawK

R.W. WILSON, P.O. Box 2012, Weirton, WV 26062/304-723-2771
Specialties: Period pieces; working knives. **Patterns:** Straight working knives; Bowies and tomahawks and patch knives. **Prices:** $85 to $175; some $1,000. **Technical:** Grinds 440C; scrimshaw. **Remarks:** Part-time maker; first knife sold in 1966. Knifemaker supplier. **Mark:** Name in tomahawk

MICHAEL WINE, 265 S. Atlantic Ave., Cocoa Beach, FL 32931/407-784-2187
Specialties: Straight and folding traditional working knives. **Patterns:** Does some fish knives; has a bareheaded, linerless, mid-release locking folder. **Technical:** Grinds 440C, 154CM and Stellite. **Prices:** $100 to $175; some to $350. **Remarks:** Spare-time maker; sold first knife in 1971. **Mark:** M. WINE with palm tree

DANIEL WINKLER, P.O. Box 255DTS, Boone, NC 28607-0255/704-264-2854
Specialties: Period pieces, some made to look old, and buckskinner working knives. **Patterns:** Buckskinners, patch knives, daggers, skinners, and fighters. **Technical:** Forges and grinds D2, old files, and buys Damascus. **Prices:** $40 to $150; some to $350. **Remarks:** Full-time maker; first knife sold in 1984. **Mark:** DW connected

TRAVIS A. WINN, 558 E. 3065 So., Salt Lake City, UT 84106/801-467-5957
Specialties: Fancy working knives and customer designs. **Patterns:** Hunters, fighters and fancy daggers; some miniatures; tantos and fantasy knives. **Technical:** Grinds 01, D2 and 440C. Does own embellishment. **Prices:** $80 to $200; some to $1,000. **Remarks:** Part-time maker; first knife sold in 1976. **Mark:** TRAV stylized

EARL WITSAMAN, 3957 Redwing Circle, Stow, OH 44224/216-688-4208
Specialties: Miniatures of straight knives and fantasy pieces. **Patterns:** Wide variety—Randall to D-guard Bowie. **Technical:** Grinds 01, 440C and 300 stainless; commercial Damascus; mirror finishes; greatly detailed. **Prices:** $40 to $70. **Remarks:** Part-time maker; first knife sold in 1974. **Mark:** EW

W-K Knives (See Votaw)

BARRY B. WOOD, 38 S. Venice Blvd., Venice, CA 90291/213-823-5637
Specialties: High-tech working folders based on patented lock. **Patterns:** Twenty-two variations of four designs. **Technical:** Blades 154CM/ATS34; handles 17-4HP investment castings. **Prices:** $175 to $500, and up. **Remarks:** Full-time maker; first knife sold in 1969. **Mark:** bw in script within triangle of arcs

LARRY B. WOOD, 6945 Fishburg Rd., Huber Heights, OH 45424/513-233-6751
Specialties: Fancy working knives in his own designs. **Patterns:** Hunters, buckskinners, Bowies, tomahawks, folding lockers and Damascus miniatures. **Technical:** Forges 1095, file steel, and his own Damascus. **Prices:** $125 to $500; some to $2,000. **Remarks:** Full-time maker; first knife sold in 1974. **Mark:** Variations of Wood, sometimes with blacksmith logo

OWEN DALE WOOD, P.O. Box 515, Honeydew 2040 (Transvaal), SOUTH AFRICA/International + 2711 + 795-1050
Specialties: Fancy working knives. **Patterns:** Hunters and fighters; big knives of many types; sword canes. **Technical:** Forges and grinds 440C, 154CM and his own Damascus. Uses rare African handle materials. **Prices:** $280 to $450; some to $3,000. **Remarks:** Full-time maker; first knife sold in 1976. **Mark:** An O encircling a W

WEBSTER WOOD, 4726 Rosedale, Clarkston, MI 48016/313-394-0351
Specialties: Fancy working knives. **Patterns:** Hunters, survival knives, folding lockers and slip joints. **Technical:** Grinds 01, 440C and 154CM; does all engraving and scrimming. **Prices:** $100 to $500; some to $3,000. **Remarks:** Full-time maker; first knife sold in 1980. **Mark:** Initials inside shield and name

WILLIAM W. WOOD, P.O. Box 877, Vera, TX 76383/817-888-5832
Specialties: Exotic working knives with Middle-East flavor. **Patterns:** Fighters, boots; some utility knives. **Technical:** Grinds D2, 440C and buys Damascus; hand rubbed satin finish; only natural handle materials. **Prices:** $300 to $600; some to $2,000. **Remarks:** Full-time maker; first knife sold in 1977. **Mark:** Name, city, state

HAROLD E. WOODWARD, Rt 3, Box 64A, Woodbury, TN 37190/615-563-4619
Specialties: Period pieces and working knives. **Patterns:** Hunters, Bowies, swords, sword canes and tomahawks. **Technical:** Grinds A2, D2 and 440C; does his own engraving. **Prices:** $75 to $350; some much more. **Remarks:** Full-time maker; first knife sold in 1972. **Mark:** WOODWARD

AL WOODWORTH, RR #1, P.O. Box 13, Plainville, IL 62365/217-656-3591
Specialties: Working straight knives and miniatures in his personal designs. **Patterns:** Bowies, fighters, daggers, and hunters. **Technical:** Grinds 01, D2, 440C, 154CM, ATS34; buys Damascus; uses natural handles. **Prices:** $125 to $250; some to $450. **Remarks:** Full-time maker; sold first knife in 1987. **Mark:** AW with cross, Libra sign

directory/custom knifemakers

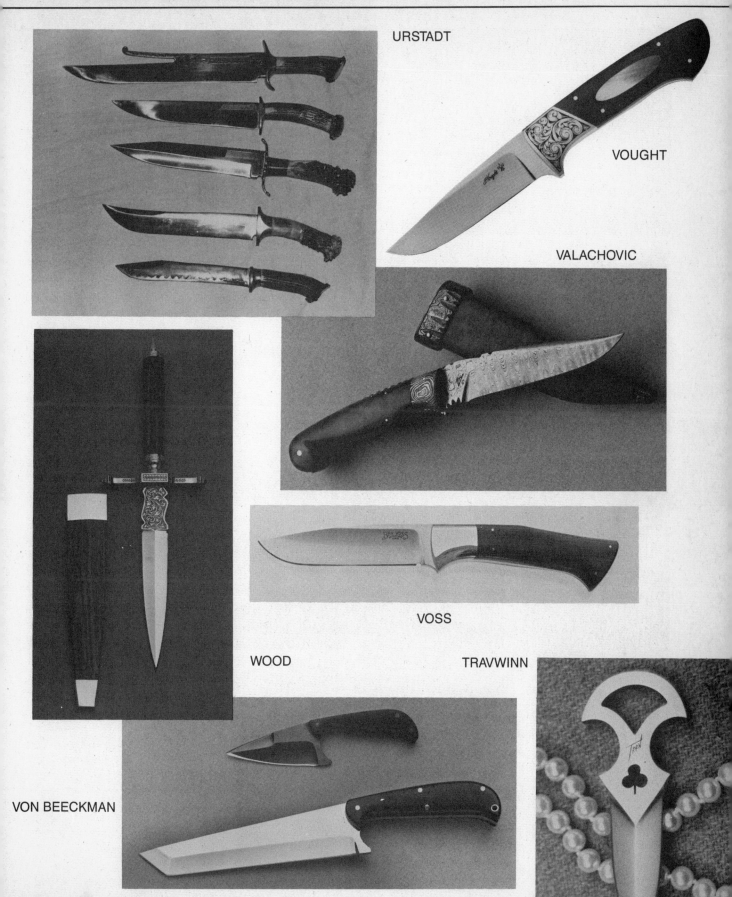

URSTADT

VOUGHT

VALACHOVIC

VOSS

WOOD

TRAVWINN

VON BEECKMAN

directory/custom knifemakers

WHITE

WINKLER

WARD

WOOD

ZIMA

WARREN

WALDROP

WEINAND

JOE WOREL, 3040 N. LaPorte, Melrose Park, IL 60164/312-455-8243 **Specialties:** Straight working knives, some fancy. **Patterns:** Hunters, Bowies and survival knives. **Technical:** Grinds 1095, 440C and F8. **Prices:** $80 to $225; some to $500. **Remarks:** Full-time maker; first knife sold in 1937. **Mark:** WOREL

WORM (See Pittman)

HAROLD C. WRIGHT, 1710 Bellwood Drive, Centerville, TN 37033/615-729-4444 **Specialties:** Fancy or plain straight working knives. **Patterns:** Hunters, small Bowies and fighters. **Technical:** Grinds L6, ATS34, and commercial Damascus; likes hollow grinds, filework and exotic wood handles. **Prices:** $50 to $150. **Remarks:** Part-time maker; first knife sold in 1982. **Mark:** Name and town logo

KEVIN WRIGHT, 671 Leland Valley Rd. W, Quilcene, WA 98376-9517/206-765-3589 **Specialties:** Fancy working knives in standard patterns. **Patterns:** Hunters, boots, buckskinners, swords, even miniatures. Enjoys customer designs. **Technical:** Forges and grinds L6, 440C and his own Damascus. **Prices:** $50 to $300; some to $1,000. **Remarks:** Part-time maker; first knife sold in 1978. **Mark:** W in anvil

TIMOTHY WRIGHT, 4100 W. Grand Ave., Chicago, IL 60651/312-489-4436/4186 **Specialties:** High-tech working folders; high-tech household knives. **Patterns:** Folding lockers in interframes; fixed hunters and kitchen cutlery. **Technical:** Grinds A2, ATS34 and M4-CPM; works with new steels, careful grinds; makes folders to disassemble, furnishes parts, tools. **Prices:** $75 to $300; some to $1,000. **Remarks:** Full-time maker; first knife sold in 1975. **Mark:** WRIGHT

YASUTOMO (See Louis G. Mills)

DAVID C. YORK, P.O. Box 1342, Crested Butte, CO 81224/303-349-5826 **Specialties:** Working knives, both folding and fixed. **Patterns:** Prefers small hunters and skinners. Offers folding lockers, buckskinner and survival knives. **Technical:** Grinds D2, 440C; buys Damascus. **Prices:** $75 to $300; some to $600. **Remarks:** Part-time maker; first knife sold in 1975. **Mark:** YORK

BUD YOUNG, Box 336, Port Hardy, BC V0N 2P0, CANADA/604-949-6478 **Specialties:** Working straight knives, some fancy. **Patterns:** Hunters from drop-points to skinners. **Technical:** Grinds 01, L6, 1095 and 5160, uses 154CM and ATS34 when available; likes mirror polish, natural handles. **Prices:** $200 to $400; some higher. **Remarks:** Spare-time maker; sold first knife in 1985. **Mark:** Name

CLIFF YOUNG, R.R.#1, Cotnams Island, Pembroke, Ont. K8A 6WZ, CANADA/613-735-6401 **Specialties:** Working knives for users; some display pieces. **Patterns:** Hunters, fighters, locking folders, and fish knives. **Technical:** Grinds mostly; some forging; offers D2, 440C and 154CM. **Prices:** $165 to $350; some to $800. **Remarks:** Part-time maker; first knife sold in 1980. **Mark:** Name, city, province

ERROL YOUNG, 4826 Storey Land, Alton, IL 62002/618-466-4707 **Specialties:** Straight and folding working knives in traditional styles. **Patterns:** Wide range, including tantos and Bowies, miniatures and multi-blade folders. **Technical:** Grinds D2, 440C, and ATS34. **Prices:** $75 to $650; some to $800. **Remarks:** Part-time maker; sold first knife in 1987. **Mark:** Last name with arrow

YAMIL R. YUNES, P.O. Box 573, Roma, TX 78584/512-849-1001 **Specialties:** Folding and straight knives in traditional patterns. **Patterns:** Folding lockers, slip joints, hunters, fighters and utility knives. **Technical:** Grinds 440C, 01 and D2. Has patented cocking design for folders. **Prices:** $45 to $140; some to $300. **Remarks:** Part-time maker; first knife sold in 1975. **Mark:** YUNES

MIKE YURCO, 260 E. Laclede Ave., Youngstown, OH 44507/216-788-7310 **Specialties:** Working straight knives. **Patterns:** Hunters, utility knives; some Bowies and push knives; makes buckle knives and other hideouts. **Technical:** Grinds 440C;

likes mirror finishes and Pakkawood. **Prices:** $35 to $150; some higher. **Remarks:** Part-time maker; sold first knife in 1983. **Mark:** NAME, steel, serial number

Z CUSTOM KNIVES (See Zollan McCarty)

DON ZACCAGNINO, P.O. Box 583, Pahokee, FL 33476/407-924-7844 **Specialties:** Working knives and some period pieces in his own style. **Patterns:** Heavy-duty hunters, axes, Bowies, daggers and fantasy miniatures. **Technical:** Grinds 440C and 17-4-PH—highly finished in complex handle and blade treatments. **Prices:** $150 to $500; some to $1,000. **Remarks:** Full-time maker; first knife sold in 1969. **Mark:** ZACK, city and state

DENNIS J. ZELLER, 1791 South West Lilyben Ave., Gresham, OR 97030/503-667-7869 **Specialties:** Working knives. **Patterns:** Daggers and fighters and boots are first; survival knives and such second. **Technical:** Grinds L6, 440C and A514. **Prices:** $125 to $475; some to $875. **Remarks:** Full-time maker; first knife sold in 1984. **Mark:** Zeller

JOE ZEMITIS, 14 Currawong Rd., Cardiff Hts./2285 Newcastle, AUSTRALIA/049-549907 **Specialties:** Traditional working straight knives. **Patterns:** Hunters, Bowies, tantos, camp knives, all in heavy-duty construction; embellishing available. **Technical:** Grinds 01, D2, 440C. **Prices:** $65 to $800. **Remarks:** Part-time maker; sold first knife in 1983. **Mark:** Name

MICHAEL F. ZIMA, 732 State St., Ft. Morgan, CO 80701/303-867-6078 **Specialties:** Working straight and folding knives in his design or to customer order. **Patterns:** Hunters, locking folders, utility and fish knives. **Technical:** Grinds D2, 440C, and ATS34. **Prices:** $50 to $225; some higher. **Remarks:** Full-time maker; first knife sold in 1982. **Mark:** Zima

TIM ZOWADA, 23583 Church Rd., Battle Creek, MI 49017/616-965-3461 **Specialties:** Working knives, some fancy. **Patterns:** Hunters, camp knives, boots, fighters and tantos, and locking folders. **Technical:** Forges 01, L6 and his own Damascus. **Prices:** $180 to $600; some to $2,000. **Remarks:** Part-time maker; first knife sold in 1980. **Mark:** Lower case gothic letters "tz"

MICHAEL ZSCHERNY, 2512 "N" Ave. NW, Cedar Rapids, IA 52405/319-396-3659 **Specialties:** Fancy working knives in standard patterns. **Patterns:** Hunters, folders, boots, and folders. **Technical:** Grinds 440C and 154CM; prefers natural handle materials. **Prices:** $150 to $1,000; some to $1,700. **Remarks:** Part-time maker. Not taking orders. **Mark:** ZSCHERNY

We have lost touch with these knifemakers:

BILL BAGWELL	EDWARD LAWLESS
RODERICK CHAPPEL	ANTHONY LOUIS, JR.
DANNY COURTNEY	C.O. McCLUNG
JIM CUNNINGHAM	JERRY POLETIS
STEVE DAVENPORT	WILLIAM J. RICHARDSON
ROGER GLEASON	G. ROCHA
CHARLES W. GRAHAM	HAROLD F. ROLLINS
	JIM SASSER
V.E. "GENE" HARRISON	ADAM SMITH
DON & RON ISAACS	JOHN T. SMITH
DON KARLIN	KEN STEIGERWALT
KIOSHI KATO	WELDON WHITLEY
JON KIRK	ART WIMAN
KURT LANG	BRUCE WOOD
GARY LANGLEY	RICHARD WORTHEN

Knifemakers
State-By-State

ALABAMA

Batson, James	(Madison)
Bell, Frank	(Huntsville)
Bryan, Jack and Morgan	(Gardendale)
Conn, C.T., Jr.	(Attalla)
Dorough, Dick	(Gadsden)
Edwards, Fain	(Jacksonville)
Fuller, Jim	(Burnwell)
Fuller, W.T. Jr.	(East Gadsden)
Gilbreath, Randall	(Dora)
Hammond, Jim	(Arab)
Hodge, J.B.	(Huntsville)
Howard, Durvyn M.	(Gadsden)
Morris, C.H.	(Atmore)
Pardue, Melvin M.	(Repton)
Pearce, Hill Everett, III	(Gurley)
Roe, Red D. Jr.	(Huntsville)
Sinyard, Cleston S.	(Elberta)
Sonneville, W.J.	(Mobile)

ALASKA

Amoureux, A.W.	(Anchorage)
Breuer, Wayne	(Wasilla)
Broome, Thomas A.	(Kenai)
Bucholz, Mark A.	(Eagle River)
Cannon, Raymond W.	(Wasilla)
Chamberlin, John A.	(Anchorage)
Dempsey, Gordon W.	(N.Kenai)
DuFour, Arthur J.	(Anchorage)
England, Virgil	(Anchorage)
Gouker, Gary B.	(Sitka)
Grebe, Gordon S.	(Anchorage)
Jirik, Sid	(Anchorage)
Kubaiko, Hank	(Big Lake)
Levine, Bob	(Anchorage)
Robertson, Ron	(Anchorage)
Stegall, Keith	(Anchorage)
Trujillo, Thomas A .	(Anchorage)
Whitman, Jim	(Chugiak)

ARIZONA

Beaver, Devon	(Phoenix)
Bloomfield, L.H.	(Kingman)
Cheatham, Bill	(Phoenix)
Dagget, Dan	(Flagstaff)
Edwards, Thomas W.	(Phoenix)
Goo, Tai	(Tempe)
Hendricks, Lorenzo Larry	(Mesa)
Hoel, Steve	(Pine)
Hull, Michael J.	(Cottonwood)
McFall, Ken	(Lakeside)
McLane, Thomas	(Tucson)

Oliver, Milford	(Phoenix)
Poletis, Jerry	(Scottsdale)
Tamboli, Michael	(Glendale)
Weiler, Donald E.	(Yuma)
Weiss, Charles L.	(Phoenix)

ARKANSAS

Crawford, Pat	(West Memphis)
Crowell, James L.	(Mountain View)
Dozier, Robert Lee	(Springdale)
Dungy, Lawrence	(Little Rock)
Duvall, Fred	(Benton)
Ferguson, Lee	(Hindsville)
Fisk, Jerry	(Lockesburg)
Flournoy, Joe	(El Dorado)
Foster, Al	(Dogpatch)
Frizzell, Ted	(West Fork)
Grigsby,Ben	(Batesville)
Hicks, Vernon G.	(Bauxite)
Lile, James B.	(Russelville)
Loflin, Bob	(Fayetteville)
Maringer, Tom	(Springdale)
Ogg, Robert G.	(Paris)
Polk, Clifton	(Ft. Smith)
Price, Jerry L.	(Springdale)
Ramey, Marshall F.	(West Helena)
Ree, David	(Van Buren)
Russell, A.G.	(Springdale)

CALIFORNIA

Barlow, Ken	(Fortuna)
Bear, Charles	(Sebastopol)
Benson, Don	(Escalon)
Besic, Leroy	(Hemet)
Blum, Chuck	(Brea)
Blum, Ronald	(Agoura Hills)
Bochman, Bruce	(El Granada)
Boyd, Francis	(San Francisco)
Brack, Douglas	(Ventura)
Breshears, Clint	(Redondo Beach)
Browne, Rick	(Upland)
Brown, L.E. Red	(Downey)
Brown, Ted	(Downey)
Casey, Dennis E.	(Redwood City)
Chelquist, Cliff	(Arroyo Grande)
Cohen, Terry A.	(Santa Cruz)
Collins, A.J.	(Burbank)
Cross, Tim	(Long Beach)
Detloff, Larry	(Santa Cruz)
Dias, Jack	(Palermo)
Dillon, Earl E.	(Arleta)
Dion, Greg	(Oxnard)

Dion, Malcolm C.	(Goleta)
Donovan, Patrick	(San Jose)
Doolittle, Mike	(Novato)
Eaton, Al	(Clayton)
Eaton, Rick	(Oakley)
Emerson, Ernest R.	(Torrance)
Engnath, Bob	(Glendale)
Essegian, Richard	(Fresno)
Faulkner, Al	(Marysville)
Ferdinand, Don	(San Rafael)
Fisher, Ted	(Montague)
Foust, Roger	(Modesto)
Freeman, Arthur F.	(Citrus Heights)
Funderburg, Joe	(Los Osos)
Gamble, Frank	(Gilroy)
George, Tom	(Magalia)
Gofourth, Jim	(Santa Paula)
Golding, Robin	(Ripon)
Goodwin, Butch	(Vista)
Hartsfield, Phill	(Garden Grove)
Henry, D.E.	(Mountain Ranch)
Herndon, Wm. R. Bill	(Acton)
Hilker, Tom	(Santa Maria)
Horn, Jess	(Redding)
Hornby, Glen	(Glendale)
Hrisoulas, Jim	(Sylmar)
Humenick, Roy	(Rescue)
Jacks, Jim	(Covina)
Jones, Curtis J.	(Palmdale)
Kreibich, Donald L.	(San Jose)
Kruse, Martin	(Reseda)
Kuykendall, Jim	(Tulare)
Lawson, Stephen M.	(Placerville)
Levine, Norman	(Victorville)
Likarich, Steve	(Carmichael)
Lockett, Sterling	(Burbank)
Loveless, R.W.	(Riverside)
McLeod, James	(Oroville)
Mecchi, Richard	(North Hollywood)
Mendenhall, Harry E.	(Milpitas)
Morgan, Emil	(Thousand Oaks)
Morgan, Jeff	(Santee)
Morgan, Justin	(Thousand Oaks)
Morlan, Tom	(Hemet)
Pendleton, Lloyd	(San Pablo)
Phillips, John	(Santa Barbara)
Phillips, Randy	(Bloomington)
Quinn, George	(Julian)
Rust, Charles C.	(Palermo)
Salpas, Bob	(Homewood)
Samson, Jody	(Burbank)
Scarrow, Will	(El Cerrito)
Schneider, Herman J.	(Laguna Niguel)

Schroen, Karl (Sebastopol)
Sornberger, Jim (Volcano)
Stapel, Chuck (Glendale)
Stapel, Craig (Glendale)
Stefani, Randy (Montrose)
Steinberg, Al (San Bruno)
Swain, Rod (South Pasadena)
Tamboli, Michael (Glendale)
Terrill, Stephen (Lindsay)
Tinker, Carolyn D. (Whittier)
Ward, Ken (Sacramento)
Warren, Al (Porterville)
Wesolowski, Mike (Petaluma)
Whitehead, James D. (Durham)
Williams, Sherman A. (Simi Valley)
Wood, Barry B. (Venice)

COLORADO

Appleton, Ray (Byers)
Belk, Jack (Marble)
Brock, Kenneth L. (Allenspark)
Campbell, Dick (Conifer)
Davis, Don (Loveland)
Dawson, Dane and Barry (Marvel)
Dennehy, Dan (Del Norte)
Genge, Roy E. (Eastlake)
High, Tom (Alamoso)
Hodgson, Richard J. (Boulder)
Hughes, Ed (Grand Junction)
Kitsmiller, Jerry (Montrose)
Lampson, Frank G. (Fruita)
McWilliams, Sean (Bayfield)
Miller, Hanford J. (Evergreen)
Nolen, R.D. and George (Estes Park)
Olson, Wayne C. (Wheat Ridge)
Owens, John (Parker)
Pogreba, Larry (Lyons)
Renner, Terry Lee (Estes Park)
Robbins, Howard P. (Estes Park)
Rollert, Steve (Keenesburg)
Teichmoeller, Lou (Dolores)
Timberline Knives (Mancos)
Wilson, James G. (Estes Park)
York, David C. (Crested Butte)
Zima, Michael F. (Ft. Morgan)

CONNECTICUT

Granquist, William R. (Bristol)
Haggerty, George S. (Monroe)
Hubbard, Arthur J. (Monroe)
Jean, Gerry (Manchester)
Nelson, Roger S. (Central Village)
Pankiewicz, Philip R. (Lebanon)
Rainville, Richard (Salem)
Turecek, Jim (Shelton)

DELAWARE

Willey, Geri L. (Greenwood)
Willey, W.G. (Greenwood)

FLORIDA

Anderson, Charles B. (Ft. Myers)
Barry, James J. (West Palm Beach)
Benjamin, George Jr. (Kissimmee)
Blackton, Andrew (Bayonet Point)
Brown, E.H. (Eustis)
Brown, Harold E. (Arcadia)
Burns, Dave (Boynton Beach)
Centofante, Frank and Mark (Tampa)
Cox, Colin J. (Apopka)
Daniels, Alex (Lynn Haven)
Ellerbe, W.B. (Geneva)
Enos, Thomas M. III (Orlando)
Garner, William O. Jr. (Pensacola)
Griffin, Howard A. Jr. (Davie)
H&W Knives (Pace)
Harless, Walt (Lake Worth)
Hodge, John III (Palatka)
Hoffman, Kevin L. (Orlando)
Hughes, Dan (West Palm Beach)
Jernigan, Steve (Milton)
Johnson, W.C. Bill (Okeechobee)
Kelly, Lance (Edgewater)
King, Bill (Tampa)
Levengood, Bill (Tampa)
Lovestrand, Schuyler (Apopka)
Lyle, Ernest L. III (Orlando)
Miller, Chris Jr. (Sebring)
Miller, Ronald T. (Largo)
Ochs, Charles F. (Largo)
Outlaw, Anthony L. (Panama City)
Pendray, Alfred H. (Williston)
Price, Joel Hiram (Palatka)
Randall, W.D. and Gary T. (Orlando)
Rose, Alex (New Port Richey)
Schwarzer, Stephen (Palatka)
Simons, Bill (Highland City)
Smith, Glenn L. (Hialeah)
Stephens, Kelly Lee (St. Petersburg)
Tomes, P.J. (Jacksonville)
Vunk, Robert Bob (Orlando)
Waldrop, Mark (Lady Lake)
Weiland, J. Reese Jr. (Tampa)
Wine, Michael (Cocoa Beach)
Zaccagnino, Don (Pahokee)

GEORGIA

Bradley, Dennis (Blairsville)
Buckner, Jimmie H. (Putney)
Cheatham, Don E. (Savannah)
Crockford, Jack (Chamblee)

Dearhart, Richard (Lula)
Ford, Allen (Smyrna)
Fuller, John W. (Douglasville)
Harmon, Jay (Woodstock)
Harris, Ralph Dewey (Grovetown)
Hawkins, Rade (Red Oak)
Hegedus, Lou Jr. (Cave Spring)
Hegwood, Joel (Summerville)
Hensley, Wayne (Conyers)
Hinson, R. and Son (Columbus)
Johnson, Harold Harry C. (Chickamauga)
Kilby, Keith (Jefferson)
Kormanik, Chris (Athens)
Love, Ed (Stockbridge)
McCarty, Zollan (Thomaston)
McGill, John (Blairsville)
Mitchell, James A. (Columbus)
North and Prater (Chickamauga)
Pittman, Leon (Pendergrass)
Poplin, James L. (Washington)
Rogers, Robert P. Jr. (Acworth)
Roper, Mark H. Jr. (Martinez)
Royal, B.M. "Red" (Helen)
Sharpe, Philip S. (Austell)
Small, Jim (Madison)
Smith, James B. Red Jr. (Morven)
Snell, Jerry L. (Fayetteville)
Stafford, Richard (Warner Robins)
Walters, A.F. (Tifton)

HAWAII

Evans, Vincent K. (Honolulu)
Fujisaka, Stanley (Kaneohe)
Lui, Ronald (Honolulu)
Mayo, Thomas H. Jr. (Waialua)
Nishiuchi, Melvin S. (Kaneohe)

IDAHO

Andrews, Don (Coeur D'Alene)
Hibben, Daryl (Pocatello)
Kranning, Terry L. (Pocatello)
Mullin, Steve (Sandpoint)
Nealy, Evan F. (Mountain Home)
Oda, Kuzan (Hailey)
Quarton, Barr (Hailey)
Rohn, Fred (Coeur d'Alene)
Sawby, Scott (Sand Point)
Sparks, Bernard (Dingle)
Towell, Dwight L. (Midvale)

ILLINOIS

Abbott, William M. (Chandlerville)
Atkinson, Dick (Decatur)
Bloomer, Allan T. (Maquon)
Brannan, Ralph (West Frankfort)

Bridgnardello, E.D. (Beecher)
Bumpus, Steve (Collinsville)
Detmer, Phillip (Breese)
Guth, Kenneth (Chicago)
Hargis, Frank L. (Flora)
Hill, Rick (Edwardsville)
Kovar, Eugene (Evergreen Park)
Lane, Jerry I. (Carbondale)
Leone, Nick (Pontoon Beach)
Meier, Daryl (Carbondale)
Myers, Paul (Wood River)
Pritchard, Ron (Dixon)
Rados, Jerry F. (Grant Park)
Smith, John M. (Centralia)
Stalter, Harry L. (Trivoli)
Tompkins, Dan (Peotone)
Turnbull, Ralph A. (Rockford)
Veit, Michael (LaSalle)
Werth, George W. (Cary)
White, Robert J. Bob (Gilson)
White, Robert J. "Butch" Jr. (Gilson)
Worel, Joe (Melrose Park)
Wright, Timothy (Chicago)
Young, Errol (Alton)

INDIANA
Allen, Joe (Princeton)
Birt, Sid (Nashville)
Brewer, Jack (Lafayette)
Fitzgerald, Dennis (Fort Wayne)
Flynn, Bruce (Middletown)
Imel, Billy Mace (New Castle)
Johnson, C.E. Gene (Portage)
Keeton, William L. (Laconia)
Kreimer, James J. (Milan)
Largin, Ken (Batesville)
Ledford, Bracy R. (Indianapolis)
Lutes, Robert (Nappanee)
Mayville, Oscar (Indianapolis)
Poag, James (New Harmony)
Porter, James E. (Bloomington)
Rigney, Willie (Shelbyville)
Rubley, James A. (Angola)
Welch, William H. (Fort Wayne)

IOWA
Brooker, Dennis (Derby)
Brower, Max (Boone)
Clark, Howard (Runnells)
Lainson, Tony (Council Bluffs)
Miller, James P. (Fairbank)
Myers, Mel (Spencer)
Trindle, Barry (Earlham)
Voss, Ben (Davenport)
Zscherny, Michael (Cedar Rapids)

KANSAS
Chard, Gordon R. (Iola)
Courtney, Eldon (Wichita)

Dugger, Dave (Westwood)
Dunn, Melvin T. (Rossville)
Green, L.G. (Prairie Village)
Harrington, Mike (Abilene)
Hegwald, J.L. (Humboldt)
Herman, Tim (Overland Park)
Kennelley, J.C. (Leon)
Kraft, Steve (Abilene)
Ray, Michael (Wichita)

KENTUCKY
Baskett, Lee Gene (Elizabethtown)
Brandstetter, Larry (Paducah)
Bugden, John (Murray)
Bybee, Barry J. (Almo)
Carson, Harold J. Kit (Radcliff)
Clay, J.D. (Greenup)
Downing, Larry (Bremen)
Fister, Jim (Finchville)
Hibben, Gil (Louisville)
Howser, John C. (Frankfort)
Keeslar, Joseph F. (Almo)
Pease, W.D. (Ewing)
Pierce, Harold L. (Louisville)
Pulliam, Morris C. (Shelbyville)
Smith, Gregory H. (Louisville)

LOUISIANA
Berzas, Larry (Cut Off)
Blaum, Roy (Covington)
Caldwell, Bill (West Monroe)
Culpepper, John (Monroe)
Douglas, Dale (Ponchatoula)
Durio, Fred (Opelousas)
Faucheaux, Howard J. (Loreauville)
Ki, Shiva (Baton Rouge)
Marks, Chris (Breaux Bridge)
Mitchell, Max and Dean (Leesville)
Provenzano, Joseph D. (Chalmette)
Roath, Dean (Baton Rouge)
Sanders, Michael M. (Ponchatoula)
Vought, Frank Jr. (Hammond)
Wehner, Rudy (Violet)
Wiggins, Horace (Mansfield)
Wiggins, James C. (Hammond)

MAINE
Bohrmann, Bruce (Yarmouth)
Fuegen, Larry (Wiscasset)
Kemal (D. Fogg & M. Sayen) (Bryant Pond)
Munro, Paul (Franklin)
Oyster, Lowell R. (Kenduskeag)

MARYLAND
Antonio, William J. (Warwick)
Barnes, Gary L. (New Windsor)
Bauchop, Peter (Hunt Valley)
Beers, Ray (Monkton)
Fielder, William V. (Westminster)

Freiling, Albert J. (Finksburg)
Goff, Darrel W. (Baltimore)
Hendrickson, E.J. (Jay) (Frederick)
Hudson, Robbin C. (Rock Hall)
Kremzner, Raymond L. (Baltimore)
Kretsinger, Philip W. Jr. (Boonsboro)
McCarley, John (Keymar)
McGowan, Frank (Sykesville)
Merchant, Ted (White Hall)
Moran, Wm. F. (Braddock Heights)
Nicholson, Kent R. (Baltimore)
Sontheimer, Douglas G. (Silver Spring)
Urstadt, E.W. (Deer Park)

MASSACHUSETTS
Dailey, G.E. (Seekonk)
Fikes, Jimmy L. (Orange)
Gaudette, Linden L. (Wilbraham)
Grossman, Stewart (Clinton)
Gwozdz, Bob (Attleboro)
Khalsa, Jot Singh (Millis)
Lapen, Charles (Ware)
Reed, Dave (Brimfield)
Sheehan, Paul P. (Sandwich)
Siska, Jim (Westfield)
Sloan, John (Foxboro)
Tsoulas, Jon J. (Peabody)

MICHIGAN
Beckwith, Michael R. (New Baltimore)
Behnke, William (West Bloomfield)
Buckbee, Donald M. (Warren)
Cousino, George (Woodhaven)
Dilluvio, Frank J. (Warren)
Dodge, Robert Orr (Saginaw)
Enders, Robert (Cement City)
Erickson, Walter E. (Warren)
Gottage, Dante and Judy (St. Clair Shores)
Hartman, Arlan (N. Muskegon)
Hughes, Daryle (Nunica)
Lankton, Scott (Ann Arbor)
Leach, Mike J. (Swartz Creek)
Mills, Louis G. (Yasutomo) (Ann Arbor)
O'Leary, Gordon (Ypsilanti)
Serven, Jim (Mayville)
Sigman, James P. (Three Rivers)
Stewart, Charles (Chuck) (Lake Orion)
Stites, Kay (Bloomfield Hills)
Wardman, Dave (Ossineke)
Warzocha, Stanley (Warren)
Whitworth, Ken J. (Sterling Heights)
Wood, Webster (Clarkston)
Zowada, Tim (Battle Creek)

MINNESOTA
Dingman, Scott (International Falls)
Goltz, Warren L. (Ada)
Hagen, Philip L. (Pelican Rapids)

Johnson, Robert B. (Clearwater)
Knipschield, Terry (Rochester)
Preuss, Robert (Cedar)
Sharp, Robert G. (Anoka)

MISSISSIPPI
Craft, Richard C. (Jackson)
Davis, Jesse W. (Walls)
Greco, John (Bay St. Louis)
LeBatard, Paul M. (Vancleave)

MISSOURI
Bolton, Charles B. (Jonesburg)
Cover, Raymond A. (Mineral Point)
Craig, James H. (Manchester)
Davis, W.C. (Raymore)
Driskill, Beryl (Braggadocio)
Duvall, Larry E. (Gallatin)
Frese, William R. (St. Louis)
Gilmore, Jon (St. Louis)
Glaser, Ken (Purdy)
Holland, Dale J. (Kansas City)
Lane, Ed (Kansas City)
Mason, Bill (Excelsior Springs)
May, James E. (Auxvasse)
McCrackin and Son, V.J. (House Springs)
Newcomb, Corbin (Moberly)
Rardon, A.D. (Polo)
Weddle, Del Jr. (Stewartsville)

MONTANA
Brooks, Steve R. (Big Timber)
Brunkhorst, C. Lyle (White Sulphur Springs)
Crowder, Robert (Thompson Falls)
Dunkerley, Rick (Cameron)
Ellefson, Joel (Bozeman)
Fassio, Melvin G. (Missoula)
Forthofer, Pete (Whitefish)
Frank, Heinrich H. (Whitefish)
Hill, Howard (Polson)
Moyer, Russ (Havre)
Petersen, Dan L. (Billings)
Peterson, Eldon G. (Whitefish)
Pursley, Aaron (Big Sandy)
Reh, Bill (Missoula)
Ruana Knife Works (Bonner)
Simonich, Bob (Clancy)
Smith, Harry R. (Missoula)
Treutel, Terry A. (Hamilton)
Weinand, Gerome W. (Lolo)

NEBRASKA
Brown, David B. (Fairbury)
Jensen, Carl A. Jr. (Blair)
Jokerst, Charles (Omaha)
Miller, Terry (Seward)
Schepers, George B. (Chapman)
Suedmeier, Harlan (Nebraska City)

Syslo, Chuck (Omaha)

NEVADA
Duff, Bill (Virginia City)

NEW HAMPSHIRE
Valachovic, Wayne (Hillsboro)

NEW JERSEY
Defeo, Robert A. (Mays Landing)
Hetmanski, Thomas S. (Trenton)
MacBain, Kenneth (Norwood)
McGovern, Jim (Oak Ridge)
Polkowski, Al (Chester)
Slee, Fred (Morganville)
Viele, H.J. (Westwood)
Weber, Fred E. (Forked River)

NEW MEXICO
Black, Tom (Albuquerque)
Coleman, Keith E. (Los Lunas)
Cordova, Joseph G. (Bosque Farms)
Digangi, Joseph M. (Santa Cruz)
Duran, Jerry T. (Albuquerque)
Hethcoat, Don (Clovis)
Holder, D'Alton (Farmington)
Jones, Bob (Albuquerque)
Lewis, Ron (Edgewood)
Lewis, Tom R. (Carlsbad)
McBurnette, Harvey (Eagle Nest)
Miller, Ted (Santa Fe)
Norton, Don (Farmington)
Nymeyer, Earl (Hobbs)
Stumpff, George Jr. (Glorieta)
Terzuola, Robert (Santa Fe)
Walker, Michael (Taos)
Wescott, Cody (Las Cruces)
Wescott, Jim (Las Cruces)

NEW YORK
Anderson, Edwin (New Hyde Park)
Coleman, Ken (Brooklyn)
Cumming, R.J. (New York)
Cute, Thomas (Cortland)
Davis, Barry L. (Castleton)
Maragni, Dan (Georgetown)
Rappazzo, Richard (Latham)
Rotella, Richard A. (Niagara Falls)
Scheid, Maggie (W. Webster)
Schmidt, James A. (Ballston Lake)
Stahl, John (Baldwin)
Wahlers, Herman F. (Austerlitz)

NORTH CAROLINA
Addison, Ed (Asheboro)
Bonner, Jeremy (Asheville)
Busfield, John (Roanoke Rapids)
Fox, Paul (Valdese)

Gross, W.W. (High Point)
Gurganus, Melvin H. (Colerain)
Guthrie, George B. (Bessemer City)
McCullough, Larry E. (Mocksville)
Neal, Jerry C. (Banner Elk)
Norris, Mike (Albemarle)
Parrish, Robert (Hendersonville)
Patrick, Chuck (Brasstown)
Rece, Charles V. (Troy)
Shuford, Rick (Statesville)
Tedder, Mickey (Conover)
Wade, J.M. (Wade)
Wagaman, John K. (Fayetteville)
Winkler, David (Boone)

OHIO
Busse, Jerry (Wauseon)
Collins, Lynn M. (Elyria)
Corwin, Don (Monclove)
Cottrill, James I. (Columbus)
Darby, Rick (Youngstown)
Downing, Tom (Cortland)
Downs, Jim (Londonderry)
Franklin, Mike (Aberdeen)
Geisler, Gary (Clarksville)
Glover, Ron (Cincinnati)
Imboden, Howard L.II (Kettering)
Koutsopoulos, George (La Grange)
Koval, Michael T. (Columbus)
Longworth, Dave (Bethel)
McCarty, Harry (Hamilton)
Morgan, Tom (Beloit)
Papp, Robert Bob (Elyria)
Salley, John D. (Tipp City)
Shoemaker, Scott (Miamisburg)
Spinale, Richard (Lorain)
Stoddart, W.B. Bill (Forest Park)
Strong, Scott (Beaver Creek)
Thourot, Michael W. (Napoleon)
Trabbic, R.W. (Toledo)
Votaw, David P. (Pioneer)
Warther, Dale (Bolivar)
Witsaman, Earl (Stow)
Wood, Larry B. (Huber Heights)
Woodworth, Al (Ashville)
Yurco, Mike (Youngstown)

OKLAHOMA
Baker, Ray (Sapulpa)
Englebretson, George (Oklahoma City)
Guess, Jack (Tulsa)
Jones, Gomer G. (Tulsa)
Kennedy, Bill Jr. (Yukon)
Naifeh, Woody (Tulsa)
Nibarger, Charlie (Tulsa)
Sanders, Athern Al (Norman)
Spivey, Jefferson (Oklahoma City)
Stice, Douglas (Norman)

OREGON

Alverson, Tim	(Keno)
Anderson, Virgil W.	(Portland)
Bell, Michael	(Coquille)
Buchman, Bill	(Bend)
Buchner, Bill	(Idleyld Park)
Corrado, Jim	(Glide)
Davis, Terry	(Sumpter)
Dowell, T.M.	(Bend)
Goddard, Wayne	(Eugene)
Harsey, William W.	(Creswell)
Huey, Steve	(Junction City)
Hunnicutt, Robert E.	(Forest Grove)
Kelley, Gary	(Aloha)
Lake, Ron	(Eugene)
Lindsay, Chris A.	(La Pine)
Little, Gary M.	(Broadbent)
Lum, Robert W.	(Eugene)
Murphy, Dave	(Gresham)
Pitt, David	(Klamath Falls)
Reed, Del	(Beaverton)
Thompson, Leon	(Forest Grove)
Wahlster, Mark David	(Silverton)
Zeller, Dennis J.	(Gresham)

PENNSYLVANIA

Bartrug, Hugh E.	(Elizabeth)
Candrella, Joe	(Warminster)
Clark, D.E. Lucky	(Mineral Point)
Frey, W. Fredrick Jr.	(Milton)
Gottschalk, Gregory J.	(Carnegie)
Nealy, Bud	(Stroudsburg)
Skirchak, Samuel Jr.	(Midland)
Taglienti, Antonio J.	(Darlington)
Valois, A. Daniel	(Walnutport)
Whittaker, Robert E.	(Mill Creek)

RHODE ISLAND

Allen, Steve	(Riverside)
Bardsley, Norman P.	(Pawtucket)

SOUTH CAROLINA

Barefoot, Joe W.	(Easley)
Beatty, Gordon H.	(Seneca)
Beck, P.F.	(Barnwell)
Branton, Robert	(Awendaw)
Brend, Walter J.	(Walterboro)
Bridwell, Richard A.	(Taylors)
Burnette, Skip	(Spartanburg)
Cannady, Daniel L.	(Allendale)
Davis Brothers Knives	(Camden)
Davis, Dixie	(Clinton)
Defreest, William G.	(Barnwell)
Easler, Russell O. Jr.	(Woodruff)
Fecas, Stephen J.	(Clemson)

Gaston, Ron	(Woodruff)
George, Harry	(Aiken)
Gillenwater, E.E. Dick	(Aiken)
Gregory, Michael	(Belton)
Herron, George	(Springfield)
Kessler, Ralph A.	(Elgin)
Langley, Gene H.	(Florence)
Lee, Tommy	(Gaffney)
Montjoy, Claude	(Clinton)
Owens, Dan	(Blacksburg)
Owens, Danny	(Blacksburg)
Page, Larry	(Aiken)
Poston, Alvin	(Columbia)
Reeves, Winfred M.	(West Union)
Smith, Ralph L.	(Greer)
Whitmire, Earl T.	(Rock Hill)

TENNESSEE

Bartlow, John	(Norris)
Canter, Ronald E.	(Jackson)
Cargill, Bob	(Oldfort)
Casteel, Douglas	(Hillsboro)
Clay, Wayne	(Pelham)
Conley, Bob	(Jonesboro)
Coogan, Robert	(Smithville)
Copeland, George A. Steve	(Alpine)
Corby, Harold	(Johnson City)
Crisp, Harold	(Cleveland)
Ewing, John H.	(Clinton)
Grigsby, John D. Butch	(Corryton)
Harley, Larry W.	(Bristol)
Hurst, Jeff	(Rutledge)
Moore, Tom W. Jr.	(Columbia)
Rhea, David	(Lynnville)
Rial, Douglas	(Greenfield)
Sampson, Lynn	(Jonesboro)
Smith, Newman L.	(Gatlinburg)
Smith, W.F. Red	(Gatlinburg)
Taylor, C. Gray	(Kingsport)
Taylor, David	(Kingsport)
Von Boeckman, R.	(Memphis)
Walker, John W.	(Bon Aqua)
Ward, W.C.	(Clinton)
Woodward, Harold E.	(Woodbury)
Wright, Harold C.	(Centerville)

TEXAS

Allen, Mike Whiskers	(Malakoff)
Barbee, Jim	(Ft. Stockton)
Barr, A.T.	(Denton)
Birch, Robert F.	(Huntsville)
Brayton, Jim	(Burkburnett)
Broadwell, David	(Wichita Falls)
Brooks, Michael	(Littlefield)
Carter, Fred	(Wichita Falls)
Cellum, Tom S.	(Willis)
Champion, Robert	(Amarillo)

Chapman, Mike	(Houston)
Chase, John E.	(Aledo)
Connor, Michael	(Winters)
Costa, Scott	(Spicewood)
Crain, Jack W.	(Weatherford)
Crawford, Larry	(Rosenberg)
Davidson, Rob	(Lubbock)
Davis, Syd	(Richmond)
Davis, Vernon	(Waco)
Dean, Harvey J.	(Rockdale)
DiTommaso, Larry	(Longview)
Donaghey, John	(Garland)
Ferguson, Jim	(San Angelo)
Fischer, Clyde E.	(Nixon)
Gartman, M.D.	(Gatesville)
Gault, Clay	(Lexington)
Gonzalez, Jean	(Roma)
Green, Roger M.	(Joshua)
Griffin, Rendon and Mark	(Houston)
Hajovsky, Robert J.	(Scotland)
Hipp, Charles (Bone Knife Co.)	(Lubbock)
Hudson, Robert	(Humble)
Hueske, Chubby	(Bellaire)
Hughes, Lawrence	(Plainview)
Johnson, Brad	(El Paso)
Johnson, Gorden W.	(Houston)
Johnson, Ruffin	(Houston)
Johnson, Ryan M.	(Hixson)
Kious, Joe	(Alamo)
Krouse, Al	(Humble)
Ladd, Jim	(Deer Park)
Ladd, Jimmie L.	(Deer Park)
LaPlante, Brett	(Richardson)
Laughlin, Don	(Vidor)
Lay, L.J.	(Burkburnett)
Lovett, Mike	(Killeen)
Luckett, Bill	(Weatherford)
Madsen, Jack	(Wichita Falls)
Malitzke, Jeffrey G.	(Wichita Falls)
Marshall, Glenn	(Mason)
McConnell, Loyd A. Jr.	(Odessa)
McDearmont, Dave	(Lewisville)
McKissack, Tommy II	(Sonora)
Merz, Robert L. III	(Katy)
Miller, R.D.	(Dallas)
Mills, Andy	(Fredricksburg)
Moore, James B.	(Ft. Stockton)
Osborne, Warren	(Waxahachie)
Overeynder, T.R.	(Arlington)
Parrish, Dwayne	(Palestine)
Pate, Lloyd D.	(Georgetown)
Pugh, Jim	(Azle)
Pullen, Martin	(Granbury)
Sams, Joseph D.	(El Paso)
Shearer, Robert A.	(Huntsville)
Sims, Bob	(Meridian)
Sloan, Shane	(Newcastle)

Spencer, John E. (Harper)
Stone, G.W. (Richardson)
Stout, Johnny (New Braunfels)
Thuesen, Ed (Houston)
Thuesen, Kevin (Houston)
Watson, Daniel and Bill (Driftwood)
Watt, Freddie III (Big Spring)
Watts, Wally (Gatesville)
Wood, William W. (Vera)
Yunes, Yamil R. (Roma)

UTAH
Black, Earl (Salt Lake City)
Bryner, Barry R. (Price)
Ence, Jim (Richfield)
Erickson, Curt (Ogden)
Erickson, L.M. (Liberty)
Johnson, Steve R. (Manti)
Maxfield, Lynn (Layton)
Rapp, Steven J. (Salt Lake City)
Smith, David Lynn (Vernal)
Warenski, Buster (Richfield)
Winn, Travis A. (Salt Lake City)

VIRGINIA
Barber, Robert E. (Charlottesville)
Beverly, Larry H. II (Hartwood)
Blakley, William E. II (Fredricksburg)
Callahan, Errett (Lynchburg)
Davidson, Edmund (Goshen)
Frazier, Ron (Powhatan)
Goldenberg, T.S. (Herndon)
Hedrick, Don (Newport News)
Holloway, Paul (Norfolk)
Jones, Enoch (Chantilly)
Scott, Winston (Huddleston)
White, Gene E. (Alexandria)

WASHINGTON
Baldwin, Phillip (Snohomish)
Ber, Dave (Nooksack)
Blomberg, Gregg (Lopez)
Boguszewski, Phil (Tacoma)
Conti, Jeffrey D. (Bremerton)
Davis, K.M. Twig (Monroe)
Goertz, Paul S. (Renton)
Mosser, Gary E. (Renton)
Reynolds, Dave (Lacey)
Rice, Adrienne (Lopez Island)
Wright, Kevin (Quilcene)

WEST VIRGINIA
Bowen, Tilton and James (Baker)
Cantini, Don (Weirton)
Dent, Douglas M. (South Charleston)
Hedgecock, Walter R. (Glen Daniel)

Maynard, Larry Joe (Helen)
McConnell, Charles R. (Wellsburg)
Quenton, Warner (Peterstown)
Sigman, Corbet R. (Liberty)
Small, Ed (Keyser)
Tokar, Daniel (Shepherdstown)
Wilson, R.W. (Weirton)

WISCONSIN
Brandsey, Edward P. (Edgerton)
Brdlik, Dan E. (Prescott)
Dahl, Cris (Lake Geneva)
DeYong, Clarence (Racine)
Hembrook, Ron (Neosho)
Kolitz, Robert (Beaver Dam)
Lary, Ed (Mosinee)
Maestri, Peter A. (Spring Green)
Ricke, Dave (West Bend)
Rochford, Michael R. (Dresser)

WYOMING
Alexander, Darrel (Big Piney)
Ankrom, W.E. (Cody)
Fowler, Ed A. (Riverton)
Friedly, Dennis (Cody)
Montegna, John C. (Sheridan)
Reynolds, John C. (Gillette)
Walker, George A. (Alpine)

FOREIGN COUNTRIES
AFRICA
Burger, Pon (Zimbabwe)

AUSTRALIA
Brown, Peter (Ryde)
Butler, Gary (Perth)
Green, William (Rosanna)
Harvey, Max (Perth)
Jones, John (Brisbane)
Rowe, Stewart G. (Kangaroo Point)
Simmonds, Kurt Barnes (Castlemaine)
Zemitis, Joe (Cardiff Hts.)

CANADA
Downie, James T. (Thedford)
Dublin, Dennis (Enderby)
Freeman, John (Toronto)
Grenier, Roger (Saint Hubert)
Haynes, Chap (Tatamagouche)
Jobin, Jacques (Lauzon)
Langley, Mick (Qualicum Beach)
Leber, Heinz (Hudson Hope)
Loerchner, Wolfgang (Bayfield)
Lyttle, Brian (High River)

Macri, Mike (Churchill)
Maneker, Kenneth (Galiano Island)
Marzitelli, Peter (Surrey)
Moeller, Harald (Thornton)
Niro, Frank (Mackenzie)
Pepiot, Stephan (Edmonton)
Peterson, Jack (Nanaimo)
Price, Steve (Kamloops)
Ross, Tim (Thunder Bay)
Schoenfeld, Matthew A. (Galiano Island)
St. Amour, Suzanne (Hillsburgh)
Young, Bud (Port Hardy)
Young, Cliff (Pembroke)

ENGLAND
Henry, Peter and Son (Wokingham)
Hitchmough, Howard (London)
Jones, Charles Anthony (No. Devon)
Moorby, Keith (South Yorkshire)

JAPAN
Aida, Yoshihito (Tokyo)
Fujimoto, Yasuhiro (Tokyo)
Fukuta, Tak (Seki-City)
Furukawa, Shiro (Tokyo)
Hirayama, Harumi (Warabi City)
Takahashi, Masao (Tokyo)
Tasaki, Seiichi (Kawaguchi-City)

NETHERLANDS
Van Eldik, Frans (Loenen)

NEW ZEALAND
Reddiex, Bill (Palmerston North)

NORWAY
Sellevold, Harald (Dreggen)

SOUTH AFRICA
Reeve, Chris (Gillitts)
Wood, Owen (Honeydew)

SWEDEN
Lundstrom, Jan-Ake (Dals-Langed)

WALES
Elliott, Marcus (Llandudno)

WEST GERMANY
Becker, Franz (Marktl/Inn)
Hehn, Richard Karl (Waldbronn)
Kressler, D.F. (Puchheim)

Official Knifemakers Membership Lists

Not all knifemakers are organization types, but those listed here are in good standing with these organizations.

Knifemakers Guild
1988 Voting Membership

R. V. Alverson, Ed Anderson, W.E. Ankrom, Dick Atkinson.

Phillip Baldwin, Norman Bardsley, Joe Barefoot, Gary Barnes, Gene Baskett, Butch Beaver, Franz Becker, Raymond Beers, Leslie Berryman, Leroy Besic, Sid Birt, Paul Bizal, Earl Black, Andrew Blackton, Philip Boguszewski, Edward Brandsey, Walter Brend, Clint Breshears, Richard Bridwell, Ed Brignardello, Tim Britton, David Broadwell, David Brown, Rick Browne, John Busfield.

Bill Caldwell, Ronald Canter, Don Cantini, Bob Cargill, Fred Carter, Frank & Mark Centofante, Gordon Chard, William Cheatham, Wayne Clay, Gerald Click, Keith Coleman, Vernon Coleman, Alex Collins, Walter Collins, Bob Conley, C. T. Conn, Harold Corby, Joe Cordova, Leonard Corlee, Jim Corrado, Eldon Courtney, George Cousino, Raymond Cover, Colin Cox, Jack Crain, Pat Crawford, James Crowell.

Cris Dahl, Alex Daniels, Barry Davis, Jesse Davis, W.C. Davis, Bill DeFreest, Robert Dodge, Patrick Donovan, Dick Dorough, T.M. Dowell, Larry Downing, Tom Downing, Bill Duff, Melvin Dunn, Larry Duvall.

Russell Easler, Joel Ellefson, Jim Ence, Robert Enders, Robert Engnath, Curt Erickson, L. M. Erickson, Walter Erickson.

Allan Faulkner, Stephen Fecas, Lee Ferguson, Joe Flournoy, Pete Forthofer, Paul Fox, Henry Frank, Ron Frazier, Dennis Friedly, Tak Fukuta, John Fuller, Shiro Furukawa.

Frank Gamble, Ronald Gaston, Clay Gault, Roy Genge, Randall Gilbreath, E.E. (Dick) Gillenwater, Kenneth Glaser, R. G. Glover, Wayne Goddard, Warren Goltz, Dante & Judith Gottage, Larry Green, Michael Gregory, Rendon & Mark Griffin, Kenneth Guth.

Doc Hagen, Robert Hajovsky, Jim Hammond, Rade Hawkins, Richard Hehn, Larry Hendricks, Wayne Hensley, Tim Herman, George Herron, Don Hethcoat, Gil Hibben, Vernon Hicks, Howard Hill, Harumi Hirayama, J.B. Hodge, Richard Hodgson, Steve Hoel, Kevin Hoffman, D'Alton Holder, Dale Holland, Jess Horn, Glen Hornby, Arthur Hubbard, Chubby Hueske.

Bill Imel.

Jim Jacks, Steve Jernigan, Gorden Johnson, Ronald Johnson, Ruffin Johnson, Steve Johnson, William Johnson, Enoch D. Jones, Robert Jones.

Don Karlin, William Keeton, Gary Kelley, Kemal (Sayen-Fogg), Bill Kennedy, J. C. Kennedy, Ralph Kessler, Jot Khalsa, Shiva Ki, Bill King, Joe Kious, Mike Koval, D.F. Kressler.

Ron Lake, Frank Lampson, Ed Lane, Gene Langley, Scott Lankton, Don Laughlin, M. Leach, Tommy Lee, Norman Levine, James Lile, Dave Longworth, Ed Love, Schuyler Lovestrand, William Luckett, Robert Lum, Ernest Lyle.

Mickey Maddox, Dan Maragni, Tom Maringer, James May, Harvey McBurnette, Charles McConnell, Loyd McConnell, David McDearmont, Chris Miller, James Miller, Terry Miller, Louis Mills & Jim Kelso, Jim Minnick, Claude Montjoy, William Moran, Jeff Morgan, Steven Mullin, Paul Myers.

Corbin Newcomb, R.D. Nolen.

Kuzan Oda, Gordon O'Leary, Milford Oliver, Wayne Olson, Warren Osborne, T.R. Overeynder.

Robert Papp, Melvin Pardue, W.D. Pease, Lloyd Pendleton, Alfred Pendray, Eldon Peterson, Randy Phillips, David Pitt, Leon Pittman, Clifton Polk, James Poplin, Stephen Price, Joe Prince, Ron Pritchard, Jim Pugh, Martin Pullen, Morris Pulliam.

George Quinn.

Jerry Rados, A. D. Rardon, David Ree, Winfred Reeves, John Reynolds, Douglas Rial, Ron Richard, David Ricke, Willie Rigney, Dean Roath, Howard Robbins, Fred Roe, Mark Roper, A.G. Russell.

Masaki Sakakibara, John Salley, Lynn Sampson, Scott Sawby, George Schepers, James Schmidt, Herman Schneider, Matthew Schoenfeld, Maurice & Alan Schrock, Steve Schwarzer, James Serven, Corbet Sigman, Norman Simons, Jim Siska, Fred Slee, Ralph Smith, Jim Sornberger, Harry Stalter, Ken Steigerwalt, Charles Stewart, Charles Syslo.

Gray Taylor, Seiichi Tasaki, J.M. Tedder, Stephen Terrill, Robert Terzuola, Leon Thompson, Timberline Knives, Carolyn Tinker, Pat Tomes, Dan Tompkins, Dwight Towell, Ralph Turnbull.

Wayne Valachovic, Frans Van Eldik, Michael Veit, Howard Viele, Frank Vought.

George Walker, Michael Walker, Brian Walters, Kenneth Ward, Buster Warenski, Dale Warther, Del Weddle, Charles Weiss, Mike Wesolowski, Robert White, Weldon Whitley, Ken Whitworth, Horace Wiggins, R.W. Wilson, Webster Wood, William W. Wood, Harold Woodward, Joe Worel, Tim Wright.

Tom Zowada, Michael Zscherny.

1988 Probationary Members Eligible for Voting Membership in 1990
Chuck Anderson, Steven Rapp.

Alaska Knifemakers Association

A. W. Amoureux, Robert Ball, J. D. Biggs, Lonnie Breuer, Mark Bucholz, Irvin Campbell, John Chamberlin, Bob Cunningham, Gordon S. Dempsey, Art Dufour, Gordon Grebe, Hank Kubaiko, Bob Levine, Ron Robertson, Steve Robertson, Red Rowell, Keith Stegall, Jim Stow, Thomas Trujillo, Ulys Whalen, Jim Whitman, Bob Willis.

American Bladesmith Society

M. Ian Adams, Gary D. Anderson, Norman B. Anderson, Marvin C. Arneson.

Bill Bagwell, Aubrey G. Barnes, Gary L. Barnes, Wayne M. Barnhart, Jay L. Barron, Hugh Bartrug, Dave Ber, W. T. Biskamp, Leon E. Borgman, Robert Branton, Jack Brewer, Jimmy Buchner, Jay Burger.

Chris Cawthorne, Tommy S. Cellum, R.B. Cervin, Dave Chrisholm, Mike Conner, James R. Cook, Joseph Cordova, Barry Crandall, James L. Crowell.

Terry Davis, Harvey Dean, Jed Dee, Ray Demers, Gordon S. Dempsey, Michael Denis, Mike de Punte, Ted M. Dowell, Fred Durio.

Amos D. Ewing.

Bill Fielder, Jerry Fisk, Allen D. Flashing, Joe Flournoy, T. Scott Forbes, Edward A. Fowler, Wendell Fox, Larry Fuegen, Jack Fuller.

Mark Gardner, Ray Garrison, Sal Glesser, Wayne L. Goddard, Frank Gunn.

P.L. (Doc) Hagen, Bruce A. Hapeman, Charles E. Haynes, Lou Hegedus, Jesse L. Hemphill, Jay Hendrickson, Carl Henkle, Bill Hicks, Roger Hockwalt, Robert A. Holmas, C. Robert Hudson, Daryle J. Hughes, Jimmy Hyde.

Paul R. Inman.

C.R. Johnson, Ryan Joynson, Jacques R. Juarer.

Joseph F. Keeslar, Kevin Keller, Keith Kilby, Dick Kimberley, George Kirtley, Raymond Kremzner, Philip Kretsinger, Jr.

Donald G. Lange, Mick Langley, David L. Lassio, John C. Leigh, Nick Leone III.

Dan Maragni, J. Chris Marks, Oscar L. Mayville, Harry McCarty, Kevin McCrackin, Victor J. McCrackin, Henry "Ted" Merchant, James D. Michels, Hanford J. Miller, Robert S. Monroe, William F. Moran Jr., Keith More, Russell A. Moyer, Jack Muse.

Bruce Nelson, R. Kent Nicholson, Robert Nicholson.

Lee A. Oberg, Charles F. Ochs III, Randy W. Ogden, Michael J. Oles III, Rodney Olsen, Michael Osbourne.

Joseph Page, Dwayne Parrish, Michael R. Parsons, Alfred H. Pendray, James Porter, Morris C. Pulliam.

Thomas C. Quakenbush.

Jerry Rados, W.D. "Bo" Randall, Scott Reymiller, James D. Rhodes, Steven L. Rick, Michael R. Rochford II.

Albert A. Sanders, Margaret R. Scheid, Norman F. Schenk, James S. Schippnick, James A. Schmidt, Stephen C. Schwarzer, Malcolm Tiki Shewan, Mark O. Shogar, James P. Sigman, Cleston Sinyard, Patrick M. Small, Bob Stevens, Glenn C. Stockton, Arthur Swyhart.

Lou Teichmoeller, John Teslow, Thomas Theill, Robert Timm, P.J. Tomes, Lester A. Twigg.

Edger Waine Urstadt.

Wayne Valachovic, Michael Veit, Gene Velek.

Joseph C. Wadeson, Mark Waldrop, Bill Walker, Roger Wallace, Daniel Watson, Donald E. Weiler, James F. West, Ray R. Wheelington, Daniel J. White, Charles E. Williams, David Williamson, Wayne Willson, David Wilson.

William H. Zeanon.

California Knifemakers Assn.*

Arnie Abegg, Elmer Art.

Leroy Besic, John Bevans, Bruce Bochman, Doug Brack, Clint Breshears, Ted Brown.

Lock Cameron.

Mark DeFelice, Bill Duff.

Bob Engnath.

Jim Ferguson, Ted Fisher.

William Herndon, Glen Hornby, Jim Hrisoulas, Eppy Huertas.

Jim Jacks, Ann Jensen, Jeff Juric.

John Knapp, John Kray, Don Kreibich, Martin Kruse, Jim Kuykendall.

Mike Lyons.

Leo Mason, Tom Mayo, Rick Mecchi, Harry Mendenhall, Jim Merritt, Bob Miller, Emil Morgan, Jeff Morgan.

Thomas Orth.

Barry Posner.

Leroy Remer, Bob Roberts, Thomas Ross.

Will Scarrow, Herman Schneider, Ed Serra, Ray Shepard, Chuck Stapel, Al Steinberg.

Steve Terrill.

Stan Urbanski.

Al Warren, Sherman Williams, Harold Wilson, Barry Wood.

*CAL- Knives

Arizona Knifemakers Association

D. "Butch" Beaver, Jack Busfield, Bill Cheatham, Dan Dagget, Tom Edwards, Anthony Goddard, Larry Hendricks, Steve Hoel, Ken McFall, Milford Oliver, Jerry Poletis, Merle Poteet, Mike Quinn, Elmer Sams, Jim Sornberger, Glen Stockton, Bruce Thompson, Sandy Tudor, Charles Weiss.

The New England Bladesmith's Guild

Jimmy Fikes, Don Fogg, Dan Maragni, Louis Mills, Jim Schmidt.

South Carolina Association of Knifemakers

Joe Barefoot, Walter Brend, Richard Bridwell, Bob Burdette, Skip Burnette, Dan Cannady, Charles Cox, Davis Bros., Dixie Davis, William DeFreest, Russell Easler, Hal Gainey, Ron Gaston, Harry George, Dick Gillenwater, Mike Gregory, George Herron, Randy Hughes, Ralph Kessler, Gene Langley, Tommy Lee, Claude Montjoy, Larry Page, Alvin Poston, Joe Prince, Winfred Reeves, Duncan Rutherford, Pat Schwallie, Ralph Smith, Rocky Thomas.

Tennessee Knifemakers Association

John Bartlow, Doug Casteel, Harold Crisp, Larry Harley, John W. Walker, Harold Woodward, Harold Wright.

Knife Photo Index
To Previous Editions

As a service to readers, we have here compiled an alphabetical guide to photos of handmade knives, listed according to their makers. THIS INDEX DOES NOT INCLUDE KNIVES PUBLISHED IN THIS ISSUE.

A

Ed Addison: K'86:103; K'88:82
Yoshihito Aida: K'82:74; K'85:114; K'86:64,67; K'87:51,109
Mike "Whiskers" Allen: K'87:69,89; K'88:171
Steve Allen: K'87:96; K'88:52,63
A.W. Amoureux: K'84:92; K'88:60
Charles B. Anderson: K'86:60,170; K'87:121,233; K'88:145
Edwin Anderson: K'83:85,149; K'84:69,173; K'85:157; K'86:229; K'88:171
Don Andrews: K'88:124,127,152
E.R. (Russ) Andrews, II: K'81:18,71,102
W.E. Ankrom: K'81:36,37,94; K'82:77,90; K'83:149; K'86:63,229; K'87: 171
William J. Antonio, Jr.: K'83:149; K'85:157; K'87:58,97,107
Ray Appleton: K'87:117; K'88: Cover 1,93
Dick Atkinson: K'81:39; K'82:71,93,97; K'83:66,75,149; K'84:Cover, 173; K'86:87,229; K'87:52

B

Bill Bagwell: K'81:123; K'82:103; K'83:117; K'84:85,173; K'85:100
Ray Baker: K'87:171
Phill Baldwin: K'82:123; K'83:108; K'84:73,121,134; K'85:157; K'86:54,118; K'87:92; K'88:83
James Barbee: K'83:149; K'84:130
Norman P. Bardsley: K'83:44,138,149; K'84:136; K'85:69; K'86:110; K'87:49,113,119,171; K'88: 63,74,80,110,137,171
Joe W. Barefoot: K'84:67,173; K'85:49,73; K'87:171
John Barlow: K'86:120
Tom Barminski: K'84:173; K'85:55
Mike Barna: K'87:130
Gary L. Barnes: K'82:104; K'83:112,115; K'84:55,56,77,111,119; K'85:Cover, 79,125; K'86:78,107,151,229; K'87:71,73,77,121,132; K'88:139
Richard W. Barney: K'82:46,61,81,123
A.T.Barr: K'82:97,123
Jack Barrett: K'81:30,123; K'85:159
James J. Barry: K'82:46,123; K'83:41,87,105; K'84:57,84,99,175; K'85:66,101; 'K'87:155,173; K'88:57
John Bartlow: K'87:121; K'88:65,173
Hugh E. Bartrug: K'87:Cover, 109,140; K'88:47,74,76,140,143
Lee Gene Baskett: K'84:175; K'85:56,118,159; K'86:92; K'87:54,101; K'88:80,115
John Bassney: K'81:125; K'82:55,91
Bear Claw (See B.R. Bryner.)
Norman Beardsley: K'85:75
Devon (Butch) Beaver: K'82:24,52; K'83:39,63,67,86,90; K'84:Cover, 56,62,70,82,89,95,116,145,175; K'85:54,72,133,159; K'86:56; K'87:91,125,148,173; K'88:51,71,117,119,126
Judy Beaver: K'87:125
P.F. Beck: K'81:125; K'82:96; K'83:74
Ethan Becker: K'88:114
Michael R. Beckwith: K'84:93,175
Ray Beers: K'81:22,125; K'82:72,78; K'83:55,90,151; K'84:72,97,110; K'85:72,159; K'86:148,152; K'87:49,121,173; K'88:75,109,147,151
Jack Belk: K'82:78,112,125 K'83:76
Frank Bell: K'87:82, 109; K'88:154
Michael Bell: K'85:71,159; K'86:54,229; K'87:112,173; K'88:108
William N. Bennett: K'82:45,125; K'83:77,151; K'84:66; K'85:90
Don Benson: K'88: 173
Dave Ber: K'88: 173
Andrew G. Berendt: K'82:56
Leslie L. Berryman: K'81:18; K'85:112

Leroy Besic: K'85:161; K'86:55; K'87:52
Sid Birt: K'82:102; K'83:105,106,111,112,116,151; K'84:89; K'85:50,79,94,161; K'86:70,113,117; K'88:69,70,94
Paul W. Bizal: K'83:41
Earl Black: K'84:55; K'85:161; K'86:254; K'87:92,175; K'88:173
Black Oak (See KEMAL.)
Andrew Blackton: K'82:46,80,125; K'83:83,151; K'84:67,177; K'85:115; K'86:59; K'88:173
Roy Blaum: K'82:125; K'84:177; K'87:60,123; K'88:82,97
Block: K'85:140
Gregg Blomberg: K'87:34,35; K'88:140
Bob-Sky (See Hajovsky.)
Bruce Bochman: K'88:175
Phil Boguszewski: K'85:108,161; K'88:87,88,91,145
Bruce Bohrmann: K'85:113
Charles B. Bolton: K'88:67,175
Bone Knife Co., Inc.: K'81:64,75,99,125; K'82:41,45,51,61,79,125; K'83:153; K'86:62
Jeremy Bonner: K'85:45; K'86:51,52
Lew Booth: K'81:125
James and Talon Bowen: K'85:99,161
Tilton and James Bowen: K'87:175
Francis Boyd: K'88:85,175
Dennis Bradley: K'85:163; K'86:72,80; K'87:69,175
Edward Brandsey: K'85:62,163; K'86:122,244; K'87:108; K'88:71,175
Larry Brandstetter: K'81:63;110; K'82:90,127; K'86:77
Jim Brayton: K'88:175
Dan Brdlik: K'87:53,107
Walter J. Brend: K'83:88,153; K'85:132,163; K'86:229
Clint Breshears: K'85:163; K'86:59,229
Brian: K'85:139
Richard A. Bridwell: K'82:74,84,94,119; K'83:47,53,58; K'84:79,143,177
E.D. Brignardello: K'82:44; K'83:83,153; K'84:91,177; K'85:67,163; K'86:147
G.M. (Tim) Britton: K'81:81,127; K'82:94; K'83:52,76
David Broadwell: K'85:73; K'86:100,253; K'87:113,175; K'88:50
Dennis Brooker: K'81:38,40,113,127; K'82:112
Steve R. Brooks: K'87:155; K'88: 51,175
Mark Brower: K'87:175
David B. Brown: K'83:30,87,153; K'85:163; K'88:65,177
E.H. Brown: K'85:163
Floyd E. Brown: K'82:127; K'83:130,146; K'84:179
Harold E. Brown: K'86:171; K'87:123,177; K'88:130
L.E. "Red" Brown: K'81:127; K'82:45; K'84:179
Peter Brown: K'88:65,177
Ted Brown: K'88:65
Rick Browne: K'81:100; K'83:63; K'84:96,179; K'85:77,165; K'86:57
Barry R. Bryner: K'84:179; K'86:75; K'87:177
Bill Buchner: K'83:128; K'84:75,85,133,179; K'85:71; K'88:139,177
R.E. Buebendorf: K'83:153; K'85:165
John Bugden: K'87:49,105
Skip Burnette: K'87:177
Dave Burns: K'85:254
John Busfield: K'82:97,127; K'83:56; K'84:76,139; K'86:82,144; K'87:61,67,146,177; K'88:87,95,142
Jerry Busse: K'87:50

C

Bill Caldwell: K'85:56; K'86:89; K'87:96,179; K'88:177
Errett Callahan: K'88:127,149
Dick Campbell: K'81:Cover, 61,93,97,127; K'82:48,57,98,127; K'84:67,88
Joe Candrella: K'87:179; K'88:55
Daniel L. Cannady: K'87:179; K'88:177
Ronald E. Canter: K'81:127; K'82:81; K'84:179; K'88:177
Bob Cargill: K'81:85,92,93,127; K'83:44,56,77,155; K'84:78,134,179; K'85:108,143,151,165; K'86:93,94,95,123,161,162; K'88:89
W.R. Carnes: K'84:138

Fred Carter:K'81:6,16,47,48,50,53,63,70,73,96,116,118,119,121,129;
K'82:Cover, 41,50,64;K'83:40,41,64,65,134,155;K'84:81,91,114,140;
K'85:40,43,94,142,165;K'86:61,98;K'88:179
Douglas Casteel: K'88:70
Tom S. Cellum: K'88:179
Frank and Mark Centofante: K'81:29,120,129; K'82:129; K'83:Cover, 35,36,61;
K'84:181;K'85:136;K'86:144;K'87:Cover, 68,149; K'88:88
Gordon Chard: K'86:57,177; K'87:85,148,179; K'88:118
John E. Chase: K'81:129; K'82:109; K'83:155; K'84:51; K'86:56,124
Bill Cheatham: K'81:22,129;K'82:56,61,93,129; K'83:122,145; K'84:133,181;
K'85:76,141;K'88:179
D.W. Childress: K'82:83,119
D.E. (Lucky) Clark: K'81:129; K'82:129
J.D. Clay: K'82:64,75,78,86,129; K'85:107,113,167
Wayne Clay: K'83:50,75,155; K'84:64,181; K'85:167; K'86:57; K'87:31,70,105;
K'88:74,147,179
Keith E. Coleman: K'84:181; K'85:49,57,73; K'87:181; K'88:123,179
Ken Coleman: K'87:119
A.J. Collins: K'82:87,93,129; K'84:85,97,100,181; K'85:87,89,90; K'87:119
Lynn M. Collins: K'84:93,181; K'85:133
Michael Collins: K'82:119
Walter "Blackie" Collins: K'81:171; K'82:95,173; K'83:40; K'85:151
Paul E. Compton: K'81:25,129; K'83:84,129; K'84:183
Bob Conley: K'85:106,114,167; K'86:76,230
C.T. Conn, Jr.: K'83:155; K'84:70,105,183; K'85:167; K'86:79,124,229; K'88:85,88
Michael Connor: K'81:6,25,84; K'82:67,103,129; K'84:81; K'85:115,167
Robert Coogan: K'86:51; K'87:73,79,121,181; K'88:75,85
George J. Cooper: K'82:56
Harold Corby: K'81:69,74,130; K'82:62,118; K'83:35,36,47,157; K'84:95,144;
K'85:95,169; K'87:181
Joseph G. Cordova: K'82:67,73,85; K'84:92; K'85:76
Leonard Corlee: K'81:17,92,130; K'82:41,52,62; K'83:43,157; K'84:77,183
Jim Corrado: K'83:Cover 2,30,50,59,111,114,115; K'84:83
Danny Courtney Jr.: K'83:157
Eldon Courtney: K'81:130; K'82:45,63,80,92,131; K'83:40,61,157; K'84:85,183;
K'85:54,63,130,169; K'86:90,112; K'87:181
George Cousino: K'83:143; K'84:183; K'85:141,169; K'86:230; K'87:181; K'88:181
A.E. Cover: K'81:24,29,78,131; K'82:62,131; K'83:78; K'84:111,183
Ray Cover: K'86:149; K'88:50,91,181
Colin J. Cox: K'83:157; K'85:55,73,107; K'86:121; K'87:53,95,101,143;
K'88:62,126,145,181
Sam Cox: K'87:250
James H. Craig: K'83 157; K'84:185; K'88: 62,126,145,181
Jack W. Crain: K'83:157; K'84:93,153,185; K'85:53,98,142,167; K'86:91,230;
K'87:94,95,135,181; K'88:54
Larry Crawford: K'87:81
Pat Crawford: K'81:36,37,62,73,75,78,79,82,93,131; K'82:44,131;
K'83:90,120,123,127,129,157; K'84:86,115; K'85:49,118; K'86:78,80,122,142;
K'87:73,137;K'88:63,102,111,125,181
Harold Crisp: K'82:131; K'84:91,101,134,152; K'85:82,115,169; K'88:77
Jack Crockford: K'82:71; K'83:53,157; K'84:67,185; K'86:79; K'88:103,105
W.W. Cronk: K'81:110
James L. Crowell: K'83:113,116,117,147; K'84:71,185; K'85:41,71,78,171;
K'86:110,118; K'88:50,98,102,181
W. Daniel Cullity: K'82:119
John Culpepper: K'81:131
R.J. Cumming: K'83:41; K'84:116,185; K'85:139,171
Jim Cunningham: K'81:131; K'83:159

D

Dan Dagget: K'81:85,86,103,115,132; K'82:52,53,75,111; K'83:Cover, 64,159;
K'84:83,185; K'85:66,104; K'86:99,230; K'88:102
Cris Dahl: K'84:185; K'86:147; K'87:105; K'88:61,147
George Dailey: K'85:85; K'86:113; K'87:90,183
Alex Daniels: K'85:171; K'87:55,105,183; K'88:181
Art A. Darakis: K'81: Cover, 32,34,56,132; K'82:117; K'83:143,159;
K'84:75,115,187
Rick Darby: K'83:81,159; K'84:110,187
Steve Davenport: K'82:133; K'83:51; K'84:187; K'87:62,183
Edmund Davidson: K'88:62,183
Rob Davidson: K'85:97,121,135; K'86:118; K'87:85; K'88:183
Davis Brothers Knives: K'82:133; K'83:159; K'84:110; K'85:171; K'87:183;
K'88:97
Davis Custom Knives: K'81:22,46,47,50,67,133
Barry Davis: K'84:68,79,81,187; K'85:171; K'86:61,71,78; K'87:81,183; K'88:183

Dixie Davis: K'85:171
K.M. "Twig" Davis: K'82:Cover; K'83:44,159; K'84:67,187; K'88:78
Syd Davis: K'84:105
W.C. Davis: K'81:93; K'82:75,133; K'83:114,159; K'84:79,88,103,187; K'86:Cover,
77,85; K'88:84,91,113,183
Dane and Barry Dawson: K'82:133; K'83:121,159; K'84:105
Richard Dearhart: K'82:133
Robert DeFeo: K'86:101; K'87:185; K'88:183
William G. DeFreest: K'82:60,61,83,119,133; K'83:79; K'85:100,173
Frank D'Elia: K'83:40,161
Gordon S. Dempsey: K'85:98,173; K'88:102
Dan Dennehy: K'86:101; K'88:149
Douglas M. Dent: K'82:135; K'85:173
Larry Detloff: K'82: 114; K'83:145,161; K'84:66,141; K'85:88; K'88:85
Phillip Detmer: K'88:183
Jack Dias: K'84:189,K'85:173
Joseph M. DiGangi: K'88:100
Carl Dillon: K'87:70
Frank J. Dilluvio: K'88:185
Malcolm Dion: K'86:58; K'87:59,79,185; K'88:185
Larry DiTommaso: K'88:Cover 1, 140
Robert Orr Dodge: K'84:83,106
Patrick Donovan: K'86:99,144; K'88:101,169,185
Dick Dorough: K'81:34,133; K'82:51,135; K'83:55; K'84:75; K'87:146
T.M. Dowell: K'81:13,17,37,41,55,65,67,71,78,96,103,112,135; K'82:Cover,
39,48,79; K'83:134,137,138,139; K'84:52,94,117,150; K'85:31,97,116,175;
K'86:24; K'87:109,185; K'88:65,99
James T. Downie: K'88:105
Larry Downing: K'83:47,161; K'84:84,87,105,109,111,189; K'85:Cover, 48,89;
K'86:83
T.M. Downing: K'86:56,181; K'87:50,58,82; K'88:185
Dubba (See E.W. Schulenberg.)
Bill Duff: K'81:135; K'82:87; K'86:145,230; K'87:187
Dave Dugger: K'84:189; K'85:48,135,175; K'86:59
Roy Dunlap: K'83:95
Melvin T. Dunn: K'83:209; K'84:61,189; K'85:57; K'86:66
Larry Duvall: K'86:109

E

R.O. Easler: K'83:161; K'84:189; K'85:106,175; K'86: 84,230; K'88:185
Al Eaton: K'87:85,95,109,148,187; K'88:69,104,122
Rick Eaton: K'87:187
Fain E. Edwards: K'82:51,135; K'83:87,90,116; K'84:73,116,191; K'85:60,61
Tom Edwards: K'86:126; K'87:87
Joel Ellefson: K'83:161; K'84:93,191; K'85:140; K'86:121; K'87:187; K'88:74
W.B. Ellerbe: K'85:175
Marcus Elliott: K'84:191
Don Ellison: K'83:48,61,161; K'84:103
Brad Embry: K'81:135
Jim Ence: K'81:53,54,55,58,65,76; K'82:25,48,49,66; K'83:43,84,86,163;
K'84:Cover; K'85:175; K'86:63,185; K'88:68,187
Robert Enders: K'86:79; K'87:187; K'88:Cover 2, 91,123,187
Mike England: K'82:74; K'83:94,131,163; K'85:46,54,79,83,177; K'86:88,121;
K'88:187
Virgil England: K'82:87
George Englebretson: K'85:115,177
Bob Engnath: K'86:54,128,129,132,133; K'87:109,112
Thomas M. Enos III: K'82:135; K'83:96,163
Curt Erickson: K'84:56,191; K'85:177; K'86:61,67,99,169; K'87:110,149,187;
K'88:111,187
L.M. Erickson: K'84:191; K'86:230; K'88:57,187
Walter Erickson: K'86:122,255; K'87:72; K'88:52,187
Vincent K. Evans: K'88:71

F

Melvin Fassio: K'86:80; K'87:62,68,189; K'88:57
Howard J. Faucheaux: K'84:136; K'85:67; K'87:189
Allan Faulkner: K'86:67; K'88:60,92,125,187
Stephen H. Fecas: K'82:60,96,119,137; K'83:84,94,163; K'84:115; K'85:75,177;
K'86:79,186; K'88:187
Vince Feragotti: K'81:21,135; K'84:65
Lee Ferguson: K'85:177; K'86:109; K'88:51
William V. Fielder: K'84:76; K'86:118; K'88:68,83

Jimmy L. Fikes: K'83:111; K'84:86,119,121,133,136; K'85:64,78,115; K'86:140; K'88:102
L.C. Finger: K'83:Cover, 129; K'84:193; K'87:75
Clyde E. Fischer: K'82:87,137; K'85:31; K'87:72; K'88:90
Theo (Ted) Fischer: K'88:189
Jerry Fisk: K'88:189
Jim Fister: K'87:81,189; K'88:48,189
Joe Flournoy: K'82:63; K'84:193; K'86:231; K'87:189
Don Fogg (See Kemal)
Allen Ford: K'85:179
Pete Forthofer: K'85:108; K'86:82; K'87:53,64; K'88:94
Roger Foust: K'83: 87,163; K'84:193; K'85: 56,61,83,91,179; K'86: 105
Ed A. Fowler: K'83:79; K'84:193; K'85:179; K'86:231
J. Paul Fox: K'81:85,93,136; K'82:137; K'83:50; K'85:108,179; K'86:78,106,231; K'87:66,116; K'88:110
Wendell Fox: K'87:130
Ed Fowler: K'87:130,189
Heinrich H. Frank: K'81:136; K'82:117,137; K'83:138; K'84:149; K'85:109; K'86:74; K'87:71; K'88:93
Andrew Frankland: K'84:116; K'87:93,136
Mike Franklin: K'81:136; K'82:73,95; K'83:35,36; K'88:189
Ron Frazier: K'81:7,67,137; K'82:48; K'84:53,81,193; K'85:72; K'87:152; K'88:49,76,131,189
Art Freeman: K'85:68,114
A.J. Freiling: K'83:50,107; K'85:64,139
Dennis Friedly: K'85:98,129; K'86:100
Larry Fuegen: K'88:140
Yasuhiro Fujimoto: K'86:79; K'87:118; K'88:92
S.M. Fujisaka: K'86:57; K'87:52,78,191; K'88:59,75,104,189
Burt Fuller and Hall: K'81:25,80
Jim Fuller: K'86:Cover, 104; K'87:32,76; K'88:62,89
John W. Fuller: K'81:30,137; K'82:72,137; K'83:105,165; K'85:179; K'88:191
W.T. Fuller, Jr.: K'81:30,137; K'82:137; K'83:54,165; K'85:179
R. Fulton: K'85:181
Joe Funderburg: K'82:25,26; K'83:43,139; K'86:64
Shiro Furukawa: K'84:195; K'87:63; K'88:87,118

G

Frank Gamble: K'82:80,97; K'84:96; K'85:74,102,181; K'88:111,191
Chuck Garlits: K'87:56,191; K'88:88
Willard O. Garner: K'87:107,191; K'88:59,191
M.D. Gartman: K'88:92
Ron Gaston: K'83:82; K'84:195; K'85:181; K'86:124; K'87:54; K'88:64,67,143,191
Linden L. Gaudette: K'88:66,191
Clay Gault: K'81:36,139; K'83:74,165; K'84:195; K'85:112; K'86:58,75,143; K'87:61,72,103,111; K'88:86
Roy E. Genge: K'82:139; K'83:165; K'84:195; K'88:113
Rick Genovese: K'81:12,139; K'83:165
Tom George: K'88:191
Randall Gilbreath: K'85:181; K'86:75; K'87:49,63,95,191
E.E. "Dick" Gillenwater: K'82:78,119,139; K'83:35,36,79; K'84:195; K'85:Cover; K'87:77,103,152,191
Jon Gilmore: K'87:Cover, 75,193
Ken Glaser: K'86:90; K'87:193
Roger Gleason: K'84:131
Ron Glover: K'84:65,95,195; K'85:68,109; K'86:231; K'87:155; K'88:127,191
Wayne Goddard: K'82:79; K'83:35,36,165; K'84:62; K'85:61,69,181; K'86:136,137; K'87:130; K'88:105,122,140
Jim Gofourth: K'87:61
T.S. Goldenberg: K'85:181
Warren L. Goltz: K'88:60,148
Tai Goo: K'83:117,165; K'84:197; K'85:91; K'86:139; K'87:137,141,193; K'88:73
Butch Goodwin: K'87:110,129; K'88:76,193
Gordon (See DeFreest)
Butch Gordon: K'87:58
Dante and/or Judy Gottage: K'83:167; K'84:78,197; K'85:73,83,107,183; K'86:82,189; K'87:104,193,65; K'88:89,100,109,193
Greg Gottschalk: K'85:183; K'87:Cover, 109,151
Charles W. Graham: K'81:42
William R. Granquist: K'83:167
Gordon S. Grebe: K'88:50
L.G. Green: K'82:139; K'83:47,51,167; K'84:76; K'85:108,183; K'86:55,145; K'87:68; K'88:76,193
Michael Gregory: K'83:41,73; K'84:61,109,197; K'85:114,183
Roger Grenier: K'84:103,197; K'87:151,153

Mark Griffin: K'85:183
Rendon Griffin: K'81:6,17,19,52,93,139; K'82:75; K'83:52,121,122,167; K'84:66,77,136; K'85:107,110; K'87:61; K'88:89,193
Larry Grigg: K'86:147
George B. Guthrie: K'83:81,167; K'84:197; K'85:185
Bob Gwozdz: K'85:132,185; K'86:125; K'88:147

H

Phillip L. (Doc) Hagen: K'83:45,167; K'84:197; K'85:62,185; K'86:83; K'87:65,195; K'88:93,102,193
George S. Haggerty: K'84:67,108,199; K'85:90; K'86:60; K'87:69,104,195
Robert J. Hajovsky: K'81:12,61,69,73,74; K'82:61,66; K'83:44,46,88,129; K'84:72,199; K'88:193
Lloyd A. Hale: K'81:47,52,65,79; K'83:Cover, 35,36,167; K'85:31; K'86:66,117
Joe R. Hales: K'82:77
Jim Hammond: K'81:8,14,55,74,78,98,105,139; K'82:64,119; K'83:65,79,131,169; K'84:61,96; K'85:185; K'86:91,145,231; K'87:59
Royal H. Hanson: K'82:139; K'83:44,51,142; K'85:108,137
Jim Hardenbrook: K'81:6,48,65,141; K'82:48,50,52; K'83:41,44,169; K'84:63,81,151; K'85:14,66
Frank L. Hargis: K'83:86,169; K'84:94,199; K'85:98,103,185; K'86:Cover; K'87:195; K'88:195
Walt Harless: K'88:72,195
Larry W. Harley: K'85:185; K'87:54,83,87,121,195; K'88:129
Ralph Dewey Harris: K'87:61,111; K'88:52,87,195
V.E. "Gene" Harrison: K'84:68; K'85:84; K'87:137; K'88:122
William W. Harsey: K'85:35,136; K'87:106,130; K'88:62,86,104
Arlan (Lanny) Hartman: K'87:195; K'88:49,195
Phill Hartsfield: K'81:8; K'82:44,68,141; K'83:98,169; K'85:37,187; K'87:49,59,92; K'88:102,113,195
M.C. Harvey: K'86:89
Don Hastings: K'81:66,70,75,84,102; K'82:103; K'83:112; K'84:49,51,52,68,199; K'85:97,187; K'86:62,90
Rade Hawkins: K'81:141; K'83:86,169; K'84:106; K'87:103,195; K'88:104
Chap E. Haynes: K'87:107,135,140; K'88:73,80,98,114,195
Don Hedrick: K'84:60; K'85:187; K'86:65,106; K'87:54,86,135; K'88:142,195
Lou Hegedus: K'84:68,199; K'86:90,140; K'87:59
Richard Karl Hehn: K'87:61,83,139,147,197; K'88:144,151,195
Lorenzo "Larry" Hendricks: K'81:38; K'82:141; K'83:107,169; K'84:151; K'87:147
E.J. (Jay) Hendrickson: K'88:62,72,197
D.E. Henry: K'81:65; K'83:80,84,85,124; K'84:12,13,14,15,16,17,18,19; K'87:110
Wayne Hensley: K'81:62,141; K'83:45,83,130,169; K'86:141
Tim Herman: K'82:55,141; K'83:66,113,169; K'84:51,88; K'85:49,109,155,187
Bill Herndon: K'87:76,115,125; K'88:103,197
George Herron: K'81:76; K'82:79,119,141; K'83:35,36; K'84:63,201; K'85:124; K'86:57,81; K'88:Cover 1
Don Hethcoat: K'83:171; K'84:63,93,201; K'87:57
Thomas S. Hetmanski: K'85:109,189; K'86:122,126; K'87:86,101,197,238; K'88:117,119
Daryl Hibben: K'87:56,197; K'88:197
Gil Hibben: K'81:43,93; K'82:42,54,68,77,141; K'83:35,36,91,108,171; K'84:Cover, 56,57,58; K'85:55,76,86,102,103,118; K'86:55,106,122; K'87:56,89,90,121,137; K'88:110,197
Vernon W. Hicks: K'81:31,34,141; K'83:56,121,171; K'84:201
Howard E. Hill: K'83:57; K'84:101,109,201; K'85:117; K'86:69,191; K'87:97,197
Rick Hill: K'87:90,197; K'88:197
Harumi Hirayama: K'86:51; K'88:Cover 2,93
Howard Hitchmough: K'82:118; K'8:55,126,142,171; K'84:64,141,145,201; K'85:97,189; K'88:143
J.B. Hodge: K'81:19,28,30,85,100,141; K'82:114; K'83:51; K'84:139; K'85:134; K'87:Cover
John Hodge (III): K'84:134,201
Steve Hoel: K'81:34,35; K'82:49; K'83:55; K'84:75,201; K'85:110,189; K'86:84; K'87:146; K'88:94
Donald B. Hoffmann: K'82:Cover
Kevin L. Hoffman: K'83:80,130,171; K'84:70,89,92,203; K'85:39,50,68,76,115,189; K'86:101; K'87:59,78,96; K'88:28,78
D'Alton Holder: K'81:16,54,64,77,84,104,109,114,143; K'82:25,26; K'83:35,36,47,66,142,171,202; K'84:68,122,203; K'85:Cover, 44,50,121; K'86:62,71,231; K'88:66
Dale J. Holland: K'85:110; K'86:82
Paul Holloway: K'85:67,90,93,189; K'86:113; K'87:51,110,120,199; K'88:113
Ron Holstrom: K'85:39,189; K'86:145,231; K'87:105,143,199
M.E. Holze and R.K. Hehn: K'82:85,143

Jess Horn: K'81:28; K'82:69,77,87,98; K'83:54,61,108,134,171; K'84:51,79; K'85:136,141; K'86:77,79; K'87:146,151; K'88:85,88,145,199

Glen Hornby: K'82:44,143; K'83:143,171; K'84:203; K'85:57; K'86:63,88,116,120,121

Durvyn M. Howard: K'82:69,143; K'83:54,60; K'84:88; K'85:191; K'88:87

David M. Howie: K'81:16,26,29,55,79; K'82:95,143; K'83:173; K'84:203

John Howser: K'86:64

Arthur J. Hubbard: K'81:143; K'82:63,143; K'83:42,64,173; K'84:86,203; K'85:74,91,117,132,191; K'86:90,100,125; K'87:67,81,83,123,143,199; K'88:Cov 1

C. Robbin Hudson: K'84:85,203; K'85:93; K'87:55; K'88:60,100,199

Chubby Hueske: K'81:15,114; K'82:84; K'83:35,36,40,173; K'84:78; K'86:60,63,80; K'87:121; K'88:121,130,199

Ed Hughés: K'88:199

Lawrence Hughes: K'84:203; K'85:191; K'87:154,155; K'88:152

Roy Humenick: K'87:199; K'88:66

Bob Hunnicutt: K'86:63,142

I

Billy Mace Imel: K'81:22,27,57,73,143; K'82:60,91,143; K'83:53,60,74,122,138,139,173; K'84:144,150; K'85:103,106,121,191; K'86:196; K'87:33,137; K'88:70,199

J

Jim Jacks: K'88:199

Gerry Jean: K'82:95,145; K'83:102,129,139,140; K'85:193; K'87:59

Steve Jernigan: K'85:79; K'86:197; K'88:71

Sid Jirik: K'83:80; K'85:75,98,193; K'86:60,232

Robert Job (See Wootz Int'l.)

S.R. Jobs: K'81:67,143

Rob Johns and John Damagala: K'88:108

C.E. "Gene" Johnson: K'88:90, 201

Gorden W. Johnson: K'81:144; K'83:81,173; K'88:151

Harold "Harry" C. Johnson: K'83:175

Ronald B. Johnson: K'83:143,173; K'85:193; K'86:149

Ruffin Johnson: K'81:11,25,68,70,71,105,112,113; K'82:68,145; K'83:173; K'84:104,153,205; K'87:126,137,141,201; K'88:78

S.R. Johnson: K'81:Cover, 13,62,78,144; K'82:67,85,91,115,120,145; K'83:43,83,95,175; K'85:193; K'86:63,231; K'87:149; K'88:51,59,67,201

W.C. "Bill" Johnson: K'83:41,77,142; 1K'84:205; K'85:112,193; K'86:147; K'87:83,201; K'88:105

Bob Jones: K'84:111,205; K'85:63; K'86:80; K'87:66; K'88:57

Charles Anthony Jones: K'88:63,201

Curtis Jones: K'88:5

Enoch Jones: K'88:201

K

Koichi Kagawa: K'88:94

Robert A. Kapela: K'81:44,92,144

Lee Karkruff: K'84:114

Don Karlin: K'81:42,103; K'82:145; K'83:175; K'86:100,125

Kioshi Kato: K'82:104; K'84:95,119

Joseph F. Keeslar: K'87:55,140,203; K'88:50,139,201

William L. Keeton: K'81:15,33,42,145; K'82:78,92,145; K'84:62,64,85; K'85:69; K'86:67,81; K'87:32,51,110,201; K'88:64,201

Gary Kelley: K'81:51; K'84:56,86,98,99,113,136,205; K'85:86; K'86:103,126; K'87:84,86,87,201; K'88:116

Lance Kelly: K'81:33,56,57,86,92,120,145; K'82:117; K'83:121,143; K'84:141,207; K'85:137; K'86:Cover, 61; K'87:201

Jim Kelso: K'85:Cover, 71,86,203; K'86:55

Kemal: K'81:41,48,71,81,103,119,144; K'82:102,147; K'83:90,113,127; K'84:52,71,81,114,123; K'85:43,73,78; K'86:70,98; K'87:108,139; K'88:50,70,150

Bill Kennedy, Jr.: K'85:117; K'87:85; K'88:124

J.C. Kennelley: K'86:125

Ralph A. Kessler: K'88:64,201

Jot Singh Khalsa: K'81:21,51,70,71,75,145; K'82:45,63,66,90; K'83:Cover, 99,106,127,175; K'84:84,94; K'85:95,195; K'86:89,232; K'87:91,92; K'88:203

Shiva Ki: K'84:207; K'85:56,72,74,195; K'86:65,78,100,151,198; K'87:47,77,113; K'88:57,62,65,75,203

Bill King: K'82:147; K'83:175; K'86:75; K'87:69

Joe Kious: K'82:50,52,115; K'83:60,66,122,175; K'84:122,207; K'85:44,95,97,106; K'86:75,98,232; K'87:155; K'88:203

Jon W. Kirk: K'81:147; K'83:175; K'84:207

George Kirtley: K'83:175; K'84:91

Jerry Kitsmiller: K'88:203

K.K.K. Co. (See A.J. Collins.)

W. Kneubuehler: K'85:61,63

George Koutsopoulos: K'85:195; K'86:116; K'87:73,203; K'88:203

Michael T. Koval: K'81:60,62,63,65,66,147; K'82:86,93,147; K'84:84,207; K'88:68

Terry L. Kranning: K'85:82,83; K'87:86,87,203; K'88:116,118,119

James J. Kreimer: K'88:98

D.F. Kressler: K'84:60,207; K'86:59,64; K'87:51,106,116; K'88:61,143

Al Krouse: K'88:203

Martin Kruse: K'87:50,90,203; K'88:82,139,203

Jim Kuykendall: K'85:195; K'86:55

L

Ron Lake: K'85:107,112; K'86:25,57,77,231; K'87:64,146; K'88:63,94

Frank G. Lampson: K'83:177; K'84:66,137,139,207; K'85:139; K'87:203

Ed Lane: K'83:177

Kurt Lang: K'83:63,101,109,115; K'84:51; K'86:52

Gary Langley: K'84:209; K'86:80,232

Mick Langley: K'87:205; K'88:69

Scott Lankton: K'84:132; K'85:79,85,87,121,122,197; K'87:91,135,140,141; K'88:71,109,121

Ken Largin: K'83:95,177; K'84:99,106; K'85:74,81,89,197; K'86:67,71,114,115; K'87:58,93,205; K'88:205

L.J. Lay: K'88:205

Milo J. (Mike) Leach: K'81:64,93; K'82:42,92,147; K'83:46,146; K'84:209; K'85:109,197; K'86:60,88; K'88:51,205

Paul M. LeBatard: K'88:104,205

Tommy Lee: K'81:15,27,64,69,80,81,106,107,121,147; K'82:109,119,147; K'83:135,177; K'84:83,209; K'86:62,92; K'87:108,121; K'88:64,69,148,205

Charles Lejcek: K'87:73,140

E. Lenaz: K'84:139; K'85:135

Norman Levine: K'82:42,96; K'83:94,121,130; K'84:56,89,144,209; K'85:139,197; K'87:205; K'88:123,151,205

Wendell Liggett: K'85:82,83

Jimmy Lile: K'81:31,55,56,57,61,82,84,110,147; K'83:50,61,64,83,94; K'84:52,114,143; K'85:31,46,53,197; K'86:91,116,120; K'87:64,101,107,119; K'88:49,59,80,205

Chris A. Lindsay: K'87:205

Steve Lindsay: K'88:94

Gary M. Little: K'85:113,197; K'86:58; K'87:111

Wolfgang Loerchner: K'87:52,59,89,149,205; K'88:70,105,207

Bob Lofgren: K'81:54; K'84:114

Bob Loflin: K'88:207

Dave Longworth: K'84:209; K'85:50; K'86:76,200; K'87:Cover,68; K'88:69,111

Tony Louis: K'84:56,209; K'85:199; K'86:63,91,112,119

A.C. Love: K'84:209; K'88:97

Ed Love: K'83:87,88,177; K'84:62; K'85:113,199,237

R.W. Loveless: K'81:12,73,96,170; K'82:Cover, 79,120; K'83:103; K'86:22,24; K'87:Cover,2,14-17,19; K'88:57

Schuyler Lovestrand: K'86:64; K'87:152,207

Bill Luckett: K'82:42,67,149; K'83:67,105,177; K'84:58,72,122,211; K'85:74,102,137; K'88:111

Robert W. Lum: K'81:40,147; K'82:64,97; K'83:Cover 2,79,80,98,130,179; K'84:63,72; K'85:71,77; K'86:56,139; K'87:53,79,126; K'88:73,207

Robert Lutes: K'87:150,207; K'88:110,123,153,207

Ernest L. Lyle: K'82:149; K'83:179; K'86:232; K'88:50

M

Mike Macri: K'87:51,113,207; K'88:67,73

J.M. "Mickey" Maddox: K'81:147; K'83:53,60

Jack Madsen: K'83:98,117; K'87:91

Jeffrey G. Malitzke: K'85:93

Mike Manrow: K'81:10,45,46,57,74,83,92,93,97,118; K'83:42,45; K'85:103

Dan Maragni: K'82:102,149; K'83:179; K'84:82; K'85:93,129; K'86:71,89,151; K'87:126,207; K'88:52

Tom Maringer: K'81:43,49; K'82:54,149; K'83:39,89,90,91,129,179; K'84:73,135; K'85:75,85,87,103,117,199; K'86:Cover 2,101,109,110, 111,116,126,142; K'87:93,126; K'88:68,107,109,110

Glenn Marshall: K'83:94,179; K'84:211; K'85:90,113,199; K'86:72; K'87:105,143

Bill Mase: K'82:149

Lynn Maxfield: K'84:211; K'87:137,207; K'88:86,207

Tom Mayo: K'85:99,201; K'87:79,82,123; K'88:83,209

Harvey McBurnette: K'81:21,36,93,98,149; K'82:51,69,116,151; K'83:52,121,126,179; K'84:79,89; K'85:136,201; K'86:76; K'87:62,66,121,147; K'88:95

Harry McCarty: K'85:62
Zollan McCarty: K'84:106
C.O. "Mac" McClung: K'81:106; K'82:151
Loyd A. McConnell, Jr.: K'82:151; K'84:145; K'85:91,201; K'86:56,64; K'87:49,120,209; K'88:153,209
V.J. McCrackin and Son: K'88:98
Larry E. McCullough: K'84:211
Dave McDearmont: K'85:201; K'87:209; K'88:59
Ken McFall: K'87:209; K'88:117,209
Jim McGovern: K'88:209
Tommy McKissack II: K'88:129
Thomas McLane: K'82:97,151; K'83:98,127; K'84:71; K'85:78; K'88:120
John McLeod: K'86:72; K'87:148,209
Sean McWilliams: K'85:89,94,115,141,201; K'86:71,99,109; K'87:93,104; K'88:147
John Meeks: K'85:49,118,201
Daryl Meier: K'84:83; K'86:139
Harry E. Mendenhall: K'87:209; K'88:144,209
Larry B. Merical: K'83:202
Chris Miller, Jr.: K'81:81,92,149; K'82:66,68; K'84:93; K'85:100; K'86:232; K'87:59
Hanford J. Miller: K'83:181; K'84:63,82,96; K'85:85,129,203; K'86:65; K'87:55,81,111
J.P. Miller: K'83:117,181; K'84:119; K'87:149; K'88:209
Ronald T. Miller: K'88:211
Terry Miller: K'82:43,111,151; K'83:181; K'84:213; K'85:203; K'86:124; K'87:97
Andy Mills: K'88:66,79,211
Louis G. Mills (Yasutomo): K'84:71,135; K'85:Cover, 71,86,203; K'86:54; K'87:112,116,154; K'88:76,153
Jim Minnick: K'81:85; K'82:50,86,151; K'83:79; K'85:135; K'88:143
Max & Dean Mitchell: K'84:53,100,106,213; K'85:60,82,108,203; K'86:91,103,115,232; K'87:87; K'88:211
Harald Moeller: K'84:213; K'85:203
Claude Montjoy: K'84:213; K'85:102,139,203; K'86:83,148; K'87:63; K'88:211
Keith Moorby: K'84:213; K'85:203
James B. Moore: K'85:205; K'87:211
Tom Moore: K'87:121
Wm. F. Moran, Jr.: K'81:Cover, 59; K'82:28,29,30,31,32,33,34, 68,77,101,120,153; K'83:33,34,92,100,101,102,103,111; K'84:82,127,150; K'85:43,68,77; K'86:120; K'87:Cover 2,55,80,106,111,120; K'88:73,119,130
Emil Morgan: K'85:205; K'86:232; K'87:106,211
Jeff Morgan: K'84:145; K'85:137,205; K'86:203; K'87:123,148,211; K'88:67,98
Justin Morgan: K'88:123
Tom Morgan: K'85:63; K'86:118; K'87:86,211
Tom Morlan: K'84:139; K'88:211
Morseth (See A.G. Russell)
Gary E. Mosser: K'88:126,211
Steve Mullin: K'83:107,189; K'84:105,215; K'85:109,205; K'86:74,83; K'87:62,70,108; K'88:86
Dave Murphy: K'83:22,23,24,25,26; K'84:215; K'85:Cover; K'87:141
John Myakowa: K'87:110
Mel Myers: K'85:205
Paul Myers: K'81:32,93; K'85:82,86,205; K'86:80,148; K'87:86,150,153; K'88:93,121,122

N

Woody Naifeh: K'82:153; K'85:110
Jerry Neal: K'85:91,205; K'86:124
Budd Nealey: K'84:215
Keith Nelson: K'86:91,122,207,234; K'88:213
R. Kent Nicholson: K'87:81
Melvin S. Nishiuchi: K'88:126
R.D. and Roger and George Nolen: K'81:24,28,33,40,44,55,56,93,109,118,151; K'82:55; K'83:67,126; K'84:96,215; K'85:207,239; K'86:109,112,233; K'87:155,213; K'88:61
N. Nomoto: K'88:127
Don Norton: K'88:146,147,148,213

O

Charles Ochs: K'87:108,135,136,213; K'88:63,92,126,147,213
Robert G. Ogg: K'81:31,56,57,120,151; K'82: 110; K'85:137
Gordon O'Leary: K'83: 40,183; K'84: 93,215; K'86:233; K'87:53,148,213
Robert Oleson: K'81:48,84,92,98,151; K'82:74
Milford Oliver: K'84:100; K'86:83
Rod Olson: K'88:148

Wayne C. Olson: K'85:114; K'86:145,208; K'88:104
Warren Osborne: K'86:58,76,100,232; K'87:213; K'88:142,213
Anthony (Tony) L. Outlaw: K'88:213
T.R. Overeynder: K'82:114,153; K'83:145,183; K'84:145,217; K'85:207; K'86:76,84,144; K'87:71,87; K'88:128,213
Danny Owens: K'88:213
Lowell Oyster: K'86:104; K'87:123; K'88:92,126

P

Larry Page: K'85:207; K'86:58
Robert "Bob" Papp: K'82:60,153; K'83:43,63,139; K'84:140,217; K'85:207; K'86:233; K'87:88,215; K'88:61,86,148
Melvin M. Pardue: K'81:22,93,117; K'82:98,115; K'83:52,54,80,183; K'84:66,140; K'85:76; K'86:144; K'88:88,91,102
Robert Parrish: K'85:56; K'86:120; K'87:95,101; K'88:62,108
W.C. Pass: K'83:39
Lloyd D. Pate: K'88:215
Hill Pearce: K'83:Cover 2,43,65,183; K'84:121; K'85:78; K'87:125,126,215
W.D. Pease: K'81:14,36,84,93,115,151; K'82:67,75; K'83:53,120,183; K'84:53,114,217; K'85:209; K'86:144; K'87:146; K'88:95,215
Lloyd Pendleton: K'81:16,114; K'82:60,92,94,155; K'83:78,183; K'84:52; K'85:99; K'87:50; K'88:72
Alfred H. Pendray: K'84:112,217; K'86:81; K'88:133,134,135
Stephan Pepiot: K'87:215
Pepper Knives (See J. Culpepper.)
Dan L. Peterson: K'88: 152,215
Eldon G. Peterson: K'81:18,29; K'83:55,66; K'84:217; K'86:80,209; K'87:64,66,72,215; K'88:215
Jack Peterson: K'88:119
Harold "Bud" Phillips: K'82:72
Randy Phillips: K'85:209; K'86:99,121,233; K'87:108; K'88:215
Larry Pickering: K'84:92,152,217; K'85:40
Harold L. Pierce: K'88:50
David Pitt: K'86:116
Leon Pittman: K'81:20,93; K'82:Cover; K'83:60,185; K'87:65,73; K'88:95
James Poag: K'88:90
Paul W. Poehlmann: K'81:171; K'84:77,219
Larry Pogreba: K'88:74
Jerry Poletis: K'81:23,66,82,153; K'82:56,155; K'83:185
Clifton Polk: K'82:155; K'83:51,202; K'84:103,111; K'85:209; K'86:115; K'87:72
Rusty Polk: K'84:219
L.T. Pomykalski: K'86:102,104
James L. Poplin: K'81:20,79,95,97,153; K'82:83; K'83:185; K'84:143
James E. Porter: K'88:96
Alvin Poston: K'84:219; K'85:209
J. Merle Poteet: K'85:211
Jerry L. Price: K'83:129,185
Joel Hiram Price: K'87:82,106,215
Steve Price: K'86:55,120; K'87:96,217; K'88:141
Joe M. Prince: K'82:119; K'84:79,219; K'85:211
Ron Pritchard: K'82:155; K'83:39,77,185; K'84:219; K'87:139,217
Jim Pugh: K'81:21,50,81,121,153; K'82:55,56; K'85:104,142; K'87:127,217; K'88:100,116
Morris C. Pulliam: K'85:211; K'86:65,81,139; K'87:62,107,132; K'88:217
Aaron Pursley: K'82:116; K'83:122,133; K'84:75; K'85:211; K'87:121,217; K'88:121,130

Q

Barr Quarton: K'83:44,46,63,76,185; K'85:211; K'87:111,113
George Quinn: K'85:211; K'86:99,212

R

Jerry F. Rados: K'83:41,75,187; K'84:221; K'85:49,103,130,211; K'86:110,139,233; K'87:66,140; K'88:117,149,152
W.D. and (Bo) Gary T. Randall: K'81:23,58,64,69,102,117,153; K'82:41,71,92,120,157; K'83:93; K'85:54; K'86:22,126,149; K'87:Cover 2; K'88:6-13,151
Steve Rapp: K'87:154; K'88:68,108,152,217
Rick Rappazzo: K'87:68,217
A.D. Rardon: K'88:90
Michael Ray: K'81:153; K'82:60,61,84,91,157; K'84:53,144,221; K'85:213
Mike Ream: K'82:88
Chris Reeve: K'88:28,71
Chris Reeves: K'87:96; K'88:142

Winfred M. Reeves: K'83:79; K'84:70
Bill Reh: K'84:65,221; K'85:213; K'87:52,123
John Reynolds: K'86:233; K'88:126
David Rhea: K'86:Cover,107
Adrienne Rice: K'88:217
Ron Richard: K'84:76,221
Sam Richards: K'86:52
Dave Ricke: K'83:187; K'84:137,140; K'86:74; K'88:219
Willie Rigney: K'84:84; K'85:67,94,213; K'86:65,98,233; K'88:70,142
Dean Roath: K'81:14,40,82,106,107,108,155; K'82:64,86; K'83:187; K'84:139
Howard P. Robbins: K'88:219
J.B. Robbins: K'86:212
G. Rocha: K'84:112; K'85:113,121
Michael R. Rochford: K'88:66,219
Fred D. Roe, Jr.: K'83:74,187; K'84:63,109,221; K'85:213; K'86:88; K'87:83,68;
K'88:75,219
Fred Rohn: K'81:15,80,112,113,114,155; K'82:157; K'83:78,94,187; K'85:213
Steve Rollert: K'86:126
Harold F. Rollins: K'82:49; K'84:221
Mark H. Roper, Jr.: K'83:187; K'84:61,93; K'85:105,215
Alex Rose: K'84:101,223; K'87:85,219
Rudolph H. Ruana: K'83:93; K'86:22,24
James A. Rubley: K'88:139
A.G. Russell: K'81:23,149,171; K'82:72,97,120; K'83:39,88; K'84:61; K'85:48;
K'86:60,117,147; K'87:76
Roger J. Russell: K'81:72,110,113,155,171; K'82:51,53,80,96,157;
K'83:123,134,189; K'85:215
Charles C. Rust: K'83:189,202; K'85:215

S

Suzanne St. Amour: K'86:51,52
John D. Salley: K'83:142; K'84:110,223; K'85:57,86,215; K'86:110; K'87:Cover,
77,90,219; K'88:75
Bob Salpas: K'85:141,215; K'86:56
Lynn J. Sampson: K'85:114; K'86:234; K'87:63; K'88:78
Jody Samson: K'84:223; K'85:67,215; K'87:50,92,151,219; K'88:108
Bill Sanders (See Timberline Knives.)
Michael M. Sanders: K'87:219
Jim Sasser: K'81:32; K'82:44,159; K'83:93,102,105; K'84:106
Scott Sawby: K'83:107,189; K'85:217; K'86:81,144; K'88:85,221
Murad Sayen (See Kemal.)
Will Scarrow: K'87:122,126
George Schepers: K'86:118,234
Carl Schlieper: K'87:45
James A. Schmidt: K'81:49,50,51,52,62,76,101,102,115,155; K'82:99,101,159;
K'83:102,113,114,116,126; K'84:Cover, 75,223; K'85:44,50,94; K'86:84,97; K'88:95
Herman J. Schneider: K'81:46,48,61,157; K'82:24,53,118,159; K'83:35,36;
K'84:57,115,151; K'85:104,134,217; K'87:120; K'88:221
Matthew A. Schoenfeld: K'81:38,41; K'82:54; K'83:189; K'84:57,97,225;
K'85:74,129,217; K'87:58,219; K'88:100,221
Maurice and Alan Schrock: K'81:40
Stephen Schwarzer: K'82:104,105; K'83:101,102,107,112,114,127;
K'84:82,114,137,225; K'85:63,66,110,217; K'86:116,140; K'88:95
Tasaki Seichi: K'88:118
Peter Semich: K'88:148
Jim Serven: K'81:20,42,72,85,92,157; K'82:50,73,159; K'83:52,191; K'84:88,225;
K'85:106,217; K'86:77,234; K'87:67; K'88:90,151
Robert G. Sharp: K'82:80,161; K'83:53,88,191; K'84:109,225; K'85:217
Phil Sharpe: K'85:62,217
David L. Shaw: K'81:79,157; K'82:51,58,63,113,161; K'83:191
Scott Shoemaker: K'87:55,89,92,131; K'88:80,114,116,221
William E. Shulenberger: K'82:161; K'83:191
Corbet R. Sigman: K'81:19,99,105,108,109,114,117,157; K'82:73,79,97,120,161;
K'83:35,36,42,65,74,191; K'84:Cover 2,
62,64,110,126; K'86:139; K'87:52,107; K'88:66,104,221
Rod Simonich: K'88:78,85
Cleston S. Sinyard: K'85:60,92,217; K'86:90,101; K'87:50,219; K'88:221
Jim Siska: K'85:140; K'87:58,97,152,219; K'88:100
David Sites: K'81:157
Samuel Skirchak, Jr.: K'88: 223
Fred Slee: K'86:233; K'88:49,223
John Sloan: K'83:77,108,191
Shane Sloan: K'88:223
Ed Small: K'85:60; K'86:118; K'87:81

Jim Small: K'82:161; K'84:112,121,225; K'87:145,223
Adam Smith: K'81:83; K'83:191; K'84:227
Gregory H. Smith: K'88:60,148
Harry Smith: K'86:74
John T. Smith: K'81:14,28,39,159; K'82:67,98; K'83:193
Ralph L. Smith: K'82:96,110,119; K'83:76,193; K'84:78,92,227; K'87:63,69
W.F. (Red) Smith: K'83:86,193
W.J. Sonneville: K'81:159
G. Douglas Sontheimer: K'88:55
Jim Sornberger: K'81:14,45,59,66,159; K'82:49,53,87,117,163;
K'83:48,63,85,106,142,193; K'84:83; K'85:Cover, 77,100,132,219; K'86: 111;
K'87:81,136,143; K'88:98,116,144,150
Bernard Sparks: K'81:23,79,159
John Spencer: K'85:219; K'87:103
Dale Spendlove: K'84:78,227
Richard Spinale: K'82:117,163; K'83:143; K'84:75,115; K'85:221; K'87:71; K'88:93
Jefferson Spivey: K'88:106
Richard Stafford: K'85:98; K'87:53,223
Harry L. Stalter: K'86:145; K'87:136,152,223; K'88:117
Chuck Stapel: K'82:96,163; K'83: 39,42,85,129,193;
K'84:65,72,112,125,144,152,227; K'85:75,151,221; K'86:121; K'87:58,70,136;
K'88:54,55,105,113,144,223
Craig Stapel: K'87:223
Richard S. Staples: K'82:41,62,85,163; K'83:193; K'84:65
John Stapleton: K'85:99,221
Keith Stegall: K'88:72
Ken Steigerwalt: K'83:193; K'84:227; K'85:221; K'86:74,214; K'87:64,67
Kelly Lee Stephens: K'82:42,60,67; K'88:223
Charles (Chuck) Stewart: K'83:41,57,75; K'84:55,89,227; K'85:57,76,107,221;
K'86: 77,98; K'87:65,70,169
G.W. Stone and Jim Erickson: K'82:119; K'88:59,225
Johnny Stout: K'86:59
Scott Strong: K'86:59; K'87:133,219
Stud (Custom Knives Ltd.): K'82:176
George Stumpff, Jr.: K'88:89,225
Rod Swain: K'85:221
Chuck Syslo: K'84:229; K'85:223

T

Antonio J. Taglienti: K'88:225
Masao Takahashi: K'85:114; K'86:50; K'87:109
C. Gray Taylor: K'81:47,63,82,159; K'82:49,50; K'83:Cover, 46,134,195;
K'84:83,93,110; K'85:32,94,104,223; K'86:82; K'87:72
David Taylor: K'83:107; K'84:86,110,229; K'85:223; K'86:81,85; K'87:65; K'88:129
Mickey Tedder: K'85:48; K'88:109
Lou Teichmoeller: K'82:43,104,163
Stephen Terrill: K'83:195; K'84:91,229; K'85:100,136,223; K'86:67; K'87:51,225
Robert Terzuola: K'83:195; K'84:64,91; K'85:72,99,223; K'87:91,112,136,225;
K'88:225
David Thompson: K'87:130
Leon Thompson: K'81:13,27,64,84,161; K'83:56,61,84,195; K'84:64,76,229;
K'87:68,225
Danny Thornton: K'81:161; K'83:93; K'84:111; K'88:225
Michael W. Thourot: K'88:125,225
Timberline Knives: K'84:63,229
Carolyn D. Tinker: K'81:12,99,107,161; K'83:78,195; K'84:229; K'86:55
Robert E. Tison: K'81:37,100,161
Pat Tomes: K'82:98; K'83:76,84,116; K'85:97,223; K'87:91,155,225;
K'88:61,125,227
Tomlinson: K'88:149
Dan Tompkins: K'84:67,231; K'85:223; K'86:151
Dwight L. Towell: K'81:Cover, 161; K'83:35,36,86,99,195; K'84:62,76,94,231;
K'85:66,225; K'86:66; K'87:125,225; K'88:49,152,227
R.W. Trabbic: K'81:19,36; K'82:46,165; K'84:231; K'85:225
Terry A. Treutel: K'87:104
TRO Knives (See Overeynder.)
Thomas A. Trujillo: K'87:82
Jon J. Tsoulas: K'88:227
Ralph A. Turnbull: K'81:86,122; K'82:43,69,86,98,115; K'83:57,197; K'84:Cover,
94; K'85:110,112,121; K'86:77,219; K'87:54,113,227; K'88:68,90,143,227
Twig (See K.M. Davis.)

U

W.L. Underwood: K'84:231

V

Wayne Valachovic: K'82:91,105,165; K'83:58,114; K'84:88,231; K'85:67,77,93,225; K'86:84,221; K'87:32,66,83,121,125,126; K'88:79,227
A. Daniel Valois: K'85:58
Frans Van Eldik: K'84:103; K'85:225; K'86:58; K'87:51,119; K'88:60,142
Michael Veit: K'87:139,227; K'88:227
H.J. Viele: K'81:22,39,40,82,83,85,86,98,99,161; K'82:49,96,165; K'83:98,99; K'84:96; K'85:69,143; K'86:149
Ben Voss: K'88:57,64
David Votaw: K'83:106,197; K'85:225
Frank Vought, Jr.: K'82:43,62,78,165; K'84:61,110,231; K'85:50,79,85,132,225; K'86:92,107,112,142,234; K'87:Cover, 227; K'88:74,79,105,114,227

W

J.M. Wade: K'84:231; K'85:225; K'88:52
John K. Wagaman: K'85:225; K'86:66; K'87:56,82,97,227; K'88:52
Mark Wahlster: K'87:115; K'88:91,116,229
Mark Waldrop: K'84:78,86; K'85:97,110,225; K'86:75; K'87:90
George A. Walker: K'82:74,110,165; K'83:197; K'84:75,104,141; K'86:74,125; K'87:63,129,147; K'88:140,147
John Walker: K'87:123
Michael L. Walker: K'83:123,197; K'84:70,75,77,105,111,140,231; K'85:122,227; K'86:Cover 2,85,141; K'87:61,67,79,121,147,227; K'88:Cover 1,117,137
Ken Ward: K'88:51,64,229
David Wardman: K'83:93,197; K'85:227
J.D. Ware: K'84:60
Buster Warenski: K'81:12,47,50,54,55,66,67; K'82:23,26,52,57,83,167; K'83:35,36,83,219; K'84:149; K'85:44,150,227; K'88:69
Al Warren: K'88:229
Stanley Warzocha: K'83:197; K'85:227
Daniel and Bill Watson: K'86:109; K'87:89,93,120; K'88:109
Freddie Watt III: K'85:227; K'86:62,234
Fred E. Weber: K'82:66,84,95; K'83:41,133,197; K'85:98
Gerome W. Weiland: K'88:229
J. Reese Weiland, Jr.: K'88:152
Donald E. Weiler: K'81:108; K'82:167; K'83:103,199; K'84:233; K'85:129,227; K'86:69; K'87:55,78,229; K'88:56,229
Charles L. Weiss: K'81:46,48,49,70,163; K'82:54; K'85:95,99; K'86:Cover, 151; K'87:229; K'88:51
William H. Welch: K'81:13,39,80,163; K'83:97; K'84:233; K'85:68,227; K'86:234
George W. Werth: K'88:231
Cody Wescott: K'86:76
Mike Wesolowski: K'81:13,62,163; K'85:81
Gene E. White: K'85:136
Bob White, Jr.: K'87:86
Robert J. "Bob" White: K'82:72; K'83:56,75; K'84:89,109,143; K'85:90,229; K'86:49,56,83,92; K'87:100,123,229
Robert J. "Butch" White, Jr.: K'88:118
Weldon Whitley: K'81:24; K'82:119; K'83:199; K'84:233
Earl T. Whitmire: K'88:231
Ken Whitworth: K'82:86,115,167; K'83:45,61,199; K'84:78,94,233; K'85:107,229
James C. Wiggins: K'84:60,233; K'85:106,229
H.L.Wiggins: K'87:123
L.R. Wilding: K'81:78,163
Gery L. Willey: K'87:231
W.G. Willey: K'82:112,167; K'83:199; K'86:234; K'87:231
W.C. Williams: K'81:20,33,34,163; K'82:119
Lowell Wills: K'83:130,199
James G. Wilson: K'87:109
R.W. Wilson: K'82:114
Art Wiman: K'83:56,199; K'86:115
Bill Winn: K'81:18,21,164
Travis A. Winn: K'84:235; K'85:75,104,112; K'86:101; K'87:155,231
Earl Witsaman: K'82:56; K'83:106,199; K'84:99; K'85:81; K'86:126; K'87:86; K'88:Cover 1, 116
W-K Knives (See Votaw)
B.B. Wood: K'83:131; K'86:81
Bruce Wood: K'84:235; K'85:100
Owen Wood: K'83:55,85,201; K'87:152,231; K'88:231
Webster Wood: K'83:201; K'84:73; K'85:55; K'86:78,85; K'87:83; K'88:79
William W. Wood: K'81:41,81,100,165; K'82:64,169; K'83:201; K'85:78,231; K'86:222; K'87:124; K'88:61
Harold E. Woodward: K'85:231; K'87:121; K'88:231

Wootz International: K'83:118
Joe Worel: K'85:231; K'86:66
Worm (See L. Pittman.)
Richard Worthen: K'85:75
Harold Wright: K'87:103,104
Kevin Wright: K'85:89; K'87:87,231; K'88:57,118,127
Timothy Wright: K'82:85,94,168; K'83:122,201; K'84:77; K'86:Cover 2,141

Y

T.J. and Ann Yancey: K'81:17,50,72,97,112,114,165; K'82:111,169; K'83:201,203
Cliff Young: K'83:201; K'84:66,92,235; K'85:100
Yamil R. Yunes: K'86:76,226; K'87:53,64; K'88:89
Mike Yurco: K'88:67,124,127

Z

Z Custom Knives (See Zellon McCarty.)
Zack (See D. Zaccagnino.)
Don Zaccagnino: K'81:24,46,61,119,165; K'83:35,36,84,201; K'85:255; K'86:227; K'87:82,232
Tim Zowada: K'85:72,93; K'86:70; K'87:70,136; K'88:73
Michael Zscherny: K'83:45,201; K'84:65,97,112; K'85:48,118,231; K'86: 234; K'88:143

ENGRAVERS

Sam Alfano: K'84:60,139; K'85:135,136
Ralph Alpin: K'87:107
Raymond Babtiste: K'88:141
Billy Bates: K'84:63,139; K'85:134; K'86:145; K'88:142
Earl Bertrand: K'88:123
Tim Bina: K'87:147
Gary Blanchard: K'86:55,77; K'88:121,142,145
Carl Bleile: K'82:114; K'83:139; K'84:140
C. Roger Bleile: K'84:140
Dale Boster: K'87:61
Gary Bouchard: K'84:60
Rudolph Bochenski: K'85:135
Dennis R. Brooker: K'82:112; K'85:117,135
Byron Burgess: K'82:114; K'84:66,141; K'85:88; K'86:145; K'87:148
Martin Butler: K'86:144; K'87:Cover, 52,89,149; K'88:70,105
Frank Clark: K'85:135; K'88:152
Fred Clark: K'87:154,155
Larry Cole: K'87:111
Lester Davis: K'82:45
Ed Delorge: K'88:144
Melissa Dibben: K'85:135; K'86:55,82
W.R. Dilling: K'87:149
Rick Eaton: K'87:148; K'88:144
Ken Eyster: K'86:Cover
Terry Flowers: K'87:148
Firmo Fracassi: K'82:113
Foster: K'83:51
Fred A.Harrington: K'82:50,86,115; K'83:143; K'84:83,88,89,94,140; K'85:39; K'86:74,145; K'87:123; K'88:123,143
Fred D. Henderson: K'82:114; K'83:51; K'84:138
Frank Hendricks: K'86:75,143; K'87:103
Tim Herman: K'85:135; K'86:85,98; K'87:148
Benno Heune: K'86:145
Domingos Joaquim: K'87:96
Bill Johns: K'87:150
Lancy Kelly: K'81:33,56,57,86,92,120,145; K'82:117; K'83:121,143; K'84:57,141,207; K'85:137; K'86:72
Jim Kelso: K'82:Cover; K'83:104,111; K'84:82; K'85:Cover,71,136; K'87:154; K'88:76,128,153
Max Kissler: K'83:51
Joe Kostenik: K'87:151
John M. Kudlas: K'83:143; K'88:145
Tom Leschorn: K'88:151
Harry Limings, Jr.: K'83:82,221; K'84:140; K'85:49; K'86:Cover, 67,113; K'87:54,148; K'88:143
Steve Lindsay: K'82:49,115; K'84:75,139; K'85:110,141; K'86:82,144; K'87:61,67,146,149; K'88:94,142
Simon M.Lytton: K'84:141; K'85:136; K'86:144; K'87:146

Robert Maki: K'84:137,140
George Marek: K'85:90,140
Franz Marktl: K'82:27; K'88:51
Lynton McKenzie: K'81:52,54,55,65,66; K'82:50,115; K'84:139,149,151;
K'85:110; K'86:84
Dave Morton: K'88:61
Mitchell Moschetti: K'86:145
F. Oberndorfer: K'87:139,147; K'88:144
Old Dominion Hand Engravers: K'88:142
Marcello Pedini: K'82:53
Rolf Peter: K'88:143
Wayne Potts: K'81:Cover, 93
Aaron Pursley: K'86:75
Martin Rabeno: K'85:98; K'86:145; K'87:146; K'88:145
Andrew Raftis: K'85:137; K'86:145; K'87:146; K'88:143
Jon Robyn: K'88:61
Bob Rosser: K'87:146
Lewis Sanchez: K'88:145
E. Seifert: K'87:61
Bruce Shaw: K'83:143; K'84:139; K'85:135; K'87:61,70,149;
K'88:61,85,113,144,145
George Sherwood: K'81:Cover, 54,93; K'82:Cover, 115; K'83:142; K'84:114;
K'85:137; K'87:110; K'88:60
Ben Shostle: K'82:50; K'85:135,137,140; K'88:143
W.P. Sinclair: K'82:118; K'83:142; K'84:64,145; K'88:143
R.E. Skaggs: K'81:50,55; K'82:Cover, 24,48,118; K'84:84,150,151; K'85:134;
K'86:61,144; K'87:149; K'88:70,99
Robert Skaggs: K'87:92
Jim Small: K'88:104
Ralph Smith: K'87:71
Ron Smith: K'82:114; K'83:67; K'84:145; K'85:137; K'86:143; K'88:128,142
Jim Sornberger: K'85:100; K'88:51,144,150
James Stewart: K'81:55,56,57
Shigetoshi Takeuchi: K'85:114; K'86:67
Robert Valade: K'81:170; K'84:57
George Vartanian: K'85:135
Eduard Vos: K'88:142
George Walker: K'87:149
Patricia Walker: K'83:123; K'84:70,75,77,140,143; K'85:140; K'86:Cover 2,85;
K'87:61,67,147; K'88:Cover 1
Buster Warenski: K'87:110
Kenneth W. Warren: K'87:123
Claus Willig: K'82:115,190
H. Wood: K'86:77,98
Mel Wood: K'81:45,56,57,59,66; K'82:25,26,61,115; K'83:66,67;
K'84:Cover,62,83,137,139; K'85:137; K'87:123; K'88:93,141

SCRIMSHANDERS
John Alward: K'83:67,142; K'88:151
Terry Jack Anderson: K'81:58; K'82:108
C.M. Barringer: K'82:110
Connie Bellet: K'84:143; K'85:140
R. Bochenski: K'85:139
Benita Bonshire: K'85:137,140
Rick Bowles: K'86:65,106,147; K'87:152
Sandra Brady: K'86:56; K'87:108; K'88:148
Bob Burdette: K'82:108,109; K'84:65; K'85:69
Mary Gregg Byrne: K'84:144
Jerry Cable: K'82:108
Lynda Capocci: K'86:147
Michael Collins: K'82:119; K'84:61,96
Andy Cook: K'85:139
Ray Cover: K'86:149; K'88:148
Barbara Cricchio: K'88:71
Jean Curtis: K'85:141; K'86:60
Guy Dahl: K'86:147; K'88:147
Georgia Davenport (Gigi): K'82:108; K'83:145; K'84:144; K'87:151
Richard DiMarzo: K'86:147; K'88:147,151
Jean E. DeSavage: K'85:141; K'87:126
Joni Elbourn: K'86:149; K'87:151,153
Bob Engnath: K'86:148; K'87:151; K'88:75,147

Linda Erickson: K'85:67
Rick Evans: K'84:64
Rick B. Fields: K'83:142; K'84:144; K'86:148,149; K'87:152; K'88:68,149
Dale Fisk: K'87:153
Adam Funmaker: K'81:54,55; K'83:145
Gigi: K'88:149
Jim Gullette: K'82:110; K'84:143
Charles Hargraves: K'85:139,141; K'88:146,148,149
Stan Hawkins: K'86:148
Bob Hergert: K'87:86
H. Harve Hildebrand: K'82:107; K'83:65; K'86:70
Dennis Holland: K'88:146,147,148
Alan Jiranek: K'87:119 K'88:149
Ann Jordan: K'83:145
Patty Kostelnick: K'87:151
John Land: K'82:107
Ben Lane, Jr.: K'83:142
George Marek: K'87:152
Berni McFadden: K'86:144
Gayle McGrath: K'87:150; K'88:123
Tommy McKissack, II: K'87:153
Carole McWilliams: K'85:141; K'87:86; K'88:147
Anita Miller: K'82:111
Joyce Minnick: K'82:50,111
J.B. Moore: K'85:140
Don Myrer: K'86:100
Michelle Ochonicky: K'88:149
Belle Ochs: K'88:147
Vaughn Parrish: K'84:65
Larry Peck: K'83:145; K'84:Cover
Lou Peterson: K'84:143
Bob Purdy: K'82:107
Tom Radant: K'84:94
Joe Rundell: K'81:58; K'82:109; K'83:146
Bob Satre: K'86:148; K'88:148
Pat Schwallie: K'86:148; K'87:63
Patricia Schwallie: K'85:139,140,141; K'87:63
Laura Schwarz: K'84:144,145; K'86:147
Alice Semrich: K'88:148
George Seymour: K'82:109
Larry Seymour: K'84:143
Peggy Smith: K'85:139; K'88:78
John Stahl: K'82:107,108; K'87:152 K'88:147
Harry Stalter: K'87:152
Glen Stearns: K'81:58; K'82:110
Don Swasey: K'85:139
Oranda Tahl: K'86:71
Mary Austin Talley: K'86:148,149; K'87:150,153
Gerald Tisdale: K'81:58; K'82:109; K'85:139
Karen Walker: K'86:146; K'88:147
Al Warren: K'88:149

ETCHERS/CARVERS
Larry DiTommaso: K'88:151
Mary Ann Eubanks: K'87:155
Dennis Holland: K'87:154,155; K'88:152
Rick Jenkins: K'88:151
Leonard Leibowitz: K'86:151; K'87:155; K'88:153
Rothenburger Waffeneck: K'88:151
Shaw-Leibowitz: K'81:57,65,85; K'82:58,91; K'83:141; K'84:114

HANDLE ARTISANS
John Alward: K'86:151
R. Hill: K'85:140,141
Mike Ochonicky: K'84:142
Tom Patterson: K'83:146
Chris Reed: K'86:127,151
Robert Schaber: K'82:46; K'83:146
Steve Schwarzer: K'86:150
Gary Vann Ausdle: K'84:137; K'85:119,132; K'87:155; K'88:150

Specialty Cutlers

The firms listed here are special in the sense that they make or market special kinds of knives made in facilities they own or control either in the U.S. or overseas, or because the knives are special because of unique design, or function.

B&D TRADING COMPANY
3935 Fair Hill Rd.
Fair Oaks, CA 95628
Phone: 916-965-0555
Specialties: Carries the full line of Executive Edge—Brazil's locking folders.

BARTEAUX & SONS
P.O. Box 66464
Portland, OR 97266/
17520A S.E. Marie St.
Portland, OR 97236
Phone: 503-665-2577
Specialties: Machetes in seven different sizes. Also carries a cane knife. Some models already in use by highway maintenance. Neil O. Marks, President.

BAUSKA MANUFACTURING CORP.
P.O. Box 2270
Kalispell, MT 59903-2270
Phone: 406-752-8080
Specialties: Sportsmen knives in Bowies, hunters, skinners, and utility styles. Offered custom or semi-custom made.

BECKER KNIFE and TOOL CO.
255 Newton Rd.
Cincinnati, OH 45244
Phone: 513-231-9710
Specialties: The Machax, a kukri-shaped machete intended to do light ax work.

BENCHMARK KNIVES (See Gerber/General Cutlers)

BERETTA U.S.A. CORP.
17601 Indian Head Highway
Accokeek, MD 20607
Phone: 301-283-2192
Specialties: A variety of Beretta-only designs, including their Classic Daggers, and folders.

BROWNING
Rt. 1
Morgan, UT 84050
Phone: 801-543-3200
Specialties: Has its own name on sports knives of all kinds, all in Browning finish.

BRUNTON/LAKOTA
620 E. Monroe
Riverton, WY 82501
Phone: 307-856-6559
Specialties: Heavy-duty sports knives, straight and folding, on a distinctive design theme.

CATTLE BARON LEATHER
P.O. Box 100724, Dept. K9
San Antonio, TX 78201
Phone: 512-697-8900
Specialties: Adventure knives from overseas; others made to Jerry Ardolino's design by Tommy McKissack; color catalog $3.

CHARTER ARMS CORP.
430 Sniffens Lane
Stratford, CT 06497
Phone: 203-377-8080
Specialties: Makes the Skatchet, a special hunter's belt tool that can chop, gut and skin.

COLD STEEL, INC.
2128 Knoll Dr., Unit D
Ventura, CA 93003
Phone: 800-255-4716 (in CA: 800-624-2363)
Specialties: Variety of urban survival instruments—big in tantos. Outdoorsman series and a new Bowie.

CONDOR (See Hoffman)

CROSMAN BLADES
250 N. St. Francis
Wichita, KS 67201
Phone: 316-261-3211
Specialties: Crosman Airguns in the sports knife business.

EK COMMANDO KNIFE CO.
601 North Lombardy St.
Richmond, VA 23230
Phone: 804-257-7272/800-468-5575
Specialties: Military fighting and survival knives, combat proven in three wars. All made in USA.

H&B FORGE CO.
Rte. 2, Geisinger Rd.
Shiloh, OH 44878
Phone: 419-895-1856
Specialties: Tomahawks and throwing knives.

HAPPY JACK CUTLERY
P.O. Box 577
Rosman, NC 28772
Phone: 704-884-2823
Specialties: Production-line pocket knives to include: sway back jack, two-blade trappers, and hunters. Most are limited production or commemoratives. All knives made of 440C, jigged bone handles, and satin finished.

HOFFMAN DESIGN
2851 Dorothy Dr.
Agoura Hills, CA 91301
Phone: 818-991-5291
Specialties: The Condor upscale sports knives now on the market.

DAN HONEYCUTT (See Ozark Knife)

KERSHAW/KAI CUTLERY CO.
25300 S.W. Parkway
Wilsonville, OR 97070
Phone: 503-682-1966
Specialties: Former Gerber designer's heavy-duty sports knives made overseas; also smaller "pocket jewelry;" handsome scrimshaw; new designs in using knives.

LAKER KNIFE WORKS
3360 Bendix Ave.
Eugene, OR 97401
Phone: 503-484-2683
Specialties: Fillet knife designed for production by Ron

Lake—piercing point, handle features, etc. Offers now Hip-mate model with mortised style handle construction.

LAKOTA CORP. (See Brunton)

LEATHERMAN TOOL GROUP, INC.
10300 N.E. Marx St.
P.O. Box 20595
Portland, OR 97220
Phone: 503-253-7826
Specialties: All-in-one pocket tool; has two sizes.

LEE BENCH MADE
P.O. Box 1777
Gaffney, SC 29342
Phone: 803-489-6699
Specialties: Fighters, boots and hunters, made at bench by group of craftsmen; offers knives in American Damascus steel in several standard models.

AL MAR KNIVES, INC.
5755 SW Jean Rd., Suite 101
Lake Oswego, OR 97034
Phone: 503-635-9229
Specialties: Designer in production oversees foreign manufacture of his own knives—first class in all respects.

HARRY K. McEVOY (See Tru Balance Knife Co.)

MORTY THE KNIFE MAN
60 Otis St., Unit C
West Babylon, NY 11704
Phone: 516-491-5764
Specialties: Everything for the fish trade; own make and both U.S. and import brands; includes many working knives not easily found, as well as chain mesh protection gloves and aprons.

MOTENG INTERNATIONAL, INC.
8696 Production Ave.
San Diego, CA 92121
Phone: 619-271-8790
Specialties: Kitchen and outdoors cutlery; markets Stapel's Outside Knife; U.S. Bali-Song knives, other high ticket survival gear.

MURPHY COMBAT KNIFE CO.
(Dave Murphy Blades)
P.O. Box 256
Gresham, OR 97030
Phone: 503-665-8634
Specialties: Currently supplying knives for the American Historical Foundation.

MUSEUM REPLICAS LTD.
2143 Gees Mill Rd./Box 840XJ
Conyers, GA 30208
Phone: 800-241-3664 to order, or 404-922-3703
Specialties: Authentic edged weapons of the ages, battle-ready—over 20 models; subsidiary of Atlanta Cutlery; catalog $1.

MYERCHIN MARINE CLASSICS
P.O. Box 911
Rialto, CA 92376
Phone: 714-875-3592

Specialties: The Myerchin Offshore. System—a quality cutlery package for the yachtsman or deep water sailor.

OLSON INDUSTRIES, INC./HANK ROBERTS
4550 Jackson St.
Denver, CO 80216
Phone: 303-399-4623
Specialties: Walton's Thumb—a multi-tool folder, and a line of hunter knives.

OUTDOOR EDGE CUTLERY CORP.
2888 Bluff St., Suite 130
Boulder, CO 80301
Phone: 303-444-0937/800-365-EDGE
Specialties: An all-in-one tool for preparing game, and all-purpose field use.

OZARK KNIFE
3165 So. Campbell, Suite A2
Springfield, MO 65807
Phone: 417-886-2888
Specialties: Shining Wave Damascus steel billets, U.S.-made in two patterns; Randall knives.

PILTDOWN PRODUCTIONS
Errett Callahan
Cliffside
2 Fredonia Ave.
Lynchburg, VA 24503
Phone: 804-528-3444
Specialties: Makes obsidian scalpels and knives; replicates Stone Age tools and weapons—all types—for museums and for academia. $3 for catalog.

RIGID KNIVES
P.O. Box 186, Hwy. 290E
Lake Hamilton, AR 71951
Phone: 501-525-1377
Specialties: Rugged styling and size in mostly full-tang straight knives and big folders made in Arkansas.

SANTA FE STONEWORKS, INC.
1209 Calle de Comercio
Sante Fe, NM 87501
Phone: 800-257-7625/505-471-3953
Specialties: Knives handled in gem stones and exotic woods in jewelry fashion.

SIMMONS OUTDOOR CORP.
14205 Southwest 119th Ave.
Miami, FL 33186
Phone: 305-252-0477
Specialties: "Old Ern" sports knives.

JOHN STAHL
2049 Windsor Rd.
Baldwin, NY 11510
Phone: 516-223-5007
Specialties: Miniature knives.

SPYDERCO, INC.
P.O. Box 800
Golden, CO 80402
Phone: 303-279-8383/800-525-7770
Specialties: Clipit folding knives; sharpening gear.

TEKNA DESIGN GROUP
101 Twin Dolphin Drive
Redwood City, CA 94065

Phone: 415-593-1410
Specialties: Flashlight maker with several slick boot knife systems.

TRA-R, INC.
P.O. Box 1056
DeRidder, LA 70634-1056
Phone: 318-462-6036
Specialties: Sells "Electric Fillet Knife," comes with cigarette lighter adapter and 12-Volt D.C. battery clips. The knife has three speeds, and comes with 10-ft. cord.

TRU-BALANCE KNIFE CO.
2155 Tremont Blvd., N.W.
Grand Rapids, MI 49504
Phone: 616-453-3679
Specialties: Harry McEvoy's full line of throwers—a design for any throwing job.

WENOKA CUTLERY/SEASTYLE
P.O. Box 8238
West Palm Beach, FL 33407-0238
Phone: 305-845-6155
Specialties: First a full line of divers' knives, and now a beefy folder.

WYOMING KNIFE CORP.
101 Commerce Drive
Ft. Collins, CO 80524
Phone: 303-224-3454
Specialties: A tool for dealing with game animals—gutting and skinning. Also makes a short folding saw, and the Powder River folders.

General Cutlers

These are, plain and simple, knife factories. Some are giants; some not so big; some a century old; some just two decades in existence. All market very complete lines of knives, generally through standard mercantile channels.

ALCAS CUTLERY CORPORATION
1116 E. State St.
P.O. Box 810
Olean, NY 14760
Phone: 716-372-3111
Specialties: Broad line of knives includes high quality household knives, as well as hunting and pocketknives. Brands are Cutco and Wear-ever; has Solution and Solution's Spirit, and the Fisherman's Solution.

BUCK KNIVES
1900 Weld Blvd.
El Cajon, CA 92020
Phone: 619-449-1100
Specialties: Creators of the belt folder syndrome; sturdy, solid working knives widely sold.

CAMILLUS CUTLERY CO.
52-54 W. Genesee St.
Camillus, NY 13031-0038
Phone: 315-672-8111
Specialties: Long-time competitor in all phases of cutlery, military knife contractor, some neat pocketknife designs.

W.R. CASE & SONS CUTLERY CO.
Owens Way
Bradford, PA 16701
Phone: 814-368-4123 or 24
Specialties: Big Daddy for pocketknife collectors, but makes full line of sports and commercial cutlery. Handsome knives.

CHICAGO CUTLERY CO.
5420 N. County Rd. #18
Minneapolis, MN 55428
Phone: 612-533-0472
Specialties: Solid utility knives, branching into sports knives.

COLEMAN-WESTERN CUTLERY
1800 Pike Rd.
P.O. Box 1539
Longmont, CO 80501
Phone: 303-772-5900
Specialties: Working pocket and belt knives. Upgraded Westmark belt knives. New locking folders.

COLONIAL KNIFE CO. INC.
P.O. Box 3327
Providence, RI 02909
Phone: 401-421-1600
Specialties: Commercial pocketknives for competitive pricing; some belt knives. Offering six new models this year; also has new logo.

CUTCO INTERNATIONAL
P.O. Box 810
Olean, NY 14760
Phone: 716-372-3111
Specialties: Kitchen cutlery—American-made shears, steak knife sets, some sportsman knives. Parent company—ALCAS.

FISKARS MANUFACTURING CORP.
14200 SW 72nd Ave.
Portland, OR 97223
Phone: 503-639-6161
Specialties: Best known for their scissors—now have cutlery and sharpening devices within their sheaths. In 1987 Fiskars bought Gerber Legendary Blades.

GERBER LEGENDARY BLADES (See Fiskars)

IMPERIAL SCHRADE CORP.
1776 Broadway
New York, NY 10019
Phone: 212-757-1814
Specialties: Probably the biggest; owns Imperial and Schrade. Sells many labels in several brands, U.S. made and imported.

IMPERIAL KNIFE COMPANY, INC.
60 King St.
Providence, RI 02909
Phone: 401-861-4700

Specialties: Pocket and hunting knives; Jackmaster; Diamond Edge; Frontier Double Eagle; others.

KA-BAR CUTLERY, INC.
5777 Grant Ave.
Cleveland, OH 44105
Phone: 216-271-4000/800-321-1630
Specialties: Makes working sports cutlery and always has. Made the first WW II Marine Corps knife, a design still in service. Imports Sabre knives.

KA-BAR KNIVES, COLLECTORS DIVISION
434 No. 9th St.
Olean, NY 14760
Phone: 716-372-5611
Specialties: Commemoratives and special models are this KA-BAR branch's business.

ONTARIO KNIFE COMPANY
P.O. Box 145
Franklinville, NY 14737

Phone: 716-676-5527/800-222-5233
Specialties: Some pocketknives; many styles of utility knives for household and restaurant use. Brands, both Hickory and Colonial Forge. Excellent values.

QUEEN CUTLERY
P.O. Box 500
Franklinville, NY 14737
Phone: 800-222-5233
Specialties: Old name. The line is shorter than once, but there are good Queen knives to be had.

SCHRADE CUTLERY CORP.
Rte. 209 North
Ellenville, NY 12428
Phone: 914-647-7600
Specialties: Widely sold pocketknives in several degrees of finish; slick own designs in belt knives. Old name.

SPORTING IMAGES
P.O. Box 8391
8659 Olive St. Dr.
St. Louis, MO 63132
Phone: 314-432-3565
Specialties: They offer all steel construction pen knives with wildlife scenes etched—some colored etched on slab.

UTICA CUTLERY COMPANY
820 Noyes St.
Utica, NY 13503
Phone: 315-733-4663/800-448-9246
Specialties: Nice line of pocketknives, including Barlows and hunters and working pattern knives. Brands: Kutmaster, Walco.

WESTERN CUTLERY (See Coleman)

Importers & Foreign Cutlers

Knives are imported these days by almost every sort of commercial cutler, but the names here are those whose specialty is importing, whether it be their own brand, famous overseas brands, or special knives for special purposes best made overseas. Every effort is made to keep the list up to date, but importing is sometimes an uncertain endeavor.

ADAMS INTERNATIONAL KNIFEWORKS
1369 Niedringhaus, Suite 114
Granite City, IL 62040
Phone: 618-931-7601
Specialties: Currently the largest dealer of Linder-Solingen hunting knives. Also carries: Muela, Al Mar, Kershaw and Commando. Catalog $3; Barry A. Adams, owner.

ATLANTA CUTLERY CORP.
2143 Gees Mill Rd., Box 839 XW
Conyers, GA 30208
Phone: 404-922-3700/800-241-3595
Specialties: Carefully chosen inventory from all over the world; selected Indian, Pakistani, Spanish, Japanese, German, English and Italian knives; often new ideas—now a principal source for kukris, kindjals and Khyber knives.

B&D TRADING CO.
P.O. Box 1023; 3935 Fair Hill Rd.
Fair Oaks, CA 95628
Phone: 916-965-0555 or 967-9366
Specialties: The Executive Edge, a folder made in Brazil.

B.W. BAKER
Smith Rd., Rd. 2
Waiuku, South Auckland
NEW ZEALAND
Phone: 085-58846
Specialties: New Zealand private outlet makes belt knives and commercial knives in high carbon steel and very sharp.

BLACKJACK KNIVES
21620 Lassen St.

Chatsworth, CA 91311
Phone: 818-902-9853
Specialties: Imports exclusive high-tech self-defense and adventure patterns with names like Mamba, Marauder.

BOKER USA, INC.
14818 W. 6th Ave. #17A
Golden, CO 80401
Phone: 303-279-5997
Specialties: Tree Brand knives and a host of new knives in the Boker USA label.

CAM III ENTERPRISES
425-A Merchant St.
Vacaville, CA 95688
Phone: 707-448-1892
Specialties: Sports folders and straight knives in modern designs; utility belt buckle; knife kits and pouches.

CATOCTIN CUTLERY
P.O. Box 188; 17 S. Main St.
Smithsburg, MD 21783
Phone: 301-824-7416
Specialties: Full line of Aitor knives from Spain, others from Italy, Germany and the Philippines.

CHARLTON LTD. (See Damascus U.S.A.)

CHINA IM/EX
Steven Schneider
69 Rockaway Ave.
San Francisco, CA 94127
Phone: 415-665-5857
Specialties: Specializes in sports cutlery from the Far East.

COLUMBIA PRODUCTS COMPANY
P.O. Box 1333
Sialkot-1. PAKISTAN
Phone: (0432)86921
U.S. Branch:
P.O. Box 1481

Flushing, NY 11354
Phone: 718-463-4180
Specialties: Lockblade and slip-joint folders in old and new U.S.-style patterns; heavy-duty belt knives; all at very low prices.

COMPASS INDUSTRIES, INC.
104 E. 25th St.
New York, NY 10010
Phone: 212-473-2614 or 800-221-9904
Specialties: Imports for dealer trade from all over at many price and quality levels; two hot brands are Silver Falcon and Sportster.

CONSOLIDATED CUTLERY CO., INC.
696 NW Sharpe St.
Port St. Lucie, FL 34983
Phone: 407-878-6139/800-288-6288
Specialties: Hunting knives, woodcarving tools, stag handled steak/carving sets, camping axes, knife sharpening steels.

CRAZY ROW TRADING POST
P.O. Box 314
Denison, TX 75020
Phone: 214-463-1366
Specialties: Mountain men cutlery and fixings.

CUCHILLERIA DEL NORTE, S.A.
P.O. Box No. 1
48260 Ermua (Viscaya)
SPAIN
Phone: 943-17-08-50
Specialties: Full range of products of Aitor from jungle knives to folding pocket knives.

DAMASCUS U.S.A.
P.O. Box 220
Howard, CO 81233
Phone: 719-942-3527
Specialties: Finished forged Damascus knives in period styles and replicas of American patterns; military sgian dubhs and dirks; some swords.

EXECUTIVE EDGE (See B&D Co.)

R.H. FORSCHNER CO., INC.
14 Progress Dr.
Shelton, CT 06484
Phone: 203-929-6391
Specialties: Imports professional cutlery by Victorinox, Solingen special-orders; Sheffield butcher steels, many other specialties, Sabinox cutlery from France.

FREDIANI COLTELLI FINLANDESI
Via Lago Maggiore 41
I-21038 Leggiuno, ITALY
Phone: 0039 332 647362
Specialties: Purveyors from Italy of fine Finnish knives, some with Italian decorative touches.

G96 DESIGNTECH INC.
Rt. 116 at Keeler Lane
North Salem, NY 10560
Phone: 916-669-5672
Specialties: Mass-marketing practical sports cutlery. Makes much of the G-96; has own designs, some pretty special.

GOODWIN ENTERPRISES
P.O. Box 4124
Chattanooga, TN 37405
Phone: 615-267-5071
Specialties: Imports German cutlery, including exclusive Red Stag pocketknives—jigged bone, etched blades in colors, and more.

GREEN HEAD GAME CALL CORP.
R.R. 1, Box 33
Lacon, IL 61540
Phone: 309-246-2155
Specialties: Distributor or Canadian-made D.H. Russell belt knives; some two-bladed folders. Game calls also.

GUTMANN CUTLERY CO., INC.
120 S. Columbus Ave.
Mt. Vernon, NY 10553
Phone: 914-699-4044/800-CUTLERY
Specialties: Puma, Edge Mark, Explorer, Hen & Rooster, Opinel and Russell Green River are the leading names in a selection of over 300 knives sold through retail stores and through the mail.

HARTKOPF MKTG. CO. AMICUS, INC.
1830 So. Robertson Blvd.
Los Angeles, CA 90035
Pnone: 213-559-1832/800-433-4367
Specialties: Solingen-made pocket knives in wide variety, with Teflon-coated stainless steel blades; Swiss-type army knives in non-traditional textures and color.

J.A. HENCKELS ZWILLINGSWORK, INC.
9 Skyline Dr., Box 253
Hawthorne, NY 10532
Phone: 914-592-7370
Specialties: U.S. office of world-famous Solingen cutlers—high quality pocket and sportsman's knives with the "twin" logo.

HOFFRITZ
515 W. 24th St.
New York, NY 10011
Phone: 212-924-7300
Specialties: Selected chef's kitchen and carving cutlery; elegant gentlemen's pocketknives; sports knives of all kinds, most with Hoffritz's; own name; all sold in Hoffritz stores and through catalog.

C.A.S. IBERIA INC./Muela
54 Patricia La.
So. Setauket, NY 11720
Phone: 516-698-9349
Specialties: Knives made in Spain by people with an eye on U.S. custom makers.

IMPEX TRADING CORP.
9400 Business Dr.
Austin, TX 78759
Phone: 512-477-1800
Specialties: Mexican-made hunting and fishing knives under the label of ONEIDA.

INTCO (Intl. Netting Co., Inc.)
P.O. Box 2180
Paso Robles, CA 93447
Phone: 805-238-6702
Specialties: Full line of sports cutlery—dozens of models—with Zest trademark in 440-A steel.

JET-AER CORP. (See G-96 Designtech Inc.)

JOY ENTERPRISES
801 Broad Ave; P.O. Box 314
Ridgefield, NJ 07657
Phone: 201-943-5920
Specialties: Martial arts, sporting and combat-style cutlery under the Fury label—full range.

KEN'S FINN KNIVES
P.O. Box 126
Republic, MI 49879
Phone: 906-376-2132
Specialties: Puukkos and other Finnish knives.

KNIFE IMPORTERS, INC.
P.O. Box 2122
Austin, TX 78768
Phone: 512-282-6860/800-531-5301
Specialties: Eye Brand cutlery.

KRIS CUTLERY (Formerly Cecil Quirino)
P.O. Box 133
Pinole, CA 94564
Phone: 415-758-9912
Specialties: Importer and designer of Philippine edged weapons.

LIBERTY ORGANIZATION INC.
P.O. Box 306
Montrose, CA 91020
Phone: 800-423-2666, Ext. 24
Specialties: Wide range of Spain, Finland, Brazil, Japanese and German imports. Sells to dealers. Has hundreds of models.

H.G. LONG & CO.
1142 W. Grace St.
Richmond, VA 23220
Phone: 804-358-1112
Specialties: Sheffield cutlery including military, hunting, pocket and carving knives.

MARTTIINI KNIVES
P.O. Box 44
96101 Rovaniemi 10, FINLAND
Phone: 358-91-21751
Specialties: Finnish knives straight from Finland's biggest cutler. Includes fancy Finn-type hunters. Line has been repriced.

MATTHEWS CUTLERY
4401 Sentry Dr.
Tucker, GA 30084
Phone: 404-939-6915

Specialties: Are wholesalers only. Carries all major brands which include over 2000 patterns.

MILITARY REPLICA ARMS INC.
P.O. Box 360006, Dept. D
Tampa, FL 33673
Phone: 813-237-0764
Specialties: Ron Hickox picks out dandies to copy Ames naval cutlasses, Krag Bowie bayonets, a wide variety of U.S. sabers and such and prices them pretty low. Catalog $2.

MIRANDA IMPORTS and EXPORTS
1524 E. Santa Clara St.
San Jose, CA 95116
Phone: 408-923-6894
Specialties: Working cutlery and sports knives in Iberian traditions.

MUELA (See C.A.S. Iberia Inc.)

MUSEUM REPLICAS LIMITED
2143 Gees Mill Rd., Box 839 XW
Conyers, GA 30208
Phone: 404-922-3700/800-241-3595
Specialties: Battle ready hand forged edged weapons. They carry swords, daggers, halberds, dirks and axes. Catalog $1.

MUSKETEER (See Liberty Organization)

NEW PATHS, INC.
300 E. 74th St., #88
New York, NY 10021-3713
Specialties: Direct importers of Norwegian cutlery, including folding Norseax hatchet, deluxe dress knives, more.

NORLANTIC INTERPRISE
200 High St.
Windsor, CT 06095
Phone: 203-688-0102
Specialties: Purveyors of advertising knives from pen knives to lockback hunters—your logo, your message, gift-wrapped if you like. EKA brand.

NORMARK CORP.
1710 E. 78th St.
Minneapolis, MN 55423
Phone: 612-869-3291
Specialties: Scandinavian-made sturdy knives for fishermen; puuko-style belt knives for hunters; filet knives. Good stainless steel.

ONEIDA (See Impex)

PARKER CUTLERY
2837 Hickory Valley Rd.; P.O. Box 22668
Chattanooga, TN 37422
Phone: 615-894-1782
Specialties: Collector quality pocketknives.

PRECISE INTERNATIONAL
3 Chestnut St.
Suffern, NY 10901
Phone: 914-357-6200
Specialties: Wenger Swiss Army knives; many American patterns in current style with Precise name; fish and marine knives—in all, hundreds of knives.

PRIMA KNIVES USA, INC.
4000 Kruse Way Place #2-225
Lake Oswego, OR 97035
Phone: 503-697-3175
Specialties: Pocketknives, outdoors specialty knives; private labels and OEM production knives manufactured in Hong Kong.

PROFESSIONAL CUTLERY
9712 Washburn Road
Downey, CA 90241
Phone: 213-803-8778
Specialties: Wholesale only. Imports historical medieval and samurai swords; armor and weapons, over 100 different models.

PUUKKO CUTLERY (See Suomi Shop)

CECIL QUIRINO (See Kris Cutlery)

A.G. RUSSELL CO.
1705 Highway 471 North
Springdale, AR 72764
Phone: 501-751-7341
Specialties: Morseth knives; Russell-marked special designs, as the "Woods Walker," Sting, CIA letter opener, Russell One-Hand knives.

STAR SALES CO., INC.
1803 N. Central St.; P.O. Box 1503
Knoxville, TN 37901
Phone: 615-524-0771
Specialties: New collector pocketknives; imports Star knives and Kissing Crane knives.

SUOMI SHOP
Rte. 2, Box 305
Fergus Falls, MN 56537
Phone: 218-739-9013
Specialties: A full and complete Finnish cutlery line, including the Puukko cutlery line, all custom/hand forged.

SWISS ARMY KNIVES, INC.
P.O. Box 846
Shelton, CT 06484
Phone: 203-929-6391
Specialties: This is the Victorinox headquarters in the U.S.; all current production comes through here; manages service center also.

TAYLOR CUTLERY MFG. CO.
806 E. Center St., P.O. Box 1638
Kingsport, TN 37662
Phone: 615-247-2406
Specialties: Taylor-Seto folders and butterfly and straight knives, plus the Elk Horn brand.

TOLEDO ARMAS S.A.
302 Ponce de Leon Blvd.
St. Augustine, FL 32084
Phone: 904-829-9671

Specialties: Spanish-made finished cutlery and blades.

UNITED CUTLERY CORP.
P.O. Box 586, Hwy. 66
Sevierville, TN 37862
Phone: 615-428-2532
Specialties: Full lines of knives at wholesale.

VALOR CORPORATION
5555 N.W. 36th Ave.
Miami, FL 33142
Phone: 305-633-0127
Specialties: Emphasizes lockback folders from overseas in popular styles. Over 100 knife models imported.

RUDOLF WEBER, JR.
P.O. Box 160106
D-565 Solingen 16
WEST GERMANY
Phone: 0212/592136
Specialties: Hunting and sports knives.

ZAKHAROV KNIVES (See B&D Trading Co.)

Knifemaking Supplies

The firms listed here specialize in furnishing knifemaker supplies in small amounts. Knifemakers—professionals—have their own sources for much of what they use, but often patronize some of these firms. All have catalogs. Send self-addressed and stamped envelope for information.

We list firms in this category upon request. New firms may be listed upon receipt of catalogs or the like. We cannot guarantee their performance. Several charge for their catalogs.

AC ENTERPRISES (See Damascus U.S.A.)

ANDERSON CUTLERY & SUPPLY CO.
Shepard Hill, Box 383
Newtown, CT 06470
Phone: 203-426-8623
Specialties: A complete selection of knifemaking supplies and equipment; $2 for catalog.

ART JEWEL ENTERPRISES, LTD.
Eagle Business Center
460 Randy Rd.
Carol Stream, IL 60188
Phone: 312-260-0400; 800-323-6144 (orders only)
Specialties: Handles—stag, ivory, pearl, horn, rosewood, ebony.

ATLANTA CUTLERY CORPORATION
Box 839XW
Conyers, GA 30207
Phone: 404-922-3700/800-241-3595
Specialties: Many blades and fixings to choose from; occasional special buys in cutlery handles, pocketknife blades, and the like; complete kits for buckskinner knives, small pocket knives. Catalog $1.50.

BDL ENTERPRISES
dba Johannsen Industries, Inc.
68-487 E. Palm Canyon Dr., Suite 56
Cathedral City, CA 92234

Phone: 619-328-7722
Specialties: 2001 blade sharpener.

BOONE TRADING CO., INC.
562 Coyote Rd.
Brinnon, WA 98320
Phone: 206-796-4330
Specialties: Exotic handle materials including elephant, fossil walrus, mastodon, warthog and hippopotamus ivory. Also sambar stag, oosik, impala and sheep horn.

CHARLTON, LTD. (See Damascus U.S.A.)

E. CHRISTOPHER FIREARMS CO., Inc.
Rt. #128 & Ferry St.
Miamitown, OH 45041
Phone: 513-353-1321
Specialties: Blades and supplies, including modern guthook hunters; classic Bowies.

CUSTOM KNIFEMAKER'S SUPPLY
Bob Schrimsher
P.O. Box 308
Emory, TX 75440
Phone: 214-473-3330
Specialties: Big catalog full of virtually everything for knifemaking. In business a long time.

DAMASCUS U.S.A.
P.O. Box 220
Howard, CO 81233
Phone: 719-942-3527
Specialties: Imports forged-to-shape Damascus blades and steel billets. (Formerly Charlton Ltd.)

DAN'S WHETSTONE CO., INC.
207 Remington Dr.
Hot Springs, AR 71913
Phone: 501-767-9598
Specialties: Traditional sharpening materials.

DIAMOND MACHINING TECH., INC.
85 Hayes Memorial Dr.

Marlborough, MA 01752
Phone: 617-481-5944
Specialties: Sophisticated sharpening gear.

DIXIE GUN WORKS, INC.
P.O. Box 130
Union City, TN 38261
Phone: 901-885-0700 (Info.)/800-238-6785 (Orders only)
Specialties: Knife supplies for buckskinners; much early American hardware; blades; catalog.

EZE-LAP DIAMOND PRODUCTS
15164 Weststate St.; P.O. Box 2229
Westminster, CA 92683
Phone: 714-847-1555
Specialties: Diamond-coated sharpening instruments, various sizes.

RICK B. FIELDS
330 No. Durango Ave.
Ocoee, FL 32761
Phone: 407-877-2339
Specialties: Ancient ivories—fossilized mastodon, etc.

FLITZ INTERNATIONAL, LTD.
821 Mohr Ave.
Waterford, WI 53185
Phone: 414-534-5898
Specialties: General line of polishers.

FORTUNE PRODUCTS, INC.
P.O. Box 1308
Friendswood, TX 77546
Phone: 713-996-0729
Specialties: "Accu-sharp" sharpeners.

GILMER WOOD CO.
2211 N.W. St. Helens Rd.
Portland, OR 97210
Phone: 503-274-1271
Specialties: They list 112 varieties of natural woods.

GOLDEN AGE ARMS CO.
Box 283; 14 W. Winter St.
Delaware, OH 43015
Phone: 614-369-6513
Specialties: Blades, many types; stag for handles; cast items—much for the buckskinner. Catalog $3.

HAWKINS CUSTOM KNIVES & SUPPLIES
P.O. Box 400
Red Oak, GA 30272
Phone: 404-964-1177
Specialties: Various size steel blanks, belts, buffing compounds and wheels, stag, and drill bits.

BILL R. HOLT
1253-F Birchwood Dr.
Sunnyvale, CA 94089
Phone: 408-745-0306
Specialties: Special buys on steel; complete furnishings for the trade; heat treaters; catalog $3.

HOUSE OF MUZZLELOADING
1019 East Palmer; P.O. Box 6217
Glendale, CA 91205
Phone: 818-241-0455
Specialties: Full line of supplies and equipment, including excellent selection of tropical woods. Does big business in custom-ground heat-treated blades in dozens of shapes.

INDIAN RIDGE TRADERS (See Koval Knives)

JOHNSON WOOD PRODUCTS
Route 1
Strawberry Point, IA 52076
Phone: 319-933-4930
Specialties: Midwestern woods, including black ash burl, walnut burl and the like.

STANLEY A. JONES
7702 E. Hopi
Mesa, AZ 85208
Phone: 602-986-4822
Specialties: Quality iron wood.

KNIFE & CUTLERY PRODUCTS, INC.
P.O. Box 54275
Tulsa, OK 74155
Phone: 918-252-2190
Specialties: Offers 14 pages of knifemaking supplies, like: exotic woods, wheels, bar stock, and blades in a variety of shapes. Catalog $1.

KNIFE AND GUN FINISHING SUPPLIES
P.O. Box 13522; 624 E. Abram
Arlington, TX 76013
Phone: 817-274-1282 or 817-261-9386
Specialties: Complete line of machine and materials for knifemaking and metal finishing. Specializing in rare and exotic handle materials—oosic, ivory, rare hard woods, horn, stag. Catalog $2.

KNIVES, ETC.
2314 North Meridian
Oklahoma City, OK 73107
Phone: 405-943-9221
Specialties: Exotic woods; variety of blade steels; carry stag.

KOVAL KNIVES/IRT
P.O. Box 26155
Columbus, OH 43226
Phone: 614-888-6486
Specialties: Full range Micarta, other materials for handles; brass, nickel-silver, steels; machines and supplies for all knife making; some knife kits; catalog.

KWIK-SHARP
350 N. Wheeler St.
Ft. Gibson, OK 74434
Phone: 918-478-2443

Specialties: Ceramic rod knife sharpeners.

CHRIS A. LINDSAY
16237 Dyke Rd.
La Pine, OR 97739
Phone: 503-536-2386
Specialties: Handle materials; abrasives; grinders. Catalog 50 cents.

LOG CABIN SPORTS SHOP, INC.
8010 Lafayette Rd.; P.O. Box 275
Lodi, OH 44254
Phone: 216-948-1082
Specialties: Muzzle-loading-style blades and fixings, to include tomahawk heads and handles.

MARKS FORGE
Rt. 2, Box 879-R
Breaux Bridge, LA 70517
Phone: 318-332-3930
Specialties: Offers forged-to-shape blade blanks and precision-ground billets of Damascus. Provides five different patterns.

MASECRAFT SUPPLY CO.
P.O. Box 423, 902 Old Colony Rd.
Meriden, CT 06450
Phone: 203-238-3049/800-682-5489
Specialties: Handle materials.

DARYL MEIER
RR 4
Carbondale, IL 62901
Phone: 618-549-3234
Specialties: Supplier and creator of "Meier Steel." Contact for available sizes and prices on his Damascus.

MID-EAST MFG., INC.
2817 Cameron St.
Melbourne, FL 32901
Phone: 407-724-1477
Specialties: Damascus blades and axe heads hardened and blemish free.

MOTHER OF PEARL CO.
P.O. Box 445
Franklin, NC 28734
Phone: 704-524-6842
Specialties: Dave Culpepper's knife handle supplies.

OPTRONICS, INC. (See Kwik-Sharp)

OZARK KNIFE
3165 So. Campbell, Suite A2
Springfield, MO 65807
Phone: 417-887-2888
Specialties: Shining Wave Damascus steel billets, U.S.-made in two patterns; Randall knives.

JAMES POPLIN/POP KNIVES & SUPPLIES
103 Oak St.
Washington, GA 30673
Phone: 404-678-2729
Specialties: Buffing compounds, sanding belts, buffing wheels, handle screws, belt splitters and counterbores, to name a few.

JIM PUGH
P.O. Box 711, 917 Carpenter St.
Azle, TX 76020
Phone: 817-444-2679
Specialties: Leather hides.

PURDY'S, INC.
2505 Canterbury Rd.
Hays, KS 67601
Phone: 913-628-3043
Specialties: All kinds of ivory.

R & R SALES
P.O. Box 498
Sycamore, IL 60178

Phone: 815-895-4995
Specialties: Makes soft zip knife cases in several sizes.

RAMCO
Box 175
Portage, MI 49081
Phone: 616-323-3570
Specialties: Wood products makers; make exotic woods knife handle scales.

SANDPAPER, INC. OF ILLINOIS
838 Hill Ave.
Glen Ellyn, IL 60137
Phone: 312-469-3320
Specialties: Coated abrasives in belts, sheets, rolls, discs or any coated abrasive specialty.

SCHEP'S FORGE
Box 83
Chapman, NE 68827
Phone: 308-986-2444
Specialties: Damascus steel made in Nebraska.

SHEFFIELD'S KNIFEMAKER'S SUPPLY
P.O. Box 141
Deland, FL 32720
Phone: 904-775-6453
Specialties: Wood, stones, steel, brass, Micarta and more; catalog $2.

SHINING WAVE METALS
P.O. Box 563
Snohomish, WA 98290
Phone: 206-334-5569
Specialties: Phil Baldwin makes and sells mokume, Damascus and a variety of Japanese alloys (for furniture, not blades) either to order or from stock.

SMITH WHETSTONE, INC.
1500 Sleepy Valley Rd.
Hot Springs, AR 71901
Phone: 501-321-2244/800-221-4156 (orders only)
Specialties: Sharpeners of every kind, ceramic sharpeners, oils, kits and polishing creams.

TEXAS KNIFEMAKERS SUPPLY
10649 Haddington, Suite 190
Houston, TX 77043
Phone: 713-461-8632
Specialties: Bar stock, factory blades, much handle material; they offer heat-treating; catalog $1.50.

TRU-GRIT
11231 Thienes Ave., #A
So. El Monte, CA 91733
Phone: 818-444-5192
Specialties: Complete selection of 3M, Norton, Klingspor and Hermes belts and discs for grinding and polishing, also excellent line of machines for knifemakers; ATS34 steel.

R.W. WILSON
P.O. Box 2012
Weirton, WV 26062
Phone: 304-723-2771
Specialties: Full range of supplies, but sells nothing he doesn't use himself.

A WORLD OF KNIVES
3376 Kietzke Lane
Reno, NV 89502
Phone: 702-826-9300
Specialties: Blades, blade material, handle materials and knife parts. Free catalog.

YAUN FORGE
31240 Highway 43
Albany, LA 70711
Phone: 504-567-2187
Specialties: Damascus steel in at least five patterns from a fourth generation smith.

Mail-Order Sales

The firms listed here are the firms that have come to our attention over a period of years. All publish lists or catalogs. Their specialties are shown; it's a good idea to send a self-addressed and stamped envelope for information. We will list firms in this category upon request. New firms may be listed upon receipt of catalogs or the like. We cannot guarantee their performance.

A&J ENTERPRISES
P.O. Box 1343 S.S.S.
Springfield, MO 65805
Phone: 417-335-2170
Specialties: Buy, sell, trade collector-grade knives by mail and at major shows.

AMERICAN HISTORICAL FOUNDATION
1142 West Grace St.
Richmond, VA 23220
Phone: 804-353-1812
Specialties: Limited editions of replica military knives in collector and presentation grades; serve as headquarters for the Military Knife and Bayonet Collectors Club International.

ATLANTA CUTLERY
Box 839XW
Conyers, GA 30207
Phone: 404-922-3700/800-241-3595
Specialties: Catalog on request; wide selection of types; aims to provide working quality knives and give good value; showroom.

ATLANTIC BLADESMITHS
c/o Peter Stebbins
8 Hawthorne Village
Concord, MA 01742
Phone: 617-369-3608
Specialties: Factory and custom-made knives, over 100 in stock at all times, for immediate sale.

BALLARD CUTLERY
1495 Brummel Ave.
Elk Grove Village, IL 60007
Phone: 312-228-0070
Specialties: Special-purchase knives, all types. Tries for good buys.

BLUE RIDGE KNIVES
Rte. 6, Box 185
Marion, VA 24354
Phone: 703-783-6143
Specialties: Wholesale only; top brand knives.

BOONE TRADING CO., INC.
562 Coyote Rd.
Brinnon, WA 98320
Phone: 206-796-4330
Specialties: Ivory, catalog features scrimshawed and carved ivory-handled knives.

CARMEL CUTLERY
Dolores & 6th; P.O. Box 1346
Carmel, CA 93921
Phone: 408-624-6699
Specialties: Knife retailer

CASANOVA GUNS, INC.
1601 W. Greenfield Ave.

Milwaukee, WI 53204
Phone: 414-672-3040 (Info.)/800-627-4570 (Orders only)
Specialties: Factory and handmade collector knives. Has list.

CATOCTIN CUTLERY
P.O. Box 188, 17 Main St.
Smithsburg, MD 21783
Phone: 301-824-7416
Specialties: Wholesaler. Popular lines of domestic cutlery to dealers, as well as many import brands.

CRAZY CROW TRADING POST
P.O. Box 314
Denison, TX 75020
Phone: 214-463-1366
Specialties: Knife blades, books, knifemaking supplies; $3 for catalog.

CREATIVE SALES & MFG.
Box 556
Whitefish, MT 59937
Phone: 406-862-5533
Specialties: Patent knife sharpeners.

CUSTOM PURVEYORS
P.O. Box 886
Fort Lee, NJ 07024
Specialties: Overseas: 19, Pinewood Gdns, Boxmoor, Hemel Hempstead, Herts, HP1 1TN, England (0442 55542). Dealers in best-grade custom knife collections; generally have a big selection.

CUTLERY SHOPPE
5461 Kendall St.
Boise, ID 83706
Phone: 208-376-0430/800-231-1272
Specialties: Discounts; custom and unusual Bali-Songs; fighting and military type knives; catalog $1.

ED'S ENGRAVING
121 East Main St.
Statesboro, GA 30458
Phone: 912-764-4409
Specialties: Broker for Randall-made knives, as well as Buck, Puma, Gerber and Case.

FALCON SUPPLY
28 Halsey St.; P.O. Box 1056
Trumansburg, NY 14886
Phone: 607-387-6666
Specialties: Victorinox and Henckels.

FROST CUTLERY CO.
P.O. Box 21353
Chattanooga, TN 37421
Phone: 615-894-6079
Specialties: Discontinued domestic and imported cutlery, especially folders and pocketknives.

HARTKOPF MKTG. CO. AMICUS, INC.
1830 So. Robertson Blvd.
Los Angeles, CA 90035
Phone: 213-559-1832/800-433-4367
Specialties: Solingen-made pocket knives in wide variety, with Teflon-coated stainless steel blades;

Swiss-type army knives in non-traditional textures and color.

INTERNATIONAL CUTLERY CORP.
3902 Croporex Pk. Dr., Suite 550
Tampa, FL 33619
Phone: 813-626-0028/800-624-3545
Specialties: Name brands.

INTERNATIONAL CUTLERY PURVEYORS
P.O. Box 1525
Royal Oak, MI 48068
Phone: 313-547-5699
Specialties: Dealer in Randalls and specialize in custom-made folders. Publish lists three times a year, $2 per list.

KEN'S FINN KNIVES
P.O. Box 126
Republic, MI 49879
Phone: 906-376-2132
Specialties: Puuko and Finnish-made knives. Brochures and price lists available to readers on request.

DOUG KENEFICK
29 Leander St.
Danielson, CT 06239
Phone: 203-774-8929
Specialties: Excellent selection of Randall Made knives, and custom knives at list prices; catalog on request.

KNIFE-AHOLICS UNANIMOUS
P.O. Box 831
Cockeysville, MD 21030
Phone: 301-628-6262
Specialties: David Cohen—purveyor of custom knives, as well as exclusive agent for Gary Barnes knives.

KNIFE & CUTLERY PRODUCTS, INC.
P.O. Box 54275
Tulsa, OK 74155
Phone: 918-252-2190
Specialties: Sells brand name commercial cutlery, some collectables, has 14-page list. Dale Gerschutz, President.

KNIFE & GUN FINISHING SUPPLIES
P.O. Box 13522; 624 E. Abram
Arlington, TX 76013
Phone: 817-274-1282
Specialties: Complete line of machine and materials for knifemaking and metal finishing. Specializing in rare and exotic handle materials—oosic, ivory, rare hard woods, horn, stag. Catalog $2.

KNIFE IMPORTERS, INC.
P.O. Box 2122
Austin, TX 78768
Phone: 512-282-6860
Specialties: Eye Brand cutlery.

KNIFE WORLD, INC. (JOE DAVIS)
5152 So. Broadway
Englewood, CO 80110
Phone: 303-781-0322
Specialties: Custom knives for collectors.

LOG CABIN SPORTS SHOP INC.
8010 Lafayette
Lodi, OH 44254
Phone: 216-948-1082
Specialties: Buckskinner knives in proper style, including Mexican type, ready to go.

JEFF MARNELL'S KNIVES
52 Edmund Ave.
Uniontown, PA 15401
Phone: 412-437-3931
Specialties: Survival, discounted major brands; catalog $2.

MORTY THE KNIFE MAN
60 Otis St.
West Babylon, NY 11704
Phone: 516-491-5764/800-247-2511
Specialties: The world's fish knives—all of them.

NORDIC KNIVES
1634CZ Copenhagen Dr.
Solvang, CA 93463
Phone: 805-688-3612
Specialties: Custom and Randall knives; custom catalog $3; Randall catalog $2; both catalogs $4.

NORTH AMERICAN KNIFE ASSOC., LTD. (See International Cutlery Purveyors)

OZARK KNIFE
3165 S. Campbell, Suite A2
Springfield, MO 65807
Phone: 417-886-2888
Specialties: Offers list of custom knives for sale, plus general cutlery collectables; Randall knives.

PARKER CUTLERY
2837 Hickory Valley Road
P.O. Box 22668
Chattanooga, TN 37422
Phone: 615-894-1782
Specialties: Collector quality pocket knives and a new line of American-made knives.

PLAZA CUTLERY INC.
333 Bristol, South Coast Plaza
Costa Mesa, CA 92626
Phone: 714-549-3932
Specialties: List ($1) of custom knives for collectors, many top names every time. Other knives, too, of course, at two stores.

R&C KNIVES AND SUCH
P.O. Box 1047
Mantera, CA 95336
Phone: 209-239-3722
Specialties: Custom knives for collectors. Wide variety. Send stamps; can call anytime. Catalog $2.

R&R SALES
P.O. Box 498
Sycamore, IL 60178
Phone: 815-895-4995
Specialties: Hand-made soft zip knife cases in several sizes.

A.G. RUSSELL CO.
1705 Hiway 471N
Springdale, AR 72764
Phone: 501-751-7341
Specialties: Regularly lists custom knives by all makers; sold on consignment; also commemoratives, Russell and Morseth knives.

SAN DIEGO KNIVES
P.O. Box 326; 11280 Posthill Rd.
Lakeside, CA 92040
Phone: 619-561-5900
Specialties: All brand names, most all types; most all discounted. Further volume discounts, each order. Lists.

SAN FRANCISCO COLLECTOR KNIVES
624 Stanyan St.
San Francisco, CA 94117
Phone: 415-668-3360
Specialties: High-tech collector Wolf Schulz-Tatten-

pach will share his goodies with qualified buyers—Paul, Walker, Appleton are some of the names.

SHOFNER'S WORLD OF KNIVES
2104 Prestonwood Ctr.
Dallas, TX 75240
Phone: 214-661-2298
Specialties: Collector grade custom knives at two Dallas stores.

SHOFNER'S WORLD OF KNIVES
2501 West Memorial Road
Oklahoma City, OK 73134
Phone: 405-752-1447
Specialties: Collector grade knives.

SMOKY MOUNTAIN KNIFE WORKS
P.O. Box 4430
Sevierville, TN 37864
Phone: 615-453-5871
Specialties: Retail and wholesale all kinds of knives and supplies.

SPORTS HUT
1311 Bell Ridge Dr.
Kingsport, TN 37665
Phone: 615-247-3987 or 378-3232
Specialties: Discounts all major brands of pocket knives and military-related cutlery.

UNITED STATES CUTLERY
P.O. Box 418
Wyckoff, NJ 07481-0418
Phone: 800-345-0710
Specialties: Top line of Precise knives.

A WORLD OF KNIVES
3376 Kietzke Lane
Reno, NV 89502
Phone: 702-826-9300
Specialties: Major brands, imported and domestic, and RANDALL MADE knives.

Knife Services

Engravers

SAM ALFANO
Rt. 1, Box 365
Pearl River, LA 70452
Phone: 504-863-3364

GARY ALLARD
Creek Side
Fishers Hill, VA 22626
Phone: 703-465-3903

BILLY BATES
2905 Lynnwood Circle S.W.
Decatur, AL 35603
Phone: 205-355-3690

JAMES P. BINA
P.O. Box 6532
Evanston, IL 60204
Phone: 312-475-6377

LAWRENCE T. BLAKESLEE
1650 El Cerrito Court
San Luis Obispo, CA 93401
Phone: 805-544-5182
(After 5 PM PCT)

GARY BLANCHARD
720 Holly Ave.
P.O. Box 1123
Burney, CA 96013
Phone: 916-335-5343

C. ROGER BLEILE
5040 Ralph Ave.
Cincinnati, OH 45238
Phone: 513-251-0249

BENITA BONSHIRE
1121 Burlington
Muncie, IN 47302
Phone: 317-282-9073

BRYAN BRIDGES
6350 E. Paseo San Andres
Tucson, AZ 85710
Phone: 602-886-9146

DENNIS B. BROOKER
Rte 1, Box 12A
Derby, IA 50068
Phone: 515-533-2103

BYRON BURGESS
710 Bella Vista Dr.
Morro Bay, CA 93442
Phone: 805-772-3974

MARTIN BUTLER
162 Metcalfe St. West
Strathroy, Ont.
CANADA NOL 1WO
Phone: 519-245-5833

FRANK CLARK
3714 - 27th St.
Lubbock, TX 79410
Phone: 806-799-1187

LARRY R. COLE
HC84, Box 10303
Broadbent, OR 97414

JIM DASHWOOD
255 Barkham Road
Wokingham
Berkshire RG11 4BY
ENGLAND
Phone: 0734-781761

BRUCE DEAN
13 Tressider Ave.
Haberfield, N.S.W. 2045
AUSTRALIA
Phone: 02-797-7608

ED DeLORGE
2231 Hwy. 308
Thibodaux, LA 70301
Phone: 504-447-1633

ROD DILLING
105 N. Ridgewood Dr.
Sebring, FL 33870
Phone: 813-385-0647

MARK DRAIN
S.E. 3211 Kamilche Pt. Rd.
Shelton, WA 98584
Phone: 206-426-5452

RICK EATON
1847 Walnut Grove Ct.
Oakley, CA 94561
Phone: 415-625-4218

KEN EYSTER
Heritage Gunsmiths Inc.
6441 Bishop Rd.
Centerburg, OH 43011
Phone: 614-625-6131

TERRY FLOWERS
P.O. Box 96
Midland, OR 97634
Phone: 503-882-1323

FRED A. HARRINGTON
2107 W. Frances Road
Mt. Morris, MI 48458
Phone: 313-686-3008

FRED D. HENDERSON
569 Santa Barbara Dr.
Forest Park, GA 30050
Phone: 404-968-4866

BENNO HEUNE
934 Jack London Dr.
Santa Rosa, CA 95405
Phone: 707-539-1747

RALPH W. INGLE
#4 Missing Link
Rossville, GA 30741
Phone: 404-866-5589

BILL JOHNS
1113 Nightingale
McAllen, TX 78504
Phone: 512-682-6602
(Business)
512-682-2971
(Evenings)

LANCE KELLY
1824 Royal Palm Dr.
Edgewater, FL 32032
Phone: 904-423-4933

JIM KELSO
RD 1, Box 5300
Worcester, VT 05682
Phone: 802-229-4254

JOE and PATTY KOSTELNIK
RD #4, Box 323
Greensburg, PA 15601
Phone: 412-832-0365

JOHN M. KUDLAS
622 - 14th St. S.E.
Rochester, MN 55901
Phone: 507-288-5579

RAY LEE
341 Alleghany Ave.
Lynchburg, VA 24501
Phone: 804-841-4955

FRANZ LETSCHNIG
620 Cathcart, Suite 422
Montreal, P. Que. H3B1M1
CANADA
Phone: 514-875-4948

HARRY LIMINGS, JR.
5030 Patrick Rd.
Sunbury, OH 43074
Phone: 614-965-3272

STEVE LINDSAY
RR2 Cedar Hills
Kearney, NE 68847
Phone: 308-236-7885

SIMON M. LYTTON
19 Pinewood Gardens
Hemel Hempstead
Herts. HP1 1TN
ENGLAND
Phone: UK# 04442-55542

ROBERT E. MAKI
P.O. Box 947
Northbrook, IL 60065
Phone: 312-724-8238

GEORGE MAREK
P.O. Box 213
Westfield, MA 01086
Phone: 413-568-9816
(Evenings)

LYNTON McKENZIE
6940 N. Alvernon Way

Tucson, AZ 85718
Phone: 602-299-5090

HARRY E. MENDENHALL
1848 Everglades Dr.
Milpitas, CA 95035
Phone: 408-263-0677

DAVID A. MORTON
1110 W. 21st St.
Lorain, OH 44052
Phone: 216-245-3410

MITCH MOSCHETTI
P.O. Box 27065
Denver, CO 80227
Phone: 303-936-1184

**OLD DOMINION HAND
ENGRAVERS**
Brett Irby, David Perdue,
Jon Robyn, Lisa Tomlin
10119 Timberlake Rd.
Lynchburg, VA 24502
Phone: 804-239-4928

SCOTT PILKINGTON
P.O. Box 125
Dunlap, TN 37327
Phone: 615-592-3786

JON POULAKIS
Rt. 11, Box 260, Pinehaven Dr.
Sevierville, TN 37862
Phone: 615-453-1311

MARTIN RABENO
Box 37F, RD #1
Ellenville, NY 12428
Phone: 914-647-4567

ANDREW RAFTIS
2743 N. Sheffield
Chicago, IL 60614
Phone: 312-871-6699

CHRIS REED
4399 Bonny Mede Ct.
Jackson, MI 49201
Phone: 517-764-4387

J.J. ROBERTS
166 Manassas Dr.
Manassas Park, VA 22111
Phone: 703-330-0448

BOB ROSSER
142 Ramsey Dr.
Albertville, AL 35950
Phone: 205-878-5388

LEWIS B. SANCHEZ
11711 Gillette St.
Tampa, FL 33617
Phone: 813-988-2772

BRUCE SHAW
P.O. Box 545

Pacific Grove, CA 93950
Phone: 408-646-1937

GEORGE SHERWOOD
Box 735
Winchester, OR 97495
Phone: 503-672-3159

BEN SHOSTLE
1121 Burlington
Muncie, IN 47302
Phone: 317-282-9073

W.P. SINCLAIR
46 Westbury Road
Edington, Wiltsh. BA13 4PG
ENGLAND
Phone: U.K. Code then
(0380) 830494

R.E. SKAGGS
P.O. Box 34, 114 Miles Court
Princeton, IL 61356
Phone: 815-875-8207

RON SMITH
3601 West 7th St.
Ft. Worth, TX 76107
Phone: 817-732-4623

ROBERT D. SWARTLEY
2800 Pine St.
Napa, CA 94558
Phone: 707-255-1394

TERRY THEIS
P.O. Box 252
Harper, TX 78631
Phone: 512-864-4384

ROBERT VALADE
931 - 3d Ave.
Seaside, OR 97138
Phone: 503-738-7672

GEORGE A. WALKER
Star Route
Alpine, WY 83128
Phone: 307-883-2372

PATRICIA WALKER
P.O. Box 2343
Taos, NM 87571
Phone: 505-758-0233

TERRY WALLACE
385 San Marino
Vallejo, CA 94589
Phone: 707-642-7041

KENNETH WARREN
c/o Mountain States Engraving
8333 E. San Sebastian Dr.
Scottsdale, AZ 85258
Phone: 602-991-5035

CLAUS WILLIG
Siedlerweg 17
8720 Schweinfurt
WEST GERMANY
Phone: 09721-41446

MEL WOOD
P.O. Box 1255
Sierra Vista, AZ 85636
Phone: 602-455-5541

Scrimshanders

JOHN ALWARD
879 Watkins Road
Allen, MI 49227
Phone: 517-869-2454

TERRY JACK ANDERSON
430 E. 1st North
Richfield, UT 84701
Phone: 802-896-6803

ART OF SCRIMSHAW
(See Gil Velasquez)

DUANE BAKER
1656 Vilardo Lane
Columbus, OH 43227
Phone: 614-236-0915

C.M. BARRINGER
244 Lakeview Terr.
Palm Harbor, FL 33563
Phone: 813-785-0088

MILES BARROWS
524 Parsons Ave.
Chillicothe, OH 45601
Phone: 614-775-9627

CONNIE BELLET
P.O. BOX 111
Ringling, MT 59642
Phone: 406-547-2272

BENITA BONSHIRE
1121 Burlington
Muncie, IN 47302
Phone: 317-282-9073

BOONE TRADING CO., INC.
562 Coyote Rd.
Brinnon, WA 98320
Phone: 206-796-4330

JUDY BOUCHARD
1808 W. Pleasant Ridge Rd.
Hammond, LA 70403
Phone: 504-345-2456

SANDRA BRADY
9608 Monclova Rd.
P.O. Box 104
Monclova, OH 43542
Phone: 419-866-0435

BOB BURDETTE
4908 Maplewood Dr.
Greenville, SC 29615
Phone: 803-288-0976

MARY GREGG BYRNE
P.O. Box 2394
Bellingham, WA 98227
Phone: 206-676-1413

JERRY CABLE
332 Main St.
Mt. Pleasant, PA 15666
Phone: 412-547-8282

LYNDA CAPOCCI-CHRISTMAN
RR 4, Box 289A
Wabash, IN 46992
Phone: 219-563-4634

LYLE CAUDILL
720 W. Walnut St.
Felicity, OH 45120
Phone: 513-876-2212

MICHAEL COLLINS
Rte. 4, Batesville Rd.
Woodstock, GA 30188
Phone: 404-475-7410

RAYMOND A. COVER, JR.
Rt. 1, Box 194
Mineral Point, MO 63660
Phone: 314-749-3783

BARBARA CRICCHIO
P.O. Box 656
Ringwood, NJ 07456
Phone: 201-962-6674

JEAN E. CURTIS
2809 Midwood
Lansing, MI 48910
Phone: 517-393-9316

GUY M. DAHL
Box 308
Horsefly, BC VOL 1LO
CANADA
Phone: 604-620-3349

MARY E. DAVIDSON
2419-25th St.
Lubbock, TX 79411
Phone: 806-762-1901

JEAN E. DeSAVAGE
9168 Redwood
Fontana, CA 92335
Phone: 714-822-6050

RICHARD DiMARZO
2357 Center Place
Birmingham, AL 35205
Phone: 205-252-3331

KYLE DUNCAN
2034 Sidney
St. Louis, MO 63104
Phone: 314-664-7103

JONI ELBOURN
P.O. Box 404, Hudson P.O.
Hudson, Que. JOP 1HO
CANADA
Phone: 514-458-2663

BOB ENGNATH
1217 Apt. B Crescent Dr.
Glendale, CA 91205
Phone: 818-241-3629

RICK M. EVANS
2717 Arrowhead Dr.
Abilene, TX 79606
Phone: 915-698-2620

RICK B. FIELDS
330 No. Durango Ave.
Ocoee, FL 32761
Phone: 407-877-2339

B.J. FISCHER
P.O. Box 310
Nixon, TX 78140
Phone: 512-582-1353

DALE FISK
Box 252
Council, ID 83612
Phone: 208-253-4582

TERRY FLOWERS
(See Engravers)

W.C. FRAZIER
1029 Kavanaugh St.
Mansfield, LA 71052
Phone: 318-872-1732

GIGI
P.O. Box 624
Clovis, CA 93613
Phone: 209-298-0685

VICKI and DARREL W. GOFF
5725 New Holme
Baltimore, MD 21206
Phone: 301-488-2230

JIM GULLETTE
Rte. 8, Box 265
Greer, SC 29651
Phone: 803-877-7727

CHARLES HARGRAVES, SR.
1839 Kingston Rd.
Scarborough, Ont., M1N 1T3
Canada
Phone: 416-699-6791

STAR HARLESS
P.O. Box 5913
Lake Worth, FL 33466-5913
Phone: 305-964-3325

FRED HARRINGTON
(See "Engravers")

STAN HAWKINS
2230 El Capitan
Arcadia, CA 91006
Phone: 818-445-3054

BOB HERGERT
12120 S.W. 9th
Beaverton, OR 97005
Phone: 503-641-6924

TOM HIGH
5474 S. 112.8 Rd.
Alamosa, CO 81101
Phone: 719-589-2108

DAVID R. HIMMELHEBER
6841 Southern Blvd.

West Palm Beach, FL 33413
Phone: 407-683-0863

DENNIS K. HOLLAND
4908-17th Place
Lubbock, TX 79416
Phone: 806-799-8427

HARVEY HOOVER
1263 Nunneley Rd.
Paradise, CA 95969
Phone: 916-872-1154

IMAGES IN IVORY
(See John Stahl)

HOWARD L. IMBODEN, II
4216 Barth Lane
Kettering, OH 45429
Phone: 513-293-1552

ALAN JIRANEK
9065 Van Emmon Rd.
Yorkville, IL 60560
Phone: 312-553-0302

LINDA K. KARST
P.O. Box 171
Coppell, TX 75019
Phone: 214-462-9006

JIM KELSO
(See "Engravers")

SUSAN B. KIRK
1019 Poseyville Rd.
Midland, MI 58640
Phone: 517-839-9131

JOE and PATTY KOSTELNIK
(See "Engravers")

JOHN W. LAND
P.O. Box 917
Wadesboro, NC 28170
Phone: 704-694-5141
Home: 704-694-2001

ERIK LOVESTRAND
325 Rolfe Dr.
Apopka, FL 32703
Phone: 305-886-0494

GEORGE MAREK
(See "Engravers")

LARRY E. McCULLOUGH
Rte. 4, Box 556
Mocksville, NC 27028
Phone: 704-634-5632

BERNI McFADDEN
2524 N. 16th
Coeur d'Alene, ID 83814
Phone: 208-664-2686

FRANK McGOWAN
12629 Howard Lodge Drive
Sykesville, MD 21784
Phone: 301-489-4323

GAYLE McGRATH
904 S.E. 24th Ave,
Cape Coral, FL 33904
Phone: 813-574-9463

LOU McLARAN
603 Powers St.
Waco, TX 76705
Phone: 817-799-2234

CAROLE McWILLIAMS
4334 C.R. 509
Bayfield, CO 81122
Phone: 303-884-9854

HARRY E. MENDENHALL
(See Engravers)

ANITA MILLER
450 S. 1st
Seward, NE 68434
Phone: 402-643-4726

PETRIA MITCHELL
R.D. 1, Box 244
Brattleboro, VT 05301
Phone: 802-257-4021

MARY MUELLER
3124 W. 64th
Anchorage, AK 99502
Phone: 907-248-5697

MICHELLE OCHONICKY
4059 Toenges Ave.
St. Louis, MO 63116
Phone: 314-351-2612

BELLE OCHS
124 Emerald Lane
Largo, FL 34641
Phone: 813-536-3827

VAUGHN PARISH
103 Cross St.
Monaca, PA 15061
Phone: 412-495-3024

LARRY H. PECK
14 Patricia Lane
Hannibal, MO 63401
Phone: 314-221-5994

LOU PETERSON
514 S. Jackson St.
Gardner, IL 60424
Phone: 815-237-8432

LINDA A. PETREE
Rte. 14 Box 2364A

Kennewick, WA 99337
Phone: 509-586-9596

TRENA POLK
3526 Eller St.
Fort Smith, AR 72904
Phone: 501-782-1396

JON POULAKIS
(See Engravers)

BOB PURDY
2505 Canterbury Rd.
Hays, KS 67601
Phone: 913-628-3043

NANCY QUINN
P.O. Box 692
Julian, CA 92036
Phone: 619-765-1415

CHARLES V. RECE
Wildwood Studios
P.O. Box 1465
Albemarle, NC 28002
Phone: 704-982-2572

J.J. ROBERTS
(See "Engravers")

JOE RUNDELL
6198 Frances Rd.
Clio, MI 48420
Phone: 313-687-0559

ROBERT SATRE
518-3rd Ave. N.W.
Weyburn, Sask. S4H 1R1
CANADA
Phone: 306-842-3051

ROBERT SCHABER
3710 No. Palm
Sebastian, FL 32958
Phone: 305-589-8609

PATRICIA SCHWALLIE
217 Parliament Rd.
Greenville, SC 29615
Phone: 803-268-0182

LURA SCHWARZ
8033 Sunset Blvd., Suite 233
Hollywood, CA 90046
Phone: 805-251-0400

GEORGE SHERWOOD
(See "Engravers")

R.E. SKAGGS
(See "Engravers")

PEGGY SMITH
Rt. 1, Box 119A Glades Rd.
Gatlinburg, TN 37738
Phone: 615-428-0811

RON SMITH
(See "Engravers")

JOHN STAHL
2049 Windsor Rd.
Baldwin, NY 11510
Phone: 516-223-5007

HARRY L. STALTER
2509 Trivoli Rd.
Trivoli, IL 61569
Phone: 309-362-2306

MARY AUSTIN TALLEY
2499 Countrywood Parkway
Cordova, TN 38018
Phone: 901-372-2263

LARRY THOMPSON
23040 Ave. 197
Strathmore, CA 93267
Phone: 209-568-2048

GERALD TISDALE
6 Aurora St.
Laredo, TX 78041
Phone: 512-723-2549

GIL VELASQUEZ
7120 Madera Dr.
Goleta, CA 93117
Phone: 805-968-7787

KAREN WALKER
Star Route
Alpine, WY 83128
Phone: 307-883-2372

PATRICIA WALKER
(See "Engravers")

GARY WILLIAMS
221 Autumn Way
Elizabethtown, KY 42701
Phone: 502-765-6963

BECKY WILSON
8080 Greenwood Ct.
Denver, CO 80221
Phone: 303-650-6338

MARY YOUNG
4826 Storeyland Dr.
Alton, IL 62002
Phone: 618-466-4707

RUSSELL ZIMA
4725 Raleigh St.
Denver, CO 80212
Phone: 303-433-6469

Leatherwork

DON BAKER
1656 Vilardo Lane
Columbus, OH 43227
Phone: 614-236-0915

JOHN BUCKELEW
P.O. Box 5913

Lake Worth, FL 33466-5913
Phone: 305-964-3325

CATTLE BARON LEATHER CO.
P.O. Box 100724, Dept. K8
San Antonio, TX 78201
Phone: 512-697-8900

GRANT CHERAMIE
4260 West Main
Rt. 3, Box 940
Cut Off, LA 70345
Phone: 504-632-5770

CHINA IM/EX
Steven Schneider
69 Rockaway Ave.
San Francisco, CA 94127
Phone: 415-665-5857

CHAS. CLEMENTS
1741 Dallas St.
Aurora, CO 80010
Phone: 303-364-0403

COW CATCHER LEATHERWORKS
(See W. Barry Wilder)

JOE DAVIS
5152 S. Broadway
Englewood, CO 80110
Phone: 303-781-0322

J.R. EDMONDSON
13424 Abinger Drive
Little Rock, AR 72212
Phone: 501-225-4698

TOM HARRIS
617 S. 1st St.
Mount Vernon, WA 98273
Phone: 206-336-2413

BRIAN KATZ
2043 N. Hoyne
Chicago, IL 60647
Phone: 312-235-5518

TIM KENNEDY
1428 S. Morningside Dr.
Melbourne, FL 32901
Phone: 305-676-2396

CHRIS KRAVETT
Tree Stump Leather
18 State St.
Ellsworth, ME 04605
Phone: NA

JIM LAYTON
2710 Gilbert Ave.
Portsmouth, OH 45662
Phone: 614-353-6179

FRANK McGOWAN
12629 Howard Lodge Drive
Sykesville, MD 21784
Phone: 301-439-4323

GEORGE S. NOONE
THE ASTORIAN LTD.
8533 Gray Ct.
Arvada, CO 80003-1337
Phone: 303-429-4132

JIM PUGH
P.O. Box 711-L
917 Carpenter
Azle, TX 76020
Phone: 817-444-2679

RAVON INC.
P.O. Box 670
311 N. Locust
Denton, TX 76201
Phone: 817-382-1831

NORM RINEY
6212 S. Marion Way
Littleton, CO 80121
Phone: 303-794-1731

RUIZ INDUSTRIES INC.
3829 San Fernando Rd.
Glendale, CA 91204
Phone: 213-242-4131

ROBERT G. SCHRAP
7024 W. Wells St.
Wauwatosa, WI 53213
Phone: 414-771-6472

SHERMAN CUSTOM LEATHER
Landon Hill Rd.
Chestertown, NY 12817
Phone: 518-494-2057

JESSEE W. SMITH SADDLERY
No. 307 Haven St.
Spokane, WA 99202
Phone: 509-534-3229

JOHN R. STUMPF
John's Custom Leather
525 So. Liberty St.
P.O. Box 402
Blairsville, PA 15717
Phone: 412-459-6802

MIKE TIERNEY
447 Rivercrest Dr.
Woodstock, ON N4S 5W5
Phone: 519-539-8859

GIL VELASQUEZ
7120 Madera Dr.
Goleta, CA 93117
Phone: 805-968-7787

WALT WHINNERY
1947 Meadow Creek Dr.
Louisville, KY 40218
Phone: 502-458-4361

W. BARRY WILDER
3006 Industrial Dr.
Raleigh, NC 27609
Phone: 919-833-8262

TAMI WORTHINGTON
86 Ensenada
Los Alamos, NM 87544
Phone: 505-672-3309

MICHAEL F. ZIMA
732 State St.
Fort Morgan, CO 80701
Phone: 303-867-6078

Photographers

Peter L. Bloomer
Horizons West
427 S. San Francisco
Flagstaff, AZ 86001
Phone: 602-779-1014

STEVEN BRADLEY
Integrated Arts
P.O. Box 3252
Taos, NM 87571
Phone: 505-758-1281

DEAN R. BROWN
Diamond Portrait Gallery
423 S. Buchanan
Edwardsville, IL 62025
Phone: 618-656-4338

BUCKMAN & MARSH
P.O. Box 4541
Oceanside, CA 92054
Phone: NA

BYRON BURGESS
710 Bella Vista Dr.
Morro Bay, CA 93442
Phone: 805-772-3974

ART CARTER
818 Buffin Bay Rd.
Columbia, SC 28210
Phone: 802-772-2148

JOHN D. CATALANO
56 Kingston Ave.
Hicksville, NY 11801
Phone: 516-938-1356

JOHN E. CHASE
("See Heat Treaters")

ROBERT COMBS
1386 Rambling Rd.

Ypsilanti, MI 48197
Phone: 313-482-6629

BILL DeSAVAGE
9168 Redwood Ave.
Fontana, CA 92335
Phone: 714-822-6050

DAVID EVERETT
White Lotus Studio
12 Jefferson Ave.
West Hartford, CT 06110
Phone: 203-236-5783

ALLAN FEDORAK
28 W. Nicola St.
Amloops, B.C. V2C 1J6
CANADA
Phone: 604-372-1255

DAN FITZGERALD
P.O. Box 198
Beverly Hills, CA 90213
Phone: 818-507-8418

BOB GLADSTONE
6623 Sedan Ave.
Canoga Park, CA 91307
Phone: 818-348-9255

RONALD E. GODBY
204 Seven Hollys Dr.
Yorktown, VA 23692
Phone: 804-898-4445

JOHN HANUSIN
3306 Commercial
Northbrook, IL 60062
Phone: 312-564-2706

JIM HAYS
7118 McGee
Kansas City, MO 64114

Phone: 816-363-1344

TOM HODGE
P.O. Box 401
Belle Mead, NJ 08502
Phone: 201-359-8386

DAVID HUTSON
8120 Juniper
Prairie Village, KS 66208
Phone: 913-383-1123

STEPHEN JACOBSON
2336 Archwood Ln. #60
Simi Valley, CA 93063
Phone: 805-581-2178

C.A. JONES
36 Broadgate Close
Bellaire
Barnstaple, N. Devon
EX 31 4AL, England
Phone: 0271-75328

ERIC KLINEFELTER
10963 Hickory Ridge Rd.
Columbia, MD 21044
Phone: 301-964-0273

LENZ PHOTOGRAPHY
2810 S. 24th St., Suite 111
Phoenix, AZ 85034
Phone: 602-275-1005

GARY W. LONG
Rt. 2, Box 169
Hillsboro, TN 37342
Phone: 615-596-2275

JIM MOAKE
18 Council Ave.
Aurora, IL 60504

Phone: 312-898-7184

THOMAS D. NEWTON
136 1/2 W. 2nd St.
Reno, NV 89501
Phone: 702-232-0971

RICHARD OWLETT
P.O. Box 169
Trumansburg, NY 14886
Phone: 607-387-5202

C. H. PIPES
718 Alpine Dr.
Sevierville, TN 37862
Phone: 615-453-4595

ERIC L. RASMUSSEN
5735 N. 4700 W.
Bear River, UT 84301
Phone: 801-279-8578

TIM RICE
P.O. Box 85
Whitefish, MT 59937
Phone: 406-862-5416

TOM RUBY
Holiday Inn University
11200 E. Goodman Rd.
Olive Branch, MS 38654
Phone: 601-895-2941

DAVID V. SCADLOCK
P.O. Box 1702
Lacrosse, WI 54602-1702
Phone: 608-787-6126

CHARLES SEMMER
7885 Cyd Dr.
Denver, CO 80221
Phone: 303-429-6947

RANDALL SMITH
1720 Oneco Ave.
Winter Park, FL 32789
Phone: 407-628-5447

MARK SURLES
Route 1 Box 70-A
Wade, NC 28395
Phone: 919-483-8814

ALLAN I. TEGER
248 Tremont St.
Newton, MA 02158

Phone: 617-527-0798

THIRD EYE PHOTOS
140 E. Sixth Ave.
Helena, MT 59601
Phone: 406-443-4688

BILL THOMAS
412 B 6th Ave.
Salt Lake City, UT 84103
Phone: 801-364-7153

TONY TOCCI

41 Ellwood Rd.
East Brunswick, NJ 08816
Phone: 201-238-2289

STEVEN L. TOWELL
2852 Iholani St.
Pukalani, HI 96768
Phone: 808-572-1207

CYNTHIA VANNOY-RHOADES
Box 195
Clearmont, WY 82835
Phone: 307-758-4460

WEYER INTERNATIONAL
Mail: 333 14th St.
Shpg.: 324 15th St.
Toledo, OH 43624
Phone: 419-241-5454

HOLLY WORLEY
6545 S. Balsom Ct.
Littleton, CO 80123
Phone: 303-973-1337

Heat Treaters

JIM BARBEE
P.O. Box 1173
Fort Stockton, TX 79753
Phone: 915-336-2882

**BAY STATE METAL
TREATING CO.**
6 Jefferson Ave.
Woburn, MA 01801
Phone: 617-935-4100

PAUL BOS
1900 Weld Blvd.
El Cajon, CA 92020
Phone: (Shop) 619-562-2370
(Home) 619-445-4740

RICHARD BRIDWELL
801 Milford Ch. Rd.
Taylors, SC 29687
Phone: 803-895-1715

JOHN E. CHASE
217 Walnut
P.O. Drawer H
Aledo, TX 76008
Phone: 817-441-8331

EL MONTE STEEL
355 S.E. End Ave.
Pomona, CA 91766
Phone: NA

HAUNI RICHMOND INC

2800 Charles City Rd.
Richmond, VA 23231
Phone: 804-222-5262

BILL R. HOLT
1253-F Birchwood Dr.
Sunnyvale, CA 94089
Phone: 408-745-0306

METAL TREATING, INC.
710 Burns St.
Cincinnati, OH 45204
Phone: 513-921-2300

JIM PUGH
P.O. Box 711-H
917 Carpenter St.

Azle, TX 76020
Phone: 817-444-2679

TEXAS KNIFEMAKERS SUPPLY
10649 Haddington, Suite 190
Houston, TX 77043
Phone: 713-461-8632

THE TINKER SHOP
1120 Helen
Deer Park, TX 77536
Phone: 713-479-7286

R.W. WILSON
P.O. Box 2012
Weirton, WV 26062
Phone: 304-723-2771

Miscellaneous

Etching

AURUM ETCHINGS
601 E. Walnut Circle
Garland, TX 75040
Phone: 214-276-8551

BARON TECHNOLOGY, INC.
62 Spring Hill Rd.
Trumbull, CT 06611
Phone: 203-452-0515

FOUNTAIN PRODUCTS
492 Prospect Ave.
West Springfield, MA 01089
Phone: 413-781-4651

LEONARD LEIBOWITZ
1202 Palto Alto St.
Pittsburgh, PA 15212
Phone: 412-231-5388

SHAW-CULLEN, INC.
212 East 47th St.
New York, NY 10017
Phone: 212-759-8460

Custom Handle Artisans

JOHN ALWARD
(See "Scrimshanders")

GARY BLANCHARD
(See Engravers)

CHAS. CLEMENTS
(See Leatherwork)

JAMES M. COOPER
2148 Cook Place
Ramona, CA 92065
Phone: 619-789-9170

RICHARD DI MARZO
2357 Center Pl. So.
Birmingham, AL 35205
Phone: 205-252-3331

ED HARRISON
10125 Palestine
Houston, TX 77029
Phone: 713-673-6893

RUSSELL S. HILL
2384 Second Ave.
Grand Island, NY 14072
Phone: 716-773-0084

DENNIS K. HOLLAND
(See Scrimshanders)

BRIAN KATZ
(See Leatherworkers)

JIM KELSO
Rt. 1, Box 5300
Worcester, VT 05682
Phone: 802-229-4254

MEL KEMP
c/o Scottsdale Casting Inc.
3949 N. Buckboard Trail
Scottsdale, AZ 85251
Phone: 602-941-4938

RAY LEE
(See Engravers)

ROBERT SATRE
(See Scrimshanders)

PETE and ALICE SEMICH
Rt. 4, Box 502
Murfreesboro, TN 37130
Phone: 615-890-5146

SHAW-CULLEN, INC.
(See Etching)

GLENN L. SMITH
1307 Custer Ave.
Billings, MT 59102
Phone: 406-252-4064

GARY VANN AUSDLE
R.R. 1, Box 50
Wingina, VA 24599
Phone: 804-263-5303

Other

BILL'S CUSTOM CASES
Wm. C. Mittelman
P.O. Box 555
Boyes Hot Springs, CA 95416
Phone: 707-996-5091
(knife cases)

NELSON GIMBERT
P.O. Box 787
Clemmons, NC 27012
Phone: 919-766-5216
(custom display chests)

THE LONG ISLAND SUTLERS
2836 Grand Ave.
Bellmore, NY 11710
Phone: 516-742-9495
        516-781-5515
(display boxes)

CHARLES R. (DICK) McDONALD
1918 Leavenworth
Manhattan, KS 66502
Phone: 913-539-9572
(custom made display cases)

FRANCES OLIVER
3832 W. Desert Park Lane
Phoenix, AZ 85021
Phone: 602-841-7038
(pouches for folding knives)

Custom Grinders

R&S SHARPENING SCHOOL, INC.
604 Phyllis Ct.
Conroe, TX 77303
Phone: 409-756-6127
(knifemaking, sharpening, correspondence courses)

BOB ENGNATH
1217 Crescent Dr. Apt. B
Glendale, CA 91205
Phone: 818-241-3629

KELGIN KNIVES
Ken Largin
110 W. Pearl
Batesville, IN 47006
Phone: 812-934-5938

Knife Appraisers

CHAS. CLEMENTS
1741 Dallas St.
Aurora, CO 80010
Phone: 303-363-0403

BERNARD LEVINE
P.O. Box 2404
Eugene, OR 97402
Phone: 503-484-0294

A.G. RUSSELL
1705 Hwy. 471 N.
Springdale, AR 72764
Phone: 501-751-7341

Organizations/ Publications

KNIFEMAKERS GUILD
c/o Frank Centofante, President
P.O. Box 17587
Tampa, FL 33682
Phone: 813-961-0637

This continues to be the big one. The times have been sometimes tough and the atmosphere strained, but the Guild has prospered, as have its members. It screens prospects to ensure they are serious craftsmen; and it runs a big show (heretofore in Kansas City and Dallas, now in Orlando) each July where over 250 Guild members show their best work, all in one room. Not all good knifemakers belong; some have joined and later left for their own reasons; the Guild drops some for cause now and again. The Knifemakers Guild is an organization with a function. A list of Guild members appears on page 234.

AMERICAN BLADESMITH SOCIETY
c/o William F. Moran, Jr.
P.O. Box 68
Braddock Heights, MD 21714
Phone: 301-371-7543

If you're interested in the forged blade, you are welcome here. The Society has a teaching program, East and West, and awards stamps to Journeymen and Master Smiths after they pass tests—tough tests at a hot forge. You don't have to make knives to belong. A list of knifemaker members appears on page 234.

REGIONAL ASSOCIATIONS
There are an increasing number of state and regional associations with goals possibly more directly related to promotion of their members' sales than the Guild and the ABS. Among these known to us are the Arizona Knifemakers Association; the California Knifemakers Association; South Carolina Association of Knifemakers; the Midwest Knifemakers Association; Professional Knifemakers Assn; New England Bladesmiths Guild; and the Association of Southern Knifemakers. Lists of members of most of these may be found on page 234.

CANADA
One umbrella organization—the Canadian Knife Collectors Club—serves collectors and craftsmen alike. The CKCC holds its own shows and has a semi-annual newsletter. Address CKCC president W. C. White, 148 Islington Ave., Apt. 208, Toronto, ON M8V 3B6, Canada or telephone 416-251-4552.

AMERICAN CUTLERY MFRS. ASSOCIATION
1133 15th St. N.W.
Washington, DC 20005
Phone: 202-429-9440

The ACMA does for its over three dozen member firms what manufacturers associations of many kinds do—provide neutral ground for meetings between competitors, legitimately combined interests for representation to government and provide a forum for the sharing of technical information. It is in no sense a public association; membership is held by companies, not individuals.

THE BLADE MAGAZINE
P.O. Box 22007-K9
Chattanooga, TN 37422
Phone: 615-894-0339

Editor/Publisher: Bruce Voyles. Six Times. Special show, fishing, hunting issues. Official magazine of the Knifemakers Guild. $2.95 on newsstand; $11.95 per year. Also publishes EDGES, a tabloid published bi-monthly ($9.95 for 2 years). Membership in the American Blade Collectors Assn. with either.

KNIFE WORLD
P.O. Box 3395
Knoxville, TN 37927
Phone: 615-523-3339

Editor and Publisher: Houston Price. Monthly. Tabloid size on newsprint. Covers custom knives, knifemakers, collecting, old factory knives, etc. General coverage for the knife enthusiast. Subscr. $12 year.

KNIVES ILLUSTRATED
2145 W. LaPalma Ave.
Anaheim, CA 92801
Phone: 714-635-9040

Editor: Bud Lang. Quarterly. $3.50 on newsstands; $10 for four issues. Plenty of four-color, all on cutlery; concentrates on hand-made knives.

NATIONAL KNIFE MAGAZINE
7201 Shallowford Rd.
Chattanooga, TN 37421
Phone: 615-899-9456

Editor: James Maples. Monthly. Four-color cover. For members, National Knife Collectors Association. Lots of ads. Emphasis on pocketknife collecting, but has broadened coverage to include all phases of knife interest. Membership $15 year.

SPECIALTY BOOK PUBLISHERS

DBI BOOKS, INC.
4092 Commercial Ave.
Northbrook, IL 60062
Phone: 312-272-6310

In addition to this KNIVES annual, DBI publishes *Gun Digest Book of Knives*, by Jack Lewis and Roger Combs, and *Levine's Guide to Knives And Their Values*, by Bernard Levine.

J.E. SMITH, JR.
121 East Main St.
Statesboro, GA 30458
Phone: 912-764-4836

After *Survival Knives*, both first and second, there is *Combat/Fighting Knives*.

WEYER INTERNATIONAL BOOK DIVISION
333 14th St.
Toledo, OH 43624
Phone: 419-241-5454

Publishers of the *Knives: Points of Interest* series. Sells knife-related books at attractive prices; has other knife-publishing projects in work.